Crisis in the Classroom

Charles E. Silberman

CRISIS IN THE CLASSROOM

*The Remaking
of American Education*

VINTAGE BOOKS

A Division of Random House

New York

ISBN: 0-394-71353-2

Library of Congress Catalog Card Number: 76-102326

Acknowledgment is gratefully extended to the following for permission
to reprint from their works:
McGraw-Hill Book Company: From *The Heart Is the Teacher*, by
Leonard Covello. Copyright © 1958 by Leonard Covello.
The New Republic: For excerpts from several articles by Joseph Feather-
stone in the August 19, 1967, September 2, 1967, and September 9, 1967,
issues. Copyright © 1967 by Harrison-Blaine of New Jersey, Inc.
Prentice-Hall, Inc.: From *Up the Down Staircase*, by Bel Kaufman.
Copyright © 1964 by Bel Kaufman.
The Urban Review, a publication of The Center for Urban Education:
From "The Mass Media as an Educational Institution," by Herbert J.
Gans, February, 1967.
The Macmillan Company, Mr. M. B. Yeats, and A. P. Watt & Son Ltd.:
From "The Prayer for Old Age," by W. B. Yeats. Copyright 1934 by The
Macmillan Company, renewed 1962 by Bertha Georgie Yeats.

To David, Ricky, Jeff, and Steve

My sons,

from whom I have learned as much as I have taught,

this book is dedicated with love and pride

Foreword

Ours is an age of crisis. Some, recalling the title of my earlier book, *Crisis in Black and White,* may cringe at my use of the term; if every social problem is labeled "crisis," we risk losing the ability to distinguish the important from the merely urgent.

But our problems are both important and urgent; the multiple crises from which we suffer are no less real for being frequent. How real, and how important, became evident in late April and May of 1970, when, as my usually understated colleague Max Ways wrote in *Fortune,* "the American situation deteriorated from serious to critical. Cambodia, Kent State, the killings of blacks in Georgia and Mississippi, along with all the protests, counter-protests, and counter-counterprotests that stemmed from these, plunged the nation to a level of bewilderment and fear that it had not reached in the depth of the great depression."

The crisis in the classroom—the public school classroom, the college classroom, the national "classroom" created by the mass media and by the operation of the American political system—is both a reflection of and a contributor to the larger crisis of American society. It cannot be solved unless all who have a stake in the remaking of American education—teachers and students, school board members and taxpayers, public officials and civic leaders, newspaper and magazine editors and readers, television directors and viewers, parents and children—are alerted to what is wrong and what needs to be done.

This book is intended to do precisely that; it is addressed, therefore, to laymen and professionals alike. My motive is political, in the broadest sense of the term—as George Orwell defined it, "to push the world in a certain direction, to alter other people's ideas of the kind of society that they should strive after."

I do not expect that all will agree with me; I hope that all will find my meaning clear, and thereby be moved to clarify their own thinking.

My debts are many and great. The book would not have been written were it not for the Carnegie Corporation of New York and its former Vice-President, Dr. Lloyd N. Morrisett, now President of the John and Mary R. Markle Foundation, who invited me to serve as Director of the Carnegie Study of the Education of Educators. Dr. Morrisett's invitation and the Corporation's funding made it possible for me to devote three and a half years to research and writing, with the assistance of a research and administrative staff of four; for this I am deeply grateful. I am even more grateful to Dr. Morrisett and to Dr. Lawrence A. Cremin, Frederick A. P. Barnard Professor of Education at Teachers College, Columbia University, who served as Chairman of the Advisory Commission to the Carnegie Study, for their courage in giving me complete autonomy in writing this book, which constitutes my report as Director of the Carnegie Study. By conceiving of and appointing a Commission of distinguished educators and scholars with powers of advice but not consent, they provided me with the best of two worlds. I had the advantage of invaluable advice, criticism, and support from the members of the Advisory Commission, who convened as a formal body for two-day meetings with me and my research staff at various points in the course of the study; but I was free from the inhibitions and restraints inherent in writing a committee report.

I am deeply indebted to the members of the Advisory Commission: Dr. Herman Branson, President, Central State University, Wilberforce, Ohio; Dr. Charles Brown of the Ford Foundation, formerly Superintendent of Schools in Newton, Mass.; Dr. Lee J. Cronbach, Vida Jacks Professor of Education, Stanford University; Dr. Wayne H. Holtzman, Dean of the College of Education, University of Texas at Austin; Dr. Douglas Knight, former President of Duke University, now Vice-President of RCA Corporation; Dr. Edward H. Levi, President, University of Chicago; Dr. Robert K. Merton, Giddings Professor of Sociology, Columbia University; Dr. Martin Meyerson, President, University of Pennsylvania, former President of the State University of New York at Buffalo; Dr. Charles Odegaard, President, University of Washington; Dr. Martin Trow, Professor of Sociology, University of California, Berkeley; and Drs. Cremin and Morrisett. I shall always be grateful to them for their collective friendship and support.

I am even more deeply indebted to the Commission members as individuals. Lawrence Cremin carried out the difficult, and I suspect deeply frustrating, role of Chairman of the Advisory Commission with tact and grace, offering his always cogent and valuable suggestions and criticisms without ever forcing them upon me. While this is not the book he conceived or would have written, it owes much to him and is far better because of him. The book is better, too, because of Lee Cronbach, an indefatigable letter writer, whose criticisms of countless drafts forced me to reexamine my own position and arguments. The book could not have taken its present shape had I not enjoyed the friendship and counsel of Robert Merton, who taught me to look for models of success as well as of failure, and who commented on each draft with wit and wisdom. Martin Trow's knowledge of comparative education and his sociological imagination were invaluable at a number of points, as were Charles Brown's sensitive judgments about schools and schooling in the United States; their friendship and encouragement, together with Martin Meyerson's, helped me through a number of difficult moments. Wayne Holtzman's comments on each draft were always helpful, saving me from many errors of fact or emphasis. Herman Branson brought to the Study the perspective of the physicist as well as of the humanist; Charles Odegaard, who opened my eyes to the world that exists west of the Hudson River, also helped delimit the study to what could be managed in a single volume.

In no period of my adult life have I learned so much as in these nearly four years of intensive study, travel, research, and writing about teaching and learning; in no period have I been privileged to have so many gifted teachers. In addition to the members of the Advisory Commission, university scholars and administrators; public and private school teachers, principals, and superintendents; lawyers, doctors, theologians, social workers, and engineers; journalists, filmmakers, and television directors; and government officials in three continents generously shared their time and knowledge with me and the members of my research staff. To thank them all would require a chapter of its own. Some, moreover, to whom I owe the greatest debt—elementary and secondary school teachers in my own community and elsewhere, who taught me that islands of decency and humanity can be created and maintained in the most repressive and inhumane of public schools—cannot be thanked here, or in any public forum; to do so would subject them to reprisals from vindictive school boards or administrators.

It is easy to appreciate the relative handful of outstanding teachers. What I hope distinguishes my indictment of the public schools from that of other critics is an empathy for the far greater number of teachers who work hard and long at one of the most difficult and exacting of jobs, but who are defeated by institutions which victimize them no less than their students. For this understanding, I am deeply indebted to Professor David Riesman of Harvard, who rescued me from the arrogance and intellectual and social snobbery toward teachers that has become almost a hallmark of contemporary critics of education. He has taught me other lessons as well, through his generosity of spirit as well as through his detailed comments on the early drafts.

This book, and I, owe much to Professor Lillian Weber of the City College of New York. By sharing the manuscript of her own book on the English Infant School and her sensitive insights into teaching, learning, and schooling in England and the United States, she profoundly influenced the course of my own thinking and hence the shape of this book. I am indebted also to David Silberman, a devoted son and sensitive and thoughtful critic, who broadened my perspective and deepened my understanding through his detailed comments on every draft; to Frank G. Jennings, a wise man and good friend, for suggestions and comments at every stage of the research and writing; and to Philip W. Jackson, Christopher Jencks, and Leonard G. W. Sealey, for their valuable criticisms of individual chapters.

I should like to pay special tribute to my wife, Arlene Silberman, the most gifted, and far and away the most influential, teacher I have had. In twenty-two years of sharing life together, there has hardly been a day when I have not learned from her— lessons about how to love and how to give of oneself, which is to say, how to live as a sensitive and caring human being. For these past four years, in which she put aside her own career to serve as Senior Research Associate to the Carnegie Study, we have been colleagues as well as husband and wife. Drawing upon her graduate studies in education and her experience and expertise as a classroom teacher and, more recently, journalist and free-lance writer, she profoundly influenced the shape of the research and the content and tone of the writing. This is her book as well as mine.

Thanks are due a number of other people who shared their knowledge with me in person or through correspondence and who gave me access to their unpublished papers and files: David Armington, Ben Bagdikian, Dean Merle L. Borrowman, Dr. John Bremer, Mrs. Mary Brown, Dr. Bettye Caldwell, Geoffrey K. Caston, Martin S. Dworkin, Peter F. Drucker, Miss Eleanor Duckworth, Mrs. Martha Froelich, Professor Herbert J. Gans, Miss Dorothy E. M. Gardner, Professor Roger Garrison, Miss Nora L. Goddard, Professor Miriam L. Goldberg, Dr. Arne H. Gronningsater, Dr. A. H. Halsey, Professor Marie Hughes, Professor Willard Hurst, John Haydn Jones, Anthony Kallet, Professor Lawrence Kohlberg, Professor Harry Levin, Dr. Alvin P. Lierheimer, George D. MacIver, I. McMullen, Professor Herbert Passin, Dean Vito Perrone, Mrs. Lore Rasmussen, Professor Vincent R. Rogers, Robert Schwartz, Dr. Harvey Scribner, Dean John Silber, Professor Saul Touster, Professor Mary Alice White, Tadashi Yamamoto, and Edward Yeomans.

I am deeply indebted to the other members of the Carnegie Study staff as well. Sybil H. Pollet and Joan Titus, resourceful Research Associates, served as extra eyes and ears, making it possible for me to be in several places at once. In particular, Miss Titus' skillful reporting and Mrs. Pollet's lucid summaries of the scholarly literature in a number of fields added breadth and depth to the study. Gloria Scott, my administrative assistant in name, was far more than that in fact. During my many field trips, she assumed responsibility for the Carnegie Study, making certain that no significant newspaper or journal article went unnoticed. In between tracking down innumerable facts, books, and periodicals, and correcting my grammar and syntax, she typed more drafts of this book than she or I care to remember, kept track of my correspondence and appointments, and performed the prodigious feat of making order out of the chaos I always managed to create.

I wish to express my thanks, also, to Louis Banks, Managing Editor of *Fortune,* and Hedley Donovan, Editor-in-Chief of Time Incorporated, for their graciousness in giving me (and twice extending) a leave of absence, at considerable inconvenience to themselves, to direct the Carnegie Study and to write this book. I am grateful also to Ronald L. Unger and Elliott J. Solomon, good and patient friends, who provided invaluable assistance with the manuscript.

No one has been more patient and understanding—or more

helpful—than my four sons, David, Ricky, Jeff, and Steve. From David, the oldest, whose specific contributions have been acknowledged above, to Steve, the youngest, who acted as a fourth research associate, supplying countless anecdotes and insights, they were a continuing source of instruction and help. This book is dedicated to them, and properly so; in an age in which cynicism and despair are hard to avoid, they continually renew my faith in the future. Commenting on a verse from Isaiah, "All your children shall be taught of the Lord, and great shall be the peace of your children," the Talmud suggests that the word *banayich,* "your children," be read instead as *bonayich,* "your builders." My sons are my builders; if their sensitivity, concern, and thoughtfulness were widely shared, great would be the peace of all the world.

Perhaps it would be most appropriate to end at the beginning, by acknowledging my profound indebtedness to my late parents, Cel. L. and Seppy I. Silberman. This book reflects their immortality; my insistence that education must involve a fusion of thought, feeling, and action is nothing more than a restatement of the beliefs they held, the lessons they taught, and the lives they led.

I hope that this book will serve as partial repayment of my intellectual and moral debts.

C.E.S.

Mount Vernon, N.Y.
June 1970

Contents

I

The Educating
Society

I

Introduction: Education for What?

The education I propose includes all that is proper for a man, and is one in which all men who are born into this world should share. . . . Our first wish is that all men should be educated fully to full humanity; not only one individual, nor a few, nor even many, but all men together and single, young and old, rich and poor, of high and lowly birth, men and women—in a word, all whose fate it is to be born human beings; so that at last the whole of the human race may become educated, men of all ages, all conditions, both sexes and all nations. Our second wish is that every man should be wholly educated, rightly formed not only in one single matter or in a few or even in many, but in all things which perfect human nature. . . .

—JOHN AMOS COMENIUS,
The Great Didactic, *1632*

"The leap of a poem into its final form will always have a certain mystery about it," the critic M. L. Rosenthal has written about the notebooks of Dylan Thomas. "Hence it would be a treacherous enterprise to try to explain that final version by earlier drafts, shed like snakeskins as the poem discovers itself."

As with poems, so with books, and this is no exception; it has become something other—something more—than what it started out to be. Some of that process of change will always be mysterious, to the writer no less than to the reader. Much of it can be discerned, and should be if the writer is to be sure that his result is one with his intent. And if it be true, as has often been said, that all theories of education are autobiographical, it is incumbent on the writer on education to sort out for the reader, as best he can, the process by which his book discovered itself.

Given the range and focus of this book, there may have been a certain inevitability about the successive shedding of each draft, even as there is inevitability about the shedding of each snakeskin as it becomes too constrictive. Commissioned by the Carnegie Corporation of New York, *Crisis in the Classroom* was initially conceived as a study of teacher education. It quickly became something more than that: to look only at teachers and schools was clearly too restrictive in an age of television and mass higher education, hence *that* skin was shed even before we began. The awkward name we gave the study—The Carnegie Study of the Education of Educators—reflected our determination to go beyond what any other study of teacher education had attempted in a number of respects: in our definition of whom we regard as educators; in our conception of how people are educated; and in our proposals for change.

Our point of departure, in fact, came from Rousseau's Preface to *Émile:*

> People are always telling me to make PRACTICAL suggestions. You might as well tell me to suggest what people are doing already, or at least to suggest improvements which may be incorporated with the wrong methods at present in use.

Our bias, it should be emphasized, was not that everything now being done is necessarily wrong; it was simply that everything now being done needs to be questioned. In an era of radical change such as the present, no approach is more impractical than one which takes the present arrangements and practices as given, asking only, "How can we do what we are now doing more effectively?" or "How can we bring the worst institutions up to the level of the best?" These questions need to be asked, to be sure; but one must also realize that the best may not be good enough and may, in any case, already be changing. And so we chose to work on two levels simultaneously: a level of short-run reform, where one works within the existing system, and a longer-run concern with the transformation of the system.

Several propositions followed. In terms of our initial concern, for example, it seemed self-evident that one cannot reform teacher education without having some clear notion of what the schools themselves are going to be like—and what they *should* be like. Hence a study of teacher education cannot start with the teachers college or the university school or department of education. It must start with the school itself: with what should be taught, in what manner, and to what purpose. And these judgments, in turn, cannot be made apart from the most fundamental judgments about values and purposes—the values of the society as well as the purposes of education. For what we teach reflects, consciously or unconsciously, our concepts of the good life, the good man, and the good society.

But if our concern is with *education,* we cannot restrict our attention to the schools and colleges, for education is not synonymous with schooling. Children and adults learn outside as well as—perhaps more than—in school. To say this is not to denigrate the public schools: as the one publicly controlled educating institution with which virtually every child comes into close and prolonged contact, they occupy a strategic, perhaps critical, position in American society. Nor is it to denigrate the colleges and universities, which for different reasons occupy a position of great and growing importance. It is simply to give proper weight to all the other educating institutions in American society: television, films, and the mass media; churches and synagogues; the law, medicine, and social work; museums and libraries; the armed forces, corporate training programs, boy scout troups. From Plato to Rousseau to Jefferson to the early John Dewey, as Lawrence A. Cremin points out in *The Genius of American Education,* almost everybody who wrote about education took it for granted that it is the community and the culture—what the ancient Greeks called *paideia* that educates. The contemporary American is educated by his *paideia* no less than the Athenian was by his. The weakness of American education is not that the *paideia* does not educate, but that it educates to the wrong ends.

To study American education, therefore, means, in part, to study American society and culture. But only in part. The traditional Platonic or Jeffersonian notion of education as *paideia* is inherently ambiguous; carried to its logical conclusion, "education" all but disappears, for the definition makes education synonymous with what the anthropologists call enculturation. This would have condemned us to study every one of the myriad ways by which American society and culture shape the individual, much as the historian in Norman Douglas' *South Wind* felt compelled to ascertain the history of every pebble before he could know the history of his beloved island.

In the view taken here, therefore, education is defined some-what more narrowly, as the deliberate or purposeful creation, evocation, or transmission of knowledge, abilities, skills, and values. To emphasize the deliberate and the purposeful is not to deny that non-deliberate influences may be more powerful; it is to assert that man cannot depend upon a casual process of learning. Unless men are to be forced to rediscover all knowledge for themselves, they must be educated, which is to say that education, to be education, must be purposeful.

It is one thing to say that education must be purposeful; it is another to say what those purposes should be. The fashion in contemporary American writing about education holds that talk about purpose is a frightful bore. Dr. James B. Conant, probably the most prestigious and influential contemporary student of education, has confessed that "a sense of distasteful weariness overtakes" him whenever he hears someone discussing educational goals or philosophy. "In such a mood," he writes, "I am ready to define education as what goes on in schools and colleges"—a definition that has prevented him from asking whether what now goes on should go on. Martin Mayer, an influential educational journalist, is equally disdainful of talk about goals. "It is well to rid oneself of this business of the 'aims of education,' " he states flatly in his book *The Schools*. "Discussions on this subject are among the dullest and most fruitless of human pursuits."

But philosophical questions neither disappear nor resolve themselves by being ignored. Indeed, the question of purpose kept intruding itself throughout the course of the research, and even more, through the course of the writing. Writing is always painful, for it is a continuous process of dialogue with oneself, of confrontation with one's thoughts, ideas, and feelings. "As is true of any writing that comes out of one's own existence," Lillian Smith has said—and no serious writing can entirely avoid that source—"the experiences themselves [are] transformed during the act of writing by awareness of new meanings which settled down on them . . . the writer transcends her material in the act of looking at it, and since part of that material is herself, a metamorphosis takes place: *something happens within:* a new chaos, and then slowly, a new being." [Emphasis hers]

It was not until I was well into the writing, therefore—not until I had, over a summer, completed and abandoned a first crude draft—that I began to realize what a metamorphosis had taken place in me and in my thinking about education. In struggling to find my theme, I discovered that my views had changed profoundly. I had not thought hard enough about educational purpose until the agony of writing forced me to; I thought I *knew* what the purpose of education should be: namely, intellectual development. "The United States today is moving away from progressivism," I had argued in 1961, and still believed when I started the study, "not because it is 'false' in some absolute sense, but because it badly serves the needs of our own time. The growing complexity of organization and the explosive pace of technological and social change are creating an enormous demand that is without historical precedent. Society has always needed a few men with highly developed and disciplined intellects; industrial society needed masses of literate but not necessarily intellectual men. Tomorrow requires something that the world has never seen—*masses of intellectuals.*" [Emphasis in the original][1]

I was wrong. What tomorrow needs is not masses of intellectuals, but masses of educated men—men educated to feel and to act as well as to think. "There is a horrible example in history of what the Educated Society might easily become," Peter F. Drucker has written, "unless the [society] commits itself to the education of the whole man. It is the destruction of one of the world's greatest and most creative civilizations, the China of the T'ang and Sung periods, by the imposition of a purely verbal, purely intellectual, purely analytical education on man in society, the Confucian canon. Within a century this commitment to the purely intellectual in man destroyed what had been the world's leader in art as well as in science, in technology as well as in philosophy. We are today in a similar danger . . ."

We don't have to go back that far to see the danger inherent in an education designed to cultivate the intellect alone. "One thing is essential to becoming a human being," according to Robert M. Hutchins, the foremost contemporary exponent of that view, "and that is learning to use the mind. A human being acts in a human way if he thinks."[2]

But he doesn't! The experience of the German university under Hitler should provide evidence enough, if evidence were

[1] Charles E. Silberman, "The Remaking of American Education," *Fortune,* April 1961.
[2] Robert M. Hutchins, *The Learning Society,* New York: Frederick A. Praeger, 1968. The writer is drawing as well on a long conversation with Hutchins.

needed, that thinking alone does not make a human being human.[3] Feeling is also needed, as in Yeats's lines:

> *God guard me from those thoughts men think*
> *In the mind alone;*
> *He that sings a lasting song*
> *Thinks in a marrow-bone.*

This is a lesson we may have learned to excess; the current tendency to celebrate the unthinking marrow-bone is as dangerous as the exaltation of the antiseptic mind, and as mistaken. The insistence that systematic and disciplined intellectual effort is a waste of time—the worship of uninhibited sensation and feeling that constitutes a newly fashionable anti-intellectualism of the intellectuals—at its best is sentimental foolishness.

More important, both this view and its opposite, the emphasis on disembodied intellect, represent badly mistaken conceptions of the nature of mind, which encompasses feeling no less than intellect, and intellect no less than feeling. The ancient Hebrews understood this well; the Biblical verb *yadah,* "to know," signifies a unification of intellect, feeling, and action. (In some contexts, it denotes sexual union as well, as in the familiar "And Adam knew [*yadah*] Eve, his wife.") Contemporary psychologists have the same understanding; in Jerome Bruner's phrase, "the scientist and the poet do not live at antipodes." On the contrary, the artificial separation of these aspects or modes of knowing—the false dichotomy between the "cognitive" and the "affective" domain—can only cripple the development of thought and feeling. If this be so, then poetry, music, painting, dance, and the other arts are not frills to be indulged in if time is left over from the real business of education; they *are* the business of education.

Giving the arts a central place is not enough, either; the crematoria were presided over by men who loved Wagner—some, even, by men who loved Mozart. What we must also realize—what I should have known from my own upbringing, and what three and a half years of sitting in on public school and college classes and immersing myself in the mass media drove home to me—is that education is inescapably a moral as well as in-

---

[3] In fairness to Hutchins, it should be noted that he dismisses the German experience as irrelevant, insisting that one should argue from the ideal, not from its corruption.

tellectual and esthetic enterprise. "The moral purpose," as John Dewey emphasized in his neglected little classic, *Moral Principles in Education,* is "universal and dominant in all instruction—whatsoever the topic."

This is not to say that education is or ever should be moralistic. There is a world of difference, as Dewey also pointed out, between "moral ideas"—ideas internalized so as to affect and improve conduct, to "make it better than it otherwise would be"—and "ideas about morality"—the pieties we acknowledge verbally and then proceed to ignore. Talking *about* morality, honesty, or kindness in no way insures that people will act morally, honestly, or kindly. The job of the educator is to teach in such a way as to convert "ideas about morality" into "moral ideas." In the words of a Talmudic axiom, "Let not thy learning exceed thy deeds. Mere knowledge is not the goal, but action."

What educators must realize, moreover, is that how they teach and how they act may be more important than what they teach. The way we do things, that is to say, shapes values more directly and more effectively than the way we talk about them. Certainly administrative procedures like automatic promotion, homogeneous grouping, racial segregation, or selective admission to higher education affect "citizenship education" more profoundly than does the social studies curriculum. And children are taught a host of lessons about values, ethics, morality, character, and conduct every day of the week, less by the content of the curriculum than by the way schools are organized, the ways teachers and parents behave, the way they talk to children and to each other, the kinds of behavior they approve or reward and the kinds they disapprove or punish. These lessons are far more powerful than the verbalizations that accompany them and that they frequently controvert.

To say that this book is about educational purpose, therefore, is not to say that it is an exercise in academic philosophy, still less to suggest that it is concerned with abstractions and exhortation. My intent, at least—how successfully, only the reader can judge—is to discuss "moral ideas," not "ideas about morality"; to discuss, in concrete detail, the ways in which schools, colleges, and mass media educate: not only *what* they teach, but *how* they teach, and in particular the manifold and frequently unconscious ways in which how they teach determines what it is that people actually learn. This is, in addition, a book about how the schools should be improved, about how they *can* be improved, the case for change being argued in the main through descriptions of schools in operation now; and it is a book about how colleges and universities might help bring these changes about by educating new kinds of educators and by developing the knowledge on which their performance might be based.

It is also, I should add, an indignant book. I am indignant at the banality of the mass media: no one concerned with the quality of American life can avoid a sense of sickening disappointment over the Vast Wasteland that public as well as commercial television has turned out to be. Nor can much more satisfaction be derived from contemplating the rest of the mass media. I am indignant, too, at the narcissism of so many college professors and administrators who, at least until prodded by student rebels, refused to think about the nature and content of liberal education, particularly about the ways in which knowledge may have to be reordered to make it teachable to a new generation. And I am indignant at the smug disdain with which most academicians view the problems of the public schools.

Most of all, however, I am indignant at the failures of the public schools themselves. "The most deadly of all possible sins," Erik Erikson suggests, "is the mutilation of a child's spirit." It is not possible to spend any prolonged period visiting public school classrooms without being appalled by the mutilation visible everywhere—mutilation of spontaneity, of joy in learning, of pleasure in creating, of sense of self. The public schools— those "killers of the dream," to appropriate a phrase of Lillian Smith's—are the kind of institution one cannot really dislike until one gets to know them well. Because adults take the schools so much for granted, they fail to appreciate what grim, joyless places most American schools are, how oppressive and petty are the rules by which they are governed, how intellectually sterile and esthetically barren the atmosphere, what an appalling lack of civility obtains on the part of teachers and principals, what contempt they unconsciously display for children as children.

And it need not be! Public schools *can* be organized to facilitate joy in learning and esthetic expression and to develop character—in the rural and urban slums no less than in the prosperous suburbs. This is no utopian hope; as I shall argue and demonstrate in the chapters that follow, there are models now in existence that can be followed.

What makes change possible, moreover, is that what is mostly wrong with the public schools is due not to venality or indifference or stupidity, but to mindlessness. To be sure, teaching has its share of sadists and clods, of insecure and angry men and women who hate their students for their openness, their exuberance, their color or their affluence. But by and large, teachers, principals, and superintendents are decent, intelligent, and caring people who try to do their best by their lights. If they make a botch of it, and an uncomfortably large number do, it is because it simply never occurs to more than a handful to ask *why* they are doing what they are doing—to think seriously or deeply about the purposes or consequences of education.

This mindlessness—the failure or refusal to think seriously about educational purpose, the reluctance to question established practice—is not the monopoly of the public school; it is diffused remarkably evenly throughout the entire educational system, and indeed the entire society. "The problem of policy-making in our society," Henry A. Kissinger has said, "confronts the difficulty that revolutionary changes have to be encompassed and dealt with by an increasingly rigid administrative structure. . . . an increasing amount of energy has to be devoted to keeping the existing machine going, and in the nature of things there isn't enough time to inquire into the purpose of these activities. The temptation is great to define success by whether one fulfills certain programs, however accidentally these programs may have been arrived at. The question is whether it is possible in the modern bureaucratic state to develop a sense of long-range purpose and to inquire into the meaning of the activity." Kissinger was talking about the problems of government; he might just as well have been talking about higher education and the mass media.

If mindlessness is the central problem, the solution must lie in infusing the various educating institutions with purpose, more important, with thought about purpose, and about the ways in which techniques, content, and organization fulfill or alter purpose. And given the tendency of institutions to confuse day-to-day routine with purpose, to transform the means into the end itself, the infusion cannot be a one-shot affair. The process of self-examination, of "self-renewal," to use John Gardner's useful term, must be continuous. We must find ways of stimulating educators—public school teachers, principals, and superintendents; college professors, deans, and presidents; radio, television, and film directors and producers; newspaper, magazine, and TV journalists and executives—to think about what they are doing, and why they are doing it. And we must persuade the general public to do the same.

2

American Education: Success or Failure?

The observer who is desirous of forming an opinion on the state of instruction among the Anglo-Americans must consider the same object from two different points of view. If he singles out only the learned, he will be astonished to find how few they are; but if he counts the ignorant, the American people will appear to be the most enlightened in the world. The whole population . . . is situated between these two extremes.

—ALEXIS DE TOCQUEVILLE,
Democracy in America, *1837*

I

To study American education in this last third of the twentieth century is to be struck by a paradox. On the one hand, the system would appear to be in grave trouble, with the very concept of public education coming under question, from critics on the left as well as the right. In most large cities and a good many smaller ones, for example, the public schools are in disarray, torn apart by conflicts over integration, desegregation, decentralization, and community control. Writing in a *New York Times Magazine* article, later expanded into a book, Martin Mayer described a 1968 teachers' strike as "the worst disaster" New York had experienced in his lifetime, "comparable in its economic impact to an earthquake that would destroy Manhattan below Chambers Street, much worse in its social effect than a major race riot," and likely to reduce the New York City school system "to the condition of a Boston or an Alabama." While many would disagree with Mayer's version of what happened, few would question the seriousness of the conflict.

Nor are the large urban centers alone. In a good many placid cities, towns and suburbs, seemingly sheltered, however temporarily, from racial conflict, schools have been closed by taxpayer revolts, teacher strikes, or student dissent. All three are growing. In a four-month period, for example (November and December of 1968 and January and February of 1969), Professor Alan Westin, director of the Center for Research and Education in American Liberties at Columbia University's Teachers College, has reported, some 348 high schools in thirty-eight states and the District of Columbia experienced serious disruption as a result of student protests. The disruptions occurred in every kind of school in every kind of community in every part of the country—in Tucson, Arizona; Edcouch, Texas; Middletown, Connecticut; Billings, Montana; Minneapolis, Minnesota; and Brooklyn, N.Y., to name only a few. Some 60 percent of a sample of high school principals surveyed at their annual convention in March 1969, in fact, reported that they had experienced significant student protests in their schools during the school year.

Colleges and universities would seem to face equally serious, if somewhat different, problems. As the 1960s were ending, hardly a major institution of higher education had escaped student demonstrations and disturbances, some on a scale amounting almost to insurrection, with acts of violence and sabotage becoming more frequent. The base of this dissent is much broader than had generally been assumed; the relative handful of activists draws support from a surprisingly large minority of students—perhaps as many as 40 percent.[1] Threats, demands, and defections from faculty members were also increasing, sometimes involving faculty grievances unrelated to, or in opposition to, student demands.

At the same time, student and faculty dissent was evoking a growing backlash on the part of alumni and contributors, state legislatures and boards of trustees, the United States Congress,

[1] Cf. Daniel Seligman, "A Special Kind of Rebellion," *Fortune,* January 1969, and the special survey, "What They Believe," in the same issue. (The articles have been reprinted in book form under the title *Youth in Turmoil,* New York: Time-Life Books, 1969.)

and the public at large—including, most prominently, the President of the United States and the governor of its most populous state. This backlash draws on, and enlarges, the anti-intellectualism that has been endemic to American society since its very beginnings. If it were to continue, therefore, the backlash could threaten not just the financial stability but ultimately the independence of the nation's colleges and universities, and through them the intellectual life and cultural tone of the whole society.

Sociologists like to distinguish between "important" problems—the sometimes undramatic and usually intractable problems that persist for some time—and those that are merely "urgent," catching the headlines of the moment but giving way fairly rapidly to some newer concern. The problems now affecting the public schools and the colleges and universities are both urgent and important, involving as they do the most basic conflicts over purpose, structure, and power.

And yet from another perspective, the United States educational system appears to be superbly successful—on almost any measure, performing better than it did ten, twenty, fifty, or a hundred years ago. Consider the United States system of higher education, which educational reformers in almost every European country now regard as their model. The United States has succeeded in doing what, until very recently, almost every European educator and a good many Americans insisted could *not* be done. It has managed to insure intellectual excellence and creative scholarship in a system of mass higher education. It has combined what the sociologist Martin Trow calls the traditional or "elite" function of the university—the transmission of high culture and the creation of new knowledge—with its "popular" functions, i.e., educating large numbers of students, particularly for professions and vocations, and providing other services to the society.[2]

Certainly the vast expansion and democratization of higher education in the 1950s and 1960s is an extraordinary achievement in and of itself, however one judges its ultimate significance or value. College attendance, once the almost exclusive prerogative of those with wealth, social position, or extraordinary talent and ambition, is coming to be viewed as the right of every American youth, and social mobility from generation to generation increasingly takes the form of providing one's children with more education than the parents received. Access to higher

[2] Cf. Martin Trow, "Reflections on the Transition from Mass to Universal Higher Education," *Daedalus,* Winter 1970.

education is not yet universal, by any means—race and social class are still significant factors—but the United States has taken giant steps in that direction. The national bill for higher education came to more than $20 billion in 1969–70, when more than 7,500,000 students—triple the number of the mid-1950s and more than five times the pre–World War II figure—were attending one or another of the 2,500 institutions of higher education. These institutions now enroll more than 40 percent of the population of college age, compared with 14 percent in 1939 and 8–10 percent in Great Britain today.

This explosion in numbers has been accompanied by an equally extraordinary expansion in the university's active participation in the affairs of society. James B. Conant tells of offering his services to Newton D. Baker, then Secretary of War, when the United States entered World War I; Dr. Conant, at the time, was president of the American Chemical Society. Baker very graciously thanked Conant and told him he would inquire where he might fruitfully serve. The next day he called back to say, "Thank you, Dr. Conant, but the War Department tells me they already have a chemist." They have more than one now.

The university serves more than just the military, of course; as the French journalist and editor J. J. Servan-Schreiber has written, Americans have worked out "a close association between business, universities, and the government which has never been perfected nor successful in any European country." There is a close association, too, between the universities and the professions (medicine, law, engineering, teaching, architecture, journalism, social work), not to mention the pseudo-professions (public relations, traffic management, hotel management). "Our universities," Martin Trow writes, "are deeply involved in the life of the society, and contribute much to the efforts to solve its problems, from social medicine to the problems of the inner city."

Whether universities *should* be this deeply involved in the affairs of society is something else again. Should universities and colleges retain or rebuild their ivy walls, or should they breach the walls and immerse themselves in the affairs of their immediate neighborhoods or the larger communities they serve? Should they serve business and the military, or should they limit their service activities to problems of urban decay, poverty, health, and the like? Should they prepare students for a wide variety of professions and occupations, or should they limit themselves to more traditional, or liberal, education? These questions are central to the future of higher education, and they defy simple answers.

What is critical at this point is the fact, contrary to most expectations, that this vast expansion in the American university's "popular" functions has *not* come at the expense of its "elite" functions. Quality has turned out to be compatible with quantity; some of the greatest American universities, e.g., Berkeley, Wisconsin, Michigan, Texas, are among the largest, and the most deeply immersed in service functions.

Most institutions, from the lowliest municipal or state colleges to the most elite liberal arts colleges and universities, have been able to raise the level of instruction and of their students' academic performance over the course of the last twenty years. The reasons are clear enough. The democratization of college education and the general reduction in religious and ethnic prejudice inside the university and out have vastly expanded the pool of talent from which both faculty members and students are drawn. While the proportion of college-age students attending college has increased dramatically, the increase thus far has come largely from the top of the academic talent pool. In 1953, for example, only 48 percent of high school students graduating in the top quarter of their class went to college; by 1960, the proportion had jumped to 80 percent.[3] During that same period, there was no increase at all in the proportion of students in the bottom half going to college. As a result, the elite institutions have been able to be more selective as they fished in a larger pool; there was more truth than jest to the warning Nathan Pusey gave a few years ago to a group of Harvard alumni: "Unless your sons are a lot brighter than you, they won't be able to get into Harvard." And increasing selectivity by the elite institutions has made it possible, in turn, for institutions of lesser prestige to raise their admission standards, and so on down the line.

The most spectacular improvement in the university's performance, however, and in many ways the least expected, has been in its creation of new knowledge through scholarship and research. With all the talk about the "brain drain" to the United States from Western Europe and the underdeveloped nations, it comes as a surprise to remember that forty years ago, any serious American student of the sciences *had* to go to Europe for

---

[3] The corollary, of course, is that future increases in the proportion of high school graduates going on to college will have to come predominantly from the second, third, and fourth quarters rather than from the top.

his graduate or postgraduate education. When he studied in Germany in the 1920s, the great physicist and Nobel Laureate I. I. Rabi has recalled, so little of consequence was happening in United States research that German universities used to arrange to get an entire year's set of the *Physical Review* from the United States at one time, in order to save postage.

And in these days when critics, quite rightly, flail the universities for subordinating the teaching of undergraduates to graduate training and research, it is useful to reread Abraham Flexner's great polemic of 1930, *Universities: American English German,* in which he called upon United States universities to stop coddling undergraduates in order to get on with their main task of training scholars and adding to the store of knowledge. The democratization of higher education that had already begun, Flexner argued—the creation of university schools of business, social work, journalism, library service, etc.—had turned American universities on a disastrous downward course, in contrast to the German universities, whose "most serious" problem he reported to be "lack of money." As a result, the United States had no university worthy of the name—"neither Columbia, nor Harvard, nor Johns Hopkins, nor Chicago, nor Wisconsin." In Flexner's view, the decline was calamitous. "Fifty years ago," he wrote, "the degree of Ph.D. had a meaning in the United States; today it has practically no significance. The same is true of research." Yet when Flexner wrote, as Clark Kerr points out, only 5 percent of the Nobel Prizes were held by Americans; today the figure is upwards of 40 percent.[4]

The improvement in elementary and secondary education has been substantial, if less dramatic. The public schools are enrolling more youngsters, both absolutely and as a proportion of population, than ever before—more than any other society save Japan has ever tried to educate. In the 1969–70 school year, for example, the public schools enrolled more than forty-five million students, at an annual cost of more than $35 billion; the schools employed an instructional staff (teachers, principals, librarians, guidance counselors, etc.) of 2,100,000 or thereabouts. Expenditures *per pupil* have more than doubled since the end of World War II, after adjusting for changes in the purchasing power of the dollar. Three students out of four now finish high school; in 1929, three out of four did not go beyond the eighth grade.

4 Clark Kerr, "Remembering Flexner," Introduction to Abraham Flexner, *Universities: American English German,* New York: Oxford University Press, paperback edition, 1968.

Contrary to popular impression, the high school "dropout rate" is declining; the proportion finishing high school has risen from 58 percent as recently as 1955 to the current rate of 75 percent or thereabouts, and is expected to reach 85 percent by the mid-1970s. The gap between the quantity, if not the quality, of education offered whites and blacks has also been declining; between 1952 and 1968, the proportion of Negroes completing four years of high school or more increased two and a half times. Hence the locus of Negro discontent is shifting from the "dropout problem" to preparation for and admission to college.

Longer and more expensive schooling does not necessarily mean better schooling. The critical question is whether students are learning any more as a result of their longer exposure to the public schools. The answer would appear to be yes. Evidence is fragmentary; for reasons that lie deep both in the nation's psyche and in the politics of its educational system, we have remarkably little information on how much students learn from school, or on how much they know, whatever the sources of their knowledge.[5] The U.S. Office of Education's annual *Digest of Educational Statistics* for 1969, for example, contains 128 pages with 170 tables, only one of which contains data on what students are learning.

It is possible to piece some information together, however. The Educational Testing Service, for example, has assembled some 186 instances in which comparable tests had been given to large and roughly representative national samples of students at two different times during the postwar period. In all but ten of these 186 paired comparisons, the group tested at the later date scored higher than the group tested earlier; the results suggest an improvement, on average, of about 20 percent.[6] The results are hardly definitive, but neither can they be dismissed out of hand. "Until better evidence is presented," the Department of Health, Education and Welfare argues, "the tentative judgment must be that American children in the sixties are learning more than their older brothers and sisters learned in the fifties."

---

[5] A major effort to develop such information on a systematic basis is now under way under the auspices of the Committee on Assessing the Progress of Education, a non-profit body funded by the Carnegie Corporation of New York, the Ford Foundation, and the U.S. Office of Education.
[6] U.S. Department of Health, Education and Welfare, *Toward a Social Report*, pp. 66–70, Washington, D.C.: U.S. Government Printing Office, 1969.

II

Why, then, the pervasive sense of crisis? How explain the fact that an educational system that appears to be superbly successful from one standpoint appears to be in grave trouble from another? The question cannot be answered with regard to education alone; it is, in fact, the central paradox of American life. In almost every area, improvements beyond what anyone thought possible fifty or twenty-five or even ten years ago have produced anger and anxiety rather than satisfaction.[7] In the decade of the 1960s alone, national output increased by nearly 50 percent, after adjusting for changes in the purchasing power of the dollar; the average American's spendable income increased by nearly one-third, after allowing for both price increases and higher taxes. Unemployment declined by 40 percent while the number of jobs increased by ten million, or 15 percent. The number of people living below the poverty line (an income of $3,335 for a non-farm family of four) declined from nearly forty million in 1960 to 25.4 million in 1968. Yet despite the diffusion of affluence, the United States in 1969 was a nation wracked by conflicts over poverty, race, unemployment, slums, and crime.

One reason, without question, is that the improvements themselves, together with the spate of social legislation passed in the 1960s, generated expectations for further improvements—improvements of a sort and at a rate that the society was unable, or unwilling, to fulfill. The "revolution of rising expectations" is not limited to the United States, of course, nor to the present moment of history. On the contrary, social discontent and rebellion frequently are the products of social improvement rather than of stagnation. The "conservatism of the destitute," as it has been called, tends to be deeper and more profound than the conservatism of the privileged.

It is only when men sense the possibility of improvement, in fact, that they become dissatisfied with their situation and rebel against it. And "with rebellion," as Albert Camus put it, "awareness is born," and with awareness, an impatience "which can extend to everything that [men] had previously accepted, and which is almost always retroactive." This retroactive impatience over things previously accepted in turn leads men to miscon-

[7] Cf. for example, Kermit Gordon, ed., *Agenda for the Nation,* New York: Doubleday, 1969.

strue improvement in their condition as deterioration, for the improvement rarely keeps pace with their expectations. "The evil which was suffered patiently as inevitable seems unendurable as soon as the idea of escaping from it crosses men's minds," Tocqueville observed. "All the abuses then removed call attention to those that remain, and they now appear more galling. The evil, it is true, has become less, but sensibility to it has become more acute."

If this were so 130 years ago, and it was, how much more so it must be today, with the compression of time and space and the expansion of human possibility that modern technology has brought about. For generations, to "reach for the moon" was to aspire foolishly after the impossible; in the 1960s, reaching for the moon became an obsessive national purpose; in the summer of 1969, it was reached. The impact on our imaginations, on our sense of the possible, is beyond measure. If man can reach the moon, if he can "walk" in outer space, if he can harness the power of the cosmos, people began to ask and their leaders to suggest, why could he not also abolish poverty and injustice, eradicate slums, eliminate crime, cure cancer, educate everyone, and so on. The United States and Soviet achievements in space thus became a lever to raise expectations of every sort, and to create a sense of disappointment, of anger, of betrayal, when they were not immediately or fully realized.

Yet contemporary technology has contributed to a pervasive sense of helplessness and impending doom at the same time that it has evoked expectations of nirvana. Man as Victim of Technology has emerged as one of the most insistent themes of our time. The theme is hardly new; men have always felt an irresistible urge to master nature and have always harbored a deep-seated fear that the attempt would anger the gods and bring about their own downfall. This ambivalence is one of the most persistent themes of mythology and legend. The price of eating of the Tree of Knowledge—of daring "to be as God"—was expulsion from Eden. For daring to give man the gift of fire, Prometheus was condemned to savage torture. And every age has had its own variation on the theme of the sorcerer's apprentice: the young apprentice, too lazy to fill his master's water barrel by his own labor, invokes some fragments of an incantation he has overheard and puts the broom to work fetching water. The broom does so with dispatch; but soon the barrel begins to overflow, and the lad, ignorant of the incantation needed to stop the broom, is powerless to intervene. In the traditional version, the sorcerer returns in time to stop the broom and save the boy from drowning. In the contemporary myth, disaster seems to be unavoidable.[8]

The apocalyptic vision extends beyond technology; a new consensus of anxiety seems to have taken hold of the nation. "Societies, perhaps more than individuals," the journalist and social critic Max Ways has written, "are susceptible to mysterious disorders arising from discrepancies between what exists and what the society perceives." In the nineteenth and early twentieth centuries, we tended to see things as better than they were; our vision was clouded by an unquestioning optimism, a naïve faith in the inevitability and beneficence of Progress. As a result, we tended to ignore the realities of poverty, injustice, and racial oppression. Now, Ways argues, the old euphoric "Bright Perception" has been replaced by an equally unquestioning and unrealistic "Dark Perception" that makes us ignore or deprecate the improvements that do occur. A society that used to see the proverbial glass as half full now sees it as half empty.[9]

It is more complicated than that, and it would be a serious mistake to conclude that our current difficulties are in ourselves alone and not in our institutions. Some of the current pessimism is exaggerated and misdirected; few things are more irritating than the mindless insistence that our problems represent a fall from some prior state of grace, a state of grace that never existed except in the critics' romantic imaginings. "Why, in order for people to say that what is going on now is bad," David Riesman plaintively asks, "do they have to say that it was once better?" With rare exceptions, it was not.

But to say that it was once worse—to point out that things are better than they used to be, better even than anyone had thought they might be—is not to demonstrate that they are as good as they should or could be. In part, what Ways calls the "Dark Perception" is simply a long overdue sensitivity to social ills that should have troubled us all along. Here, the mass media have played a powerful role in forcing poverty and bloodshed over the threshold of our awareness; we are the first nation in history to watch a war in the comfort of our bedroom. The impact on the disadvantaged may be even greater. If the poor, as Michael Harrington has it, are invisible, the affluent certainly

[8] Cf. Charles E. Silberman and the Editors of *Fortune, The Myths of Automation,* New York: Harper & Row, 1966.
[9] Max Ways, "O Say Can You See? The Crisis in Our National Perception," *Fortune,* October 1968.

are not; through commercials as well as the programs themselves, television daily projects the poorest Negro American
into the living rooms and patios of the comfortable middle class.

In good measure, too, the consensus of anxiety that afflicts us
grows out of a new and growing concern with the quality of life
—a belated discovery, if you will, that man does not live by
bread alone, that affluence leaves some old problems unsolved
and at the same time creates some new ones. Thus, economic
growth reduces poverty, but it also produces congestion, noise,
and pollution of the environment. Technological change widens
the individual's range of choice and makes economic growth
possible; it also dislocates workers from their jobs and their
neighborhoods. Affluence plus new technology frees men from
slavery to the struggle for existence, from the brutalizing labor
that had been man's condition since Adam; it thereby forces
them to confront the questions of life's meaning and purpose
even while it destroys the faith that once provided answers. Our
anxiety is of the spirit.

It is not only affluence that poses problems or causes anxiety,
however. The enormous widening of choice that contemporary
society makes possible also appears as something of a mixed
blessing, enhancing our sense of individuality, but contributing,
too, to the pervasive sense of uneasiness and malaise. In past
ages, and in much of the world today, as the sociologist Edward
Shils writes, "hunger and imminence of death, work such as we
in the West would regard as too burdensome even for beasts,
over very long hours, prevented the development of individuality."[10] Men inherited their occupations, their status, their religion, and their life style; their wives were selected for them;
and their struggle to survive gave them little time to question
anything. Today, by contrast, they are presented with a bewildering range of options; they are forced to choose their occupations, jobs, places to live, marital partners, number of children, religion, political allegiance and affiliation, friendships,
allocation of income, and life style. This widening of the range
of choice and enhancement of individuality have had the effect
of reducing the authority of tradition, which in turn requires
still more choices to be exercised.

The burden is heavy. The choices are frightening, for they

[10] Edward Shils, "Daydreams and Nightmares: Reflections on the Criti-
cism of Mass Culture," *Sewanee Review,* Vol. 65 (1957), pp. 587–608.
Cf. also Emmanuel Mesthene, *Technological Change,* Cambridge, Mass:
Harvard University Press, 1970.

require the individual, perhaps for the first time in history, to choose, and in a sense to create, his own identity. The young rebels understand this well, even though their rhetoric sometimes obscures it. The rebels, that is to say, complain about their loss of identity and individuality, about their helplessness in the face of manipulative large organizations and technologies. But their actions, as Peter Drucker points out, make it clear that it is the burden of choice that really torments or frightens them, and which many understandably try to postpone as long as possible. It is not coincidental that rebellion among white students is concentrated among youngsters from the upper middle class, second- or third- or fourth-generation college students who take it for granted that they will be able to earn a comfortable living without difficulty. This lack of concern about money, more than anything else, distinguishes the rebels from their less affluent, less rebellious, and more vocationally oriented fellow students.[11]

What these "new" students understand, far better than their parents, is that the choice of a career involves far more than a choice of how to earn a livelihood. They understand, viscerally if not intellectually, that the question, "What shall I do?" really means "What shall I do with myself?" or rather, "What shall I make of myself?" And that means asking "Who am I?" "What do I want to be?" "What values do I want to serve?" "To whom, and to what, do I want to be responsible?" As Drucker rightly observes, "These are existential questions, for all that they are couched in secular form and appear as choices between a job in government, in business, or in college teaching."[12] That the students' answers are not always relevant is less important than the fact that they are forcing us to confront the most fundamental questions of value and purpose.

Part of what we must confront is the fact that many of the young are rejecting values, goals, and identities we have always taken for granted—values, goals, and identities we have regarded as intrinsic parts of the social fabric. What is new, it must be understood, is not the generational conflict itself; four thousand years before Christ, an Egyptian priest carved in stone what contemporary parents are lamenting: "Our earth is degenerate . . . children no longer obey their parents." Nor is there anything new in college protests—not even in the vio-

[11] Daniel Seligman, "A Special Kind of Rebellion."
[12] Peter F. Drucker, *The Age of Discontinuity,* New York: Harper & Row, 1969.

lent ones. The first, and most successful, "student power" movement was organized at the University of Bologna in the twelfth
and thirteenth centuries, and student riots were endemic to the
medieval university.[13] In eighteenth- and nineteenth-century
American colleges, too, students were constantly waging war
with the faculty, whom they generally viewed as the enemy, and
violence was almost commonplace. "Among the victims of the
collegiate way," Frederick Rudolph writes, "were the boy who
died in a duel at Dickinson, the students who were shot at
Miami in Ohio, the professor who was killed at the University
of Virginia, the president of Oakland College in Mississippi who
was stabbed to death by a student, the president and professor
who were stoned at the University of Georgia, the student who
was stabbed at Illinois College, the students who were stabbed
and killed at the University of Missouri and the University of
North Carolina."[14] Large-scale student rebellions took place,
moreover, at Princeton, Miami University, Amherst, Brown,
University of South Carolina, Williams, Georgetown, University
of North Carolina, Harvard, Yale, Dartmouth, Lafayette, Bow-
doin, City College of New York, Dickinson, and DePauw.[15]
And since 1870, at the least, there has been "a steady stream of
serious student protests" in high schools in such cities as New
York, Chicago, and Gary, Indiana.[16]

In the United States, however, unlike such countries as Russia,
Germany, China, and Japan, young people rarely challenged
the legitimacy of their parents', or their university's, or their
government's authority. They claimed that authority had been
abused or that the wrong people were exercising it; at times they
simply defied authority. They rarely questioned the legitimacy of
authority itself.

They are questioning it now! Indeed, they are questioning not
only the legitimacy but the very concept of authority. "The most
dangerous intellectual aspect of the contemporary scene," the
sociologist Robert A. Nisbet states, is the refusal of the young,

[13] Hastings Rashdall, *The Universities of Europe in the Middle Ages,*
New York: Oxford University Press, 1936 edition.
[14] Frederick Rudolph, *The American College and University,* New York:
Vintage Books, 1962.
[15] Lewis S. Feuer, *The Conflict of Generations,* New York: Basic Books,
1969.
[16] Alan F. Westin, "Civic Education in a Crisis Age," paper delivered at
the Conference on the School and the Democratic Environment, sponsored by the Danforth Foundation and the Ford Foundation, April 10,
1969 (mimeographed).

and of the would-be-young, "to distinguish between authority and power. They see the one as being as much a threat to liberty as the other. But this way lies madness," for "there can be no possible freedom in society apart from authority." Authority, after all, is "built into the very fabric of human association," being rooted in the relationships and loyalties of the members of a group, whether family, church, university, or state, and derived from the function the group or institution performs. Power is necessary to authority only when the function from which it derives has been weakened or when, for whatever reasons, allegiance has been shifted to some other institution.[17]

There are, moreover, many forms of authority besides the ones we generally think of—the state, the church, the school, the university—when we use the term. As Nisbet states, "There is the authority of learning and taste; of syntax and grammar in language; of scholarship, of science, and of the arts. In traditional culture there is an authority attaching to the names of Shakespeare, Montaigne, Newton, and Pasteur in just as sure a sense of the word as though we were speaking of the law. There is the authority of logic, reason, and of genius. Above all, there is the residual authority of the core of values around which Western culture has been formed"—among them, the values of justice, reason, equity, liberty, charity, morality, which until the sixties, conservatives, liberals, and radicals alike recognized. "It was culture and its authority on which minds as diverse as Newman, Spencer, Marx, and even Proudhon rested their causes." Indeed, anarchist that he was, Nisbet writes, "no one could have surpassed Proudhon in his recognition of the necessity of authority in the social order; the authority of the family, the community, the guild; above all the authority of morality that he, as a member of the European community, recognized as the indispensable framework of culture and of social justice."

Contemporary radicals of the over-thirty variety have continued in this tradition. "We are not only free organisms but parts of mankind that has historically made itself with great inspirations and terrible conflicts," Paul Goodman, the contemporary Proudhon, writes, in attacking A. S. Neill of Summerhill fame for his "latitudinarian lack of standards," e.g., his insistence that Beethoven and rock 'n roll are equivalent. "We cannot slough off that accumulation, however burdensome,"

[17] Robert A. Nisbet, "The Twilight of Authority," *The Public Interest,* Number 15, Spring 1969.

Goodman adds, "without becoming trivial and therefore servile."[18]

But what the young rebels are trying to do is precisely that—to "slough off" the accumulation of past achievements, creations and discoveries that constitutes contemporary culture and, for the older generation, gives it its authority. Indeed, we cannot understand the crisis in education—the crisis in society and culture as a whole, in the United States and in virtually every other advanced industrial society—except in terms of the fact that many of the young are questioning, and some rejecting altogether, the authority of culture and morality as well as of law. "I can't make clear to a young lady at the Antioch-Putney School of Education," Goodman plaintively reports, "that a child has an historical right to know that there is a tie between Venus and the Sun and thanks to Newton we know its equation, which is even more beautiful than the Evening Star; it is *not* a matter of taste whether he knows this or not."

But the most rebellious among the young insist that it *is* a matter of taste, for they do not recognize the authority of knowledge, of skill, of simple truth; to a frightening degree, they do not even understand the concept. When they question the college administration's authority, say, to make parietal rules or take disciplinary action for infractions of other rules, they are challenging the legitimacy of there being any rules at all. More to the point, when they question the administration's or the faculty's right to make or enforce academic regulations, they frequently are denying that there are, or can be, standards of learning or of scholarship. "The disinterested ideals of science and art are hardly mentioned and do not seem to operate publicly at all," Goodman writes, with only partial exaggeration, "and the sacredness of these ideals no longer exists even on college campuses. Almost no young person of college age believes that there are autonomous professionals or has even heard of such a thing."

It was his experience in teaching a course on "Professionalism" at The New School for Social Research in 1967, in fact, that first made Goodman aware of the degree to which the new generation which he had helped produce did not share—did not even understand—the assumptions about knowledge and society

---

[18] "The Present Moment in Education," *New York Review of Books*, April 10, 1969. This essay and another by Goodman ("The New Reformation," *New York Times Magazine*, September 14, 1969) constitute a most illuminating explanation of the new generation gap.

that he took for granted. The professionals whom Goodman brought to class to explain "the obstacles that stood in the way of honest practice, and their own life experience in circumventing them," were uniformly and unanimously rejected by the students, who called them "liars, finks, mystifiers, or deluded," repeating, by way of explanation, what the guests had themselves pointed out. In exploring why the students had not listened, Goodman "came to the deeper truth, that they did not believe in the existence of real professions at all; professions were concepts of repressive society and 'linear thinking.' I asked them to envisage any social order they pleased—Mao's, Castro's, some anarchist utopia—and wouldn't there be engineers who knew about materials and stresses and strains? Wouldn't people get sick and need to be treated? Wouldn't there be problems of communication? No, they insisted; it was important only to be human, and all else would follow." Goodman continues:

> Suddenly I realized that they did not really believe that there was a nature of things. Somehow all functions could be reduced to interpersonal relations and power. There was no knowledge, but only the sociology of knowledge. They had so well learned that physical and sociological research is subsidized and conducted for the benefit of the ruling class that they did not believe there was such a thing as simple truth. To be required to learn something was a trap by which the young were put down and co-opted. Then I knew that I could not get through to them. I had imagined that the worldwide student protest had to do with changing political and moral institutions, to which I was sympathetic, but I now saw that we had to do with a religious crisis of the magnitude of the Reformation in the fifteen-hundreds . . .[19]

There is a risk, to be sure, in generalizing too loosely about "the young." Goodman, after all, is talking about the most alienated among them, and as he points out, styles in student rebellion follow one another with bewildering speed, the young rebels being as ignorant of their own history as they are of everyone else's. "I am often hectored to my face," he writes, "with formulations that I myself put in their mouths, that have become part of the oral tradition two years old, author prehistoric."[20] But when all the qualifications are made, it is hard

[19] "The New Reformation," *New York Times Magazine*, September 14, 1969.

[20] One of the measures of the rebels' alienation, of the degree to which they have cut themselves off from everything but their own insistent

to escape the conclusion that the *zeitgeist* Goodman describes is shared more widely than we have so far dared to acknowledge or face. As noted earlier, at least 40 percent of college students share some of the attitudes of the active dissidents, and all the evidence suggests that their number is rising. It is also clear that dissent and alienation are moving rapidly into the high school and even the junior high. And the extraordinary rock festivals in the summer of 1969—in Bethel, New York, Texas, Washington, the Isle of Wight—gave some hint of the reservoir of alienation that may lie beneath the surface.

In short, the crisis is real, involving as it does the most basic questions of meaning and purpose—the meaning and purpose of life itself. It may well be a religious or spiritual crisis of a depth and magnitude that has no parallel since the Reformation. Certainly it is akin to the profound personal predicament John Stuart Mill describes in his autobiography:

> Suppose that all your objects in life were realized: that all the changes in institutions and opinions which you are looking forward to could be completely effected at this very instant: would this be a great joy and happiness to you? And an irrepressible self-consciousness answered, 'No!' At this my heart sank within me: the whole foundation on which my life was constructed fell down.

There is little comfort, therefore, in the fact that the crisis stems more from the successes of American society than from its failure. As one student put it to the psychologist Kenneth Keniston, "You have to have grown up in Scarsdale to know how bad things really are." His comment "would probably sound arrogant, heartless and insensitive to a poor black," Keniston remarks, but it reflects the realization that "even in the Scarsdales of America, with their affluence, their upper-middle-class security and abundance, their well-fed, well-heeled children and their excellent schools, something is wrong."[21] Just *how* wrong

---

present, is the fact that they now seem to find Goodman "irrelevant." Having argued, in his most influential book, that the young were "Growing Up Absurd," Goodman now discovers his prediction was all too accurate.

[21] Kenneth Keniston, "You Have to Grow Up in Scarsdale to Know How Bad Things Really Are," *New York Times Magazine,* April 27, 1969. Cf. also Kenneth Keniston, *Young Radicals,* New York: Harcourt, Brace & World, 1968.

became evident a few months after Keniston's article appeared, when a substantial majority of Scarsdale's leading citizens expressed strong opposition to the board of education proposal to bus fifty—*50*—black first-graders from a neighboring community into Scarsdale's schools.

Nor is the sense that something is wrong limited to the Scarsdales of America. It is equally strong in the Brooklyns and Queenses, Dearborns, Chicagos, and Pittsburghs—the cities, suburbs, and towns that house the great middle class, the $5,000–$15,000-a-year blue- and white-collar workers who told a 1969 Gallup poll that the United States had changed for the worse during the preceding five years, and who expressed doubt about whether the nation could solve its problems at all.

The need of the moment, clearly, is not to celebrate our successes but to locate and remedy the weaknesses and failures. The test of a society, as of an institution, is not whether it is improving, although certainly such a test is relevant, but whether it is adequate to the needs of the present and of the foreseeable future. Our educating institutions fail that test: schools, colleges, churches, newspapers, magazines, television stations and networks, all fall short of what they could be, of what they *must* be if we are to find meaning and purpose in our lives, in our society, and in our world.

What follows, then, is one man's attempt to say what education should be—what education and particularly schooling *can* be in this eighth decade of the twentieth century. The criticisms of what is, and the recommendations for what should be, do not derive from any utopian vision of a world that exists only in the writer's imagination. On the contrary, the case for a transformation of the schools is argued throughout by way of detailed descriptions of schools that are operating now, in England and in almost every part of the United States, though theoretical arguments are used where pertinent. To remake the schools in these ways, it goes without saying, will be difficult in the extreme. Hence the last part of this book is concerned with the ways in which colleges and universities might use their considerable leverage for change by educating new kinds of educators, developing new knowledge, and providing assistance in other ways.

As we have already argued, education is not synonymous with schooling. There are other educating institutions, e.g., the mass media, whose power equals or exceeds that of the schools and colleges. To try to deal with all of them in anything like equal

detail would give this book a length and structure that would
make it unmanageable for any but the hardiest or most dedicated reader. The remaking of these other, less formal educating
institutions will have to be the subject, therefore, of another
volume. Before turning to the schools, in Parts II and III, and to
the colleges and universities, in Part IV, however, it might be
useful to provide at least a cursory sketch of the weaknesses and
failures of these other educating institutions, and some hint of
possible remedies.

III

"When we look realistically at the world in which we are living
today and become aware of what the actual problems of learning
are," the anthropologist Margaret Mead wrote in 1958, "our
conception of education changes radically. . . . We are no
longer dealing primarily with the *vertical* transmission of the
tried and true by the old, mature, and experienced teachers to
the young, immature, and inexperienced pupil. This was the
system of education developed in a stable, slowly changing culture. In a world of rapid change, vertical transmission of knowledge alone" is not enough. "What is needed," Dr. Mead argued,
"and what we are already moving toward is the inclusion of
another whole dimension of learning: the *lateral* transmission,
to every sentient member of society, of what has just been discovered, invented, created, manufactured, or marketed." The
need is acute: "the whole teaching-and-learning continuum,
which was once tied in an orderly and productive way to the
passing of generations and the growth of the child into a man—
this whole process has exploded in our faces."[22]

To be sure, Dr. Mead has exaggerated the degree of change
and, as a consequence, the obsolescence of our formal educational institutions. It simply is not true that "a subject taught to
college freshmen may have altered basically by the time the same
students are seniors," except conceivably in one or more of the
more esoteric branches of biology or biochemistry (and these
are not subjects which freshmen are likely to study). Nor is ours
the first society that has required lateral as well as vertical transmission of knowledge. Since the Reformation and the introduc-

[22] Margaret Mead, "Thinking Ahead: Why Is Education Obsolete?",
Harvard Business Review, XXXVI (November–December 1958), re-
printed in Ronald Gross, ed., *The Teacher and the Taught,* New York:
Dell Publishing, 1963.

tion of the printing press, at least, i.e., since the breakup of traditional society began, one of the functions of literature and the arts has been to make people aware of the discontinuities in life and society—in Marshall McLuhan's metaphor, to serve as an "early warning system." The novel, for example, developed at least in part as a means of "bringing the news" about changes in the social fabric. (Fielding's *Tom Jones* and Stendhal's *The Red and the Black* are particularly good examples.)

The distinction is crucial nonetheless. However much Dr. Mead may exaggerate, one can hardly doubt that the lateral transmission of knowledge has become, and will continue to become, more important relative to the vertical. It is this change that makes the mass media so important, for the lateral transmission of knowledge is what they are all about. No matter how well educated people may be in the traditional sense, they cannot understand the world in which they live and operate unless journalism gives them some understanding of what is happening outside their own sphere of knowledge and action.[23] In response to this need, the postwar period has seen a remarkable proliferation of journalistic media and an enormous extension of their range and power. (A fifth of mankind is reported to have watched the television coverage of astronauts Aldrin and Armstrong walking on the moon). These quantitative changes have been accompanied by an equally striking improvement in quality, reflecting both the rise in the mass audience's educational level and the fact that contemporary journalists are themselves better educated, more skillful, and far more serious about their work than their predecessors of even a decade or two ago. Compare, for example, the daily half-hour "Huntley-Brinkley Report" with the fifteen-minute "Camel News Caravan" with John Cameron Swayze and his carnation, which it replaced in 1956. (Some forty-four million people watch Huntley-Brinkley and Walter Cronkite each night.) Or compare a current issue of *Time, Newsweek, Life,* or *Look* with an issue of twenty years ago; both the advertising and the editorial content are more sophisticated.

And yet the media do not begin to meet the contemporary need. By and large, they do a competent job of reporting on the "urgent" problems of the day, which is to say they handle their

[23] We are using the term "journalism" in a broad sense, to include newspapers, newsmagazines, radio and television newscasts, documentaries, and informational programs, the press services, specialized magazines, trade union and corporate periodicals—all the media that report and comment on one or more segments of the current scene.

traditional function reasonably well. They do a poor job of dig-
ging out and analyzing the "important" problems before they become urgent; witness the way in which journalism, even after the
Supreme Court school desegregation decision of 1954, ignored
the problem of race until it erupted into violence,[24] or the superficiality and frequent distortion with which it has reported on the
rise of computers and of automation. They do an even poorer
job of sorting out and ordering the mass of data that bombards
us daily, of cutting through the babble that prevents or impedes
conversation between men in different countries, fields, or disciplines to create a community of discourse—in short, of finding
the *meaning* of the changes that confront and assault us on every
side. The result, as Max Ways has written, is that "even the most
powerful nation, with the highest production of new knowledge
. . . becomes pervaded by a sense of its own ignorance and
helplessness because it feels—correctly—that it has no adequate
view of its own direction."[25]

Nor are the failures limited to the journalistic media. As already mentioned, art and the entertainment media also play an
important role in the lateral transmission of knowledge. In our
time, films and, more recently, television have taken over the
largest part of that function. With 57.5 million homes—96.9
percent of all American homes—owning a total of 78 million
television sets and keeping them turned on an average of six and
a half hours a day, commercial television is the educational medium par excellence. Indeed, it is estimated that students being
graduated from high school today will have spent more time in
front of the video tube than in the classroom.

Students probably learn more about certain subjects from
television than from the schools, moreover; as the sociologist
Herbert J. Gans of Columbia University has suggested, television
and to a lesser extent the other mass media play a major role in
"bringing the news" about how to live in contemporary society.

[24] In all fairness, it should be pointed out that the journalists' myopia
was shared even more strongly by the historians, sociologists, political
scientists, psychologists and other members of academe. One measure of
the scholars' appalling failure even to recognize the existence of the
problem is the fact that Project Talent, a massive study of American
high school students, one of the largest social science surveys ever
conducted, did not even collect, let alone tabulate or analyze, data on
race. And yet the project began in 1960, six years after the Supreme
Court decision in *Brown v. Board of Education.*
[25] Max Ways, "What's Wrong with News? It Isn't New Enough," *Fortune,*
October 1969.

Television has taken over the mythic role in our culture; soap operas, situation comedies, Westerns, melodramas, et al., are folk stories or myths that convey and reinforce the values of the society. These programs and, equally important, the commercials that accompany them transmit a large amount of information relevant to these values or world view: what people are wearing, how the status system works, which occupations have status or promote mobility, how to outsmart authority, what products to consume and how, and so on. They convey a great deal of information relevant to—perhaps necessary for—socialization of the adult as well as of the child. "Almost all TV programs and magazine fiction teach something about American society," Gans writes.

For example, "Batman" is, from this vantage point, a course in criminology that describes how a superhuman aristocrat does a better job of eradicating crime than public officials. Similarly, the "Beverly Hillbillies" offer a course in social stratification and applied economics, teaching that with money, uneducated and uncultured people can do pretty well in American society, and can easily outwit more sophisticated and more powerful middle-class types. Television series such as "Bonanza" and "The Virginian," and most popular films and fiction, are in reality morality plays that show how a hero confronts a moral dilemma and how he finally makes a moral choice. These dilemmas are often quite contemporary and controversial; I have seen "Bonanza," one of the most popular TV programs, deal with questions of racial intolerance and intermarriage, albeit in a 19th century Western setting. Programs such as "Law and Mr. Jones," "East Side–West Side," and "The Defenders" have discussed pertinent social issues in contemporary settings, although they have been less popular from a rating standpoint. And even the innocuous family situation-comedies such as "Ozzie and Harriet" deal occasionally with ethical problems encountered on a neighborhood level, for example, how to help the socially isolated child or the unhappy neighbor.[26]

26 Herbert J. Gans, "The Mass Media as an Educational Institution," *The Urban Review*, Vol. 2, No. 1 (February 1967). Cf. also Herbert J. Gans, *The Uses of Television and Their Educational Implication: Preliminary Findings from a Survey of Adult and Adolescent New York Television Viewers*, New York: Center for Urban Education, 1968; and Herbert J. Gans, "Popular Culture in America: Social Problems in a Mass Society or Social Asset in a Pluralist Society?", in Howard S. Becker, ed., *Social Problems: A Modern Approach*, New York: John Wiley & Sons, 1966.
For other important discussions of the educating role and impact of

The fact that the programs Gans cites may have been replaced by others is irrelevant to the point he is making: that television, like the popular entertainment forms that preceded it, e.g., Horatio Alger, Frank Merriwell, the Rover Boys, Jack Armstrong, The Lone Ranger, the Green Hornet, is a powerful means of conveying a set of values, attitudes, and behaviors. In particular, the mass media teach people how to consume and play in this increasingly consumer- and pleasure-oriented society, in sharp contrast to the schools, which still emphasize the nineteenth-century virtues of work and thrift. Unlike the schools, too, the media are able to respond to changes in taste or in life style, for example, inducting young people into the new youth culture and legitimizing parts of it for the adult population. "We want to see things the way they really happen now and the way they really are," a Philadelphia high school student explained in the spring of 1969. "I think the first step toward that in television has been the 'Mod Squad.' It's a bit entertaining, I watch it myself; it shows that young people have problems and that if they work at it they can be figured out."[27]

The trouble is that television does *not* enable its audience "to see things the way they really happen now and the way they really are." On the contrary; while more current and realistic than the schools, television nonetheless presents a partial and, in important ways, distorted view of contemporary society. No television program or series, for example, has even begun to deal adequately or realistically with the new problems and opportunities of life in a world of large organizations. TV either ignores the large organization altogether, or presents a simplistic and

---

the mass media, see the following: David Riesman with Nathan Glazer and Reuel Denney, *The Lonely Crowd*, New Haven: Yale University Press, 1950 (paperback, 1961); David Riesman, *Individualism Reconsidered*, Glencoe, Ill.: Free Press, 1954; Reuel Denney, *The Astonished Muse*, New York: Grosset & Dunlap (Grosset's Universal Library), 1964; Norman Jacobs, ed., *Culture for the Millions? Mass Media in Modern Society*, Boston: Beacon Press paperback, 1964; Bernard Rosenberg and David Manning White, eds., *Mass Culture*, New York: The Free Press (paperback edition), 1964; Stuart Hall and Paddy Whannel, *The Popular Arts*, Boston: Beacon Press, 1964; Raymond Williams, *Communications*, Penguin Books, 1968; Harold Mendelsohn, *Mass Entertainment*, New Haven: College & University Press, 1966.
[27] The "Mod Squad"—two young men, one black, and a young woman—are what might be called scrubbed-up hippies who work for the Los Angeles police department. The weekly program shows them solving problems and cracking "cases" that are beyond the talents of conventional detectives.

obsolescent picture of the individual as a cog in a big machine, or an equally obsolescent picture of the individual battling, and triumphing over, the organization. But pluralism in our society increasingly means a pluralism of organizations as well as of individuals; and organizations are becoming less hierarchical as knowledge replaces muscle as the principal factor in production. "The young are right when they protest against the tendency of organization to look upon an individual as a tool," Peter Drucker writes. "But they are wrong when they blame organization for this. They have never asked themselves: 'How can I make this or that organization serve *my* end and *my* needs?' 'How can I make it enable *me* to perform, to achieve, to contribute?' " The young have never asked these questions because no one has ever suggested that these are pertinent questions to ask—because no one has ever suggested that they *can* make organization serve their own purposes and values, or provided the information they need in order to do it. Young people today, Drucker suggests, will have to "learn organization" the way their forefathers "learned farming."

Nor has television attempted to deal with a number of other important aspects and problems of contemporary life. It has made no attempt, for example, to explore the complex relations between man and machine or between man, society, and an exploding technology. Some aspects of the problem may be difficult to deal with, to be sure, but others are not. The anxiety young people feel about The Bomb and about the computer is the stuff of which drama and melodrama are made; so are the kinds of new ethical and moral as well as political and economic dilemmas that technology poses—when (and whether) to terminate or prolong life, how to allocate organs for transplant, how to balance competing interests in the use of the environment.

Until very recently moreover, one could never have known from watching television that there are social classes in the United States, still less that the United States is a society of ethnic, racial, and religious groups as well as of individuals. Except for an occasional commercial for Italian spaghetti or spaghetti sauce, ethnicity was ignored, and acknowledgment of racial and religious differences was taboo, except on the news programs and an occasional documentary. There are signs of change: for example, the school depicted weekly in "Room 222" has a Jewish principal and two unstereotyped black teachers, and a program shown in the late fall of 1969 involved a Mexican-American student and the conflict in values between his home culture and the dominant white middle-class culture. But television has a long way to go before it can be said to prepare Americans to live in a world in which group identity and group conflicts are becoming more important.

The fatal flaw, in short, is that television and, to a greater or lesser degree, the other mass media reinforce the status quo in a world in which the status is never quo—in which people desperately need to know how to deal with change. The media fail to provide the knowledge and insights that adults and young people alike require if they are to understand the world in which they live. TV and film, to be sure, report on some of what is new, but they make no attempt to distinguish between the evanescent and the enduring, or between what is inevitable and what can be changed. Nor do they attempt to find the elements of continuity with the past—essential if we are to be more than flotsam and jetsam on the currents of history. "There are two principles inherent in the very nature of things," Alfred North Whitehead wrote nearly half a century ago in *Science and the Modern World*—"the spirit of change, and the spirit of conservation. There can be nothing real without both. . . . Mere conservation without change cannot conserve," he argued, while "mere change without conservation is a passage from nothing to nothing." A dramatic improvement in the performance of the mass media is essential if we are to escape that passage to nothingness.

Why the failure of the mass media? The answer is at once simple and complex. What is mostly wrong with television, newspapers, magazines, and films is what is mostly wrong with the schools and colleges: mindlessness. At the heart of the problem, that is to say, is the failure to think seriously about purpose or consequence—the failure of people at every level to ask why they are doing what they are doing or to inquire into the consequences.

To begin with, journalists, editors, television writers, directors, and producers, network executives, newspaper publishers, filmmakers, et al., rarely think of themselves as educators. "If it had not been for the communications revolution, he might have remained an educator," Fred W. Friendly has written of Edward R. Murrow, one of the great educators of our time. Certainly the television men rarely think of the educational consequences of either the subjects they choose or the way in which they report or portray them, whether the program be news, comedy, soap opera, or drama. Even more rarely do they think about the criteria by which they make decisions: what constitutes "news"; how the medium affects the definition; what values or lessons are being conveyed, consciously or unconsciously. They portray the "wrong" values, as Herbert Gans suggests, not because of venality (though venality there is) but because the people who write and direct and produce the programs are representative Americans, men who mirror the values of the society but who have never thought about the values they are conveying.

Nowhere is this mindlessness more evident than in the communications sector that is supposed to remedy it: public television. Witness the fiasco of the Public Broadcasting Laboratory, whose generously financed coast-to-coast Sunday night programs were supposed to demonstrate the magnificent potential of public television. The main assumption on which PBL was organized was that what is principally wrong with commercial television is that it is commercial, and that removing the restraints and constraints generated by advertising sponsorship, and the consequent need to aim for the largest possible audience, would automatically unleash enormous creative powers.

PBL's assumption was, and is, widely shared. It was the thesis, of course, of the polemical volume *Due to Circumstances Beyond Our Control* by Fred W. Friendly, who conceived of PBL and persuaded the Ford Foundation to underwrite it. The PBL assumption was shared, too, by the members of the Carnegie Commission of Educational Television, whose report proposed creation of a fourth, federally financed network for public television. "If we were to sum up our proposal with all the brevity at our command," the Commission wrote in conclusion, "we would say that what we recommend is freedom. We seek freedom from the constraints, however necessary in their context, of commercial television. We seek for educational television freedom from the pressures of inadequate funds . . ."[28]

The PBL programs made clear the sterility of the conventional view of the problem. With a few notable exceptions—for example a *cinéma vérité* examination of a young couple during the wife's pregnancy and childbirth, and of a lonely old man getting ready to die—PBL did virtually nothing that commercial television has not done, and does not regularly do, and do a lot better.[29] Its greatest failures, in fact, were in the area in which

[28] *Public Television: A Program for Action,* The Report of the Carnegie Commission on Educational Television, New York: Bantam Books, 1967.
[29] The Carnegie Commission, similarly, despite pages of purple prose about the golden age that public television would open up, suggested

Friendly and his colleagues had promised the greatest distinction
—reporting and explaining the great issues, problems, and
changes of contemporary life. In straining to prove the advantage of non-commercial television, paradoxically enough, PBL
frequently did no more than display the faults of commercial
television journalism in exaggerated form.

No one should have been surprised. What is mostly wrong
with journalism is *not* the fact that it is commercial (although
certainly commercialism exacerbates the problem) but the fact
that journalists have an obsolete view of their role. "Conditioned
by its own past," as Max Ways writes, "journalism often acts as
if its main task were still to report the exceptional and dramatically different against a background of what everybody knows."[30]
Hence the news the mass media handle best is the great dramatic, discontinuous event: a moon landing, a riot, a presidential assassination, an election. The news the media handle poorly,
or ignore altogether, is the undramatic event that may, as much
as or more than the dramatic one, shape the future.

The problem goes even deeper, involving a whole set of
largely unexamined assumptions not only about what constitutes
news but about where and how to look for it, and how to report
it. There is, firstly, the cult of objectivity that still dominates
American journalism—the naïve conviction that the journalist
can and should avoid making any judgments of his own. Thus,
Herbert Brucker, former director of the Professional Journalism
Fellowships Program at Stanford (a West Coast Nieman program), argues that the difference between good and bad journalism can be found in the motive: "whether you are trying to
persuade the reader or stick to reporting." And so *Newsweek*
boasts that it separates fact from opinion, as if that were hu-

---

little by way of programming that did not already exist. The one exception—the Commission's proposal that public television "give great attention to the informal educational needs of preschool children, particularly
to interest and help" children from so-called disadvantaged (i.e., poor)
homes—is turning out to be public television's most spectacular success.
The program "Sesame Street," initially funded by the Carnegie Corporation to carry out the Educational Television Commission's proposal, is
providing (at least in its first year) a daily demonstration of what a
powerful educational medium television can be when it is used purpose-
fully and imaginatively.
[30] Max Ways, "What's Wrong with News? It Isn't New Enough," *Fortune*, October 1969. Cf. also Herbert J. Gans, "The Shaping of Mass
Media Content: A Study of the News," paper delivered at the American
Sociological Association's Annual Meeting, 1966.

manly possible; poor Walter Lippman, the magazine's advertisements suggest, deals only in opinions, in contrast with the *Newsweek* staff writers and correspondents, who specialize in fact. "Our only commitment is to our readers," *Esquire* proclaimed, in a curious ad promoting an issue containing Roy Cohn's version of "the truth about the Army-McCarthy Hearings." *"Esquire* takes no sides. We've got room for both sides of every interesting coin."

But truth is not a coin, nor does every controversial question have two sides. Some may have only one, others may have a half-dozen. In any case, objectivity—the avoidance of judgments —is impossible. The decision regarding which stories to print, where to place them (on the first page, or in the back, with the maritime news? on the right-hand column of the first page, or on the bottom of the page?), in what detail and at what length to discuss them are the most important expressions, by far, of an editorial point of view; the decisions cannot be made "objectively," for they depend on judgments, however unconscious, of what is important and what is not. Indeed, *Newsweek*, for all its insistence on separating fact from opinion, takes justifiable pride in its efforts to persuade Americans to take note of, and try to solve, the problems of poverty and racial injustice. What journalists must recognize, in short, is that while *objectivity* is not possible, *fairness* is. As Irving Kristol argued in an incisive critique of the *New York Times* (and through it, of American journalism in general), "To keep a reporter's prejudices out of a story is commendable; to keep his judgment out of a story is to guarantee that the truth will be emasculated."[31]

When allied with a conception of the journalist as reporter rather than as educator, moreover, the cult of objectivity produces an art form grossly unsuited to handling complexities. The form has several conventions. One is that the journalist's job is to report what other people—the "experts"—think or say about a problem, not what he thinks or has discovered on his own. Another is that the journalist's responsibility is to juxtapose opposing points of view without indicating which he feels is correct, without even indicating the errors or exaggerations of what he puts down. More than anything else, the late Senator Joseph McCarthy's keen understanding of this convention, together with his knowledge of the way deadlines operated, provided the basis of his power and influence. He knew that the

31 Irving Kristol, "The Underdeveloped Profession," *The Public Interest,* No. 6, Winter 1967.

dramatic charge of treason and subversion would make headlines; he knew that if the charge were made close enough to the
deadline, newspapers would report the charge without a reply to
it; and he knew that in any case reporters would print the charge
without comment *even when they knew it was false*. Indeed, the
New York Times acknowledged the problem but shrugged it off
as not the paper's responsibility. "It is difficult, if not impossible,
to ignore charges by Senator McCarthy just because they are
usually proved false," the *Times* explained. "The remedy lies
with the reader." But as Richard Rovere observed, "to many
people, this was rather like saying that if a restaurant serves
poisoned food, it is up to the diner to refuse it."[32] It was no
accident, therefore, that McCarthy's fall did not begin until
Edward R. Murrow violated most of these canons with his brilliant television documentary of March 9, 1954.

Another unfortunate convention of journalism—a natural outgrowth of an art form that sees the reporter's responsibility as
reporting what others say—is the assumption that journalists
need no special expertise of their own, that a good reporter can
handle any subject. He can't. In more and more areas the
journalist needs some of the scholar's expertise and some of his
dedication to the search for truth.[33] This is not to denigrate the
journalist's honesty; it is to recognize that the journalist has a
different commitment than the scholar; his mandate is to tell an
interesting story. When he is dealing with very complex matters,
therefore, he runs a peculiar risk: that he will find an interesting
story line too soon—that he will commit himself to a story line
before he has completely penetrated his subject. He is not being
dishonest; his story line is "true." But it may not be the whole
truth or the highest truth or the most relevant truth. He needs
the voice of the scholar prodding him on.

There are few precedents for what the times require: journalists today need to have the depth of knowledge of the specialist
and the ability to communicate of the generalist. As the news
media have come to appreciate the importance of science, a
small corps of able science writers and reporters—men like
Walter Sullivan, Francis Bello, Lawrence Lessing, Earl Ubell—

[32] Quoted by Irving Kristol in *The Public Interest,* Winter 1967.
[33] By the same token, the scholar needs the journalist's passion for the
relevant and the immediate. Too often, the scholar fails to remember
what the journalist can never forget—that life can never wait until all
the evidence is in, that important decisions must always be made on
the basis of incomplete information.

have developed new forms in which to report and explain the developments at the frontiers of science.[34] But journalism has done very badly in dealing with the economic, social, and political implications of the advances in science and technology, or with the increasingly political nature of decisions about the nature and direction of scientific research and the allocation of research funds and personnel.

The demand for clarity, together with the lack of expertise, means that the media tend either to ignore complex issues or to distort them through oversimplification. Journalists would do well to follow the maxim advanced by the Nobel Laureate in Physics Hans Bethe: "I resolve never to write more clearly than I think." They would also profit by following a maxim of the late Henry R. Luce, Jr., the founder of *Time, Life,* and *Fortune:* "Never overestimate how much the American public knows—but never underestimate its ability to learn."

The weakness of television journalism is that it inherited the weaknesses of print journalism while adding a few of its own. Aiming at the widest possible audience, and recognizing that the simple subject can be communicated more easily than the complex, television has developed a preference for dramatic conflict: a demonstration makes a better television story than a debate, and a shrill debate a better story than a quiet discussion. The biggest failure, however, has been in television's reluctance to examine its impact on the events it is reporting, particularly the way in which its own, perhaps inherent, artistic bias affects the behavior of the "actors" in the news themselves, from the President down to the student demonstrators.[35]

[34] Their experience, however, suggests that journalistic specialization, while solving some problems, creates others. The great hazard of specialization is that the journalist may begin to be more and more concerned with, and responsive to, the judgments of the scholars from whom he gets his information than of the audience for whom he is ostensibly reporting. In the case of the science reporter, for example, this means that he begins to write for the scientists themselves rather than for the wider audience which depends on his ability to "humanize" or popularize knowledge. The danger is not unique to the specialist; one of the problems with which the political reporter has always grappled (and not always successfully), is that of becoming the captive of his sources.

[35] That reluctance has come back to haunt the networks, for it gave a surface plausibility to Vice-President Spiro Agnew's attack on TV news in the fall of 1969. The Vice-President lumped soundly based criticism of the networks together with a naïve call for "objectivity" and a cynical demand that TV reporters and commentators conform to the politics and point of view of the Administration. He appealed to the Administration's

IV

To suggest that journalists, editors, television writers, directors, and producers, filmmakers, and publishers are educators does not really stretch the conventional definition of education very far. Nor would people have any difficulty regarding museum directors, librarians, or ministers, priests, and rabbis as educators. If we are to create a new American *paideia,* however, the definition of education will have to be broadened to include a great many occupations not generally thought of under that rubric.

Legal philosophers understand this well. The law, the legal historian and philosopher Willard Hurst points out, is an important—perhaps decisive—adult educating institution. As much as any single institution, the law shapes the values and therefore the ethical and moral tone of the community. The law does this through its preoccupation with what Professor Hurst calls "the substantive importance of procedure,"[36] i.e., the recognition that means shape and even determine ends—that the way men do things determines what kind of men they are, as much as the other way around. This recognition, Hurst argues, is "the most basic lesson that constitutional legal order can teach." Since means shape ends, the kinds of legal procedures the society develops shape the goals and values and indeed the whole character and ethos of the society. A society willing to risk damage to itself in order to protect the rights of accused criminals, for example, is different from one that subordinates the rights of the accused to the safety of the state or of the public.

If lawyers are to regard themselves, and to act, as educators, they must themselves be educated to this conception of the law and of their role in it. "The study of law," as Professor Charles Reich of Yale Law School has written, "must be a study of so-

---

supporters to enforce that point of view by bringing pressure to bear on the networks; his appeal was couched in terms designed to evoke the old Populist fear and hatred of Eastern Big City types.

[36] I am enormously indebted to Mr. Hurst, professor of law at the University of Wisconsin School of Law, and to Merle Borrowman, Dean of the School of Education at the University of California in Riverside, for opening my eyes to this conception of the law and of education. The conception, which Hurst derived from Brandeis, goes back to the Greeks. "In the Athenian state," Werner Jaeger writes, "law was not only the 'king' but the school of citizenship." Indeed, law was "the highest teacher of every citizen; for law is the most universal and final expression of current moral standards." (*Paideia,* Vol. I)

ciety in the moral sense of ought and should." Most law schools
—some critics would say all law schools—do *not* turn out
lawyer-educators. They tend, rather, to train high-level technicians who take the ends—indeed the system itself—as given.
Yet virtually every major law school has some faculty members
struggling to imbue their students with purpose, and trying to
remold their schools accordingly.

Their efforts have received considerable impetus from the
burgeoning interest in providing legal services to the poor.[37]
The attempt to provide such services radically changes the
lawyer's role. For one thing, he becomes an educator in a much
more specific way, since the first (and perhaps most important)
part of his job may be to educate the poor to what their rights
are. To do this, moreover, he may have to go out into the community, in effect advertising for clients, thereby bringing himself into direct violation of—and confrontation with—the traditional code of legal ethics. Two other canons are also likely to
be violated by "neighborhood law firms": the prohibition on
the use of lay intermediaries, and the prohibition on the un-
authorized practice of law by laymen. One of the main services
the poor need, for example, is advocacy—before landlords,
welfare administrators, creditors—a function that, in many cases,
can be performed as well by an informed layman as by a lawyer.

Brief and limited as they are, the various attempts to provide
legal services to the poor have raised even more fundamental
questions about the inadequacy of the legal system itself. Most
of these programs have been based until now on the assumption
that the heart of the problem was the way in which lawyers' work
is organized: that the poor are denied equal justice because they
do not have equal access to legal services. Ergo the way to secure
legal justice for the poor is to find new ways of making legal
services available to them.

This assumption is now being challenged. "The ends of justice
will not be served if all that neighborhood law firms do is foist
on the poor a legal system which the middle class has rejected

37 The proliferation of "neighborhood law firms" and other means of providing legal services to the poor provides an interesting case history of
the role of the university in social change. While a number of law schools
are now deeply immersed in this area, they played a minor role in the
development of poverty law. The initial impetus came from foundation-
and government-financed projects in New York (Mobilization for Youth)
and New Haven (Community Progress, Inc.), and the rapid diffusion
was the result of the encouragement and financing offered by the
Office of Economic Opportunity.

as obsolete, cumbersome, and too expensive in money, psychological strain, and investment of time," Edgar S. and Jean
Camper Cahn, among the earliest advocates of the neighborhood
law firm concept, now argue. "The difficulties now being experienced by neighborhood law firms go to deficiencies in the nature
of our legal system itself—deficiencies experienced by the middle
class as well as the poor."[38]

The deficiencies are of several sorts. One involves an inadequate or irrelevant conceptual framework. For example, a number of fields of law—contract law, landlord-tenant law, domestic
law, and tort law—are built around the concept of negligence—
"a quest for fault, for 'who did what when' as a way of deciding
how the risk should be borne and who should pay, perform, and
provide remedy." But the concept of negligence may be irrelevant in most automobile accident, industrial injury, and domestic
relations cases, and the quest for fault serves to clog the courts,
and delay or obstruct justice. It also makes expansion of legal
services virtually impossible. If all the attorneys in the United
States did nothing but legal aid work, according to Gary Bellow,
deputy director of the California Rural Legal Assistance Program, the manpower would still be grossly inadequate, given the
present legal system.

Another deficiency involves the near-total absence of institutions capable of monitoring the discretionary actions of government officials and of compelling accountability. This absence
stems from the independence of the Executive Branch from the
Congress and the courts. The threshold of congressional awareness is too high to provide redress for, or even scrutiny of, the
bulk of injuries; it takes a stark injustice, a scandal, gross mal-
administration, or a clearly demonstrable failure to activate congressional concern. The courts, too, are ineffective. Test cases
may vindicate the rights of one individual, but they do not
generally revise administrative rules and regulations or prescribe
new ones, nor do they bring administrative behavior into conformity with official policy. The result is that the poor—recipi-

[38] Edgar S. and Jean Camper Cahn, "What Price Justice: The Civilian
Perspective Revisited," *Notre Dame Lawyer*, Vol. 41. Cf. also Edgar S.
Cahn, Abram Chayes, et al., "Proposal for a Citizens' Rights and Complaint Center," unpublished; Jerome E. Carlin, Jan Howard, and S. L.
Messinger, *Civil Justice and the Poor*, Center for the Study of Law and
Society, University of California at Berkeley; Gary Bellow, "The Extension of Legal Services to the Poor—New Approaches to the Bar's Responsibility," address to the Harvard Law School Sesquicentennial Celebration.

ents of welfare, residents of public housing projects, etc.—find themselves in a no-man's land which is off-limits to the courts and beyond the concern of the legislature.

Clearly, therefore, new legal and political institutions and new legal concepts and processes are necessary if the poor—and in many cases, the middle classes—are to secure justice. New concepts of the lawyer's role and function are also needed: lawyers, and law professors, must concern themselves not just with providing more and more legal service to more and more people; they must concern themselves with the goals of that service and with the institutional changes necessary to achieve those goals.

It will not do, therefore, for law schools to deal with the problem by simply adding a new course of study for lawyers who plan to go into public service instead of into private practice. Such a course, as Supreme Court Justice William Brennan warned in his address to the Harvard Law School Sesquicentennial Celebration in September 1967, would rapidly produce a "bifurcated profession," half devoted to public service, half concerned exclusively with private interests. "And the two halves will not make a whole." Whether it is possible, as Justice Brennan urged, to create a two-way traffic between the two sectors remains to be seen.

The more important task in legal education, in any case, is to make the embryo corporate lawyer and private practitioner conscious of the law's educating role: to give him a real understanding of how the legal system works, what values it incorporates and advances, how the system is changing, how it can be changed, and to what ends—in short, to make him an educator rather than a mere technician.

v

Doctors, too, are—or should be—educators; etymologically, in fact, the term doctor *means* teacher. To be sure, most doctors do not think of themselves in this way. But a good many medical reformers are now talking about changing medical education in order to produce men who are doctors in this etymological sense. Medicine, they argue, must shift its focus from disease to health. If it does so—if the doctor's responsibility becomes the maintenance of health rather than the treatment of disease—the doctor's role changes profoundly. He must be preoccupied with phenomena now relegated to the margins of medical interest under the labels "preventive medicine," "community medicine," and "environmental medicine," which is to say, he must educate not only his patients but their families and their communities as well.

Indeed, the whole concept of what constitutes the practice of medicine changes when the doctor's role is defined as maintaining health rather than curing disease. To maintain health, the doctor must be concerned not only with germs, viruses, and the organs they inhabit but with the entire environment—social, economic, and psychological as well as physical—in which the individual patient lives. "The real measure of health," René Dubos of Rockefeller University writes, "is not the Utopian absence of all disease, but the ability to function effectively within a given environment. And since the environment keeps changing, good health is a process of continuous adaptation to the myriad microbes, irritants, pressures and problems which daily challenge men." The point is that few diseases are caused by a germ alone. "Thousands of people carry with them the microbes of influenza, staphylococcus infections and many other illnesses," Dr. Dubos explains, "but this single factor does not make them develop the disease. However, inclement weather or starvation or even a family quarrel may provide the trigger that makes the disease flare up. Every illness, no matter what its nature, is usually the consequence of a variety of causes, not just one—and no two people react to any one cause in the same way. Thus disease itself is a failure of homeostasis—a failure to respond appropriately to challenge."[39]

Even if he is to treat disease, therefore, the doctor must be an educator as well as a physician. "Human behavior," Dr. George James, dean of New York's Mount Sinai Medical College, writes, "is deeply implicated in the four leading causes of death in the United States: heart disease, cancer, stroke, and accidents." Thus, Dr. James suggests that an elementary or secondary school teacher who can persuade her students not to smoke cigarettes when they grow up is practicing medicine a lot more effectively than the chief of lung surgery at Mount Sinai, who can save only about one patient in ten. Similarly, he argues, rheumatoid arthritis, one of the most crippling diseases today, might leave people less disabled if they could be educated to avoid obesity and to take reasonable and regular exercise

[39] René Dubos, Maya Pines, and the Editors of *Life, Health and Disease*, New York: Time Incorporated (Life Science Library), 1965.

throughout their lives.[40] Doctors must be concerned with education at the most elementary level, Dr. Cecil Sheps, director of the Center for Health Services Research at the University of North Carolina, points out, since studies indicate that 40 percent of patients do not take the drugs prescribed for them. To provide medical care, therefore, the doctor must take the time and effort to make sure that his patient understands what the problem is, and what he has to do to recover or to prevent more serious illness.

Any serious attempt to provide medical care to the urban and rural poor, moreover, broadens and changes the conception of medicine even more.

ITEM: The pediatricians from Albert Einstein Medical College who staffed a Neighborhood Health Center in New York City's South Bronx, were puzzled by the prevalence of diarrhea among Puerto Rican infants. A social anthropologist on the staff, making a study of attitudes toward food, discovered that Puerto Ricans classify foods as "cold" and "hot," a categorization having little to do with either temperature or spiciness, and that evaporated milk, the usual base for infants' formula, was defined as hot. Since Puerto Rican folklore also held that children should not be fed hot foods, mothers were substituting whole milk, which acts as a cathartic for newborns. With the help of local residents being trained as health aides, the doctors were able to educate the mothers to stick to evaporated milk.

ITEM: When a public housing project in Boston was found to have virtually no medical care at all—the project was surrounded by new superhighways, which cut it off from the rest of the city—the Tufts University Medical School opened a full-time clinic in the development, staffed with doctors, interns, nurses, and social workers. The most widespread, and in some respects most serious, health problem, the clinic members quickly discovered, was severe back pains; the reason, they discovered almost as quickly, was that the impoverished residents had jobs that usually involved their being on their feet most of the day, and because of their poverty, their shoes tended to fit poorly. The clinic brought in some podiatrists to handle the serious problems and to train residents to handle the routine complaints.

[40] *The Journal of the Mount Sinai Hospital,* Vol. XXXIV, May–June 1967.

This view of the physician as educator—a return, in a sense, to the nineteenth and early twentieth century, or pre-Flexner, view of medicine—draws strength from the recent realization that the great contemporary advances in "scientific medicine" have not produced any comparable improvement in the health of the population. The life expectancy of Americans, for example, has barely increased in the last twenty years, while the budget of the National Institutes of Health was exploding from $2.5 million a year to $1.4 *billion*. In the same period, the American position in international comparisons of national health standards (infant mortality rate, maternal mortality rate, life expectancy, etc.) has dropped sharply.[41] By contrast, there was a dramatic improvement in health and a substantial lengthening of life expectancy in the late nineteenth and the first half of the twentieth centuries. But these changes, as René Dubos and others have pointed out, were due less to the growth of scientific medicine than to the increase in the standard of living, combined with the various public health measures—e.g., sanitary engineering, chlorination of drinking water, mass immunization and vaccination, draining of swamps—that Abraham Flexner and his followers relegated to second-class citizenship within the medical fraternity.

VI

Doctors and lawyers are not the only professionals who need to view themselves as educators. Certainly social workers educate, although the profession is wracked by conflict over what the purpose should be. In the dominant casework approach, the social worker's task is to teach the client to adjust to the world as it is. The social worker may teach a poor in-migrant Negro mother how to budget her limited income, how to buy more nutritious and less expensive foods, how to resist the blandishments of door-to-door salesmen, how to apply for medicaid or other social services of whose existence she is unaware—in short, how to function in a crowded, harsh, impersonal city. In more psychiatrically oriented casework, the social worker may teach a middle-class family how to cope better with an emotionally disturbed child, or teach an unmarried pregnant girl how to

[41] Walsh McDermott, "Medical Institutions and Modification of Disease Patterns," *The American Journal of Psychiatry*, Vol. 122, No. 12 (June 1966); David Rutstein, *The Coming Revolution in Medicine*, Cambridge, Mass.: The M.I.T. Press, 1967.

deal with her unwanted baby, as well as with her feelings about the child, the pregnancy, etc.

A small but rapidly growing and increasingly influential minority, however, argues that the social worker's most important educating function should be to teach the poor—and the rest of us—how to change the conditions that produce poverty and the tangle of pathology surrounding it, rather than how to adjust to conditions as they are. The emphasis, therefore, is on community organization and social and political action and on development of social policy rather than on individual casework—a return to the reformist, Progressivist tradition of the founders of social work. Settlement workers, Jane Addams wrote, not only needed "scientific patience in the accumulation of facts, but they also had to arouse and interpret the public opinion of their neighborhoods . . . furnish data for legislation, and use their influence to secure it." "The dominant idea," Edward T. Devine, general secretary of the Charity Organization Society, wrote in 1911, was "to seek out and strike effectively at . . . those particular causes of dependence and intolerable living conditions which are beyond the control of individuals whom they injure and often destroy."

If there is anything to the Churchillian aphorism that "we shape our buildings, and then our buildings shape us," architects should also see themselves as educators. So should engineers; we need engineer-educators at least as much as architect-educators—engineers who have some understanding of, and some interest in, the consequences of the technologies they manipulate. And we need businessmen concerned with the ways in which business enterprise affects and shapes the society.

It is not stretching the concept of education as *paideia* too far, in fact, to suggest that almost every profession has some educating role to play, and that its members must be made more conscious of that role. "What professional men should carry away with them from a university is not professional knowledge," John Stuart Mill suggested a century ago in his Inaugural Address at the University of St. Andrews, "but that which should direct the use of professional knowledge, and bring the light of general culture to illuminate the technicalities of a special pursuit. Men may be competent lawyers without general education, but it depends on general education to make them philosophic lawyers." Or, we might add, philosophic doctors, social workers, engineers, architects, and businessmen.

II

---

*What's Wrong with
the Schools*

3

Education
and Equality

They, then, who knowingly withhold sustenance from a newborn child, and he dies, are guilty of infanticide. And, by the same reasoning, they who refuse to enlighten the intellect of a rising generation, are guilty of degrading the human race! They who refuse to train up children in the way they should go, are training up incendiaries and madmen to destroy property and life, and to invade and pollute the sanctuaries of society.

—HORACE MANN, *1846*

I

"What the best and wisest parent wants for his own child," John Dewey suggested in 1899, in the first of the lectures that formed *The School and Society,* "that must the community want for all of its children. Any other idea for our schools is narrow and unlovely; acted upon, it destroys our democracy."

Our democracy is not destroyed, but it is in danger. Not the least of the reasons is the fact that the community has *not* wanted for all its children what the best parent wants for his own child. As a result, the public schools are failing dismally in what has always been regarded as one of their primary tasks— in Horace Mann's phrase, to be "the great equalizer of the conditions of men," facilitating the movement of the poor and disadvantaged into the mainstream of American economic and social life. Far from being "the great equalizer," the schools help perpetuate the differences in condition, or at the very least, do little to reduce them. If the United States is to become a truly just and humane society, the schools will have to do an incomparably better job than they are now doing of educating youngsters from minority-group and lower-class homes.

The failure is not new; it is one the United States has tolerated for a century or more. The public school never has done much of a job of educating youngsters from the lower class or from immigrant homes. For one thing, as Lawrence A. Cremin has pointed out, we have greatly exaggerated the "commonness" of the common school, which has always been essentially a middle-class or upper middle-class institution.[1] "By the theory of a common school system scholars of every rank are supposed to come within the sphere of its operation," Bishop James Fraser reported to the English Schools Inquiry Commission in 1866, following a visit to the United States. "As a matter of fact, social distinctions do tell with a very marked effect upon American schools. Speaking generally, they are in the possession of the great middle class, the artizans, storekeepers, farmers." In a large part of the United States, to be sure—in the rural and small-town communities west of the Alleghenies—the reality did approach the myth. Where there was considerable homogeneity of social class, religion, ethnic background, and race, that is to say, the schools were common. But where heterogeneity prevailed—in the South as well as in the larger cities of the East and the Midwest—the schools were not very common, and they served the lower classes badly, if at all.

It is not only the "commonness" of the common school that we have exaggerated, however; we have also greatly romanticized the role the schools have played in stimulating social and economic mobility for immigrant and native-born lower-class people. For some groups, to be sure—the Japanese Americans, the Greeks, and the Eastern European Jews, in particular—the schools have been the critical means of mobility, and so have served to enlarge the democratic base of society. But these really were exceptions—ethnic groups whose cultures placed a heavy premium on individual achievement.

For most immigrant groups, however—for the Irish, the Italians, the Poles, the Slavs, the groups which comprised the bulk of the immigration of the middle and late nineteenth and early twentieth centuries—education was *not* an important

[1] Lawrence A. Cremin, *The Genius of American Education*, New York: Vintage Books, 1966.

means of mobility. On the contrary; as the historian Stephan Thernstrom of UCLA has demonstrated, mobility frequently "was achieved by sacrificing the education of the younger generation." Wages were so low and unemployment so frequent that the immigrants, mostly unskilled laborers, depended on their children's earnings as well as their own and their wives'; Thernstrom estimates that nearly 20 percent of laboring families' incomes came from the labor of children under the age of fifteen. The only way in which most nineteenth-century workmen could save enough to buy a home was to withdraw their children from school at age ten or twelve and put them to work.[2] As a result, mobility frequently was short-lived; fathers had difficulty transmitting their relative prosperity to their uneducated sons, who had to begin as laborers at the bottom, as their fathers had done.

Necessity aside, most immigrants viewed the schools with suspicion if not outright hostility. The South Italian immigrants, for example, came from villages in which schools had been only for the children of the upper class; their children would have been unwelcome had they attempted to send them—a notion that would have struck them as ridiculous. "Education," as Nathan Glazer has written, "was for a cultural style of life and professions the peasant could never aspire to." The peasants' culture, in any case, ruled out any desire for change; "intellectual curiosity and originality," Glazer continues, "were ridiculed or suppressed. 'Don't make your child better than you are,' runs a South Italian proverb. Nor, despite a strong desire for material improvement, did the Italian family see a role for education in America. One improved one's circumstances by hard work, perhaps by a lucky strike, but not by spending time in a school, taught by women, who didn't even beat the children."[3]

School was feared, too, as a threat to the solidarity of the family; to the extent to which Italo-Americans aspired to social and economic mobility, it was construed in terms of family rather than individual mobility. From the family's standpoint, the rebellious son or daughter was the one who insisted on remaining in school, not the youngster who insisted on dropping out. Contrariwise, for the youngster intent on using school and

[2] Stephan Thernstrom, *Poverty and Progress,* Cambridge, Mass.: Harvard University Press, 1964.
[3] Nathan Glazer, "The Italians," in Nathan Glazer and Daniel Patrick Moynihan, *Beyond the Melting Pot,* Cambridge, Mass.: The M.I.T. Press and Harvard University Press, 1963.

college as the route to the middle class, the price was estrangement from both family and friends.[4]

What was true of the Italo-Americans was true, in greater or lesser degree, of the Irish and of most of the members of the "new immigration"—the predominantly peasant ethnic groups who came here from Southern and Eastern Europe during the late nineteenth and early twentieth centuries. For the most part, they did not begin to view education as important, either in itself or as a means of mobility, until *after* they had become middle class—a process that, for some groups, is only just beginning. Middle-class status was achieved not through education but through politics or business, and to a considerable extent through crime, whose close relation to both politics and business has been recognized by only a few writers.[5]

[4] Cf. William Foote Whyte, *Street Corner Society*, University of Chicago Press, second edition, 1955; Leonard Covello, *The Heart Is the Teacher*, New York: McGraw-Hill, 1958; and *The Social Background of the Italo-American School Child*, unpublished doctoral dissertation, New York University. Cf. also Fred L. Strodtbeck, "Family Interaction, Values, and Achievement," in David C. McClelland, et al., *Talent and Society*, Princeton, N.J.: Van Nostrand, 1958; Herbert J. Gans, *The Urban Villagers*, New York: Free Press, 1962; Bernard C. Rosen, "Race, Ethnicity, and the Achievement Syndrome," in Bernard C. Rosen, H. J. Crockett, and C. Z. Nunn, eds., *Achievement in American Society*, Cambridge, Mass.: Schenckman Publishing Co., 1969.

[5] In *Street Corner Society*, for example, William F. Whyte shows in considerable detail the critical importance of the organized rackets, especially those involving gambling, e.g., numbers and bookmaking, to the economy of Boston's "North End" Italian immigrant community. Many small businesses, e.g., barbershops, variety stores, lunchrooms, poolrooms, depended on the revenues from selling "numbers" to break even. Perhaps more important, racketeers provided the principal source of investment capital to young entrepreneurs, and to young doctors and lawyers needing help in setting up practice; the combination of prejudice and an unwillingness to see the newcomers compete with the established businesses and professional men made the local commercial and investment bankers unwilling to lend to young Italians.

As Daniel Bell has suggested, crime has played an important role for almost every immigrant group seeking mobility, racketeers of one ethnic background succeeding those of the preceding group as it found its niche in American society. In New York, for example, Jews like Arnold Rothstein succeeded the earlier Irish racketeers in the 1920s, in turn being replaced by Italians in the 1940s. One of the recurrent complaints of Negroes and Puerto Ricans in recent years has been their inability to gain control of the rackets in their neighborhoods, as earlier ethnic groups had been able to do. Cf. Daniel Bell, *The End of Ideology*, New York: Free Press, 1960. Cf. also St. Clair Drake and Horace R. Cayton, *Black Metropolis*, New York: Harcourt Brace, 1945; Dan Wakefield, *Island in*

If the immigrants viewed the schools with suspicion, teachers and administrators more than returned the compliment in kind. By and large, American schools had taken over the curriculum and the instructional methods of the European schools, which had developed to instruct mainly the upper class; they made little attempt to understand the special needs of their new students. All of the adjustment was expected to be on the students' part. Dr. Leonard Covello, the first Italo-American to become a principal in the New York City schools, describes the methods in use at the turn of the century in vivid detail:

> I was sitting in class trying to memorize and pronounce words written on the blackboard—words which had absolutely no meaning to me. It seldom seemed to occur to our teachers that explanations were necessary.
>
> "B-U-T-T-E-R—butter—butter," I sing-songed with the rest of the class, learning as always by rote, learning things which often I didn't understand but which had a way of sticking in my mind.
>
> Softly the door opened and Mrs. Cutter entered the classroom. For a large and heavy-set woman she moved quickly, without making any noise. We were not supposed to notice or even pretend we had seen her as she slowly made her way between the desks and straight-backed benches. "B-U-T-T-E-R," I intoned. She was behind me now. I could feel her presence hovering over me. I did not dare take my eyes from the blackboard. I had done nothing and could conceive of no reason for an attack, but with Mrs. Cutter this held no significance. She carried a short bamboo switch. On her finger she wore a heavy gold wedding ring. For an instant I thought she was going to pass me by and then suddenly her clenched fist with the ring came down on my head. . . .
>
> Every day before receiving our bowl of soup we recited the Lord's Prayer. I had no inkling of what the words meant. I knew only that I was expected to bow my head. I looked around to see what was going on. Swift and simple, the teacher's blackboard pointer brought the idea home to me. I never batted an eyelash after that. . . .
>
> Silence! Silence! This was the characteristic feature of our existence at the Soup School. You never made an unnecessary noise or said an unnecessary word. Outside in the hall we lined up by size, girls in one line and boys in another, without uttering a sound. Eyes front and at attention. Lord help

the City, New York: Citadel Press (Corinth Books), 1960; Gus Tyler, ed., *Organized Crime in America,* University of Michigan Press, 1962.

you if you broke the rule of silence. I can still see a distant relative of mine, a girl named Miluzza, who could never stop talking, standing in a corner behind Mrs. Cutter through an entire assembly, with a spring-type clothespin fastened to her lower lip as punishment. Uncowed, defiant—Miluzza with that clothespin dangling from her lip . . .

The constant drilling and the pressure of memorizing, the homework, and detention after school raised havoc with many students . . .

During this period the Italian language was completely ignored in the American schools. In fact, throughout my whole elementary school career, I do not recall one mention of Italy or the Italian language or what famous Italians had done in the world, with the possible exception of Columbus. . . . We soon got the idea that "Italian" meant something inferior, and a barrier was erected between children of Italian origin and their parents. This was the accepted process of Americanization. We were becoming Americans by learning how to be ashamed of our parents.[6]

"We were becoming Americans by learning how to be ashamed of our parents." Covello's comment is a summary of what the schools tended to do to most of the immigrant children in their charge. The effect was almost inescapable, when so many teachers and principals shared the view of William Henry Maxwell, Superintendent of Schools in New York in the early years of the century, that immigrant parents were "ignorant, prejudiced and highly excitable people."[7] In their refusal to meet the immigrants' alien cultures halfway—in their refusal to adjust the school to the children as well as the children to the school—teachers and administrators, as the historian Michael B. Katz writes, "all said to the child and parent from the working class, 'You are vicious, immoral, shortsighted and thoroughly wrong about most things. We are right; we shall show you the truth.' "[8] The result "has been the estrangement of the school from the life of the working-class community" since the middle of the nineteenth century. There were exceptions, of course—

[6] Leonard Covello, *The Heart Is the Teacher*. Cf. also "Interview with Leonard Covello, *The Urban Review*, Vol. 3, No. 3, January 1969.
[7] Cf. Selma C. Berrol, "The Schools of New York in Transition, 1898–1914," *The Urban Review*, Vol. 1, No. 5, December 1966. Cf. also Colin Greer, "Immigrants, Negroes, and the Public Schools," *The Urban Review*, Vol. 3, No. 3, January 1969.
[8] Michael B. Katz, *The Irony of Early School Reform*, Cambridge, Mass.: Harvard University Press, 1968.

schools here and there that managed to welcome, and to educate, children whom other schools found to be uneducable. These
exceptions aside, the United States, as Professor Katz argues,
"has never, on any large scale, known vital urban schools"—
schools "which embrace and are embraced by the mass of the
community, which formulate their goals in terms of the joy of
the individual instead of the fear of social dynamite or the im-
peratives of economic growth."

Some reformers, of course, did try to make the schools more
responsive to the needs of their students. After visiting schools in
England, Ireland, Scotland, Germany, Holland, Belgium, and
France in the spring of 1842, Horace Mann, in his capacity as
secretary of the Massachusetts State Board of Education, reported glowingly on the "beautiful relation of harmony and
affection which subsisted between teacher and pupils" in the
schools of Prussia [*sic*], which at the time were using the methods
of the Swiss educational reformer Pestalozzi. During the six
weeks he spent in Prussia, Mann wrote, "I never heard a sharp
rebuke given, I never saw a child in tears, nor arraigned at the
teacher's bar for any alleged misconduct. . . . The teacher's
manner was better than parental, for it had a parent's tenderness
and vigilance, without the foolish doatings [*sic*] or indulgences
to which parental affection is prone. I heard no child ridiculed,
sneered at, or scolded for making a mistake." Mann urged adoption of these methods.[9]

The schoolmen, however, would have none of it. "That the
method pursued by the Prussian instructor is calculated to interest the mind of the pupil we would not deny," a group of thirty
one Boston grammar school masters wrote in a violent attack on
Mann's report; "for the variety of information and illustration
must, without fail, gratify his curiosity, and for the time arrest
his attention . . ." That was precisely the problem with the
child-centered approach Mann was urging: to make learning
pleasurable would be to destroy the habits of discipline and
obedience the schools were intended to foster. Nothing was likely
to yield more "mischief" or to be more "subversive of real
happiness," the masters wrote, "than mistaking what may afford
the child present gratification, for that which secures him lasting
good." To place the child's needs and interests first could only
threaten "the welfare, both of the individual and society, by

[9] Seventh Annual Report, in Lawrence A. Cremin, ed., *The Republic and
The School: Horace Mann on the Education of Free Men*, New York:
Teachers College Press, 1957.

sending forth a sickly race, palsied in every limb, through idleness" and determined "to gratify a morbid thirst for pleasure."[10]

The masters were only reflecting the opinion of those to whom they were responsible: that the purpose of public education was to give the lower classes the habits of obedience and submission necessary for public peace, a docile labor force, and the protection of property. "In this day of agitation and violence," the Newburyport, Massachusetts, School Committee warned in 1844, the ignorance of the mob threatened "the permanence of that system to which we are indebted for the security of our rights—the defense of our property, our persons and character." The remedy was public schooling designed to "diminish the vice, crime and moral degradation" resulting from the Irish immigration. "School days," the committee went on to say, "are those emphatically in which the individual is taught obedience." And "a proper sense of obedience and submission," Professor Thernstrom observes, "could not be instilled in the pupil by coddling him." "Pupils need governing," the School Committee wrote, "and this, in the last analysis, always means coercing, compelling."[11]

And so the schools did not learn how to adopt and accommodate themselves to immigrant or native lower-class cultures. "The very success of the public school tended to remove it further from the very class of children for whose benefit it was originally established," one observer wrote in 1833. "Theoretically, the public school is for all; practically, it is conducted with less regard to the very lowest stratum of society than is desirable. Our public schools are now the best schools to be found, but they are surrounded by a set of rigid rules, customs, and traditions which have a tendency to keep out the very children that these schools were established to educate."

For all the changes that the progressive revolution brought in its wake in the earlier part of the century,[12] the schools never did learn how to be effective with children from lower-class or minority homes; they remained institutions in which these youngsters felt alien and estranged. Writing at the height of the progressive movement in education, for example, in a book about New York City's Greenwich Village, one of the centers of progressivism, Caroline Ware reported that "the local schools

[10] Quoted in Katz, *The Irony of Early School Reform.*
[11] Quoted in Stephan Thernstrom, *Poverty and Progress.*
[12] Lawrence A. Cremin, *The Transformation of the School,* New York: Alfred A. Knopf, 1961.

were indifferent to the loyalties and customs of the Italian group and did not consider it necessary to be familiar with the ethnic background of the children in order to prepare them for their role in American life."[13]

Nor were the Greenwich Village schools unusual in this regard. In their pioneering study of Muncie, Indiana, Robert and Helen Lynd described in some detail the ways in which the schools, reflecting the dominant middle-class ethos, served to suppress the educational aspirations of children from the lower social classes.[14] The Lynds's judgment of the schools was repeated in a series of other studies of communities in New England, the Deep South, and the Midwest by W. Lloyd Warner and others. As Warner, Robert Havighurst, and Martin Loeb argued in a volume drawing on all these studies, the main function of the schools appeared to be that of sorting and certifying students for mobility, a process that tended to doom lower-class students to remain lower class. "One large group," they wrote, "is almost immediately brushed off into a bin labelled 'non-readers,' 'first-grade repeaters,' or 'opportunity class,' where they stay for eight or ten years and are then released through a chute to the outside world to become 'hewers of wood and drawers of water.' "[15] And in his more sophisticated analysis, August B. Hollingshead argued that while lower-class family life and culture did not prepare adolescents to adjust to the school, neither did the school adjust itself to the needs of lower-class students; for the most part, administrators and teachers enforced their own middle-class values by "putting down" lower-class adolescents.[16]

[13] Caroline F. Ware, *Greenwich Village, 1920–1930: A Comment on American Civilization in the Post-War Years*, Boston: Houghton-Mifflin, 1935.
[14] Robert S. Lynd and Helen M. Lynd, *Middletown: A Study in American Culture*, New York: Harcourt, Brace & World, 1929.
[15] W. Lloyd Warner, Robert J. Havighurst, and M. B. Loeb, *Who Shall Be Educated?*, New York: Harper & Row, 1944. For a summary of the literature, Cf. W. B. Brookover and David Gottlieb, "Social Class and Education," in W. W. Charters, Jr., and N. L. Gage, eds., *Readings in the Social Psychology of Education* (A Project of the Society for the Psychological Study of Social Issues), Boston: Allyn and Bacon, 1963.
[16] August B. Hollingshead, *Elmstown's Youth,* New York: John Wiley, 1949. Cf. also Howard S. Becker, "Social Class Variations in the Teacher-Pupil Relationship," *Journal of Educational Sociology*, Vol. 25, 1952, reprinted in B. C. Rosen, H. J. Crockett, and C. Z. Nunn, *Achievement in American Society;* Robert E. Herriott and Nancy Hoyt St. John, *Social Class and the Urban School,* New York: John Wiley, 1966; and A. H.

II

The schools have changed substantially in the postwar period; on almost any measure they are doing a better job of educating minority-group and lower-class children now than a generation ago. But not enough better; on almost any measure, the schools are still failing to provide the kind of education Negroes, Indians, Puerto Ricans, Mexican Americans, Appalachian whites —indeed, the poor of every color, race, and ethnic background —need, and deserve. It would be a serious mistake to assume that the schools are succeeding with the rest of the population. As we shall argue at length in the next chapter, the failures of the urban and rural slum schools are in large part an exaggerated version of the failures of American schools as a whole—a failure, in Comenius' phrase, to educate all men to full humanity; and as we shall argue in Part III, the remedy for the defects of slum schools is the remedy for the defects of all schools: namely, to transform them into free, open, humane and joyous institutions.

But the slum schools are failing in a way that middle-class schools are not. One of the purposes of schooling—not the only purpose but a critical one nonetheless—is to teach the intellectual skills and academic knowledge that students need if they are to be able to earn a decent living and to participate in the social and political life of the community. This the slum schools are failing to do.

It would be unreasonable, perhaps, to expect absolutely equal results from different schools. Lower-class youngsters start school with severe educational deficiencies for which the school cannot be blamed; moreover, the school as we have already argued, is only one of a number of educating institutions and influences that affect a youngster's academic achievement. It is not unreasonable, however, in a society that prizes (or claims to prize) equality of opportunity, to expect the schools to be a *significant* influence—to expect them to make the opportunities open to its students less dependent on their social origins. And that means making it possible for students from every social class and every ethnic and racial group to acquire the necessary basic skills.

One way to assess the schools' performance, therefore, is to

Halsey, Jean Floud, and C. Arnold Anderson, eds., *Education, Economy, and Society*, New York: Free Press, 1961.

measure how well they accomplish this end. The U.S. Office of Education did just this in its mammoth and controversial study, "Equality of Educational Opportunity," the so-called Coleman Report, named after its principal author, Professor James S. Coleman of Johns Hopkins University.[17] Standardized achievement tests measuring students' skill in reading, writing, calculating, and problem-solving were given to some 645,000 children in grades 1, 3, 6, 9, and 12 in some 4,000 schools in all fifty states and the District of Columbia. These tests, Coleman and his colleagues argue in the report, do not measure students' intelligence, attitudes, or character; they do measure skills that "are among the most important in our society for getting a good job and moving up to a better one, and for full participation in an increasingly technical world. Consequently, a pupil's test results at the end of public school provide a good measure of the range of opportunities open to him as he finishes school—a wide range of choice of jobs or colleges if these skills are very high; a very narrow range that includes only the most menial jobs if these skills are very low."

For the average minority-group student, the range of choice is very narrow; on all the tests administered, students from minority groups—Indian Americans, Mexican Americans, Puerto Ricans, and blacks—scored substantially below white students. Table 1 summarizes the test results by showing the median scores (the score dividing the group in half) for first-grade and twelfth-grade students. The test scores were handled statistically so that the average score for the country as a whole was 50, and the standard deviation was 10; that means that two-thirds of the total sample scored between 40 and 60, with about 16 percent scoring above 60, and 16 percent below 40.

As the table indicates, the disparity either remains the same or widens as each group goes through school. The average Negro score, for example, tends to be about one standard deviation below the white average, meaning that about 85 percent of the Negro scores fall below the white average. (But 50 percent of the white students, it must be remembered, also score below the white average.) Puerto Rican and Mexican-American scores are almost as far below the white average, with Indian-American scores only slightly higher.

[17] James S. Coleman, et al., *Equality of Educational Opportunity,* Washington, D.C.: U.S. Government Printing Office, 1966. The controversies surrounding the report involve other parts of its analysis and will be discussed later in the chapter.

TABLE 1

Nationwide Median Test Scores for 1st- and 12th-Grade Pupils,
United States, Fall 1965

Test	Puerto Ricans	Indian Americans	Mexican Americans	Oriental Americans	Negro	White
			Racial or Ethnic Group			
1st Grade:						
Nonverbal	45.8	53.0	50.1	56.6	43.4	54.1
Verbal	44.9	47.8	46.5	51.6	45.4	53.2
12th Grade:						
Nonverbal	43.3	47.1	45.0	51.6	40.9	52.0
Verbal	43.1	43.7	43.8	49.6	40.9	52.1
Reading	42.6	44.3	44.2	48.8	42.2	51.9
Mathematics ...	43.7	45.9	45.5	51.3	41.8	51.8
General Information	41.7	44.7	43.3	49.0	40.6	52.2
Average of the 5 tests	43.1	45.1	44.4	50.1	41.1	52.0

NOTE: This table presents the results of standard achievement tests of certain intellectual skills such as reading, writing, calculating, and problem-solving. The tests were designed to measure the skills which are the most important in our society for getting a good job and moving up to a better one, and for full participation in an increasingly technical world.

The scores in each test were standardized so that the average over the national sample equaled 50 and the standard deviation equaled 10. This means that for all pupils in the Nation, about 16 percent would score below 40 and about 16 percent would score above 60.

SOURCE: Coleman, et al., *Equality of Educational Opportunity*, Table 9, reprinted in *Digest of Educational Statistics*, 1968.

Another way of measuring the relative achievement of different groups of students is in terms of grade-level achievement. On this measure, the disparity between the achievement of minority- and majority-group students widens as they go through school.[18] In the third grade, for example, the average Negro in

[18] The two measures give different results because a standard deviation means different things at different grades. A rule of thumb used by many elementary school teachers, for example, holds that the dispersion of verbal and reading skills in any class is roughly equal to the grade, so that a third-grade teacher is likely to find a three-year spread; a sixth-grade teacher, a six-year spread. In relative terms—relative, that is, to the dispersion of white students—Negroes in the metropolitan Northeast are

the metropolitan Northeast is one year behind the average white student in reading ability; by grade six, he is more than a year and a half behind; by grade nine, he is more than two and a half years behind; and by the twelfth grade, he is nearly three years behind the average white. Much the same is true for Mexican Americans—their lag goes from nearly two and a half years in the sixth grade to three and a third in the twelfth—and for Puerto Ricans and Indian Americans, who end up 3.7 and 3.2 years, respectively, behind the white average in the twelfth grade.[19]

For Negroes in the rural South, the most disadvantaged group, by far, both the relative and the absolute gap widens as they go through school; by twelfth grade, they are almost two years behind Negroes in the metropolitan Northeast (and nearly five years behind whites in the metropolitan Northeast). For all groups, the figures understate the discrepancy: they measure the scores only of those students still in school in the twelfth grade, and large numbers of minority-group students leave school before then.

Some scholars, it should be pointed out, question the significance of these measures, arguing that academic achievement is a less important source of social and economic mobility than Coleman suggests, especially for blacks. Professor Otis Dudley Duncan of the University of Michigan, for example, has demonstrated that Negroes, at least until now, have received a substantially lower return than whites on an "investment" in education. At least one-third of the income gap between whites and blacks arises, Duncan writes, "because Negro and white men in the same line of work, with the same amount of formal schooling, with equal ability, from families of the same size and same socio-economic level, simply do not draw the same wages and salaries."[20] In short, Negroes have had great difficulty converting gains in education into gains in occupational achievement, income, and social status.

---

the same distance below white students in the twelfth as in the third grade, i.e., the average Negro scores below about 85 percent of white students in each grade. But since the dispersion of white students is much greater in the twelfth than in the third grade, the constant *relative* gap means a widening *absolute* gap.

19 *Equality of Educational Opportunity*, Table 3.121.2, page 274.

20 Otis Dudley Duncan, "Inheritance of Poverty or Inheritance of Race," in Daniel P. Moynihan, ed., *On Understanding Poverty,* New York: Basic Books, 1969.

Professor Duncan is raising an important point, one that suggests that dropping out of school may be more rational than educators and others have been willing to admit. At the same time, however, it must be recognized that his analysis reflects the heritage of the past, when most decent occupations and jobs were barred to Negroes, and when union contracts permitted, or even mandated, lower pay to blacks than to whites performing the same jobs. While prejudice has hardly disappeared, overt discrimination is declining; governments, corporations, and non-profit institutions are all taking active measures to increase the number of blacks in skilled, technical, professional, and managerial positions, with white workers beginning to complain of reverse discrimination. The experience of other ethnic groups, moreover—especially Japanese Americans and American Jews —suggests that there may be a lag of one or two decades between gains in educational attainment and their translation into gains in income and occupational status. During the 1920s and 1930s, for example, American Jews tended to be substantially overeducated for the positions they held, but when the barriers against them were lowered during and after World War II, they were able to convert their educational attainment into jobs and income with great speed.[21] The same phenomenon appears to be happening now to American Negroes. In a number of fields, black college graduates, who used to earn no more than whites with an eighth-grade education, now command salaries equal to, or higher than, those offered to whites. Indeed, few groups in the United States are in as good a bargaining position as Negro Ph.D.'s, especially in the social sciences. There is good reason to believe, therefore, that the disparity in the "return on education" may be narrowing.

Other critics argue that what prevents minority-group students from moving up the socioeconomic ladder is not their lack of academic ability but their failure to acquire middle-class habits of punctuality and reliability. "Despite much popular rhetoric," Professor Christopher Jencks of the Harvard Graduate School of Education writes, "there is little evidence that academic competence is critically important to adults in most walks of life. If you ask employers why they won't hire dropouts, for example, or why they promote certain kinds of people and not

21 Cf. Walter Fogel, "The Effect of Low Educational Attainment on Incomes: A Comparative Study of Selected Ethnic Groups," *The Journal of Human Resources,* Vol. 1, No. 2, Fall 1966; Nathan Glazer and Daniel Patrick Moynihan, *Beyond the Melting Pot,* pp. 42–44.

others, they seldom complain that dropouts can't read. Instead, they complain that dropouts don't get to work on time, can't be counted on to do a careful job, don't get along with others in the plant or office, can't be trusted to keep their hands out of the till and so on."[22] Hence it is the school's failure to develop such " 'middle-class virtues' as self-discipline and self-respect," Jencks insists, and "not its failure to teach history or physics or verbal skill" that is the real problem.

But students are not likely to develop self-respect if they are unable to master the reading, verbal, and computational skills that the schools are trying to teach. Children must have a sense of competence if they are to regard themselves as people of worth; the failure that minority-group children, in particular, experience from the beginning can only reinforce the sense of worthlessness that the dominant culture conveys in an almost infinite variety of ways, and so feed the self-hatred that prejudice and discrimination produce. Chronic failure makes self-discipline equally hard to come by; it is these children's failure to learn that produces the behavior problems of the slum school, as we shall argue later, and not the behavior problems that produce the failure to learn.

Jencks is exaggerating, moreover, when he claims that dropouts' inability to read is not a factor in employers' reluctance to hire or promote them. Indeed, the contrary is true. A fair degree of literacy—for example, the ability to read the safety instructions on machinery, or the instruction manuals for repairing automobiles or other machines—is essential for even routine jobs on an assembly line or in an automobile repair shop, let alone an office. When, for example, as is the case in Atlanta, Georgia, the median reading score in the eighth grade in Negro schools is slightly below the fourth-grade level, which means that half the black eighth graders are reading *below* the fourth-grade level, a great many jobs are bound to be beyond their capacity. In fact, virtually every firm that has attempted any large-scale hiring of so-called "disadvantaged" or "unemployable" men and women has found it necessary to provide, among other kinds of training, teaching in basic skills of reading and computation. And educational requirements will continue to increase, reflecting the long-run trend toward the substitution of brainpower for muscle power. The students now starting

[22] Christopher Jencks, "A Reappraisal of the Most Controversial Educational Document of Our Time," *New York Times Magazine,* August 10, 1969.

school may still be in the labor force in the year 2030; they need an education that will prepare them, or enable them to be prepared, for jobs whose very nature cannot now even be imagined.

In the meantime, employers are demanding more and more education on the part of prospective employees—more education, in fact, than is required to perform most of the jobs being offered to them. Certainly the growing tendency to reject anyone lacking a high school diploma, and in some cases, education beyond high school, bears little relation to the technical requirements of the present occupational structure; if existing jobs required that much education, half the present labor force would be unemployable.[23] What happened, in part, was that during the long period of labor surplus in the 1950s and early 1960s, employers made a diploma a prerequisite for employment as a screening device, i.e., as a means of cutting down on the number of people who had to be interviewed, or of insuring "a better class of employees." By the time the labor surplus had ended, the screening device had become a traditional job requirement.

But the demand for more education also reflects a major cultural change. The United States is becoming more and more of a "credential society," a kind of pseudo-meritocracy in which a person is judged by his credentials—his high school or college diploma—rather than by his performance on the job. These tendencies have been aggravated by the various campaigns designed to persuade youngsters to finish high school. Constant repetition of the thesis that to get a job, students need at least a high school diploma (former Secretary of Labor Willard Wirtz insisted that two years of schooling beyond high school was the minimum) has helped persuade employers that "dropouts" are indeed unemployable. The fact that there seems to be little correlation between people's performance on the job and either the amount of education they have had or the marks they have received does not help the young man who has been turned down, on the grounds of insufficient education, before he can demonstrate his competence or before he can develop that competence on the job itself.[24]

---

[23] Cf. Charles E. Silberman and the Editors of *Fortune, The Myths of Automation,* New York: Harper & Row, 1966, Chapters 1, 2, and 3. Cf. also A. J. Jaffe and Joseph Froomkin, *Technology and Jobs,* New York: F. A. Praeger, 1968, especially Chapter 8.

[24] Cf. Ivar Berg, *Education and Jobs: The Great Training Robbery,* New York: Frederick A. Praeger, 1970.

Whether spurious or real, the effects are substantially the same: at the very least, a high school diploma, and now increasingly, a junior college certificate or college diploma, is becoming the prerequisite to a decent job. Thus, education is becoming the gateway to the middle and upper reaches of society, which means that the schools and colleges thereby become the gatekeepers of the society. And this transforms the nature of educational institutions. They are inevitably politicized, for whoever controls the gateways to affluence and social position exercises political power, whether he likes it or not, and whether he is conscious of the fact or not. This is a central theme of Michael Young's brilliant and disturbing reverse-utopian novel, *The Rise of the Meritocracy;* it is also one of the genuine insights of the New Left.

What has produced such profound disappointment with the public school as an institution, and such burning anger at public school teachers and administrators, is the fact that recognition of the importance of education has coincided with a profound change in expectations, especially among Negro Americans, but now increasingly among Puerto Ricans, Mexican Americans, and Indian Americans as well. They are furious because the schools are not moving their children into the middle class rapidly enough. The concept of "rapidly enough" has also changed. To the extent that they were interested in mobility, earlier ethnic groups took it for granted that the movement would be one-by-one, over a fairly long time span. Negroes, by and large, are unwilling to wait that long; they have waited too long already, and they quite rightly want rapid and collective mobility. And the society as a whole places far less premium on deferred pleasure; even the banks now advertise, "Why wait?" Television has also projected black demonstrators into the homes of poor Mexican Americans and Indian Americans, persuading them, too, to demand changes for which they have been waiting patiently, and vainly.

III

But *can* the schools do more? Can they make educational outcomes less dependent—substantially less dependent—on social class, ethnicity, and race than they now are? The liberal response has been an automatic yes, but it is by no means clear that this is so. Indeed, it must be confessed that the weight of

evidence runs the other way—that at the moment, at least, the
burden of proof rests on those of us who claim that schools *can*
make a difference.

The largest bloc of evidence is contained in the Coleman Report itself, which found that the wide disparities in academic
achievement referred to above could not be attributed to differences in the quality of the schools minority-group students attended. Coleman and his collaborators had expected to find the
reverse. They had expected, that is to say, to find gross inequalities in the quality of the schools attended by majority- and
minority-group students, as measured by such factors as age of
school buildings, number of textbooks, library facilities, and
average class size, as well as teachers' education and background,
and they had assumed that these inequalities would explain the
inequalities in academic achievement. This has also been the
principal basis for federal policies and most other educational
programs: on the assumption that differences in school inputs
largely explained the differences in outputs, i.e., student achievement, the main thrust of educational policy has been to equalize
the inputs—to provide the resources and programs necessary to
bring below-average and average schools up to the level of the
best.

Much to his surprise, Coleman found nothing of the sort. The
survey revealed that black schools do not spend significantly less
money per pupil than white schools, do not have substantially
larger classes, do not operate in older and more crowded buildings,[25] do not have fewer or less adequate textbooks, and so on.
The assumption that there were gross disparities between the
resources put into black and white schools had apparently been
based on comparisons between Northern ghetto schools and
schools in the most affluent suburbs or city neighborhoods.
"What all such comparisons evidently ignore," Jencks explains,
"is the fact that most white Americans live in smaller (and
poorer) cities and towns, where the school facilities, curriculum
and teachers evidently leave almost as much to be desired as
they do in the big-city ghettos, where most blacks live." While
black students are short-changed, so are large numbers of white
students.

More important, Coleman and his colleagues found that differ-

[25] Except in the urban North, where the schools are older. In the South,
Negro schools tend to be newer than white schools, reflecting white
Southerners' willingness to pay to keep schools segregated.

ences in school quality were not very closely related to differences in student achievement; the cause-and-effect relationship between low student achievement and inadequate educational inputs that they expected to find simply did not materialize. On the contrary, neither black nor white nor Mexican-American, Puerto Rican, Indian American, or Oriental children from a given socioeconomic background did significantly better in schools with high per-pupil expenditures, modern plants, large libraries, up-to-date curricula, and the like than in schools with low expenditures, outdated plants and curricula, and small libraries. (The authors did conclude that minority-group students did slightly better in schools with articulate and experienced teachers, but the difference was small, and the evidence rather shaky.)

This finding has been misinterpreted as meaning that schools have *no* effect on students' learning. It means nothing of the sort. The evidence suggests only that the schools are remarkably uniform in their effects on students' learning. Differences in student achievement from school to school seem to be due more to differences in the students' own family background and in the backgrounds of their fellow students than to differences in the quality of the schools themselves. "Taking all these results together," the authors concluded, "one implication stands out above all: That schools bring little influence to bear on a child's achievement that is independent of his background and social context; and that this very lack of an independent effect means that the inequalities imposed on children by their home, neighborhood, and peer environment are carried along to become the inequalities with which they confront adult life at the end of school."

The Coleman Report is not the last word, by any means. It came into being because of a little-noticed section of the Civil Rights Act of 1964, which directed the U.S. Commissioner of Education to "conduct a survey . . . concerning the lack of availability of equal educational opportunity for individuals by reason of race, color, religion, or national origins," the findings to be reported to the President and to Congress within two years. The survey was delayed for nearly a year, in part by bureaucratic wrangling, in part by uncertainty and disagreement over how to go about the task. As a result, Coleman and his colleagues had very little time in which to design and administer the survey and analyze the results, and no time to consider objections to either their methods or conclusions, or even to correct a few mistakes that crept in. The report, consequently, has been subjected to a great deal of criticism, some of it quite heated and bitter, on a variety of methodological and substantive grounds.[26]

A number of the criticisms were quite valid. There were defects in the sample because of the refusal of some school districts, e.g., Chicago and Los Angeles, to participate, together with the fact that many "cooperating" districts failed to return important data. (Complete returns were received from only about 60 percent of the schools in the original sample.) The authors also used a number of questionable statistical techniques and made a number of errors in handling the data. But as Jencks points out, "they also recognized that such errors were likely, given the extreme haste with which they worked, and they were generous in helping others reanalyze the data more meticulously." Reanalyses have been made by staff members and outside consultants preparing the U.S. Civil Rights Commission Report on *Racial Isolation in the Public Schools,* by members of the Harvard University Seminar on the Equality of Educational Opportunity Report, which included scholars from other institutions as well as Harvard, and by Jencks and his colleagues at the Center for Educational Policy Research, which continued the analyses after the Seminar formally ended. The reanalyses indicate that while a number of important details were wrong, the main conclusions of the Coleman Report were correct. "In particular, and contrary to what some critics have argued," Jencks sums up, "the net effect of the report's various errors was to *under*-estimate the importance of family back-

---

[26] Cf. Samuel Bowles and Henry M. Levin, "The Determinants of Scholastic Achievement: An Appraisal of Some Recent Evidence," *The Journal of Human Resources,* Vol. 3, No. 1, Winter 1968, and Coleman's Reply in the Spring 1969 issue; Robert C. Nichols, "Schools and the Disadvantaged," *Science,* Vol. 154, December 9, 1966, and replies in the issue of May 12, 1967; review symposium by William H. Sewall, Leonard A. Marascuilo, and Harold W. Pfautz in *American Sociological Review,* Vol. 32, No. 3, June 1967; Harvard Educational Review, *Equal Educational Opportunity,* Harvard University Press, 1969 (an expansion of the Winter 1968 Special Issue of the *Harvard Educational Review*); Jeannette Hopkins, "Some Critical Questions About the 'Coleman Report' on *Equality of Educational Opportunity,* New York: Metropolitan Applied Research Center, mimeographed.

For a lucid summary and critique of both the Coleman Report and the various criticisms of it, cf. Christopher Jencks, "A Reappraisal of the Most Controversial Educational Document of Our Time," *New York Times Magazine,* August 10, 1969.

ground and *over*-estimate the importance of school in determining achievement."[27] [Emphasis in the original]

In any case, Coleman's most important and most controversial
conclusion—that variations in school inputs seem to have little
effect on students' academic achievement, while variations in
their family background have substantial impact—does not rest
on the Coleman Report's data alone. On the contrary; the Coleman Report is the largest but by no means the only study of its
sort. Surveys conducted for the English "Plowden Report,"
which avoided most of the methodological weaknesses and limitations of the Coleman Report, reached the same conclusion.[28]
So have other studies in the United States. Using the economist's
technique of input-output analysis, for example, Professor Jesse
Burkhead of Syracuse University traced the relationships between
the allocation of resources and other school inputs and the output
in terms of student achievement in high schools in five large
cities. His "most important finding" was "that variations in
educational outcomes in large-city high schools, measured in
terms of test scores, are almost wholly conditioned by the socioeconomic environment of the neighborhood. The income class
of the neighborhood, housing conditions, occupation of parents,
ethnic status—these are the important determinants of variations
in educational outcomes."[29]

[27] "A Reappraisal of the Most Controversial Educational Document of
Our Time." Cf. also Harvard Educational Review, *Equal Educational
Opportunity*, Harvard University Press, 1969; U.S. Civil Rights Com-
mission, *Racial Isolation in the Public Schools,* esp. Vol. 2, Appendix
C-1, Washington, D.C.: U.S. Government Printing Office, 1967.
[28] Central Advisory Council for Education (England), *Children and
Their Primary Schools*, London: Her Majesty's Stationery Office, 1967
(2 volumes). Cf. also, M. L. K. Pringle, N. R. Butler, and R. Davie,
11,000 Seven-Year Olds, London: Longmans, Green, 1966; Douglas
Pidgeon, ed., *Achievement in Mathematics,* National Foundation for
Educational Research in England and Wales, 1967.
[29] Jesse Burkhead with Thomas G. Fox and John W. Holland, *Input and
Output in Large-City High Schools*, Syracuse University Press, 1967.
Cf. also Alan B. Wilson, "Educational Consequences of Segregation in
a California Community," in U.S. Civil Rights Commission, *Racial Isola-
tion in the Public Schools,* Vol. 2; and "Social Stratification and Academic
Achievement," in A. Harry Passow, ed., *Education in Depressed Areas*,
New York: Teachers College Press, 1963; W. W. Charters, Jr., and N. L.
Gage, eds., *Readings in the Social Psychology of Education*, Boston:
Allyn & Bacon, 1963, esp. Section I; Robert E. Herriott and Nancy Hoyt
St. John, *Social Class and the Urban School*, New York: John Wiley,
1966; Harvard Educational Review, *Equal Educational Opportunity,* esp.
papers by Irwin Katz and Alan B. Wilson.

What is surprising, in fact, is not that Coleman found what he found but that so many people were so surprised, and so angered, by the finding. "The remarkable constancy of educational results in the face of widely differing deliberate approaches," J. M. Stephens writes in *The Process of Schooling*, "is one of those things that everybody knows. It is part of the folklore that, in educational investigations, one method turns out to be as good as another and that promising innovations produce about as much growth as the procedures they supplant, but no more. . . . In truth this has been a refrain ever since [Joseph Mayer] Rice discovered the surprising constancy of spelling attainment in the face of marked variations in the time devoted to study"—in 1897.[30] In a chapter entitled "The Constancy of the School's Accomplishment," Stephens summarizes research studies indicating that academic achievement is unaffected by class size, size of the school, administrative organization of the school, amount of time given to instruction, teacher's ability and personality, teaching method (e.g., lecturing versus class discussion), homogeneous or heterogeneous grouping, and so on.

Those who doubt that the schools can overcome the handicaps of poverty point also to the apparent failure of compensatory education. The U.S. Commission on Civil Rights, after reviewing a number of the most widely publicized programs, including New York City's Higher Horizons Program, St. Louis' Banneker District Project, and Syracuse's Madison Area Project, concluded that "none of the programs appear to have raised significantly the achievement of participating pupils, as a group, within the period evaluated by the Commission."[31] The Commission itself argued that schools *can* reduce the disparities between white and black students through integration. Evidence from the Coleman Report and other studies suggests that when black students are in predominantly white, and predominantly middle-class, schools, their academic achievement is higher. But the differences are modest, and the evidence by no means unequivocal. The gains are realized, moreover, only if the school is predominantly middle class, for the benefits of integration come almost entirely from the fact that integrated schools also tend to be middle class. Placing black students in lower-class white schools does not help their achievement at all.

---

[30] J. M. Stephens, *The Process of Schooling*, New York: Holt, Rinehart and Winston, 1967.
[31] *Racial Isolation in the Public Schools*, Vol. 1, Chapter 4.

The apparent failure of compensatory education, therefore, and the disappointing results of Head Start and other preschool programs—initial gains seem to wash out by the second or third grade—has led some scholars to raise the ugly question of genetic explanations for the schools' failure to educate Negro youngsters. "In other fields," Professor Arthur R. Jensen of Berkeley has written in a storm-provoking article in the *Harvard Educational Review*, "when bridges do not stand, when aircraft do not fly, when machines do not work, when treatments do not cure, despite all conscientious efforts on the part of many persons to make them do so, one begins to question the basic assumptions, principles, theories, and hypotheses that guide one's efforts. Is it time to follow suit in education?" he asks rhetorically, and then proceeds to answer in the affirmative for some 123 pages.[32]

What created the storm, of course, was the fact that Jensen went on to argue that genetic rather than environmental factors are largely responsible for Negroes' lower average IQ scores and poorer scholastic performance. As a result, Jensen suggested that schools teaching black children place less emphasis on abstract thinking and more emphasis on rote learning. The Pandora's Box having been opened, it is essential that we examine Jensen's argument.[33]

The bulk of Jensen's article is devoted to an exposition of the thesis that *individuals* with low IQ typically differ genetically from individuals with high IQ's. It is, as Jencks suggests, the clearest statement of this thesis ever published—a thesis that most of Jensen's critics either accept or make no real attempt to refute. Stated this way, in fact, the argument is almost unexceptionable, since Jensen concedes that environmental factors are also involved in IQ differences, and that the question is not the old one of heredity versus environment (genetic factors can

[32] Arthur R. Jensen, "How Much Can We Boost IQ and Scholastic Achievement?", *Harvard Educational Review*, Winter 1969.

[33] The analysis draws heavily on the author's earlier discussion of the question in *Crisis in Black and White*, Chapter 9, New York: Random House, 1964; and on the critiques of Jensen's article by Christopher Jencks ("Intelligence and Race," *The New Republic*, September 13, 1969), Lee J. Cronbach ("Heredity, Environment, and Educational Policy," *Harvard Educational Review*, Vol. 39, No. 2, Spring 1969), and Martin Deutsch ("Happenings on the Way Back to the Forum," *Harvard Educational Review*, Vol. 39, No. 3, Summer 1969). Cf. also the discussions of Jensen's article by Jerome S. Kagan, James F. Crow, and David Elkind in the Spring 1969 *Harvard Educational Review*, and the Reply by Jensen in the Summer 1969 issue.

only take effect through interaction with the environment), but rather of assessing the relative importance of each.

Unfortunately, Jensen does not stop there. He proceeds to measure the relative importance of heredity and environment, concluding that in contemporary white America, environmental factors account for no more than 20 percent of the variation in individual IQ's, with genetic factors accounting for the rest. More important, he goes on to argue that genetic factors account not only for the great bulk of the IQ differences among individuals *within* a given group, but also for the great bulk of the IQ differences *between* groups—in particular, between white and black Americans, whose IQ's differ, on average, by fifteen points. (While both white and black IQ's have risen over time, the difference between them has held pretty constant.)

But Jensen's evidence—a reorganization of existing data—is drawn in its entirety from studies of whites, mostly in England and the United States. He relies in particular on studies of identical twins reared in different homes and of unrelated children reared in the same home. In general, identical twins, who have identical genes, have very similar IQ's when reared in different homes, while unrelated children reared in the same home have quite different IQ scores. These studies are interesting and useful but hardly conclusive. They cover very few children; most of the studies were conducted abroad, since little serious research of this sort has been conducted in the United States for a generation; different investigators have measured IQ in different ways; and most important, a number of the studies are in disagreement, with the importance of environment varying from one study to another, a fact that Jensen tends to ignore or suppress. Without question, his data demonstrates that heredity has an important effect on IQ; but they do not permit precise estimates of the proportion of the variations of IQ within a given group that is determined by heredity.

More important, Jensen's data permit no conclusions at all about the role of heredity in explaining the IQ differences *between* the races. It is quite possible, to be sure, that the genes affecting IQ are distributed differently among whites and blacks, since the two groups differ genetically in a number of other respects—bone structure and configuration, facial characteristics, amount and texture of hair, susceptibility to certain kinds of diseases, and so on, as well as skin color. The fact that something is possible, however, does not thereby make it so. Given the present state of knowledge among geneticists, biologists, psychologists, and anthropologists, we simply do not know whether blacks and whites have different gene pools with respect to IQ—nor do we know whether such differences, if they exist, favor one group or the other.[34] Indeed, given the social and cultural environment with which black Americans have had to contend, it is quite possible that they are genetically "superior" to whites.

In any case, Jensen's argument that black-white IQ differences are largely genetic in origin simply does not stand. As Jencks points out, something like one-sixth of the white identical twins reared in separate homes have as large a difference in IQ —fifteen points or thereabouts—as that between the average white and the average black. The differences between the twins can be due only to environment, since identical twins always have the same genes. If a sixth of the white families raising these twins differed enough to produce a fifteen-point IQ difference, it is plausible to assume that the average black home, family, community, and culture may differ enough from the average white home, family, community, and culture to produce the same disparity.

Jensen's whole treatment of environment, in fact, is simplistic almost to the point of caricature. He makes a great deal of the fact, for example, that middle-class black children have lower IQ and achievement scores than middle-class white children, as though socioeconomic status were the only environmental factor involved.

But socioeconomic status is neither the only nor the most important element in environment. Indeed, Jensen has ignored a substantial scholarly literature suggesting that what inhibits the academic development of lower-class children relative to that of middle-class children is not poverty per se, but a complex of cultural factors frequently, but not necessarily, associated with poverty and low social status. These include the nature of the language used, the child-rearing practices, and a whole range of unconsciously transmitted values and attitudes, all of which may vary substantially from one ethnic, racial, or religious group to another within the same socioeconomic class.

[34] There is no more basis for statements that the distribution of intelligence is identical in all races than for statements that one race is superior to another. Social scientists who have argued that the distribution is identical are guilty of sloppy, if well-intentioned, polemics that have done the cause of racial justice a grave disservice. Their refusal to acknowledge the reality, or even the possibility, of racial differences suggests a fear on their part that differences must connote inferiority.

In the instance at hand, as Jencks points out, "the fact that a black and white child both have fathers who do the same kind of work or mothers who spent the same number of years in school does not mean the two children are treated the same way, either at home or elsewhere. Jewish children also do better on IQ tests than Christians at the same socioeconomic level, but very few people conclude that Jews are genetically superior to Christians. Instead, we conclude that Jews treat their children differently from Christians, even when their occupations, incomes, and education are the same."

The environmental effect is even more complex than Jencks's comparison suggests. Within the same religious or ethnic group, for example, subtle differences in cultural traditions may have profound effects on children's IQ and academic performance. In a carefully controlled comparison of native-born, middle-class American Jewish children coming from Ashkenazic (Western European) and Sephardic (in this instance, Syrian) descent, for example, Professor Morris Gross of Hunter College found substantial differences in IQ and academic performance between the two. The groups were matched in a variety of ways: they all lived in the same neighborhood; the children as well as the mothers were all native born; English was the language spoken in all the homes; and all the parents were religiously oriented, to the extent of sending their children to a private religious school rather than to the local public school. Despite these similarities, the Sephardic youngsters, on average, had IQ's seventeen points below the Ashkenazic average.

The difference cannot be attributed to socioeconomic background. "The Sephardic mothers in this study were not 'deprived,' however one defined the term," Professor Gross writes. "In many cases, they had minks, maids, and country homes. Similarly, the sensory, linguistic, and experiential deprivation, commonly associated with slum conditions and economic poverty, were not apparent; the Sephardic mothers were all native born, high school graduates, and none worked."[35] As the sociologist John Seeley writes in his introduction to Gross's paper, the results suggest "both the virtually invisible persistence of cultural traditions ('ethnic differences') for very long periods even under ostensibly like social conditions, and the depth to which such differences reach right into something so profound in the ontogenetic process as 'measured intelligence.' "

[35] Morris Gross, *Learning Readiness in Two Jewish Groups*, New York: Center for Urban Education, Occasional Paper, 1967.

Moreover, differences in cultural tradition, language, child-rearing practices, and so on, do not exhaust the environmental factors that may affect intellectual performance. To assess the influence of environment, it is necessary to look beyond the subculture of a particular race or ethnic or religious group to the larger culture of the society as a whole, and particularly to the way it impinges on the group in question. Certainly American society does not treat all individuals alike. To discuss Negro intelligence and achievement with no reference to the manifold ways in which American society systematically stripped blacks of their connection to their past or to the ways in which it still destroys ambition and suppresses the sense of self, as Jensen does, is to turn one's back on what may be the most important environmental influences of all. Anyone who seriously believes that low IQ is the cause of Negroes' problems or that higher IQ's might solve them, as Jencks suggests, "should simply ask himself whether he would trade the genes which make his skin white for genes which would raise his IQ 15 points."

However important genetic factors may be in explaining individual differences in IQ, therefore, there is no basis at present for arguing that they explain the differences between the races; at the very least, the question must be considered open. In any event, as Lee Cronbach points out, "the educator's job is to work on the environment; teaching him about heredity can do no more than warn him not to expect easy victories." Clearly the victories will not be easy. They *are* possible.

IV

There is ample evidence, in any case, that the learning difficulties from which lower-class and minority-group children suffer have their origins in the school as well as in the home. As Basil Bernstein of the University of London has written, with typical English understatement, "we have failed to think through systematically the relationship between the pupil's background and the educational measures appropriate to successful learning."[36]

To be sure, a great deal of thought has been given to the rela-

[36] Basil Bernstein, "Social Structure, Language, and Learning," reprinted in A. Harry Passow, Miriam Goldberg, Abraham J. Tannenbaum, *Education of the Disadvantaged*, New York: Holt, Rinehart & Winston, 1967. Cf. also B. Bernstein, "Social Class and Linguistic Development: A Theory of Social Learning," in Halsey, Floud, and Anderson, *Education, Economy and Society*.

tionship between the "disadvantaged" pupil's background and his failure to learn. Research by a number of scholars—for example, Basil Bernstein, Roger Brown, Carl Bereiter, Sheldon L. White—suggests that the difficulties lower-class children have in school are directly related to their language structure and usage. Others—e.g., J. McV. Hunt, Benjamin S. Bloom, Martin Deutsch, Robert D. Hess, Fred L. Strodtbeck, Burton White—stress the "environmental deprivation" of the lower-class home, reflected not only in the language used but also in the ways in which adults, especially the mother, interact with the child, the absence of books and other artifacts of middle-class culture, the view of life that develops, and so on. The result, in this view, is that lower-class children enter school lacking a wide variety of attitudes and cognitive and affective skills which are crucial to success in school, and which middle-class children acquire from their environment more or less by osmosis. Still others, influenced by David C. McClelland's work on "achievement motivation," place their emphasis on the failure of some ethnic cultures to develop the complex of attitudes—future orientation, a stress on individual rather than collective mobility, an emphasis on individual achievement, a sense of control over one's own destiny—needed for academic (as well as social and economic) achievement.

This literature has contributed a great deal to our understanding of why "disadvantaged" children fail; with a few exceptions, it has contributed very little to our understanding of why *schools* fail, or of how they might be changed in order to make learning successful for children from these backgrounds.[37] Indeed, the question hardly even comes up in most of the scholarly literature. It is taken for granted that if children fail to learn, the fault must lie with them rather than with the school. Yet schools that place the blame for students' failures on their "poor home environment" or "lack of motivation" do not hesitate to take full credit when these same students succeed.

ITEM: A black student does poorly in a Northern high school for three years. When he expresses interest in college, his guidance counselor assures him that he is not "college material."

---

[37] The most notable exception is the work of Martin Deutsch, one of the first American scholars to argue that lower-class children's failure in school was rooted in the school as well as in the home and community environment. Cf. Martin Deutsch and associates, *The Disadvantaged Child*, New York: Basic Books, 1967.

Through the intercession of some white friends, and over the objection of the guidance counselor, he is admitted into the federally financed Upward Bound program at a nearby college, which provides an intensive remedial program during the summer, and special tutoring during his senior year. His grades shoot up so rapidly that the Upward Bound officials recommend him for a special Transitional Year program at Yale University, designed to give "underachieving students" with high potential the academic skills and the self-confidence they need to realize their potential. The counselor begrudgingly supplies the necessary transcripts, after remarking to the boy, "What, you at Yale? Don't make me laugh."

But when the student is admitted—one of sixty selected, out of 500 applicants—the school system's public relations apparatus springs into action. The boy's picture appears in the local newspaper in an article reporting the high school's success story; the superintendent of schools introduces him to the public at an open meeting of the board of education; and when a group of local black leaders meet with school officials to press some of their complaints about the system, they are told that the boy's admission to the Yale program shows how well the school is serving black students.

Schools fail, however, less because of maliciousness than because of mindlessness. Like Procrustes stretching his guests or cutting off their limbs to make them fit the standard-sized bed his inn provided, educators and scholars, frequently with the best of intentions, have operated on the assumption that children should be cut or stretched or otherwise "adjusted" to fit the schools, rather than adjusting the schools to fit the children. And most of us have tended to accept this without question.

Much of the current emphasis on preschool education, for example, grows out of the unconscious assumption that the school is fixed and immutable, and the solution therefore is to change the child to fit the school. Research indicates that lower-class children do not learn because they enter school lacking the attitudes and the linguistic, cognitive, and affective skills that are crucial to success in school. Ergo, teach these skills to lower-class children before they enter school![38]

---

[38] The writer has been as guilty of this reasoning as anyone else. Cf. C. E. Silberman, *Crisis in Black and White*, Ch. 9; and "Let's Give Slum Children a Chance: A Radical Proposal," *Harper's*, May 1964.

It is at least theoretically possible, however, that a better solution would be to change the school, too. While most preschool programs do boost their students' IQ and achievement test scores, the gains, as we noted before, are only temporary. The fact that these gains are dissipated within a year after the intervention stops suggests that they may have been caused by the intervention itself, and not by the fact that it came at some critical stage in the children's development.[39] This hypothesis draws support from some recent reports that when the intervention continues in the public school itself, the children seem to maintain their initial advantage.[40]

The evidence is fragmentary, of course, but the question is real. "Now that more and more evidence on the impermanence of enrichment effects appears to be accumulating," Dr. Bettye Caldwell, editor of the *Journal of Child Development*, writes (in a letter to the author), "I find myself thinking that the critical period hypothesis in this context was naïve to begin with. That is, if behavior at any point of time is a function both of the individual genetic potential, his pool of accumulated experiences and skills, and of the current situation in which the behavior will occur, then it is naïve to assume that one could ever assume that the work of the environment is completed. . . . If the slight gains we are able to produce evanesce in the bump and grind of the existing elementary school levelling process," Dr. Caldwell adds, "then in all honesty we should advocate forgetting about preschool programs and concentrate instead on improving the later educational programs."

[39] There are, of course, other explanations for the fact that the gains wash out so rapidly. It is possible, for example, that the fall-off occurs because the intervention did not come early enough; some researchers suggest intervention as soon as the child is born, some even before that, i.e, *in utero*. It is possible, too, that the fall-off occurs because the intervention was not massive enough, or was not in the right sequence, or did not have the appropriate character. It is also possible that the intervention fails because it is not reinforced by the child's home life. "I personally believe that the family is the primary educational institution and that the schools are secondary," Earl Schaefer of the National Institute of Mental Health writes, and "that until we succeed in training and motivating parents and future parents in early and continuing child care and education we will not solve our educational problems."

[40] Institute for Developmental Studies, School of Education, New York University, Interim Progress Report—Part II, November 1968 (mimeographed); Martin Deutsch, "Happenings on the Way Back to the Forum," *Harvard Educational Review*, Vol. 39, No. 3, Summer 1969.

What is it in the schools that leads to failure? Professor Robert K. Merton of Columbia University, one of the most distinguished American sociologists, suggested the answer in 1948, in his theory of the "self-fulfilling prophecy."[41] Stated as simply as possible, the theory holds that in many, if not most, situations, people tend to do what is expected of them—so much so, in fact, that even a false expectation may evoke the behavior that makes it seem true. As Merton formulated the theory in his essay, "men respond not only to the objective features of a situation, but also, and at times primarily, to the meaning this situation has for them. And once they have assigned some meaning to the situation," their subsequent behavior, and the behavior of others, are both determined by it. Whether the meaning they ascribe to the situation is initially true or false is beside the point; the definition evokes the behavior that makes it come true. "The specious validity of the self-fulfilling prophecy," as Merton put it, "perpetuates a reign of error."[42]

Thus, a teacher's *expectation* can and does quite literally affect a student's *performance*. The teacher who assumes that her students cannot learn is likely to discover that she has a class of children who are indeed unable to learn; yet another teacher, working with the same class but without the same expectation, may discover that she has a class of interested learners. The same obtains with respect to behavior: the teacher who assumes that her students will be disruptive is likely to have a disruptive class on her hands. "You see, really and truly, apart from the things anyone can pick up [the dressing and the proper way of speaking, and so on]," Eliza Doolittle explains in Shaw's *Pygmalion*, "the difference between a lady and a flower girl is not how she behaves, but how she's treated. I shall always be a flower

[41] Robert K. Merton, "The Self-Fulfilling Prophecy," *The Antioch Review*, Summer 1948 (reprinted in Merton, *Social Theory and Social Structure*, New York: Free Press, revised and enlarged edition, 1957).
[42] For a review of the voluminous literature documenting the phenomenon, cf. Robert Rosenthal and Lenore Jacobson, *Pygmalion in the Classroom*, New York: Holt, Rinehart, and Winston, 1968, Chapters 1 to 4. The rest of the volume is a report of an experiment designed to show that raising teachers' expectations about some children's intellectual capacity results in higher achievement by these children. The hypothesis is reasonable and probably correct; unfortunately, the data presented are defective and contradictory, and so do not, by themselves, support the conclusion. Cf. the review by Robert L. Thorndike in the *Teachers College Record*, Vol. 70, No. 8, May 1969.

girl to Professor Higgins, because he always treats me as a flower girl, and always will; but I know I can be a lady to you, because you always treat me as a lady, and always will."

In most slum schools, the children are treated as flower girls. One cannot spend any substantial amount of time visiting schools in ghetto or slum areas, in fact, be they black, Puerto Rican, Mexican American, or Indian American, without being struck by the modesty of the expectations teachers, supervisors, principals, and superintendents have for the students in their care.

Consider, for example, James Herndon's description of his first day of teaching in an all-black California junior high school. Walking up the stairs to his first class, he receives his first bit of advice from a fellow teacher:

> Jim, you ever work with these kids before?
> No, I admitted.
> I thought so. Well, now, the first thing is, you don't ever push 'em, and you don't expect too much. If you do, they'll blow sky-high and you'll have one hell of a time getting them down again. May never do it. Now, it's not their fault, we all know that. But you have to take them as they are, not as you and me would like them to be. That means, you find out what they can do, and you give it to them to do.[43]

Later in the semester, Herndon is visited by the language and social studies consultant for the district:

> Mrs. X didn't visit my classes. She met me in the teacher's room during my free period and opened the conversation by telling me that she came, as she did with all the new teachers, to offer any help or advice she could. . . . She asked me if I had any problems I cared to mention. Did I? I began to outline them . . .
> Before I'd gotten fairly started, she interrupted. Now, we all have our problems, she said, and sometimes we're tempted to consider our own problems as being unique. But with *these* children (leaving out The Word, as usual) I've found that a simpler, more direct approach works best. I feel already that you may be making it all too complicated for yourself. In my experience, the best advice I can give you beginning teachers is, hold out a carrot.
> A carrot? I didn't get it.
> You know, she said brightly, the carrot, or perhaps we

---

[43] James Herndon, *The way it spozed to be,* New York: Simon & Schuster, 1968.

should say a sugar cube. If you want the goat to pull the cart, but he doesn't want to, you hold a carrot out in front of him. He tries to reach the carrot because he does want it. In doing so he pulls the cart. *If,* she said with a kind of wink, *if* you've attached the carrot to the cart.

I must have seemed a little stupid to her. Seeing that I just sat there, she tried to explain. *Teaching these children is like training animals. For each task you want them to do, you must offer them a carrot. . . .* Of course the reward must vary. There are individual differences as we know. A carrot for one, a sugar cube for another. [Emphasis added]

Herndon's supervisor's advice to treat the children like animals —to train them rather than to educate them—was no isolated incident. The metaphor is widespread and explains, as much as any other factor, the way in which expectations fulfill themselves. "I attended to teachers' conversations, listened to them abuse the children until I could no longer go into the teacher's lunchroom," Herbert Kohl, perhaps the most sensitive of the recent crop of teachers who have written anguished accounts of their experiences in ghetto schools, reports. "The most frequent epithet they used in describing the children was 'animals.' " He goes on to describe the self-fulfilling prophecy in action:

After a while the word "animal" came to epitomize for me most teachers' ambiguous relations to ghetto children—the scorn and the fear, the condescension yet the acknowledgment of some imagined power and unpredictability. I recognized some of that in myself, but never reached the sad point of denying my fear and uncertainty by projecting fearsome and unpredictable characteristics on the children and using them in class as some last primitive weapon. It was pitiful yet disgusting, all the talk of "them," "these children," "animals." I remember a teacher from another school I taught in, a white Southerner with good intentions and subtle and unacknowledged prejudices. He fought for the good part of a semester to gain the children's attention and affection. He wanted the children to listen to him, to respond to him, to learn from him; yet never thought to listen, respond, or learn from the children, who remained unresponsive, even sullen. They refused to learn, laughed at his professed good intentions, and tested him beyond his endurance. One day in rage and vexation it all came out.

"Animals, that's what you are, animals, wild animals, that's all you are or can be."

His pupils were relieved to hear it at last, their suspicions confirmed. They rose in calm unison and slowly circled the raging trapped teacher, chanting, "We are animals, we are animals, we are animals . . . ," until the bell rang and mercifully broke the spell. The children ran off, leaving the broken, confused man wondering what he'd done, convinced that he had always been of goodwill but that "they" just couldn't be reached.[44]

Prejudice is not the only problem; expectations can be lowered by empathy as well as by distaste. Indeed, one has the uneasy feeling that many of the books, courses, and conferences designed to sensitize teachers and administrators to the problems of the "disadvantaged" have backfired. By learning why black (or Puerto Rican, Mexican American, or Indian American) youngsters fail through no fault of their own, teachers learn to understand and to sympathize with failure—and thereby to expect it. James C. Conant's widely hailed volume, *Slums and Suburbs*, which called attention to the "social dynamite" contained in the failures of ghetto education, provides a nice case in point, for the book amounted to a plea to educators to lower their sights. "One lesson to be drawn from visiting and contrasting a well-to-do suburb and a slum is all important for understanding American public education," Dr. Conant announced on the first page. *"The lesson is that to a considerable degree what a school should do and can do is determined by the status and ambitions of the families being served."* [Emphasis his]

When schoolmen do try to adjust the school to fit the students' needs, therefore—for example, by creating separate curricula for the "disadvantaged"—all too often they compound rather than relieve the problem. Thus many schools have tried to follow Conant's recommendation that "in a heavily urbanized and industrialized free society the educational experiences of youth should fit their subsequent employment." But as James Coleman points out, the recommendation "takes as *given* what should be problematic—that a given boy is going into a given post-secondary occupational or educational path. It is one thing to take as given that approximately 70 percent of an entering high school freshman class will not attend college; but to assign a *particular child* to a curriculum designed for that 70 percent closes off for that child the opportunity to attend college."[45] [Emphasis his]

[44] Herbert Kohl, *36 Children*, New York: New American Library, 1967.
[45] James S. Coleman, "The Concept of Equality of Educational Opportunity," in Harvard Educational Review, *Equal Educational Opportunity*.

The problem begins well before high school; it starts, in fact, in the first grade. The anthropologist Eleanor Burke Leacock has described with exquisite detail how different are the expectations regarding both academic achievement and behavior among teachers in middle-class and lower-class schools, and how, in all kinds of subtle ways, these expectations serve to teach lower-class children *not* to learn.[46] In the study she directed, teams of observers studied classrooms and interviewed teachers and students in schools representing four socioeconomic categories: low-income black, low-income white, middle-income black, and middle-income white. They discovered, as Professor Leacock writes, that "even with the best will in the world and the application of considerable skill" in their teaching, teachers "unwittingly help perpetuate a system of inequalities" by transmitting to the children "in myriad ways the message: 'This is your station in society; act, perform, talk, *learn* according to it and no more.' " [Emphasis hers]

The difference in expectations is summed up in these responses to an interviewer's question, "What kinds of things do you think these children should be getting out of school?" A fifth-grade teacher in a low-income black school answered:

> First of all, discipline. They should know that when an older person talks to them or gives a command that they should respond, they should listen. That there are times when we do things—there's a time for fun, there's a time for play, then there is a time when we should get down to work. I feel they should learn values, moral values, social values. . . . That a teacher is not here as a policeman but as someone to help. That maybe they might not remember everything they have learned in school, but I think they should remember a broad concept. They should remember the nice things that happened in school.

A teacher in a middle-income white school answered this way:

> As I say to the children, the most important thing is to be able to get along with one another and to have acceptable standards of behavior. In other words to develop into a good human being. That comes first. I think that is the main reason they come to school, because they can learn how to spell at home with anybody. But the fact that they're working in a

[46] Eleanor Burke Leacock, *Teaching and Learning in City Schools,* New York: Basic Books, 1969.

group and that they are learning acceptable standards of behavior is very important. I count that number one. And secondly, the intellectual development of the child. That they
progress intellectually is very important, but that they become
decent and intelligent human beings, that's most important as
far as I'm concerned.

Asked what they do when children aren't doing what they're supposed to be doing, the teachers' answers are equally revealing.
The teacher in the low-income school uses learning as a punishment.

> Oh, I call their names. It depends on what the offense is.
> Under no circumstances will I allow talking on a fire drill.
> If there is talking, they'll have to come back and maybe write
> something. One of my pet things has been getting the dic-
> tionary and beginning to write. . . . Even the thought of it,
> the dictionary and writing—you have to look back and forth
> —it's tedious. It's not the "I must behave myself on the fire
> drill" type of thing. . . . What else? I might write a note in
> their notebooks to their mothers, I might change their seat.
> . . . I might have them stand for a certain length of time.

The teacher in the middle-income school takes a different tack:

> If somebody talks and I don't want to say, now you're rude
> for talking while I'm talking, I just hold my hand up and I say
> "No. 4," or just four fingers, and they'll know that some-
> body's being rude. It works. . . . You would like to know,
> I'm sure, how I handle a great deal of disorder. I find some-
> body that is sitting quietly, and I say, "I like the way whosit's
> sitting. I like the way Evelyn is working." They get the mes-
> sage. Immediately they want to be praised. They want me to
> like them for something so that it usually works magic.

These expectations are transmitted to the children in all sorts
of ways. Like almost everyone who studies ghetto schools, Leacock and her observers were struck by the liveliness and eager
interest children in the lower grades displayed, and by the passivity and apathy that is evident later on; in the schools they
studied, the children's interest and eagerness had disappeared
by the fifth grade.

The reason was not hard to find: the teachers in the low-
income black school did remarkably little to evoke the children's

interest. A careful count of the frequency and nature of teacher-student interchanges, for example, showed that teachers in the low-income classrooms discussed the curriculum with their students less than half as often as did the teachers in the middle-income rooms. There is considerable truth, in short, to Kenneth Clark's insistence that black children do not learn because they are not taught.[47]

Low-income students are discouraged from learning in another way. The teachers in the low-income black school not only taught less, they also evaluated their students' work less than half as frequently as the teachers in the middle-class rooms. More important, perhaps, their evaluations were almost always negative; in the low-income black classes, teachers made negative comments about their students three times as often as they made positive ones. In the middle-class rooms, by contrast, teachers offered positive evaluations more often than negative ones. The result, as Leacock writes, is that by the fifth grade, "the low expectations for their achievement, combined with the lack of challenge in the classroom, had taken their toll. The children fidgeted listlessly, looked distractedly and aimlessly here and there, and waited until something captured their attention." The classroom observers, Professor Leacock writes, "were struck by the fact that standards in the low-income Negro classrooms were low for both achievement and behavior." This was not what they had expected to find, for "they had assumed that the middle-income schools would stress achievement and that the lower-income schools would emphasize behavior. Yet it was in the middle-income schools, both Negro and white," the researchers discovered, "that the strictest demands were made" on behavior, as well as on achievement, with students expected to adhere to high standards for everything from "self-control" and "being nice" to posture and such inane teacher idiosyncrasies as "Are our thumbs in the right place?" In the low-income schools, the demands were fewer and more modest, with the emphasis, as noted earlier, on "learning to take orders," and the expectation was that disorder would prevail. As often as not, it did.

It can be argued, of course, that teachers in low-income schools have no choice—that they must spend less time teaching because they have to spend more time maintaining order. One study of classroom procedures in Negro slum schools, for exam-

[47] Kenneth B. Clark, *Dark Ghetto*, New York: Harper & Row, 1965.

ple, indicated that teachers spend as much as 75 percent of their time maintaining, or trying to maintain, order, leaving only 25 percent of the time for actual instruction.[48]

The question, of course, is why so much time has to be devoted to maintaining order. One reason, certainly, is that much of the pathology of the ghetto which Kenneth Clark describes spills over into the school; teachers must be on guard to prevent violence, to stop some youngsters from extorting money from younger or weaker children, to monitor the use of, and traffic in, narcotics, and so on.

For the most part, however, particularly in elementary schools, the misbehavior that keeps teachers from teaching is of a milder, more familiar sort: children talking when they are supposed to be silent, moving about when they should be sitting still, daydreaming when they should be paying attention, and so on. This is what might be termed misbehavior by definition; what would be considered normal behavior in almost any other environment is defined in school as misbehavior. For schools—wealthy suburban schools, as we shall argue in the next chapter, no less than slum schools—are obsessed with silence and lack of motion. It is, indeed, this unnatural insistence on silence and lack of motion that forces teachers to devote so much time and energy to maintaining "control," and that makes it so difficult for them to achieve it.

ITEM: From a description of a second-grade class in a big city slum.

The class is one that the principal himself warned visitors, with a kind of negative pride, to be one of the "wild" classes. He was not at all reluctant that visitors should witness the problems his school faced. The class is in ill repute throughout the school; several teachers commented on it, one calling it "a zoo." There are twenty-four students on roll, fifteen boys and nine girls. They are all in the reading readiness stage [kindergarten level]. . . . On this day there are only eighteen of the twenty-four students present . . .

The song is over and the teacher, attempting to drill them on the days of the week, asks them, "What day is today? What day was yesterday? What day will tomorrow be?" As the chil-

[48] Martin Deutsch, "Minority Group and Class Status as Related to Social and Personality Factors in Scholastic Achievement," *Society for Applied Anthropology Monograph*, No. 2, 1960.

dren call out the names of the various days, she stops to correct them: "Give your answers in sentences!"

Meanwhile several children are noisily running around the room hitting one another. Others sit in a stupor, apparently quite unaware of their surroundings. In the space of the first ten minutes, the teacher has used physical force and actually hurts the children in an attempt to control them. Yet she has not achieved control of the class, nor does she at any time during the morning. She frequently addresses her noisy, restless class, saying, "When I have everyone's attention and your hands are folded, then I will listen to what you're really trying to say." Since this never happens, she never really listens to any of the children during the morning, yet many of them do seem to want to say something to her.[49]

The question of why teachers have more trouble maintaining control in lower-class than in middle-class schools remains. A piece of the answer may be that lower-class children are more physical (and less verbal) than middle-class children, and so find it much more difficult to sit still for five hours a day. A far more important reason, the Leacock study suggests, is "the reign of error" which the self-fulfilling prophecy sets in motion.

It is a gross oversimplification, therefore, to attribute the failures of the slum school to lower-class students' inability to understand or unwillingness to accept middle-class values. What teachers and administrators communicate to lower-class students, Leacock suggests, in what is perhaps her most useful insight, is not middle-class *values* but middle-class *attitudes* toward lower-class people and their role in society. The school, she writes, conveys *"a middle-class image of how working-class children are and how they should be*—an image which emphasizes obedience, respect, and conscientiousness . . . rather than ability, responsibility, and initiative, and which expects . . . unruliness with regard to behavior and apathy with regard to curriculum." [Emphasis hers] By conveying this image to their students, "teachers perpetuate the very behavior they decry." And the behavior, in turn, confirms the teachers' initial expectations, thereby perpetuating the reign of error for still another generation of students.

The teachers whom Leacock & Company interviewed and observed, it is important to realize, "were all experienced, hard-

[49] From G. Alexander Moore, Jr., *Realities of the Urban Classroom*, Garden City, N.Y.: Doubleday Anchor Books, 1967.

working, and capable people who were trying to do their best for the children in their classrooms within the limits of their training and situations."[50] So far as the observers could tell, the teachers were free from racial prejudice (as free, that is to say, as anyone growing up in the United States can be). Some of the teachers were themselves black; those who taught in low-income black schools expected as little from their students as did their white colleagues. Their prejudices, in short, were prejudices of class.

Where racial and ethnic prejudice exists, however, the vicious circle of low expectations = low achievement = low expectations becomes even more vicious. And such prejudice does exist; there is little reason to expect teachers to be any freer from prejudice than the rest of us. In all too many schools, therefore, minority-group children are exposed to a steady flow of insult and humiliation that blocks their learning in a number of ways. Experiencing prejudice reinforces the sense of inferiority, even of worthlessness, which the culture and society outside the school instills. It destroys the incentive to learn, persuading students that there is no use trying, since the cards are stacked against them anyway. And it evokes a burning anger and hostility against the school that makes students want to leave as soon as they can, and that diverts their energies from learning into a search for ways of striking back.

Teachers and administrators convey their prejudice in a variety of ways, some subtle, some not so subtle, all damaging.

ITEM: A sixth-grade class in a racially mixed school. A black girl calls out the answer to a question the teacher had asked of the entire class. "Don't you call out," the teacher responds. "You sit where I put you and be quiet." A few minutes later, when a blond-haired, blue-eyed girl calls out an answer to another question, the teacher responds, "Very good, Annette; that's good thinking."

ITEM: A fifth-grade class in a racially-mixed school. A black youngster has his hand raised to ask a question; before the teacher can respond, the principal, who is visiting, tells the child, "Put your dirty hand down and stop bothering the teacher with questions."

[50] Just how limited that training usually is will be discussed in Chapter 10, with possible remedies discussed in Chapter 11.

Sometimes—more frequently than those outside the schools realize, and more frequently than those inside the schools are willing to admit—prejudice manifests itself in harsh and even brutal ways.

ITEM: An assistant principal, monitoring the main corridor in a large urban high school, sees a black student, one leg in a cast, hobbling along on crutches. He waits until the student has reached his destination, and then orders him to return to the other end of the two-block-long corridor and retrace his steps. The student had been walking on the left side of the corridor, and an obscure and never-before enforced school regulation requires students to walk on the right side.

ITEM: A fifteen-year-old black boy is suspended from high school, accused of having put his hand up a white girl's skirt as she passed his table in the cafeteria. Since the boy is afraid to upset his mother, who is about to undergo major surgery, the writer intercedes in his behalf, and so pays a call on the high school's vice-principal in charge of discipline. The vice-principal explains that the boy's guilt is clear: the girl had two witnesses (i.e., friends) who confirmed her story. Asked why he had not also questioned the boy's witnesses—the youngster had been lunching with the writer's son, and was sitting with several black friends at the time of the alleged incident—the vice-principal explains that it wasn't necessary, since the girl had also reported that the boy had made obscene remarks to her a few months earlier, while boarding the school bus to return home.

But the latter incident, which had not been reported at the time, could not have taken place at all; the boy in question did not ride that particular school bus. (As a member of the wrestling team, he remained in school until five or six o'clock.) When the writer pressed the matter further, pointing out that the girl's parents appeared to be emotionally disturbed—they had disrupted a public meeting a few nights before with charges of sexual assault against their daughter, the father at one point announcing that he offered prayers for his daughter's virtue every night—the vice-principal confessed that he had no reason to think the boy was guilty. The girl, whom he described as a "floozie," had been making charges of this sort for two years, he explained; after the last charge, the parents had harangued him for two hours, and then, dissatisfied with his failure to act, had taken their tale to sympathetic members of the board of education, who made known their dissatisfaction with his "soft" handling of the matter. "What could I do?" he plaintively asked. "I had to get those parents off my back."

Black children are not the only ones who are harmed in these ways. In California and the Southwest, prejudice against Mexican Americans is almost as great; teachers, administrators, school boards, and even state legislatures and boards of education convey their contempt for these youngsters and their parents by forbidding the use of Spanish anywhere in the schools. Until it was repealed in the late 1960s, Section 288 of the Texas State Penal Code made it illegal for a teacher, principal, or school superintendent to teach or conduct school business in any language but English; Texas tradition makes it illegal for students to use Spanish.[51]

ITEM: In a South Texas school, children are forced to kneel in the playground and beg forgiveness if they are caught talking to each other in Spanish; some teachers require students using the forbidden language to kneel before the entire class.

ITEM: In a Tuscon, Arizona, elementary school classroom, children who answer a question in Spanish are required to come up to the teacher's desk and drop pennies in a bowl—one penny for every Spanish word. "It works!" the teacher boasts. "They come from poor families, you know."

ITEM: In a school in the Rio Grande Valley, teachers appoint students as "Spanish Monitors." Their job: to patrol the corridors, writing down the names of any fellow students they hear talking Spanish.

V

The reasons for failure are clear enough. But is success possible? Are there any grounds, other than blind faith, for believing that the schools *can* educate children from lower-class and minority-group homes, that they *can* reduce the disparities in academic achievement attributable to poverty and ethnicity?

The answer is yes. "In the world laboratory of the sociologist,

[51] Stan Steiner, "La Raza: The Mexican-Americans," *The Center Forum*, Vol. 4, No. 1, September 1969. The following items are also taken from that article.

as in the more secluded laboratories of the physicist and chemist," Robert Merton wrote, in concluding his essay on "The Self-Fulfilling Prophecy," "it is the successful experiment which is decisive and not the thousand-and-one failures which preceded it. More is learned from the single success than from the multiple failures. A single success proves it can be done. Thereafter, it is necessary only to learn what made it work." In the face of widespread doubt about the schools' ability to educate black (or Mexican American, Puerto Rican, or Indian American) children, therefore, it is useful to recall the "law" of human society that Merton laid down: "Whatever is, is possible."

One need only look at what is, therefore, to discover that it *is* possible to educate the "uneducable," "disadvantaged," "culturally deprived" children of poverty. If "a single success proves it can be done," as Merton suggests, there is ample proof that schools can substantially reduce the disparity in academic achievement between lower-class and middle-class youngsters.

In New York City and Chicago, for example, privately operated schools are demonstrating that "uneducable" dropouts are highly educable. They are showing that alienated, hostile, bitter, semiliterate or illiterate young people who had been living off the streets can become articulate, sensitive, highly motivated learners—that many of them not only can finish high school but can go on to college.

Take Chicago's CAM Academy, for example. Sponsored by a consortium of eight Protestant and Catholic churches, CAM (Christian Action Ministry) is located in a decaying neighborhood that turned from all white to all black in the early 1960s. The local high school has a dropout rate of 50–65 percent; its *graduates* read, on average, at the seventh-grade level. CAM's students—dropouts whose age ranges from fifteen to twenty-five —enter with less than a sixth-grade reading ability; about 85 percent of the boys have police records, and many of the girls have had children out of wedlock. Students may enter at any time during the year (if there is a vacancy) and stay as long as they wish. CAM offers three "degrees": a certificate demonstrating completion of work through the tenth-grade level, which means students are ready for job-training programs or for direct entry into the labor market; a high school equivalency diploma; and a college preparatory diploma.

ITEM: One CAM student had been classified as an "educable mentally handicapped" student by the Chicago public schools, a label given youngsters with IQ's in the 50–75 range. He proved to be educable all right, but hardly handicapped. When he entered CAM, his reading was at the second-grade, his math at the fifth-grade level. In twelve weeks he was reading at the eighth-grade level and doing tenth-grade math. By the time he left for college, he was writing sensitive poetry and short stories, and his oil paintings were hanging all over the school.

CAM Academy has had its failures, too; not every student can be enticed to leave the street culture, and some are hopelessly hooked on drugs. But the school has managed to arouse the interest of most of its students, and to produce substantial, and in a good many cases, spectacular gains in learning and in academic achievement. Of the first thirty graduates, for example, twenty received scholarships to colleges around the country.

Housed in a remodeled supermarket, New York's Harlem Prep has also had striking success in demonstrating the untapped reservoir of talent that exists in the black ghetto. Unlike CAM Academy, Harlem Prep offers only a college preparatory program, albeit of an unconventional sort. The school is ungraded, with students moving at their own pace; teachers are free to develop their own curriculum. The accent is on informality, "relevance," and black pride. "Walk tall, think straight. You are black, you are beautiful. We love you, we dig you," Edward Carpenter, the black headmaster told the first graduating class in bidding them farewell. The school is demonstrating that informality, relevance, and black pride are fully compatible with academic rigor; Plato's *Crito* and Sophocles' *Oedipus Rex* are read, and are seen to be relevant to the students' problems, along with Eldridge Cleaver's essays and *The Autobiography of Malcolm X*.

Initially sponsored by the Urban League of Greater New York, but now independent of it, Harlem Prep is the third tier of a remarkable private educational system that has been developing in Harlem and other depressed neighborhoods in New York. The first tier consists of a series of thirteen "street academies" in Harlem, the Lower East Side, the South Bronx, and Brooklyn; sponsored by the Urban League and initially financed by the Ford Foundation, they now get most of their funds from a group of large corporations, each of which has taken responsibility for one academy. The street academies are small storefront schools, manned by one or two teachers in addition to a street worker, who recruits the students from the streets and acts as "motivator, counselor, friend, father disciplinarian, and companion." The schools are quite informal, the purpose being to get the dropouts "hooked" on education, and to provide some skill in the three R's. From the street academy, students may enter a job-training program (some of the sponsoring corporations provide on-the-job training along with the academic preparation), or go to work full time. If students are academically motivated, they may go on to one of several "academies of transition," which form the second tier of the system, and which aim to prepare students for Harlem Prep, or for some other college preparatory school.

Why do these schools succeed where the public schools fail? One reason is that they attract unusually able and dedicated teachers, a factor that gives them an edge over the public schools, which because of the huge numbers involved must of necessity rely on people of more or less average, rather than extraordinary, endowments. Many of the teachers in Harlem Prep and CAM Academy, however, are essentially indistinguishable from many idealistic college graduates who have been entering public school teaching with a strong desire to teach in ghetto schools (and an understandable desire to avoid military service in Vietnam). The difference is that Harlem Prep and CAM Academy are free to use whatever materials and whatever teaching methods they think will excite their students—to develop what Mario Fantini and Gerald Weinstein call a "contact curriculum"— one that starts where the student is and takes him someplace else. "The big mistake most schools have made," they write, "is in showing reluctance to meet the child in his home territory and then to take him for the ride. Until now we have been asking the child to meet us in *our* territory and then to begin the ride from there."[52]

The Harlem Prep and CAM teachers meet their students in the students' home territory, but they are not content to let them stay there. Adapting curricula and teaching methods to the students' interests and learning styles is a means of getting them hooked on learning, not—as it is with many well-meaning teachers—an excuse for not teaching. In the last analysis, what makes these programs, and others like them, succeed is less their

[52] Mario D. Fantini and Gerald Weinstein, *Toward a Contact Curriculum*, New York: Anti-Defamation League of B'nai B'rith. Cf. also Fantini and Weinstein, *The Disadvantaged: Challenge to Education*, New York: Harper & Row, 1968.

teachers' talent or novel curriculum than the teachers' unshak-
able conviction that their students *can* learn. The self-fulfilling
prophecy works in a positive as well as negative direction.

In every successful program in fact, a major reason for success is the fact that project directors and teachers expect their
students to succeed, and that they hold *themselves*—not only
their students—accountable if the latter should fail. "He believes so much in you he gives you confidence in yourself," a
black University of Oregon freshman, who a year earlier had
been living off the streets, says of Professor Arthur Pearl, director of the University's Upward Bound program, which prepared
him for the university. "Pearl builds something in you—
strength," another student explains. "He expects you to do it
right, but he's honest; he doesn't con you or mollycoddle you if
you do it wrong."[53]

The same theme emerges as an explanation of the success of
the Defense Department's Project 100,000, a program that takes
men who previously had been rejected as unfit for military service because of their low educational level. (The Project 100,-
000 inductees had a median reading ability barely at the sixth-
grade level, compared with almost an eleventh-grade level for a
control group of inductees.) "The instructors are optimists; they
assume that the young man's personality can be modified and
his ability level improved regardless of the deficiencies in prior
background," I. M. Greenberg, director of Project 100,000,
writes. "When the recruit or student arrives for training, the
instructor assumes he is educable." And when students fail, as
some do, the instructor—most are professional military men
with no previous experience as teachers—generally assumes
"that the student's failure occurred because somehow he, as an
instructor, was unable to motivate the student to try harder. The
instructor rarely attributes the student's failure to cultural deprivation or genetic limitations."[54]

The question, of course, is whether this can happen in the
public schools—whether existing institutions can reverse the
reign of error that leads to failure, or whether success depends
on the creation of new institutions. The answer is that it *can*
be done in the public schools.

There are at least three public schools in New York's Harlem,

---

[53] For a description of Pearl's approach, see Chapter 8.
[54] I. M. Greenberg, "Project 100,000: The Training of Former Re-
jectees," *Phi Delta Kappan*, June 1969.

for example, where students' academic achievement approximates or even surpasses the city-wide and national norms, and where students are having a full, rich, varied, happy school experience. P.S. 129, or the John H. Finley School, as it prefers to be known (using the school's name, the principal feels, gives the school an individuality with which students, teachers, and parents can identify; it's hard to make "P.S. 129" sound very personal), is located in West Harlem and has a student body that is 89 percent black, 10 percent Puerto Rican, and 1 percent "other," i.e., white. In P.S. 192, also located in West Harlem, 30 percent of the students are black and 10 percent "other"; 60 percent have Spanish-speaking backgrounds—Puerto Rican, Dominican, and Cuban. P.S. 146 in East Harlem is 45 percent black and 50 percent Puerto Rican. Achievement is high in all three schools, but without the grim, almost martial environment sometimes associated with academic achievement. On the contrary, all three schools have a relaxed, warm atmosphere. A visitor is immediately struck by the spontaneity and laughter that characterize the environment. The children are visibly happy and engaged; disruptive behavior, if evident at all (on some visits, there was none), is at a minimum—comparable to the best middle-class suburban schools. In all three schools, moreover, parents come and go freely and are visible everywhere.

There are worse neighborhoods in Harlem, to be sure (and in Bedford-Stuyvesant and Brownsville), than the ones these schools are located in—a fact that some defensive teachers and administrators have cited to derogate the schools' accomplishments. But their neighborhoods are poor enough. One index of socioeconomic status, for example, is the proportion of a school's register eligible for the free lunch program; the New York State Education Department regards anything over 25 percent as an indication that the school is serving a low socioeconomic population. At the Finley School, 78 percent of the students are eligible for free lunch; the proportion is 65 percent at P.S. 192 and 60 percent at P.S. 146.

All three schools, in short, serve impoverished minority-group communities; their students enter with all the social handicaps and cognitive deficits that characterize lower-class youngsters. A recent, and typical, first grade at the Finley School was given the New York State Reading Readiness Test when they entered in the fall, for example; all the children scored below the national median. But when the same children were given the New York Tests of Growth in Reading at the end of the school year, considerably more than three-fourths of them scored *above* the national median.[55] The Finley first graders' median score was 2.4 (four months into the second grade), compared with a national median of 1.9; the lowest quartile of Finley students had a median of 2.1. This class, to be sure, showed particularly striking gains; the lowest quartile usually scores at the national median rather than above it, with the median for the entire grade ranging from 2.1 to 2.3.

More important, the children continue to learn; their reading scores do not dip in the upper grades, as is the case in most ghetto schools. (Nor is there any significant drop from spring to fall, as would be the case if the reading scores merely reflected the fact that the children had become "test-wise." At Finley, the spring-fall scores are remarkably stable.) In the spring of fourth grade, for example, the median scores of the other seventeen schools in the Finley district average 4.0, seven months behind the national median of 4.7; the Finley median is 4.8.[56] In fifth grade, the gap widens, the other schools in the district showing median reading scores of 4.7, a full year behind the national norm. The Finley median is 5.9, two months ahead of the national norm.

The results at P.S. 192 and P.S. 146 are also impressive. At 146, for example, where half the student body comes from Spanish-speaking homes, the most recent tests showed the fourth grade reading three months above the national median—5.0 versus 4.7—and more than a year above the median (3.9) of the fifteen other East Harlem schools. Fifth- and sixth-grade students, who had started their schooling in other, more typical ghetto schools, were still reading below the national norms, but they were catching up. The sixth graders, for example, who had

[55] These scores are all the more striking in the light of the fact that before the school's remarkable principal, Mrs. Martha Froelich, took over in 1962, fewer than half of the children in the first grade read well enough to take the test. More than half the youngsters, that is to say, read so badly at the end of first grade that it was not even possible to test their reading ability.

[56] The Finley median is closer to the national median in the upper grades than in the first two grades in part, at least, because of differences in the tests used. In the upper grades, the Metropolitan Achievement Tests are used, which slower readers find more difficult than the New York Tests of Growth in Reading. On the latter tests, for example, a recent second grade had a median of 3.3, with the lowest quartile scoring at the national norm of 2.9. On the Metropolitan test, the Finley median was at the national norm of 2.8; the lowest quartile scored five months below that (2.3), the highest quartile, a year above it (3.8).

been reading seven months below the norm in fourth grade, were only one month behind the norm in the spring of sixth grade; their median reading scores had shown a twenty-six-month gain in a period of only seventeen months.

How are these results achieved? Not, certainly, at the expense of other values, or with any obsessive preoccupation with reading instruction. It takes a strong effort of will, for example, to get Mrs. Martha Froelich, principal of the Finley School, to discuss her students' reading scores—not because she regards reading as unimportant, and certainly not out of any lack of pride. Rather, her resistance stems from her conviction that reading scores are simply one measure, albeit a crucially important one, of how she fulfills her real objective: educating children who feel good about themselves and about their school. Reading is an important means to that end; without the ability to read, no child is likely to feel good about himself. But reading is not the only means of building self-esteem. Mrs. Froelich hastens to tell visitors, therefore, that her students also took every prize in a Harlem-wide art contest sponsored by Harlem Hospital, and that they won three prizes in a city-wide garden contest. "School," she says, "should be a place to laugh and dance and sing and have fun."

All three schools are such places.

ITEM: A second-grade classroom in the Finley School. On entering the room, the visitor is struck by a large display, headed as follows:

> We had our pictures taken by a photographer.
> She used a camera.
> How do you think you look?

Underneath were the answers:

> "Pretty," said Yolanda (and her snapshot was pasted next to the sentence).
> Keith said, "Nice" (and his snapshot was there).
> "Handsome," said Alvin (and his snapshot was there).

And so it went, with each child's picture and self-description. Underneath the display of pictures and comments was the question, "Which words describe how we look?"

attractive   lovely   pretty   charming
handsome   cute   nice   beautiful

ITEM: A class at P.S. 192 put on its own musical version of *You're a Good Man, Charlie Brown,* which the class called "Happiness." A visitor the next day sees a beaming principal walking down the hall carrying a huge, colorfully iced cake bearing the message, "Thanks for Happiness." Paper plates, napkins, utensils, and fudge ripple ice cream are also supplied. As the food is disappearing, the teacher, on the spur of the moment, swings a desk into position; a parent-aide, catching her signal, starts playing the hit song on an old piano; and the boy who had had the lead climbs up on the "stage" and belts out the number, the principal and the rest of the class clapping their hands to the beat.

ITEM: A second-grade classroom at P.S. 146, which is organized along more informal lines (see Chapters 6 and 7) than the other two schools. As the principal and his visitor enter, two children rush over and offer to read to them. The other children hardly take notice. One girl is typing (a bulletin board is covered with typed New Year's resolutions); a boy is painting; another girl is listening to a record, using earphones to keep it quiet. A group of children are putting together a display for the bulletin board, entitled "We Do Research on Life in Washington, D.C."; some are writing captions, e.g., "The President," "The White House," "Printing Money," while others are cutting out pictures to go under them; one child is making a map showing the Lincoln Memorial, Washington Monument, and other places of interest, and another is writing a report.

Elsewhere in the room, children are involved in a variety of activities connected with reading. Two youngsters are using film-strip machines; two boys with limited command of English are chanting the letters of the alphabet, using a long pointer to touch the letters displayed on the blackboard. One girl is "fishing"; she has a fish tank filled with pieces of paper, each with a single word written on it and a paper clip attached. Dangling a horseshoe magnet on a string, she fishes for the words, reading each one as she "catches" it. And so it goes.

The three schools' success is all the more striking, moreover, in view of the fact that they are representative New York City ghetto schools. To be sure, each of the principals—Mrs. Froelich at Finley, Matthew Schwartz at P.S. 146, and Seymour Gang at P.S. 192[57]—is exceptional (but in different ways; it would be hard to imagine three more distinct personalities or administrative styles), and the schools' success is due directly to them. Yet the principals are also representative of New York City principals as a whole: each is white, Jewish, and middle class, and each has spent his or her entire career in the New York public schools, coming up through the ranks in the usual manner, if more rapidly than most.

In any case, the principals are operating with much the same resources, and much the same problems and obstacles, as their less successful colleagues. They are not operating small experimental programs like Harlem Prep (250 students) or CAM Academy (100 students), in which intimacy is an important factor. On the contrary, their schools are all quite large, with enrollments of 1,000 to 1,400. Only one of the three—P.S. 146, which is part of New York's "More Effective Schools" program —has a lower student-teacher ratio than the one which prevails in "special service," i.e., slum schools generally. The faculties are more experienced, and perhaps a bit abler, than one normally finds in ghetto schools—not because they were initially handpicked, but because teacher turnover is unusually low. Teachers, like children, find success gratifying, and so they are eager to teach in these schools and reluctant to leave them. It takes only a few minutes in the teachers' lounges, however, for an experienced observer to discover that in terms of socioeconomic status, ethnic background, and education, the teachers are a representative cross-section of New York City teachers. If these schools succeed, therefore, it is not because they are staffed by extraordinary teachers, but because ordinary teachers are performing in an extraordinary way.

Why? Several factors seem to be responsible. For one thing, the atmosphere is a good bit warmer and more humane, and the environment both freer and more supportive, than in most schools. Like Messrs. Schwartz and Gang, for example, Martha Froelich will not accept unkindness on the part of her staff. A new teacher who punished a child by refusing to let him have lunch was reprimanded and told that she would not be defended if the parents came to complain, and warned not to use that, or

---

[57] Dr. Gang is now a district superintendent in charge of New York City's District 5. Since he was principal of P.S. 192 during the time the research on which this section is based was being conducted, the descriptions that follow refer to the school during his tenure.

any other cruel punishment, again. "I back up my teachers whenever possible," Mrs. Froelich explained, "but this behavior just couldn't be justified." She distinguishes, however, between meanness or harshness, which she will not tolerate, and mere ineptness, which she tries to correct.

ITEM: A first-grade teacher, her first-grade students lined up in the hall, ready to go somewhere else in the building, cautions them to "walk quietly like soldiers." Mrs. Froelich, happening by, softly asks if the children mightn't walk like butterflies instead. "Butterflies are quiet, too," she says, "but they are so much prettier and gentler."

This insistence on kindness and gentleness is evident throughout the school; on three separate visits, the Carnegie researcher saw little that smacked of harshness or insensitivity. And in contrast to the ghetto schools Eleanor Leacock describes, in which teachers were almost always responding to the children in negative terms, teachers in the Finley School have been trained to respond positively. Even those children who are not yet succeeding receive a continuous flow of encouragement: "I like the way you're sitting, Marie"; "Jimmy is paying such close attention"; "Mario is trying very hard."

Disruptive behavior is also handled more gently and more positively. When teachers use the traditional punishment of sending a child to the principal's office, for example, as often as not the reason is less that the child has done anything horrendous than that the teacher, for whatever reason, has reached the end of her rope, and so has "blown" at behavior she normally handles without strain. When they determine that this is what probably happened, therefore, Mrs. Froelich and Dr. Gang offer the youngster a comfortable chair to curl up in, and some books to read or toys to play with. Mrs. Froelich keeps a supply in her office for just such occasions. "Teachers need a breathing spell from time to time," she explains; "Keeping a child out of her way is usually all that is needed, so we try not to turn a visit to the principal's office into a nightmare."

Sometimes, of course, the problem *is* with the child and not the teacher. At P.S. 192, "acting out" children may come to Gang's office of their own accord. "If they feel the need to 'pop,'" Gang says, "they know they can just walk out of the class and come down here to unwind." At P.S. 146, on the other hand, Matthew Schwartz does not permit teachers to send children to his office for punitive purposes. If a child is so disruptive that the teacher can't handle the situation, the child is sent to the guidance counselor—one of the luxuries of a "More Effective School"—for a determination of what the problem is and how the child can be helped. Like Mrs. Froelich and Dr. Gang, however, Schwartz keeps his office door open at all times so that children, teachers, and parents can seek his advice or register a complaint.

In all three schools, moreover, love is freely given—and received.

ITEM: Seated in a big leather club chair, his back to the open door, Seymour Gang is talking to a visitor. A black sixth-grade boy walks in, tip-toes over to Dr. Gang's chair, and kisses him on the top of his bald pate, saying, "I'm going to miss you next year, Dr. Gang!"

But love is not enough. An accepting, sympathetic environment is not necessarily one in which children learn very much. What is needed as well is a conviction that "disadvantaged" children can learn. The conviction is present in all three schools; more important, it is genuine. The three principals are not merely reciting liberal rhetoric when they voice the expectation; they really *believe* that their students can learn.

But what happens when teachers do not share this conviction? Since the three schools have representative faculties, their teachers probably share the conscious and unconscious biases of class and race that most middle-class white Americans possess. Many of the teachers, moreover, had had teaching experience before Mrs. Froelich and Messrs. Schwartz and Gang had taken over, and experience in slum schools tends to confirm teachers' negative expectations. How, then, do the principals' positive expectations prevail?

The answer is at once simple and complex. "The self-fulfilling prophecy, whereby fears are translated into reality," Robert Merton points out, "operates only in the absence of deliberate institutional controls." The three principals supply such controls—controls designed to transform the self-fulfilling prophecy from a negative to a positive one. For the principals not only expect their students to succeed, *they hold themselves and their teachers accountable if their students fail.* "There's no excuse for our kids not succeeding," Matthew Schwartz tells his teachers. "I don't want to hear any talk about apathetic parents or hungry children or sleepy children or anything else. We have enough riches to overcome such handicaps, and *we* are accountable if these children fail." Martha Froelich and Seymour Gang talk in similar terms. Indeed, Gang recommends that principals be given three-year contracts instead of tenure, to underline their accountability for their students' success. "A school in which there is failure is a failing school."

The schools are run accordingly: the expectation of success, and accountability for failure, are built into their structure, despite their wide differences in administrative style and approach. Seymour Gang's approach, for example, is heavily managerial, and his conversation is filled with terms like "production controls," "output," and the like. "It's our responsibility to turn out a good product," he says, "much as it's Ford's responsibility to turn out a good car." But he also regards creating and maintaining a humane atmosphere as his responsibility. "Education is a quality of living that teachers transmit to children," he says. "There must be a mutuality of respect between teachers and children."

Atmosphere aside, Gang does not concern himself with the curriculum or the teaching methods and indeed is hard put to describe just how reading is taught or even what texts are used in his school. In general, instruction in reading is the joint responsibility of the regular classroom teachers and a team of nine reading specialists, created in large part by reshuffling teacher assignments and increasing class size somewhat; more time is spent on reading instruction than in most schools. Nonetheless most observers seem unable to find anything in the reading program itself to explain the school's success.[58]

Gang's emphasis, in any case, is on what he calls "production management"—devising and maintaining "production controls" that produce the "output," i.e., the reading scores he wants. One wall of his office is lined with "production charts" showing each child's progress. Reading tests are administered every two to three months; each student's score is charted, and a projection is made of what his score should be on the next test. If the child's score falls below the projection, the teachers involved are held accountable; they are expected to figure out why, and to take whatever measures they deem necessary to bring the score up to par by the next go-round. Gang's charge to them is simple and

[58] Cf. George Weber, "How One Ghetto School Achieves Success in Reading," Council for Basic Education *Bulletin*, Vol. 13, No. 6, February 1969.

blunt: "I don't care what you do as long as the children are reading at the norm." As a result, the approach varies widely from teacher to teacher, with (from this observer's standpoint, at least, and that of two members of his research staff) a good deal of undesirable teaching in evidence.

At the Finley School, on the other hand, there is a distinct school-wide approach to reading instruction that bears Martha Froelich's imprint from start to finish and that clearly explains much of the school's remarkable success. Mrs. Froelich is interested in how the results are achieved as well as what they are, and she supervises every aspect of the curriculum and teaching methods used in her school, insisting that every one of her fifty-five teachers submit a weekly lesson plan to her, which she reads and returns, with comments. If the comment is affirmative, Mrs. Froelich writes it in the lesson book; if she has anything negative to say, she discusses it with the teacher in person. ("I don't want to put something down that might sting every time she opens the book.") While some teachers obviously are better than others, the approach is much the same, with comparatively little bad teaching in evidence.

Reading instruction begins with an "experience story," which children and teacher jointly compose each day. The story is usually three lines long and concerns something the class is doing, with the children's names worked in for added involvement. The teacher writes the story on the board in large letters, and then runs off a copy for each child, who pastes it into his notebook, illustrates it as he sees fit, and as his writing skills progress, copies it over in his own handwriting.

ITEM (in one first-grade class):

> *Our class got new library books.*
> *We will put them on the library table.*
> *Linda said that she will take care of the books.*

ITEM (in another first-grade room):

> *We made a birthday cake.*
> *We sang Happy Birthday to Melvin.*
> *Melvin wore a birthday crown and got a cupcake with
> a candle.*

Written on the board, the experience story becomes the occasion for a variety of games. Children begin taking turns reading a line at a time. "Read the sentence that tells you what the class got." "Which sentence tells us the name of the person who will take care of our books?" and so on, the teacher calling on one child after another. After a time, the game shifts. "Who can frame the word that shows us where we are going to put our books?" A child then goes to the blackboard and puts his hands on each side of the correct word to "frame" it. "Who will underline a word that begins with the same sound as Carol's name?" the teacher asks, and another child scurries to the front. The game continues, involving many different children through the use of their names, through their being able to move about the room, discharging energy, using their hands as well as words to answer.

The experience story is only one way children learn to read; they are surrounded with words on every side. Every wall has charts of one sort or another, with slots into which children insert prepared slips with the appropriate response: there is a chart of those who have library cards, a chart of those who have been to the dentist, a weather chart, a calendar, an attendance chart, a "duties of helpers" chart, a special news chart, and so on. Thus, word, phrase, sentence, and paragraph comprehension are introduced through reading and talking about the wall charts and providing the correct slip for the insert.

While many schools use some of these techniques, and have some of these kinds of charts around the room, few (if any) formal schools have the richness and variety of verbal stimulation one finds in every Finley School classroom. Nor is the verbal stimulation limited to the routine; almost any occasion that impinges on the children's lives may be used as an opportunity for talking, writing, and reading. When Senator Robert F. Kennedy was assassinated, for example, every class wrote condolence letters to his widow and his children, as well as letters to the President urging the passage of gun-control legislation.

As the children progress, the experience stories and work charts are supplemented by the use of reading primers and then of other books. Precisely when a particular child begins using the primer, however, and, equally important, which primer he uses depends on a judgment (by the classroom teacher and reading supervisor) concerning what pacing would be best for that child and what text would be most appropriate to his interests and skills. The judgment is based partly on "feel" and partly on formal evaluation, which begins on the first day, when each child is given a Beginning Reading Profile devised by the school; an adaptation of another standard test (the Harris Sample Graded Word List) is given once a month to each first grader and once every six weeks to second graders.

The testing is not done for the sake of testing, however, but to provide the "fine tuning" needed to individualize the reading program—essential if each child is to experience success at every step. Thus, the school stocks some three hundred titles—trade as well as text books—in the pre-primer to second-reader range; the books are classified according to the school's experience with its students, which frequently differs from the publisher's classifications. Once they start with books, therefore, the children's reading is increasingly individualized. They move as rapidly as they can, but no child is hurried; some may need exposure to a number of books at a given reading level, others may be able to skip that level altogether. By spring of first grade, one may find as many as fifteen different titles in use in a single first-grade classroom.

Children are encouraged to go beyond the primers. Reading involves more than mastering a set of skills, Mrs. Froelich insists; it also means grappling with concepts and abstractions. To broaden the children's reading—to dramatize to them that reading is not something one does only during the reading period—students keep track of the books they read by coloring in the spokes of a "reading wheel." The wheel is simply a large mimeographed circle divided into sixteen sections, each representing a different kind of book: myths and fairy tales, legends, mystery, humor, history, science, biography, sports, animals, and so on. The children take great pride in their reading wheels, which become colorful evidence of the extraordinary amount of reading they do in the course of a year.

ITEM: As principal, Mrs. Froelich moves in and out of classrooms with great frequency, serving as what the English call a "head teacher" (see Chapter 6), who models desirable teaching behavior in the classroom itself. In one room a youngster did not have his reading wheel with him when the teacher asked him to show it to Mrs. Froelich and her guest. Instead of scolding the child for not having his work in class, as so typically happens in schools across the nation, Mrs. Froelich asked the child if he had a reason for leaving his reading wheel at home. He did. "I never had a picture and my reading wheel looked so nice I hung it over my bed." Ever since, each child has two reading wheels: one to keep in school and the other to hang over his bed or wherever.

There are other indications of the remarkable amount of reading that is done at the John H. Finley School. In an average week, about 500 books are borrowed from the stockroom; the school's enrollment is 1,100. A typical second grade, for example, is likely to read anywhere from fifty to eighty different books in a single year, judging by past experience.

The breadth of the reading the students do helps explain why their reading scores do not fall off in the upper grades, as is the case in other schools serving similar populations. Finley youngsters not only can handle the standardized reading tests that, in the early grades, are geared to the primers; they can also cope with the tests which, in the upper grades, call for a much broader range of reading ability and comprehension.

Another element in the Finley School's success is Mrs. Froelich's efforts to involve the parents in their children's education; she regards herself as an educator of parents as well as of children and teachers.[59] Meetings for parents are held with some frequency—in the daytime for parents who do not work, in the evenings for those who do. Mrs. Froelich has prepared several video-taped demonstrations for parents, grandparents, older sisters and brothers, suggesting ways of encouraging children to talk (in one tape, she plays a grandmother helping a kindergarten child get dressed for school) and ways of helping children to study at home. Each child is expected to do some "home-study" each night, and parents are asked to sign a form placed in each book a child brings home, indicating the pages to be read and the words to be checked; the proportion of parents cooperating in this way ranges from 75 to 90 percent. And parents receive a staggering flow of personal letters. Before each vacation, for example, each parent gets a letter suggesting things his or her child might do during vacation—both home-study and things to see or do in the neighborhood. (Letters to Spanish-

[59] Besides the "modeling" she does in the classroom, Mrs. Froelich provides more formal in-service education for her teachers. Once every two weeks, for example, all the children in a given grade are brought to the Assembly Room so that Mrs. Froelich or one of her two assistant principals can work with their teachers on some aspect of instruction. From time to time, moreover, two classes in the first or second grade may be combined for part of the day, to give a new teacher an opportunity to watch a more experienced one in action.

speaking parents are written in both Spanish and English.)
Parents also receive letters if their child is doing something particularly well, if the child might benefit from some local event,
and so on; when children are having difficulty, individual conferences are arranged. And Mrs. Froelich is in her office at 7:45
every morning to see any parent who wants to drop by; she also
returns in the evening whenever necessary.

At both Finley and P.S. 146, moreover, great stress is placed
on developing pride in the children's racial and ethnic identity—
an aspect of the more general insistence on respect for each
child's integrity as an individual. "Under the most hopeful circumstances," Basil Bernstein writes, "the educational process
increases the risk of the [student's] alienation from his origins."
These schools try to minimize that risk, but without the sentimentality that leads so many radical reformers to urge, with
unconscious patronization, that lower-class children not be
"lured" into the middle class.

ITEM: A second-grade classroom in the Finley School. A large
poster announcing an exhibition of Afro-American artists dominates one wall; under it, in primer-sized print, are these sentences:

> We went to see the Afro-American art show.
> We saw many paintings there.
> We saw pieces of sculpture, too.
> All of the artists were Afro-American.
> Would you like to be an artist?

ITEM: Another room in the Finley School is known as the
Negro History Museum; the walls are covered with student-made
portraits of such famous Negroes as Harriet Tubman and
Frederick Douglass, with silhouettes of great poets like James
Weldon Johnson and Langston Hughes, with reports the students
researched and wrote to accompany their art work and with auto-
graphs of famous Negroes who have visited the Finley School,
such as Manhattan Borough President Percy Sutton, who left a
card bearing the gold seal of his office and his personal inscrip-
tion for each child.

P.S. 146's principal, Matthew Schwartz, insists that every
classroom have at least one visual display to help develop ethnic identity, and he asks each teacher to try to work some meaningful and positive ethnic reference into each day's class work.

Every other week or thereabouts, a black or Puerto Rican lawyer, doctor, chemist, accountant, businessman, social worker, or what have you visits with the sixth grade, discussing the nature of their work and telling their own life stories. For the most part, the visitors are not famous men; they are simply men who have been successful in some occupation or profession. Since materials on Puerto Rican culture are much scarcer than those on black culture—there is, for example, no Puerto Rican counterpart to *Ebony* magazine or *The Negro Digest*—the school also has an annual Puerto Rican Discovery Week featuring, among other events, an "Eat-in," in which various Puerto Rican foods, prepared by the mothers, are served.

To Robert Merton's "law" that "whatever is, is possible," let us, then, add Ralph Waldo Emerson's reminder: "Our chief want in life is someone who will make us do what we can."

4

Education for
Docility

*Teachers almost invariably take their pupils as they find
them; they turn them, beat them, card them, comb them,
drill them into certain forms, and expect them to become
a finished and polished product; and if the result does not
come up to their expectations (and I ask you how could
it?) they are indignant, angry, and furious. And yet we
are surprised that some men shrink and recoil from such
a system. Far more is it a matter for surprise that any one
can endure it at all.*

—JOHN AMOS COMENIUS,
The Great Didactic, 1632

I

Our preoccupation with the urban crisis must not be permitted
to blind us to the important, if less urgent, defects of public
schools everywhere. In good measure, the defects and failures
of the slum schools are but an exaggerated version of what's
wrong with *all* schools. To be sure, the schools in middle-class
neighborhoods seem to do a better job of teaching the basic
skills of literacy and computation, hence their students are
better equipped to earn a living. But this "success" is due far
less to the schools themselves than to what has been called "the
hidden curriculum of the middle-class home."

Moreover, students need to learn far more than the basic
skills. For children who may still be in the labor force in the
year 2030, nothing could be more wildly impractical than an
education designed to prepare them for specific vocations or

professions or to facilitate their adjustment to the world as it is. To be "practical," an education should prepare them for work that does not yet exist and whose nature cannot even be imagined. This can only be done by teaching them how to learn, by giving them the kind of intellectual discipline that will enable them to apply man's accumulated wisdom to new problems as they arise—the kind of wisdom that will enable them to *recognize* new problems as they arise. "The qualities essential to employability and productivity," Francis S. Chase, former dean of the Graduate School of Education of the University of Chicago, has written, with some exaggeration, "are coming closer and closer to the characteristics that have long been attributed to the educated person."

More important, education should prepare people not just to earn a living but to live a life—a creative, humane, and sensitive life. This means that the schools must provide a liberal, humanizing education. And the purpose of liberal education must be, and indeed always has been, to educate educators—to turn out men and women who are capable of educating their families, their friends, their communities, and most importantly, themselves. "Though we cannot promise to produce educated men and women," says the catalogue of the College of the University of Chicago, whose faculty has thought harder about educational purpose than most faculties, "we do endeavour to bring each student . . . to a point beyond which he can educate himself." This must also be the purpose of the public schools.

Of what does the capacity to educate oneself consist? It means that a person has both the desire and the capacity to learn for himself, to dig out what he needs to know, as well as the capacity to judge what is worth learning. It means, too, that one can think for himself, so that he is dependent on neither the opinions nor the facts of others, and that he uses that capacity to think about his own education, which means to think about his own nature and his place in the universe—about the meaning of life and of knowledge and of the relations between them. "To refuse the effort to understand," Wayne Booth, dean of the College of the University of Chicago, argues, "is to resign from the human race." You cannot distinguish an educated man, he continues, "by whether or not he believes in God, or in UFO's. But you can tell an educated man by the way he takes hold of the question of whether God exists, or whether UFO's are from Mars."[1]

1 Wayne C. Booth, "Is There Any Knowledge That a Man Must Have?", in Wayne C. Booth, ed., *The Knowledge Most Worth Having*, University

To be educated in this sense means also to know something of the experience of beauty—if not in the sense of creating it or discoursing about it, then at the very least, in the sense of being able to respond to it, to respond both to the beauty of nature and to the art made by our fellow men. "To find and appreciate beauty in the ordinary and the extraordinary is the right of every child," the Ontario, Canada Provincial Committee on Aims and Objectives of Education, has written, "for esthetic experience is a basic need of all men in their universal struggle to add meaning to life. We owe to children the freedom to explore the full range of their senses; to appreciate subtle differences; to be aware of beauty wherever it is found; to see, to touch, to smell, to hear, to taste, so that each in his own way will strive to find and express the meaning of man and human destiny."[2]

To be educated also means to understand something of how to make our intentions effective in the real world—of how to apply knowledge to the life one lives and the society in which one lives it. The aim of education, as Alfred North Whitehead has written, "is the acquisition of the art of the utilization of knowledge." Indeed, "a merely well-informed man is the most useless bore on God's earth."

The schools fail to achieve any of these goals. They fail in another and equally important way. Education is not only a preparation for later life; it is an aspect of life itself. The great bulk of the young now spend a minimum of twelve years in school; with kindergarten attendance, and now preschool programs, becoming more widespread, more and more of the young will have spent thirteen to fifteen years in school by the time they receive their high school diploma.

The quality of that experience must be regarded as important in its own right. A good school, as the English "Plowden Committee" insists in its magnificent report on *Children and Their Primary Schools,* "is a community in which children learn to live first and foremost as children and not as future adults."[3] The Committee is exaggerating, to be sure, when it goes on to insist that "the best preparation for being a happy and useful

of Chicago Press, 1967. Booth's essay and his introduction to the volume represent the best brief statement about liberal education in recent years.
[2] *Living and Learning: A Report of the Provincial Committee on Aims and Objectives of Education in the Schools of Ontario,* Ontario, Canada: Department of Education, 1968.
[3] Central Advisory Council for Education (England), *Children and Their Primary Schools,* London: Her Majesty's Stationery Office, 1967.

man and woman is to live fully as a child"—an exaggeration
from which many American progressive schools of the 1920s
and 1930s suffered. "Merely to let children live free, natural,
childlike lives," as Carleton Washburne, one of the giants of
American progressivism, warned in 1925, "may be to fail to
give them the training they need to meet the problems of later
life." Thus Washburne insisted on a dual focus. "Every child
has the right to live fully and naturally as a child," he wrote.
"Every child has the right also to be prepared adequately for
later effective living as an adult."[4] In the grim, repressive, joyless places most schools now are, children are denied both those
rights.

The notion that children have rights, particularly the right to
happiness, is fairly recent, in part because the concept of childhood itself is so recent. In medieval society, as the French
historian Philippe Ariès documents in fascinating detail in *Centuries of Childhood,* there was no childhood.[5] The concept of
childhood as a separate stage of life, as a psychological and
social as well as biological phenomenon, simply did not exist;
children moved directly from infancy into adulthood. Almost as
soon as the child was weaned, and certainly from the age of
seven or thereabouts, infancy ended; the child was regarded
as, and in fact became, a small adult, who mingled, worked,
competed, and played with adults on even terms. Even schools
and colleges, such as they were, enrolled students of all ages; to
go to school was a mark of a special purpose or status, not a
special stage in life. Hence it is not surprising that medieval
artists always portrayed children as scaled-down adults rather
than as children, not because they lacked the skill, but because
the modern image of childhood had no reality for them. In the
view of the great sixteenth-century French essayist Montaigne,
children had "neither mental activities nor recognizable bodily
shape."

It was not until the infant mortality rate declined enough to
permit parents to risk loving their children, in fact, that it became possible to recognize childhood as a separate stage of life.
"People could not allow themselves to become too attached to
something that was regarded as a probable loss," Ariès remarks.
Hence Montaigne's observation, shocking to modern sensibilities but not to those of his time: "I have lost two or three chil-

[4] *Progressive Education,* July–September 1925.
[5] Philippe Ariès, *Centuries of Childhood,* New York: Vintage Books,
1962.

dren in their infancy, not without regret, but without great sorrow."

The change began in the seventeenth century, when upper-class parents started coddling their young and dressing them in special clothes, and religious reformers like Comenius, concerned with the moral instruction of the young, developed the notion that the "innocent" child had to be quarantined, so to speak, against the corruption of the adult world. The result was the invention of the modern school—the creation, that is to say, of a special institution for the instruction of the young, carefully insulated from the rest of society—and the development of religious orders like the Jesuits, devoted to instruction.

Even so, childhood and schooling remained limited to the upper and middle classes; until well into the nineteenth century, in fact, poor children had little if any schooling and little if any childhood—a fact of which any reader of Charles Dickens is aware. It was not until industrial societies could afford to defer productive work until puberty, in fact, that childhood became universal; even then, compulsory school attendance laws, together with laws prohibiting child labor, were needed to "persuade" the working class to recognize childhood.

Adolescence is an even more recent invention. Every society, to be sure, recognizes the physiological changes that mark the onset of adolescence through puberty rites of one sort or another. But these rites usually served to hasten the assumption of adult status; girls married at twelve or thirteen, and boys began working or serving in the army at that age. Romeo and Juliet, after all, were only thirteen; Shakespeare could not have imagined a Holden Caulfield, or even a Penrod Schofield. Adolescence, in the sense of an extended period of intellectual and emotional growth and self-exploration, is possible only in a society prosperous enough to permit adolescents to be unproductive. Adolescence did not become universal until compulsory school attendance was extended to the age of fifteen or sixteen.

And now our generation is adding still another stage, what Kenneth Keniston calls "the stage of youth," in which full entry and submergence into the adult world is delayed until the early or mid-twenties, and in increasing numbers of cases, until the thirties.[6] The spread of affluence frees more and more young people from the need to seek gainful employment through the

[6] Kenneth Keniston, *Young Radicals*, Chapters 7–8. Cf. also "You Have to Grow Up in Scarsdale to Know How Bad Things Really Are," *New York Times Magazine*, April 27, 1969.

college, and now the graduate or professional school, years, thus prolonging their disengagement from society. Keniston sees this extension of youth as an advance, "a good thing for the student. Put in an oversimplified phrase," he writes, "it tends to free him—to free him from swallowing unexamined the assumptions of the past, to free him to express his feelings more openly and to free him from irrational bondage to authority"—to make it possible for him to criticize his society "from a protected position of disengagement."

There is reason to fear, however, that prolonging the stage of youth may delay the assumption of adult roles too long. In several scholarly fields, for example, the most significant work tends to be done by men in their late twenties; in most fields, men do their most creative work before the age of forty. But the proliferation of specialties, and the consequent extension of professional and graduate study, keeps them in the ambiguous status of student until their late twenties—in the case of medicine, until age thirty or thereabouts.

Too long a disengagement from society, moreover, may cripple young people's ability to become engaged. In a number of important respects, the new stage of youth represents an extension of adolescence, which, as Keniston also writes, "is characterized by an absence of enduring commitments, by a continuing focus on questions of philosophy, morality and ideology, by a lack of readiness for work and intimacy with others, and, above all, by a preoccupation with questions of identity, inner intactness, and wholeness." If continued too long, this preoccupation with self may make it impossible for the young to develop the enduring commitments and readiness for work that are essential if youths are to become adults. Indeed, Keniston describes the young radicals whom he admires as unwilling to move directly into adulthood. "Although many doors are open to them," he writes, "they lack the will to enter any of them, fearing that once inside they will be trapped and robbed of their freedom to change and be themselves. Despite the dazzling vista of jobs, life-styles, mates, ideologies, recreations, and avocations before them, they question them all, fearing fixity. Some have an inner calling so strong that they can find no niche in society where they can follow it. Others have no calling and are unwilling to settle for a job; although they may possess many skills, talents, and interests, they are unwilling to stake their selves on any one or any set of them."

What young people may need, therefore, is the chance to

break out of the constraints that keep them disengaged, without sacrificing the stage of youth altogether. As Peter Drucker suggests, they need opportunities "to do what the child of yesterday did without special efforts: to work with adults as a young adult," instead of as an adolescent. And that means that we must "build exposure to areas of experience and performance" as part of the normal process of growing up; "we must make it possible for the young person to test himself in work."[7]

Our concern here, however, is with the nature of childhood and adolescence, and with the growing insistence, on the part of the young themselves, that the schools make these years rewarding in their own right, and not merely a preparation for the next stage of life. Let us turn, then, to a systematic analysis of what is wrong with the schools before considering how the defects can be remedied.

II

Every society educates its young. Until fairly recently, however, few societies saw fit to educate many of their young in schools. For most of man's history, most children have received most of their education informally and incidentally. Family and community, and in some societies, the church, were the primary educating institutions, shaping young people's attitudes, forming their behavior, endowing them with morals and manners, and teaching them the vocational and other skills needed to get along in their physical and social environments. The processes of education were informal, traditional, and largely unconscious and unarticulated; children learned in the main by being included in adult activities.[8]

Much education is still carried on in this way. During their first years of life, children—all children—manage perhaps the most complicated bit of learning that humans do: they learn to talk, to use language. And they learn this through processes so informal, yet so complex, that we can barely describe, let alone understand, them. What we *are* beginning to understand is the enormity of the accomplishment. Learning to speak involves far more than simply absorbing, through constant repetition, the patterns of speech the child has heard around his home.

[7] Peter F. Drucker, *The Age of Discontinuity*, Chapter 14.
[8] Cf., for example, the description of education in colonial America in Bernard Bailyn, *Education in the Forming of American Society*, New York: Vintage Books, 1960.

On the contrary, much of what the child who has learned to talk says in the course of ordinary conversation is entirely new. His conversation is not a repetition of anything he has heard before. The same is true of what he hears: the number of sentences we are all able to understand, immediately and with no sense of strangeness, is almost infinite.[9]

Looking at the success of the informal processes of learning to talk—Paul Goodman calls it "the archetype of successful education"—and contrasting it with the widespread failures of formal schooling, a growing number of critics have begun to wonder if *all* education should not be carried on informally and incidentally.[10] These critics are part of a tradition several centuries old. "Go, my sons . . . burn your books . . . buy yourselves stout shoes, get away to the mountains, search the valleys, the deserts, the shores of the sea, and the deepest recesses of the earth . . ." Peter Severinus urged,[11] expressing sentiments that might have been lifted from any number of Paul Goodman's essays and books. The warning that "our pedantic mania for instruction is always leading us to teach children things which they would learn better of their own accord" sounds like John Holt; it was Rousseau's.

There is another tradition of criticism, however, typified by John Amos Comenius, a seventeenth-century Czech religious leader. Comenius was as harshly critical of the schools of his day—"slaughterhouses of the mind," he called them—as Rousseau was of the schools of his, but Comenius proposed to reform rather than abolish them. To Rousseau, as to Goodman and Holt, Nature made formal education unnecessary; the best education was to let Nature unfold, to permit the child to follow

[9] Cf. Noam Chomsky, *Language and Mind*, New York: Harcourt, Brace & World, 1968.

[10] Cf. John Holt, *How Children Fail*, New York: Pitman Publishing Corp., 1964; Paul Goodman, "The Present Moment in Education," *New York Review of Books*, April 10, 1969, and *Compulsory Mis-Education*, New York: Horizon Press, 1965; Fred M. Newmann and Donald W. Oliver, "Education and Community," *Harvard Educational Review*, Winter 1967; Edgar Z. Friedenberg, *The Dignity of Youth & Other Atavisms*, Boston: Beacon Press, 1965, and *Coming of Age in America*, New York: Random House, 1964; George Dennison, *The Lives of Children*, New York: Random House, 1969; A. S. Neill, *Summerhill*, New York: Hart Publishing Company, 1960.

[11] Thomas Woody, "Historical Sketch of Activism," in National Society for the Study of Education, 33rd Year Book, Part II, *The Activity Movement*, 1934.

his own instincts and desires. Comenius, on the other hand, saw Nature as providing the basis for education, but not education itself. "While the seeds of knowledge, of virtue, and of piety are naturally implanted within us," he wrote, "the actual knowledge, virtue and piety are not so given. These must be acquired." Hence "all who are born to man's estate have need of instruction" if they are to fulfill their potential as men. Comenius has been succeeded by a long roster of reformers—Pestalozzi, Froebel, Herbart, Horace Mann, John Dewey—who railed against the evils of the schools and tried to reform them.

The persistence of the same kinds of criticisms of the schools over several centuries makes it clear that despite profound differences in cultures, technologies, languages, and the like, there are remarkable uniformities in the way schools are organized and run. "In a fundamental sense," as Philip W. Jackson of the University of Chicago, one of the most sensitive and subtle contemporary students of schooling, concludes, "school is school, no matter where it happens."[12] This is so because of a number of characteristics virtually all schools share in common. (Other institutions, of course, e.g., factories, offices, the armed services, share some or all of these characteristics.)

1. There is, to begin with, the element of compulsion, the fact that children are in school involuntarily. In the United States, school attendance is required by law. But even when attendance is not legally required, the decision to attend school, especially for younger children, generally is made not by the child but by his parents. Whether compulsion is by the state or by his parents is largely immaterial to the child; what matters to him is that he *must* be in school whether he wants to or not— and that there are likely to be penalties for not being there.

2. Children not only must be in school, they must be in school for long periods of time. School generally lasts five to six hours a day, five days a week, thirty to forty weeks a year, for twelve or more years.

3. School is a collective experience, since the economies of scale require a student-teacher ratio of more than one. This is crucial for the child: being in school means being in a crowd.

---

[12] Philip W. Jackson, *Life in Classrooms*, New York: Holt, Rinehart & Winston, 1968. Jackson offers a devastating picture of how repressive and stultifying schools are—all the more devastating, in view of the fact that Jackson, who is principal of the University of Chicago's Nursery School as well as professor of education, essentially approves of the way schools are run, on the grounds that there is no other way.

And it is crucial for the teacher, who is always responsible for
a group of students.

4. School is almost always evaluative. Going to school means
living under a constant condition of having one's words and
deeds evaluated by others. Given the way in which evaluation
is usually handled, this in turn means a sharp demarcation of
power and authority between student and teacher. The teacher
not only is the one who keeps the child in school, he is also the
one who evaluates him.

Most of the characteristics that make school school, no matter where it is, flow out of these four constants. Indeed, they
produce patterns of behavior so uniform and constant over
time and across cultures as to suggest that schools form almost
a subculture of their own. Schools differ, of course, according
to the nature of the community they serve, the education of the
children's parents, the school's own history and tradition, the
outlook of its teachers and administrators, and so on. But the
differences tend to be differences in degree, not in kind; in any
case, they are relatively trivial compared to the uniformities and
similarities. Thus, the vignettes of school life that illustrate this
chapter and the ones that follow are drawn from classroom
visits by the writer and members of the Carnegie Study research
staff, from the scholarly and popular literature on education, and
from fiction and documentary films. They describe senior and
junior highs as well as elementary schools, private as well as
public schools—every kind of public school serving every racial
and ethnic group and social class in every part of the country.
And if the quotations from Philip Jackson make school sound
unduly oppressive, it should be understood that most of the
classroom visits on which his book is based were made, as he
puts it, "in so-called advantaged schools whose teachers were
proud of their 'progressive' educational views." A large portion
of them, in fact, occurred in the University of Chicago's Laboratory School—the school John Dewey founded.

III

The most important characteristic schools share in common is a
preoccupation with order and control. In part, this preoccupation grows out of the fact that school is a collective experience
requiring, in the minds of those who run it, subordination of
individual to collective or institutional desires and objectives. "It

is only because teachers wish to force students to learn that any unpleasantness ever arises to mar their relationship," Willard Waller observed nearly four decades ago, in his classic *The Sociology of Teaching*. "We have defined the school as the place where people meet for the purpose of giving and receiving instruction. If this process were unforced, if students could be allowed to learn only what interested them, to learn in their own way, and to learn no more and no better than it pleased them to do, if good order were not considered a prerequisite to learning, if teachers did not have to be taskmasters, but merely helpers and friends, then life would be sweet in the school room. These, however," Waller adds, "are all conditions contrary to fact. The conditions of mass instruction and of book instruction make it necessary that learning be forced."[13] Or as Philip Jackson puts it, "If students were allowed to stick with a subject until they grew tired of it on their own, our present curriculum would have to be modified drastically. Obviously, some kinds of controls are necessary if the school goals are to be reached and social chaos averted."

One of the most important controls is the clock; as Jackson puts it, "school is a place where things often happen not because students want them to, but because it is time for them to occur." This in turn means that a major part of the teacher's role is to serve as traffic manager and timekeeper, either deciding on a schedule himself or making sure that a schedule others have made is adhered to.

Several things follow from this. Adherence to a timetable means that a great deal of time is wasted, the experiencing of delay being one of the inevitable outcomes of traffic management. No one who examines classroom life carefully can fail to be astounded by the proportion of the students' time that is taken up just in waiting. The time is rarely used productively. Hence in the elementary grades, an able student can be absent from school for an entire week and, quite literally, catch up with all he has missed in a single morning.

More important, adherence to a rigid timetable means that activities, as Jackson puts it, "often begin before interest is aroused and terminate before interest disappears. Adherence to the schedule also means that lessons frequently end before the students have mastered the subject at hand. As Herbert Kohl

[13] Willard Waller, *The Sociology of Teaching*, New York: John Wiley & Sons Science Editions, 1965.

points out, "the tightness with time that exists in the elementary school has nothing to do with the quantity that must be learned or the children's needs. It represents the teacher's fear of loss of control and is nothing but a weapon used to weaken the solidarity and opposition of the children that too many teachers unconsciously dread."[14]

ITEM: An elite private school in the East, once a bastion of progressive education. A fifth-grade teacher is conducting a mathematics class, demonstrating a technique for quick multiplication and division by recognizing certain arithmetic patterns. A few students grasp the concept instantly, a few ignore the teacher altogether; most struggle to understand. Just as they are beginning to catch on—"oohs" and "ahs" and mutterings of "I think I see, I think I see," "I think I have it," "Oh, that's how it works" can be heard all over the classroom—the lesson ends. No bell has rung; bells would violate the school's genteel progressive atmosphere. But the time schedule on the board indicates that math ends and social studies begins at 10:40, and it is now 10:37; the teacher tells the children to put away the math worksheets and take out their social studies texts. Some of the children protest; they're intrigued with the patterns they are discovering, and another five or ten minutes would enable them to consolidate what they have only began to grasp. No matter; the timetable rules.

ITEM: All over the United States, that last week of November 1963, teachers reported the same complaint: "I can't get the children to concentrate on their work; all they want to do is talk about the assassination." The idea that the children might learn more from discussing President Kennedy's assassination— or that like most adults, they were simply too obsessed with the horrible event to think about anything else—simply didn't occur to these teachers. It wasn't in that week's lesson plan.

It is all too easy, of course, for the outsider to criticize. Unless one has taught (as this writer and members of his staff have), or has studied classroom procedures close-up (as we have also done), it is hard to imagine the extent of the demands made on a teacher's attention. Jackson's studies of teacher-student interchange, for example, indicate that "the teacher typically

14 Herbert Kohl, *36 Children*, New York: New American Library, 1967.

changes the focus of his concern about 1,000 times daily," with many lasting only a few seconds, most less than a minute.[15] One of the hard facts of teaching (and teaching is a very hard occupation), therefore, as Professor Lee J. Cronbach of Stanford suggests, is that "there will always be some momentary distraction; habitually pursuing the spur-of-the-moment theme reduces the curriculum to a shambles." There are occasions when it is wise to depart from the lesson plan—surely the assassination of a President, a distinguished civil rights leader and Nobel Laureate, and a senator contending for the Presidency are such occasions—but there are also times when the teacher may be well advised to resist the seduction of talking about the day's headlines.

The trouble, then, is not with the schedule or the lesson plan *per se*, but with the fact that teachers too often see them as ends in themselves rather than as means to an end. As Professor Joseph C. Grannis of Teachers College puts it, the lesson plan tends to be regarded not as a convenient device for regulating classroom decisions, but as a "moral contract that a teacher is *obliged* to deliver on." [Emphasis his] Even when children are excited about something directly related to the curriculum, therefore, teachers ignore or suppress the interest if it is not on the agenda for that period.

ITEM: A scholar studying curriculum reform visits a classroom using a new elementary science curriculum. Arriving a few minutes before the class was scheduled to begin, he sees a cluster of excited children examining a turtle with enormous fascination and intensity. "Now, children, put away the turtle," the teacher insists. "We're going to have our science lesson." The lesson is on crabs.

The tyranny of the lesson plan in turn encourages an obsession with routine for the sake of routine. School is filled with countless examples of teachers and administrators confusing means with ends, thereby making it impossible to reach the end for which the means were devised.

[15] Philip W. Jackson, "The Way Teaching Is," in Association for Supervision and Curriculum Development and the Center for the Study of Instruction, *The Way Teaching Is,* Washington, D.C.: National Education Association, 1966. Cf. also Herbert M. Kliebard, "The Observation of Classroom Behavior—Some Recent Research," in the same pamphlet.

ITEM: A West Coast elementary school student is discovered by his parents to have abandoned reading E. B. White and the Dr. Doolittle books in favor of Little Golden Books, at his teacher's request. The teacher explains that students are required to submit a weekly book report on a 4 x 6 filing card. If the student were to read books as long as *Charlotte's Web* or *Dr. Doolittle*, he would not be able to submit a weekly report, and his reports might be too long to fit on the file card. "I urged him to continue reading those books on his own," the teacher explains, "but not for school."

ITEM: A surburban community boasts of its new $3 million elementary "school of the future," opened in September 1969, in which the classrooms are all built around a central library core—"the nerve center of all educational processes in the school," as one piece of promotional literature describes it. During the school's first year of operation, children are permitted to use the library only during a weekly "library period," when they practice taking books from the shelves and returning them. They are not permitted to *read* the books they take off the shelves, however; they are there to learn "library skills," and the spelling teacher who doubles as "librarian" will not permit them to "waste time." The following year, children are not permitted to enter "the nerve center of all education processes in the school" at any time; the "librarian" has returned to teaching spelling.

Administrators tend to be even guiltier of this kind of mindlessness and slavish adherence to routine for the sake of routine. It is, in a sense, built into their job description and into the way in which they view their role. Most schools are organized and run to facilitate order; the principal or superintendent is considered, and considers himself, a manager whose job is to keep the organization running as efficiently as possible.[16]

ITEM: A high school principal talking: "Maybe the public may think the schools are democratic. They are democratic as far as the rights of the individual, but as far as the operation, they are not democratic. In order to get efficiency in a school system,

[16] Cf. Raymond E. Callahan, *Education and the Cult of Efficiency*, University of Chicago Press, 1962. This myopia is not limited to school administrators. Cf. Peter F. Drucker, *The Effective Executive*, New York: Harper & Row, 1967, on the need to distinguish between effectiveness (getting the right things done) and efficiency (getting things done right).

there has to be a clear pattern of operation, behavior, rules and regulation. Then there's not time for a group of people to sit down and thrash out a variety of ideas and to come up with a quick, clear-cut and efficient policy. There has to be one individual who has been selected because of his training, because of his experience, because of his drive and know-how, that is put in charge. And within reason, then, his philosophy would be interpreted into a policy which would be the policy of that school. Now I believe that's basic—how you get an efficient school."[17]

ITEM: From the opening sentences of an appraisal of the reorganization of a comprehensive high school, ostensibly designed to reduce the impersonality inherent in a large institution by creating, in effect, smaller schools within the school.

> Halls are clearer, attendance-keeping is speedier, and the general flow of administration is easier on both students and staff at the Mount Vernon High School now that the "division" system has gone into effect.
> The school was divided this fall into five campus-like houses of some 700 students. The houses, or divisions, are designed to look after a student, counsel him, check up on him, and claim his loyalty through his four years at the comprehensive high school.
> Attendance procedures, parent consultation, guidance services, and most administrative and disciplinary activity take place within each of the five divisions. *For every major school function with the exception of plant management and instruction itself*, in fact, there are now five schools within the Mount Vernon High School, each with its own guidance and secretarial staff, and its own cross-section of students . . . [Emphasis added]

The appraisal continues:

> The greatest immediate gain seems to be in the matter of keeping attendance.

But there are other gains as well:

> . . . that a division principal and his homeroom teachers are in charge of a particular part of the building has rationalized

---

[17] From the Canadian Broadcasting Company film, *What They Want to Produce, Not What We Want to Become.*

hall supervision and rendered the school's halls demonstrably quieter . . .[18]

This preoccupation with efficiency, which is to say with order and control, turns the teacher into a disciplinarian as well as a timekeeper and traffic manager. In the interest of efficiency, moreover, discipline is defined in simple but rigid terms: the absence of noise and of movement. "When we ask children *not* to move, we should have excellent reasons for doing so," an English psychologist and educator, Susan Isaacs of the University of London, argued in 1932. "It is stillness we have to justify, not movement." But no justification is offered or expected. Indeed, there is no more firmly rooted school tradition than the one that holds that children must sit still at their desks without conversing at all, both during periods of waiting, when they have nothing to do, and during activities that almost demand conversation. Yet even on an assembly line, there is conversation and interaction among workers, and there are coffee breaks and work pauses as well.

ITEM: A new suburban elementary school is being hailed in architectural circles for its "open design." The building has no corridors; the sixteen classrooms open instead onto "project areas" equipped with work tables, sinks, easels, and the like. What the architects do not know, however, is that in most classrooms the project areas go unused. As the principal explains, "If some children are in the project area while others are in the regular classroom, the teacher can't watch every child, and some of them might start talking."

ITEM: In lecturing the assembled students on the need for and virtue of absolute silence, an elementary school principal expostulates on the wonders of a school for the "deaf and dumb" he had recently visited. The silence was just wonderful, he tells the assembly; the children could all get their work done because of the total silence. The goal is explicit: to turn normal children into youngsters behaving as though they were missing two of their faculties.

ITEM: A high school in a New England city is very proud of its elaborately equipped language laboratory, with a new "Random Access Teaching Equipment" system touted as "tailored to the individual student's progress, as each position permits the

[18] From the Mount Vernon, New York *Daily Argus*, October 1, 1969.

instructor to gauge the progress of all students on an individual basis." To make sure that its expensive equipment is used properly, the high school gives students careful instructions, among them the following:

• "No one is an individual in the laboratory. Do nothing and touch nothing until instructions are given by the teacher. Then listen carefully and follow directions exactly.

• "The equipment in the laboratory is not like ordinary tape recorders. The principles involved are quite different. Please do not ask unnecessary questions about its operation.

• "You will stand quietly behind the chair at your booth until the teacher asks you to sit. Then sit in as close to the desk as possible."

The instructions for the lab assistants are equally explicit. They include the following:
"1. Keep watching the students all the time.
  a) By standing in the middle of the lab on window side you can see most of the lab.
  b) Walk along the rows to make sure all arms are folded; politely but firmly ask the students to do this."[19]

The obsession with silence and lack of movement is not limited to American schools, of course; it is a characteristic of schools everywhere.

ITEM: From *Socialist Competition in the Schools*, a Soviet manual for "school directors, supervisors, teachers, and Young Pioneer leaders" prepared by the Institute on the Theory and History of Pedagogy at the USSR's Academy of Pedagogical Sciences. The manual begins with instructions for the teacher standing before the class on the first day of school:

> It is not difficult to see that a direct approach to the class with the command, "All sit straight," often doesn't bring the desired effect since a demand in this form does not reach the sensibilities of the pupils and does not activate them.

In order to "reach the sensibilities of the pupils" and "activate them" according to principles of socialist competition, the teacher should say, "Let's see which row can sit the straightest."[20]

[19] From Anthony G. Oettinger with the collaboration of Sema Marks, *Run, Computer, Run*, Cambridge, Mass.: Harvard University Press, 1969.
[20] Quoted in Urie Bronfenbrenner, "Soviet Methods of Character Education," in *Review of Recent Research Bearing on Religious and Charac-*

In the United States, training in sitting still begins in kinder-garten, the function of which is, in large measure, to instill the behavior patterns the rest of the school demands.

ITEM: The report card that a well-to-do suburban school sys-tem uses for kindergarteners grades the five-year-olds on their "Readiness for First Grade Work." Readiness involves some seventeen attributes, the first three of which read as follows:

1. Sits still and works at assigned task for 15 to 20 minutes.
2. Listens and follows directions.
3. Displays good work habits.

The fourth attribute is "Has intellectual curiosity."

Silence is demanded, moreover, despite the fact that school children work in very close quarters. "Even factory workers are not clustered as close together as students in a standard class-room," Jackson observes. "Once we leave the classroom we seldom again are required to have contact with so many people for so long a time." Yet despite the close contact, students are required to ignore those around them. They "must try to behave as if they were in solitude, when in point of fact they are not. They must keep their eyes on their paper when human faces beckon. Indeed, in the early grades it is not uncommon to find students facing each other around a table while at the same time being required not to communicate with each other." To become successful students, they "must learn how to be alone in a crowd."

Silence is demanded even when students are moving from one class to another.

ITEM: From an article in the National Education Association's journal, *Today's Education*, giving an experienced teacher's ad-vice to new teachers. "During the first week or two of teaching in an inner-city school, I concentrate on establishing simple routines, such as the procedure for walking downstairs. I line up the children, and after appointing two line leaders and ex-plaining to the entire class the school's rules about walking and speaking softly in the halls, I have them practice walking up

---

ter Formation (Research Supplement to *Religious Education,* July–August 1962), reprinted in Robert J. Havighurst, ed., *Comparative Perspectives on Education,* Boston: Little, Brown and Company, 1968.

and down the stairs. Each time the group is allowed to move only when quiet and orderly."[21]

ITEM: A visitor asks a junior high school principal why his school's twelve-, thirteen-, and fourteen-year-old students are required to "line up" in each classroom before being permitted to leave for the next class. "Didn't you notice how narrow our halls are?" he replies. "No. I did not," the visitor answers. "But I did notice that the youngsters abandon the single lines as soon as they leave the classroom." The principal thinks for a minute, then announces his solution: "I guess we'll have to get more marshalls to patrol the halls."

ITEM: In that same school system, the principal of the elementary school serving the city's wealthiest neighborhood insists that all students carry their books in their left hand when going from room to room. Asked why, the principal looks surprised, and after some hesitation and fumbling, explains that the children need to have their right hand free to hold on to the banisters to avoid falling when going up or down stairs. And besides, he adds, if children were permitted to carry books in their right hand, they might bang them against, and thus damage, the steel coat lockers that line some of the halls. (The students are also required to walk only on the right side of the corridors and stairs.)

The ban on movement extends to the entire school. Thus, students in most schools cannot leave the classroom (or the library or the study hall) without permission, even to get a drink of water or to go to the toilet, and the length of time they can spend there is rigidly prescribed. In high schools and junior highs, the corridors are usually guarded by teachers and students on patrol duty, whose principal function is to check the credentials of any student walking through. In the typical high school, no student may walk down the corridor without a form, signed by a teacher, telling where he is coming from, where he is going, and the time, to the minute, during which the pass is valid. In many schools, the toilets are kept locked except during class breaks, so that a student not only must obtain a pass but must find the custodian and persuade him to unlock the needed facility. Indeed, the American high school's "most memorable

[21] Eugene D. Ruth, Jr., "The Benevolent Dictator in the Inner-City Schools," *Today's Education*, October 1969.

arrangements," as Edgar Z. Friedenberg puts it, "are its corridor passes and its johns; they dominate social interaction."[22] There are schools, of course, where some of these arrangements have a rational basis—where school authorities are legitimately concerned about the intrusion of outsiders, where traffic in heroin and other narcotics is brisk. But the same regulations have obtained for as long as anyone can recall. (For further discussion, see Chapter 8.) Even during periods when students do not have a class, they must be in a study hall or some other prescribed place. It is a rare school, for example, in which students are permitted to go to the library if they have a free period; the library is open to them only if they have an assigned "library period," or if they manage to wangle a pass for that purpose from the librarian or some other person in authority.

ITEM: From *Up the Down Staircase*.

> NO WRITTEN PASSES ARE TO BE ISSUED TO LAVATORIES, SINCE THEY ARE EASILY DUPLICATED BY THE STUDENTS. ONLY WOODEN LAVATORY PASSES ARE TO BE HONORED.
> James J. McHabe, Adm. Asst.

ITEM: From an article in the September 1969 *Today's Education*, one of a series "presenting the handling of a troublesome classroom incident by a teacher":

> Last year the faculty of our high school adopted a plan to control excessive loitering in the halls. Each teacher received a hall pass for his room—a good-sized piece of wood, painted bright yellow, marked with the room number. No student was allowed to leave the room without the pass, and the pass was issued only for trips to the rest room or the nurse's office. . . . In a few minutes, a boy got the pass from me in order to go to the rest room. I would never have noticed that he hadn't returned within a reasonable period of time if another student hadn't asked for the pass. [The boy was delayed because he had to use a toilet at the opposite end of the building; workmen were making repairs on the one nearby.]

ITEM: Over an elementary school's p.a. system comes the principal's announcement: "Children are not using the lavatories correctly. No child may be out of his room for more than three minutes."

22 Edgar Z. Friedenberg, *Coming of Age in America*, New York: Random House, 1965.

These petty rules and regulations are necessary not simply because of the importance schoolmen attach to control—they like to exercise control, it would seem, over what comes out of the bladder as well as the mouth—but also because schools, and school systems, operate on the assumption of distrust. "The school board has no faith in the central administration, the central administration has no faith in the principals, the principals have no faith in the teachers, and the teachers have no faith in the students," Christopher Jencks has observed. "In such a system it seems natural not to give the principal of a school control over his budget, not to give the teachers control over their syllabus, and not to give the students control over anything. Distrust is the order of the day."

ITEM: From an N.E.A. volume on *Discipline in the Classroom.*

> May an old hand give a beginning teacher some tips about keeping classroom discipline? I have found these procedures helpful:
>
>   . . . *Plan the lesson.* Be ready to use the first minute of class time. If you get Johnny busy right away, he has no time to cook up interesting ideas that do not fit into the class situation.[23] [Emphasis in original]

The result, of course, is that the classroom becomes a battleground, with students and teachers devoting an inordinate amount of energy to the search for ways of outwitting one another.

ITEM: From *Up the Down Staircase.*

> INTRASCHOOL COMMUNICATION
> From: 508
> To: 304
>   Dear Syl—Serves you right! Never turn your back to the class when writing on the board—learn the overhead backhand. Never give a lesson on 'lie and lay.' Never raise your voice; let *them* stop talking to hear you. Never give up. And to thine own self be true.
>   (There is no such thing as a Social Intercourse Period!)
>   "Bea"

[23] Martha W. Hunt, "Tips for Beginning Teachers," in *Discipline in the Classroom: Selected articles of continuing value to elementary and secondary school teachers*, Washington, D.C.: National Education Association, 1969.

ITEM: From the N.E.A.'s *Discipline in the Classroom.*

> Avoid standing with your back to the class for any length
> of time. If you do, you may invite disorderly conduct. Learn
> to write on the board with only your right shoulder toward the
> board. Student attention tends to be focused on what you are
> writing if the words are not obscured by your body. Whenever
> possible, anything you need to put on the board should be
> written before class time . . ."

> Avoid emotion-charged topics. Discussing them may lead to
> an argument so explosive that fighting can result. Until a group
> has achieved enough maturity to keep itself under control, it
> is better to risk boredom than pandemonium.[24]

IV

But how can a group "achieve enough maturity to keep itself
under control" if its members never have an opportunity to exercise control? Far from helping students to develop into mature,
self-reliant, self-motivated individuals, schools seem to do everything they can to keep youngsters in a state of chronic, almost
infantile, dependency. The pervasive atmosphere of distrust, together with rules covering the most minute aspects of existence,
teach students every day that they are not people of worth, and
certainly not individuals capable of regulating their own behavior.

ITEM: A group of fifth graders decide to put out a class newspaper as an English project. The principal refuses to permit the
paper to be distributed to the other fifth graders unless the ten-
year-old editor rewrites his signed editorial to conform to the
principal's view. The editorial reads as follows:

> Many of us feel strongly that we have a lack of freedom in
> school. Maybe adults don't realize what it feels like to be ten
> or eleven or twelve years old and have to ask permission to go
> to the bathroom or to throw away a piece of paper, or talk
> to a teacher. When we are not permitted to leave our seats to
> go to the project area or the library we know you are saying
> you don't trust us.

> Teachers may be thinking "If we give you this freedom you
> will just be noisy and fight." But if we students had more free-
> dom we would also accept more responsibility.

[24] Elizabeth Bennett, "An Ounce of Prevention," in *Discipline in the
Classroom.*

School would be a more pleasant place for all of us if there weren't so many unnecessary rules. Just think, if we had the freedom to talk or whisper while we work. The teacher wouldn't have to yell and scold so much. What a great place Traphagen School would be if we had more freedom and responsibility.

Even when schools set out to develop self-direction, moreover, they seem incapable of letting go of the traces.

ITEM: A Southern high school has received a national award as its state's "Pacemaker School of the year" for its innovative climate in which the school "seeks to provide an atmosphere in which the student will be motivated toward self-direction." As the school's handbook adds, "Self-direction cannot be taught but must be experienced." Discipline is regarded "as a learning process by which the student is guided in the development of self-control and in the recognition of his responsibilities to himself and to the group." But the school's regulations include the following:

Students should move from one area to another within a four-minute period following the module tone. There will be no movement through the halls, nor will any student be in the halls, except by written permission from a teacher, at any time other than during the four minutes following the module tone. . . .

General propriety rules out boisterousness, excessively loud talking in the talking commons, failure to be seated while in the commons area (not more than four at a small table, eight at large tables), running in the building, throwing trash on the floor, and all other areas displaying lack of self-discipline.

More important, schools discourage students from developing the capacity to learn by and for themselves; they make it impossible for a youngster to take responsibility for his own education, for they are structured in such a way as to make students totally dependent upon the teachers. Whatever rhetoric they may subscribe to, most schools in practice define education as something teachers do to or for students, not something students do to and for themselves, with a teacher's assistance. "Seated at his desk, the teacher is in a position to do something," Jackson reports. *"It is the teacher's job to declare what that something shall be."*

[Emphasis added] "It is the teacher who decides who will speak and in what order," and it is the teacher who decides who will have access to the materials of learning.

ITEM: From *Up the Down Staircase.*

> There is a premium on conformity, and on silence. Enthusiasm is frowned upon, since it is likely to be noisy. The Admiral [the administrative assistant] had caught a few kids who came to school before class, eager to practice on the typewriters. He issued a manifesto forbidding any students in the building before 8:20 or after 3:00—outside of school hours, students are "unauthorized." They are not allowed to remain in a classroom unsupervised by a teacher. They are not allowed to linger in the corridors. They are not allowed to speak without raising a hand. They are not allowed to feel too strongly or to laugh too loudly.

The result is to destroy students' curiosity along with their ability—more serious, their desire—to think or act for themselves.

ITEM: A large suburban high school informs its juniors that they will be able, the following year, to pursue a course of independent study on a topic of their own choosing, under faculty guidance, in lieu of a conventional course. In a class of eight or nine hundred, half of whom will be going to college, and in a year in which "relevance" has become an almost universal student catchword and demand, only three students bother to apply. The school has done its job well!

The vignette is not an isolated instance. "Schools that experiment with independent study," J. Lloyd Trump and Dorsey Baynham of the National Education Association reported in 1961, "find it difficult to stimulate even the most able students to do truly creative, independent work. They are accustomed to doing only what the teacher assigns and little more. Teachers' assignments have left little room in many cases for the exercise of initiative." Even when teachers, principals, and curriculum designers seriously try to give students room "for the exercise of initiative," they cannot drop the habit of looking over the students' shoulders (for details, see Chapters 5 and 8). In many of the schools Trump and Baynham examined, for example, "what was supposed to be independent study looked quite similar to the homework that usually occurs."[25]

It is understandable that that be so, for Trump himself, in one of the "supporting papers" he sends schoolmen interested in participating in the N.E.A.'s National Association of Secondary School Principals' "Model Schools Project," defines independent study "simply as what pupils do when their teachers stop talking. It is sometimes done individually," he goes on to explain, "more often in various sized groups. Pupils read, view, listen, write, think, and do both what their teachers require and what is described as working in greater depth or being creative." Indeed, one of the purposes of regular classroom meetings, Trump explains, is to give the teacher an opportunity to make "assignments so that each pupil may engage successfully in independent study."[26]

The reluctance to turn children free—to let them follow their own curiosity—is understandable in the context of the way schools operate. "Truly creative, independent work can be messy, expensive, and time-consuming," as Anthony G. Oettinger observes. "Schools are organized for neatness, low budgets and time compression." Hence most of the great experiments in "individualized instruction" define individualization in the narrowest terms; as Oettinger describes it, "each pupil is free to go more or less rapidly where he's told to go." (The failures of individualized instruction will be described in detail in Section V of the next chapter, "The Failures of Educational Reform." Successful modes of individualization are described in Chapters 6, 7, and 8.)

At the heart of the schoolmen's inability to turn responsibility over to the students is the fact that the teacher-student relationship in its conventional form is, as Willard Waller states, "a form of institutionalized dominance and subordination. Teacher and pupil confront each other in the school with an original conflict of desires, and however much that conflict may be reduced in amount, or however much it may be hidden, it still remains. The teacher represents the adult group, ever the enemy of the spontaneous life of groups of children. The teacher represents the for-

25 J. Lloyd Trump and Dorsey Baynham, *Guide to Better Schools*, Chicago: Rand McNally, 1961.
26 J. Lloyd Trump, "Needed Changes for Further Improvement of Secondary Education in the United States," and "How Excellent Are Teaching and Learning in Your School," National Association of Secondary School Principals, mimeographed.

mal curriculum, and his interest is in imposing that curriculum upon the children in the form of tasks; pupils are much more interested in life in their own world than in the desiccated bits of adult life which teachers have to offer. The teacher represents the established social order in the school, and his interest is in maintaining that order, whereas pupils have only a negative interest in that feudal superstructure. Teacher and pupil confront each other with attitudes from which the underlying hostility can never be altogether removed." There is a kernel of truth, in short, as well as a large element of self-pity in the young rebels' fondness for the metaphor of the "student as nigger."

A major source of the underlying hostility is the preoccupation with grades. "Tests are as indigenous to the school environment as are textbooks or pieces of chalk," Jackson observes. "But tests, though they are the classic form of educational evaluation, are not all there is to the process." Indeed, the use of tests "is insufficient to explain the distinctively evaluative atmosphere that pervades the classroom from the earliest grades onward," for almost anything and everything the student does is likely to be evaluated and graded.

The teacher, of course, is the chief source of evaluation. "He is called upon continuously to make judgments of students' work and behavior and to communicate that judgment to the students in question and to others. No one who has observed an elementary classroom for any length of time can have failed to be impressed by the vast number of times the teacher performs this function. Typically, in most classrooms students come to know when things are right or wrong, good or bad, pretty or ugly, largely as a result of what the teacher tells them."

Evaluation per se is not the problem. As we shall argue in greater detail in Chapter 8, evaluation is an important and indeed intrinsic part of education—essential if teachers are to judge the effectiveness of their teaching, and if students are to judge what they know and what they are having trouble learning. The purpose should be diagnostic: to indicate where teachers and students have gone wrong and how they might improve their performance. And since students will have to judge their own performance, they need experience in self-evaluation.

But schools rarely evaluate in this way. They make it clear that the purpose of evaluation is rating: to produce grades that enable administrators to rate and sort children, to categorize them so rigidly that they can rarely escape. "Each teacher," Professor Benjamin S. Bloom of the University of Chicago writes, "begins a new term (or course) with the expectation that about a third of his students will adequately learn what he has to teach. He expects about a third of his students to fail or to just 'get by.' Finally, he expects another third to learn a good deal of what he has to teach, but not enough to be regarded as 'good students.' This set of expectations, supported by school policies and practices in grading, becomes transmitted to the students through the grading procedures and through the methods and materials of instruction. The system creates a self-fulfilling prophecy such that the final sorting of students through the grading process becomes approximately equal to the original expectations. This set of expectations, which fixes the academic goals of teachers and students," Bloom adds, "is the most wasteful and destructive aspect of the present educational system," reducing students' motivation to learn and systematically destroying the ego and sense of self of large numbers of students.[27]

The assault on the student's self-esteem and sense of self is frequently overt, with teachers virtually demanding failure from some children.

ITEM: A fourth-grade math teacher writes a half-dozen problems on the board for the class to do. "I think I can pick at least four children who can't do them," she tells the class, and proceeds to call four youngsters to the board to demonstrate, for all to see, how correct the teacher's judgment is. Needless to say, the children fulfill the prophecy.

ITEM: An elementary school in a wealthy Northeastern suburb whose name is almost synonymous with concern for education. Three children are in a special class for children with perceptual problems. The teacher insists on talking with the visitor about the children in their presence, as though congenital deafness were part of their difficulty. "Now, watch, I'm giving them papers to see if they can spot the ovals, but you'll see that this one"—he nods in the direction of a little boy—"isn't going to be able to do it." A few seconds later, he says triumphantly, "See, I told you he couldn't. He never gets that one right. Now I'll put something on the overhead projector, and this one"— this time, a nod toward a little girl—"won't stay with it for

[27] Benjamin S. Bloom, "Learning for Mastery," in *Evaluation Comment,* Vol. 1, No. 2, May 1968, published by the UCLA Center for the Study of Evaluation of Instructional Programs.

more than a line." Five seconds later, with evident disappointment: "Well, that's the first time she ever did *that*. But keep
watching. By the next line, she'll have flubbed it." The child gets
the next one right, too, and the teacher's disappointment mounts.
"This *is* unusual, but just stick around . . ." Sure enough, the
child goofs at line five. "See, I told you so!"

The problem is compounded by the misuse of IQ and other
standardized tests. "Although the validity and reliability of all
standardized tests is far from perfect," David A. Goslin of the
Russell Sage Foundation writes, "a precise numerical score
frequently takes on a kind of absolute validity when it appears
on a child's record card. Teachers and administrators alike,
when confronted with a child's IQ score or his percentile rank
on an achievement test like the Iowa Test of Basic Skills, often
tend to disregard the considerable degree of imprecision that is
inherent in such measures." The result, Goslin adds, "is that in
a variety of ways we are tending to put individuals into cubby
holes."[28]

A corollary of teacher dominance is the teacher's role in dol-
ing out privileges from which status flows. "In elementary classrooms, it is usually the teacher who assigns coveted duties, such
as serving on the safety patrol, or running the movie projector,
or clapping erasers, or handing out supplies," Jackson observes.
"Although the delegation of these duties may not take up much
of the teacher's time, it does help to give structure to the activities of the room and to fashion the quality of the total experience
for many of the participants."

The phenomenon is not limited to elementary schools. "The
concept of privilege is important at Milgrim," Edgar Z. Friedenberg observes of one of the representative high schools he describes in *Coming of Age in America*. "Teachers go to the head
of the chow line at lunch; whenever I would attempt quietly to
stand in line the teacher on hall duty would remonstrate with
me. He was right, probably; I was fouling up an entire informal
social system by my ostentation. Students on hall patrol also,
when relieved from duty, were privileged to come bouncing up
to the head of the line; so did seniors. Much of the behavior
Milgrim depends on to keep it going is motivated by the reward

---

[28] David A. Goslin, *The School in Contemporary Society*, Glenview, Ill.:
Scott, Foresman, 1965.

of getting a government-surplus peanut butter or tuna fish sandwich without standing in line for it."

Still another by-product of teacher dominance, one that has profound consequences for children's attitudes toward learning, is the sharp but wholly artificial dichotomy between work and play which schools create and maintain. Young children make no such distinction. They learn through play, and until they have been taught to make the distinction ("Let's stop playing now, children; it's time to start our work"), they regard all activities in the same light. But the dichotomy grows out of the assumption that nothing can happen unless the teacher makes it happen. "Work entails becoming engaged in a purposeful activity that has been prescribed for us by someone else, an activity in which we would not at that moment be engaged if it were not for some system of authority relationships," Jackson explains. "The teacher, with his prescriptive dicta and his surveillance over the student's attention, provides the missing ingredient that makes work real. The teacher, although he may disclaim the title, is the student's first 'Boss.' "

v

Why are schools so bad?

To read some of the more important and influential contemporary critics of education—men like Edgar Friedenberg, Paul Goodman, John Holt, Jonathan Kozol—one might think that the schools are staffed by sadists and clods who are drawn into teaching by the lure of upward mobility and the opportunity to take out their anger—Friedenberg prefers the sociological term *ressentiment*, or "a kind of free floating ill-temper"—on the students.[29] This impression is conveyed less by explicit statement than by nuance and tone—a kind of "aristocratic insouciance," as David Riesman calls it, which these writers affect, in turn reflecting the general snobbery of the educated upper middle class toward the white collar, lower-middle-class world of teachers, social workers, civil servants, and policemen. In recent years this snobbery has become a nasty and sometimes spiteful form of bigotry on the part of many self-made intellectuals, who seem to feel the need to demonstrate their moral and cultural superi-

---

[29] Edgar Z. Friedenberg, "The Gifted Student and His Enemies," in Friedenberg, *The Dignity of Youth & Other Atavisms,* Boston: Beacon Press, 1965.

ority to the lower middle class from which they escaped. A number of critics of American culture, moreover, such as Friedenberg, who is a conscious elitist, Paul Goodman, Norman Mailer, and Leslie Fiedler seem to be particularly attracted by the virility and violence of lower-class life, which they tend to romanticize. They seem unable to show empathy for the problems of the lower-middle-class teacher, whose passivity and fear of violence they deride as effeminate and whose humanity they seem, at times, almost to deny.[30]

But teachers *are* human. To be sure, teaching—like the ministry, law, medicine, business, and government—has its share of angry, hostile, and incompetent people. Most teachers, however, are decent, honest, well-intentioned people who do their best under the most trying circumstances. If they appear otherwise, it is because the institution in which they are engulfed demands it of them. As we shall see in Part III, especially Chapters 7 and 8, transforming the school transforms teacher as well as student behavior. If placed in an atmosphere of freedom and trust, if treated as professionals and as people of worth, teachers behave like the caring, concerned people they would like to be. They, no less than their students, are victimized by the way in which schools are currently organized and run.

Certainly nothing in the way most schools are built or run suggests respect for teachers as teachers, or as human beings. After visiting some 260 classrooms in 100 elementary schools in thirteen states, for example, John Goodlad, dean of the UCLA Graduate School of Education, concluded that the schools are "anything but the 'palaces' of an affluent society." On the contrary, he writes, they look "more like the artifacts of a society that did not really care about its schools, a society that expressed its disregard by creating schools less suited to human habitation than its prisons."[31] Goodlad and his colleagues had hoped to conduct long interviews with the teachers they observed, but few schools had either quiet or attractive places in which to meet; they held their interviews on the run, therefore, unless they were able to meet the teachers for breakfast or dinner. Nor was Goodlad's experience atypical. Teachers rarely have offices of their own, and if there is a teachers' lounge, more often than not

---

[30] Cf. David Riesman, Introduction to the Grosset Universal Library edition of Reuel Denney's *The Astonished Muse*.

[31] John Goodlad, "The Schools vs. Education," *Saturday Review,* April 19, 1969.

it is a shabbily furnished room designed to permit no more than a fast smoke.

The shabbiness of the teachers' physical environment is exceeded only by the churlishness of their social environment, a fact that educational critics and reformers tend to ignore or to acknowledge only in passing. "Reform literature," as Dean Robert J. Schaeffer of Teachers College has written, "has failed to examine the total educational experience of teachers, and has narrowly concentrated upon preservice preparation to the neglect of the educative or the debilitating effects of the job itself." And the job *is* debilitating. In a section on "What Teaching Does to Teachers" in *The Sociology of Teaching*, Willard Waller talks about "that peculiar blight which affects the teacher mind, which creeps over it gradually, and possessing it bit by bit, devours its creative resources."

This "peculiar blight" is a product of a number of forces. There is the low regard in which teachers are held by the rest of the community, reflected not only in the salaries and physical plants teachers are provided, but also in the unflattering stereotypes of teachers with which American literature (and films and TV programs) are filled.[32] There is the atmosphere of meanness and distrust in which teachers work; they punch time clocks like factory workers or clerks and are rarely if ever consulted about things that concern them most, such as the content of the curriculum or the selection of textbooks. And there are the conditions of work themselves: teaching loads that provide no time for reflection or for privacy, and menial tasks such as "patrol duty" in the halls or cafeteria that demean or deny professional status. "Whatever becomes of our method, the conditions stand fast—six hours, and thirty, fifty, or a hundred and fifty pupils," Ralph Waldo Emerson observed more than a century ago.

---

[32] In a study of occupational prestige conducted by the National Opinion Research Center, teaching ranked thirty-fifth from the top—just below the building contractor and just above the railroad engineer. Cf. W. W. Charters, Jr., "The Social Background of Teaching," in N. L. Gage, ed., *Handbook of Research on Teaching,* Chicago: Rand McNally, 1963. The status problem mainly affects male teachers, the great majority of whom teach in secondary schools. For women, teaching is a highly prestigious occupation; indeed, teaching is a low-status and low-paying occupation for men in large part because it traditionally has been dominated by women and so is regarded as a female occupation. Cf. Dan C. Lortie, "The Balance of Control and Autonomy in Elementary School Teaching," in Amitai Etzioni, ed., *The Semi-Professions and Their Organization,* New York: Free Press, 1969.

"Something must be done and done speedily, and in this distress the wisest are tempted to adopt violent means, to proclaim martial law, corporal punishment, mechanical arrangements, bribes, spies, wrath, main strength and ignorance. . . . And the gentle teacher, who wishes to be a Providence to youth, is grown a martinet, sore with suspicions . . . and his love of learning is lost in the routine of grammar and books of elements."

Despite the continuous contact with children, moreover, teaching is a lonely profession. Teachers rarely get a chance to discuss their problems or their successes with their colleagues, nor do they, as a rule, receive any kind of meaningful help from their supervisors, not even in the first year of teaching. "When we first started working in the schools," members of the Yale University's Psycho-Educational Clinic report, "we were asked in several instances in the early weeks not to go into several classrooms *because* the teachers were new."[33] [Emphasis in the original]

If teachers are obsessed with silence and lack of movement, therefore, it is in large part because it is the chief means by which their competence is judged. A teacher will rarely, if ever, be called on the carpet or denied tenure because his students have not learned anything; he most certainly will be rebuked if his students are talking or moving about the classroom, or—even worse—found outside the room, and he may earn the censure of his colleagues as well. Nor will teachers receive suggestions from their supervisors as to how to improve their teaching methods and materials; they will receive suggestions for improving "discipline." Thus, the vows of silence and stillness are often imposed on teachers who might prefer a more open, lively classroom.

ITEM: From *Up the Down Staircase.*

There was one heady moment when I was able to excite the class by an idea: I had put on the blackboard Browning's "A man's reach should exceed his grasp, or what's a heaven for?" and we got involved in a spirited discussion of aspiration vs. reality. Is it wise, I asked, to aim higher than one's capacity?

---

[33] Seymour B. Sarason, Murray Levine, I. Ira Goldenberg, Dennis L. Cherlin, and Edward M. Bennett, *Psychology in Community Settings: Clinical, Educational, Vocational, Social Aspects,* New York: John Wiley, 1966.

Does it not doom one to failure? No, no, some said, that's ambition and progress! No, no, others cried, that's frustration and defeat! What about hope? What about despair?—You've got to be practical!—You've got to have a dream! They said this in their own words, you understand, startled into discovery. To the young, clichés seem freshly minted. Hitch your wagon to a star! Shoemaker, stick to your last! And when the dismissal bell rang, they paid me the highest compliment: they groaned! They crowded in the doorway, chirping like agitated sparrows, pecking at the seeds I had strewn—when who should appear but [the administrative assistant to the principal].

"What is the meaning of this noise?"

"It's the sound of thinking, Mr. McHabe," I said.

In my letter box that afternoon was a note from him, with copies to my principal and chairman (and—who knows?— perhaps a sealed indictment dispatched to the Board?) which read:

> "I have observed that in your class the class entering your room is held up because the pupils exiting from your room are exiting in a disorganized fashion, blocking the doorway unnecessarily and *talking*. An orderly flow of traffic is the responsibility of the teacher whose class is exiting from the room."

The cardinal sin, strange as it may seem in an institution of learning, is talking.

ITEM: A sixth-grade science teacher in a highly regarded suburban school, learning that one of his pupils is the son of a local butcher, obtains the heart and lungs of a cow. Next day, elbow-deep in tissue and blood, he shows the class how the respiratory system operates. When he returns from lunch, he finds a note from the Superintendent, who had looked in on the class that morning: "Teachers are not supposed to remove their jackets in class. If the jacket must be removed, the shirt-sleeves certainly should not be rolled up."

If schools are repressive, then, it is not the teachers' fault, certainly not their fault alone. Nearly two-thirds of the high school students' parents surveyed in early 1969 for *Life* by Louis Harris, for example, believe that "maintaining discipline is more important than student self-inquiry"; the comparable figure among teachers is only 27 percent. The United States, in short, has the kinds of schools its citizens have thus far demanded. The role of taskmaster is thrust upon the teachers, some of whom accept it willingly, some reluctantly; all are affected by it. "The teacher-pupil relationship," Waller writes, "is a special form of dominance and subordination, a very unstable relationship and in quivering equilibrium. . . . It is an unfortunate role, that of Simon Legree, and has corrupted the best of men."

VI

What schools do to both students and teachers can be understood best if one realizes that in a number of respects, schools resemble "total institutions" like hospitals, armed services, and even prisons. In all of these, as Philip Jackson puts it, "one subgroup of their clientele (the students) are involuntarily committed to the institution, whereas another sub-group (the staff) has greater freedom of movement and, most important, has the ultimate freedom to leave the institution entirely. Under these circumstances it is common for the more privileged group to guard the exits, either figuratively or literally." Even when teachers operate "democratic" classrooms, Jackson insists, "their responsibilities bear some resemblance to those of prison guards. In 'progressive' prisons, as in most classrooms, the inhabitants are allowed certain freedoms, but there are real limits. In both institutions the inmates might be allowed to plan a Christmas party, but in neither place are they allowed to plan a 'break.' "[34]

To survive in school, as in other "total institutions," the students, like the teachers, are forced to develop a variety of adaptive strategies and attitudes. And survival—getting through and compiling a good record or avoiding a bad record—does become the goal. It is inevitable that this be so, given the obsession with routine and given also the frequency with which students are evaluated, the arbitrariness and mysteriousness (at least to the students) of the criteria by which they are judged, and the importance attached to these evaluations by parents, teachers, colleges, graduate and professional schools, and prospective employers.

ITEM: A high school student talking: "School is just like roulette or something. You can't just ask: 'Well, what's the point of it? . . . The point of it is to do it, to get through and

---

[34] Cf. Willard Waller, *The Sociology of Teaching*, especially Chapters 2 and 14; and Gertrude H. S. McPherson, *The Role-Set of the Elementary School Teacher: A Case Study*, unpublished Ph.D. dissertation, Columbia University Library.

get into college. But you have to figure the system or you can't win, because the odds are all on the house's side."[35]

Unfortunately, survival has little to do with learning in the sense of cognitive development. "For children," as John Holt documents in some detail, "the central business of school is not learning, whatever this vague word means; it is getting those daily tasks done, or at least out of the way, with a minimum of effort and unpleasantness. Each task is an end in itself."[36] This is so, as Mary Alice White of Teachers College has explained with great sensitivity, because "the view from the pupil's desk" bears little resemblance to the view from the teacher's or the curriculum designer's desk. "What the pupil is going to learn is to him far away in time and entirely mysterious," Professor White writes. "All he knows is what he *has* been taught, and he only remembers part of that, often in an isolated fashion. Why he is made to learn this and not that, or this before that, is another mystery to him; nor does he know what the alternative choices might be. Since little of what he is asked to learn makes much sense to him, except perhaps the more visible skills of reading, writing, and computation, he rarely asks why he has been asked to learn them. He also senses that he is going to be taught whatever the teacher has decided she is going to teach, so the question is useless."[37]

In any case, the student has no cognitive map to guide him through the labyrinth of knowledge he is asked to master. He is guided instead, Professor White suggests, by his map of school experience. Thus, elementary school students almost invariably regard mathematics as the most important subject in the curriculum—not because of its structure or its elegance, but because math has the most homework, because the homework is corrected the most promptly, and because tests are given more frequently than in any other subject. The youngsters regard spelling as the next most important subject, because of the frequency of spelling tests. "To a pupil," Professor White explains, "the workload and evaluation demands obviously must reflect what the teacher thinks is important to learn."

[35] Quoted in Kathryn Johnston Noyes and Gordon L. McAndrew, "Is This What Schools Are For," *Saturday Review,* December 21, 1968.
[36] John Holt, *How Children Fail,* New York: Pitman, 1964.
[37] Mary Alice White, "The View from the Pupil's Desk," *The Urban Review,* Vol. II, No. 5, April 1968.

It is not simply the students' ignorance of the purposes of what they are asked to learn that makes them subordinate learning to survival. Almost from the first day, students learn that the game is not to acquire knowledge but to discover what answer the teacher wants, and in what form she wants it; there are few classroom scenes more familiar than that of the teacher brushing aside or penalizing correct answers that don't happen to be the ones she had in mind. "It is soon clear to students what types of responses are likely to be successful at playing the school game," a group of dissident Maryland students write in a biting critique of their county's schools. "And so, before long, a student's approach to questions and problems undergoes a basic change. It quickly becomes clear that approaching a question on a test by saying 'What is my own response to this question?' is risky indeed, and totally unwise if one covets the highest grade possible (and the school system teaches the student that he should). Rather, the real question is clear to any student who knows anything about how schools work: 'What is the answer the teacher wants me to give? What can I write that will please the teacher?' "[38]

These tendencies are almost built into the way most classrooms operate. "In training a child to activity of thought," Alfred North Whitehead wrote, "above all things we must beware of what I will call 'inert ideas'—that is to say, ideas that are merely received into the mind without being utilised, or tested, or thrown into fresh combinations."[39] In most classrooms, however, the teacher sits or stands at the front of the room, dispensing "inert ideas" to his passive students, as if they were so many empty vessels to be filled.

ITEM: "A high-school teacher displays the following sales pitch on his bulletin board: 'FREE. Every Monday through Friday. Knowledge. Bring your own containers.' " (From *Reader's Digest,* October 1969.)

Without realizing it, moreover (few have been exposed to any other way of teaching), most teachers dominate the class-

[38] Montgomery County Student Alliance, *Wanted: A Humane Education: An Urgent Call for Reconciliation Between Rhetoric and Reality,* Bethesda, Md.: Montgomery County Student Alliance, 1969 (mimeographed), reprinted in Ronald and Beatrice Gross, eds., *Radical School Reform,* New York: Simon and Schuster, 1969.
[39] Alfred North Whitehead, *The Aims of Education,* New York: New American Library Mentor Books, 1949.

room, giving students no option except that of passivity. Exhaustive studies of classroom language in almost every part of the country, and in almost every kind of school, reveal a pattern that is striking in its uniformity: teachers do almost all the talking, accounting, on average, for two-thirds to three-quarters of all classroom communication. There are differences, of course, from teacher to teacher, but the differences are surprisingly small. In the most child-centered classroom in a private school known for its child-centeredness, for example, Philip Jackson found that the teacher initiated 55.2 percent of the conversation; in the most teacher-dominated room, the ratio was 80.7 percent. Equally significant, analyses of the nature of student and teacher conversation indicates that the student's role is passive, being confined, for the most part, to responses to teacher questions or statements. In almost all the systems of "interaction analysis" that have been devised to analyze the different kinds of classroom communication—there are now several dozen—three-quarters or so of the "talk" categories refer to teachers.[40]

Small wonder, then, that students seem unable to take responsibility for their learning; the following description of a Massachusetts school system could apply to almost any other in the United States.

Watertown's young people do not find school an intellectually exciting place. Although the Study Staff observed some

[40] Herbert M. Kliebard, "The Observation of Classroom Behavior," in *The Way Teaching Is,* Washington, D.C.: Association for Supervision and Curriculum Development and National Education Association, 1966; Arno Bellack, Herbert M. Kliebard, Ronald T. Hyman, and Frank L. Smith Jr., *The Language of the Classroom,* New York: Teachers College Press, 1966; Donald M. Medley and Harold F. Mitzel, "Measuring Classroom Behavior by Systematic Observation," in N. L. Gage, ed., *Handbook of Research in Teaching,* Rand McNally, 1963; Ned A. Flanders, "Interaction Analysis: A Technique for Quantifying Teacher Influence," paper delivered at American Educational Research Association, Chicago, February 1962; Edmund J. Amidon and Ned A. Flanders, "The Role of the Teacher in the Classroom: A Manual for Understanding and Improving Teachers' Classroom Behavior," Minneapolis, Minn.: Paul S. Amidon & Associates, 1963; John B. Hough, "Training in the Control of Verbal Teaching Behavior—Theory and Implications," paper read at A.E.R.A. Convention, New York City, 1967; Philip M. Jackson, "Teacher-Pupil Communication: An Observational Study, paper read at A.E.R.A. Convention, February 1965; Marie N. Hughes, "The Utah Study of the Assessment of Teaching," in A. A. Bellack, ed., *Theory and Research in Teaching,* Teachers College Press, 1963; Cf. *Interaction Analysis Newsletter* for complete bibliography of past and new studies.

good schools staffed in part by able, hard-working, creative teachers, instructing youngsters who were happy, vibrant, and actively engaged in the learning process, these bright spots are overshadowed by evidence that too often Watertown's students look without enthusiasm upon their schools and the learning required in them. In many of the classes observed by the Study Staff, students remained passive and uninvolved in their own education.

Watertown's schools do not give the student many opportunities to assume responsibility for his own learning. The student is not encouraged to explore, to stretch his thinking, to pursue an independent line of inquiry. The program of studies is defined by the school, and the student is expected to learn what the school decides he should learn. Rarely does the student in Watertown have the chance to make meaningful decisions; rarely does he have a chance to discover for himself what learning is all about.

The pervasive method of instruction consists of lectures and teacher-dominated activities. The teacher talks; the students are expected to listen or recite in response to the teacher's cues. The emphasis is on the acquisition of factual information untempered by reflective thought. Textbooks determine course content and organization, and many courses are untouched by current thought in curriculum development. In Watertown, the student succeeds by being quiet, by following directions, and by memorizing the information which the teacher doles out. The teacher succeeds by following textbook instructions.[41]

The phenomenon is not limited to elementary and secondary schools. Because college students' academic relationship to faculty and administration is also one of subjection, Howard S. Becker, Blanche Geer, and Everett C. Hughes argue, "students seek only the information faculty wants, and direct their efforts toward producing whatever impression is required to get a good grade," and "learning for its own sake flies out the window." In medical school, too, the goal is to get through.[42]

One of the ways of getting through is by cheating. "Learning

[41] *Watertown: The Education of Its Children,* Harvard Graduate School of Education Center for Field Studies, 1967.
[42] Howard S. Becker, Blanche Geer, and Everett C. Hughes, *Making the Grade: The Academic Side of College Life,* New York: John Wiley, 1968; Howard S. Becker, Blanche Geer, Everett C. Hughes, and Anselm Strauss, *Boys in White: Student Culture in Medical School,* University of Chicago Press, 1961. For a somewhat different view of medical school, see Robert K. Merton, George C. Reader, and Patricia L. Kendall, eds., *The Student Physician: Introductory Studies in the Sociology of Medical Education,* Harvard University Press, 1957.

how to make it in school," as Jackson observes, "involves, in part, learning how to falsify our behavior." Some of the forms of falsification involve little more than the petty dissembling common to adult social discourse, e.g., feigning interest in what another is saying. Some involve outright cheating, e.g., copying on a test. In their classic studies of character education of forty years ago, Hartshorne and May discovered that children's tendency to cheat depended on the risk of detection and the effort required rather than on intrinsic notions of morality; noncheaters were more cautious than the cheaters, but not more honest.[43]

These findings, which have been confirmed by a number of subsequent studies, reflect the primitive morality which the culture of the school actively cultivates. "While most elementary school children are aware of, and concerned about, the harm done others by acts of aggression or theft," Professor Lawrence Kohlberg of Harvard, the leading contemporary student of moral education, writes, "their only reason for not cheating is their fear of being caught and punished. Even at older ages, teachers give children few moral or mature reasons to think cheating is bad. Sixth-grade children tell us their teachers tell them not to cheat because they will get punished"—the most primitive level of moral judgment—"or because 'the person you copied from might have it wrong and so it won't do you any good,'" a level of judgment only one step up on Kohlberg's hierarchy. Teachers are always and unavoidably moralizing to children about rules, values, and behavior, but they rarely think about the values they are communicating. "Many teachers would be most mortified and surprised to know what their students perceive to be their moral values and concerns," Kohlberg observes.

Getting through school also involves learning how to suppress one's feelings and emotions and to subordinate one's own interests and desires to those of the teachers. Up to a point, this, too, is useful—a necessary aspect of learning to live in society. But schools tend to turn what could be a virtue into a fault by in effect excluding the child's interests altogether. The result, Peter Marin, a former high school principal suggests, is to create "a

[43] H. Hartshorne and M. A. May, *Studies in the Nature of Character,* quoted in Lawrence Kohlberg, "Moral Education in the Schools: A Developmental View," *The School Review,* Vol. 74, No. 1, Spring 1966; Lawrence Kohlberg, *The Development of Children's Orientations to a Moral Order,* New York: Holt, Rinehart and Winston, Inc., expected to be published late 1971.

cultural schizophrenia in which the student is forced to choose between his own relation to reality and the one demanded by the institution." Children frequently respond by learning to live in two worlds. "Children acquire great dexterity in exhibiting in conventional and expected ways the *form* of attention to school work," John Dewey observed, "while reserving the inner play of their own thoughts, images, and emotions for subjects that are more important to them, but quite irrelevant."

Some students, however, survive by withdrawing into apathy, whether feigned or real; in the constantly evaluative atmosphere of the school, one way for them to avoid the pain of failure is to persuade themselves that they do not care. But those who do care, and who do do well on tests, are not free from pain, either; they may bear the marks of caring for the rest of their lives, particularly if they go on to college and graduate or professional school. One of the first discoveries that Sigmund Freud made when he began studying the significance of dreams was the near-universality, among people with advanced degrees, of what he called the "examination dream." In it, the dreamer imagines himself back at school and about to take an examination for which he is hopelessly unprepared and almost certain to fail. The dream—still common among university graduates— is marked by acute anxiety; the dreamer often awakens in a cold sweat.

The most important strategy for survival is docility and conformity. "Most students soon learn that rewards are granted to those who lead a good life. And in school the good life consists, principally, of doing what the teacher says," Jackson observes. "Every school child quickly learns what makes teachers angry. He learns that in most classrooms the behavior that triggers the teacher's ire has little to do with wrong answers or other indicators of scholastic failure. Rather, it is violations of institutional expectations that really get under the teacher's skin"; for example, "coming into the room late, or making too much noise, or not listening to directions, or pushing while in line. Occasionally, teachers do become publicly vexed by their students' academic shortcomings, but to really send them off on a tirade of invective, the young student soon discovers, nothing works better than a partially suppressed giggle during arithmetic period."

This encouragement of docility may explain why girls tend to be more successful in school than boys: passivity and docility are more in keeping with the behavior the culture expects of girls outside of school than the behavior it expects of boys. The phenomenon is cumulative and self-reinforcing: the behavior demanded in school is more feminine than masculine; girls adapt better; therefore school, and an interest in school affairs, tends to be defined as feminine, particularly among ethnic and social groups that place a high premium on masculinity. Perhaps as a result—or perhaps also because boys develop at a different rate than girls, a fact that the schools ignore—boys tend to do less well in school than girls, and are vastly more susceptible to learning and emotional problems. Thus, boys account for three-quarters of all referrals to reading clinics; more than two-thirds of the children who are "retained" (left back) in a grade for one or more years are boys; between three and four times as many boys as girls are stutterers.[44]

Docility is not only encouraged but frequently demanded, for teachers and administrators seem unable to distinguish between authority and power. "The generalization that the schools have a despotic political structure," Waller writes, "seems to hold true for nearly all types of schools, and for all about equally, without very much difference in fact to correspond to radical differences in theory."

ITEM: The director of physical education for girls in a well-regarded suburban school system insists that a thirteen-year-old girl change into gym shorts and sit on the sidelines each time her class has gym, despite the fact that the girl has been excused for medical reasons. "There's no reason you can't watch, or keep score if the other girls are playing a game," the director tells the child, whose cancerous right leg has just been amputated at the hip, and who cannot yet be fitted with an artificial limb. Not until her mother carries the appeal to the superintendent of schools is the youngster spared this thrice-weekly humiliation.

ITEM: A boy, being put on detention, protests his innocence, politely but insistently presenting his version of what happened. (The incident in question had involved another teacher.) The

[44] Frances Bentzen, "Sex Ratios in Learning and Behavior Disorders," *The National Elementary Principal,* Vol. XLVI, No. 2, November 1966; M. L. Kellmer Pringle, N. R. Butler, R. Davie, *11,000 Seven-Year-Olds,* London: Longmans, Green, 1966; Patricia Sexton, *The Feminized Male,* New York: Random House, 1969.

teacher giving the punishment responds each time by telling the boy how important it is to respect his elders, insisting that he should go on detention first and then tell the teacher involved why he thought the punishment was unfair. "You have to prove you're a man and can take orders." The boy finally agrees to go to detention, "but under protest." The scene ends with the teacher smirking as the boy walks away.[45]

Docility is demanded outside the school as well as inside; students learn fairly rapidly that their participation in civic affairs is not welcome, except for one ceremonial day a year when they are allowed to play at being superintendent of schools, principal, or teacher for the photographers from the local newspaper.

ITEM: A high school senior—eighth in a class of 779, active in a host of extracurricular activities (student marshalls, General Organization, Key Club, after-school tutoring program, president of the Debate Society, among others), and described on the school's record as "intelligent, highly motivated and mature" with "excellent leadership and academic potentials"— is barred from the school's chapter of the National Honor Society on the grounds of poor character. At an open meeting of school board candidates the preceding spring, he had politely asked a question that implied some criticism of the high school. In the opinion of eight of the Honor Society's fifteen faculty advisers, none of whom had been present at the meeting in question and none of whom knew the boy, criticism of the high school is equivalent to disloyalty, and disloyalty constitutes bad character. The seven faculty advisers who know the youngster fight for his admission but are overruled.

ITEM: Memorandum to teachers from the principal of a high school in a Washington, D.C., suburb: "If you see any copies of the *Washington Free Press* [a local student "underground" newspaper] in the possession of a student, confiscate it immediately. Any questions from the student regarding this confiscation should be referred to the administration. If you see a student selling or distributing this paper, refer them [sic] to an administrator and they will be suspended."[46]

[45] From the film *High School*, produced by Frederick Wiseman.
[46] Montgomery County Student Alliance, *Wanted: A Humane Education: An Urgent Call for Reconciliation Between Rhetoric and Reality,* Be-

ITEM: The principal of a Queens, N.Y., high school went further: every student *"seen reading or carrying—or even suspected of possessing*—copies" of *The High School Free Press,* a New York underground paper, was suspended.[47] [Emphasis added]

The tragedy is that the great majority of students do not rebel; they accept the stultifying rules, the lack of privacy, the authoritarianism, the abuse of power—indeed, virtually every aspect of school life—as The Way Things Are. "All weakness tends to corrupt, and impotence corrupts absolutely," Edgar Friedenberg sardonically observes. Hence students "accept the school as the way life is and close their minds against the anxiety of perceiving alternatives. Many students like high school; others loathe and fear it. But even these do not object to it on principle; the school effectively obstructs their learning of the principles on which objection might be based . . ."

ITEM: A high school student talking. "The main thing is not to take it personal, to understand that it's just a system and it treats you the same way it treats everybody else, like an engine or a machine or something mechanical. Our names get fed into it—*we* get fed into it—when we're five years old, and if we catch on and watch our step, it spits us out when we're 17 or 18. . . ."[48]

The sociologist Buford Rhea, who set out to study high school students' alienation, discovered that most students are not alienated and do not want power because they feel they would not know what to do with it if they had it. They have remarkable faith in the high schools' paternalism and so see no need to question what their teachers are doing or why. "It is the teacher's job to know what to tell the student to do, and it is therefore the teacher's responsibility to know *why* the student should do it," Rhea reports. Indeed, academically ambitious students quite literally will themselves into believing in their teachers' ability.

---

thesda, Md.: Montgomery County Student Alliance, 1969, in R. and B. Gross, eds., *Radical School Reform.*
[47] Nicholas Pileggi, "Revolutionaries Who Have to Be Home by 7:30," *Phi Delta Kappan,* June 1969.
[48] From Noyes and McAndrew, "Is This What Schools Are For?", *Saturday Review,* December 21, 1968.

"Unable to withdraw or rebel (this route leads to failure), these ambitious students seem eager to detect, and perhaps even to fantasy, competence and concern among the staff."[49]

As a result, schools are able to manipulate students into doing much of the dirty work of control under the guise of self-government. As Waller pointed out nearly forty years ago, "Self-government is rarely real. Usually it is but a mask for the rule of the teacher oligarchy," or "in its most liberal form the rule of a student oligarchy carefully selected and supervised by the faculty." (For a description of high schools where self-government *is* real, see Chapter 8.)

ITEM: "A GENERAL CODE OF BEHAVIOR FOR STUDENTS"

(Submitted by the George Washington Student Council)

The students of George Washington High School have many privileges and are not bound to a set of regulations as traditional students. The goal of each student is to be purely self-motivated in his academic pursuits. To make self-direction successful, the student must keep a high standard of behavior. This must be maintained in the classrooms as well as in unscheduled time. *Since our privileges can be removed by the administration at any time, the student must stay within the realms of this general code.*

Be courteous to the administrative staff and faculty.

Be considerate of upperclassmen and their privileges.

Refrain from littering by using the trash cans.

- Return all trays in the cafeteria.
- Use trash receptacles for waste paper, candy wrappers, milk cartons, etc.
- Do not use waste receptacles as chairs.
- Keep books neatly on tables and do not put them on the floors.

Do not deface the walls or destroy any school property.

Keep movement in the halls between modules at a minimum. Remember that even moderate talking while changing classes could disturb classes in session. Keep conversation to a minimum on quest and seminar corridors.

Use lockers only before and after school and at lunch when it is necessary.

Maintain silence while in the library or a quiet study area.

Be seated in the quiet commons at all times.

[49] Buford Rhea, "Institutional Paternalism in High School," *The Urban Review*, February 1968.

- No more than four should be seated at small tables.
- No more than eight should be seated at large tables.

Refrain from boisterous conduct.
Do not talk in the quiet commons.
Do not leave the school building, except during lunch modules, without permission of a member of the administrative staff.
Do not use the balcony area outside the quiet commons except during the lunch modules.
Do not loiter in the halls.[50] [Emphasis added]

To be sure, students are less pliable now than they were even a few years ago. Dissent and protest are becoming widespread high school phenomena, and in his 1969 survey of high school students' attitudes, Louis Harris discovered a large reservoir of discontent with adult authority. Even so, the discontent was rather narrowly focused. Two-thirds of the students Harris surveyed felt that they should have more say in making rules and in deciding on curriculum, but fewer than half felt they should have more say in determining discipline.

More important, while students want some role in making the rules, surprisingly few of them question either the rules themselves or the way they are enforced. A clear majority, for example, think the school regulations are "about right," including rules on dress, haircuts, and use of free time. Three times as many students think the rules are enforced too leniently than feel enforcement is too severe; the great majority (two-thirds) think enforcement is about right. Students are equally satisfied with the curriculum: 50 percent of them think they "learn a lot" in high school, nearly two-thirds think the grading system is fair (they voted over two to one against abolishing grades), and 81 percent rate their teachers as good to excellent.[51] Belief in the beneficence of the paternalism to which they are subject exists, Buford Rhea suggests, "because there is a need for faith of this sort"; without it, students might find school intolerable. It is "the myth of institutional paternalism," in short, that keeps students from being alienated. Whether this is a virtue is something else again.

---

[50] From the *George Washington High School Student Handbook,* Charleston, West Va.
[51] "What People Think About Their High Schools," *Life,* May 16, 1969. Additional data courtesy of *Life* and Louis Harris and Associates, Inc.

5

The Failures of
Educational Reform

For more than a hundred years much complaint has been made of the unmethodical way in which schools are conducted, but it is only within the last thirty that any serious attempt has been made to find a remedy for this state of things. And with what result? Schools remain exactly as they were.

—JOHN AMOS COMENIUS,
The Great Didactic, *1632*

I

". . . the decade which began in 1955, and through which we are still churning," Professor Robert H. Anderson of Harvard predicted in the early sixties, "may ultimately come to be regarded as one of the major turning points in American public education."[1] Anderson's optimism was widely shared: the 1950s and '60s saw one of the largest and most sustained educational reform movements in American history, an effort that many observers, this writer included, thought would transform the schools.[2]

Nothing of the sort has happened; the reform movement has

[1] Robert H. Anderson, "Team Teaching in the Elementary and Secondary Schools," in Alfred de Grazia and David A. Sohn, eds., *Revolution in Teaching: New Theory, Technology, and Curricula,* New York: Bantam Books, 1964.

[2] Cf. C. E. Silberman, "The Remaking of American Education," *Fortune,*

produced innumerable changes, and yet the schools themselves are largely unchanged. In a study referred to in Chapter 4, John I. Goodlad, dean of the UCLA Graduate School of Education, along with several colleagues, visited some 260 kindergarten-through-first-grade classrooms in 100 schools in thirteen states to determine the extent to which the reform movement had changed the schools. He found what this writer and his colleagues found: that things are much the same as they had been twenty years ago, and in some respects not as good as they were forty years ago, when the last great school reform movement was at its peak. "We were unable to discern much attention to pupil needs, attainments, or problems as a basis for individual opportunities to learn," he reports. "Teaching was predominantly telling and questioning by the teacher, with children responding one by one or occasionally in chorus. In all of this, the textbook was the most highly visible instrument of learning and teaching. . . . Rarely did we find small groups intensely in pursuit of knowledge; rarely did we find individual pupils at work in self-sustaining inquiry . . . we are forced to conclude that much of the so-called educational reform movement has been blunted on the classroom door."[3]

Goodlad's gloomy picture contrasts sharply with the unbridled optimism with which the "Education Decade," as he calls it, began. "Never before in history have our schools engaged in such widespread experimentation to meet the new educational requirements," Dr. James E. Allen, then New York State Commissioner of Education, and at this writing, U.S. Commissioner of Education, wrote in his foreword to Arthur D. Morse's 1960 volume, *Schools of Tomorrow—TODAY*. "Never before have so many hopeful new approaches developed in such a relatively short period. An intense self-examination is now under way on a national scale," Dr. Allen went on to say; and "In the process, we are learning that many of the old ways of operating our schools are not necessarily the best ways. New methods of organization, the use of new technological devices and new con-

---

April 1961. Cf. also *Innovation and Experiment in Education*, A Progress Report of the Panel on Educational Research and Development, Washington, D.C.: U.S. Government Printing Office, March 1964.
[3] John Goodlad, "The Schools vs. Education," *Saturday Review*, April 19, 1969. Cf. also John Goodlad, "Thought, Invention, and Research," in *The Schools and the Challenge of Innovation*, Supplementary Paper No. 28, Committee for Economic Development, 1969; and "Curriculum: A Janus Look," *Teachers College Record*, Vol. 70, No. 2, November 1968.

cepts of the role of the teacher provide answers that numbers alone cannot provide."

If the schools are to be transformed in the 1970s, we need to understand why they were so immune to change in the 1950s and '60s. Morse's book provides a useful starting point. *Schools of Tomorrow—TODAY* was commissioned by the New York State Department of Education and underwritten by the Ford Foundation's Fund for the Advancement of Education; it offered a wide-eyed and enthusiastic description of ten "hopeful new approaches," selected, as Dr. Allen's foreword explains, "because they represent a cross-section of experimentation, they are in operation *now,* and their early results appear to be hopeful." [Emphasis in original]

They appear a lot less hopeful now. Indeed, most of Morse's schools of tomorrow look strangely like the schools of yesterday and today. Compared to the schools described in the volume whose title Morse borrowed, John and Evelyn Dewey's *Schools of Tomorrow,* first published in 1915, Morse's schools are remarkably conventional; for the most part, what are hailed as new methods of organization, new technologies, and new concepts of the role of the teacher turn out, on examination, to be more gimmickry and packaging than substantive change. More important, perhaps, only one of the innovations Morse describes, the ungraded primary, seems to grow out of or reflect any serious thought about the nature of childhood or the nature or purposes of education. Most of the others, such as team teaching, instructional television, and teacher aides, were techniques to increase efficiency which left both the content of the curriculum and the process of instruction untouched and, for the most part, unexamined.

Team teaching, for example, which Morse hails in his first chapter, is a useful but essentially limited device. In team teaching at the elementary school level, which Morse describes, all the children in a single grade are pooled together. Instead of each teacher being assigned to a single self-contained class of twenty-five or thirty youngsters for the entire year, teaching them every subject, the teachers in that grade operate as a team, under the direction of a team leader. The youngsters are divided into smaller groups as the teachers see fit; e.g., they may be brought together in large lecture halls for some purposes, small discussion groups for others, conventionally sized classes for others. The teachers may divide the work in any number of ways. Those who are particularly skilled at lecturing, for example, may concentrate on large-group instruction, while teachers with a talent for Socratic dialogue may handle only the small groups. Or they may divide the workload according to subject matter. In any case, team members are supposed to spend a good bit of time together, deciding what is to be taught, and how.

By itself, however, putting teachers together in teams does not necessarily mean that the curriculum or the teaching will be improved, only that a new kind of division of labor will be put into effect. Indeed, all sorts of inanities can be perpetrated under the rubric of team teaching.

ITEM: From Morse's description of team teaching at the Franklin Elementary School in Lexington, Massachusetts. "This constant exchange of views strengthens the Beta team. For Billy at the moment it means carefully planned lessons in farming." Indeed, each member of Billy's second-grade teaching team, Morse reports, "chose an area of concentration." The team leader "boned up on the subject, 'How soil determines what is raised locally.' Other teachers singled out weather effects on soil, regional and national factors in crop growth and area influences in lumbering." But why a second grader or his teachers in a Boston suburb should devote quite that much attention to lessons on "area influences in lumbering" and the like is not a question Morse answers, or even asks.

On the other hand, team teaching, if taken seriously and literally, can generate questions that normally do not get raised, for it brings teachers together in a collegial relationship that would not otherwise exist in an elementary school. In the school Morse describes, team teaching was taken seriously, with time set aside for the teams to meet and discuss their work. The more team members discussed what they were teaching, the more the question of why they were teaching it began to intrude, and with it the realization that the curriculum was a mishmash of unrelated and frequently inane details. The ultimate result, therefore, was substantial curriculum reform—a result that had not been anticipated when the experiment began.[4]

Curriculum reform had not been anticipated because team teaching had not been introduced in Lexington as a means of improving instruction, except indirectly. The authors of the idea,

[4] Ethel B. Bears, *Team Teaching,* Lexington, Mass.: Lexington Public Schools, mimeographed.

members of the faculty of the Harvard Graduate School of Education, regarded team teaching as a device to hold able teachers in the classroom. Under the conventional system, ambitious teachers have no option but to leave the classroom for administration if they are to increase their salary and improve their status. Team teaching was designed to create another option by making it possible for a teacher to begin as an assistant, move up to a job as a regular teacher, and then, if particularly well qualified, become a team leader. The Harvard men hoped that this sort of differentiated career ladder, with gradations in salary and status, would attract abler people into teaching in the first place and keep them there longer.

This has not happened to any noticeable extent; on the contrary, most schools purporting to use team teaching do not distinguish either the role or the salary and status of the various team members. As often as not, in fact, "team teaching" is simply a new label for old-fashioned departmentalization.

ITEM: An elementary school in one of the wealthiest suburbs in the United States claims to be using team teaching in its fifth grade. What this means is that some teachers are handling math and science, others English and social studies. It is called team teaching because the teachers allegedly "get together and discuss all the children." "Isn't that kind of conference difficult to fit into a full teaching schedule?" a visitor asks with feigned innocence. "Well, you know how it is," comes the reply. "We fit it in during lunch hour, or we stay around after three for a few minutes."

Another innovation Morse discussed with considerable enthusiasm was instructional television, devoting two chapters to two separate experiments. His enthusiasm was understandable: in the late 1950s and early '60s, a great many educational reformers saw the new medium as a panacea for any number of educational ills, and the Ford Foundation and its Fund for the Advancement of Education poured millions into a variety of experiments to show the medium's potential. TV was expected to solve the teacher shortage by enabling teachers to reach more students; with master teachers handling the televised instruction, it was argued, class size could rise substantially. Television was also expected to reduce some of the inequities in the allocation of educational resources, enabling students in small rural schools, or in outlying suburban areas, to receive the same (high) quality of instruction as students in more favored urban and suburban areas, and making available to them instruction in foreign languages, sciences, and other specialized subjects that small school systems could not afford to provide on their own. And it was hoped that the new medium would increase learning on the part of all students by giving everyone that "exposure to greatness" which Whitehead felt was essential to good education.

Thus Morse concludes his chapter on the Ford Foundation–financed Southwestern Indiana Educational Television Council by quoting the Evansville, Indiana, superintendent of schools' enthusiastic assessment. "Television," the superintendent told Morse, "has succeeded beyond our expectations in the quality of courses taught, in the enthusiastic acceptance by communities it has touched and by the self-improvement it has stimulated."

There is a lot less enthusiasm now. The Council's tenth annual report begins with these sobering words: "The tenth year of telecasting by the Southwestern Indiana Educational Television Council may be summed up as one of frustration." It continues:

> From the very beginning of the year when the Council programming was dropped by Channel 7, through the problem of driving to Vincennes, Indiana, to put on live programs from the studio of Channel 22, Vincennes University, the entire 1967–68 school year was one unusual experience after another. The statistical report shows that the student enrollment was 21,661, a drop of 11% from last year. [6 percent below the number reported by Morse for 1959.] These students were enrolled in 458 classes, a drop of 17% from last year. With the use of radio as a replacement for television; and then radio and Channel 22, and then radio, Channel 22, and translator Channel 70—there developed some reception problems that, for some schools, were impossible to solve. . . . The staff is looking forward to year eleven. This will be the year educational television takes its big step in our area.

The Council's frustration is widely shared. To the disappointment of its early enthusiasts, instructional television has not yet produced any economies or reduced the number of teachers required for a given number of students. Nor has it produced any noticeable improvement in students' learning; the best that can be said is that students learn about as much—no more, no less—from televised as from live instruction.[5]

Thus, Alvin C. Eurich, one of the most ardent advocates of instructional television in the years he directed the Ford Foundation's education program, confesses that "This is not a success story. After a decade and more of intensive effort and the expenditure of hundreds of millions of dollars, television has *not* made a decisive impact on schools and colleges in this country. . . . Whether measured by the numbers of students affected, by the quality of the product, or by the advancement of learning, televised teaching is still in a rudimentary stage of development."[6] [Emphasis in the original]

Eurich's 1969 assessment contrasts sharply with the optimism of the decade before. "Today the question is no longer *whether* television can play an important role in education," an anonymous 1959 Ford Foundation monograph on *Teaching by Television* flatly declared. "That question has been answered in the affirmative. . . . The question that now needs fuller exploration is *what* kind of a role television can play most effectively." [Emphasis in the original]

The question that needs to be explored now is why the new medium has proved so disappointing. To see instructional television at its best—as exemplified, for example, in "Sesame Street," the daily program for preschool children, or the British Broadcasting Company's film "The Battle of Cullodin"—is to know the power the medium can exert when it is used imaginatively and well. One reason, perhaps, that television remains marginal is that its proponents and users have so little understanding of the nature of the medium. "Television is only a pipeline to carry teaching and demonstration," Wilbur Schramm insists. "Television is in itself merely a medium of communication," declares the superintendent of the school district which is one of the largest users of TV. And indeed this is how it usu-

[5] Cf. the review of the evidence by Wilbur Schramm in a paper prepared for the Ford Foundation and submitted by the Foundation as part of its presentation to the Federal Communications Commission in support of its proposal for educational television transmission by satellite. In underdeveloped countries, on the other hand, where teachers simply are not available, instructional TV does seem to produce some gains in learning. Cf. W. Schramm, "Instructional Television Here and Abroad," in Committee for Economic Development, *The Schools and the Challenge of Innovation,* Supplementary Paper No. 28.

[6] Alvin C. Eurich, *Reforming American Education,* New York: Harper & Row, 1969.

ally is used in practice—as a pipeline carrying the same dull curriculum via the same dull lectures.

ITEM: A ninth-grade teacher is teaching a class over closed-circuit television in a "core" course combining American history and literature. For thirty-five minutes she drones on about *Moby Dick,* discussing the novel for the light it throws on the development of the New England whaling industry. The unit is on the Industrial Revolution.

To see television this way is to guarantee failure; *no* medium —neither the book nor the lecture nor the seminar nor the film nor the drama—is "only a pipeline." One need not be a McLuhanite to agree that the medium is at least part of the message. At the very least, each medium makes demands and imposes limitations; it has its own grammar that requires the material to be altered to fit the medium. To paint in oil is not the same as to paint in watercolor; to write is not to lecture; and to teach via television is not the same as to teach in the classroom.[7]

Nor should anyone be surprised that television has not produced the economies that had been predicted. For one thing, television cannot do the entire teaching job; it can carry lectures and demonstrations, but it cannot direct a class discussion. Hence the TV lecture usually has to be followed immediately by a teacher-directed discussion or drill. Televised classes, moreover, cost considerably more than conventional teaching, because teachers need and demand a lot more time to prepare televised than conventional lessons. "Television makes great demands on teachers who appear on it," Schramm reports, "not because it is especially difficult to use, but rather because it opens the classroom to critical view from the outside. If a lecture is dull, an explanation foggy, an approach to a subject out of date, the performance is not hidden behind the classroom doors, but rather exposed pitilessly to the view of a teacher's colleagues and superiors and the parents of his pupils." This is the same Schramm who argued—two paragraphs earlier in the essay in question—that television is only a pipeline! Note, moreover, his use of the word "performance" to describe the televised

[7] For a lucid analysis of the technical differences between the classroom and television and film, cf. Stephen White, "Educational Television and Films," *The American Behavioral Scientist,* Vol. VI, No. 3, November 1962 (reprinted in de Grazia and Sohn, eds., *Revolution in Teaching: New Theory, Technology, and Curricula*).

lecture, a term not generally used to describe conventional teaching.

Only one of the experiments Morse describes, the ungraded or nongraded primary, had the potential to transform the school; if fully implemented, it would require radical changes in both the aims and the methods of schooling. In the conventional graded school, children are grouped according to age, with all the children in a given grade following a set curriculum. (If the children within a given grade are subdivided horizontally according to ability, the set curriculum may come in two or three slight variations.) Schools have been organized this way for so long that most people take it for granted, as if there were no other way.

The fact is, however, that most American schools were ungraded until the second half of the nineteenth century, the graded school having been introduced in the United States in 1848, when the Quincy Grammar School in Boston, Massachusetts, opened its doors. A number of educators, impressed with the graded schools they had seen in Germany, had been proposing adoption of the technique in this country. The Quincy School was the first built for that purpose; it contained twelve rooms of equal size, four to a floor, in which a teacher and some fifty-five children would meet for a year at a time. The men who created the school predicted that it would set the pattern of American schooling for another fifty years. Their estimate was clearly conservative.

With public school attendance mushrooming, the graded school was an important advance. It gave schoolmen a means of sorting and classifying the hordes of children pouring into the schools, along with a way of subdividing the knowledge to be taught. It thus made it easier to prepare the teachers who were now being demanded in unprecedented numbers: teachers could be taught no more than what they needed to know to teach a specific grade.

It was not very long, however, before the graded school came under attack for its rigidity and its inability to take account of individual differences. "The stereotyped patterns of the graded school system demands a stereotyped individual as learner," Charles W. Eliot and William Rainey Harper, the presidents, respectively, of Harvard and the University of Chicago, declared at the turn of the century. "The class system has been modelled upon the military," Frederick Burk, first president of San Francisco State Normal School, the predecessor of San

Francisco State College, wrote in 1912, in *Remedy for Lock-Step Schooling*. "It is constructed upon the assumption that a group of minds can be marshalled and controlled in growth in exactly the same manner that a military officer marshalls and directs the bodily movements of a company of soldiers. In solid, unbreakable phalanx the class is supposed to move through all the grades, keeping in locked step. This locked step is set by the 'average' pupil—an algebraic myth born of inanimate figures and an addled pedagogy. The class system," Burk argued, "does injury to the rapid and quick-thinking pupils, because these must shackle their stride to keep pace with the rate of the mythical average." But "the class system," he went on to say, "does a greater injury to the large number who make progress slower than the rate of the mythical average pupil. . . . They are foredoomed to failure before they begin. . . . Could any system be more stupid in its assumptions, more impossible in its conditions, and more juggernautic in its operation?" Burk asked. "Every one of its premises is palpably false; every one of its requirements is impossible and every one of its effects is inefficient and brutal. Nevertheless this system has endured and has been endured for centuries."

It still endures—in many cases, under the "ungraded" or "nongraded" label. "Since the first appearance of *The Nongraded Elementary School*," John Goodlad and Robert H. Anderson wrote in 1963, in the introduction to the revised edition of their volume, "the authors have witnessed with mixed awe and pleasure a remarkable surge of national interest in nongrading. Hundreds of cities, including some of America's largest, have announced themselves committed to nongraded organization at least for the primary years. Secondary schools and even colleges have begun to follow nongraded patterns, and such agencies as the United States Office of Education and the National Education Association have reported a widespread adoption of nongraded practices. One such report went so far as to state that, in a sample of wealthy suburban schools, nongraded classrooms 'have become almost conventional practice.' "[8]

The authors drew something less than satisfaction from the trend. "While we are heartened by the lively interest that has been shown," they went on to say, "we confess to deep concern over the superficiality and inadequacy of much that is being done

[8] John I. Goodlad and Robert H. Anderson, *The Nongraded Elementary School,* New York: Harcourt, Brace & World, revised edition, 1963.

in the name of nongrading. *Many of the so-called nongraded programs are little different from the graded plans they replaced, and except for a 'levels' scheme in reading there are few changes of real significance to children."* [Emphasis added]

Six years later Goodlad was even more disheartened by what he and others observed schools doing under the name of nongraded organization. "I should have known better," he confessed, in pointing out that most schoolmen had completely misunderstood what he and Anderson had proposed. He should have realized, he said, "that teachers and administrators would reach eagerly for the catchy, innovative label and that nongrading soon would be used to describe pitifully old practices of interclass achievement grouping."[9]

To be sure, a number of schools have made serious attempts to develop curricula, teaching techniques, methods of evaluation, and administrative arrangements that would permit students to move at their own pace irrespective of grade. The Appleton, Wisconsin, elementary schools, which Morse describes, have experimented with what the English call "family" or "vertical" grouping (see Chapter 6) in which children covering a three-grade spectrum are grouped together. But most of the schools claiming to have adopted nongraded programs have not done so at all. What they *call* nongrading is nothing more than conventional homogeneous grouping of students by ability *within* the same grade; the vertical grade organization is left unchanged, along with the curriculum, teaching methods, and everything else.

II

The most significant part of the reform movement of the 1950s and '60s is hardly mentioned in Morse's book. This was the great effort at reforming the curriculum that was already well under way when Morse was conducting his research and writing his book. Education, Professor Jerrold Zacharias of MIT had suggested in a 1956 memorandum which led to the creation of the Physical Sciences Study Committee, is like high fidelity. To have good hi-fi, you need a good performer on a good day, a good recording, a good pressing of it, and a good pickup and

[9] John I. Goodlad, "Thought, Invention, and Research in the Advancement of Education," in Committee for Economic Development, *The Schools and the Challenge of Innovation.*

amplifier; you need a room with good acoustical qualities and a person with the intent to listen. "But most important of all," Zacharias argued, "is the composition itself; without a great composition, everything else is pointless." It was to the attempt to supply the schools with "great compositions" that the most serious and influential reformers gave their time and energies, and attached their greatest hopes.

One of the myths about American education, so deeply rooted as to be unextinguishable, is the one that explains the curriculum reform movement as a response to Sputnik. To be sure, the launching of Sputnik was a great shock to the American ego, producing much wringing of the hands over the state of American education and lending apparent support to school critics like Admiral Rickover, who had been predicting intellectual and moral decay as a result of the softness of our schools. And so it was, as Lawrence Cremin writes, that "when the Russians beat us into space, the public blamed the schools, not realizing that the only thing that had been proved, as the quip went at the time, was that their German scientists had gotten ahead of our German scientists."[10]

But "it didn't all start with Sputnik," to use Frank Jennings' phrase.[11] The University of Illinois Committee on School Mathematics, for example, began its revisions of the secondary school mathematics curriculum in 1952, and the Physical Sciences Study Committee's development of a new high school physics course began in 1956. Sputnik's effect, in the main, was to accelerate these developments, generating public support, and therefore much larger federal funding, for projects that were already under way or being discussed when the satellite went into orbit. "The Russian satellites, and the furor that followed them," the Physical Sciences Study Committee stated in its first annual report in 1958, "came into being while this process [the Committee's development of the new physics course] was in full course. The principal effect of these events has been to bring the work of the Committee to the attention of the public a good

---

[10] Lawrence A. Cremin, *The Genius of American Education.*
[11] Frank G. Jennings, "It Didn't All Start with Sputnik," *Saturday Review,* September 16, 1967. Cf. also John I. Goodlad, "Curriculum: A Janus Look," *Teachers College Record,* Vol. 70, No. 2, November 1968; John I. Goodlad with Renata von Stoephasius and M. Frances Klein, *The Changing School Curriculum,* New York: Fund for the Advancement of Education, 1966; Robert W. Heath, ed., *New Curricula,* New York: Harper & Row, 1964, especially Chapters 2, 3, 5, and 13.

deal more sharply than the Committee would normally have anticipated, and to make it easier to attract support from bodies responsive to public opinion. *But neither the goals the Committee had established for itself, nor the process by which these goals are being attained, was affected measurably by Sputnik. The Committee's course has been set not by Sputnik but by the realities of today's culture and today's environment, of which Sputnik and Explorer are equally a product."* [Emphasis added]

The curriculum reform movement had its origins outside the schools; indeed, it began as an attack on the intellectual flabbiness of the schools. Progressive education had grown soft, as Dewey had warned against and feared. (See discussions of progressive education in Chapters 6 and 7.) The softness was compounded by the vulgarities of the "life adjustment curriculum," with its distinctly un-Deweyan and anti-democratic assumption that no more than 20 percent of the student population could benefit from an intellectually oriented education. The great majority of students, the U.S. Office of Education declared in 1946, needed "functional experiences in the areas of practical arts, home and family life, health and physical fitness, and civic competence."[12]

From the beginning, moreover, leadership was largely in the hands of university scholars concerned with the schools' failure to reflect and incorporate advances in knowledge. The scholars were concerned, too, with the schools' failure to adjust to the so-called knowledge explosion as well as to the increasingly important role of knowledge in the economy and in society at large. Some of the reformers were eager to end the split between the "two cultures" by giving more students an understanding of the nature of contemporary science. Others had a more parochial interest: to increase the supply of scientists, and to give students entering university courses a more adequate preparation in their high school years.

As with the techniques of classroom management and school administration discussed in Morse's book, the curriculum reform movement has also been blunted on the classroom door. In 1960 Zacharias was confident that with $100 million a year for curriculum development, he could work a revolution in the

---

[12] U.S. Office of Education, *Life Adjustment Education for Every Youth,* quoted in Lawrence A. Cremin, *The Transformation of the School,* p. 335.

quality of United States education. By 1966 he knew better. "It's easier to put man on the moon," he confessed to this writer, "than to reform the public schools."

Certainly the new courses are used far less frequently than the scholars who developed them had hoped. A U.S. Office of Education survey of enrollments in public high school science courses in the 1964–65 school year, for example, revealed that barely 20 percent of the students taking introductory physics were using the PSSC course—99,900 out of 485,000. (The survey also indicated that the proportion of high school seniors taking *any* physics course had dropped from 25.8 percent in 1948–49 to 19.6 percent in 1964–65.)[13] Among the ablest college-bound students, the proportion is higher; some 40 percent of those taking the College Entrance Examination Board achievement test in physics in the 1965–66 school year had followed the PSSC course. But fewer than 25 percent of those taking the College Board achievement test in biology that year had used any of the three courses prepared by the Biological Sciences Curriculum Study, and less than 20 percent of those taking the chemistry test had followed either of the two major chemistry curriculum revisions.[14]

These proportions, it should be noted, are drastically lower than those reported by James B. Conant: "about half of all the schools responding have adopted the new physics, about half the new chemistry, and over a half (64.9 percent) one of the new biology courses. Thus the evidence is conclusive," he continues, "that those in charge of curricula development in at least half the schools in our category [medium-sized comprehensive high schools] are alert to innovations and have adopted them."[15] The discrepancy is almost certainly due to the way in which Dr. Conant formulated his questions, which gave the schools almost unlimited leeway in how they might answer. In the case of physics, for example, his questionnaire read as follows: "Is

[13] Fletcher G. Watson, "Why Do We Need More Physics Courses?", *The Physics Teacher,* Vol. 5, No. 5, May 1967.
[14] Raymond E. Thompson, *A Survey of the Teaching of Physics in Secondary Schools;* William Kastrinos, *A Survey of the Teaching of Biology in Secondary Schools;* Frank J. Fornoff, *A Survey of the Teaching of Chemistry in Secondary Schools*—all Princeton, N.J.: Educational Testing Service, 1969.
[15] James B. Conant, *The Comprehensive High School: A Second Report to Interested Citizens,* New York: McGraw-Hill, 1967.

Physics offered? If so, is any type of 'new or advanced' physics available? (For example, PSSC)."[16] It is hard to know, in any case, how to interpret the numbers themselves, for they refer to the proportion of *schools* answering in the affirmative, not to the proportion of *students*. A school might very well make the PSSC course "available," for example, yet have most of its physics students taking a conventional course. When compared with the precise measurements made by the Educational Testing Service and the U.S. Office of Education, therefore, Dr. Conant's data suggest that "those in charge of curricula development" are more alert to the rhetoric of innovation than to the innovations themselves.

One need only sit in the classrooms, in fact, and examine the texts and reading lists to know that, with the possible exception of mathematics, the curriculum reform movement has made a pitifully small impact on classroom practice. The criteria for deciding what should be in the curriculum, Jerome Bruner of Harvard, one of the chief architects of curriculum reform, has suggested, should be to ask "whether, when fully developed, [the subject or material] is worth an adult's knowing, and whether having known it as a child makes a person a better adult. If the answer to both questions is negative or ambiguous, then the material is cluttering the curriculum."[17]

The answer is negative to both questions for an incredibly high proportion of the elementary and secondary school curriculum. There is a great deal of chatter, to be sure, about teaching students the structure of each discipline, about teaching them how to learn, about teaching basic concepts, about "postholing," i.e., teaching fewer things but in greater depth. But if one looks at what actually goes on in the classroom—the kinds of texts students read and the kind of homework they are assigned, as well as the nature of classroom discussion and the kinds of tests teachers give—he will discover that the great bulk of students' time is still devoted to detail, most of it trivial, much of it factually incorrect, and almost all of it unrelated to any concept, structure, cognitive strategy, or indeed anything other than the lesson plan. It is rare to find anyone—teacher, principal, supervisor,

[16] Quoted in Anthony G. Oettinger with Sema Marks, *Run, Computer, Run*, Cambridge, Mass.: Harvard University Press, 1969.
[17] Jerome S. Bruner, *The Process of Education*, Cambridge: Harvard University Press, 1960. Bruner's book was perhaps the most important and influential to come out of the curriculum reform movement.

or superintendent—who has asked why he is teaching what he is teaching.

ITEM: The students in a sixth-grade English class in a school on a Chippewa Indian reservation are all busily at work, writing a composition for Thanksgiving. The subject of the composition is written on the blackboard for the students (and the visitor) to see. The subject: "Why We Are Happy the Pilgrims Came."

Much of what is taught is not worth knowing as a child, let alone as an adult, and little will be remembered. The banality and triviality of the curriculum in most schools has to be experienced to be believed. The Educational Testing Service's study of secondary school teaching of history and social studies, for example, indicated that the curriculum followed in 1965–66 "does not differ in any striking way from that which has been traditional in the United States for the past twenty-five years." More important, perhaps, the study revealed that even for the students taking college board exams—the top twenty-five percent in terms of academic ability—schools relied heavily on textbooks. Eighty-five percent of the students reported that more than half their reading in a senior American history course came from a single text; some 55 percent did three-quarters or more of their reading in the text. To know what that means, pick up almost any of the texts in widespread use!

The social studies curriculum is even worse at the elementary school level. The obsession with the explorers is one of the mysteries of American schooling; inordinate amounts of time are devoted to their exploits, and the topic may be repeated as many as three times during the elementary years. Disproportionate amounts of time are devoted to the Colonial Period and the American Revolution, too—but with no attempt to relate the ideas and issues of those days to our own time.

ITEM: A fifth-grader, asked if his social studies class had discussed any aspect of the October 15, 1969, Vietnam Moratorium Day, answers in the negative. "We're doing the American Revolution," he explains.

"Doing the American Revolution" means, of course, memorizing names, dates, places, "causes" of the Revolution, and so on—a mass of unrelated data. "Students, perforce, have a limited exposure to the materials they are to learn. How can this exposure be made to count in their thinking for the rest of their lives?" Jerome Bruner asked in *The Process of Education*. "The dominant view among men who have engaged in preparing and teaching new curricula is that the answer to this question lies in giving students an understanding of the fundamental structure of whatever subjects we choose to teach. This is a minimum requirement for using knowledge. . . . If earlier learning is to render later learning easier, it must do so by providing a general picture in terms of which the relations between things encountered earlier and later are made as clear as possible." "What education has to impart," Alfred North Whitehead declared in *The Aims of Education*, "is an intimate sense for the power of ideas, for the beauty of ideas, and for the structure of ideas, together with a particular body of knowledge which has peculiar reference to the life of the being possessing it."

ITEM: A fifth-grade test on the American Revolution given in an elementary school in the Southwest. The questions and the spaces for the answers are all contained on a standard-sized (8½" x 11") sheet of paper:

1. What was the main cause of the Revolutionary War?
2. England punished the state of Massachusetts as a result of the Boston Tea Party. What was the punishment?
3. The Revolutionary War began in _____. The colonists who fought were called _____.
4. What does this mean: "The shot heard round the world"?
5. Who came to assist the colonists? _____
   Who came to assist the British? _____
   What was another name for the British soldiers?_____
6. Name two things the Americans won by winning the Revolutionary War.
7. What did the Acts have to do with the Revolution? Name 2 Acts imposed on the colonists.
8. What was the Declaration of Independence?
9. List some of the problems that faced the Colonial Army.
10. What were the Committees of Correspondence?
11. _____ organized the first Committee of Correspondence in Boston.
12. What was the purpose of the first Continental Congress?
13. In the Revolutionary War, the colonists won their independence from _____.
14. _____ was the Commander-in-Chief of the Continental Army.

15. True _____ False _____ The Boston Tea Party took place in New York.
16. Who were the Patriots? _____
17. Another name for the Tories._____
18. Who were the Tories? _____

Another seven multiple-choice questions were read to the students because the sheet had no room for them.

ITEM: The same class, six weeks later. In a single forty-five minute period, students and teacher have a discussion that "covers" World War I, the urbanization of the United States (especially the Negro migration from South to North) during the 1920s, World War II, and the Space Program. The teacher *has* to hurry; the curriculum allows only one semester for the history of the United States from its "discovery"[18] to the present, the second semester being reserved for a study of the states (memorizing the state capitals, their major cities and products, their nicknames, and their tourist attractions).

The English curriculum is no better, and possibly worse, in most schools. Here again it is difficult for people, even those close to the schools, to appreciate the puerility of so much of the literature assigned students to read, or the banality with which it is usually handled. A friend of the writer, commenting on an earlier draft of this chapter, wrote, "I find it hard to believe that *Silas Marner* still holds sway" in the high school curriculum. "There surely is a lot of movement in the direction of Salinger, etc. Are you sure you aren't distorting?" But the writer was *not* distorting; despite the near-unanimous recommendation of scholars and curriculum specialists that *Silas Marner* be dropped from the curriculum, more than three-quarters of the high schools in the United States still require that novel, which has bored generations of American students.[19]

The point is that in most schools, the English curriculum has not changed for a long, long time. Whether good, bad, or

[18] One of the more common provincialisms of social studies textbooks and teaching is the tradition that Columbus "discovered" America, the word implying that the continent did not exist until it was inhabited by white men.

[19] James R. Squire and Roger K. Applebee, *High School English Instruction Today: The National Study of High School English Programs*, New York: Appleton-Century-Crofts, 1968.

indifferent, the curriculum is simply taken as given, with no questions asked. The Educational Testing Service's study of the teaching of English to the academically ablest college-bound students found, for example, that the traditional pattern in which American literature is studied in the eleventh grade and English literature in the twelfth is still followed by most schools, in large part because that is how the textbook anthologies are arranged. This format, the author dryly observes, is "perpetuating an arrangement that has now endured for two-thirds of a century. One wonders how many teachers and publishers know how it all started. Or why *Silas Marner* and *A Tale of Two Cities* are, shall we say, ubiquitous in today's schools."[20]

The lack of thought extends not only to what is read, but to *how* it is read—how students are taught to read and regard literature. Their view of literature is set by the way novels, plays, stories, and poems are discussed in class and, even more, by the kinds of questions they are asked to answer on tests. As in history (or geography, biology, physics, chemistry, or any other subject), the emphasis usually is on memorizing "facts." Students are expected to be able to summarize the plot, list and describe the major characters and events, and so on. They rarely are asked, or taught, to look for meaning or symbolism or style; they even more rarely are asked to think about, or discuss, the ways in which form affects content or the ways in which literary forms change from one period to the next. As the authors of the National Study of High School English Programs reported, "too many teachers seem to think that the ultimate end of instruction in literature is knowledge of and about *Macbeth* or *Silas Marner*, rather than refinement of the processes of learning to read *Macbeth* or *Silas Marner* with insight and discrimination."

The teaching of writing and composition is even worse. For one thing, their teaching loads make it impossible for most high school teachers to devote much time to instruction in writing. The average high school English teacher meets with 150 students a week; to spend just ten minutes a week reading and correcting each student's papers would consume twenty-five hours. Not surprisingly, therefore, composition and writing receive relatively little attention, accounting for about 15 percent of classroom time.

The problem runs deeper, however, for when writing *is* taught,

[20] Fred I. Godshalk, *A Survey of the Teaching of English in Secondary Schools,* Princeton, N.J.: Educational Testing Service, 1969.

the emphasis is almost wholly on mechanics—spelling, punctuation, grammar, sentence structure, width of the margins, and so on—with little attention to development, organization, or style, i.e., to anything larger than a sentence.

ITEM: Excerpts from the *Program of Studies* of a prestigious suburban New York school district—a district whose students have a median IQ of 121, with 90 percent of them going on to four-year colleges:

> English I: The ninth-grade English course, as do all the English courses, reviews and extends, emphasizing the sentence pattern with its basic varieties. Grammar and punctuation are taught as inseparable parts of sentence meaning. During the year the student is expected to master the simple paragraph form . . .
> English II: Tenth-grade English continues the study of fundamentals, strongly emphasizing usage, clarity, and variety in sentence structure, and the accurate use of words, as well as coherence in paragraph writing. Students learn to write themes several paragraphs long and simple friendly and business letters . . .
> English III: Eleventh-grade English thoroughly reviews the fundamentals after which the student is expected to concentrate on the correction of his individual errors. . . . There is practice in letter writing and an occasional personal essay . . .

ITEM: A twenty-three page guide to seventh-grade English teachers in that same system states as its goal: "Any seventh-grade English teacher can consider himself successful if most—nay, some—of his students can, by the end of the school year, write clear narrative and descriptive paragraphs."

The modesty of the goal, and the emphasis on grammar and sentence structure in the upper grades, is understandable when measured against the standard of writing the administrators themselves provide.

ITEM: A guide to the teaching of sixth-, seventh-, and eighth-grade composition contains errors in syntax and punctuation and awkward sentence structure in its first few paragraphs.

> Some axioms about the teaching of English which few teachers would challenge are [NB: no colon]
> 1. if students are to learn to write well, they must not only

write often but must be taught to write, or, in other words, though it is important that students be assigned compositions to write, assigning compositions is not the same thing as teaching writing;

2. compositions taught through a carefully planned sequence of assignments is [*sic*] likely to be more effective than a hit-or-miss approach . . .

In any case, students learn what teachers are looking for as soon as they enter the junior high.

ITEM: From a student manual in the same school system:

THE FORM OF WRITTEN WORK

Whenever you write anything that is to be read by someone else, it should be in such a form that it can easily be read. It should be *legible*. Poor handwriting and general untidiness of the manuscript take the attention of the reader away from the idea, from what you are trying to say; and, as a consequence, your writing is much less effective and will not be rated very high. This is true not only in English classes but also in mathematics, in science, in social studies, and, in fact, whenever and wherever you write.

So that your written work in the Junior High School will present a uniformly good appearance, you are asked to follow certain suggestions and forms whenever you hand a paper to any teacher for checking or for suggestions.

1. Using the first line, head your paper in the following way:

Specific Title of Paper   Your Name
English 7–3   Date

2. Capitalize the first word of the title and every other word except prepositions, conjunctions and articles. No punctuation should be used unless the title is a question or an exclamation. Use a title that suggests the specific nature of the contents of the paper; not just *English,* but rather, *Correct Use of Verbs;* not *Math,* but *Division of Fractions;* not *Social Studies,* but *The Westward Movement;* not *Science,* but *The Solar System.*

3. Use standard size paper—8½ x 11. Two-ring or three-ring notebook paper is correct. Use ruled paper for pencil and pen; unruled for typing. Double space if you type. Type only if you can type your own papers; do *not* have someone else do this for you. Do *not* tear sheets of paper from notebook.

4. Skip a line between the heading and the body of the paper. Leave proper margins on each page—left, right, and bottom. Leave an irregular margin at the right of at least one-half inch. Write against the red margin line at the left—except to indent. Do *not* write on the bottom line of any page. When you complete your paper, do not write "The End."

5. Indent the first and each succeeding paragraph.

6. On the second page or back of a page begin on top of the first ruled line, not between the first two. Don't repeat the title. Don't write "Continued" at the bottom or top of a page.
   Write your name in the upper right hand corner of the second and each succeeding sheet. Do not repeat grade and date. To the left of the name, in the top center, put an Arabic (1-2-3 etc.) page number.

7. Use a sensible ink—black, blue, blue-black. Use both sides of the paper unless your teacher directs you otherwise. Always use one side only when you type.

III

What happened? Why did a movement that aroused such great hopes, and that enlisted so many distinguished educators, exert so little impact on the schools?

A large part of the answer is that what was initially regarded as the curriculum reform movement's greatest strength—the fact that its prime movers were distinguished university scholars and teachers—has proven to be its greatest weakness. In part because the movement was based in the scholarly disciplines, in part because it grew out of the scholars' revulsion against the vulgarization of progressive education and against the anti-intellectualism that that vulgarization in turn had spawned, the reformers by and large ignored the experiences of the past, and particularly of the reform movement of the 1920s and '30s. They were, therefore, unaware of the fact that almost everything they said had been said before, by Dewey, Whitehead, Bode, Rugg, etc.; and they were unaware that almost everything they tried to do had been tried before, by educators like Frederick Burk, Carleton Washburne, and Helen Parkhurst, not to mention Abraham Flexner and Dewey himself.[21]

[21] Cf. Lawrence A. Cremin, *The Transformation of the School* and *The Genius of American Education;* John I. Goodlad, "Curriculum: A Janus Look," *Teachers College Record*, November 1968; J. Stuart Maclure,

One result of this failure to study educational history, particularly the history of progressivism's successes and failures, was that the contemporary reformers repeated one of the fundamental errors of the progressive movement: they perpetuated the false dichotomy that the schools must be *either* child-centered *or* subject-centered. Ignoring the warnings of men like Dewey, Boyd Bode, Harold Rugg, and Carleton Washburne, the progressive reformers had opted for the former; their preoccupation with child-centeredness made them content, in Dewey's phrase, "with casual improvisation and living intellectually hand to mouth." It was this "absence of intellectual control through significant subject-matter," Dewey wrote, "which stimulates the deplorable egotism, cockiness, impertinence and disregard for the rights of others apparently considered by some persons to be the inevitable accompaniment, if not the essence, of freedom."[22]

The reformers of the 1950s and '60s made the same mistake, except that they opted for the other side of the dichotomy. They placed almost all their emphasis on subject matter, i.e., on creating "great compositions," and for the most part ignored the needs of individual children. As Dewey wrote of the progressive educators whose one-sidedness he deplored, the new reformers "conceive of no alternative to adult dictation save child dictation." Reacting against the banality that child-dictated education had become, they opted for adult dictation. They knew what they wanted children to learn; they did not think to ask what children wanted to learn. Some of the reformers, however, now realize their error. Thus it was Zacharias, at the 1965 White House Conference on Education, who made a passionate plea that educators think about children and their needs.

Because the reformers were university scholars with little contact with public schools or schools of education, moreover, and because they also neglected to study the earlier attempts at curriculum reform, they also tended to ignore the harsh realities of classroom and school organization. The courses they created were, and are, vastly superior to the tepid and banal fare most

---

Curriculum Innovation in Practice, Third International Curriculum Conference, Oxford (Her Majesty's Stationery Office, 1968); Patricia A. Graham, *Progressive Education: From Arcady to Academe,* New York: Teachers College Press, 1967; Harold Rugg and Ann Shumaker, *The Child-Centered School: An Appraisal of the New Education,* New York: World Book Co., 1928.
22 John Dewey, "How Much Freedom in New Schools?", *The New Republic,* July 9, 1930.

students now receive. But without changing the ways in which schools operate and teachers teach, changing the curriculum alone does not have much effect.[23]

To some degree, this error reflected the reformers' innocence and naïveté. Because they had so little firsthand experience with the elementary or secondary school classroom (in contrast to most of the great figures of the progressive movement), they somehow assumed that students would learn what the teachers taught; that is, if teachers presented the material in the proper structure, students would learn it that way. Thus, they assumed implicitly that teaching and learning are merely opposite sides of the same coin. But they are not, as we have seen in Chapter 4.

The error reflected academic hubris as well: not content with ignoring the classroom teacher, the reformers, in effect, tried to bypass the teacher altogether. Their goal, sometimes stated, sometimes implicit, was to construct "teacher-proof" materials that would "work" whether teachers liked the materials or not or taught them well or badly. "With the kind of casual arrogance only professors can manage, when they conceived of lower schools," Dean Robert J. Schaefer writes, the curriculum reformers' goal was "to produce materials which permit scholars to speak directly to the child." They viewed teachers, if they thought of them at all, as technicians, and they conceived of the schools, Schaefer suggests, as "educational dispensaries— apothecary shops charged with the distribution of information and skills deemed beneficial to the social, vocational, and intellectual health of the immature. The primary business of a dispensary," Schaefer continues, "is to dispense not to raise questions or to inquire into issues as to how drugs might be more efficiently administered, and certainly not to assume any authority over what ingredients should be mixed."[24]

The effort was doomed to failure. For one thing, the classroom teacher usually is in an almost perfect position to sabotage a curriculum he finds offensive—and teachers are not likely to have a high regard for courses designed to bypass them. For another, many of the "teacher-proof" curricula have turned out

[23] Cf., for example, Blythe Clinchy, "School Arrangements," in Jerome Bruner, ed., *Learning About Learning: A Conference Report,* U.S. Office of Education, Cooperative Research Monograph No. 15. The Clinchy essay is one of thirty in this volume; it is the only one directly concerned with the ways in which schools and classrooms operate.

[24] Robert J. Schaefer, *The School as a Center of Inquiry,* New York: Harper & Row, 1967.

to be more difficult to teach than the courses they replaced; certainly the "discovery method" makes far more demands on the teacher than does rote drill or lecturing. But insofar as they thought about in-service education of teachers, the reformers tended to assume that the problem was to get teachers to know— to really know—the subject they were teaching. This was crucial, of course, but experience with National Defense Education Act Institutes and the like have made it painfully clear that mastering the subject matter does not begin to solve the problem of how to teach it.

The failure to involve ordinary classroom teachers in the creation and modification of the new curricula, moreover, tended to destroy, or at least inhibit, the very spirit of inquiry the new courses were designed to create. Curriculum designers are not likely to attract students to the life of the mind if they fail to entice the students' teachers as well. "How can youngsters be convinced of the vitality of inquiry and discovery," Dean Schaefer asks, "if the adults with whom they directly work are mere automatons who shuffle papers, workbooks, and filmstrips according to externally arranged schedules?" Since the spirit of inquiry "necessitates a live sense of shared purpose and commitment," the teachers *must* participate in the scholar's search if the effort is to succeed.

The most fatal error of all, however, was the failure to ask the questions that the giants of the progressive movement always kept at the center of their concern, however inadequate some of their answers may have been: What is education for? What kind of human beings and what kind of society do we want to produce? What methods of instruction and classroom organization, as well as what subject matter, do we need to produce these results? What knowledge is of most worth?[25]

There is considerable irony in the fact that the contemporary reformers did not put these questions in the foreground, for certainly they did think about them. Bruner's *The Process of Education* is full of reflections on these questions; so is his essay "Character Education and Curriculum" in *Learning About Learning,* and several of the essays in *On Learning.* Other reformers, such as Jerrold Zacharias and David Hawkins, have also thought seriously and hard about these fundamental questions. But because the reform movement was university-based

[25] Cf. especially Lawrence A. Cremin, *The Genius of American Education,* and John I. Goodlad, "Curriculum: A Janus Look."

and grew out of dissatisfaction with the teaching of specific subjects, e.g., physics, chemistry, biology, math, social studies, the reformers never really attacked the curriculum as a whole. Indeed, academic provincialism made the reform movement a good deal narrower than some of the reformers had wanted. For example, Jerrold Zacharias and Francis Friedman originally intended to create a course in the physical sciences, hence their organization was named the Physical Sciences Study Committee. But the university chemists refused to go along; they were only interested in reforming the teaching of chemistry. And so it went; as a result, the reformers never worked on more than a course at a time. But a curriculum, as Lawrence Cremin writes, "is more than a succession of units, courses and programs, however excellent; and to refuse to look at curricula in their entirety is to relegate to intraschool politics a series of decisions that ought to call into play the most fundamental philosophical principles."

IV

An important result of the reformers' failure to consider the curriculum as a whole is the fact that they left one of the most critical areas of the curriculum almost completely untouched: namely, the arts. The reformers did make some tentative moves in that direction. For example, The Panel on Educational Research and Development met with a group of musicians in late 1962 to discuss the creation of a new music curriculum for the schools, and this in turn led to a two-week seminar of musicians and teachers in June 1963 to plan the development of curricular materials. The Office of Education's Arts and Humanities Program, established in 1964, has financed a number of curriculum projects and experiments. But the effort has been small and sporadic and, with one or two exceptions, those concerned have made the mistake of the rest of the curriculum reform movement in attacking the problem piecemeal, as if what were needed were simply new courses and course materials.[26]

The need is for more than that. No course, however good, is likely to compensate for the current weakness in the arts. Most schools give their students a powerful and effective esthetic education: they teach them that interest in the arts is effeminate

---

[26] John I. Goodlad with Renata von Stoephasius and M. Frances Klein, *The Changing School Curriculum,* New York: Fund for the Advancement of Education, 1966.

or effete, that study of the arts is a frill, and that music, art, beauty, and sensitivity are specialized phenomena that bear no relation to any other aspect of the curricula or of life.

The schools teach these lessons in a variety of ways. The most important, perhaps, is the lesson that is taught by the ugliness of the buildings themselves: the barrenness of the walls, the absence of flowers, paintings, sculpture, and music; in short, the esthetic sterility of the entire environment. "The school environment sends messages to all children," as the Ontario, Canada, Provincial Committee on Aims and Objectives of Education insists in its beautifully sensitive report, *Living and Learning*. "The space that invites, the color that warms, the parkland that lures, the human accents of the planning of the school and its surroundings are intuitively grasped by every child," the Committee continues. "Children thrive when they can touch, breathe, see, hear and feel beauty. Early sensory awareness can mark significant first steps in the never-ending joy of discovery and appreciation of the esthetic. Works of visual art, sculpture gardens, fountains and trees should be an integral part of the planning of every school, for the bricks and mortar of the schools are themselves the 'silent teachers.' Through the personal experience of beauty one of the most significant dimensions of humanity is added to a child." Hence "schools should not be created as appendages to be attached to efficient administrative facilities."[27]

Children also learn to disparage the arts and to relegate them to a highly specialized and trivial segment of life by the way in which schools deal with the esthetic. If taught at all, art and music generally are taught as separate subjects, offered once or at most twice a week by specialist teachers. Beauty thus is defined as something to be concerned with for an hour or so a week, not as an intrinsic part of everything people do.

ITEM: A prestigious private elementary school boasts of its heavy emphasis on arts and crafts. Students take art or shop for at least one period a day, and both subjects are geared to the social studies curriculum, each year of which is built around a country or a period of history. Thus, during the year in which students study the Vikings, they make helmets, armor, spears,

[27] *Living and Learning,* Report of the Provincial Committee on Aims and Objectives of Education in the Schools of Ontario, Canada: Ontario Department of Education, 1968.

boats, and paint Viking pictures; in the year on the Middle Ages, they make moats and castles, armor, etc. But the regular class-room walls are absolutely bare: no pictures, no sculpture, no flowers. Art, the children quickly learn, is something you go to another room to study or do; beauty is something separate and apart from the ordinary life of the classroom.

More often than not, it might be better if art were left out of the curriculum altogether, for at least children's spontaneity and native love of beauty would not be destroyed.

ITEM: The "Center for Creative Expression" in a wealthy suburban elementary school. Each of the ten children is covering a box with a sheet of colored construction paper, and then at-taching a face, made of pipe cleaners and scraps of paper, to the box. Searching for some evidence of individual or creative ex-pression, the visitor asks a child if she had a special reason for covering her box with purple paper. The answer is simple and direct: "The teacher gave each of us one sheet of paper, and I got purple."

ITEM: A first-grade classroom in an urban school is well sup-plied with easels, paints, brushes, and paper, which go unused almost all the time. Seeing the sign hanging above the easels, the visitor understands why the children seem uninterested in painting.

BEFORE PAINTING	WHILE PAINTING	AFTER PAINTING
apron	take one color at a time	dry picture
newspaper	wash your brush between	cover paint
paper	colors	wash brushes
paints	paint a colorful picture	clean easel
brushes		wash hands
name		hang apron

The situation becomes even worse in high school, where the arts are even more specialized, i.e., they are only for people with talent, or in some schools, for students who have difficulty with the regular academic program. The schools desperately need an infusion of amateurism; in David Riesman's marvelous epigram, "Anything worth doing is worth doing badly." The problem is compounded by the schools' tendency to ignore or to derogate the popular arts, which do reach the students and which could be used to lead them to the other arts. Certainly, film is an art form—one to which the current generation responds most directly. It could be used to study the nature of literary and artistic forms, the relation of form to content, the nature of esthetic and critical criteria, and so on. Yet only a handful of schools are using films in this way.[28]

Neither the schools nor their reformers, moreover, have given much thought to how the schools might relate to, or counteract, the mass media. There is enormous grumbling, to be sure, about the corrupting effects of television, advertising, and the mass media in general, but painfully little thought about how these media affect youngsters, let alone how the schools might take account of them. This failure is bound up with teachers' and administrators' inability or reluctance to recognize that we are no longer living in a purely literary culture, that the current generation will get a large proportion of its information and values from films, television, and radio, and that they therefore need to be taught to deal critically with nonliterary as well as literary forms.

V

If the decade beginning in 1955 was "the Education Decade," the middle sixties marked the beginning of what might be called "the Educational Technology Decade." Since the middle sixties, certainly, the best-financed efforts at school reform have involved the development of one or another new instructional technology.

A great deal of money and effort, for example, have gone into experiments with computer-assisted instruction, whose advocates and prophets have made extravagant predictions of wonders to come. Lawrence M. Stolurow, director of the Computer-Aided Instruction Laboratory at Harvard, is one of the more under-

[28] Cf. Sister Bede Sullivan, *Movies: Universal Language,* Notre Dame, Indiana: Fides Publishers, 1967; A. W. Hodgkinson, *Screen Education,* UNESCO Reports and Papers on Mass Communication No. 42; John M. Culkin, S.J., *Film Study in the High School,* New York: Fordham University Film Study Center; Rodger Larson, Jr., *A Guide for Film Teachers to Filmmaking by Teenagers,* New York City Administration of Parks, Recreation and Cultural Affairs.

stated of this new breed of scholar. "Computer-assisted instruction (CAI) is not the panacea for today's educational problems," he writes. "There is no single solution to problems as complex as these." Panacea or not, Stolurow goes on to say, computer-aided instruction is "comparable to Gutenberg's invention of the printing press in terms of the potential effect it will have upon education."[29]

Professor Patrick Suppes of Stanford, who directs perhaps the most extensive experimentation with computer-assisted instruction, is less restrained. "One can predict that in a few more years millions of school children will have access to what Philip of Macedon's son Alexander enjoyed as a royal prerogative: the personal services of a tutor as well-informed and responsive as Aristotle," he told the readers of *Scientific American* in 1966.[30] A few months earlier, R. Louis Bright, then Associate Commissioner of Education in charge of the Bureau of Research, assured a Congressional Committee studying educational technology that while existing equipment could not satisfy the necessary criteria of simplicity, reliability, and economy—to be competitive, he indicated, costs would have to come down to about 25 cents per student hour—"in about three years this price objective will indeed be reached with equipment that is simple and reliable." Pointing to one of Suppes's experiments, a computerized classroom teaching first-, second-, and third-grade arithmetic and reading in the Brentwood school district, near Stanford, Bright went on to tell the Committee that "regular operational use of such a system . . . would be competitive with traditional techniques, perhaps in the fall of 1969 and most certainly in the fall of 1970."[31]

Most certainly *not* in the fall of 1970, and most probably not for a good many years to come; the fall of 1980, or perhaps 1985, might be a better bet. Indeed, the same Suppes who in 1966 predicted "that in a few more years millions of school-children" would, through the computer, have a tutor like Aristotle, three and a half years later dismissed the notion as hope-

[29] Lawrence M. Stolurow, "Computer-Assisted Instruction," in Committee for Economic Development, *The Schools and the Challenge of Innovation*.

[30] Patrick Suppes, "The Uses of Computers in Education," *Scientific American*, September 1966.

[31] R. Louis Bright, Statement in Hearings Before the Subcommittee on Economic Progress, Joint Economic Committee, Congress of the United States, Washington, D.C.: U.S. Government Printing Office, 1966.

lessly utopian. "If we could create the best of all possible worlds for the children in our society," he wrote in the *New York Times Annual Education Review* (January 12, 1970), "we might wish that each of them would have a tutor of the quality of Socrates or Aristotle. *As a general approach to mass education, however, this is clearly prohibitive economically.*" [Emphasis added]

This is in no way to suggest that the computer is unimportant. Lawrence Stolurow may well be right in suggesting that eventually it will affect education as profoundly as did the printing press. Certainly there are close analogies between the computer and the book. By making it possible for knowledge to be stored in a readily accessible form, the "invention" of the book vastly reduced the amount of information that had to be stored in the human brain, which is to say, committed to memory. The "anti-technologists" of antiquity were as fearful of this innovation as their successors today are of the computer. The ancients, for example, were convinced that the book, by downgrading memory, would produce a race of imbeciles. "This discovery of yours," Socrates told the inventor of the alphabet in Plato's *Phaedrus,* "will create forgetfulness in the learners' souls, because they will not use their memories; they will trust to the external written characters and not remember of themselves. . . . They will appear to be omniscient and will generally know nothing."

The computer is likely to reduce once again the amount of information that has to be committed to memory, by again increasing the amount of information that can be stored in readily accessible form.[32] It will thereby alter the role of the teacher, accentuating the tendency to see education less as the amassing of a body of information and knowledge and more, in Whitehead's phrase, as "the acquisition of the art of the utilisation of knowledge." But the computer is likely to have less effect on teachers than did the book, which destroyed the teacher's monopoly of knowledge by giving students the power, for the first time, to learn in private—and to learn as much as, or more than, their masters. There is reason to believe that the computer will change the teacher's role and function rather than diminish his importance.

[32] How to get such access is as yet an unsolved problem, however. Designing "information retrieval systems" has proved more difficult than expected.

But "eventually" is a long way off. In part because of its power, we are only barely beginning to know how to use the computer, and disillusionment with it is becoming almost as widespread as enchantment was a few years ago. For example, a great many corporate executives who five years ago were talking boldly and confidently about using computers to make all sorts of managerial decisions (and to replace whole echelons of middle-level executives) are now reasserting their faith in management by hunch and rule of thumb; corporations like Westinghouse Electric that were planning to centralize top management via the computer are now decentralizing. What has happened is that the "third-generation" computers that were supposed to make all this possible have proved to be vastly more difficult, and more expensive, to operate than either the sellers or the customers had anticipated. The experience has been much the same in the attempts to use computers to control production processes. No corporation understands its production processes, or its managerial processes, well enough to turn them over to the computer, which requires a precision and specificity that human beings can manage without. In Peter Drucker's phrase, "there is no substitute for the brewmaster's nose."[33]

The problems of using computers in business are as nothing compared with those of using them in education, for even less is known about the processes of learning and instruction than about the processes of production and business management, and the variables are harder to control. As with attempts to use the computer in business, the main result of experiments in computer-assisted instruction has been to dramatize the degree of our ignorance. Suppes's main interest, for example, is in learning how to use the computer to individualize instruction. "We're increasingly aware that if we are to develop a capacity for real individualization," he told this writer, "we have to face the tough question: What do we know about individualizing?" At the present moment, he concedes, the answer is "damned little. Our technological capacity is far ahead of our knowledge." Suppes is not attempting to construct an individualized curriculum, therefore; that is well into the future. Rather, he is conducting basic research whose object is less to find the answers than to

---

[33] Charles E. Silberman, *The Myths of Automation*, Chapter 1. Cf. also Tom Alexander, "Computers Can't Solve Everything," *Fortune*, October 1969.

discover the questions, to find out "what variables will make individualization pay off." His principal finding so far: it is "hell on wheels to intervene so as to make a difference."

Most of Suppes's research involves a tiny chunk of the curriculum: drill and practice in arithmetic, in which students use computer terminals instead of the usual arithmetic workbook to practice and master skills of addition, subtraction, multiplication, and division. This kind of mechanical drill is essential to mastery of computational skills, and there is reason to assume that a computer can handle it more effectively than a teacher. The computer tells the student immediately if he is right or wrong, and it can be programmed to give some students more practice in whatever skill they are weak in, while permitting others to avoid the boredom of drill in skills they already have mastered. Using a computer in this way enables the teacher to avoid the monotony of endless supervision and correction of workbooks, allowing her to concentrate on the things a human teacher can do best. Experiments in three cities suggest that ten or fifteen minutes a day of computer-assisted drill and practice can yield significant gains in learning.[34]

Computers can be, and are, used in other ways. The exercise of simulating theoretical or real-life situations on a computer can help a student gain insight into a problem by making it possible for him to experiment, thus enabling him to see the consequences of his, or other people's, action in a much shorter time than is possible in real life. The computer also imposes a strong discipline on a student, forcing him to analyze a problem in a logically consistent manner, while freeing him from a good deal of time-consuming computation. Thus, the armed forces have been using computer simulation and computer games to teach military strategy; and the American Management Association, to teach business strategy.

Perhaps the greatest potential application of this approach is in the teaching of science at the college or university level. "A physical theory expressed in the static language of mathematics," Anthony Oettinger of Harvard writes, "often becomes dynamic when it is rewritten as a computer program; one can explore its inner structure, confront it with experimental data and interpret its implications much more easily than when it is in static

[34] Patrick Suppes, "Computerized Instruction Shows Promise in 3 Cities," *New York Times Annual Education Review*, January 12, 1970.

form."[35] But this kind of application, again, supplements and expands conventional teaching; it does not replace it. In part because of the costs involved, in part because of the kinds of skills required, e.g., a knowledge of computer language, applications of this sort are likely to be restricted to advanced undergraduate or graduate students in subjects like economics and the physical and biological sciences, which are susceptible to this kind of approach. (Research applications are more extensive, of course.)

What has created the greatest excitement, however, and the most extravagant claims, is what computer men call "the tutorial mode"—the use of the computer to handle direct instruction. Suppes's arithmetic and reading program at the Brentwood School is one of a number of experiments of this sort. The vision is exciting and seductive. "Central to the realization of quality education on a universal basis," Dr. Wayne H. Holtzman, dean of the College of Education at the University of Texas in Austin, writes, "is the development of individualized instruction which takes into account the great human diversity in cultural background, styles of life, values, goals, motivation, mental abilities, and personality of students. To keep track of a person moving at his own pace in a continuous progress environment where the particular branching of the curriculum is tailor-made for his own learning aptitudes and level, requires a computer to manage the curriculum and assist with the instruction." Under such a computer-managed education, Dr. Holtzman continues, "the student begins at that point in the curriculum where he is best capable of learning and moves at his own rate with his behavior being reinforced—rewarded or disapproved—immediately following his answer. The particular sequence of the curriculum may be controlled almost entirely by a computer or it may be completely under the control of the student, depending on the type of material to be learned, the kind of student, and the purposes of the instruction."[36]

[35] Anthony G. Oettinger with Sema Marks, *Run, Computer, Run,* Cambridge, Mass.: Harvard University Press, 1969. For a systematic analysis of the various approaches, cf. L. M. Stolurow, "Computer-Assisted Instruction," in *The Schools and the Challenge of Innovation;* and Wayne H. Holtzman, ed., *Computer-Assisted Instruction, Testing, and Guidance,* New York: Harper & Row, 1970.

[36] Wayne H. Holtzman, "Computers in Education," in Holtzman, ed., *Computer-Assisted Instruction, Testing, and Guidance.*

As Holtzman indicates, however, this kind of use of the computer is in the future. "A number of problems must be solved before computer-assisted instruction, testing, and guidance can be properly implemented as an integrated system." The problems are massive and not susceptible to easy solution. They fall into two broad categories, to use computer terminology: "hardware," referring to the equipment itself; and "software," referring to the design and programming of the curriculum itself. At the height of the great merger movement of the 1960s, when electronics manufacturers and publishing companies were forming marriages of convenience, RCA's then chairman David Sarnoff explained the trend by saying, "They have the software and we have the hardware."[37]

In fact, neither had either—nor are they likely to for some time to come. No computer manufacturer, for example, has begun to solve the problems inherent in building a computer that can respond to spoken orders; students must communicate with the computer via a typewriter or teletype keyboard, or by "writing" on a screen with a cathode-ray "light pen." More important, computers cannot respond to or correct an essay, or even a brief statement, written in natural language or containing a normal quota of misspellings and grammatical errors. Computer-assisted instruction must restrict itself, therefore, to giving students a choice of a number of preordained answers. As Oettinger writes, "Responses to requests like 'describe a relationship,' 'define a concept,' or 'explain how something works' are well beyond the realm of current computer capability. Recognizing arbitrary English sentences by computer is still beyond the frontier of either linguistic or computer science." There are grave problems of reliability as well; a wad of chewing gum can throw almost any part of the terminal out of whack.

Even with these constraints and limitations, moreover, no computer manufacturer is even close to being able to produce equipment at a cost competitive with conventional instruction. In the 1969–70 school year, for example, the public schools spent a total of $38.5 billion on the education of some 45,600,-000 students. With students attending six hours a day for an average of 180 days a year, that works out to total costs (including capital costs and interest on bonded indebtedness) of seventy-eight cents per instructional hour. Only 55 percent of

[37] C. E. Silberman, "Technology Is Knocking at the Schoolhouse Door," *Fortune,* August 1966.

that, however, goes for instruction; the remainder goes for operation and maintenance of the plant, the costs of pupil transportation, lunches, health services, and the like, as well as capital outlays and interest on indebtedness,[38] all of which would be essentially unchanged (and certainly not reduced) if teachers were replaced by computers. To gauge the competitiveness of computer-assisted instructional systems, therefore, their costs should be compared not with total costs per student hour, but with the hourly cost of instruction per se, which comes to forty-three cents. Of that total, roughly forty-one cents represents teachers' salaries; only two cents an hour goes for all instructional materials—texts, laboratory equipment, and so on.

The computers have a long way to go. Lawrence Stolurow, for example, estimates the cost of the IBM 1500, its newest CAI system, at $1.95 per hour, a sharp reduction from the $7.50 hourly cost of IBM's earlier 1401 system.[39] The trend looks promising, as Stolurow points out, even though the figure is nearly five times the current cost of an hour of conventional instruction. The trend is less promising, however, when one realizes that the $1.95-an-hour figure does not include the costs of programming the computer, nor any operating costs the school might incur, e.g., for specially trained personnel. More important, Stolurow arrived at the $1.95-an-hour figure by assuming that the computer would be operating on something close to two shifts a day. If the computer were used only during normal school hours, the cost would run to $3.80 an hour or thereabouts, rather than $1.95—nearly *ten* times present hourly instructional costs!

To be sure, widespread use of computer-assisted instruction would produce significant economies of scale in manufacturing that would bring costs down. (But not at every stage; some costs are relatively inflexible.) To determine just how such widespread use might affect costs, the Committee for Economic Development's Subcommittee on Efficiency and Innovation in Education engaged the management consulting firm of Booz, Allen & Hamilton to make a study. The results staggered the Subcommittee members, who were prepared to recommend widespread adoption of CAI. The Booz, Allen & Hamilton team calculated the cost of providing an hour a day of computer-assisted instruction (as much as any CAI advocate anticipates

[38] U.S. Office of Education, *Digest of Educational Statistics,* 1969.
[39] "Computer-Assisted Instruction," in *The Schools and the Challenge of Innovation.*

in the foreseeable future) to the 75 percent of public school students who live in metropolitan areas. The cost would range from $9 billion a year for the simplest sort of drill and practice mode to $24 billion a year for a more complex tutorial mode— several billion dollars more than the schools spent for *all* instruction in 1968–69. These costs take into account all the economies that might be achieved through mass production; they do not reflect any reductions that might come through major technological breakthroughs. For a hypothetical district of 100,000 students, hourly cost per student would run to $1.81 for the drill and practice mode and $4.79 for the more complex tutorial mode.[40]

It is quite possible, of course, that technological breakthroughs will permit drastic reductions in the cost of computer-assisted instruction. Two University of Illinois professors, for example, Donald Blitzer and D. Skaperdas, argue that it is possible to produce a computer-assisted instruction system at a cost, for central equipment and terminal devices only, of 25 cents an hour.[41] Their estimate, however, is for a system, called Plato IV, that is yet to be designed—one that would serve 4,000 student terminals, compared with only twenty in their Plato III system. The estimate assumes the economic and technical feasibility of several as yet untested technological breakthroughs, the most important being a plasma display panel "now under development," which would take the place of the cathode-ray tube display now in use, which accounts for a large part of current costs. Moreover, the twenty-five-cent-an-hour figure does not include the costs of maintaining the system, which would add 10 to 20 percent, nor does it include costs of preparing course materials or costs of administering the system.[42] In any case,

---

[40] The costs would vary somewhat according to the size of the school district. For the drill and practice mode, the hourly cost would be $2.27 for a district of 10,000 students and $1.77 for a district of 500,000. The range is greater for the tutorial mode: $7.53 an hour for a district of 10,000; $4.27 for a district of 500,000. Clyde N. Carter and Maurice J. Walker, "Costs of Instructional TV and Computer-Assisted Instruction in Public Schools," in Committee for Economic Development, *The Schools and the Challenge of Innovation.*

[41] D. Blitzer and D. Skaperdas, "The Economics of a Large-Scale Computer-Based Education System," in W. H. Holtzman, *Computer-Assisted Instruction, Testing, and Guidance.*

[42] J. G. Castle, Jr., "Design of Interactive Computer Systems for Educational Purposes: One View of the Proposal for the University of Illinois," in Holtzman, *op. cit.* Cf. also Oettinger, *Run, Computer, Run,* pp. 191–2.

the twenty-five-cent figure applies not to the first-generation system, but to Blitzer's and Skaperdas' estimate of what the cost would come down to if the system went into mass production. There are enough "ifs," in short, to suggest the low cost figure is more an expression of hope than a statement of reality.

There is no evidence, in any case, that introducing computer-assisted instruction into the schools would permit any reduction at all in the number of teachers required. Such displacement is theoretically possible, of course. But all the current CAI experiments—in part, to be sure, because they are well-financed experiments—involve substantial *increases* in the number of people. Although the Brentwood installation is described in promotional literature as "the first to be an integral part of a public school," the fact is that it is housed in a completely separate building erected for the purpose of the experiment, and it is staffed by a separate team of teachers and computer specialists from Suppes's Institute for Mathematical Studies in the Social Sciences. While displacement of teachers is theoretically possible, the current experience provides no basis for such an expectation.[43] Nor does business' experience provide much basis for anticipating a reduction in the number of teachers required. Where corporate computer installations have paid off, the pay-off usually has come not from reductions in personnel but from providing kinds of services or information that had not been possible before.

In any case, the biggest obstacle to computer-assisted instruction is not cost—not the "hardware" problem—but rather the "software" problem. "Our present and most pressing problem is the lack of an empirically validated theory of teaching," Stolurow writes, reflecting the view of every responsible CAI advocate. "In fact, we even lack a useful set of empirically validated principles of instruction that could form the basis for a theory of teaching. In effect," he adds, "CAI makes our meager knowledge of teaching patently obvious. Our ignorance cannot go unnoticed as with some other forms of instruction." As a result, research with computer-assisted instruction has greatly accelerated the search for the principles that could form the basis of a theory of instruction. Because of the mass of data computers can accumulate as a by-product of their use in instruc-

[43] As Oettinger points out, moreover, such personnel "tradeoffs" as might occur could well increase rather than reduce costs, since computer personnel are generally paid at a much higher rate than teachers.

tion, CAI researchers can analyze, in a matter of years, an amount of data that previous generations of scholars needed a lifetime to accumulate.

This has generally been regarded as a great plus for education. But is it? "What's good for educational technologists," Emmanuel Mesthene, director of the Harvard Program on Technology and Society, dryly warns, "is not necessarily good for education." The problem is part of a more general one. "Our technologies today are so powerful, so prevalent, so deliberately fostered, and so prominent in the awareness of people," Mesthene argues, "that they not only bring about changes in the physical world—which technologies have always done—but also in our institutions, attitudes and expectations, values, goals, and in our very conceptions of the meaning of existence. This means that decision-making relating to technology can not any longer—as it once could—take place without deliberate consideration of those wider ramifications of technology."[44]

To consider the ramifications of educational technology is to discover cause for concern, for they pose a number of real, and potentially serious, dangers to American education. One of the dangers grows out of what Mesthene calls "the seductiveness of rigor." "The implicit claim" of most of those working with computer-assisted instruction, he points out, "is a modest one: we are only trying to do better and faster what is now being done less well and more slowly. But much of what we are now doing in education may be wrong," he adds, "and if technology helps us to do it very efficiently, it may lead us beyond the point where we can detect and correct our errors."

Indeed, the approach to instructional technology that most researchers are following is likely to compound what is most wrong with American education—its failure to develop sensitive, autonomous, thinking, humane individuals. To program a computer, for example, one must define the instructional objectives in precise, measurable, "behavioral" terms; one must be able to specify the "behavior" to be produced with far greater precision than is needed in the conventional classroom. (Computer-assisted instruction is similar, in this regard, to programmed instruction.)

It is not enough, however, to define only the ultimate ob-

[44] Emmanuel G. Mesthene, "Computers and the Purposes of Education," in Holtzman, ed., *Computer-Assisted Instruction, Testing and Guidance*.

jectives. "An effective technology of instruction," Robert Glaser, director of the University of Pittsburgh's Learning Research and Development Center, argues, "relies heavily upon the effective measurement of subject matter competence at the beginning, during, and at the end of the educational process." Particularly if some degree of individualization is desired, behavioral objectives have to be defined at a great many steps along the way. "Well-defined sequences of progressive, behaviorally defined objectives in various subject areas must be established as guidelines for setting up a student's program of study," Glaser explains. "The student's achievement is defined by his position along this progression of advancement."[45]

Part of the difficulty is that behavioral objectives are easier to define in some curriculum areas than in others. It is not coincidental, for example, that most of the applications of programmed instruction have been in training courses for industry and the armed forces, where it is relatively easy to define the knowledge or skills to be taught in precise behavioral terms, and where the motivation to learn is quite strong. (A survey of industry's use of programmed instruction several years ago, for example, indicated that 69 percent of the programs used were "job-oriented.") It is a lot harder, however, to specify the behavior to be produced, say, by a course in Shakespeare or music or American history. Glaser acknowledges the problem. "Education," he writes, "ought to provide society with people who are capable of doing new things, rather than repeating what other generations have done, and with people who can analyze and verify so that they do not readily accept available trends of thought. To recognize these goals is one thing; to attempt to approximate them is another. As a scientist," he continues, "I am primarily concerned with the operational mechanisms by which these goals are attained. Mechanism," he adds, "is indeed

---

[45] Robert Glaser, "The Design and Programming of Instruction," in Committee for Economic Development, *The Schools and the Challenge of Innovation*. Cf. also Glaser, "The Design of Instruction," in *The Changing American School*, Sixty-fifth Yearbook of the National Society for the Study of Education, Part II, University of Chicago Press, 1966; "Adapting the Elementary School Curriculum to Individual Performance," in Educational Testing Service, *Proceedings of the 1967 Invitational Conference on Testing Problems*, Princeton, N.J., 1968; and "The New Pedagogy," statement and testimony at *Hearings on Technology in Education*, Subcommittee on Economic Progress of the Joint Economic Committee, U.S. Government Printing Office, 1966.

the right word; *it denotes the specificity required to carry out a reliable, replicable system*. It need not imply rigidity and non-humanism. These goals are difficult to measure, but *few have ever contended that the most easily measured products of education are necessarily the most valuable. . . .* On the other hand, attempts must be made to measure what we say we are after."[46] [Emphasis added]

Unfortunately, it tends to work the other way; instead of measuring "what we say we are after," there is an almost irresistible temptation to go after the things that can be measured. This tendency is clearly visible in the Individually Prescribed Instruction (IPI) approach, which Glaser and his colleagues (particularly C. M. Lindvall and John O. Bolvin) designed and have been trying out in the Oakleaf School in Whitehall, Pennsylvania, outside Pittsburgh. The IPI experiment would be important by itself, since it is perhaps the most comprehensive attempt anywhere in the United States at developing an individualized instructional technology. Its importance is heightened, however, by the fact that the U.S. Office of Education is disseminating the approach rather widely.[47]

This tendency to leap on the innovation bandwagon heightens the dangers inherent in the technological approach to education.[48] The dangers are several, starting with the concept of individualization itself. In IPI, individualization is defined as permitting students to cover the prescribed curriculum at their own rate of speed—a useful but nonetheless narrow and restricted view of individualization and of individuals.

But what Glaser and his colleagues call individualization, Oettinger suggests, is not individualization as we usually understand the term, but "rather what an industrial engineer might

[46] Robert Glaser, Discussion of Oettinger and Marks's "Educational Technology: New Myths and Old Realities," in *Harvard Educational Review*, Vol. 38, No. 4, Fall 1968.
[47] Under the auspices of Research for Better Schools, Inc., the Office of Education's Regional Laboratory in Philadelphia, the experimental application of IPI has escalated from the one school in which Glaser and his associates began working, to twenty-three schools in the 1968–69 school year and 164 schools in thirty-three states and three foreign countries in the 1969–70 school year, with some 1,000 school districts reportedly asking to be included.
[48] The critique of IPI that follows is drawn from observations made by the writer and a member of his research staff, as well as by the observations and analyses of Anthony Oettinger, which, while made a year or two later, were remarkably similar. (Oettinger's observations are reported in *Run, Computer, Run*, Chapter 3.)

call mass production to narrow specifications with rigid quality control." For IPI's version of individualization does not permit the individual student to define his own goals and attempt to reach them; it permits him only to reach someone else's goals at his own rate of speed. James W. Becker, executive director of Research for Better Schools, which is sponsoring the wide dissemination of IPI, is even more explicit on this score than Glaser. "There is no necessary definition of 'individualized instruction' which requires that the student be completely free to pursue his own ends," he wrote in response to Oettinger's critique. "IPI does *not* accept the theory that every child should do exactly what he wants. This is simply not a part of IPI; whether it ought to be is another question entirely. . . . IPI's strategy assumes that the ends are known, that somebody does in fact prescribe the goals, and that a student is supposed to reach those carefully defined goals. Indeed, it is a highly structured kind of strategy." Becker concedes that "some concepts of individualization of instruction at some times in some subject areas might include ends that the student himself defines." For himself, however, the concept is clear: *"I must reject the idea that maximum freedom is a necessary condition for something called individualization of instruction."*[49] [Emphasis added]

Few educators, however, would pose the alternatives in such stark terms: total prescription of goals by others, or total freedom for the student to pursue his own goals. Indeed, Becker's definition of the alternatives represents a complete misunderstanding of the nature of education and a perversion of its goals. As we shall argue in the next three chapters, with detailed examples from the United States and England, freedom and structure are perfectly compatible; there can be, and indeed are, schools in which students have considerable freedom to set their own goals and follow their own interests, without the teachers in any way surrendering *their* responsibility to set external goals of their own.

Our argument, however, is not with Becker, but with IPI; he is only stating his system's requirements. *What is undesirable about IPI is precisely that it does not permit any position between the two extremes Becker poses; the instructional technology can work only if those who write the programs specify every goal in the most precise and detailed terms.* A descriptive booklet on IPI published jointly by Research for Better Schools and Glaser's Learning Research and Development Center is most explicit. Under the heading "Distinguishing Fundamentals," the pamphlet states:

1. Individually Prescribed Instruction must be based on a carefully sequenced and detailed listing of behaviorally stated instructional objectives. Such listings must be used in planning most other aspects of the program and should have the following characteristics:

    (a) *Each objective should tell exactly what a pupil should be able to do* to exhibit his mastery of the given content and skill. *This should typically be something that the average student can master in such a relatively short time as one class period* . . .[50] [Emphasis added]

In short, what is crucial to the system called Individually Prescribed Instruction is not the adjective "individually" but the verb "prescribed"; and what the individual does must be prescribed in terms so narrow as to leave no room whatsoever for the exercise of individuality. The system simply cannot accommodate a student who wants to strike out on his own. If any number of students attempted to do so—if, for example, they decided to satisfy their curiosity about American history by reading everything they could find in their school or home or local public library instead of limiting themselves to the prepared programs, the whole system would break down!

In developing the IPI curriculum, moreover, Glaser disregarded his own obiter dicta about the need "to provide people who are capable of doing new things, rather than repeating what other generations have done," or the need to develop "people who can analyze and verify so that they do not readily accept available trends of thought." On the contrary, what he and his colleagues did was simply to program the existing curriculum, which meant programming the school's existing goals as well. "We haven't thought much about what kind of citizens the school is going to turn out," Glaser told this writer. "If we had started with that, we would still be designing the system." His disinclination to examine educational goals is basic to his entire approach, which is that of an engineer, not an educator.[51] "You

---

[50] "Individually Prescribed Instruction," Research for Better Schools, Inc. and The Learning Research and Development Center, undated.
[51] Cf. also Glaser's self-description in his essay, "Variables in Discovery

tell me what values you want to teach," he says, "and I'll tell you the best technology for teaching it."

But the technology changes the values, and dictates some of its own; no technology is ever neutral. When a large part of the curriculum is programmed—half or more in the case of IPI—certain values may be circumscribed, if not pushed out altogether. Since students must be able to check their own answers, for example, or have their answers checked by a clerk or a computer, questions necessarily must be in a form that can be answered briefly, e.g., by filling in a word, indicating whether a statement is true or false, or choosing which of, say, four answers is correct.

The result—the ultimate irony—is that IPI forces students into a passive, almost docile, role under the name of individualization. Because the material is presented in programmed instruction form, the student not only cannot specify his own goals, he cannot reach them in his own way; he is limited to the program, with its preordained answers. He cannot "internalize" or apply what he has learned, for he cannot reconstruct the material in his own way—he cannot express a concept in his own words or actions or construct his own applications and examples. The rigidity of the structure, moreover, implies that there is only one right answer and only one route to it; but what students (and teachers) may need to learn most is that some questions have more than one answer—and that others may have no answer at all.

The problem runs deeper still. One can argue, after all, that the rigidities and biases of IPI are due not to the concept but to the current limited "state of the art" of programming, and that further refinements of programming techniques may eliminate the objections we have raised. The argument will not stand: the weakness of IPI, and of computer-assisted instruction, is inherent in the behaviorist approach to education itself, with its insistence that the goals of education not only can, but should, be defined in precise behavioral terms. This insistence on behavioral definition of objectives, as Professor Lee J. Cronbach of Stanford points out, is a prescription for training and not for education.

The distinction is important. In both education and training,

---

Learning," in Lee S. Shulman and Evan R. Keisler, *Learning by Discovery: A Critical Appraisal,* Chicago: Rand, McNally, 1966.

goals are, or should be, specified; the difference lies in how the goals are related to the process of instruction itself. In training, the behavior to be produced is embedded in the lesson itself: as Cronbach puts it, "the lesson is the thing." Or as Glaser puts it, in a definition already quoted, "Well-defined sequences of progressive, behaviorally defined objectives in various subject areas need to be established as guidelines for setting up a student's program of study. *The student's achievement is defined by his position along this progression of advancement.*" [Emphasis added]

In education, on the other hand, the student's achievement is defined by what he does—and what he is—*after* the lessons have all ended. The lesson, as Cronbach suggests, is merely "a vehicle by and through which one develops values, self-confidence, abilities to reason, analyze, and learn." The lesson is *not* the thing; on the contrary, "one can forget the lesson itself, and indeed must, when it is rendered obsolete." As the old aphorism has it, education is what remains when the lessons have been forgotten. Or in Whitehead's phrase, "your learning is useless to you till you have lost your textbooks, burnt your lecture notes, and forgotten the minutiae which you learnt by heart for the examination."

Education can, and almost certainly should, include training; in almost every field, there are skills that have to be mastered, concepts that have to be learned. But the converse does not hold; education cannot be subsumed under training. "The person who wants us to 'specify the acts the learner is to perform as a result of instruction' is deluding himself when he talks of history, science, or other nonskill subjects," Cronbach writes. "He is a confederate of the static society."[52]

But ours is not a static society; it is education that we need, not training. William James saw this and warned against the tendency to substitute training for education in 1892, in his *Talks to Teachers.* "We are all too apt to measure the gains of our pupils by their proficiency in directly reproducing in a recitation or an examination such matters as they may have learned," he said, "and inarticulate power in them is something of which we always underestimate the value. . . . Although the ready memory is a great blessing to its possessor," he continued, "the vaguer memory of a subject, of having once had to do with it, of its neighborhood, and of where we may go to recover it again,

52 In correspondence with the author.

constitutes in most men and women the chief fruit of their education . . ."

> Be patient, then, and sympathetic with the type of mind that cuts a poor figure in examinations. It may, in the long examination which life sets us, come out in the end in better shape than the glib and ready reproducer, its passions being deeper, its purposes more worthy, its combining power less commonplace, and its total mental output consequently more important.[53]

Our most pressing educational problem, in short, is not how to increase the efficiency of the schools; it is how to create and maintain a humane society. A society whose schools are inhumane is not likely to be humane itself.

[53] William James, *Talks to Teachers on Psychology and to Students on Some of Life's Ideals,* New York: W. W. Norton (The Norton Library), 1958.

III

How the Schools Should Be Changed

6

The Case of the New English Primary Schools

Children need to be themselves, to live with other children and with grownups, to learn from their environment, to enjoy the present, to get ready for the future, to create and to love, to learn to face adversity, to behave responsibly, in a word, to be human beings.

—CHILDREN AND THEIR PRIMARY SCHOOLS
A Report of the Central Advisory Council
for Education (England), 1967.

I

"That is common knowledge, so common in fact, that it may not even be true," one of the characters in Donald Barthelme's ribald "black humor" version of *Snow White* observes. Alexis de Tocqueville made the point more elegantly 140 years ago. "What we call necessary institutions," he wrote, "are often no more than institutions to which we have grown accustomed."

So it is with schools in their traditional form. The "necessity" that makes schooling so uniform over time and across cultures is simply the "necessity" that stems from unexamined assumptions and unquestioned behavior. The preoccupation with order and control, the slavish adherence to the timetable and lesson plan, the obsession with routine qua routine, the absence of noise and movement, the joylessness and repression, the universality of the formal lecture or teacher-dominated "discussion" in which the teacher instructs an entire class as a unit, the emphasis of the verbal and de-emphasis of the concrete, the inability of students to work on their own, the dichotomy between work and play—none of these are necessary; all can be eliminated.

Schools can be humane and still educate well. They can be genuinely concerned with gaiety and joy and individual growth and fulfillment without sacrificing concern for intellectual discipline and development. They can be simultaneously child-centered and subject- or knowledge-centered. They can stress esthetic and moral education without weakening the three R's. They can do all these things if—but only if—their structure, content, and objectives are transformed.

These assertions represent a statement of fact, not a mere expression of hope. Schools of this sort exist in the United States on a small but rapidly growing scale; they can be found in the small cities and hamlets of North Dakota, in medium-sized cities such as Tucson, Arizona, and Portland, Oregon, in prosperous suburbs, and in the ghettos of Philadelphia and New York. (Examples at the elementary school level will be discussed in Chapter 7; Chapter 8 will be concerned with examples at the secondary level.)

Such schools exist on a much wider scale in England. Their rapid growth after World War II went largely unnoticed in this country, and to a surprising degree, in England itself, until 1967, when a Parliamentary Commission, the so-called Plowden Committee, called attention to the new approach and urged its adoption by all English primary schools.[1] The approach has a variety of labels, none of them entirely satisfactory: the "free day," the "integrated day," the "integrated curriculum," the "free school," the "open school," "informal education." The multiplicity of labels reflects the wide range of specific school practices and organization; there is no monolithic system or approach.

Indeed, the "free day," or "informal education," to use a more inclusive term, is less an approach or method than a set of shared attitudes and convictions about the nature of childhood, learning, and schooling. Advocates of informal education begin with a conception of childhood as something to be cherished, a conception that leads in turn to a concern with the quality of the

---

[1] Central Advisory Council for Education (England), *Children and Their Primary Schools*, London: Her Majesty's Stationery Office, 1967 (2 vols). The report is generally referred to as the Plowden Report, after the chairman of the Council, Lady Bridget Plowden.

school experience in its own right, not merely as preparation for later schooling or for later life. As the members of the Plowden Committee state in their report, "Children need to be themselves, to live with other children and with grownups, to learn from their environment, to enjoy the present, to get ready for the future, to create and to love, to learn to face adversity, to behave responsibly, in a word, to be human beings."

There is, in addition, a conviction that learning is likely to be more effective if it grows out of what interests the learner, rather than what interests the teacher. This is a truism to any adult: we *know* how rapidly we can learn something that really interests us, and how long it takes to master something that bores us, or for which we have a positive distaste. Formal schools, whether in England or the United States, tend to ignore the truism; informal schools do not. Hence they generally abandon the traditional rigid timetable which divides the day into a succession of short periods. In its place there are longer periods during which, at the teacher's discretion and under his supervision, students may be engaged individually or in small groups in a wide variety of activities.

To suggest that learning evolve from the child's interests is not to propose an abdication of adult authority, only a change in the way it is exercised. "With our foolish and pedantic methods," Rousseau wrote, "we are always preventing children from learning what they could learn much better by themselves, while we neglect what we alone can teach them." Teachers in the informal English schools try to make this distinction, but they have no doubt about their responsibility to teach. "From the start," the Plowden Committee firmly declares, "there must be teaching as well as learning: children are not 'free' to develop interests or skills of which they have no knowledge. They must have guidance from their teachers." Since what children are interested in is a function of their environment as well as of their native endowment, it is the teacher's responsibility to structure that environment in the best possible way, and to help it change and grow in response to each child's evolving interests and needs.

What chiefly distinguishes the contemporary English informal schools, then, from the American child-centered progressive schools of the 1920s and '30s, which they resemble in many ways, or from the kind of education that romantic critics like John Holt, George Dennison, and Paul Goodman now advocate, is the absolute clarity of this understanding, the hard-headed recognition of and indeed insistence on the teacher's central role.[2] It would be impossible for a teacher acting in accord with the Plowden Report to respond as a teacher in New York's Walden School, one of the citadels of American progressivism, did in the 1920s. Asked if he were the teacher, the young man, who was standing with his back to the room, speaking only when children addressed a question to him, replied, "Well, you can call me that; at least I'm here."[3]

With rare exceptions, the teachers and administrators with whom I talked and whose informal classrooms I observed were more than simply "here"; they were very much in charge. "It's easy to be a sweet nothing and just say, 'Oh, that's nice,' " one London "head" (headmistress) remarked, "but we are here to teach, not just to let children discover." The teacher "must know clearly what she's trying to do and how and why," Nora Goddard, Chief Inspector of Infant Schools in London, insists. It is not enough to create a rich environment, as teachers of the progressive era were content to do. The teacher must know when, and how, to intervene if she is to achieve the main objective—as Miss Goddard defines it, "helping children learn how to think, to form judgments, to discriminate."

With rare exceptions, too, teachers and administrators were careful to avoid confusing sentiment *for* children with sentimentality *about* them. "We must avoid being sentimental," declares Sir Alec Clegg, Chief Education Officer of the West Riding of Yorkshire and one of the most child-centered English educators. "Happiness has got to derive from achievement and success, not just having a good time." Concern for the needs of each child, writes John Blackie, a former Chief Inspector of Primary Schools, "does not mean being sentimental about children ('dear little things') or foolishly indulgent ('the child is always right') or forcing them into premature and precocious importance, mistakes that many have made in England and elsewhere. It means regarding them as our responsibility."[4] And that responsibility means educating them: transmitting, creating, and evoking the skills, values, attitudes, and knowledge that will help them grow into mature, creative, and happy adults.

Most advocates and practitioners of informal education, in

[2] For a more detailed and systematic comparison of contemporary English informal education with American progressivism, see Chapter 7.
[3] Agnes de Lima, *Our Enemy the Child,* quoted in Lawrence A. Cremin, *The Transformation of the School,* p. 213.
[4] John Blackie, *Inside the Primary School,* London: Her Majesty's Stationery Office, 1967.

short, reject John Holt's romantic notion that children should simply be turned loose to do their own thing, that as soon as one introduces adult priorities and adult notions of what is worth learning, one destroys the fidelity of the child. "What the child wants and how much he wants is largely determined by his environment," Mary Brown and Norman Precious write, in criticism of Holt, and "the school and the teacher must play a vital role in this choice."[5]

These views of childhood and of schooling are strongly in-fluencing English primary education. A 1964 survey made for the Plowden Committee by the education inspectorate indicated that roughly one-third of English primary schools had been "substantially affected" by the new approach, with another third "somewhat affected"; the proportions have increased since then. Terms such as "substantially affected" and "somewhat affected" are ambiguous, to be sure, and statistics applying to English primary education as a whole can be misleading in view of the fact that many school authorities maintain separate infant and junior schools, the former enrolling children aged five to seven; the latter, children aged seven to eleven. (Some districts have mixed infant and junior schools with a separate infant depart-ment; others have single primary schools enrolling the whole age span.) But it is safe to say that about 25 percent of English primary schools fit the model described in this chapter, and that another third are in one or another stage of moving toward it.[6]

Informal education is more influential and widespread among infant schools and the infant departments of mixed infant and junior schools. Indeed, its growth derives in considerable meas-ure from the hundred-year-old tradition of separate schools for "infants," with an atmosphere and approach radically different from that found in schools for older children.[7] In part because they are dealing only with very young children, in part because children generally enter the infant school at four different times during the year (at the beginning of the "half term" nearest

[5] Mary Brown and Norman Precious, *The Integrated Day in the Primary School,* London: Ward Lock Educational Publishers, 1968.
[6] John Blackie, *Inside the Primary School,* p. 12; Vincent R. Rogers, *Teaching in the British Primary School,* New York: Macmillan, 1970, p. v.
[7] England is one of the three industrial nations (Israel and New Zealand are the others) in which compulsory schooling begins at age five. In the United States, schooling is not compulsory until age six (kindergarten attendance is voluntary), and in some nations, not until age seven. Cf. *Children and Their Primary Schools,* Vol. I.

their fifth birthday), infant school teachers and administrators traditionally have shown greater flexibility and informality and have been more child-centered than their colleagues in junior, grammar, and secondary schools. In any case, the majority of infant schools now follow one or another variant of informal or free day methods.[8]

The junior schools have been slower to follow suit. Most are still formal in their approach, and many are harsh and rigid— more so, perhaps, than comparable American schools. Corporal punishment is still fairly widespread; while the Plowden Committee (with one member dissenting) formally urged its legal prohibition, the Committee acknowledged the fact that the majority of teachers favored its continued use. Even so, a considerable number of junior schools have been using informal education for some time, and a great many others are moving in that direction, in part as a result of the Plowden Report, in part in response to suggestions and pressure from the local and national inspectorate.

What is crucial for our purposes, in any case, is not the precise number of informal schools but the fact that the approach is widely used in state schools (what we call public schools) in every part of England, staffed by every kind of teacher in every kind of building and serving every kind of student. I observed informal schools in London—in one of the wealthiest neighborhoods, in one of the poorest and most crime-ridden Cockney slums, and in several rapidly changing immigrant neighborhoods. I observed informal schools, too, in the depressed coal-mining towns of Yorkshire, in middle-class and lower-class neighborhoods in Leicestershire County in the industrial Midlands, and in pastoral (but increasingly industrialized) Oxfordshire; and I have drawn on accounts by others of informal schools in such diverse places as Manchester, Bristol, and Nottingham. The buildings in which these "new" schools are housed also run the gamut from spanking-new one-story glass-enclosed buildings designed specifically for informal education, to dark and dank

---

[8] One measure of the degree to which informal methods dominate the infant school is the fact that the volume *Going to School* in the popular series of "Ladybird" books describes a completely informal school. "In this book," the Preface explains to parents, "are illustrated all the interesting and enjoyable activities which to-day make school such a happy experience . . ." The book was first published in 1959. Cf. M. E. Gagg, *Going to School,* A Ladybird Learning to Read Book, Loughborough, Eng.: Wills and Hepworth Ltd., 1959.

three-story buildings erected in Queen Victoria's reign and designed for the most rigid formal schooling. The teachers and "heads" ranged from veterans of forty years of teaching to miniskirted young women fresh out of training school. In order to present as clear a picture as possible of what schooling *can* be, the descriptions that follow represent the best of English practice rather than the average. At a number of points, however, the potential weaknesses and dangers of informal education will be discussed.

II

The trend toward informal education in England is not a sudden departure from the past. On the contrary, it has developed gradually over the last half century, out of the insights and experiments of innumerable teachers, "heads" (principals), local and national school inspectors and advisors, and college and university professors.[9] "I should love to be able to believe that the primary teachers who in the past three decades have brought about such important changes in outlook did so from a base of deeply considered educational policy coupled with splendid practical foresight concerning the needs of society in the future," Sybil Marshall of the University of Sussex, herself an important figure in the change, has written; "but looking back myself over thirty-plus years of teaching I cannot honestly do so." Like Kanga in *Winnie-the-Pooh,* these teachers, out of simple concern for the children in their care, "did a Good Thing without knowing it." The revolution came about, as Miss Marshall puts it, because "teachers in infant classes everywhere began to act on a professional instinct that told them a happy child actively involved in something he wanted to do was getting more out of his educational opportunities than a passive, bored child politely

[9] The roots go much deeper—all the way back, in fact, to the infant school Robert Owen established at New Lanark in 1816. For an account of how informal education has evolved over the past century and a half, see Lillian Weber, *The English Infant School: A Model for Informal Education,* scheduled to appear as a Center for Urban Education publication, and "The English Infant School" in C. W. Harris, ed., *The Encyclopedia of Educational Research,* The Macmillan Co., 1970. The writer is deeply indebted to Professor Weber for sharing her manuscript and her insights and judgments. Cf. also W. A. C. Stewart and W. P. McCann, *The Educational Innovators, 1750–1880,* New York: St. Martin's Press, 1967; and W. A. C. Stewart, *The Educational Innovators, Vol. 2: Progressive Schools, 1881–1967,* New York: St. Martin's Press, 1968.

resisting most of the instruction dished out to him in 30-minute parcels."

That "professional instinct" gained official encouragement in 1934 with the publication of the "Hadow Committee" Report on *Infant and Nursery Schools,* which some advocates of informal education regard as the best piece of educational writing of the century.[10] The "instinct" was heightened again during World War II, when urban teachers and their pupils were evacuated because of the bombing raids. "Teachers who had taught the same stuff in the same city classrooms for fifteen years found themselves in the fens, or the hills, or the farm-lands," John Blackie recalls, where they were "the only link with the children's background, and they simply had to re-think what they were doing."[11]

The rethinking was made all the more necessary by the fact that the teachers found themselves with the children twenty-four hours a day; forced into a new relationship with their students, they began to see them in a different light. Learning clearly was something that went on all the time, not just during school hours, hence the teachers were persuaded that it is fruitless to try to segment and compartmentalize children or learning. They were even more persuaded when the war ended. Back in their traditional classrooms, teachers found themselves confronting a roomful of children who had been dispersed all over England, some of whom, consequently, could read fluently, some poorly, and some not at all. Faced with a range of background, knowledge and ability several times the prewar norm, teachers once again found it necessary to improvise.

While the change in primary education grew out of the pragmatic responses of a great many teachers, it is backed by a substantial body of theory about the nature of children and the ways in which they grow and learn, as well as about the nature of knowledge, the processes of instruction, and the aims of education. Like Molière's *bourgeois gentilhomme,* the teachers discovered after the fact that they had been speaking prose all along. Their intuitive responses have strong theoretical support in the writings and work of Rousseau, Friedrich Froebel, the nineteenth-century "inventor" of the kindergarten, Maria Montessori, John Dewey, Rachel Macmillan, Susan Isaacs, Jerome Bruner, and most importantly, the Swiss biologist-psychologist-

[10] Report of the Consultative Committee on Infant and Nursery Schools, London: Her Majesty's Stationery Office, 1934.
[11] Blackie, *Inside the Primary School.*

epistemologist, Jean Piaget—the "giant of the nursery," as he has been called—whose forty-odd years of study of the development of children's mental processes are just beginning to be appreciated in the United States. It may be useful, therefore, before turning to a detailed description of the schools themselves, to sketch out in summary form the theories which inform and justify informal schooling. (Instead of filling these next pages with footnotes, there will be a Note on Sources at the end of this chapter.)

So far as educational practice is concerned, Piaget's most important contribution has been his demonstration that the child is the principal agent in his own education and mental development. To be sure, mental development occurs through an enormously complex and continuous process of interaction between the child and his environment that begins at birth. But the critical factor is the child's own activity in assimilating his experiences and accommodating to them; the child is continually forming mental images or structures within his mind corresponding to his experience of the world outside, and continually modifying these structures as a result of new experiences.

At each stage in development, that is to say—indeed, at each moment of time—the child has *some* mental apparatus, however primitive, that is the result of the interaction that has already occurred between the unfolding of his innate or "wired-in" mental structures and his experiences. And at each stage or moment of time, the child is extending that apparatus through probing and testing his environment—in infancy, exploring with his eyes, his mouth, his hands, his feet, his lungs; later on, through babbling, walking, talking, playing, reading, etc. He not only stores information in his mental "files," he continually modifies and reconstitutes the filing system or mental apparatus through using it. In John Dewey's phrase, he learns through doing—*his* doing, and no one else's. Thus, the child learns to hear, and then to speak, by hearing and speaking, and not, until much later, by being told *how* to speak; he learns to think mathematically or in terms of cause and effect through his engagement with things that embody causal or mathematical relationships; it is only much later, after he has learned to think causally, that he can begin to think *about* causality.

The sequence is not random, however; all children go through the same series of stages as, bit by bit, they construct their mental images of the world. Each stage sees the development of new mental abilities that determine the nature, but also set the limits, of what the child can learn at that point. "The essential conclusion, as far as education is concerned," Piaget writes, is that "learning cannot explain development, but that the stage of development can in part explain learning. Development follows its own laws, as all of contemporary biology leads us to believe, and although each stage in the development is accompanied by all sorts of new learning based on experience, this learning is always relative to the developmental period during which it takes place, and to the intellectual structures, whether completely or partially formed, which the subject has at his disposal during this period." In Piaget's view, the sequence is invariant for all children in all cultures, and is generally related to age, although the precise age at which a given stage emerges varies from child to child according to his native endowment and the environment and culture in which he has been reared. "Maturation," Piaget argues, "simply opens up possibilities, and never is sufficient in itself to actualize these possibilities."[12]

What "actualizes these possibilities," to use Piaget's phrase—what enables the child to progress from one stage to another—is his own activity. Learning, indeed the development of intelligence itself, is a continuous process of assimilating the external facts of experience and integrating them into the individual's internal mental structures. The activity is crucial: the child, or for that matter, the adult, must discover understanding for himself. He must actively invent and re-invent what he wants to understand, for understanding, as Piaget puts it, is a transformation of reality. To know something is not merely to be told it or to see it but to act upon it, to modify and transform it and to understand the process, and consequences, of the transformation. In the words of an old Chinese proverb,

> I hear, and I forget;
> I see, and I remember;
> I do, and I understand.

[12] This argument, perhaps Piaget's most controversial, has been widely questioned, in part on the grounds that Piaget's own researches have been confined to middle-class Swiss children. But a number of cross-cultural studies by other scholars, using Piaget's methods but involving children in the United States, China, Britain, India, Iran, Algeria, Somali, and Senegal, among other countries, seem to confirm Piaget's theory of stages. Cf. John H. Flavell, *The Developmental Psychology of Jean Piaget,* Princeton, New Jersey: Van Nostrand, 1963; David Elkind, "Piaget and Montessori," *Harvard Educational Review,* Fall 1967; Lawrence Kohlberg, *The Development of Children's Orientation to a Moral Order,* New York: Holt, Rinehart and Winston, to be published 1971.

This does not mean that the child develops in isolation. "The human being is immersed right from birth in a social environment which affects him just as his physical environment," Piaget has written. "Society, even more, in a sense, than the physical environment, changes the very structure of the individual, because it not only compels him to recognize facts, but also provides him with a ready-made system of signs, which modify his thoughts; it presents him with new values and it imposes on him an infinite series of obligations. It is therefore quite evident that social life affects intelligence." Thus, Piaget insists on the fundamental unity of the cognitive and affective domains; feeling is an aspect of thought. The infant's egocentricity, for example, is a function of the crudity of his mental structure; it is "nothing more than a lack of coordination, a failure to 'group' relations with other individuals as well as with other objects"—an inability to distinguish between what is internal and what is external.

The implications for educational practice could not be more profound, although it would be an error—one that Piaget himself has cautioned against—to assume that *any* theory can specify precisely what a teacher should do. "You make a great, a very great mistake," William James told the Cambridge, Massachusetts, teachers nearly eighty years ago, in a warning that still holds, "if you think that psychology, being the science of the mind's laws, is something from which you can deduce definite programmes and schemes and methods of instruction for immediate classroom use. Psychology is a science," James argued, "and teaching is an art; and sciences never generate arts directly out of themselves. An intermediary inventive mind must make the application, by using its originality." Yet science must be understood; it plays a major role, for it "lays down the lines within which the rules of the art must fall, laws which the follower of the art must not transgress. . . . Everywhere the teaching must *agree* with the psychology, but need not necessarily be the only kind of teaching that would so agree."

What kind of teaching, then, agrees with Piaget's psychology? What lines do his theories lay down which teachers must not transgress?

A big part of the teacher's artistry, clearly, must be to find and provide an appropriate relationship between what is to be learned, the way it is to be learned, and the stage the child is in—what the American psychologist J. McV. Hunt calls "the problem of the match." This requires a high degree of individualization. Since developmental age corresponds only very roughly with chronological age—as already mentioned, precisely when a child moves from stage to stage is a function of both his native endowment and his experience—any school class will contain a wide range; the spectrum of "developmental ages" is bound to be wider than the chronological ages.

The problem is compounded by the fact that children rarely develop on all fronts simultaneously; a given child may be in one stage in one conceptual area, e.g., reading, and in quite another stage in a different area, e.g., mathematics. Finding the right match is crucial. On the one hand, learning cannot be forced—a child cannot learn what he is not yet capable of learning—but on the other hand, children will become restless and bored if the material is too familiar or the learning skills too easy. "The teacher's task," as the Plowden Committee puts it, "is to provide an environment and opportunities which are sufficiently challenging for children and yet not so difficult as to be outside their reach. There has to be the right mixture of the familiar and the novel, the right match to the stage of learning the child has reached."

The teacher's role must change in other and equally profound ways. There must be far less telling on the part of the teacher, and far more doing on the part of the student. "Teaching," Piaget argues, "means creating situations where structures can be discovered; it does not mean transmitting structures which may be assimilated at nothing other than a verbal level." At least until youngsters are old enough to handle verbal abstractions easily (what Piaget calls the stage of "formal operations," which for most children develops between the twelfth and fifteenth years) the teacher's job is to present the child with situations that encourage him to experiment, to manipulate things and symbols, trying them out to see what results they produce.

But the child must "do" at his own rate, with the teacher arranging the classroom environment in such a way as to permit children to learn at their own pace as well as in their own way. "Children have real understanding only of that which they invent themselves, and each time we try to teach them something too quickly, we keep them from reinventing it themselves," Piaget warns. "Thus, there is no good reason to accelerate this development too much." The time that seems to be "wasted" in personal investigation, he argues, is really time gained, i.e., time devoted to securing deeper understanding, which is what we want, or should want. "The principal goal of education," Piaget insists, "is to create men who are capable of doing new things, not simply of repeating what other generations have done— men who are creative, inventive, and discoverers," who have "minds which can be critical, can verify, and not accept everything they are offered."

> The great danger today is of slogans, collective opinions, ready-made trends of thought. We have to be able to resist individually, to criticize, to distinguish between what is proven and what is not. So we need pupils who are active, who learn early to find out by themselves, partly by their own spontaneous activity and partly through material we set up for them; who learn early to tell what is verifiable and what is simply the first idea to come to them.

This means providing young children with an abundance of concrete materials they can explore, manipulate, and handle— materials they can play with, for play is a child's work. Certainly "the distinction between work and play is false, possibly throughout life, certainly in the primary school," the Plowden Committee observes. "We know now that play—in the sense of 'messing around' either with material objects or with other children, and of creating fantasies—is vital to children's learning, and therefore vital in school." For "play is the principal means of learning in early childhood. It is the way through which children reconcile their inner lives with external reality"—the way in which they "gradually develop concepts of causal relationships, the power to discriminate, to make judgments, to analyze and synthesize, to imagine and to formulate."

The emphasis on play and on the individual child's activities and interests in no way implies anarchy; quite the contrary. "When I say 'active,' " Piaget declares, "I mean it in two senses. One is acting on material things. But the other means doing things in social collaboration, in a group effort . . . where children must communicate with each other. This is an essential factor in intellectual development. Cooperation," he adds, "is indeed co-operation."

The philosopher David Hawkins of the University of Colorado, an active figure in American curriculum reform and a close student of English informal schooling, suggests that the teaching-learning process of the informal classroom can be understood best in terms of a triangular relationship, consisting of the child, the teacher, and the "stuff," as the English call the wealth of concrete materials that fill the informal classroom.[13] These three points correspond to Martin Buber's "I," "thou," and "it." As the child (I) becomes involved with the stuff (it), the teacher shares his involvement, so that it becomes "we" confronting "it."

The process never should, indeed never can, involve the child's confronting the stuff alone. "It is simply a product of abstraction, of adult reflection when we try to separate experiences into two parts, and distinguish what the child learns from things and from other people," John Dewey argued. "As a matter of fact, there is no contact with things excepting through the medium of people. The things themselves are saturated with the particular values which are put into them, not only by what people say about them, but more by what they do about them, and the way that they show that they feel about them and with them."[14]

The informal English schools demonstrate in practice what Dewey argued in theory: that a deep and genuine concern for individual growth and fulfillment not only is compatible with but indeed demands an equally genuine concern for cognitive growth and intellectual discipline, for transmitting the cultural heritage of the society. "The educative process," Dewey wrote, is the interaction of "an immature, undeveloped being" with "certain social aims, meanings, values incarnate in the matured experience of the adult." And the intellectual disciplines of language, arithmetic, history, music, science, et al., Dewey also argued, "are themselves experience," experience that embodies "the cumulative outcome of the efforts, the strivings, and the successes of the human race generation after generation." Their value is that they say to the teacher, "Such and such are the capacities, the fulfillments, in truth and beauty and behavior, open to these children. Now see to it that day by day the conditions are such that *their own activities* move inevitably in this direction, toward such culmination of themselves. Let the child's

[13] David Hawkins, "I, Thou, It," Newton, Mass.: Educational Development Center, Inc., Elementary Science Study Reprint (Reprint of a paper given on April 3, 1967, at the Primary Teachers' Residential Course, Loughborough, Leicestershire).
[14] John Dewey, *Lectures in the Philosophy of Education,* New York: Random House, 1966, p. 47. Cf. also David Hawkins, "Teacher of Teachers," *New York Review of Books,* February 29, 1968.

nature fulfill its own destiny, revealed to you in whatever of science and art and industry the world now holds as its own."[15]

III

To enter an informal classroom for the first time is a disorienting experience for an American (or for that matter, an Englishman) accustomed to traditional formal schooling. To begin with, the classroom does not *look* like a classroom. It is, rather, a workshop in which "interest areas" take the place of the familiar rows of desks and chairs and in which individualized learning takes the place of what informal English educators now disparagingly call "the talk and chalk" method, i.e., the teacher conducting a lesson for all the children simultaneously from her vantage point at one of the "chalkboards" lining the front and side of the room. To be sure, American kindergartens bear a superficial resemblance to this kind of classroom; children are usually seated at groups of tables instead of rows of desks, and there may be interest areas of sorts. But the informality of the kindergarten is abandoned once children enter the first grade.

In any case, not even the most informal American kindergartens (with exceptions to be noted in Chapter 7) have the incredible richness and variety of materials found in the average informal English infant or junior school classroom. The reading corner, for example, typically is an inviting place, with a rug or piece of old carpet on which children may sprawl, a couple of easy chairs or perhaps a cot or old couch for additional comfort, and a large and tempting display of books at child's height. The arithmetic (or "maths," as the English call it) area most likely will have several tables pushed together to form a large working space. On the tables, in addition to a variety of math texts and workbooks, will be a box containing rulers, measuring tapes and sticks, yardsticks, string, and the like; other boxes, containing pebbles, shells, stones, rocks, acorns, conkers (the acorn of a chestnut tree), bottle tops, pine cones, and anything else that can be used for counting, along with more formal arithmetic and mathematical materials, such as Cuisenaire rods, Dienes blocks, Stern rods, and Unifisc cubes. There will be several balance scales, too, with boxes of weights, as well as more peb-

[15] John Dewey, *The Child and the Curriculum,* University of Chicago Press. Cf. also John Dewey, "Progressive Education and the Science of Education," in Martin S. Dworkin, ed., *Dewey on Education,* Teachers College Press (Classics in Education No. 3), 1959.

bles, stones, rocks, feathers, and anything else that can be used for weighing.

Near the maths area is an infant school room, and frequently in the lower grades of a junior school, there is likely to be a large table-height sandbox and a specially constructed table, at about the same height, for water play. The water table comes "equipped" with an assortment of empty milk cartons and bottles, plastic detergent bottles, pitchers, plastic containers, and the like, all with their volume (⅓ pint, ½ pint, quart, gallon) marked on them, for practice in maths. There may also be an oven; following a recipe for muffins or cookies provides still another application of simple mathematical notions, along with practice in reading.

Nearby will be a table, or perhaps several cartons on the floor, some with blocks, tinkertoys, and the like, some containing "junk" (so marked), i.e., empty cereal and soap boxes, egg cartons, toilet paper and paper towel rollers, cardboard, pieces of wood, scraps of wallpaper and fabric, oaktag, cigar boxes— anything children might use for constructing things (airplanes, trucks, cars, steamrollers, robots, spaceships, houses, office buildings, bridges) or for making collages or murals. Somewhere in the room, or perhaps in the hall outside, there will be some large easels with jars of paints and large brushes. In one corner, or perhaps in a converted closet, will be a "Wendy House," a child-size play house, furnished with dolls, furniture, dishes, kitchenware, and a pile of castoff adult clothing for children to dress up in.

To complete the general picture, and without allowing for the idiosyncratic arrangements that distinguish one teacher's classroom from another even in the same school, there typically is a music area with xylophones, drums, cymbals, castanets, recorders, and other (sometimes homemade) instruments. Somewhere or other, too, there is a science area, with rocks and shells, leaves and other local flora, candles and jars, perhaps some small motors, batteries, bulbs, and wire, and in all probability, an animal or two or three, be it rabbit, turtle, hamster, or kitten. And this in classrooms which more often than not contain as many as forty children.

How do they find room? In good measure by replacing the desks and chairs with a smaller number of tables and chairs. There is no need to have a seat and desk for each child: the teacher seldom instructs the class as a whole, and when she does, the children simply gather around her, pulling up chairs or sitting on the floor. But teachers also create space for the various interest areas and activities by using closets, cloakrooms, indeed, every conceivable nook and cranny, and by spilling over into the halls, lobbies, playgrounds, and other common space. "An infant school classroom is too small and too confined for all the things children need to do," the Plowden Committee observed. "They overflow into the open air where there are no walls to shut off one class from another; they stray into corridors which are not marked out into pens like sheep folds."

Indeed, a visitor accustomed only to formal classrooms is likely to be disoriented by the sound and movement of an informal classroom even more than by its physical arrangements. To photograph a formal classroom in action, one needs only a still camera with a wide-angle lens; to photograph an informal classroom for infant and younger junior school children, one needs a motion-picture camera with sound, for the initial impression is that the children are all in motion. At any one moment, some children may be hammering and sawing at a workbench, some may be playing musical instruments or painting, others may be reading aloud to the teacher or to a friend, still others may be curled up on a cot or piece of carpet, reading in solitary absorption, oblivious to the sounds around them. (They belong to a generation, after all, that does its homework with the "telly" or a transistor radio blaring away.)

Elsewhere in the room, moreover, there are likely to be children seated at a table or sprawled on the floor, writing a story. Other children are in the maths area, counting or weighing acorns, bottle caps, pebbles, cones, shells, and what have you, or measuring the perimeter of the room, or the teacher's desk, or the length of a visitor's shoes, or one another's height, and writing it all down; others are measuring the ingredients of a cookie recipe, getting them ready for the oven. There are children playing in the sandbox, and others at the water table, filling the various-sized containers and enjoying the feel of the water, and there are children acting out various roles as they play at being grownups. And always there is the sound of children talking— to themselves, to their friends, to the teacher, to the headmistress as she walks around, to the visitors from America, in sharp contrast to the United States (or to formal classrooms in England), where children and visitors usually are carefully segregated from each other.

The sound and movement are not limited to the classroom it-self. There is a continuous ebb and flow of children into and out of the room—into the halls and corridors, the stairs, the cloak-rooms, the library, the hall,[16] the head's office, other classrooms, the lobby or entrance hall; and in halfway decent weather (half-way decent, that is to say, by English rather than American standards), out of doors, as well; into the playground, if it is a city school, and perhaps even into the surrounding fields, if it is a rural school. In the seventy- and eighty-year-old buildings that seem almost standard in London, for example, the corridors are almost always used, not just as a passageway, but as part of the classroom, as part of the total learning environment. They contain easels, workbenches, water tables, and displays and activities of every sort.

ITEM: A school in Leicestershire. In a corner, where two main corridors meet, is a large table with a sign in large letters read-ing, "Smell everything on this table." On the table are a number of jars, of rose petals, of mixed flowers, of vanilla, coffee, cloves, and various other herbs and spices.

ITEM: An infant school, circa 1890, in a London working-class neighborhood rapidly turning into a slum. The corridor walls are covered with materials designed to attract and engage the chil-dren. There is an "information corner," with a host of construc-tion-paper booklets to which children add a picture or story at will; among the titles are "Fast and Slow," "Big and Little," "Sound We Hear," "Shapes." There is the "Ambler Art Gallery," with the work of a different artist featured each month. (This month's artist is Degas.) The "Ambler News Shop" features newspaper and magazine pictures and articles about the Ameri-can astronauts, under the heading, "Ambler Salutes Brave Men."

In some schools, the "hall" provides a focal point from which activity radiates all over the building.

ITEM: An infant school, also in a rapidly changing immigrant neighborhood in London. At one side of the hall, a small wooden

---

[16] The "hall" (the term derives from the great hall of medieval castles and public buildings) is a large room, usually centrally located, which serves as auditorium, gymnasium, cafeteria, meeting place, and even classroom.

platform serves as a stage for two splendidly costumed little girls, recent immigrants from the West Indies, who are improvising a ballet for the headmistress. Two more girls, of cockney origin, join the ballet and soon eight more youngsters sit down to watch, applauding enthusiastically when the ballet ends. While this is going on, three boys are busily engaged in building a castle in one corner, while in another corner a boy and girl, playing the xylophone, are joined by four more. Somewhere else in the hall, a boy and a girl, in "grownup" clothes, are playing Mum and Dad. In the front of the hall is a "Blue Display"—a table containing a hat, mug, ribbon, jewelry, scarf, fabric, and various other objects, all in varying shades of blue, carefully and tastefully arranged and draped.

Understandably, in view of all the sound and motion, the first impression may be one of chaos. In most schools, it is a false impression. "You always have to assess the nature of the noise," the headmistress of the first school the writer visited helpfully explained. "Is it just aimless chatter, or does it reflect purposeful activity?" And as the visitor becomes acclimated, it becomes clear that the activity usually is purposeful; it does not take very long to be able to assess the nature of the noise, and to distinguish classes where the children's play is leading to learning from those where it is pleasant but aimless.

As the strangeness wears off, one becomes aware of many things. One becomes aware, for example, of the teacher's presence: in contrast to the first moments of wondering where she is, or whether she is even there at all, the visitor begins to see that the teacher is very much there and very much in charge. She seems always to be in motion, and always to be in contact with the children—talking, listening, watching, comforting, chiding, suggesting, encouraging—although from time to time she stops for a minute to jot down a comment in the record book she keeps for each child (Peter is trying to write his name for the first time, Evelyn is making much brighter pictures, John seems to be resisting maths, Susan has learned to multiply by two, James is coming out of his shell—he talked more easily and played with others for the first time . . .).

ITEM: An infant school in London. The classroom is buzzing with activity and conversation. As unobtrusively as possible, the visitor follows the teacher around, recording her conversation as she moves from cluster to cluster and from child to child. What initially appears to be casual chitchat turns out to be purposeful, if informal, teaching. As she talks to the children at the water table, absorbed with the feel of water on their hands, with pouring water from one container to another, with dropping objects in the water to see them splash, or to see whether they sink or float, the teacher casually injects words and concepts such as "sink," "float," "heavy," "light," "full," "empty," "bigger," "smaller." Talking to the children at the sand table about what they are making, she uses words like "castle," "moat," "tunnel," "mold," "shape," "sieve," "strainer," as well as "bigger," "smaller," "taller," "shorter," and the like. With the children who are painting and sculpting, the teacher discusses subtleties of color, shade, texture, and design. With the children at the junk box—one is making a tractor out of an empty cornflakes box, two paper towel rollers, and a smaller box; another is building a steamship, with a large detergent box serving as the hull and two empty cans of Heinz vegetable soup as the smokestacks—a discussion ensues about where tractors and ships are used, how they are propelled, what kinds of people use them or travel on them. And so it goes.

ITEM: A primary school in Oxfordshire. A group of three or four children have been weighing and measuring ingredients, preparatory to baking a cake. The teacher gathers them together to work through the mathematics involved: sixteen ounces make a pound, four ounces a quarter pound, etc., making sure that the ones who seemed to be having difficulty understand. The teacher moves on to another group when she sees that they understand, and the children return to their baking.

One becomes aware, too, of the sense of structure. For all the freedom the children enjoy, for all the ease and informality, for all the child-centeredness, there is no ambivalence about authority and no confusion about roles. "Children like to know where they stand and what to expect," the Plowden Committee remarks. "They must depend upon adults for their moral standards and for guidance on what behavior is tolerable in society; an adult who withholds such guidance is in fact making a decision which involves as heavy a claim for his own judgment as is made by the martinet. There may be occasions, as the children grow older, when such guidance ought to be withheld so that children can think out problems for themselves," the Committee adds, "but this only underlines the fact that the teacher has a crucial role to play at every point in the 'free' school."

ITEM: The teacher, noticing that a child has left the tape recorder after only two or three minutes, suggests that he return and listen to the entire story being played. "There are only four sets of earphones," she tells him, "and another child who wanted to listen wasn't able to because you asked first." Seeing that another child is about to leave the sandbox after just a few minutes, the teacher stops him. "I'd like to see what you made before you go on to something else," she tells him, and goes back to the sandbox with him. Later, when the child is out of earshot, she explains that he tends to flit from thing to thing and needs help in learning to stay with a game or task until he has accomplished or finished it.

ITEM: A child who has been seated at a table, writing, hurriedly leaves as she hears the call for physical education. "Come back, please, Michelle; your chair isn't put back," the teacher softly calls to her. "We don't have very many rules," the teacher tells the visitor, "but children must learn to look after the property and put things back where they belong."

The guidance extends to matters more important than taking care of property.

ITEM: A primary school in Oxfordshire. After the assembled children have sung a hymn—a morning worship service is mandatory in all English schools—the headmaster talks to them about the nature of prayer. "If we are praying—if we are asking for guidance, or saying thank you—does it mean someone is watching us?" he asks rhetorically. "I'd prefer to think we do things not because someone is watching us but because it's right —because we have a responsibility to others," he says in answer. "We are all two things: someone very special and different, and someone belonging to others."

The lesson is not only verbal, however. "It has long been characteristic of the English educational system that the teacher has been expected to carry the burden of teaching by example as well as by precept," the Plowden Committee says. "He is expected to be a good man and to influence children more by what he is than by what he knows or by his methods." A half-hour in the school makes it clear that this is such a man.

And yet control is rarely harsh or punitive. An American visitor is struck, for example, by the atmosphere of civility that prevails; teachers are as polite to the children as they are to the visitors, in contrast to the United States, where it is the exception to hear a teacher say "please" or "thank you" to a student. In large measure, of course, this atmosphere simply reflects the greater civility of English society as a whole; but the fact that corporal punishment is still widely used in formal English schools suggests that at least part of it must also stem from the more relaxed atmosphere of the informal school. Because control is exercised easily, moreover, teachers and heads in informal schools use their normal speaking voice when talking to the children, in contrast to formal teachers, who tend to adopt a special "teacher's voice" when addressing a class or an individual child. (Teachers' tendency to use their teacher's voice and manner with parents or other adults is a familiar irritant and a stock source of comedy.)

ITEM: The children in a London infant school are dispersing after the morning prayer session, chattering to each other as they walk away, arm in arm. The headmistress, a gentle and maternal woman, suddenly remembers something and calls out. "Oh children, I've forgotten to tell you, would you please tell your Mums . . ." The children immediately stop talking and walking and stand there, listening attentively. Professor Lillian Weber, reporting the incident, adds, "It is hard for me to imagine, in a parallel United States situation, so easily regaining the children's attention in midstream."

What impresses an American the most, however, is the combination of great joy and spontaneity and activity with equally great self-control and order. The joyfulness is pervasive: in almost every classroom visited, virtually every child appeared happy and engaged. One simply does not see bored or restless or unhappy youngsters, or youngsters with the glazed look so common in American schools.

The joy is matched by an equally impressive self-discipline and relaxed self-confidence. There seem not to be any disruptive youngsters or even restless youngsters in informal classrooms—indeed, few of the behavior problems with which American teachers are almost always coping. The reason has relatively little to do with the fact that British culture cultivates greater respect for authority,[17] for teachers in formal English classrooms have the same problems of maintaining control that American teachers do. Indeed, in every formal classroom that I went to visit in England, children were restless, were whispering to one another when the teacher was not looking, were ignoring the lesson or baiting the teacher or annoying other children— in short, behaving just like American youngsters. The formal classroom thus seems to produce its own discipline problems. It produces them by the unnatural insistence that children sit silently and motionless, by the unreasonable expectation that they will all be interested in the same thing at the same moment and for the same length of time, by the lack of trust the plethora of rules implies, which produces the misbehavior that is expected. It is not the children who are disruptive, it is the formal classroom that is disruptive—of childhood itself.

Because informal schooling, as the Plowden Committee puts it, is "ideally suited to the needs and nature of young children and to their development as human beings," maintaining discipline is no longer a problem. The self-fulfilling prophecy works both ways: the expectation that children will behave properly produces the expected behavior; given courteous treatment, the children respond in kind.

ITEM: An infant school in an abjectly poor, crime-ridden cockney slum in London. Until a new young head converted it to the free day approach, the school had been notorious for vandalism and disciplinary problems, having gone through four heads in four years. Eleven months after the new head had taken over, I did not see a single disruptive child in a half-day of classroom observations.

This is not to suggest that every English child is perfectly adjusted; the country has its share of emotionally disturbed children. But the warmth and concern and care of the infant schools, and their flexibility in handling children according to their own individual needs, seem to mitigate the behavior problems that disturbance produces.[18] Thus, while heads occasionally identified

[17] The cultural and institutional differences between England and the United States will be discussed in Chapter 7, when we turn to American applications.
[18] Cf. Alec Clegg and Barbara Megson, *Children in Distress,* Penguin Books, 1968.

children as having one or another emotional disturbance, I did not see disruptive behavior in any of the informal classrooms I visited. This was true in London, in schools in the aforementioned slum, in changing neighborhoods with a high immigrant population, and in wealthy South Kensington. It was true in Leicestershire County, in schools serving the most depressed housing projects, and in schools serving relatively prosperous artisan and white-collar neighborhoods. It was true in semi-rural Oxfordshire, in schools containing children of the indigenous rural population and of newly migrated factory workers; and it was true in the most depressed coal-mining towns of Yorkshire. In some schools, children were learning a great deal; in others they were learning very little; in all, they clearly were happy and engaged. This last point cannot be emphasized too strongly: while I saw "bad" informal schools—bad from the standpoint of their students' academic achievement—I saw none that were destructive, none in which the children did not appear to be happy and engaged.

The children's happiness is not coincidental; the reasons go to the heart of the informal approach. "All schools," as the Plowden Report suggests, "reflect the views of society, or of some section of society, about the way children should be brought up, whether or not these views are consciously held or defined." How those sections of English society represented in the Plowden Committee view children is reflected even in the way the Committee entitled its report. It did not call the document "English Primary Education" or "The Education of Primary School Children," but rather "Children and Their Primary Schools." In the title, as in the schools the Committee admired most, the children come first, and the schools are defined as theirs—not the teachers', nor the local education authorities', nor the taxpayers'. The orientation is explicit. "At the heart of the educational process lies the child," the Committee flatly states in its opening paragraphs.

Central to the informal English primary schools, then, is a view of childhood as something precious in its own right, something to be cherished for itself and not merely as preparation for later life: there is a quality of caring, a concern for children qua children, that tends to be missing in American schools. It is not that Americans like children less—certainly we indulge them more—but rather that we tend to see childhood as a corridor through which children should pass as rapidly as possible on the way to adulthood. Hence our schools are designed not to let children be children, but to speed them on the way to adult life.

The same is true, of course, in formal English schools, to an even greater extent than in the United States. It is not coincidental that informal methods developed first in schools in working-class rather than middle-class neighborhoods. Compared to the United States, the British have always sent a tiny proportion of their children on to higher education; even now, after two decades of democratization of higher education, only 6 or 7 percent of the age group goes to college, and only about 25 percent even finish secondary school. Since examinations have played a critical role in determining which students would go on to the university, schools serving a middle-class (and especially those serving an upper-middle-class) clientele have tended to be frozen into rigid, formal patterns by the pressures to prepare students for the selective examinations. Schools serving working-class children, on the other hand, most of whom would be expected to leave school at age fifteen, have been able to relax and teach their students as they think they *should* be taught, not as the examinations require.

Now, England is being buffeted by several cross currents. On the one hand, a slow but steady increase in the proportion of students going on to college or advanced technical training has increased the number of parents concerned with whether their children are being prepared for the next stage of the educational ladder. On the other hand, there has been a strong backlash against the infamous 11+ examination, given at the end of junior school to determine which students would be admitted to the college-preparatory grammar schools, which to the dead-end secondary modern schools.[19] The latter tendency appears to be stronger at the moment; a great many school districts have eliminated the 11+ exam altogether as part of the same process that has led to the extension of informal methods in the primary schools.

Indeed, the swing from formal to informal schooling involves fundamental changes not only in the view of childhood but in the definition of the purpose of education, and consequently of the nature of society itself. Nowhere is this revealed more clearly than in the grounds on which the opponents of informal education have attacked the primary schools. "The new fashionable

[19] For a devastating critique of the meritocratic pressures surrounding the 11+ and other selective exams, see Michael Young's reverse-utopian novel, *The Rise of the Meritocracy,* Baltimore, Md.: Penguin Books (A Pelican Book), 1961.

anarchy," as one group of polemicists call the informal approach, "flies in the face of human nature, for it holds that children and students will work from natural inclination rather than the desire for reward." This is precisely what informal educators do believe; they take an optimistic view of human nature, and they attempt (with striking success, as we shall see) to help children become autonomous, self-motivated, and self-directed learners. Informal educators also have an optimistic view of the human being's—*all* human beings'—capacity for growth and fulfillment, and therefore refuse to see their role as training people to fill the existing slots in society and the economy. For this, they have also been attacked. Thus, the anti free day polemicists deplore the fact that the English primary schools have moved away from the idea "that education exists to fit certain sorts of people for certain sorts of jobs, qualifications, and economic roles to the idea that people should develop in their own way at their own pace."[20]

In any case, most informal school teachers and heads do treat children as though they are children, and likely to remain so for some time to come. Children are expected to learn, to prepare to be productive and creative adults; but it is assumed that adulthood will come in due course, and soon enough, and that in the meantime, the children must be accepted and dealt with on their own terms. "What is central to education," Tom John, headmaster of the Tower Hill Primary School in Witney, Oxfordshire, argues, is "the caring, the general caring for the child. This means caring for his intellectual development, of course, because this is what school is all about. But it also means caring for the emotional and physical and spiritual sides as well. If you are concerned with the child as a person, you must be concerned with what *he* needs, not with what the school as an organization needs."

The result is an administrative flexibility that leaves an American visitor gasping: the informal primary schools really *are* run with the children's needs foremost. In part, to be sure, administrative flexibility is made possible by the fact that English heads enjoy a degree of autonomy unheard of in the United States, and in part by the fact that schools are small enough for the head to know all the children. But the heads of formal English primary schools enjoy the same autonomy in schools of the

[20] *Fight for Education: A Black Paper,* quoted in the *New York Times,* March 27, 1969.

same size without displaying the same flexibility. The critical factor clearly is the dominant concern for the needs of children in general and each child in particular.

ITEM: The phone rings in the office of the headmaster of a primary school serving a low-income housing project in a Leicestershire County factory town. At the other end is a social worker with a problem: two children from another community who will be staying with their grandmother for an indefinite period. It seems that the boys' father is in jail, and Mum just violated her parole, so that she has to return to jail; the boys have been farmed out to their grandmother, who lives in the school district, until Mum is sprung again. "Tell Grandmum to bring the boys here tomorrow," the head tells the social worker, "and if they like it here, let them stay until they go back home." The social worker explains that she does not have any transfer papers from the boys' own school district; the head assures her that no papers are needed—he will keep the boys as long as necessary.

ITEM: A visitor to an infant school in a wealthy London neighborhood, noticing a second adult working with the children, wonders if she is a teacher aide. She is not, although the school does have aides; the woman is the mother of a five-year-old who had displayed great anxiety when he started school the month before. "The little boy is overly attached to his mother and cried whenever he was dropped off at school, so we asked Mum if she wouldn't like to stay in the class with him until he felt secure enough to be on his own," the headmistress explains. At first the child insisted that Mum be in the room all the time; now he takes no note when Mum leaves with the teacher for the morning coffee break, lunch, and the afternoon break for tea, and the head thinks that in another week or so, he will feel safe enough for Mum to leave altogether. In the meantime, as long as the mother is there, the teacher has pressed her into service.

ITEM: In another London school, this one in a deteriorating neighborhood, a five-year-old comes up to a visitor to show him a picture he had made. After he leaves, the head observes that the boy is coming along nicely. It seems that when he began school the month before, the boy had shown very aggressive tendencies. Since Mum didn't work—she had other young children at home—the head suggested that the child try attending only in the mornings for a stretch; she suspected that the full day was proving too much of a strain for him. The remedy is working well; in another week or so, the head believes, the boy will be ready for all-day attendance.

This sort of flexibility is the rule, not the exception. A great many heads, for example, do not admit all the five-year-olds on the first day of the half-term, since no teacher can get to know that many youngsters at one time. Instead, admission is staggered over a period of several weeks, to make it easier for the teachers to get to know the children, and the children to know the teachers. In some schools, moreover, especially in working-class areas where many mothers work, children are welcomed whenever the parents want to drop them off. And so the children begin coming into the classrooms as early as 7 or 7:30 A.M.; the teachers arrive shortly before 9 A.M. In some of these schools, the caretaker is in charge until the teachers arrive; in others, a single teacher will be in charge, the teachers rotating that duty among themselves.

The children respond in kind, developing a capacity for self-control and self-direction that one rarely finds in children educated in formal schools. In most informal schools, for example, every teacher leaves the classroom at about 10:30 to go to the teacher's lounge, if there is one, or else to the head's office, for a fifteen-minute coffee break. In some schools, the children go out into the playground for a break of their own at this time, with just a single teacher or teacher aide stationed there in case a child might be injured or some other emergency arise. In other schools, the children remain in their classrooms, completely unsupervised. (Even the student teachers and teacher aides, if the school has them, leave for the coffee break.) In formal classrooms, a teacher's absence is usually the signal for spitballs, loud talking, running about the room, and the like. In informal classrooms, the children simply "carry on," in the English, not the American, sense of the term.

This self-control and autonomy are evident throughout the day.

ITEM: A junior school in Leicestershire County, serving a working-class and lower-middle-class neighborhood. A class of eight- and nine-year-olds, a happy, buzzing group, are returning to their room from physical education. A visitor engages the teacher in conversation as the children are putting their shoes and socks and clothes back on. (In infant and junior schools, boys and girls quite unselfconsciously strip down to their underwear for phys. ed.) The conversation continues for a while. Suddenly the visitor becomes aware that all thirty-eight children are busily at work: some are reading, some are writing essays and poems, some are filling in answers in workbooks; one cluster of youngsters are measuring one another's height and constructing graphs of the results; several others are in the science corner, performing an experiment.

The children's self-discipline and self-direction is accompanied by a relaxed and easy self-confidence; everywhere I went, the children were open and friendly without being brash. In a formal school, youngsters feel compelled to ignore a visitor, even when they know him; a few bold ones may smile shyly or venture a half-wave of the hand; most, if they feel free to acknowledge the visitor's presence at all, will do so with no more than a flicker of recognition in their eyes. None will talk to the visitor, and the visitor will feel constrained to keep silent, too.

In the informal English schools, by contrast, there was no room in which children did not come over to chat, to show the visitor a picture or a story, to ask quite unselfconsciously if he would like to hear them read or to see something they had made, or to inquire where he came from and how he had traveled and pardon me, sir, what was the airplane like?

ITEM: A classroom in a primary school in a bitterly impoverished Leicestershire slum. (The school serves an old low-income housing project that has more than its share of "multi-problem families.") A nine-year-old redhead, small for his age and wearing his poverty not only in his shabby clothes but in the sores on his body as well, comes over to tell the visitor that "Me brrrrutherrrr was marrried yesterrrrrday." The visitor offers congratulations. " 'Twasn't me what got married; 'twas me brrrrruth-errrrr," he responds, politely but firmly correcting what he considered her misunderstanding, and then proceeding to describe the wedding.

The contact is not only social; every adult in sight, as well as every bit of "stuff," is pressed into service as part of the learning environment. Without exception in informal classrooms, one child would come over to ask how to spell a word he needed in a story he was writing, another to ask for advice in a science experiment he was conducting, another for help in some contraption he was putting together, another to check an answer in maths.

ITEM: A classroom in an infant school in a pre-1900 building located in a deteriorating London slum; the school's population is 56 percent immigrant. A six-year-old is reading to the visitor, fluently and flawlessly, while two others are on the floor, measuring the length of the visitor's shoe, and then writing their finding in a little notebook. The two argue quietly about the proper measurement, and then refer the question to the visitor for arbitration.

Children feel free to use adults in this way in good measure because their teachers and heads encourage them to do so; they, too, regard anyone in sight as a potential source of learning.

ITEM: A brand-new infant school in Melton Mowbray in Leicestershire County in which painters, carpenters, electricians, et al., are still working all over the building. "You must love that!" the American visitor sardonically remarks to the head. "Oh, I do," she responds with animation, missing, or perhaps just ignoring, the sarcasm. "The children are fascinated by the workmen, and the workmen are interested in what the children are doing." Instead of being considered an intrusion, the workmen have been made part of the learning environment.

The children's poise thus is matched by the teachers'. In the United States, it is a rare school in which a visitor is permitted, let alone encouraged, to simply roam in and out of classrooms at will; it is an even rarer school in which a visitor is permitted to observe at all without prior notification to the teachers. Almost invariably, an American principal will give the visitor a schedule of which rooms he can visit at what hours, explaining that "It would be unfair to the teachers to let you come when they're not prepared," or perhaps that "Mrs. X has reading at 10 and Mrs. Y at 10:30, and we'd like you to see our reading program." And the visitor is careful to stay in the back of the room, as unobtrusively as possible, to avoid distracting the children. (In one school—one of the oldest and most prestigious progressive schools—the visitor is explicitly told not to talk either to the teacher or the children, to sit in the back of the room, and to leave no later than 11:45.) In England, by contrast, there was no informal school in which a visitor did not have carte blanche to roam freely and to talk to the children and the teachers.

IV

But how *do* the children learn, an American inevitably and quite naturally wants to know. Or as one American principal asked me, "How do the children get any work accomplished if they do nothing but play all day?" The question, and the view of education it reflects, is not unique to Americans; it is shared by formal educators in England, too. "There is a reason for coming to school, and that's work," a London head tartly remarked, indicating his disapproval of the very informal infant school across the playground from his junior school.

But play *is* a child's work; the distinction between work and play, so central to formal schooling, is not one that children make until adults force it upon them. On the contrary, play is one of the principal ways young children learn. In the words of the Plowden Report, "it is the way through which children reconcile their inner lives with external reality. In play, children gradually develop concepts of causal relationships, the power to discriminate, to make judgments, to analyze and synthesize, to imagine and to formulate. Children become absorbed in their play, and the satisfaction of bringing it to a satisfactory conclusion fixes habits of concentration which can be transferred to other learning."

It is a mistake, however, to assume children can learn through play alone, without any assistance or "teaching" by adults. On the contrary, children need feedback from people as well as things if their random play, their "messing around"—in early infancy, with movements of the eyes, hands, arms, legs, and with sounds, later on with objects, words, concepts—is to lead to more structured or purposeful activity. We are just beginning to appreciate the critical role the mother plays in language development, for example, and to understand that middle-class children's greater facility with language is the product, in large part, of the fact that middle-class mothers have more time for reciprocal play with their children than do lower-class mothers.

In a sense, teachers in informal classrooms do consciously and deliberately what mothers do unconsciously and more or less instinctively. The teacher's job, like the mother's, is to help children make the progression from purely random activity—messing around with blocks, paints, water, or sand, or imaginative or imitative play—to more structured and purposeful activity, and then to mastery through application. To do this, the teacher must know when to intervene and when to let the child alone, which is to say, she must always be aware and "at the ready"—aware not only of what each child is doing but of what he is *capable* of doing, and ready to use whatever teaching-learning opportunity presents itself. The opportunity grows out of the child's interests and activity; the learning stems from the teacher's responses to that activity. "The educator's task," as George Baines, headmaster of the Eynsham County Primary School in Oxfordshire, puts it, "is to maximize the occasion."

It is more than that. The teacher does not just maximize the occasion; he makes the occasion possible in the first place by the kind of environment he creates and maintains. "In a sense there is no spontaneity at all," says Mary Brown, headmistress of Sherard Infant School in Leicestershire County and co-author of *The Integrated Day in the Primary School,* "since we select the materials that are available. We are structuring all the time; that is what teaching is." Indeed, the informal classroom can be termed a formal situation, in the sense of having form and structure. To be sure, the form and structure do not stem from a lesson plan imposed and carried out with little regard for the widely varying interests, abilities, attention spans, and responses of individual children—the situation described in Chapter 4, which leads to the ultimate mindlessness of the teachers' lounge, the familiar complaint that "I taught them that material, all right, but they didn't learn it." The "formality" of the informal classroom grows out of the fact that the teacher creates a highly structured environment, organized around a space rather than a time framework, and then manages it so that it changes in response to children's interests, activities, and needs. In their practice, then, if not always in their rhetoric, most informal teachers and heads reject the romantic notion that children should simply be turned loose to do their own thing.

Not all teachers and heads, however. The child-centeredness of the free day classroom creates a certain risk that teachers may interpret their role in completely passive terms and thus sit back and allow children to be "free," avoiding what they regard as the arbitrary imposition of adult values. When this happens, as it sometimes does, the result is a familiar kind of self-conscious anti-intellectualism.

ITEM: "The children don't have any reading problem," the head of a primary school serving a particularly impoverished Leicestershire County neighborhood tells the visitor with studied casualness. "It's the teachers who have the reading problem." What he means is that it is the teachers and not the children who are bothered by the children's inability to read; only when the teachers relay their feelings of disappointment and concern do the children become troubled, he insists. But the teachers *should* be troubled; the reading level is woefully poor, i.e., roughly comparable to what one would find in an average American slum school. (Unlike the American school, however, the children in this school seem happy and content.)

This kind of latitudinarian approach to learning appears to be more widespread among younger heads, whose whole experience has been in informal schools, than among the oldtimers, almost all of whom began as formal teachers. There is a danger, therefore—small but real—that the free day movement may in time repeat some of the mistakes of the American progressives of the 1920s and '30s.

Most teachers and heads, however, are aware of the danger. They recognize that to pretend that the teacher's job is to let the child follow his own interests and develop his own talents and capacities without imposition of any adult values is in fact to *prevent* the child from realizing his own nature. For the child is not an atom freely floating about without any relationship to the adult world; he is a part of that world, with its values, its past, and its present. One grows as a human being only by incorporating knowledge gained from others—teachers, parents, grandparents, friends, relatives—as well as that gained through one's own explorations.

Without such knowledge, moreover, the young are condemned to helplessness, forced to rediscover all knowledge for themselves. While "the sense of personal discovery influences the intensity of a child's experience, the vividness of his memory, and the probability of effective transfer of learning," the Plowden Committee observes, there is also a danger that if left too much to their own devices, children may discover only the trivial, the inefficient, or the incorrect. Equally important, the Committee argues, "time does not allow children to find their way by discovery to all that they have to learn."

There are some things, moreover, that children are not likely to be able to discover for themselves. "A child can write the letters t-h-e in sand or blood," a Leicestershire head observes, "but he'll never know they spell the word 'the' until someone tells him." While children can learn many mathematical principles through their own play and discovery, another head remarks, you simply cannot see "place value"[21] in the natural world, yet an understanding of the concept is crucial if children are to really understand addition and subtraction. Hence the teacher must structure it artificially, e.g., through the use of Dienes blocks.

And so most informal teachers and heads also reject the view that "one piece of learning is as good as any other." Their responsibility, as they see it, is to create an environment that will stimulate children's interest in and evoke their curiosity about all the things they *should* be interested in and curious about: reading, writing, talking, counting, weighing, measuring; art, music, dance, sculpture; the beauty and wonder of the world about them; relationships with adults and with other children; and above all, the process of learning itself. "The object of teaching," says Sir Alec Clegg, "is not so much to convey knowledge as it is to excite a determination in the child to acquire it for himself, and to teach him how to go about acquiring it."

It is also to teach the child to know what is worth knowing; there is remarkably little obfuscation among teachers and heads about their responsibility to help children learn to discriminate between the valuable and the meretricious. One of the most significant aspects of the change in primary education, as the Plowden Committee observes, "is the increasing attention given by teachers to the worth of what is taught and to the quality of the children's learning."

Most teachers in the informal schools visited, for example, were not just concerned with giving their students proficiency in the technical skills and mechanics of reading. They are equally interested in what the children use their proficiency for, and in the pleasure they derive from it. "Reading for what?" the head of a London infant school asks. "If my children get perfect reading scores and then grow up to read only the tabloids and movie magazines," she answers, "I shall have failed. My job is to develop attitudes and values as well as skills—to make

---

[21] "Place value" is the value accorded a digit by its location in a numeral, e.g., in the numeral 111, the first "1" has a value of 100; the second, a value of 10; and the third, a value of 1.

music, art, poetry, beauty, experiences they will enjoy throughout their lives. I don't want to develop a generation of proficient
readers who lack humane values."

These broad interests and concerns are reflected in the way
children learn to read and write in informal schools. The
process begins with the conviction that since children have no
inborn impulse to read, school must create an environment that
will evoke it, that will make them *want* to read and write. "Interest can be a driving power," Nora L. Goddard writes, "and
we try to get the child's absorption in what he sees and does to
overflow into reading and writing about those things. In this way
the driving force of his interest will help him through the first
steps of reading."[22]

But first the child must be comfortable with language. Hence
children are encouraged to talk, to communicate with each
other and the adults around them about the things that interest
and engage them. The incredible richness and variety of stuff
in the classroom and the great diversity of activities going on
at once provide that encouragement. Indeed, in an environment
in which so many people are doing so many different things,
communication almost becomes a necessity; how else would anyone know what you are doing? And the teachers make it clear
that they *want* to know what the children are doing, what they
are thinking, how they feel, and so on. A silent classroom, they
patiently tell American visitors, is the worst possible preparation
for learning to read and write.

Infant school headmistresses play a particularly important
role in encouraging and facilitating this free and easy conversation. English heads are regarded, and regard themselves, as head
teachers, not administrators, and they seem to spend the bulk
of their time in the classrooms, watching, listening, talking to
the children, helping the teachers with a suggestion, taking a
few children aside for some help, etc. It is a rare head, at least
in informal schools, who does not seem to know every child,
and to know a great deal about every child, e.g., this boy just
returned from a visit with Grandmum, this child comes from a
broken home, that lad is shy and needs help coming out and
this one tends to be too aggressive, this youngster just got a new
puppy, etc. In part, perhaps, because her presence is occasional

[22] Nora L. Goddard, *Reading in the Modern Infant School*, University of
London Press, second edition, 1964; Cf. also L. G. W. Sealey and Vivian
Gibbon, *Communication and Learning in the Primary School*, Oxford:
Basil Blackwell, 1963; and Lillian Weber, *The English Infant School*.

rather than constant, but in good measure because the children clearly want her to know what they are doing, want to see her enthusiasm or receive her praise, the children seem particularly eager to talk to her, to show her their painting, or their sand castle, or the dress they have sewn, or the poem they have written. Even when she sits in her office, there is a steady traffic of children coming to talk, to read to her, to ask a question or sometimes just to curl up in a corner in her office for a little solitude.

Getting children to talk about themselves and their activities is not enough, however. If richness and subtlety of language is an objective, their relatively limited experiences must be extended and supplemented. The teachers do this in a variety of ways. They read to the children with great frequency, sometimes to small groups of children, sometimes to the class as a whole. (Most infant school teachers, for example, seem to end the day, and many the morning as well, with a story.) They take the children on trips—nature walks, trips to the train station, or to a historic church or castle, or to the city hall. This is a familiar enough practice to American primary teachers, but the English seem to take trips with far greater frequency. More important, the trips are used as a springboard for every kind of classroom activity: conversation about the trip, making a drawing, painting, or sculpture about it, constructing something with "junk" or building something with blocks, and ultimately, when children have gained the skill, writing a story or poem about the trip.

ITEM: A class of eight-year-olds in a junior school in Leicestershire. On one wall is a large mural, entitled "Our Nature Walk." The grass, road, and sky are painted; the shrubbery consists of bits of hawthorne, thistle, rose hips, dog daisy, pine needles and cones, which have been pasted on; crepe paper butterflies are flying about. Next to the mural is a display of stories and essays about the nature walk, which had been taken the week before.

ITEM: An infant school in a bleak London slum. In the large hall, a group of five-year-olds are making an enormous train, complete with dining car, sleeping car, locomotive, and caboose. (The day before, they had made an expedition to one of the London railroad stations to see and go through a train; their interest had been aroused by an earlier trip to a museum which had had an exhibition on trains.) As they put the train together, the teacher engages them in conversation about what they are doing, what they had seen at the station, and so on.

Once a child is comfortable with language, the next step in teaching him how to read is to get him writing—to get him writing something *he* wants to say. Art, a major activity, often provides the opening wedge. When a teacher thinks a child is ready to start writing, she may admire a picture he is drawing and ask him what he wants to call it, or whether he would like to write something about it. If the child responds affirmatively, she will write what he dictates in large letters under the picture, e.g., "Me and Mum," "My house," "I had a party," and the child will then copy the words (*his* words, remember) letter by letter, directly under the teacher's writing. If the child lacks the co-ordination to copy, the teacher will help him trace over her letters. Later, the teacher will help him read back what he has written, to help him understand that these strange symbols communicate something he wants to say. The process continues, the rate depending on the child's interest and ability. As a rule, children begin dictating monosyllabic sentences ("Me and Mum"), move on to whole sentences ("I had a party"), and then start putting two or more sentences together ("I had a birthday party. My friends came and brought presents").

At some point, the child will begin writing in his notebook, putting down measurements he has made, describing something he has built with blocks or made with junk, describing a trip he has taken or a party he has gone to, or whatever happens to interest him. He may begin doing this on his own initiative or as a result of some gentle prodding from the teacher; or he may be trying to imitate one of the older or more advanced children in his class. Many infant and junior schools use what the English call vertical or family grouping in which children of several age levels are grouped together in a single class. Older children thus can serve as models for the younger ones, and can also provide some of the instruction—a device that not only helps the younger ones learn, but also enables the older ones to test their own knowledge in action.[23]

When writing begins in this way, the child probably will have to ask the teacher, or a teacher aide, or an older or more ad-

[23] The approach has disadvantages, too, and some schools have moved toward a modified form of family grouping in which the youngsters who will be moving on to the junior school, or from the junior school to secondary school, are grouped separately.

vanced child, to show him how to write what he wants to say, and he will then copy the letters below. As he progresses, he will write what he wants to say on his own, asking someone for help only if there is a word he doesn't know. In either case, however, he is writing what *he* wants to say, not what someone has told him to say.

In most schools, a child at this stage will have his own "word book," a blank notebook he turns into a dictionary of the words he likes to use. In addition, most teachers will make up word books for the whole class, hanging them on a wall or placing them on a table in the appropriate interest area—one may have pictures and names of musical instruments; another, "words we use for weighing and measuring"; another, pictures and names of members of the family and household objects (Mum, Dad, Grandmum, Grandpa, house, dog, cat, broom, television, radio) —so that children not yet able to use a dictionary may nonetheless find out how to write and spell the words they need.

Formal instruction is not dispensed with entirely. While the approach varies from school to school, and even sometimes from classroom to classroom within a given school, most teachers and heads agree that children need *some* training and drill in phonics and the other fundamentals of reading and writing if they are to be able to read the unfamiliar, though they tend to postpone such teaching longer and do less of it than most American teachers would think desirable.

Instruction in phonics and other reading skills is provided in a variety of ways. Most classes have all sorts of word and letter games that children may play with on their own or with the teacher or with an older child. Whether the traditional series of graded readers and workbook readers is used depends on the taste of the teacher and on her assessment of the child's own needs. "Some children may need the security of a graded series of readers and some may not," Mary Brown tells her faculty. "It is the teacher who must decide this," taking into consideration the interests of the particular child, but also the need *all* children have to make quick progress, to gain a sense of competence and achievement. ("Help should be fairly intensive or he will lose enthusiasm if learning to read becomes too drawn out a process and he does not feel success.") Some teachers may need the graded readers, too, feeling more comfortable with the structure they provide.

Instruction in phonics is carried on informally, too. A child may be looking at a book, for example, or at a caption a friend has written on a picture, and discover that the first letter of his name is the same as the first letter of the friend's name. If the teacher is there, she may remark, "Yes, that says *Mmmm* for Michael, and that says *Mmmm* for Mary; what else can you think of that begins with *Mmmm?*" She may ask him to think of proper names, of objects, of places, or suggest he find words in his book beginning with *M*. And so it goes.

Whatever the method of instruction, most classrooms are suffused with a wide variety of reading matter. "Among the most welcome changes which have accompanied the growing informality of the primary school," the Plowden Committee observes, "has been the move away from categories of books, each confined to a special time and purpose. In many schools there are now no longer class readers, supplementary readers, group readers, text books and library books: though library books were often the most exacting and rewarding of all, they were frequently relegated to odd moments when other tasks were finished." Now, by contrast, "there are simply books— to be used as and when they are needed."[24] One of the main uses is to read aloud—to the teacher, to the head, to other children, and to any visitor who will listen.

Reading is not confined to books, however, by any means. As soon as children gain some competence, they are likely to be reading all the time. Almost every object in the room is labeled. More important, reading and writing are integrated into virtually every classroom activity.

ITEM: A science corner in a Leicestershire infant school. On the table are a series of "Experiment Cards," or 7″ x 9″ cardboard instruction sheets. Two six-year-olds are studying one of the cards, which has a picture of an experiment along with the following instructions:

Things you will need:

a bucket
a balloon

---

[24] Most schools also have a central library to which children generally are permitted to come at will. For the most part, these libraries are also attractive and inviting. It probably was not entirely coincidental, therefore, that the Leicestershire school described above, in which the reading level was so markedly poor, had a big sign in its library reading "Make sure your hands are clean before you touch the books." In contrast to most schools visited, the library here was empty the entire day.

a bottle
warm water

Things to do:

1. Fit the balloon over the neck of the bottle.
2. Pour some warm water into the bucket.
3. Now place the bottle into the bucket.
4. What happens to the balloon? If you'd like, write it down
   in your notebook.

The cards thus serve a quadruple function: they provide practice in reading; they provide instruction in science; they make it possible for children to do all this on their own initiative, without having to wait for the teacher to tell them what to do; and they provide practice in writing as well.

ITEM: The maths corner in a Yorkshire infant school classroom, with a number of signs on the wall near the scales. One chart is headed, "Words to use when you are weighing." The words include "sponge," with a small piece of sponge pasted next to it; "feather," with a feather pasted next to it; "shell," with a shell pasted next to it, and so on; other words, with appropriate objects, are "cotton reel" (from a spool of thread), "stick," "bean." Another chart has a series of questions: "Which is the biggest group?" "Can you find the smallest group?" and so on.

Even activities we normally think of as "play"—activities we consider appropriate to nursery school and perhaps to the beginning of the kindergarten year, but inappropriate for the first grade and beyond—are structured to provide a great deal of experience in the three R's.

ITEM: An infant school classroom in Oxfordshire. The sandbox is standing next to the maths area, which is set apart from the rest of the room by a room divider with shelves on one side. The shelves are filled with maths stuff: seven bottles of different sizes, a jug of rulers, a cup of beans, some giant and medium-sized dice, books about numbers, telling time, etc., and a set of work cards. A boy takes out a work card and proceeds to follow its directions, which read as follows:

Fill the red mug with sand. Guess what it weighs.
Now weigh it.

Write down how much it weighs.
Draw a picture of the mug.

Another youngster is sitting at the table, following the instructions of a card that reads:

Draw a milk crate.
Measure the milk crate.
How long is it?
How wide is it?

ITEM: The cooking corner in a primary school in Oxfordshire, complete with sink, stove, cupboard, counter, mixing bowls and spoons, baking pans, measuring spoons and pitchers, scales, etc., along with a large chart with the names and pictures of the various implements and ingredients. Five children, reading a recipe card, are busy measuring, weighing, and mixing ingredients for a cake they are about to bake, with an occasional assist from a teacher.

ITEM: The water table in a London infant school. Several children are playing, following the instructions on one of the series of "Water Cards." The card reads:

1. Fill a 1 pint bottle.
2. How many 1 pint bottles of water will you need to fill the ½ gallon measure?
3. Fill a ⅓ pint bottle.[25]
4. How many ⅓ pint bottles will you need to fill a pint bottle?

Other children are also playing at the water table, but they ignore the cards, perhaps because they cannot read, perhaps because at this moment they just feel like messing around with the water, pouring it from one container to another and enjoying its feel on their hands.

Almost all the stuff in the classroom can be used in this way, over and over again at different levels of sophistication and learning. Children thus are able to keep coming back to the same materials as their understanding increases.

ITEM: A classroom in a Leicestershire infant school, as the children stroll back from gym. A freckle-faced five-year-old

---

[25] The morning milk children in English infant schools receive comes in one-third pint bottles, rather than the half-pint containers Americans are used to.

boy starts to work at the science table, filling a dish with water and inserting a candle upright, securing it in place with some plasticene. He then strikes a big kitchen match, ignoring the American visitor's only half-suppressed "Be careful!" He lights the candle, admiring the flame for a bit, and then places an empty jar over the candle until the flame goes out. He repeats the "trick," as he calls it, several times, filled with awe at the "magic" he has wrought. After the third or fourth time, he is joined by a serious-looking six-year-old, who looks for the appropriate instruction card, reads it, and then proceeds to find a stopwatch somewhere on the table. Then, very systematically, after gravely explaining to his young friend that "this is an experiment, not a trick," he lights the candle, places the jar over it, and uses the stopwatch to check how long it takes for the flame to go out. He repeats the experiment with jars of different sizes, counting the number of seconds with each size, and writing the results in his notebook.

ITEM: A primary school in Oxfordshire, in which children five to nine are in the same class, vertically grouped. There is a steady flow of children to the science corner to see Thumper, the rabbit. The younger children come to pet the rabbit, the older children to measure Thumper's body (fifteen inches in length), his ears (five inches long, one inch wide), and to write the measurements in their notebooks. The more sophisticated are keeping a chart of Thumper's growth.

The stimulation is provided by the children as well as the teachers; in maths, in particular, children love to make up problems for their classmates to do.

ITEM: The maths corner of a junior school in Leicestershire County. The table contains a variety of balance scales and boxes containing acorns, seeds, blackberries, crab apples and other stuff. Hanging up is a large graph, signed by three girls, with the legend:

> Our graph shows how many berries and nuts weigh one ounce.
> Can you answer these questions?
>   Which is the heaviest seed?
>   Which is the lightest seed?
>   Which is heavier, a blackberry or an acorn?
>   How many strawberries weigh ½ ounce?

How many crab apples weigh two ounces?
Make up some problems of your own.

And always the children are writing! "Perhaps the most dramatic of all the revolutions in English teaching is in the amount and quality of children's writing," the Plowden Committee observed. "In the thirties, independent writing in the infant school and lower junior school rarely extended beyond a sentence or two and the answering of questions, and for the older children it was usually a weekly or fortnightly composition on prescribed topics only too frequently repeated year by year." Now, anything and everything the child does may provide the occasion for an essay, story, or poem. Writing is no longer a "subject" to be studied for thirty minutes a day; it is a form of communication that pervades the entire curriculum. At first, the teacher suggests that the child write about what he has just done, that he translate one form of communication into another. And so the notebooks are filled—with the measurements a child has taken, the counting he has done, an account of a trip he has gone on, a castle he has built with sand or blocks, a game he has played, emotions he has felt, an experiment he has performed. The amount of writing the children do is staggering by American standards; the quality is even more impressive.

ITEM: A class of eight- to ten-year-olds in a Leicestershire primary school. A ten-year-old boy shows the visitor a poem he has written, which reads as follows (spelling as in the original):

The Beach

As I walk along the pebble-stricken beach
I hear my mind talking to me
Sea gulls garralously chirp into my blank imagination
The sea talks to the wind
But not to me.
I call myself an empty shell.

In the margin, the teacher has written some comments: "I think these last three poems are the best you have written. I hope you are proud of them; I think I would if I had written them.

"Look at your latest poem, 'The Beach.' Can you explain 'pebble-stricken beach'? Why do you call yourself 'an empty shell'? I should be interested to read what you have to say." Underneath the teacher's question, the boy has written, "I think the last three poems were my best. The reason I call myself an empty shell is plainly to capture the feeling that a lonely wonder filled man would have."

ITEM: An infant school in an upper-middle-class London neighborhood. The visitor admires an apron a six-year-old girl is making. A bit later, she trots over to show him the finished product, announcing, "Now I want to write about the apron." The visitor catches the hint, sits down, and writes as the girl dictates, "Today I made a beautiful apron." The teacher comes by as the girl is copying the sentence and asks if she would like to make a picture of the apron, too. "No, I only want to write," the girl responds.

ITEM: An infant school in a coal-mining town in Yorkshire. From the notebook of a six-year-old girl (spelling and punctuation as in the original):

> This is a seed and it is growing. It is me and Julies and I've got two and shes only got one. We had to plant it and put some water on it. Only a little bit of water. When it grew it got bigger and bigger and its nice. It grew a root and a shoot. The root is white and it is growing down. The shoot is green and it is growing up. The roots are down in the earth.
>
> Eleanor.

Particularly creative teachers and heads provide all sorts of props and stuff to stimulate the imagination, open the senses, and provide opportunities for writing.

ITEM: An infant school classroom in London. Hanging on a wall is a homemade scrapbook entitled "Things we like doing in the rain." The pages have been filled in by various children who drew a picture and/or wrote a caption: "Dancing through the puddles," "Letting the rain tickle my hand," "Letting the rain run down my boots," "Wearing Dad's hat and splashing through puddles," "Bouncing a football in the puddles," etc.

ITEM: A room in a Leicestershire junior school. In a corner somewhere is a table containing a piece of fur, a stick, a variety of pebbles, stones and rocks, and other objects, and a sign reading:

> *Look* at these objects.
> Think about one object.
> Now can you write a story?

There are times, of course, when the prompting can get heavy-handed and so cause children to resist. There can be something deadening in the picture always accompanied by a caption, the experiment always described in the notebook, the class news book always filled out whether there is anything to be said or not. Almost every head tells of having had the experience, in her early years of using informal methods, of approaching a child who was building something with blocks (or sand, or junk, or what have you), only to have the child knock the whole thing down and exclaim, "Now you can't ask me to write about it." Enough such experiences, the heads explain, and a teacher begins to learn when she is pushing too hard.

There are other times, of course, when children, in their wonderfully perverse way, reject even the subtlest attempt to use their play for some kind of learning the teacher has in mind.

ITEM: A primary school in Oxfordshire. In the Wendy House area, a boy and a girl are playing Mum and Dad having babies, using two dolls. The head, taking the visitor around, sees a splendid teaching-learning opportunity and asks, "Where did the babies come from?" "Oh, out of the cupboard over there," comes the answer. End of lesson.

v

"Education," Sir Herbert Read has written, "may be defined as the cultivation of modes of expression—it is teaching children and adults how to make sounds, images, movements, tools and utensils."[26] Most informal schools operate on this definition. The emphasis on communication extends beyond reading, writing, and talking to painting, drawing, sculpting, dancing, crafts—to all the forms of nonverbal expression. The arts "are not 'frills' but essentials just as much as the 3 Rs," John Blackie writes in *Inside the Primary School*. "Everything that we know about human beings generally, and children in particular, points to the importance of the arts in education. They are the language of a whole range of human experience and to neglect them is to neglect ourselves."

The Plowden Committee was even more explicit. "Art is both a form of communication and a means of expression of feeling

[26] Herbert Read, *Education Through Art*, London: Faber and Faber, 1958.

which ought to permeate the whole curriculum and life of the school," the Committee declared. "A society which neglects or despises it is dangerously sick. It affects, or should affect, all aspects of our life from the design of the commonplace articles of everyday life to the highest forms of individual expression."

And so it does. An American visitor is inevitably struck, for example, by the fact that there are flowers everywhere—in the entrance to the school, in the hall, in the head's office, and in every classroom. ("Every school is a warmer and more congenial place for the presence of flowers," Sir Alec Clegg has written.) There literally was not a school I visited, and this in October and November, that did not have flowers about—something one rarely sees in American schools—as well as attractive arrangements of autumn leaves, pine cones, acorns, and other local flora. Yet the flowers were very much taken for granted. I frequently asked, for example, who was responsible for the arrangements gracing the entrance hall. The question always took people by surprise; no one was "responsible," as such.

The concern for beauty was not limited to the floral arrangements; in the Plowden Committee's phrase, it permeated the life of almost every informal school visited. There are displays of the children's art everywhere—the freest and most imaginative kinds of paintings, murals, collages, illustrated stories, etc.

ITEM: An infant school in Melton Mowbray, a lower-middle-class and upper-working-class neighborhood in Leicestershire County. On a classroom wall is a collage—a piece of white oaktag, attached to the middle of which is a long piece of string, artfully coiled into an ever-widening series of concentric circles. In one corner of the oaktag is the legend, "I am six and I go 34 times along the string"; in another corner, the legend, "the string fits around two sides of the playground"; in another, "we have made string as long as a rocket and it is as long as the school."

ITEM: A primary school in Oxfordshire. In one classroom, there is a large wall mural, called "The Bottom of the Sea"—a collage of fishes made of old pieces of fabric, seaweed, sand, and shells, among other things, with a wide variety of textures and colors. On another wall is a collage of butterflies and fish, made out of multicolored crumpled tissue paper.

ITEM: A classroom in a school in a coal-mining town in Yorkshire. On one wall there is a large and striking mural of dinosaurs, made out of egg crates painted green and studded with little silver foil milk-bottle caps.

It wasn't always thus. Thirty or forty years ago, in fact, art instruction in English primary schools was much the same as it is in American schools today: the arid copying of objects and pictures, with every child drawing nearly identical flowers, trees, fruit, pumpkins, turkeys, Christmas trees, etc. The change began in the 1920s and '30s, under the influence of a few outstanding teachers, who substituted large sheets of kitchen paper and large brushes for the pencils, crayons, and small sheets of drawing paper the children had been using, and who turned the children free to paint whatever and however they wished. The results demonstrated that young children have far greater artistic potential than had been realized, and that it was the schools themselves, with their sterile formalism, that was destroying this native talent.

The most striking example of education as "the cultivation of modes of expression" is an activity that has no counterpart in American schools—something the English call "Movement," with a capital "M." One of the important aspects of the growth of informal education, the Plowden Committee writes, "has been the increasing recognition of the place of expressive movement in primary education. Children have a great capacity to respond to music, stories, and ideas, and there is a close link through movement, whether as dance or drama, with other areas of learning and experience— with speech, language, literature, and art as well as with music."

In its most fundamental sense, Movement is an attempt to educate children in the use of their bodies—to provide them with an ease, grace, and agility of bodily movement that can carry over into sports, crafts, and dance. "How many of us feel awkward, clumsy, self-conscious and embarrassed if we are called upon to perform any movement to which we are not accustomed?" John Blackie writes in *Inside the Primary School,* in a chapter interestingly entitled "Body and Soul." "How many of us have watched with envy the apparently effortless ease with which expert riders, skiers, fencers, divers, dancers, potters, woodcutters, etc., move their bodies and compared it with our own ineptitude?"

The procedure is a fascinating blend of formal and informal instruction. As a rule, an entire class participates under the teacher's direction; but precisely *how* the teacher's directions are carried out is left to each child. There is, after all, no right way or wrong way to move as if you were a snowflake, or a leaf fluttering down from a tree, which are the kinds of things children may be asked to do. The purpose, as the Plowden Committee explains it, is "to develop each child's resources as fully as possible through exploratory stages and actions which will not be the same for any two children. When these ends are pursued successfully," the Committee continues, "the children are able to bring much more to any situation than that which is specifically asked of them; the results transcend the limits of what can be prescribed or 'produced,' and lead to a greater realization of the high potential of young children."

A Movement lesson may be concerned with agility on the physical education apparatus, with skills in handling balls and other athletic apparatus, or with expressive movement of a dramatic and dancelike quality; the latter is what we are concerned with here. Barefoot and stripped to their underwear, the children assemble in the hall to learn to communicate through bodily movement—to express the whole range of feelings and emotions through the use of their hands, arms, heads, legs, torsos, and to do so with agility and ease and without self-consciousness or embarrassment.

ITEM: A junior school in the West Riding of Yorkshire. A class of ten- and eleven-year-old boys and girls, most of them the children of coal miners, are taking a class in Movement. The teacher, with tweed suit and British walking shoes, looking like the American stereotype of a British headmistress, calls out the directions; their execution is left to each child's imagination and ability. "Move about in a small circle, as if your body were very heavy. . . . Move about in a small circle as if your body were very light. . . . Move very quickly. . . . Move very slowly. . . . Now find a partner and make your movements in response to his, so that you are aware of what he or she is doing as well as what you are doing. . . . Speed the movements up. . . . Slow them down. . . . Make them sharp and jerky. . . . Move only your arms and body above the waist; move as if you felt very sad. . . . Move only your fingers, hands and arms, as though they were very sad. . . . Now move them as though they were very happy. . . . Find a partner and move your fingers, hands, and arms as though you were talking to each other. . . . Move about the room as though you were a butterfly. . . . Move about the room as though you were an elephant. . . . Move about in your own space as though you were a snowflake. . . . Stay in the space around you, but try to use all of it, close to the floor, above your head. . . ." All this without music, then repeated with music of various kinds. (This same school, incidentally, has the best rugby team for miles around.)

ITEM: A Movement class in an infant school in Bristol. A class of six- and seven-year-olds is performing a ballet of their own invention about a trip through outer space; they use only their own bodies and a few percussion instruments. One child is the earth, another the moon, several are stars. Several rocket ships go into orbit. A number of children are clouds, which at one point converge in a thunderstorm, which almost, but not quite, downs one of the rocket ships.

And so it goes; the specific approach and teaching technique varies from school district to school district and from school to school, depending on the tastes and talents of the teachers and heads and the influence of the local inspectors and advisors. But almost always, the children, except for an occasional shy or chubby or clumsy youngster, move with a marvelous grace and ease and apparent total lack of self-consciousness. The experience brings to mind Lillian Smith's haunting evocation of Martha Graham dancing:

> Sometimes as I have sat in the audience watching Martha Graham dance, it has seemed to me as if she were unwrapping our body image which has been tied up so long with the barbed wires of fear and guilt and ignorance, and offering it back to us: a thing of honor. Freeing, at last, our concept of Self. Saying to us, The body is not a thing of danger, it is a fine instrument that can express not only today's feeling and act, but subtle, archaic experiences, memories which words are too young in human affairs to know the meaning of.[27]

The advocates of Movement are persuaded that the activity has a profound effect on other activities. "You don't dance to get rid of something, you dance to be aware of something," Martha Graham says, and the awareness that Movement evokes seems to carry over into the children's writing, painting, and sculpture.

ITEM: An infant school in an impoverished London slum. The visitor admires the sensitivity of the poetry these cockney boys

[27] Lillian Smith, *The Journey,* New York: W. W. Norton, 1954.

are writing. "A child who has moved like a snowflake or a falling leaf is bound to write more sensitively," the headmistress explains. "He knows how it *feels* to be a snowflake or a leaf." He also knows that sensitivity to feelings and awareness of beauty are neither effeminate nor effete. The visitor wonders what it might mean for the quality of American life if this kind of schooling were widespread in the United States.

VI

To evaluate a "seminal innovation" in education, John Goodlad warns, "the researcher simply cannot go in with his stable research—his conventional criteria, his timeworn measures—and expect to contribute to the advancement of educational practice and science. By doing so, he endangers both." What the researcher must do, Goodlad argues, is "come to grips with the conceptual underpinnings of the innovation," for if it is truly radical, it will have objectives the conventional instruments of evaluation simply are not designed to measure.[28]

Indeed, the conventional instruments are usually grossly inadequate for evaluating even relatively minor innovations. "Education has many purposes, and any learning experience must be judged in terms of all those goals," Professor Lee J. Cronbach of Stanford writes. "To take a simple example, there must exist some method of teaching arithmetic that produces graduates who compute brilliantly—and who hate all work involving numbers. It would be improper to advocate the method," Cronbach continues, "on the basis of research that considers only its effect on computational skill. It is no defense for the advocate to say that computation is the only objective that concerns *him*. If he recommends an educational change, it is his responsibility to consider how that change will affect all the outcomes that reasonable men consider important."[29]

How, then, evaluate the informal English schools? Certainly they represent a seminal innovation, and the usual instruments of evaluation—standardized tests in reading, mathematics, and

[28] John Goodlad, "Thought, Invention, and Research in the Advancement of Education," in Committee for Economic Development, *The Schools and the Challenge of Innovation,* Supplementary Paper No. 28, 1969.
[29] Lee J. Cronbach, "The Logic of Experiments on Discovery," in Lee S. Shulman and Evan R. Keislar, eds., *Learning by Discovery,* Chicago: Rand McNally, 1966.

the like—measure only a small, albeit important, part of what they are trying to do.

ITEM: An American visitor asks the Education Officer of a large English school district, a man known for his passionate advocacy of informal education, whether he has any statistics on student achievement that might permit comparisons between informal and formal methods of schooling. "Here are the statistics," he says, as he opens an enormous leather portfolio lying on his conference table. The portfolio contains samples of paintings, drawings, collages, embroideries, poems, stories, and essays from schools in his district.

The Education Officer has a point. He wants his students to develop competence in reading, writing, and maths, of course. But he also seeks competence in painting, dancing, sculpting, athletics, and crafts. Equally important, his objectives go beyond competence. He wants to evoke joy in learning, excitement in reading and writing, pleasure in painting, dancing, and computing, a sense of wonder and curiosity about science and nature, ease in relationships with peers and with elders, self-confidence, and self-direction. Some of these can be measured with ease, some with difficulty, and some cannot be measured at all.

John Dewey spoke to the point more than forty years ago. "Even if it be true that everything which exists could be measured—if only we knew how," he told the Progressive Education Association in 1928, "that which does *not* exist cannot be measured. And it is no paradox to say that the teacher is deeply concerned with what does not exist. For a progressive school is primarily concerned with growth, with a moving and changing process, with *transforming* existing capacities and experiences; what already exists by way of native endowment and past achievement is subordinate to what it may become. Possibilities," he continued, "are more important than what already exists, and knowledge of the latter counts only in its bearing upon possibilities."[30] [Emphasis in the original]

Still, evaluations must be made. For forty years or more, critics of informal education, in England as well as the United

[30] John Dewey, "Progressive Education and the Science of Education," reprinted in Martin S. Dworkin, ed., *Dewey on Education,* New York: Teachers College Press (Classics in Education No. 3), 1959.

States, have charged that informality and joyousness are provided at the expense of learning the three R's in the primary grades and subject-matter in the later years. Hence parents may justifiably wonder and worry whether their children's future academic or vocational success may be harmed by informal education.

The answer would appear to be no. The most striking piece of evidence, perhaps, is the fact, as the Plowden Committee puts it, that "despite the dismal reports that appear from time to time in the press, the standard of reading in the country as a whole has been going up steadily since the war." According to standardized reading tests administered periodically by the Department of Education and Science, in 1964 eleven-year-old children on average were reading at a level seventeen months above that of eleven-year-olds in 1948. This is equivalent to a gain of almost two years of schooling: in 1964, eleven-year-olds were reading almost at the level thirteen-year-olds had reached in 1948. Furthermore, the median, or level of competence reached by half of the children tested in 1948, was reached by three-quarters of the eleven-year-olds in the 1964 testing. And corresponding gains were made by fifteen-year-old children.[31]

The evidence is indirect, of course, and far from conclusive; a great many factors besides schooling may have been responsible, including changes in income, social class, and attitudes toward learning. Moreover, the testers did not distinguish between or compare informal and formal schools. The fact remains that this "remarkable improvement in standards of reading," as the Plowden Committee terms it, occurred at the same time that informal schooling was spreading rapidly. It seems reasonable to conclude, therefore, that informal education at the very least has not impaired English children's ability to learn to read.

This conclusion is confirmed by several studies which have compared the reading attainment of matched groups of students in formal and informal schools and found no significant difference between the two at either the infant or the junior school level. In summarizing one such study, Professor K. Lovell concludes that "Overall there is no evidence whatever of any deterioration of reading standards in informal Junior Schools. Although there is no evidence that these schools bring superior

[31] *Children and Their Primary Schools*, Vol. I, p. 212, and Vol. II (Appendix 7), p. 260.

standards in reading," Professor Lovell continues, "they may well benefit their pupils in other ways."[32]

. That informal schools do indeed benefit their students in other ways without harming their progress in reading is suggested by two studies made by Dorothy E. M. Gardner during her years

[32] K. Lovell, *Informal versus Formal Education and Reading Attainments in the Junior School*, London: National Foundation for Educational Research in England and Wales, 1963. Cf. also Joyce M. Morris, *Standards and Progress in Reading*, New York University Press and National Foundation for Education Research in England and Wales, 1966.

There is one other study that might suggest some slight superiority for formal schooling were it not for the weakness in its design. The National Foundation for Educational Research studied two groups of junior schools for the Plowden Committee. Their objective was to try to determine the effects of what the English call "streaming" (and what Americans call homogeneous or ability grouping), an emotion-packed subject in England, rather than to compare the results of formal versus informal schooling. But since "unstreamed" schools tend to be less formal and more child-centered than "streamed" schools, comparing the performance of students in the two groups gives a rough—but only rough—comparison of formal and informal teaching methods.

In the study at hand, reported in Appendix 11 to the Plowden Report, tests of reading ability at age ten showed no difference between the two groups of schools; however, students in the streamed schools tested higher in arithmetic and English (comprehension and grammar). The differences were small—two or three more correct answers on tests having thirty to forty items—but statistically significant, which is to say, larger than can be attributed to chance.

The educational significance of the differences is much less clear. Students in the sample of streamed schools came from a higher socioeconomic background than did the students in the unstreamed sample, hence could have been expected to outperform the latter in academic subjects, reading ability included. In addition, the tests themselves may have been biased against the unstreamed schools, as the National Foundation itself points out. For one thing, students in the streamed schools are tested much more frequently, and so may have been "test wise." For another, the tests were geared much more closely to the teaching objectives of the streamed than of the unstreamed schools. The closer the test came to streamed schools' aims and procedures, as in the case of mechanical arithmetic, the larger the difference was between the two groups.

In the one test that was relatively neutral, on the other hand—that of reading ability—there was no difference between the two groups, a result that could be interpreted as favoring the performance of the unstreamed schools. Attitudinal measures, moreover, showed some superiority for the unstreamed schools: fewer children were classified as "social isolates," and more teachers regarded the boys in their charge as "a pleasure to have in the class." All told, the authors of the study concluded that "as they stand," the results "lend small support to the controversialists on either side."

as a member and later head of the Child Development Department of the University of London Institute of Education. In her most recent study, covering the years 1951 to 1963, Miss Gardner and her associates compared children in matched pairs of formal and informal infant and junior schools, using five tests of achievement (free drawing, spoken and written English, reading, handwriting, arithmetic, and general information) and nine tests of attitude (among them, concentration, listening and remembering, neatness and care in work, ingenuity, sociability, moral judgment). Since the free day approach was just beginning to spread in 1951, when the study began, Miss Gardner limited her sample of informal schools to those that followed informal methods for only part of the day—anywhere from a single "free hour" to half the day "free"; she excluded schools which followed an entirely "free day" program.[33]

The results clearly favor the informal school, although it must be confessed that Miss Gardner does not provide enough information about her methods to enable a reader to draw his own conclusions about the adequacy of the controls. With tests administered at the end of junior school, for example, the informal schools showed clear superiority in six of the fourteen categories that were evaluated: spoken and written English, drawing and painting, "listening and remembering," "neatness, care and skill," "ingenuity," and the breadth and depth of children's out-of-school interests. The informal schools showed some superiority, though of a less striking sort, in children's reading ability, their ability to concentrate on an uninteresting task, their moral judgment, general information, handwriting, and ability to work with other children.

The only area in which formal schools showed superiority was arithmetic, and this superiority may no longer obtain, since the approach to arithmetic and maths has been completely transformed in informal schools since 1963, with the introduction of concrete materials, the great emphasis on counting, weighing, and measuring, and the use of new curricula, especially that of the Nuffield Math Project. There are no measures of achievement since the change in curriculum, but in most of the schools I visited, children who were asked their favorite activity mentioned "maths" more often than anything else—the opposite

---

[33] D. E. M. Gardner, *Experiment and Tradition in Primary Schools,* London: Methuen, 1966. Cf. also D. E. M. Gardner, *Testing Results in the Infant Schools,* 1942.

of what one finds in formal schools in England or the United States.

Some of the most interesting differences among the two groups in the Gardner study showed up not in the test results themselves but in what the testers had to report about the way children went about taking the tests. A test measuring children's ability to concentrate on a task of their own choice, for example, showed no significant difference in results. But children in the informal schools picked a task "much more quickly" than did youngsters in the formal schools. More of the "informal" children chose tasks involving working together with others, and many would stop their own task to help other children, e.g., "Kenneth stopped work to mix paint for Edward; on seeing the tester look at him he said, 'I'm not changing you know—just doing this for him.' "[34] The children in the informal schools also volunteered with great frequency to help the tester arrange the materials and clean up afterward. And more than twice as many children in the informal schools picked reading as the task on which to be tested. These kinds of differences showed up in a great many tests; in general, children from informal schools were more relaxed, showed less anxiety and more initiative, independence, and self-confidence, and had an easier relationship with their peers and with the testers.

Interestingly enough, studies of American progressive schools in the 1920s, '30s, and '40s showed much the same pattern. Reviewing all the major studies for the *Handbook of Research on Teaching,* Norman E. Wallen and Robert M. W. Travers summarized them as indicating "no important differences in terms of subject-matter mastery and a superiority of the progressive students in terms of the characteristics which the 'progressive school' seeks to develop"—for example, "initiative, work spirit, and critical thinking" as well as language use and knowledge of current events. While the studies have a great many conceptual and methodological defects, Wallen and Travers argue, "it seems clear that one major conclusion survives the criticisms which have been discussed—namely, that reducing the amount of authoritarian control over students (in some cases rather markedly) does not necessarily result in drastic impair-

---

[34] Children in an experimental informal program in Tucson, Arizona, do the same thing, completely confounding the researchers coming in to run evaluation tests; the researchers, unprepared by American classrooms for this kind of cooperation, at first insisted they couldn't test because the children "were cheating." See Chapter 7, Section VI.

ment of their academic skills, contrary to the expectation of many."[35]

It would be satisfying, of course, to be able to point to statistical data showing clear superiority for informal schooling. The fact that such data is not at hand in no way suggests that differences in educational strategy are unimportant, only that we look in the wrong place to find their effects. As the National Foundation for Educational Research suggests in its report to the Plowden Committee, the consequences of different modes of schooling should be sought less in academic attainment than in their impact on how children feel about themselves, about school, and about learning. For three hundred years or more, schools have been denounced for their capacity to destroy children's spontaneity, curiosity, and love of learning, and for their tendency to mutilate childhood itself. To create and operate schools that cultivate and nurture all these qualities without reducing children's academic attainment—this is a magnificent achievement.

Note on Sources

The description and analysis of informal English primary schools is based in large measure on my on-the-spot study of schools in London, Leicestershire County, Oxfordshire, and the West Riding of Yorkshire in the fall of 1968, supplemented and corrected by discussions and correspondence with a great many American and English students of informal schooling, as well as by careful reading of the available literature.

The largest debt, by far, is due Professor Lillian Weber of the City College of New York, the most sensitive and best-informed American student of informal education. I am deeply indebted, too, to Leonard G. W. Sealey, a leading figure in the growth of informal schooling in Leicestershire and now a consultant to the Ford Foundation and the U.S. Office of Education; as well as to a number of others: Joseph Featherstone,

[35] Norman E. Wallen and Robert M. W. Travers, "Analysis and Investigation of Teaching Methods," in N. L. Gage, ed., *Handbook of Research on Teaching*, Chicago: Rand McNally, 1963. Cf. also J. P. Leonard and A. C. Eurich, *An Evaluation of Modern Education*, 1942; J. W. Wrightstone, *Appraisal of Newer Elementary School Practices*, 1938; Progressive Education Commission on the Relation of School and College, *Adventure in American Education*, especially Vol. I, *The Story of the Eight Year Study;* Vol. III, *Appraising and Recording Student Progress;* and Vol. IV, *Did They Succeed in College?*

who first called my attention to informal schooling in England through his articles in *The New Republic* (August 19, September 2, and September 9, 1967); Professor Vincent R. Rogers, Chairman of the Department of Elementary Education of the University of Connecticut; David Armington of the Educational Development Center of Newton, Mass.; Miss Nora L. Goddard, Inspector of Infant Schools for the Inner London Education Authority; Dorothy E. M. Gardner, former head of the Child Development Department of the University of London Institute of Education; Dr. A. H. Halsey, Chairman of the Department of Social and Administrative Studies and Fellow of Nuffield College, Oxford University; I. McMullen, formerly Coordinating Director, Resources for Learning Project, the Nuffield Foundation, London; Mrs. Mary Brown, Headmistress, Sherard Infant School, Melton Mowbray, Leicestershire County; Miss Susan Williams, Headmistress, Gordonbrock Infant School, London; Mr. Tom John, Headmaster, Tower Hill Primary School, Witney, Oxfordshire; Geoffrey K. Caston, Joint Secretary, The Schools Council, London; Sir Alec Clegg, Education Officer, West Riding of Yorkshire; T. R. Weaver, Deputy Under-Secretary of State, Department of Education and Science; Anthony Kallet, Advisory Center, Leicestershire County Education Department; Professor W. A. Campbell Stewart, Vice-Chancellor, University of Keele; and headmasters, headmistresses, and teachers too numerous to mention.

The summary of the theories of Jean Piaget and of their implications for educational practice in Section II is based on extensive reading of the major primary and secondary sources and interviews, by myself and Mrs. Sybil Pollet, a member of my research staff, with academic and professional students of Piaget's work. The statements in the text directly attributed to Piaget are drawn, for the most part, from notes that Mrs. Pollet and I took at the lectures given by Professor Piaget at Teachers College, Columbia University, in 1968, and at New York University in 1967; and from published texts of Piaget's lectures at Cornell University and the University of California at Berkeley in 1964. The author is particularly indebted to Miss Eleanor Duckworth for her translations of Piaget's lectures, and for sharing her detailed knowledge of Piaget's thought in lengthy discussions in New York and Toronto. A debt is owed, too, to Professor David Elkind of the University of Rochester and Professor Millie Almy and Frank G. Jennings of Teachers College, Columbia University.

For readers wanting a relatively brief and readable discussion of Piaget's work, especially as it bears on education, perhaps the most useful source is a small monograph, *Piaget Rediscovered,* edited by Richard E. Ripple and Verne N. Rockcastle (Cornell University Press, 1964). The monograph contains the text of Piaget's 1964 lectures at Cornell and Berkeley, along with a number of other papers commenting on the significance of Piaget's work. In addition, the following sources are recommended: Jean Piaget and Barbel Inhelder, *The Psychology of the Child,* New York: Basic Books, 1969; David Elkind, "Giant in the Nursery—Jean Piaget," *New York Times Magazine,* May 26, 1968; David Elkind, "Piaget and Montessori," *Harvard Educational Review,* Fall 1967; David Elkind, Introduction to Jean Piaget, *Six Psychological Studies,* Random House, 1967; Nathan Isaacs, *The Growth of Understanding in the Young Child: A Brief Introduction to Piaget's Work,* London: Ward Lock Educational Co. Ltd., 1961; Frank G. Jennings, "Jean Piaget: Notes on Learning," *Saturday Review,* May 20, 1967; Jerome Bruner, *The Process of Education,* Cambridge, Mass.: Harvard University Press, 1961, Chapter 3.

For more detailed and systematic explanations, analyses and critiques of Piaget, the following should be consulted: John H. Flavell, *The Developmental Psychology of Jean Piaget,* Princeton, New Jersey: Van Nostrand, 1963; David Elkind and John H. Flavell, eds., *Studies in Cognitive Development: Essays in Honor of Jean Piaget,* New York: Oxford University Press, 1969; Jean Piaget, *Six Psychological Studies,* New York: Random House, 1967; Molly Brearley and Elizabeth Hitchfield, *A Teacher's Guide to Reading Piaget,* London: Routledge and Kegan Paul, 1966; Millie Almy with Edward Chittenden and Paula Miller, *Young Children's Thinking,* New York: Teachers College Press, 1966; Jean Piaget, *The Moral Judgment of the Child,* Glencoe, Illinois: Free Press, 1948; *The Language and Thought of the Child,* London: Routledge and Kegan Paul, 1952.

7

It Can
Happen Here

*The prospect which is here held out is indeed great and
very desirable, though I can easily foresee that to many it
will appear to be an idle dream rather than the exposition
of a real possibility.*

—JOHN AMOS COMENIUS,
The Great Didactic

I

Genius among teachers, John Dewey suggested some three-
quarters of a century ago, "is as rare as genius in other realms
of human activity. Education is, and forever will be, in the
hands of ordinary men and women." But can the ordinary men
and women in whose hands American public education is
placed successfully handle informal classrooms? For an American audience, after all, the critical question is not whether informal education works well in England, but whether it can
work as well in the United States. Hearing descriptions of
informal English classrooms, Americans (especially American
teachers) naturally wonder whether genius, or at least above-
average teaching ability, is not necessary to carry the method
off. Certainly the descriptions in Chapter 6 make English teachers *sound* as though they possess extraordinary skill, sensitivity,
and energy. If this were so—if the success of informal education

were due to the fact that English primary teachers are a superior breed—then the approach would not be likely to work in the United States, at least not on a scale large enough to be significant.

Such is not the case; informal education can work as well in the United States as in England. This flat assertion is based on experience as well as theory; the approach already is in use in schools as diverse as those of New York's Harlem and the small cities, towns, and hamlets of North Dakota; of Philadelphia, Pennsylvania, and Tucson, Arizona; Washington, D.C. and Cambridge, Massachusetts; Paterson, New Jersey, San Antonio, Texas, and Johnson County, North Carolina. In some of these, e.g., North Dakota, Washington, New York, the programs now in operation represent conscious adaptations and modifications of the English experience; in others, they are indigenous developments. In all, they appear to be working well.

The free day does not depend on extraordinary talent or genius on the part of the teacher; teachers of every sort—ordinary, garden-variety teachers, not only superior ones—are able to function well in informal classrooms. "Perhaps it is in our isolated and encapsulated formal classrooms that only genius can succeed," Lillian Weber, one of the most perceptive students of informal teaching, suggests. Be that as it may, English primary teachers are not a superior breed; on the contrary, they come from much the same kinds of backgrounds as do American teachers. Some 40 percent of English female primary school teachers, for example, have fathers who are blue-collar workers, and more than half come from lower-middle-class backgrounds; as in the United States, teaching is an important avenue of social mobility, and has been for a long time.[1]

More important, perhaps, English primary school teachers tend to be younger and less experienced than their American counterparts, for teacher turnover, especially in infant schools, is

[1] Jean Floud and W. Scott, "Recruitment to Teaching in England and Wales," in A. H. Halsey, Jean Floud, and C. Arnold Anderson, *Education, Economy and Society*, New York: Free Press Paperback, 1965. Cf. also George E. Dickson, et al., *The Characteristics of Teacher Education Students in the British Isles and the United States*, Research Foundation of the University of Toledo, 1965.

Unlike the United States, however, English secondary school teachers tend to come from a somewhat higher social background than do primary school teachers. Indeed, teachers in grammar schools and public schools (the English term for private schools like Eton and Harrow) have much the same kinds of backgrounds as university faculty members.

extraordinarily high. A survey made for the Plowden Committee, for example, indicated that two-thirds of the women who had taught in infant schools during a period of two years and nine months were no longer in those schools at the end of the period. This is a turnover rate of nearly 25 percent a year, more than double the American rate. Not all of those who left their posts left teaching altogether, of course; there appears to be more movement from school to school in England than in the United States. But many did leave teaching; the annual attrition rate is roughly twice that of the United States, where some 8 percent of classroom teachers leave the profession each year.[2] (In the United States, roughly half of those who leave teaching return at some later date, e.g., when their own children have reached school age.) Taking everything together, therefore, the success of informal schooling cannot be attributed to extraordinary talent or experience on the part of English teachers.

This is not to suggest that informal teaching is easy. *No* teaching is easy, and informal teaching makes a number of demands on teachers that the conventional classroom does not. For example, it requires much more alertness. To be able to "maximize the occasion," a teacher must always be "at the ready"—aware not only of what each child is doing at any moment, but of what stage of development the child is in. Since anything and everything a child may do can provide the occasion to be maximized, teachers are *always* teaching; the intellectual and emotional demands seem relentless and unending. And teachers need to be informed about many more things; the curriculum is not limited to the teacher's lesson plan, but is as broad and unpredictable as the children's interests.

And yet teachers who have tried both approaches insist that informal teaching is no more difficult than formal teaching and is much more rewarding. For one thing, informal education relieves the teacher of the terrible burden of omniscience. In a traditional classroom, that is to say, it is difficult for any but the most secure teacher to admit ignorance—difficult, and threatening. Since the traditional classroom is organized on the assumption that the teacher is the source of all knowledge, and that learning is something the teacher makes happen to the student,

[2] Children and Their Primary Schools, Vol. II, Appendix 5; Frank Lindenfeld, *Teacher Turnover in Public Elementary and Secondary Schools,* 1959–60, United States Office of Education, Circular No. 678, 1963; National Education Association, *Teacher Supply and Demand in Public Schools,* 1968.

many teachers fear that admitting ignorance may diminish their authority. "One has become a school teacher," Willard Waller's dictum runs, "when he has learned to fear the loss of dignity."[3] To the formal teacher, admitting ignorance means loss of dignity.

In an informal classroom, by contrast, the teacher is the facilitator rather than the source of learning, the source being the child himself. Learning is something the child makes happen to and for himself, albeit with the teacher's aid, and sometimes at her instigation. The consequence is an atmosphere in which everyone is learning together, and in which teachers therefore feel comfortable saying to children, "I'm awfully sorry, I don't know much about this. Let's go to the library and get a book, and we'll find out together," or "What kind of experiment can we set up together to find the answer?" or "Where might we turn to find out?" Because the classrooms are not self-contained, moreover—because teachers are used to working with one another—they also feel free to direct a child to the head or to another teacher who may be better informed on the subject in question. And since the whole school is their orbit, children feel free to go to one teacher for help with science, another for help with art, still another for music, and so on, without losing respect for anyone. It is manifestly impossible, after all, for any one person to be an authority on everything that comes up in an open classroom.

Informal education also relieves the teacher of the obligation to try to teach the entire range of abilities at one time, a task that is as exhausting as it is futile. A typical third-grade class, for example, is likely to contain children whose reading ability ranges from nonexistent to fifth- or sixth-grade level; the spread is comparable in most other academic subjects. Of necessity, therefore, teachers in traditional classrooms tend to pitch their lessons at the middle, thereby boring the most advanced and losing those who are behind. The strain on the conscientious teacher is considerable.

Most important, however, the free day classroom relieves the teacher of the necessity of being a timekeeper, traffic cop, and disciplinarian. In a formal classroom, a large proportion of the teacher's time and an extraordinary amount of her energy are consumed simply by the need to maintain order and control. ("I cannot begin until all talking has stopped and every eye is

[3] Willard Waller, *The Sociology of Teaching.*

on me!") In the informal classroom, the discipline problem withers away, in part because children are not required to sit still and be silent. The release of the teacher's energy is incalculable; she is free to devote all her time and energy to teaching itself. The result is a kind of professional satisfaction and reward that simply is not found in the average formal classroom.

ITEM: A teacher in a North Dakota elementary school, evaluating her first semester of informal teaching after twenty years of running a tight, traditional classroom, writes the dean of the University of North Dakota's New School for Behavioral Studies in Education, where she had been retrained for the new approach: "I know there are areas in which I have worked with greater reservations perhaps than you would have liked me to. This is not because I disagree with the philosophy but because it is difficult to throw away some of the restraints I have practiced for many years." Difficult or not, her enthusiasm is clear. "As far as teaching is concerned, it's been almost like starting a new profession. I feel sorry for the older teachers who are staying at home in the same old rut. If only they knew what they were missing!"

ITEM: Another "retreaded" North Dakota teacher describes the experience this way: "It has not been painless. I've cursed and blessed the New School inwardly—sometimes simultaneously. I am not satisfied with what I am doing, but I could never go back to what I did before."

ITEM: A "Teacher Resource Center" in one of Philadelphia's black ghettos. Fifty teachers are attending a voluntary after-school workshop to learn informal teaching methods and to make "stuff" for their own classrooms. The union contract mandates payment of $6.05 an hour for any activity teachers perform after school hours; these teachers come voluntarily and without compensation. Many remain until 8:00 P.M., or whenever the lights are turned off.

It would be difficult to exaggerate the importance of this kind of response. Enjoyment of one's work and pride in one's accomplishments are important motivations in almost every occupation, and more so in teaching than in most. "An individual, having joined a given occupation, concentrates his reward-seeking energies at those points where effort makes the largest difference in his total rewards," the sociologist Dan C. Lortie of the University of Chicago writes. In teaching, effort has very little relation to extrinsic rewards such as higher salary or status, since these are geared largely to length of service and number of courses taken and degrees acquired. And while "ancillary rewards" such as job security and long vacations may attract people into teaching in the first place, they are relatively unimportant once a person has become a teacher, since they are identical for almost everyone in the field. Intrinsic rewards such as satisfaction and pride of accomplishment, on the other hand, *are* related to effort. It is not surprising, therefore, that teachers show more concern for intrinsic than for extrinsic or ancillary rewards. In Lortie's study, for example, the reward teachers consider most important, by a wide margin, is "Knowing that I have 'reached' students and they have learned."[4]

One result is that teachers may be even more sensitive to the reactions of their students than to the judgments of their colleagues, since it is the students, as Lortie emphasizes, who "have the capacity to grant or deny the responses which teachers consider their primary payment." This fact distinguishes teaching from most other professions; one of the hallmarks of a profession is that the practitioner is more concerned with his colleagues' than with his clients' approval.

Teaching is distinguished from the arts in much the same way. "The poet can at least take pleasure in his own poem, no matter whether anyone will publish him or buy his book," Lee Cronbach points out. And the artist can find some consolation in the objective reality of his painting, the composer in his symphony, even if their audience rejects or ignores the work; the "artist ahead of his time" is a familiar phenomenon. "But what does it do to a teacher," Cronbach asks, "to discover that pupils don't want what he has to teach? Can a teacher take pleasure in pursuing his vision with no takers?"[5] The answer is no, of course,

---

[4] Dan C. Lortie, "The Balance of Control and Autonomy in Elementary School Teaching," in Amitai Etzioni, ed., *The Semi-Professions*, New York: Free Press, 1969.
[5] From a letter to the author. "This has always been the tragedy of the English teacher who really wants to make pupils love Tennyson and Gray," Professor Cronbach continues. "Now it is shocking all of us university professors," as bright but rebellious undergraduates, and now, even graduate students, reject their professors' expertise, making it clear, sometimes subtly, sometimes with only half-concealed insolence, that they want to create quite different roles for themselves.

and anyone who has ever taught, or who has been close to teachers, knows the agony and bitter frustration teachers suffer when they find that students are not interested in what they have to offer.

To avoid this fate, teachers, especially teachers of the young, look for their rewards less in the information they have transmitted than in the excitement they evoke and, even more, in the quality of the relationships they establish with their students. The elementary school teachers Philip Jackson studied, for example, like the ones in Lortie's sample, found their greatest reward in "reaching" students, but they measured their success less by how well students did on tests than by their "feel" for their students' responses. Asked how they could tell when they were doing a good job, for example, teachers typically gave answers like, "Oh, look at their faces," "I can tell by the way they sound," or "Their interest; their expressions; the way they look." "There is a here-and-now urgency and spontaneous quality that brings excitement and variety to the teacher's work," Jackson comments, "though it also may contribute to the fatigue he feels at the end of the day."

Moreover, teachers set great store on creating a warm and informal atmosphere in the formal classroom and in having the freedom to teach each class as they see fit. "I have to have a lot of freedom in the way that I teach," one of Jackson's respondents says, "because each class is different. It takes each class a different length of time to learn something that you're presenting to them. I do a lot of speaking myself, oral presentation, but not formal lectures. I try to maintain a very informal atmosphere . . ." And a teacher with forty years' experience remarks, "I try to be informal. I mean, I try to make this situation as much as possible like a family group sitting around a fireplace or around a table when some question has come up and they're discussing it." The teachers' greatest concern, in fact, was loss of their professional autonomy as a result of a rigid curriculum imposed from the outside, or "invasion" of their classroom by superiors bent on evaluation.[6]

---

[6] Philip W. Jackson, *Life in Classrooms*, Chapter 4. It is the fragility of the teacher's autonomy, an autonomy that has no legitimation in official statements of authority, Lortie suggests, that explains one of the great paradoxes of teacher behavior: "why does a group which expresses so little concern for extrinsic rewards perceive them as so dangerous to peer solidarity?" The answer, in Lortie's view, is that the introduction of merit pay would strengthen the relative position of school boards and adminis-

Small wonder, then, that teachers respond so affirmatively to the introduction of informal, free day techniques, that once their initial concerns have been relieved, they insist that they could never go back to formal teaching. In the kinds of classrooms described in Chapter 6, teachers *must* be treated as professionals able to make their own decisions; it would be patently absurd, for example, to require teachers to submit lesson plans for the principal's approval. Freed of the necessity to expend time and energy on maintaining order and control, moreover, teachers can concentrate on "reaching" children individually and collectively, on getting the relationships right, on really getting to know each child as an individual, and on getting the kinds of responses from children that provide the teachers' main reward. The phenomenon of the self-fulfilling prophecy works for teachers no less than for children: if they are treated as professionals able to manage a classroom, teachers are likely to act as professionals, particularly if they are given some support and help in making the change.

II

It would be a mistake, however, to assume that the informal approach can simply be transplanted to the United States as is. For one thing, there is no such thing as *the* informal approach; there is no model or blueprint to be shipped across the ocean. There is, rather, an approach to teaching and learning and to the nature of childhood that is consistent with a wide variety of specific practices. The kinds of classrooms described in Chapter 6 represent one end of a large spectrum; they are the culmination and logical extension of practices that have been in the making for a century or more.

Equally important, educational systems always are, and by nature must be, native plants. All schools reflect the views of society about the way children should be brought up, the purposes of education, and the relations between school and society. Moreover, the institutional differences in the way schools are organized, administered, and financed, along with the cultural differences, especially in the role of the family and of adult authority in general, make it dangerous to try to transfer forms unchanged from one country to another. Before turning to a

---

trators vis-à-vis teachers, and thereby weaken whatever *de facto* autonomy teachers enjoy.

description of informal education in the United States, therefore, it may be useful to consider some of the relevant cultural
and institutional differences between England and the United
States.

To begin with, education has always been largely decentral-
ized in the United States, with the funding and supervision of the
schools the responsibility, in the main, of the individual states—
a responsibility they generally delegate, in turn, to local governments.[7] In England, on the other hand, it is the national government that sets salaries and terms of employment and that also
provides the bulk of the funds. Even the supervision of the
schools is a national as well as local concern, with a corps of
inspectors known as HMI's (Her Majesty's Inspectors) supple-
menting the local inspectors and local education authorities.

A main consequence has been to insulate the English classroom from direct social pressures, which gives English teachers
and heads far more freedom to experiment and innovate than
their American counterparts enjoy. Once appointed, a head has
almost complete autonomy over his school's organization, timetable, and curriculum. He is expected to consult with the local
education authority and the local and national inspectors before
making major changes, of course, and to listen carefully to their
suggestions; but what he does then is up to him. No American
principal experiences that degree of independence.[8]

---

[7] While management of the schools has always been local, they have
rarely been entirely free of national influences. Cf. Roald F. Campbell
and Robert A. Bunnell, eds., *Nationalizing Influences on Secondary Education*, University of Chicago, Midwest Administration Center, 1963.
Even so, it was not until 1965 that Congress first approved a program of
general federal aid for elementary and secondary schools; proposals for
such aid had been defeated with regularity for a century or more. Cf.
Philip Meranto, *The Politics of Federal Aid to Education in 1965: A
Study in Political Innovation*, Syracuse University Press, 1967.
[8] English heads are just beginning to feel the parental and social pressures that are commonplace in this country. Parents from all social
classes in England increasingly view education as the means of mobility
in what is becoming an increasingly meritocratic society. Hence Englishmen, like Americans, are coming to regard education as too important to
be left to the educators, and are asserting their right to know about and
to influence what goes on in the classroom.
Several recent factors have contributed to this change. A succession
of Parliamentary Commissions studying various aspects of English education have documented the close association between children's family
background and their academic achievement. The Plowden Committee
interpreted its research findings as indicating that parental attitudes have
an even greater impact on achievement than parental education, occupa-

Thus the English head plays a distinctive role; he is "the pivot of the English school system," as George Baron and Asher Tropp put it.[9] The head is pivotal not only because of his autonomy but also because his primary role is that of teacher—the head teacher—rather than of administrator. Indeed, the old terms "headmaster" and "headmistress" are falling into disfavor, being replaced in many schools by "head teacher," which is more accurate.

Heads function in a completely different manner than do American principals: they continue to teach. In small schools the head may have a regular class of his own, as is still the case in rural America. But even in larger schools, where the head does not have his own class, he continues to teach nonetheless, taking over a class when a teacher is absent (a substitute, or "supply teacher," as the English call it, will rarely be called unless a teacher is going to be absent for a week or more), and more important, teaching children individually, in small groups, or in whole classes, all year long. It is "essential," the Plowden Committee declared, "that head teachers of larger schools should not have to spend so much time on administrative duties and on general supervision that they are unable to teach." Testimony before the Committee suggested that head teachers should spend up to 75 percent of their time in the classroom.

Quite the opposite exists in the United States, where elemen-

---

tion, and social class. That interpretation is open to question, since much of what the Committee called "attitudes"—for example, the emphasis on literacy within the home, the kinds of books and magazines children are encouraged to read, etc.—are themselves closely related to parental education and social class. Nonetheless the Plowden Committee urged, in the strongest terms, a major expansion of contacts between parents and schools, including such radical (for England) innovations as twice-yearly meetings with parents to discuss their children's progress, and special efforts to reach parents who fail to show.

Under the Plowden Committee recommendations, to be sure, it is still the school which is taking the initiative, educating parents to their responsibilities. But once established, parent-teacher relationships are not likely to remain one-directional, a possibility which English teachers recognize and fear. Indeed, the recommendations already seem to have encouraged parents, especially those in middle-class neighborhoods, who want to play a more active role in determining educational policy. English parents are still a long way from brow-beating teachers in the manner of some prosperous American suburbs, but there is a clear tendency toward the Americanization of parent-teacher and school-community relations.

[9] George Baron and Asher Tropp, "Teachers in England and America," in Halsey, Floud, and Anderson, eds., *Education, Economy and Society.*

tary school principals spend, on average, only 4 percent of their time teaching. Some 70 percent do no teaching whatsoever, and most prefer it that way; asked how much time they would allot to teaching in an ideal schedule, principals suggested 4 percent.[10]

To some extent, heads are able to spend time teaching rather than administering because their schools tend to be a good bit smaller than American elementary schools. Most English primary schools have between one hundred and three hundred students; by contrast, only one American elementary school principal in four has fewer than four hundred students in his school, and nearly half have between four hundred and seven hundred pupils. The difference in size is not coincidental; the English have deliberately opted for small schools. (Where infant and junior schools are housed in the same plant, the English frequently have separate heads for each branch, thus holding down the number of students assigned to each.)

But school size is not the only factor affecting how a principal or head spends his time; how he views his role is even more important. A head who sees himself as an administrator will find considerably more administrative chores to perform than one who sees himself as a head teacher.

ITEM: Arriving at an American elementary school at 8:35 A.M., the start of the school day, to see the principal as per appointment, the writer is kept waiting, amidst a bevy of young children, until well after nine. Children who arrive after the "late bell" has rung are not permitted to go to their classroom until they have first seen the principal, made their explanations, and received a "late pass" from him, a procedure that takes the first half-hour of the principal's day (and that also makes children who have arrived two or three minutes late miss the bulk of their first period).

ITEM: Another elementary school with slightly less than 1,000 pupils. Touring the school with a visitor, the principal, who has four assistant principals and an administrative assistant, in addition to a passel of secretaries and clerks, sees a burnt-out bulb in one classroom and makes a notation to tell the custodian.

[10] Department of Elementary School Principals, National Education Association, "The Elementary School Principalship in 1968," Washington, D.C.: National Education Association, 1968. ("Teaching principals" have been excluded from the data.)

Asked why he needs such a large staff, the principal looks surprised and explains that he could not possibly make do with any fewer. He follows up the explanation with a letter specifying the reasons in some detail. The staff is essential, he writes, to handle the administrative workload, which includes "administrative details such as: ordering materials, supplies, and textbooks; receiving, entering and storing them; distributing and collecting them; inventorying them; arranging complex class, individual, and teacher programs and schedules; overseeing yards, basements, lunchrooms; administering standardized tests, etc." But none of these, of course, are administrative, except perhaps for arranging the schedules, which presumably is done before the school year begins. Most are routine chores that can be handled by clerks. ("Ordering textbooks," for example, does not mean *selecting* the texts—the central board of education does that—but simply determining how many books the school needs.) The rest, e.g., "overseeing yards, basements, lunchrooms," can easily be performed by teacher aides.

Thus, American principals clutter up their day with needless "administration," which is to say with chores that could easily be delegated to others, if indeed they need to be performed at all. Some, of course, are unavoidable; English heads either delegate the tasks to their teachers (a head is lucky if he or she has a full-time secretary) or perform them after school, in order to make the time in which to teach. The head's job is to get to know the children, and "the best way to get to know children," as the Plowden Committee remarks, "is to teach them, and be with them inside and outside the classroom. In this way a good head teacher can stimulate the children, inspire the staff, weld the school into a unity, and set its values." Teaching is also the means by which heads maintain their authority. "There is no better way of commending their leadership to the staff than by demonstrating their skill in the classroom," the Plowden Committee points out. British heads are able to do this because they are chosen, by and large, for their ability to teach, in contrast to American principals, who tend to be chosen for their administrative ability or their capacity to maintain discipline.

American principals spend far less time in the classroom and almost never take over a class. To do so might offend both the teacher's and the principal's sense of etiquette. A principal is supposed to be above mere teaching, and his failure to teach helps define teaching as less important than administration. In England, on the other hand, as the Plowden Committee observed, "the fact that the head continues to teach raises the whole status of teaching." The result of this distinction is that an American teacher who wants to experiment, whether with informal methods or anything else, is far less likely to get the kind of support and help that is available to most teachers in England.

Furthermore, the United States has nothing resembling the English inspectorate, which provides added assistance to both teachers and heads. As the Plowden Committee observed, "help from within the school is not enough, especially at this time of a rapidly changing curriculum, methods and organization. The freedom of the class teacher to prescribe for his students, and of the head teacher to prescribe for his school must be informed by a knowledge of the successes and failures of others." That knowledge is provided, in good measure, by the HMI's and the local inspectors and advisers.

As the name implies, "inspectors" were originally precisely that: people who visited the schools to inspect the manner in which teachers, who had little training, were using public funds. For a time, the Inspectorate served as a straightjacket. Under the system of "payment by results," which a number of people now seem to be advocating for the United States,[11] the size of the grant the national government made to the local education authorities depended on the scores children achieved on standardized tests which the HMI's supervised or administered. The result was a deadly uniformity, in which teachers inevitably taught to the tests, and to nothing but the tests.

That system was abandoned around the turn of the century, however, and the inspector's role has shifted steadily from punitive monitor to that of friendly adviser, informing teachers and heads of methods that work elsewhere, helping and supporting those who are trying new ways, offering suggestions on how to improve performance, and so on. Some local authorities have

[11] Professor James Coleman has proposed that public schools subcontract instruction in reading and other subjects to private corporations, with payment geared to the scores students achieve on standardized tests. The U.S. Office of Education has made several grants to school districts to try the notion out.

dropped the term "inspector" altogether in favor of "adviser" in order to stress this change in role. In Leicestershire, for example, where this change probably has gone the furthest, advisers may not visit a school unless the head so wishes. Heads and teachers, so the reasoning goes, are more likely to accept advice if they do not feel threatened by the person giving it.

This does not mean that there are no sanctions or controls over the schools in England, but rather that they are fewer and less direct. Promotions, for example, from teacher to deputy head to head of a small school to head of a more prestigious one are affected very much by the judgments of the inspector, whether he is called inspector or adviser. Furthermore, the inspector's approval or disapproval may be even more important to a head's professional pride and self-esteem and to his reputation among his peers. Still, the fact that heads enjoy both tenure and autonomy, the fact that an inspector can never *order* a head to do anything, means that to be effective inspectors must rely mainly on their powers of persuasion, which is to say their ability to educate the teachers and heads they supervise.[12] Their ability to persuade stems from their own expertise, for most inspectors have risen from the ranks of teachers and heads.

In any case, a number of inspectors, both HMI's and local inspectors, have influenced a whole generation of teachers and heads to adopt the new approach. Their influence was felt through personal contacts in their school visitations as well as through teaching in-service courses. The head of a primary school in Oxfordshire, for example, says that his entire approach to education changed as a result of an in-service course in "Movement, Art, and Poetry" while still a teacher. The ten-day course was given by three HMI's; the suggestion that he apply for the course came from another inspector who was encouraging him in his efforts to break away from formal teaching. "It was at that course," he recalls, "that I met the kind of people I had never met before—human beings of a very high order. They weren't just instructors or teachers. They were human beings who developed a relationship between us."

The head, a gifted and sensitive man, went on to recount how he learned the importance of relationships during those ten days, how he discovered that he could draw and paint, something he

---

[12] The other side of the coin of the head's autonomy is the fact that there is almost nothing an inspector or education officer can do about an incompetent head who does not take kindly to suggestions.

had never done in his life—how, as he put it, "a piece of me was unlocked."

> I found that I had begun to change my whole philosophy. I was putting the emphasis on learning rather than teaching. I knew that I had to grow myself, that I had to do a lot more experimenting. I had to learn a lot more about children.

American teachers are rarely offered in-service courses of this caliber. There is no analogue to the local inspectorate or the HMI, and educators who represent a high order of human beings tend to drift out of public education. Hence, the classroom teacher neither gets the support from his principal that a head is able to offer nor the opportunity to mingle with and learn from the "great" people.

England's national Department of Education and Science has also been an important force in primary education, a statement that could hardly be made of the U.S. Office of Education. England's 1952–53 revision of the recommended physical education syllabus provides an interesting case in point. It exerted considerable impact not only in "shaping the philosophy of physical education," as the Plowden Committee terms it, but in opening the way to the introduction of Movement. The 1933 syllabus which it replaced had proposed some eighteen separate "lessons" and forty-two exercises to form a uniform program of phys. ed. for all primary students. The change in approach is reflected even in the title of the new syllabus, Part I of which is called "Moving and Growing." The volume referred to "the movement period" instead of the "physical exercise lesson," and it proposed a program to develop each child's physical ability through "exploratory stages and actions which *will not be the same for any two children.*" [Emphasis added]

The great Parliamentary Commission studies of primary education, the Hadow Commission in the late 1920s and early '30s and the Plowden Committee in the '60s, have also influenced professionals in the schools in a manner that no Congressional Committee here has ever attempted. Heads have used the reports as the basis for continuing discussions with their teachers. Indeed, I cannot recall visiting a school in which well-thumbed-through copies of the Plowden Report were not available in the head's office, the teachers' lounge, or both. These reports are not dusty documents but active forces in helping to shape classroom life. In fact, it was the 1934 Hadow Report on *Infant and Nursery Schools* that served as something of a watershed in the transition from formal to informal schooling.

The English Colleges of Education and the university Institutes of Education have contributed to the change, too, in a way that American colleges and universities have not. The relation between teachers and educationists is both closer and more reciprocal in England than in the United States (see Chapter 10). The change toward more informal methods has tended to begin with the teachers in the field and to move upward to the teacher training colleges; but since the college faculties are drawn, in the main, from successful teachers and heads, the movement proceeds along a two-way street. The colleges and institutes have exerted an independent influence, moreover, through their traditional emphasis on the study of child psychology and child development, an emphasis that has no real counterpart in the United States. Thus, educationists like Susan Isaacs and Dorothy E. M. Gardner of the University of London, both of whom also taught and ran their own schools, played a major role in popularizing informal education. With rare exceptions, detailed in Chapter 11, American colleges and universities are not playing a similar role.

Some of the cultural differences between England and the United States, however—differences that might inhibit adoption of the "free day" in this country—turn out, on closer scrutiny, to be more apparent than real. Americans frequently suggest, for example, that the emphasis on art, dance, beauty, and sensitivity might be all right in England, but could never be accepted in this country. At best, it is suggested, Americans would reject these activities as unnecessary and costly frills, and at worst, as effeminate and effete. This is true enough—but the same objections were raised in England when schools first began to stress Movement and Art. The English working class, after all, is no more esthetically inclined than the American; if one were to pick an area where Movement and Art would be resisted most strongly, for example, one could hardly do better than the coal-mining towns of Yorkshire—yet this is one of the areas where Movement had its origins and where Movement and Art still receive the heaviest emphasis.

The development of Movement, and of the related approaches to physical education, in fact, provides a useful example of how parental resistance can be overcome. Admittedly, transplanting Movement and "P.E." as the English practice it would be difficult; to have even six- and seven-year-old boys and girls playing in their underwear would be regarded as provocative and immoral. A Leicestershire head who ran a "free day" program in Cleveland a few summers ago, for example, ruefully recalls the storm that ensued the first day, when she routinely asked her class of six-year-olds to strip down to their underwear for gym. It is the Americans, she learned the hard way, and not the English, who maintain a Victorian prudishness about the human body. The fact is, however, that the idea of having children play in their underwear created as big a furor in England when it was first broached in the early thirties as it would today in the United States. It took years of patient explanation and education before English parents could accept the practice.[13]

Some English educators, moreover, fear that Americans will have great difficulty accepting informal education, because of the much longer view of education the approach requires. They have a point; Americans do seem to have a greater need to define themselves, so to speak, at any given moment—to know where they stand vis-à-vis others. In the case of the schools, this means that parents want to know what their children are learning, relative to what others are learning; this puts pressure on schools to emphasize short-term goals, since these are much more easily measured than long-term goals.

And yet the point can be easily overdone. There is the growing emphasis in the United States, for example, especially among the young, on "experience," "process," "involvement," and so on, all of which tend toward greater acceptability of informal education. More to the point, informal education was widely accepted in the United States in the 1920s and '30s, when the progressive movement in education was at its height. Indeed, contemporary English informal schools may be described, with only slight exaggeration, as English adaptations of what John Dewey had in mind, but his followers did not always carry out. There are important differences, of course, between the schools Dewey envisaged and contemporary English informal schools. For example, Dewey, along with men like Harold Rugg and Boyd Bode, placed more emphasis on a formal curriculum, with sequential courses, than do the English. But Dewey also emphasized the need to know more about learning and child development, and he undoubtedly would have modified his recommen-

---

[13] John Blackie, *Inside the Primary School.*

dations as new insights, for example, those of Piaget, emerged.[14]

The reality of progressive schools, in any case, was quite different than the current stereotype would imply. That many progressive schools were perversions of the ideal can hardly be doubted. As Lawrence Cremin writes in *The Transformation of the School*, the movement "elicited not only first rate art, but every manner of shoddiness and self-deception as well. In too many classrooms license began to pass for liberty, planlessness for spontaneity, recalcitrance for individuality, obfuscation for art, and chaos for education—all justified in the rhetoric of expressionism. And thus was born at least one of the several caricatures of progressive education in which humorists reveled —quite understandably—for at least a generation." And no one, it should be recalled, attacked these excesses more vigorously than Dewey, Rugg, and Bode.[15]

At their best, however, the progressive schools were very good indeed; some of the literary intellectuals who caricatured them sent their children to the very schools they were ridiculing. And no wonder; here are Harold Rugg and Ann Schumaker's description of two schools of the 1920s:

> Picture, then, children who cannot go to school early enough, and who linger about the shops, laboratories, yards and libraries until dusk or urgent parents drag them homeward. Observe these busy and hardworking youngsters who seem to play all

[14] "The weakness of existing progressive education," Dewey wrote in 1930, "is due to the meager knowledge which anyone has regarding the conditions and laws of continuity which govern the development of mental power. To this extent its defects are inevitable and are not to be complained of." (*The New Republic,* July 9, 1930)

[15] Perhaps the most devastating and trenchant criticism of progressive schools ever written may be found in Dewey's article, "How Much Freedom in New Schools," in *The New Republic* of July 9, 1930. "Ultimately it is the absence of intellectual control through significant subject matter," Dewey wrote, "which stimulates the deplorable egotism, cockiness, impertinence and disregard for the rights of others apparently considered by some persons to be the inevitable accompaniment, if not the essence, of freedom." Cf. also Boyd H. Bode, "The New Education Ten Years After: Apprenticeship or Freedom?", *The New Republic,* June 4, 1930, in which Bode related the now-famous story of the little boy in a progressive school plaintively asking his teacher, "Do we have to do what we want to do today?" Cf., too, Harold Rugg and Ann Shumaker, *The Child-Centered School: An Appraisal of the New Education,* New York: World Book Co., 1928; Lawrence A. Cremin, *The Transformation of the School*; and Patricia A. Graham, *Progressive Education, From Arcady to Academe,* New York: Teachers College Press, 1967.

day, who do not seem to have lessons and recitations, yet who do not wait for teachers to make assignments.

Here is a group of six and seven year olds. They dance; they sing; they play house and build villages; they keep store and take care of pets; they model in clay and sand; they draw and paint, read and write, make up stories and dramatize them; they work in the garden; they churn and weave and cook.

A group is inventing dances, which we are told, are for a pageant. In a darkened room films are being shown. A high school class is teaching the seventh grade how to use the library in looking up information on a geography topic.

Or this school:

It was Monday morning in a 'new' school. The chairs—painted clear, light green by juvenile artists—were empty, while the children themselves played in the yard. Around the walls interesting pictures in bright colors were grouped—the product of creative activity of another sort.

A girl came in, quietly arranged her materials, and began to paint. Another followed and, divesting herself of her wraps, gathered her record books and stamp box and departed for the post office, where, as postmistress, it was her duty to take charge of the school mail.

Presently the group had assembled. Here were fifteen or so talkative, busy nine-year-olds. We waited to see how the day would begin. . . .

What concerns us here, however, is not whether the progressive schools of the twenties and thirties were "good" or "bad," but simply the fact that informal education did take root in American soil at about the same time, and for much the same reasons, that the approach was gaining strength in England, where Dewey's writings were also influential. Indeed, progressivism was more widespread in this country than in England in the twenties and thirties—a fact that contributed to its demise in the decades following, when the approach was vulgarized beyond recognition by teachers, principals, and superintendents who mouthed the rhetoric but understood neither the spirit nor the underlying theory. ("It has perhaps helped," Dorothy Gardner writes, "that in England reforms came more slowly than they did in the United States.") Be that as it may, progressivism was not limited to private schools and the elite suburban public schools of the Northeast, as is sometimes thought. Some of the most distinguished progressive programs of the twenties and thirties were to be found in the public schools of Des Moines, Iowa; Denver, Colorado; Winnetka, Illinois; Madison, Wisconsin; and Tulsa, Oklahoma. Aspects of progressive techniques could be found, too, in such diverse places as Battle Creek and Grand Rapids, Michigan; Raleigh, North Carolina; Norfolk, Virginia; Houston, Texas; and Seattle, Washington, as well as in New York City, Chicago, Cleveland, Detroit, and Los Angeles. The experience of history thus suggests that Americans, no less than Englishmen, are capable of accepting informal education for their children.

III

They are accepting it now; informal classrooms are operating successfully in every part of the United States.

One of the most interesting programs is in North Dakota, where elementary schools are gradually being remodeled along informal lines, under the aegis of the University of North Dakota's newly created New School for Behavioral Studies in Education. The change had its origins in a statewide study of North Dakota's educational problems, initiated by the state's Legislative Research Committee in 1965 and carried out by the Committee, the North Dakota Department of Public Instruction, the University of North Dakota, the State Board of Higher Education, the United States Office of Education, and several local school districts. The study turned up the fact, among others, that North Dakota ranked fiftieth among the states in the professional preparation of its elementary school teachers, with only two in five holding a college degree. The state ranked fiftieth, too, in the overall opportunities it provided for elementary schooling, with few children attending kindergarten, few remedial reading teachers, and no diagnosticians or teachers of the handicapped at all.

The state's prestige demanded that the elementary school teachers' lack of academic preparation be corrected. More than prestige was involved, however; students taught by teachers without a college degree were achieving lower scores on standardized tests than students taught by college graduates.[16] The result was

16 Whether the discrepancy was due to poorer teaching, or simply to a less stimulating home background, is another question. Rural children tend to score below urban children all over the United States, and North Dakota's degree-less teachers are concentrated in the state's smallest villages and towns.

a proposal to bring all the state's elementary school teachers up to standard by 1975. But the authorities vetoed what most cities and states have attempted in similar circumstances: a crash program designed simply to provide teachers with the desired credentials. There would be little value in sending experienced teachers back to college, they reasoned, unless they would become better teachers as a result of the experience.

But what *is* a better teacher? And how do you make one? How can a college program change—really change—the way people teach? To get their money's worth—to justify the costs inherent in bringing the state's experienced teachers back to the university—the North Dakotans had to face up to the ultimate questions about the nature and purpose of education. They decided that merely to train teachers to do what they had always done, only better, was inadequate to the special need the state now faced: the fact that children coming from small, stable, closed, laconic rural communities would be living their lives in a large, rapidly changing, open, and much more verbal society. "The compelling task for elementary education in the State," as one document puts it, "is to prepare essentially rural children to become productive and useful citizens in what is rapidly becoming an urban society."

What this means in practice is that North Dakota children need much greater facility and ease with language (talking, reading, writing) than they now enjoy, better arithmetic and mathematical ability, and greater powers of creative expression. (North Dakota children currently score well below national norms in standardized tests of achievement.) It also means broadening the children's horizons beyond their immediate Great Plains environment. And it means making them comfortable with themselves and with others, as well as with the process of change.

These goals had to be achieved, moreover, within a set of constraints not operative in most American classrooms. Although North Dakota is beginning to urbanize, it is still predominantly rural, with a population of 615,000 spread over 71,-000 square miles. (By contrast, New York state has seventeen million people living in 50,000 square miles.) As of the 1960 census, only fifteen places in the entire state had a population of 2,500 or more. As a result, only 270 of the state's 400 operating school districts are large enough to afford a high school, and at least 100 districts operate a single one-, two-, or three-room schoolhouse. Except in the cities—the largest, Fargo, has a population of 52,000 and the other two "large" cities, Grand Forks and Minot, have about 35,000 each—most schools are so small that the conventional graded pattern of organization is uneconomical. Teachers may have to handle several grades simultaneously, therefore, and subject specialists, let alone curriculum supervisors, guidance personnel, remedial reading teachers, psychologists, etc., simply are not available. The classroom teacher has to do, and be, everything.

The statewide study committee, therefore, was looking for an approach that would be compatible with small, ungraded schools. They wanted an approach, too, that would permit some expansion in the student-teacher ratio (sending experienced teachers back to the university was going to be an expensive proposition), and that would permit some reduction in the number of formal curriculum objectives. If a teacher with thirty children has eight formal objectives, Dr. Karl Hereford, a consultant to the statewide committee, argued, that means 240 separate objectives. This is more than any teacher can supervise and still have time left to diagnose individual children's learning problems, let alone try to deal with them. The committee also hoped to find an approach that could be handled by the young master's degree candidates who would be taking over the classrooms while the experienced teachers were back at the university—ideally, an approach that might generate enough enthusiasm among the young people to hold them in the state, instead of their leaving after they had gotten their own certification.

By a happy coincidence, one of the members of the study group happened to read Joseph Featherstone's 1967 *New Republic* articles on the revolution in English primary schools,[17] and also happened to see the relevance of the English informal approach to both North Dakota's needs and the constraints under which its schools operate. For example:

• Vertical, or family, grouping makes a virtue of what North Dakota schools had been doing of necessity, i.e., putting several grades together in a single class. By developing children's capacity to work on their own, and by encouraging younger children to imitate older children and older children to teach younger ones, the free day approach makes it possible for

---

[17] Joseph Featherstone, "Schools for Children: What's Happening in British Classrooms," *The New Republic,* August 19, 1967; "How Children Learn," *The New Republic,* September 2, 1967; "Teaching Children to Think," *The New Republic,* September 9, 1967.

teachers to cope with a two- or three-year age span instead of being overwhelmed by it.

• Informal classrooms encourage free and easy communication, which North Dakota students and teachers need. The richness of concrete materials and other stimuli foster mathematical learning, too, as well as verbal and artistic expression, which North Dakota educationists seem to feel are particularly important in making the transition to an urban society. The richness of the environment also helps open children to new experiences and points of view, encouraging each student, as an official document puts it, "to broaden his vistas beyond his immediate age group and environment, and to assimilate elements of a broader culture."

• The informal approach also appeared to the study-group members to be suitable for use by inexperienced teachers, since it makes it possible to cut back the formal curriculum objectives to the basic skills of the three R's, permitting the other objectives to grow out of the children's interests and experience. This, along with the fact that children work at their own rate, either on their own or with other children, would, it was hoped, give teachers a lot more time and energy to deal with problems of individual instruction, thereby compensating, at least in part, for the absence of diagnostic and remedial specialists. Most learning problems in elementary school, the statewide study concluded, are neither emotional nor physiological in origin; they are simply children's defensive reactions to curricula that appear irrelevant and to teachers who are overly punitive or judgmental. The openness of the informal classroom, and the fact that children's activities grow out of their own interests, will, it is hoped, sharply reduce the incidence of learning disabilities and behavior problems.

North Dakota thus adopted a far-reaching program to convert formal elementary classrooms into informal ones, in which individualized learning replaces most large group instruction, the teacher's role changing from "chalk and talk" teaching to that of "observing, stimulating, and assisting children in their learning." The axis on which the program turns is a completely new program of teacher education and re-education developed by the University of North Dakota's New School of Behavioral Studies in Education, which was established in the spring of 1968. The University already had a conventional school of education; it was felt, however, that the kinds of sweeping changes that were envisaged could be more readily accomplished by creating a new institution to prepare teachers for informal teaching. To be effective, the New School's impressive young dean, Dr. Vito Perrone, maintains, a school of education "must itself become a model of the kind of educational environment it is promoting." Students cannot learn to become informal teachers, that is to say, unless they experience informal and individualized instruction themselves.[18]

The New School enrolls regular University of North Dakota undergraduates in their junior year, in a three-year program leading to a master's degree; the school also enrolls experienced teachers, who return to the Grand Forks campus for a year or more of study leading to a bachelor's degree.[19] While they are at the university, the teachers' places are taken by the New School's master's degree candidates, who spend September to June of the master's year teaching, under close supervision from the New School faculty. Participation in the program is voluntary on the part of the teachers, who commit themselves to return to their schools for a minimum of one year, as well as on the part of their supervisors and school boards. In 1968–69, the first year of operation, fourteen school districts participated. The number more than doubled at the beginning of the 1969–70 school year, and the inclusion of Grand Forks meant that the state's three largest cities—Fargo, Grand Forks, and Minot— are all participating. Thus, the program appears to be winning support throughout the state.

The program also appears to be remarkably successful, and the impact on the teachers is quite evidently profound. So far as the children are concerned, it is, of course, too soon to measure how informal education has affected their ability in the three R's; a full-scale evaluation of the program's impact on academic skills and on the other objectives of the program will be made after it has been operating for several years. Records of some individual classes, however, indicate strikingly large gains in reading ability during the first year, and on direct observation, the quality of the writing, arithmetic, and science, while uneven, was frequently quite impressive.

What cannot be doubted is that the children are visibly happy

18 The New School's program will be described in some detail in Chapter 11, when we turn to reforms in teacher education.
19 In addition, a small doctoral program enrolls faculty members from North Dakota's four state colleges, to equip them to initiate similar teacher education programs when they return to their own institutions.

and engaged. They express as much enthusiasm for the new approach as do the teachers: school is fun, something new in this heartland of the Protestant Ethic.

ITEM: "Last year we had to work all the time. Now we can play all the time," one little boy volunteers to the visitor, as he "plays" with a complicated mathematical game.

One of the measures of the children's enthusiasm is the markedly improved attendance records at most of the schools in the program. "The children won't stay home even when they're sick," a Minot teacher reports. "Our carpet gets it every once in a while, but it does one's ego good to have parents call and tell you their child is not well but won't stay home." And a woman teaching in a wooden two-room schoolhouse wrote, in her self-evaluation, "I have had several mothers tell me that this is the first year they haven't had to fight every morning to get their youngsters to school. I think this is perhaps my greatest accomplishment."

To be sure, some children have had difficulty making the change. "I liked it better last year," one fastidious little girl informed the visitor. "Our seats were in straight rows and it never got messy." But hers is very much a minority view. Indeed, the children's evident pleasure has troubled some of their hardworking parents, who worry that the youngsters are having too much fun; work, especially school work, is *supposed* to be arduous and unpleasant.

By and large, however, parental resistance has been overcome, in part through a great deal of painstaking explanations the New School teachers have given at meetings of community organizations as well as of PTA's, in part through the parents' gradual recognition that their children were learning a great deal —that they were reading proficiently, writing fluently, and handling arithmetic with ease. (In one case, the turning point seems to have been the parents' discovery that their youngest child was mastering fractions before their older children who were still in formal classes.) By the end of the first year, parents were expressing considerable enthusiasm.

ITEM: From a father's letter to an elementary school principal. "May my son come to school earlier? There's so much he wants to do and he can't seem to fit it all in during the regular hours."

The change is visible to anyone; the New School probably is the only school of education in the United States whose graduates are easily, indeed instantly, recognizable by their teaching style. Walking into any elementary school in North Dakota, in fact, a visitor can tell at a glance whether a New School alumnus is present, and who he or she is. Or who *they* are; wherever possible, the School attempts to send its teachers out in teams of two or more, so that they can reinforce each other in what sometimes is a resistant or even hostile environment—a janitor who objects to their "messy" rooms,[20] a principal who complains about the noise or about children moving about, other teachers who deprecate the "kindergarten" atmosphere, parents who worry that their children can't be learning if they are having so much fun. The teachers also receive a good deal of support from Dean Perrone and the New School faculty, with whom they stay in close contact.

The impact the New School has had is all the more remarkable in view of the fact that the teachers observed by the Carnegie Study's researcher were the first to be sent into the field. Because the New School had just opened, the first batch of candidates for the master's degree had received only a single summer session of preparation for informal teaching, during which the regular New School faculty had been supplemented by a team of English advisers, heads, and teachers. Despite the brevity of the preparation, the teachers have transformed the look, sound, and feel of their classrooms.

Starkweather, North Dakota, provides a nice example. Appropriately named, Starkweather has a population of 250 hardy souls; its main street, when not covered by a foot and a half or more of snow, is an unpaved dirt road. There are no stores; even the bar has closed down for lack of customers, its broken windows bearing mute testimony to the community's decline. The school, a modern, attractive building, houses two hundred children, most of whom travel a number of miles to get there, in grades one through twelve. (The high school graduates fifteen students a year.) Four elementary school teachers are New

---

[20] Custodians are a critically important, and almost universally overlooked, factor in public school reform. In many school systems, especially in large cities like New York, the custodians sometimes have the power to block reforms that involve rearrangement of the classrooms—all the more so if the reforms involve use of the corridors. (See Part IV.) In almost all large schools, the custodians are a force to be reckoned with.

School master's candidates. Their classes are in many ways more exciting, and certainly more innovative, than anything one can find in the Scarsdales, Winnetkas, Shaker Heights, and Palo Altos of the United States.

ITEM: In the room housing the second and third grades, most of the children are working in and around the math area, which has a huge "number line," from 0 to 70, running along one wall, individual cardboard number lines for each child, straws and beans for counting, a number of abacuses, a cash register, a set of Cuisenaire rods, quite a few styrofoam peg boards, etc. Two boys are working together; using a 0 to 25 cardboard number line, they are counting by twos, by fours, by eights, by threes, etc. Four children and the teacher are studying fractions, using a flannel board. Another half-dozen are sprawled out on pillows, cushions, and scraps of carpet in the reading corner, partitioned off from the rest of the room by homemade room dividers.

ITEM: After watching the children for a while, the visitor is attracted to a huge display in the reading corner—a piece of corrugated board painted a brilliant blue, with the heading "Book Sharing" printed in bright red letters. Mounted to the board are a number of colored strips of oaktag, each suggesting a way of sharing one's pleasure in reading with the other members of the class. Charlotte has signed up to make a play of her book on January 21, and Kathy Ann and Becky have indicated their intention to offer a joint dramatization two days later. Nat and Lori have signed up for two other dates, to read their favorite parts of the books they have finished aloud to the class. Other children have committed themselves to read a story to the first grade, to write a letter of appreciation to the author of the book they've finished, to make a dust jacket, and to dramatize the book in dance.

ITEM: A sixth-grade classroom in Starkweather. The teacher is surrounded by a cluster of children calling out "loud" words— "bong," "boom," "scream," "crash," "screech," etc. The teacher leaves to greet the visitors; the children continue with enthusiasm undiminished. When they begin to run out of "loud" words, they start collecting "soft" words. Other children, meanwhile, are busily working in the reading area, math area, and science corner.

Nor is Starkweather unusual. All over the state, New School teachers have created exciting, open, informal classrooms.

ITEM: A third-grade classroom in Minot, the state's third largest city (population 33,477). Five children are plugged into a tape recorder, listening to a story and following it in the books in front of them. Another child is dictating a story he has written into a second tape recorder; when he finishes the dictation, he plays it back, a look of rapture on his face. Several others are watching a film strip on some aspect of Indian life; two of the children are operating the projector. Four children are painting at a huge easel made by the teacher. Others are busy reading and writing at a large homemade carrel in the middle of the reading area. One youngster, who feels the need for privacy, is reading in a booth the teacher has built for that purpose. Made out of the packing crate in which a large freezer had been shipped, the booth has a door and window, two chairs, and a light.

ITEM: The school in Lakota, North Dakota, population 1,658, where four New School teachers work with 130 fourth, fifth and sixth graders. In one classroom, the children are sprawled on the floor in groups, working on a series of murals. It is too soon to judge these murals, but the walls are covered with some lively impressionist paintings of a recent blizzard. The room itself has a verve and flair that bespeaks imagination and talent; it is subdivided into any number of sections by dividers made of corrugated paper, which the children have painted in abstract and pop styles.

ITEM: A classroom in Edmore (population 405). Three girls and two boys tell their teacher they have prepared a skit and ask if the visitors could stay to see them put it on. The teacher, after conferring with the visitors, agrees, and then teacher, visitors, and classmates see the skit for the first time. The adults are impressed by these rural youngsters' poise and style as much as by the skit itself.

In no sense, however, are the rooms mere slavish imitations of English classrooms. The similarities are readily apparent, but so are the differences. The American penchant for hardware and gadgetry is even more visible in hamlets like Starkweather and

Edmore than in the Scarsdales and the Winnetkas of the United States. It is the rare classroom in North Dakota that does not have carrels equipped with film-strip machines and screen, overhead projectors, tape recorders with a number of plug-in listening posts, record players, typewriters, and what have you.

The science areas are richer and more extensive than those in the typical English primary school, reflecting the rural American interest in the natural world and the near-universal American interest in machinery.

ITEM: The math-science area for the fourth-, fifth-, and sixth-grade class in Lakota originally had two ample-sized rooms. The teachers, working as a team, chose to have the wall separating their two rooms removed, thereby creating one enormous area. The science workshop contains, among other items:
• An incubator with twelve eggs hatching in it, which some children chose to observe systematically, once a week for the first two weeks, and every day thereafter;
• Four cages of white mice;
• Two microscopes;
• An internal combustion engine, which some boys had put into working condition;
• A rusty, dismantled motor from an old washing machine, which two other youngsters were restoring to shape;
• An old radio, which two ten-year-olds were taking apart in order to put in working condition;
• An intercom system which a fourth grader was assembling;
• Several shelves containing batteries, transformers, heating elements, magnifying glasses, electric resistors, iron filings, test tubes, Bunsen burners, and a host of other such material;
• An arrangement of every kind of shell imaginable, labeled with name and place of origin by people who may never have been outside of the land-locked state of North Dakota;
• A display of some fifty different kinds of grains and seeds, again carefully labeled;
• Another display of bark from different trees;
• A collection of carefully mounted butterflies;
• An overhead viewer and projector.

Every student was working on his individual study project. Before beginning, he had written a proposal, stating what his topic was to be, what materials he planned to use, and how he planned to go about resolving the particular problem that he had set up. Typically, although not always, the boys leaned toward mechanical and electrical problems and the girls toward nature study. In almost every instance, the work was of an impressively high level. Almost staggering in its complexity was a project showing how an automobile ignition system works, with complicated diagrams of battery, switch, coil, spark plugs, distributor, rotary switch, and more.

ITEM: A third-grade classroom in Minot. A number of children are in the science area, absorbed in watching the fish in a huge aquarium—an old-fashioned bathtub the teacher had picked up from a salvage company.

ITEM: The science area in a second- and third-grade room in Starkweather. A small group of eight-year-olds guide their visitor through a display of seashells and rocks, talking knowledge-ably as they go. Next they come to a section containing a snake-skin, jars of pickled frogs, pickled deer brains, pickled pig brains, and, the pride of their display, a pair of pig's eyes rolling wildly in a jar of formaldehyde. Oblivious to the visitor's queasy stomach, the boy who had performed the surgery on the pig calmly discusses the procedure he used. He goes on to point out the toughness of the white of the eye: how he discovered the toughness while trying to pierce it, why the white of the eye has to be tough, and how it compares to the toughness of the white of the human eye. The visitor is relieved when the group moves on to a display of brilliantly colored photographs of dinosaurs, fossils, even insects, and then to a map of the moon, a micro-scope, slides, and other more familiar material.

The biggest difference between the North Dakota and the English informal classrooms, however, is in the approach to reading. The North Dakota schools place substantially more emphasis on learning to read in the first grade, and there is con-siderably more formal instruction in reading, as well as a good bit more evaluation of children's reading progress. American parents simply cannot accept the casual approach that char-acterizes the English classroom. By and large, however, teachers have been able to emphasize reading instruction within the framework of informal, individualized instruction.

ITEM: A young third-grade teacher describes the results of the standardized reading tests the children took in September and

January. In the September tests, the children ranged from some who could barely cope with pre-primer materials to those who were comfortably reading at the third-grade level. By January, the range had widened, from youngsters about to begin the simplest first-grade readers to youngsters reading on a sixth-grade level. "How can I stand at the front of the room and assign the same level of work to all my children?" she asks rhetorically.

More important, the emphasis on reading skill has not come at the expense of concern for enjoyment in reading or ease and creativity in writing.

ITEM: A fourth-, fifth-, and sixth-grade room in Lakota. A number of youngsters are writing stories, each taking off from the opening phrase, "One frosty, frigid morning . . ." On the board is a collection of a hundred or so "winter words and phrases," which the children themselves have assembled. The buzz and chatter all over the room indicate that the children are quite verbal.

ITEM: Another fourth-fifth-sixth-grade room in Lakota, filled with devices to stimulate communication of all sorts. There are sheets posted around the reading area, where children write their own suggestions for "A Good Poem to Share," "Stories to Read Out Loud," "Suggestions for Choral Reading," "A Good Story to Read to Yourself." A "Something to Share" bulletin board is filled with the children's own snapshots, poems, stories, personal notices, etc. Other displays of the children's writing indicate a more-than-usual degree of imagination. There is a display headed, "What is . . . ?" with poems children have written on what is blue, what is gold, what is purple, etc., trying to express how a color feels, sounds, smells, etc. And there are stories on "What a Turkey Thinks of Thanksgiving" (a nice switch from "Why We Are Happy the Pilgrims Landed"), a collection of "Spooky Tales," essays on "My Dream School."

ITEM: A sixth-grade classroom in Starkweather. Three youngsters are writing a story. To help them break away from the usual rigid classroom exercise, the teacher has one child begin by writing something that is to serve as the middle of a story; a second then writes a beginning to lead up to the middle segment, and a third completes the story.

ITEM: A room in Minot. A display headed, "A Poem I Recommend" has a caption suggesting that those students who were interested might like to write down the poem's title, the book and page number where it can be found, and their reasons for liking the poem. Nineteen children were interested.

ITEM: A fourth-fifth-sixth-grade room in Lakota. On the wall are poems the children have written. One, by a farmer's son, begins, "I think my shadow is full of fears/Because when I go in the dark it disappears."

In extending informal teaching to the upper elementary grades, moreover, the New School teachers have been particularly ingenious in using math materials that will help children move from the purely concrete to the formal and abstract.

ITEM: The math area in the fourth-fifth-sixth-grade math and science room in Lakota. Several youngsters are working—or playing—with a game called "The Tower of Hanoi," a board with three upright sticks and five varying-sized discs stacked in order of size on each peg. The object is to transfer the discs from one peg to either of the other two, ending up with the discs arranged in the same order; only one disc may be removed at a time, and a larger disc may never be placed on top of a smaller one. To make sure that the game is purposeful, several exercises accompany it, which the students are trying to solve. Among the exercises:

1. To transfer three discs requires at least seven moves. Is there any way to tell the least number of moves for two discs? four discs? five discs?
2. Find the rule for the Tower of Hanoi. Let $\square$ be the number of discs and $\triangle$ the number of moves.

$\square$	$\triangle$
1	
2	
3	
4	
5	
6	

3. Get a sheet of graph paper and make a graph of your equation. Use the ordered pairs you found in exercise #2.

Pretty sophisticated math for ten- and eleven-year-olds; and the squeals of laughter and murmurs of disappointment testified to their absorption and enjoyment.

ITEM: The same classroom. Two children are absorbed in solving the problems that go with another homemade game, a piece of styrofoam with nine holes and a number of black and white golf tees. The exercises follow:

> Place the tees in the board so that the black tees are on your left and the white tees on your right.

RULES:
1. The white pegs move only to the left and the black only to the right.
2. Move only one peg at a time.
3. You can move a peg into the next hole, or
4. You can jump, but only a single peg of the opposite color.

OBJECT: To interchange all the pegs.

EXERCISES:
1. With one peg on each side of the center hole, it takes 8 moves to interchange them; how many moves would it take to interchange 3 pegs? 4 pegs?
2. If there were 5 pegs, how many moves would it take to interchange all of them? 6 pegs?
3. What is the rule for the peg game? Let the number of pegs be □ . Let the number of moves to interchange them be △ .

□	△
1	
2	
3	
4	
5	
6	

IV

Some 1,500 miles east of Starkweather, in the city of New York (population 8,000,000), a much more limited but no less significant experiment in informal education is going on in five elementary schools. The experiment had its origins in the extreme dissatisfaction that Professor Lillian Weber felt, on her return from England, in sending her City College students into conventional classrooms to do their student teaching. It made no sense, she felt, to give her students an understanding of the psychology of learning and of the nature of child development, only to have them do their student teaching in classrooms that controverted everything she had tried to teach. Such an arrangement was not only senseless but self-defeating, since a large body of research suggests that the classroom teacher with whom students do their practice teaching exerts a decisive influence on the development of their teaching style.

Placing the students in the hothouse atmosphere of a laboratory school, on the other hand, also seemed unsatisfactory; it would not, Professor Weber felt, prepare the students for the harsh realities of the classrooms and schools in which, in all probability, they would be working. If her students were to be able to exert any influence for change, Professor Weber reasoned, they would have to learn how to deal with schools as they are, and how to handle all the obstacles, frustrations, and petty irritations that change usually evokes.

The solution was to carve out a small section of P.S. 123, a Central Harlem elementary school, which Mrs. Weber served as consultant, and in which she had helped develop the pre-kindergarten program before going to England. (The school was one of four Harlem schools affiliated with City College's School of Education, where Mrs. Weber teaches early childhood education.) In the course of her eighteen months of close study of informal English schools, Mrs. Weber had come to regard the use of the hall and corridors—what she likes to call "in and out-ness" —as one of the keys to the schools' success. Her program began, therefore, by using only the corridor outside a group of five participating classrooms; the five classes included one pre-kindergarten, two kindergartens, a first-grade, and a second-grade room around the "L" at one end of the school's first floor.

Setting up the "stuff" for informal teaching in the corridor— initially, for just an hour a day, three days a week—had the further advantage of giving the five classroom teachers access to the new approach without forcing it upon them. Mrs. Weber was determined to avoid any direct challenge to the teachers or to the autonomy of their classrooms. Her object, in addition to training her students in informal teaching, was to explore how far one could go toward freeing the classroom structure and developing more intimate, humane settings, starting with the base of the existing curriculum and grade organization. Indeed, she strenuously resisted attempts by others to pin labels like "free day" or "infant school" on what she was doing. "We were Americans," she wrote in summarizing the experience, "and the point was to try to develop support for the child's learning drive in our own context, not to use terms and labels that didn't apply."

Hence the teachers, who had agreed to participate in the experiment, and who had been involved in the planning from the outset, were obliged only to schedule their classes in such a way as to provide a common hour three times a week during which the corridor could be used. They were also asked to suggest some activity they particularly wanted to do in their classrooms during the corridor hour, and which they would be willing to share with other teachers and children. One teacher chose a collection of guinea pigs and other small animals, another a phonograph and records for dancing, a third a workbench and tools, and a fourth an oven, all of which Mrs. Weber purchased with a $1,000 grant she had obtained from a small foundation.[21]

The "open corridor" came into being in the spring of 1968, after months of preparation and planning. For the rest of that school year, during the thrice-weekly corridor hour, each teacher would release five children at a time to visit the corridor or one of the other four rooms; each teacher agreed to accept up to three children from other classes. Inside the classrooms, teachers used the hour as they wished, frequently to carry on the activity for which they had gotten special equipment, e.g., dancing, cooking, woodwork. The room with the animals became a point of interest for the whole school, particularly after the second batch of guinea pigs was born. The corridor activities—a sandbox, a water table, tables with rich maths materials, blocks, easels—were supervised by Professor Weber's students.

At first, the classroom teachers tended to direct the children, or to insist that they stay with a single activity for the entire hour. Gradually, however, they become less concerned with "giving" the children "full experiences" and more content with letting them explore on their own; and the children, once the novelty of the rich environment wore off, were able to settle down with a single activity. Both teachers and children also

---

[21] For a more detailed description of how the project developed, see Arthur Tobier, "The Open Classroom," *The Center Forum*, Vol. 3, No. 6, May 15, 1969. Cf. also Center for Urban Education Programmed Reference Service, *The Open Door,* New York Center for Urban Education, 1970.

learned to talk in normal conversational tones—the children more quickly than the teachers. (In the beginning, the noise level was high, as teachers and children continued to speak with the volume needed to address a whole class.)

By the end of the semester, the impact was substantial. The children clearly enjoyed the corridor activities, greeting their teachers each morning with the query, "Is it corridor today?" The teachers learned to handle the unexpected, and became less concerned about the interruption to their planned instructions, as they discovered that the children were creative as well as active in the corridor—that they were learning as well as playing. Most important, perhaps, the teachers were won over as they realized that their discipline problems had been sharply reduced, and that they consequently had far less need to exercise conscious control.

ITEM: From a transcript of a teachers' meeting: Miss _____:

> There has been a lot of discussion about control or lack of it in our school—control over behavior—and we found in the corridor that behavior was never a problem. And I think the key to this was the fact that we were flexible. A child was not forced into something that he did not want to do. Whatever he went to, he went to because he was interested in it. And if he left it, he was always able to find something else that he was interested in. The motivation came from within and needed little external control. The control came from within each child because he was interested and excited about what he was doing. This interest was enough to keep him . . . active and creative, not a discipline problem. It was a treat to come out, and nobody wanted to spoil his chance for the next time by being unruly.

The corridor, in fact, became a magnet that attracted children from all over the building, with the older children showing particular interest. At first the teachers resented the intrusion and ordered the outsiders away. Gradually, however, some of them came to welcome the older children, inviting them to look around if they would like, and in some cases, forming close relationships with them.

ITEM: From a transcript of a teachers' meeting. Mrs. _____:

> I have found that for the most part the older children really aren't consciously out to bother you. They are really there, number one, because they're a little lost, and number two,

because they have seen something that interests them. For a short time, involving them and including them gives them reason to have some sort of contact with you, and it ends up being a much more positive thing than hurrying them up and running them off with an angry growl in your voice.

Mrs. _____: I have found the relationship developed with the older children who come in this fashion is a very different one than they have with their teachers. You and they are really friends with respect for each other. You're not trying to teach them, you are merely another person whom they may encounter, and who can expose them to something they may never have seen.

Before the semester was over, moreover, a group of parents and teachers from another school came to observe the open corridor. They were sufficiently impressed to persuade their district superintendent to invite Lillian Weber to introduce the program the following year in their school, P.S. 84, located in a racially mixed neighborhood of low- to high-income families. Before the program got underway, however, the custodian forbade the use of the corridors, claiming violation of the fire laws, and so Professor Weber and the teachers had to revamp the classrooms themselves.[22] By spring, the change was dramatic, if sometimes faltering or erratic.

ITEM: A first-grade room at P.S. 84. The science area has, among other animals, two turtles. Over the turtle pond is a poster headed, "Our Turtles. We have two turtles. We can observe them. What do they do? Can you do that, too?" Five children have written their observations, as follows.

Kathy—One of the turtles has two red spots near his eyes.
Daniel—One can stretch his neck very far.
Anthony—They can put their head and their feet in their shells.
Gordon—When I observed both turtles did not move.
Victor—The big turtle was on top of the little one.

ITEM: A girl approaches the visitor to ask, "What are you doing?" and invites her to join her in the maths area, where she picks out a game with various shapes and matching cards. Two boys, already there, are using the Cuisenaire rods, and another two are playing a game with peg boards and sticks; the teacher is working with a small group of children, holding up cards that

[22] Some of the steps in that process are described in Tobier, *The Open Classroom*.

say, "Make something with 3 black," "Make something with 2 yellow," and so on. On the bulletin board, in a child's writing, is a report reading, "Gordon and Julie weighed themselves. Gordon weighed 50. Scott weighed 43. Who weighed more? Gordon weighed more." After a few minutes, the teacher plays a xylophone to get the class's attention; the children stop and listen, as the teacher softly tells them it is time to clean up. Denise, who was about to teach the visitor a new game, says, "I'll teach it to you another day," and puts it away.

At P.S. 123, meanwhile, the project continued in the corridor, expanding from the three hours a week of the preceding spring to a "corridor period" of an hour and a half a day during the 1968–69 school year. Besides the greater time allocated to the corridor activities, the second year saw much more fluid movement of both children and teachers in and out of the corridor and the participating rooms. And while most of the concrete materials were still housed in the corridor, to be set up at the beginning of the daily period and taken down at the end, a substantial amount of stuff began to infiltrate the classrooms themselves.

ITEM: The second-grade classroom during the corridor hour at P.S. 123. A record player is providing background music from the class's collection of "soul music." A number of children are clustered around the cages of gerbils and their new offspring; some are simply watching, most are recording their observations or writing stories about the gerbils. Other children are working at an enormous workbench, fully equipped with hammers, nails, saws, planes, vises, wood, etc. Teachers elsewhere in the school had looked askance at the workbench's installation. These ghetto children, they insisted, were bound to hurt each other, if not themselves, with such "dangerous" tools—and besides, they could be counted on to steal whatever could be easily moved. A year after installation, there had been no injuries and no thefts.

It is in the corridor, however, where most of the action is and most of the stuff can be found. On a morning in March, a visitor sees the following:

A huge sheet of brown paper, on which two girls are drawing pictures of, and writing stories about, the gerbils. (By the end of the morning, the paper is hanging on the wall.)

• At another table, a little girl is attaching numbered weights to each arm of a balance scale. By the end of the corridor hour, she has determined—and written down—the fact that "4 + 3 equals 5 + 2 equals 7."

• A table with rulers and various lengths of string, which children are using to measure each other and anything else in sight. The table also contains a large "geoboard" and a box of rubber bands ("I made squares from rubber bands and screws," the boy at the geoboard writes), Cuisiniere rods, and a host of stuff for counting, almost all of it in use.

• Another table containing a box with variously colored plastic rings that fit together; mirrors and plastic shapes; boxes of discs with numbers on each; and mounds and mounds of colored cubes that children are interlocking together, making towers, apartment houses, etc. One girl is measuring herself against her tower to see if she is longer or shorter; a boy is counting how many yellows, how many reds, how many greens, etc. there are in the Rube Goldberg contraption he has put together.

• Blocks of every conceivable size, shape, and color.

• A water table, big enough for six children, with an array of different-sized and shaped plastic bottles, pitchers, and containers for measuring and pouring.

• A table with crayons, Magic Markers, pencils, writing paper, drawing paper, all in full use.

And much, much more; the movement is so fluid that the visitor finds it impossible to make a complete inventory.

More striking than the richness of materials, however, is the atmosphere of joyousness that pervades.

ITEM: A little girl, who has been flirting as she works with pencil and paper, finishes her effort and triumphantly hands it to the visitor. It reads:

PS 123   Gazella
                March 19, 1969

                I feel good

I feel good and not Bad. I met a new teacher and her name is Mrs. Silberman.

1	6	3	3	3
+ 1	+ 6	+ 3	+ 9	− 0
2	12	6	12	3

But this is Central Harlem, where children have every reason to feel bad and not good. As the teachers report the background of one child after another, the visitor understands what a tepid euphemism "disadvantaged" is. The classes participating in the corridor program include, among others, an orphan who lives with a blind grandmother, two children whose mothers are in mental hospitals, a child whose father was killed in Vietnam and whose mother is a prostitute, another orphan who had lived with his grandmother until she was incapacitated by a stroke, and who now lives with an aunt, a child who had watched her mother gradually destroyed by multiple sclerosis, and who now lives with her grandmother, a child brought to New York from Jamaica and then abandoned, a child whose father had just been killed in an automobile accident, a child whose parents have been trying to abandon him for some time. . . . And yet the visitor does not need Gazella's note to know that these incredibly resilient children are indeed happy, at least while they are in school. "You could see it in the bodies of the girls who were dancing to the soul records," she reports. "You could read it in the eyes of the boys who were building airplanes and scooters at the workbench. You could hear it in the babble of voices. (How nice it is to hear children talking in school!) And you could sense it in the purposeful comings and goings of children as they left one room for another, and then one table in the corridor for another."

And the purpose, it is clear, is learning: learning to talk comfortably, learning to read, learning to write. Every activity, in fact, seems to result in reading and writing. In some cases, the writing comes easily, in some with great difficulty. One little girl, for example, has to ask the visitor how to spell every word she wants to use, but her inability to spell does not daunt her in the least; she keeps writing and writing and writing. Clearly, these children have things they *want* to say; their impulse to communicate impels them to write, to read, to talk.

ITEM: From a composition being written in the corridor by a first grader, spelling as in the original: "I like Miss Dubovick. I like the way she likes me too and she is a good girl too me. Love Sandra H."

ITEM: Two girls offer to read their second grade's daily newspaper, entitled "The Phony News," which is written on the blackboard. (The children had picked the name, rejecting the traditional "The Happy News.") With a "Look Ma, no hands" flourish, a third child demonstrates her skill by reading the paper backwards, as does a fourth. Clearly, these children are *reading* each word, not repeating from memory or guessing words from the general context. Not surprisingly, this class tests slightly above grade norm on the city-wide standardized reading tests.

ITEM: A seven-year-old boy, having finished building an elaborate contraption of wood, cardboard, and assorted other materials, writes, with evident self-satisfaction and a little help with the spelling: "I made an astronaut. I made the door of the astronaut's capsule." Mrs. Weber reports that the boys are reading and writing as well as, or better than, the girls, breaking the usual pattern in which boys lag considerably behind girls. The reason, she suggests, is that these boys have male things to do, in sharp contrast to the femininity of the usual elementary school classroom.

These results are being achieved, moreover, in heterogeneously grouped classes taught by typical New York City teachers. While participation was voluntary, none of the teachers was handpicked for the program; almost all were profoundly affected by it. One teacher, for example, freely confessed that when the year began she saw her children—and referred to them—as "animals" and "savages"; by spring, she had a warm and close relationship with almost every child. "Let me tell you about John," she would tell the visitor, bragging about what a "monster" he had been in September and what a "doll" he now was. "The only time they act up," she explained, "is when there has been too much repression."

ITEM: From a visitor's notes on a visit to P.S. 123.

> I saw—or rather I experienced—a vivid example of how the informal approach enables teachers to develop closer relationships with their children. Specifically, a little girl named Sandra took a strong dislike to me. Every time I wandered past the mural she was working on, she threw her whole body over it so that I couldn't see her work. If I smiled at her, she covered her face or ran away. If I were a teacher standing at the front of the room and she were a student sitting at a desk all day, this inability to relate to one another almost certainly would snowball. What happened instead was that I lent my felt-tipped pen to another child who wanted to write her name;

then I wrote this child a letter, and she wrote me a letter . . . and lo and behold, Sandra happened over to watch, and I mentioned that I had another pen and more paper. Next thing, Sandra was writing a story about her gerbils, and she signed it, "Love Sandra to Mrs. Silberman." And before I left, I also had a love letter from her. The informality, the ease of movement, and the variety of "stuff" made it possible for Sandra and me to reach each other in a way that isn't ordinarily open to children and teachers.

ITEM: Sandra's story about the gerbils.

Our Gerbils.

in our classroom we have gerbils. we you like to see them today. you can see them every day. You came to this class room. and we have five baby gerbils. but one of them died and now we have six bady gerbils. and the gerbils are a good pat to have in you class room.

Love sandra to Mrs. Silberman.

ITEM: Sandra's love letter.

Dear Mrs. Silberman.

I we Like you to be my Friend. We you be a Good Friend to me. We you like to came every day and be a Good Friend to me. I Love to came and Play with you But I have to go to school.

Love Sandra for Mrs. Silberman.

Understandably, therefore, the experiment is spreading. In the 1969–70 school year, three more schools asked Professor Weber to establish informal classrooms, bringing the number to thirty-seven. And when Professor Weber, in response to some requests, established a workshop on informal teaching at City College, twenty-three teachers enrolled, paying the hundred-dollar tuition out of their own pockets.

v

While the North Dakota and New York experiments represent conscious attempts to adapt and modify English methods for American use, a number of important programs have developed independently, and without prior knowledge, of the English experience.

In 1964, for example, Mrs. Lore Rasmussen—a dynamic educator, who had, among other things, run a cooperative children's camp in Michigan and taught education at a Southern Negro college, and math in an independent school in the Philadelphia suburbs—accepted a position as a math supervisor in one of Philadelphia's poorest Negro slums. Her varied background had persuaded her that silent, rigid, authoritarian, almost purely verbal formal classrooms had to be transformed into informal, humane workshops filled with concrete materials that children could manipulate, count, move, rearrange, stack, measure, join, and separate. Like Lillian Weber, Mrs. Rasmussen recognized that she could not produce the change she wanted by simply walking into a classroom and telling a teacher what to do, or even by taking over a class herself, turning it into a model of what she had in mind; she would be defeated, she felt, by the physical arrangements themselves—the rows of desks, taking up all the floor space, facing forward toward the teacher as The Source of All Knowledge. Change would be more effective, she decided, by enticing rather than bludgeoning teachers into gradually adopting new approaches and new materials.

The solution was to set up shop in the basement of an elementary school, and to invite teachers to bring their classes for an hour a week. The room was furnished very much like the maths area of an informal English classroom. The teachers were perfectly happy to come, since Mrs. Rasmussen took over the class for the hour, giving them an unscheduled free period. A pot of coffee, the freedom to smoke, and a comfortable chair or two set up in one corner served to keep most teachers in the room for the period, thereby exposing them, as well as the children, to the new materials and approach. Another principal, impressed by what he saw during a visit, asked Mrs. Rasmussen to set up a similar workshop in his school the following year.

By 1969, nine such "Learning Centers," as they came to be called, had been established in the Philadelphia schools, their purpose broadened considerably beyond the original concern with math alone. Although each one has its own flavor, reflecting the interests and capabilities of the teachers in the school in which it is located, the Centers share a number of characteristics. In general, they are comfortable and inviting rooms, with an abundance of materials and equipment to which the children have free and easy access. Their tone is nonauthoritarian, although considerable use is made of teacher-directed individual or small-group activities as well as child-initiated play; the emphasis is on developing competence in language, math, and science, with relatively little attention given to the arts. Thus, the Learning Centers, although far less structured than the typical American classroom, tend to be a good bit more structured than English free day classrooms. In part, that greater structure reflects greater preoccupation with formal curriculum objectives. In good measure, however, it simply reflects the exigencies of scheduling; most children get to spend only an hour a week in a Learning Center.

That hour tends to be divided into four parts, beginning with the "Welcoming Minutes," when the lab teacher greets the children at the door. The explicit goal is to set a relaxed, informal tone and to make each child feel that he or she is personally expected and valued; hugs are given and returned, compliments exchanged, and secrets whispered.

The second part of the hour is typically a teacher-directed "talking and doing" session. As Mrs. Rasmussen describes it for participating teachers:

> Now the children are either sitting on the floor or in a semi-circle around the teacher and her surprise activity or toys for the day, or they are seated informally around tables in the lab classroom, each with a set of his own laboratory materials to explore under the teacher's guidance. This period is semi-structured but not rigidly pre-planned. It may last from five to thirty minutes depending on the interest and maturity of the children. Active involvement of the children is sought. They must get a chance to do much talking, acting, touching, chanting, listening, wondering, laughing—all this around some theme which is begun simply but which builds up into inter-woven thought. Because it is *their* learning session, humor, whimsy, individuality, playfulness, non-conformity, are not only tolerated, but actively encouraged as long as they represent appropriate styles of response fitting the common theme.

ITEM: A Learning Center teacher directs a first-grade class in a series of games designed to show how different kinds of language—gestures, actions, words—can portray different moods, situations, identities. "Let's look angry in as many different ways as you can," she tells the children.

"Now let's laugh in different ways," she says. "First let's giggle." "Now let's snicker." "Let me hear a belly laugh like Santa gives." As groups of children make up their own variants, the teacher begins playing a subtler game with two or three children at a time. In this game, the child must describe a toy or game or other object without naming it, listing as many characteristics as possible—size, shape, color, texture, etc.— until the teacher or another child can pick it off the shelf.

ITEM: Four second-grade children sit around a table containing four mail-order catalogues, four sets of advertisements from department stores, four pads, four pencils, and four "adding-multiplying" machines. For a time, the children select random items from the catalogues for the sheer fun of going "shopping" and then adding up costs. Then they follow a prepared "suggestion card" written by the teacher, directing each child to pretend that he has a forty-dollar budget with which to buy a complete Easter outfit, from hat to shoes, from underwear to lightweight coat. A furious amount of addition, subtraction and multiplication ensues as the children struggle to stretch the budget as far as possible. For these children, arithmetic has become "relevant."

ITEM: The teacher directs a group of children in a game about circles. The children dance into large circles, small circles, tiny circles. They intersect. They form concentric circles. Then, with pencils, paper, and compasses, the children each make a "Circle Book," no two of which are alike. It is clear that they understand terms like "connecting," "concentric," "intersecting," as well as subtle differences between "huge" and "large" or "small" and "tiny."

The third part of the hour is devoted to nondirected play and work—a time to experiment, explore, and invent. Now the scissors and colored paper and paste are seized upon, the blocks manipulated, the magnifying glasses and mirrors and microscopes scrutinized, the rubber bands stretched into every conceivable shape on geoboards, the spring scales and balance scales given a workout with pebbles and bottle caps and washers.

ITEM: Two little girls dress up in "grownup" clothes; together with a boy, they play house in a remarkably sophisticated manner. The two "mothers" decide on their marketing list, writing the order on a pad, and then dictating it over the phone to the grocery store clerk. The clerk takes down the order but tells them they will have to come and call for it; his delivery man has gone home. Off the girls trot, weaving on their high heels as they go. Everything is fine until it comes time to pay the bill; the clerk has arrived at one total, the shoppers another. The impasse is resolved by going to the "bead bank"—a table with three sealed jars, each containing beads of a different color to represent "ones," "tens," and "hundreds," and a huge open jar containing beads of all three colors. The children arrange and rearrange the beads until they agree on the (correct) answer.

ITEM: An eight-year-old third grader is fascinated with the way ordinary, everyday objects look under a microscope. After examining one item after another, she writes the following story:

> A pice of nylon under a micrscope looks like thread loosely sewn together. Sandpaper looks like tiny crystles. Under the Microscope there are a million things to see. It is like being in another world. A micrsope is something great! What would a scientist do if there wasn't a micrscope how could they see things closer?

The final segment is cleanup time: at a prearranged signal, the children stop what they are doing and put the Learning Center back in shape for the next class. Even cleaning up, Mrs. Rasmussen insists, can provide an opportunity for learning, since children are involved in sorting, matching, arranging, and separating materials, and in working with one another. When the children leave, there is a fifteen- or twenty-minute staff meeting to discuss individual children's behavior and plan activities for the next time the class visits the Center.

Bit by bit, as in Lillian Weber's corridor program, the teachers found themselves drawn into the activities, instead of merely sitting by, sipping their coffee and watching passively. They discovered that the worst punishment they could mete out to a child was to forbid him from going to the Learning Center. More important, they recognized, often to their utter astonishment, that behavior problems seemed to melt away in the open environment, that children could move about and talk freely without getting out of control, and learn a great deal in the process. As a result, teachers have begun flocking to Mrs. Rasmussen's "Teacher Resource Center," where they can learn to use the new approach,[23] and also make materials for their classrooms. Now,

[23] Although she began the program before she had heard of the English infant schools, Mrs. Rasmussen now keeps in touch with informal English educators like Leonard Sealey and Sybil Marshall.

after a trial run in a small laboratory school—120 children in five classes—Mrs. Rasmussen and her colleagues in the Learning Centers Project are planning to set up a number of "schools within schools," biting off a few rooms to explore the use of informal methods in the classroom itself.

VI

About the same time Lore Rasmussen was beginning her program in one of Philadelphia's Negro slums, Dr. Marie Hughes, professor of educational psychology at the University of Arizona and director of its Research and Development Center in Early Childhood Education, was launching an extensive experiment for disadvantaged Mexican-American children in the Tucson public schools.

In Tucson, as in the rest of the Southwest, generations of Mexican Americans have found school a hostile place that breeds failure. When they begin school at age six—Arizona provides no public kindergartens—many Mexican-American children manifest a quality that Tucson teachers call "shyness"—an apparent lack of curiosity that borders on withdrawal.

ITEM: In an effort to evoke curiosity and exploration on the children's part, Dr. Hughes, in her early days in Tucson, placed a large stuffed Mama kangaroo with a baby kangaroo in her pouch in a conspicuous place in a classroom; not a child responded to it in any way. Deciding that the kangaroo might have been too foreign to the youngsters' experience, Dr. Hughes replaced it with a striking pink hat box, tied with a huge pink bow, sure that this time the youngsters would start poking around to see what was inside. The reaction was the same; the children ignored it completely.

Equally important, the children are as inarticulate as they are passive. Their difficulty in expressing themselves is accompanied by difficulty in learning to read and write, which frequently leads to their being "retained" (educationese for "left back") in first grade at least once, and frequently twice. Tucson school officials place large numbers of Mexican-American children in special "1C" classes, which means that they automatically remain in first grade for two years—but without any significant change in the standard curriculum. Being earmarked for failure helps to produce failure, of course, along with a good deal of hostility to school and teachers, reflected in extraordinarily high absentee rates as well as a good deal of disruptive behavior. Failure also reinforces the negative view of themselves which discrimination and poverty have instilled in the children by the time they start school. By sixth grade, therefore, Mexican-American children tend to score one and a half to three years below the "Anglos" on reading and other standardized tests.

If Mexican-American or other slum children are to succeed,[24] Dr. Hughes reasoned, the school experience must help them develop a positive attitude toward themselves; they have to see themselves as people of worth, capable of dealing with their environment. This in turn provides a base on which the program's other objectives can be built. Those objectives are fourfold: developing a positive attitude toward learning; developing the children's language ability, with particular emphasis on talking freely and comfortably; developing an "intellectual base," i.e., learning how to learn, how to process information, how to solve problems, how to distinguish cause and effect and classify and label;[25] and acquiring the skills of reading, writing, and arithmetic, as well as the social skills involved in getting along with others.

Each of these objectives seemed to Dr. Hughes to require a change not only in curriculum, but in teaching methods and classroom organization as well, for each required a degree and kind of individualization not possible in the conventional classroom. To develop positive self-image, teachers would have to make clear to each child that he is a person of worth—to respond to his behavior in ways that would convey a sense of trust and affection. Moreover, since self-image grows out of a child's own activities as well as the activities and attitudes of others— to feel good about himself, a child must have a sense of competence—teachers would have to structure classroom activities to give every child frequent experiences of success. To develop a language base, teachers would have to get children talking freely. Since Mexican-American youngsters find talking in English difficult, and often threatening, this meant that teachers would have to shift the emphasis from the use of language *per se*

[24] The program includes a scattering of Indian, Negro and Anglo children as well as Mexican Americans.
[25] Professor Hughes, whose work in this area has influenced, and been influenced by, the work of the late Professor Hilda Taba of San Francisco State College, has identified some twenty separate activities and functions involved in developing an intellectual base.

to the topic of conversation itself, by getting each child to talk about things that matter to him. And so it went.

The result was a classroom structure and approach remarkably like the English free day, though with important differences as well. The rows of desks facing the front of the room have been abandoned, replaced in part by interest areas, in part by small tables with chairs grouped around them. For half the day, children are free to follow their own inclinations at the various interest areas, rich in games, blocks, toys, books, musical instruments, animals (every room seems to have, at the least, a fish tank and a collection of silk worms). Unlike the informal English schools, however, children remain in their own self-contained classrooms, without spilling over into the corridors or other rooms. There are fewer concrete materials in the math area and there is less emphasis on painting, sculpting, and building than in England.

The atmosphere, however, is much the same as in England—or in North Dakota, Philadelphia, and New York. More to the point, the contrast with the usual Mexican-American classroom, with its rows of silent, sullen, withdrawn children, is overwhelming. The visitor is immediately struck by the fact that these children are comfortable with themselves and with each other, as they move freely about the room, chattering volubly to each other and to the teacher, visibly happy and engaged. There is little "shyness" in evidence in the Hughes classrooms, and little absenteeism, too.

There is, however, a good deal of learning. While half the day is "free," the other half is highly structured, with a variety of teacher-directed activities designed to enhance the children's competence in language, cognitive development, and the three R's. Few of the activities involve the teacher's standing in front of the room, addressing the entire class. Instead, the teacher and an aide, provided for the structured half of the day, work with children in groups of five, the children seated around round tables just large enough to accommodate their number.

ITEM: A second-grade classroom. The teacher is sitting at a table with five children, the table heaped with objects—bottle caps, buttons, nails, cookie cutters—some two dozen in all. Each child has a magnet and a work sheet, listing the objects alphabetically, with spaces to be filled in, one indicating whether the object can be picked up by the magnet, another reporting what the object is made of. With an occasional question from the teacher, to direct their play in the desired direction, the children are touching, testing, comparing, classifying, as well as reading, writing, and talking. At a second table, four children are reading; at a third, the teacher aide is working with five children, using Cuisenaire rods, small cubes, and other concrete mathematical material. The five children at a fourth table are constructing things out of paper plates, tissue paper, and other assorted stuff. At a fifth, the children are writing "About Me," following a form that reads: "I was born in the month of _____. The name of my street is _____. I live in the city of _____. Our school is called _____. My teacher's name is _____. My favorite game is _____. I like most to _____ when I am at school.

ITEM: A first-grade classroom. Children at several tables are working with "intellectual kits"—homemade collections of stuff organized around some common characteristic or theme. At one table, a master teacher is "modeling" the Hughes approach for the classroom teacher. The process can be used for any kind of kit (teachers are encouraged to make up their own) or for any objects a teacher may use to get children talking, observing, comparing, classifying, etc.

Each of the five children has a kit, made out of a piece of bright red felt. The master teacher begins by asking the children if they can guess what's inside without looking. "It's something hard," one boy volunteers. "Mario thinks he feels something hard," the teacher repeats, asking for more replies. "It's noisy," another child suggests. "Carla shook her package and heard noises," the teacher responds. "I wonder what kind of material makes noises?" "I think it's metal," a third ventures. "Juan thinks the material is made of metal, Carla thinks the material makes noises, and Mario thinks he felt something hard," the teacher continues. "Hearing is a good way of finding out, and so is touching. How else can we find out about things?" "Looking," one child replies. "Well, then, why don't you open your kits and see what is inside." The children open the kits with gusto; each has a collection of keys of various shapes, sizes, and functions—assorted house keys and car keys, a big black wrought-iron decorative key, a small metal key that winds a toy car, the tiny key to a personal diary, and so on.

After the children have handled the keys for a few minutes, the teacher continues the lesson, asking if anyone can find two keys that look alike. Carlos offers two keys that are the same length but have differently shaped tops. "They certainly do have shafts of the same length," the teacher replies, rubbing her finger along the length of the shaft, but not translating the word directly and not correcting the child directly; instead, she works the word "shaft" into the conversation several times. For a half-hour the lesson continues, as teacher and children talk about the keys, comparing and differentiating them according to size, shape, color, material, weight, and use.

ITEM: At another table, five children and the teacher aide are working with a kit of hinges, including among other items a door hinge, a scissors, a purse, spectacles, and a clothespin. They discuss the fact that the door hinge and the scissors are both hinges, that the scissors has a cutting edge, just like a table knife, but that the table knife has no hinge. The point of the discussion is to establish the concept of cross-classification, i.e., that objects may have membership in more than one group, sharing some but not all the characteristics of the other objects in that group.

Learning is not confined to the classroom; there are a great many trips designed to extend the children's experience and to provide experiences that can be used as a base for both language and cognitive development. An unwritten rule provides that there must be two excursions within the *barrios* for every trip outside. This is a means of conveying interest in and respect for the children's own background (essential to developing a sense of worth), and also, hopefully, of involving parents, grandparents, and other members of the adult community in school activities.

The standard procedure following a trip or some other collective experience outside the ordinary, is for the children to create a so-called "talking mural."

ITEM: A first-grade class has visited a citrus grove north of Tucson—a new experience for the children, since oranges, lemons, and grapefruit do not grow in the city's immediate vicinity. On their return, they make a fifteen-foot-long talking mural, with huge clusters of trees painted in lovely, lush green groves. Coming out of the trees in comic-strip bubbles are comments, written by the teacher but dictated by each child. For example:

"I wish I could have one," said Yolanda V.

"I liked the yellow lemons," remarked Ethelvina.

Rebecca noticed, "The lemon trees were the smallest."

"The grapefruit is bigger and round," remarked Patricia.

"Inside the peeling there is something white and soft," exclaimed Marty.

ITEM: In a second-grade classroom, a mother had come to school and made tortillas with the children, who painted an enormous mural portraying the event with considerable zest and originality. Some of the balloon captions read:

"I wish I had some butter," Eddie said.

"And some jelly," Greg added.

"My mother," Inez recalled, "makes BIG ONES."

Juanita asked, "May I make one for Mr. A?" [the principal]

Ray noticed, "They're as thin as paper!"

Lorenzo exclaimed, "She looks like a real maza maker."

"These are Mexican tortillas," Arnold said.

"I could feel the warm," Ray commented, holding his tortilla.

The murals, as indigenous to the Hughes classrooms as the omnipresent graphs are to English informal classrooms, have several functions. They serve to get the children talking and provide a reference point for future conversations. They provide a means of "lifting" or "extending" the children's language; besides adding verbs like "noticed," "remarked," "added," and "recalled," teachers are careful to introduce a variety of speech patterns when they write the balloons. And the murals help drive home the notion that writing is, at least in part, recorded speech, and that one function of reading is to see what people, yourself included, have to say.[26] Hence teachers reproduce the children's remarks verbatim, mistakes and all. Correcting a child's speech directly, Dr. Hughes argues, would serve to discourage him from talking, while letting errors go by uncorrected would simply reinforce the error. Hence Dr. Hughes tries to train teachers to correct in subtle, nonthreatening ways. Thus, when Ray said, "I could feel the warm," the teacher responded by saying, "It

---

[26] Even sophisticated academicians, Ralph J. Wetzel, Associate Director of the Early Childhood Education Laboratory, points out, delight in reading their own words. The first thing they do when they receive a transcript of a conference they have attended is to leaf through it to read what they had to say.

feels nice to hold something warm, doesn't it? The heat feels good," and she worked the nouns "heat," "warm," and "warmth" into the conversation whenever possible.

As in the three programs already described, the Hughes program uses ordinary classroom teachers; none have been handpicked. The program differs, however, in a number of other respects. Unlike Lillian Weber and Lore Rasmussen, for example, who believe that change will be more effective and more lasting if it proceeds slowly, Marie Hughes began her program on a comparatively large scale, and is expanding it rapidly. Thus, the program was launched in the fall of 1965 in some twenty-six first-grade classrooms in a number of Tucson schools, moving upward a grade a year.[27] Although federal funding ended in June 1968, the program continued to operate during the 1968–69 school year in some sixty-eight first- to fourth-grade classrooms in eight schools, only one of them still under Professor Hughes's supervision. Most of the schools, moreover, added a fifth grade in 1969–70 and were hoping to add a sixth in 1970–71.

The expansion is geographical as well; the Hughes approach, or "The Tucson Early Education Model," as it is officially known, is also being tried in some eighteen public school systems around the country, under the U.S. Office of Education's "Follow Through" program.[28] Since Professor Hughes attempts to structure the process rather than the content of the curriculum, teachers are free to vary the materials according to the interests and needs of the children they are teaching. The schools involved include a remarkable cross-section of the United States: cities with large black populations, such as Newark, Baltimore, and Los Angeles; communities with Indian Americans, such as

[27] The approach had been in preparation for a number of years; passage of the Elementary and Secondary Education Act of 1965 provided the funds and the impetus Professor Hughes needed to get the Tucson schools to go along with her ideas.

[28] The Follow Through program was initiated when it became apparent that the preschool Head Start program was far from the panacea it had originally been advertised to be; whatever gains disadvantaged children made while enrolled in preschool programs tended to dissipate rapidly when they entered the public schools. Follow Through is designed to determine whether changing the nature of primary schooling will prove more successful. Instead of plunging into a massive program, as the Office of Economic Opportunity did with Head Start, the Office of Education is proceeding more cautiously, testing a wide range of approaches in a limited number of communities.

Chickasha, Oklahoma, and three Bureau of Indian Affairs schools outside of Philadelphia, Mississippi; other cities, like Santa Fe and Fort Worth, with large Mexican-American populations; Pikesville, Kentucky, a heartland of white Appalachia; Hoonah, Alaska, with a predominantly Eskimo, population; as well as Des Moines, Iowa; Durham, North Carolina; Lakewood, New Jersey; Vincennes, Indiana; Abbyville, Louisiana; Lafayette, Georgia; Lincoln, Nebraska; and Wichita, Kansas.

Unlike North Dakota, moreover, where the introduction of informal education is tied to an elaborate program of teacher education and re-education at the University, the teachers in the Hughes program receive little or no advance preparation. Professor Hughes would have liked to give teachers a summer of pre-service training, but funds were not available. Instead, teachers are trained in their own classrooms. To do this, Professor Hughes has created something like the English advisory system, whereby she selects a number of particularly able teachers and trains them to be "Program Assistants." Each program assistant, or "change agent," as Dr. Hughes also likes to call them, is assigned to a school to work with the teachers involved in the Hughes program, visiting the classrooms to observe and make suggestions, demonstrating (or "modeling") the various approaches and techniques by taking over groups of children herself, and showing films of brief "micro-teaching" sessions designed to illustrate a particular concept or technique. The program assistants also provide moral support for the classroom teachers, who inevitably feel insecure as they struggle to make the change.[29] Since the program assistants are not supervisors coming in to evaluate and report back to the central office, teachers do not feel threatened by their presence in the classroom, and so are better able to accept their advice.

VII

"If progressive schools become complacent with existing accomplishments, unaware of the slight foundation of knowledge upon which they rest, and careless regarding the amount of study of the laws of growth that remains to be done," John Dewey warned in 1930, "a reaction against them is sure to take place."

---

[29] In the fourteen "Follow Through" projects, the program assistants in turn receive support and reinforcement from a small corps of "field representatives," who visit each classroom at least once a month.

The warning was ignored then; it must be heeded now, for the foundation of knowledge about teaching and learning, while certainly firmer than it was in the thirties, can hardly be considered adequate. "It would be presumptuous for any of us to say that we know so much about the learning process and the educative process that we now have a program," Ralph J. Wetzel, associate director of the University of Arizona's Early Childhood Education Laboratory, says, insisting that the Tucson program is very much in flux. "We learn new things every day about children, about cultures, about the process of learning, and unless there is some process by which this new information can be incorporated and the program . . . continually changed, we are lost."

One danger is that the American penchant for fads could lead to promotion of informal education as the panacea for all educational ills. It is not. Some teachers may simply be temperamentally unsuited to the approach; a good formal teacher is to be preferred to a poor informal one. Some children, moreover, or some subjects—quite possibly, reading—may require more structure, more teacher direction, and more specificity of goals than the typical informal classroom provides. And experience is still too scanty to know what blends of formal and informal methods work best in the upper-primary and secondary grades.

There is a risk, therefore, that educators or parents may see informal education as a simple, monolithic approach—as a "model" or "plan" to be adopted without further ado. There is a sign of this already in the curious identification of the "free day" with Leicestershire County in England. For example, school conventions are holding well-attended sessions on what they call "the Leicestershire plan," as if informal education had been invented there; and summer training programs seem to be staffed almost exclusively by people from Leicestershire, although the London style and the London school conditions may be more relevant to American needs than the Leicestershire style and environment. It would be tragic, in any case, if the desire to adopt The Latest Thing in Education were to lead to hasty introduction of the English forms without an understanding of their substance or goals and without the careful preparation that is essential.

One of the great strengths of informal education in England, in fact, is that it has not been imposed from above, but has developed slowly out of the insights and experiments of innumerable teachers, heads, inspectors, and advisers. In the United States, introduction is likely to be more rapid, and the impetus is likely to come from the outside more often than from within. It is crucial, therefore, that the most careful preparations be made before the changes are introduced. As we have seen, American parents are perfectly capable of understanding and accepting informal education if it is explained to them, and American teachers can adapt informal teaching styles with grace and enthusiasm if—but only if—they receive sufficient training and support.

Reform of the public schools thus needs to be tied to drastic changes in both pre-service and in-service teacher education, a matter to be discussed in Chapter 11. Introduction of informal education is likely to be smoother, moreover, if it is accompanied by creation of some counterpart to the English inspectorate and advisory centers, as Marie Hughes has done with her program, and the Education Development Center is doing with its Follow Through program, which is also closely associated with the English approach. Teachers are bound to need a good deal of continuing help, support, and reassurance if they are to make the change comfortably and successfully. Some children may feel the need to test the limits of their new freedom, and others may have difficulty coping with choice. So may some of the teachers. "In order to free the child," Harold Rugg argued, it is necessary "first to free the teacher." The process can be unsettling. "My teachers and I do not know what to do with this freedom," a high school principal declared at a meeting during the early stages of the so-called Eight-Year Study, the great experiment to determine whether progressive education affected students' preparation for college. "It challenges and frightens us," she continued. "I fear that we have come to love our chains."[30]

Not every principal is that sensitive or understanding. Indeed, given the obsession with silence and lack of movement that so many principals, superintendents, and curriculum supervisors show, and the fact that teachers' ability tends to be judged more on their "control" than on any other attribute, it is essential that *someone* be available to relieve teachers' anxiety about what their supervisors may say if they see children talking or moving about in class. Teaching, after all, is a very lonely profession.

[30] Wilford M. Aikin, *The Story of the Eight-Year Study,* New York: Harper & Row, 1942.

In the typical American school, as Seymour B. Sarason, director
of Yale University's Psycho-Educational Clinic, has documented,
teachers are alone with their problems in the classroom. They
are not given, and normally do not expect to receive, any help
or advice from their principals or other supervisors; nor does
the culture of the school encourage teachers to discuss their
educational problems with one another except on the most
superficial level. As a result, a teacher generally, and the beginning teacher in particular, "tends to anticipate failure, is plagued
by all kinds of doubts, fearful of a negative evaluation, thankful
for her relative isolation due to fleeting and infrequent visitations
by administrative superiors, and yet acutely aware that she needs
and wants help, guidance and support uncomplicated by the implied threat of a negative evaluation."[31] Only someone who has
no evaluative function, and who is not competing with or threatening the teacher in any way, can break through the teacher's
loneliness and isolation.

The teacher re-education that accompanies introduction of
informal methods must include the supervisors as well, for they,
too, are victims of the school culture. Certainly the North
Dakota experience indicates that principals no less than teachers
will welcome the new approach if they have the opportunity to
understand it. Thus, a special 1969 summer program for principals, many of whom had been indifferent or even hostile to the
new approach, was so successful that the principals, with only
one of their number dissenting, asked the New School faculty to
provide additional workshops for them during the course of the
school year.

A certain continuing vigilance is also needed, for informal
education can be as mindless in its own sweet, well-intentioned
way as the arid formalism it replaces. Certainly there is a danger,
evident in a few of the classrooms visited in England and the
United States and perhaps inherent in the approach itself, that
the pendulum of informality and child-centeredness may swing
too far, thereby embracing the flabbiness and anti-intellectualism that characterized so many of the progressive schools of the
1920s, '30s, and '40s. "You have to be careful not to let this

31 Seymour B. Sarason, "The School Culture and Processes of Change,"
The Brechbill Lecture, University of Maryland, January 10, 1966 (mimeo-
graphed). Cf. also Chapter 6, "Teaching Is a Lonely Profession," in
S. B. Sarason, M. Levine, I. I. Goldenberg, D. L. Cherlin, and E. M.
Bennett, *Psychology in Community Settings: Clinical, Educational, Vo-
cational, Social Aspects*, New York: John Wiley, 1966.

new kind of teaching become a 'cop-out,' " a teacher in Lore Rasmussen's Philadelphia program warns. "The kids are happy, the discipline problem is nil, and it's awfully easy for a teacher to convince herself that the kids are having a 'learning experience' or some damned thing, no matter what they're doing."

Finding the right balance is never easy; there will always be a certain tension between two groups of educational objectives —those concerned with individual growth and fulfillment, and those concerned with the transmission of specific skills, intellectual disciplines, and bodies of knowledge—and finding the "right" balance is neither easy nor obvious. In the older American progressive schools, the balance certainly needed to be tipped toward the cognitive; in most American schools today, as Geoffrey Caston of the Schools Council, a leading figure in curriculum reform in England, argues, on the basis of extensive visits, "the need is to tip it very strongly back toward the affective." In doing so, there is a risk of tipping too far; fortunately, the people in charge of most of the current experiments in informal education seem to be well aware of the danger.

8

"What They Want
to Produce, Not What
We Want to Become":
Reforming the High School

*Let the main object of this, our Didactic, be as follows: To
seek and to find a method of instruction, by which teachers
may teach less, but learners learn more; by which schools
may be the scene of less noise, aversion, and useless labour,
but of more leisure, enjoyment, and solid progress . . .*

—JOHN AMOS COMENIUS
The Great Didactic

I

So far, we have been talking mainly about the reform of elementary education. In part, this is because of the intrinsic importance of the early years, in part because this is where the greatest change is occurring, and where there is the clearest evidence that schools can be humane and free without in any way sacrificing intellectual development.

But change is needed at the secondary level as much as at the primary. "Not too many of us realize how bad American schools are from the point of view of humanity, respect, trust, or dignity," Charles E. Brown of the Ford Foundation, a former Superintendent of the Newton, Massachusetts, schools, told a *Daedalus* conference on adolescence. And secondary schools are the worst of all. Because adolescents are harder to "control" than younger children, secondary schools tend to be even more authoritarian and repressive than elementary schools; the values they transmit are the values of docility, passivity, conformity, and lack of trust. These unpleasant attributes might be tolerable if one could view them, so to speak, as the price to be paid for "a good education"—good, that is to say, in academic terms. Such is not the case; as we have seen in Chapter 5, mindlessness affects the high school curriculum every bit as much as the elementary curriculum. And the junior high school, by almost unanimous agreement, is the wasteland—one is tempted to say cesspool—of American education.

Reform has been slower in the secondary than in the primary schools in part, at least, because the problems are more complex and the solutions a good deal less obvious. "Many people here," Geoffrey Caston writes, "are becoming a little concerned about the rather romantic notion that the model infant school methods can simply be carried on upwards into the junior school and beyond."[1]

Clearly they cannot. While children in informal infant schools work at what interests them, the teacher easily and decisively influences those interests through the environment she creates. Teenagers, on the other hand, arrive in school with their interests, their likes and dislikes, and their values much more clearly formed. They are far less susceptible to the teacher's influence; one of the characteristics of growth, as Jerome Bruner of Harvard emphasizes, is the "increasing independence of response from the immediate nature of the stimulus." Moreover, teenagers are subject to a far wider range of influences outside the classroom—influences from their own peer culture, as well as from the adult culture as transmitted by parents and the mass media.[2]

---

[1] From a letter to the author.

[2] Cf. David Riesman with Reuel Denney and Nathan Glazer, *The Lonely Crowd,* Yale University Press, 1950; Reuel Denney, *The Astonished Muse,* University of Chicago Press, 1957; Reuel Denney, "American Youth Today: A Bigger Cast, A Wider Screen," in Erik H. Erikson, ed., *The Challenge of Youth,* Garden City, N.Y.: Anchor Books, 1965; James S. Coleman, *The Adolescent Society,* The Free Press of Glencoe, 1961; James S. Coleman, *Adolescents and the Schools,* New York: Basic Books, 1965; Bennett M. Berger, "Adolescence and Beyond: An Essay Review of Three Books on the Problems of Growing Up," *Social Problems,* Vol. 10, No. 4, Spring 1963; Edgar Z. Friedenberg, *The Vanishing Adolescent,* New York: Dell Publishing, and *Coming of Age in America,* New York: Random House, 1965.

The problem is complicated still further by the fact that adolescents learn in different and more complex ways than young children. During adolescence, "something very special happens," as Jerome Bruner puts it, "when language becomes increasingly important as a medium of thought." It becomes increasingly important because, roughly between the ages of twelve and fifteen, young people gradually gain command over what Piaget calls formal operations—the final "stage" of cognitive development. The emergence of formal operations makes it much easier for adolescents to think about their own thoughts, to think systematically about the future, to deal with concepts, propositions, and hypotheses as well as with objects, and to understand and handle metaphors.

What they think about is a matter of considerable importance, for it is during adolescence, as the philosopher Alfred North Whitehead suggested, that "the lines of character are graven. How the child emerges from the romantic stage of adolescence is how the subsequent life will be moulded by ideals and coloured by imagination." Hence the content of the curriculum cannot be left to chance; education is a process that cannot be separated from what it is that one learns. The transcendent objective, to be sure, is not mastery of a body of knowledge per se, it is, in Jerome Bruner's formulation, "to create a better or happier or more courageous or more sensitive or more honest man." But other institutions also have that goal, among them the family and the church. The raison d'être of the school—society's ultimate justification for creating a separate, formal, educational institution, and for making prolonged exposure to it compulsory —is the conviction (the faith, if you will), that, as Bruner also puts it, "The conduct of life is not independent of what it is that one knows" nor "of how it is that one has learned what one knows."

The growth that occurs during adolescence makes possible substantial changes both in what is learned and how it is learned. Since their growing command over language, abstraction and metaphor enable high school students to transcend their own experience and environment, high school, even more than elementary school, is where they can begin to come into possession of the culture, which is to say, the world created by the perceptions, discoveries, creations, imaginations, and thoughts of men. In a way and with a subtlety and sophistication that the elementary school cannot attempt, the high school can concern itself with the transmission of culture as Matthew Arnold defined it in *Culture and Anarchy:* "to make the best that has been thought and known in the world current everywhere." No democratic society can afford to do less.

The "best that has been thought and known" is embodied in large measure in the scholarly disciplines. What is crucial about the disciplines, however, is that they are not mere bodies of knowledge or collections of information; they are conceptual models, or paradigms, which men have constructed to give meaning to experience, "to make sense out of some portion of the world or of life," as Ralph Tyler puts it. "I think that we shall have to get accustomed to the idea that we must not look upon science as a 'body of knowledge,' " Sir Karl Popper writes, but "rather as a system of hypotheses; that is to say, as a system of guesses or anticipations which in principle cannot be justified, but with which we work as long as they stand up to tests."[3]

Several things follow from this. The first is that a major emphasis must be to give students an understanding of the fundamental structure of the disciplines they study. "This is a minimum requirement for using knowledge," Jerome Bruner writes in *The Process of Education*, the most influential contemporary work on curriculum, "for bringing it to bear on problems and events one encounters outside a classroom—or in classrooms one enters later in one's training."[4] Emphasizing structure does not mean turning classes into bull sessions or derogating the importance of mastering a body of information and data. As Alfred North Whitehead, an early advocate of emphasizing structure, insisted, "There is no royal road to learning through an airy path of brilliant generalizations." On the contrary, he argued, education involves "a patient process of the mastery of details."

[3] *The Logic of Scientific Discovery,* quoted in Gerald Holton's introduction, Gerald Holton, ed., *Science and Culture,* Boston: Houghton Mifflin, 1965. Cf. also Thomas S. Kuhn, *The Structure of Scientific Revolutions,* University of Chicago Press, 1962.
[4] Jerome Bruner, *The Process of Education,* Harvard University Press, 1961. Cf. also J. Bruner, *On Knowing,* Harvard University Press, 1962; *Toward a Theory of Instruction,* Harvard University Press, 1966; and Philip Phenix, *Realms of Meaning,* New York: McGraw Hill Book Company, 1964; John Dewey, *The Child and the Curriculum,* University of Chicago Press, 1902.

But mastery of details is the means, not the end. Emphasizing structure means emphasizing the concepts that give meaning to the details, that enable students to distinguish relevant from irrelevant details and to apply their knowledge to new situations and problems. "Your learning is useless to you," Whitehead also maintained, "till you have lost your text-books, burnt your lecture notes, and forgotten the minutiae which you learnt by heart for the examination. What, in the way of detail, you continually require will stick in your memory as obvious facts like the sun and the moon; and what you casually require can be looked up in any work of reference." The function of education, he added, "is to enable you to shed details in favor of principles."[5]

To be able to "shed details in favor of principles," one needs depth of understanding and practice in its use. Hence Whitehead's "two educational commandments": "Do not teach too many subjects," and "What you teach, teach thoroughly." Or as Bruner formulated the question some four decades later, "whatever is introduced, let it be pursued continuously enough to give the student a sense of the power of mind that comes from a deepening of understanding." Respect for competence is one of the distinguishing characteristics of adolescence—witness the intense interest in sports and in driving a car, activities in which standards of competence are clearly defined. Adolescents should not be denied the satisfaction that comes from competence in intellectual and esthetic activities as well.

If students are not to regard knowledge as dogma, they must also understand something of its ephemeral character and, even more, the degree to which the "truth" of a discipline is a function of its structure and its method of inquiry. They need to understand the different kinds of evidence and proof that different disciplines use, that is to say, as well as their different degrees of dependability, and they need to understand the ways in which conceptual structures produce new knowledge and then change themselves in response to that knowledge. In short, students need to study the grammar or syntax of the disciplines, as well as their structure and content.[6]

[5] Alfred North Whitehead, *The Aims of Education,* New York: Mentor Books, 1949.
[6] Joseph J. Schwab, "Structure of the Disciplines: Meanings and Significances," in G. W. Ford and Lawrence Pugno, eds., *The Structure of Knowledge and the Curriculum,* Chicago: Rand McNally, 1964. See also

But *which* disciplines? In what sequence? With what content? Taught in what way?

To educational traditionalists, the answers are obvious. "Certain intellectual disciplines are fundamental in the public school curriculum," Professor Arthur Bestor of the University of Illinois, wrote in *The Restoration of Learning*, the most serious and thoughtful of the attacks on progressive education that appeared in the 1950s, "because they are fundamental in modern life. Reading, writing, and arithmetic are indispensable studies in the elementary school because no intellectual life worthy of the name is possible or conceivable without these particular skills. Science, mathematics, history, English, and foreign languages are essentials of the secondary school curriculum because contemporary intellectual life has been built upon a foundation of these particular disciplines. . . . In some far-distant future the list of fundamental disciplines may be somewhat different, just as it was somewhat different in the past." James D. Koerner, another thoughtful and influential advocate of "basic education," offers much the same list. "For most young people," he writes, the aims of education "are best attained through an education based . . . on the principal areas of human knowledge: English and foreign languages, history, mathematics, and the natural sciences."[7]

The questions are not that simple, nor are the answers quite so cut and dried. Apart from the fact that they omit the arts, indeed the entire esthetic realm, altogether, Bestor's and Koerner's lists raise more questions than they answer. Take history, for example. We can agree immediately that all students need some knowledge of the past if they are to understand the present and aspire to the future, and that a study of history therefore is a must. But the history of what? Taught how, with what emphases, and with what relations to other subjects or disciplines such as political science, economics, sociology, psychology? Bestor's answer is forthright and unequivocal: "His-

---

Joseph J. Schwab, "Education and the Structure of the Disciplines," a paper prepared for the National Education Association Project on the Instructional Program of the Public Schools, mimeographed, 1961; and "The Teaching of Science as Enquiry," in J. J. Schwab and Paul F. Brandwein, *The Teaching of Science,* Harvard University Press, 1962.
[7] Arthur Bestor, *The Restoration of Learning,* New York: Knopf, 1955; James D. Koerner, *The Miseducation of American Teachers,* Baltimore: Penguin Books, 1963.

tory *as history* is indispensable to education for intelligent citizenship." [Emphasis his] Indeed, history, in his view, is the quintessential discipline, "the one discipline in the traditional secondary-school curriculum which is perennially and consistently concerned with the perspective of time—with development, adaptation to change, progress, crisis, and decline. In this respect history is not one of the social sciences," he continues, "but an indispensable complement to them. It stands out against the social sciences as a critic of the errors that result from their partial view of society. . . . History co-operates with and learns from the other disciplines concerned with man and society, but it has its own tasks, its own techniques, and its own system of values."

One may question Bestor's thesis, however, without in any way succumbing to the fuzzy anti-intellectualism of the kind of "social studies" curriculum he was attacking, for it is by no means clear that the historian's traditional chronological approach—"history as history"—is in fact the best way to give students an understanding of, and feeling for, the past. Indeed, it is by no means clear that history is a discipline at all, that there is any such thing as "history as history." "Everything in our world has *a* history, and the man who wants to understand any particular thing or field is well advised to inquire into *its* history," the philosopher John Herman Randall, Jr., of Columbia writes. "Everything that is, is historical in character, and has an existence that can be measured in time. And this historical aspect which any particular thing has and possesses is an essential part of what it is. But 'just history' in general seems to have no meaning," Professor Randall continues, "unless it be taken as synonymous with knowledge as a whole. History is not a 'thing' at all; it is not a noun, a 'substance.' It is rather a character, an adjective, a predicate. Or put in somewhat more formal terms, 'history' is not a distinctive subject-matter to be inquired into. It is rather at once a trait of all subject-matters, something to be discovered and understood about each of them; and a distinctive way of inquiring into any subject-matter—though by no means the only way."[8] One consequence, Professor Randall argues, is that "for any understanding of the histories that

[8] John Herman Randall, "History and the Social Sciences," in *Freedom and Reason: Studies in Philosophy and Jewish Culture, in Memory of Morris Raphael Cohen*, Salo Wittmayer Baron, Ernest Nagel and Koppel S. Pinson, eds., Glencoe, Illinois: Free Press, 1951, pp. 287–308.

things possess, the social sciences are essential," since their subject matter is the processes of change. By the same token, a knowledge of history is essential to the study of the social sciences, since they are fundamentally historical in character, dealing as they do with temporal and therefore historical institutions and structures.

A number of historians who have been concerned with curriculum reform agree. "I find constantly that my friends in the social sciences are of greater help to me in thinking about problems in history than historians are," Professor Elting Morison of Yale reports. Organizing the materials of history on a chronological basis "has its uses and purposes," Morison argues, "but frequently if you reorganize the data in a different kind of way, or take only part of it which is relevant to a kind of question you have in mind, you find all different kinds of information coming out which you can't get from the organization of a single situation within a chronological form." If the purpose of the curriculum is "not knowing history but having an historical sense," the purpose might be served more effectively by selecting a limited number of episodes or periods or problems and treating them in greater depth.[9] In fact, this kind of "postholing" approach, used in the social studies curriculum developed by Educational Services Inc. and in the high school social science curriculum developed by the historian Edwin Fenton and his colleagues at Carnegie-Mellon University, seems to give students a far greater understanding of the ways historians work, of the nature of historical inquiry, as well as of the historical process, than does the conventional course.

Bestor's dicta are no more reliable when we turn to the sciences, where he assures us, the curriculum that was developed at the turn of the century has proven to be "the curriculum not for the year or the decade, but for the century." The study of the sciences "as organized into the systematic branches of biology, chemistry, and physics" around the turn of the century, Bestor flatly states, "represented a genuinely international consensus of views" which contained "the means of adjusting itself to the regular advances in knowledge that were occurring,"

---

[9] "Men and Ideas." ESI's Social Studies and Humanities Program: A Conversation with Elting Morison," in W. T. Martin and Dan C. Pinck, *Curriculum Improvement and Innovation: A Partnership of Students, School Teachers, and Research Scholars,* Cambridge, Mass.: Robert Bentley, Inc., 1966.

guaranteeing "that changes in the curriculum of the elementary and secondary school would be moderate and evolutionary in character. The quantum theory, Einstein's principle of relativity, and non-Euclidean geometry," he continues, "might affect certain details in certain high-school courses, but could hardly call for wholesale revision of the high-school curriculum, because, quite obviously, these advances in scientific theory could not even be apprehended without thorough knowledge of the fundamental physics and mathematics which alone the high school was concerned with teaching."

What is "quite obvious" to Bestor, however, is not at all obvious to the scientists themselves. The first of the major reforms of the science curriculum, for example, developed by the Physical Science Study Committee under the leadership of Jerrold Zacharias and Francis Friedman of MIT, began, as its name suggests, "in revolt against the fractionation of chemistry and physics at the high school level into separate disciplines," a fractionation which the Committee members felt made no sense. The revolt was abortive because it proved impossible, at that juncture in time, to get chemists and physicists to work together. Hence the PSSC devoted itself exclusively to revising the high school physics course. The changes were neither "moderate" nor "evolutionary"; on the contrary, the new course—as intellectually rigorous as one could ask for—dropped about half of the material treated in the traditional course, limiting itself to two concepts (the "wave particle duality" and the modern concept of the atom) which the PSSC members felt "lay at the heart of the modern physicist's outlook upon his universe."[10]

Despite the fact that the PSSC physics course was developed by some of the most distinguished physicists in the United States, it became clear by the mid-1960s, if not earlier, that this was not *the* curriculum for the year, the decade, or the century, as Bestor described the course it replaced. In part, this is because of the diversity of the student population to be served, in part because no single course can "cover" physics or do more than provide an introduction to it, and physicists themselves disagree on which concepts and approaches to emphasize. As a result, Educational Services Inc. (now part of Education

[10] *Innovation and Experiment in Education,* A Progress Report of the Panel on Educational Research and Development, U.S. Government Printing Office, 1964; Jerrold R. Zacharias and Stephen White, "The Requirements for Major Curriculum Revision," in Robert W. Heath, ed., *New Curricula,* New York: Harper & Row, 1964.

Development Center, Inc.), which had sponsored the PSSC course, also developed an Introductory Physical Science course for the ninth grade, to provide the framework students needed for the new physics course as well as for the new courses being developed in chemistry and biology. The National Science Foundation sponsored the creation of a wholly new high school physics course, with a more humanistic and historical approach —"Project Physics," under the direction of Professor Gerald Holton of Harvard, a philosopher and historian of science as well as a physicist. Still another group, the Secondary School Science Project at Princeton, took up the PSSC's original desire to develop an integrated approach to the physical sciences, creating a tenth-grade course on "Time, Space and Matter," which employs principles of chemistry, physics, geology, astronomy, and mathematics in trying to explain the nature of the physical world.[11]

Nor was physics a lonely exception. In approaching the revision of the high school biology course—"twenty years behind the advancing front of science, and in important respects . . . a full century in arrears"—the members of the American Institute of Biological Sciences concluded that "the life sciences are so diverse, both in point of view and in methodology, that there is no single best way to organize a high school course in biology." As a result, they created three separate courses, reflecting the three major approaches to the biological sciences: the genetic and developmental, the biochemical and physiological, and the ecological and evolutionary.[12] Two groups of chemists have been working on two different approaches to high school chemistry, neither designed as the definitive approach. And the mathematicians, of course, disagree violently over the most appropriate approach to the teaching of mathematics.[13]

In short, there is, and can be, no one curriculum suitable for all time, or for all students at a given time. "The evocation of curiosity, of judgment, of the power of mastering a tangled set of circumstances, the use of theory in giving foresight in special cases," Whitehead declared—"all these powers are not to be

[11] John I. Goodlad with Renata von Stoephasius and M. Frances Klein, *The Changing School Curriculum,* New York: The Fund for the Advancement of Education, 1966.
[12] Bentley Glass, "Renascent Biology: A Report on the AIBS Biological Sciences Curriculum Study," in Heath, *New Curricula.*
[13] Cf. Goodlad, et al., *The Changing School Curriculum;* Benjamin De Mott, "The Math Wars," in Heath, *New Curricula.*

imparted by a set rule embodied in one set of examination sub-jects." To insist that there is only one curriculum is to confuse the means of education with the end.

This is in no way to suggest, however, that any one piece of learning is as good as any other, and that high school students therefore might just as well study whatever interests them. Knowing one thing is *not* the same as knowing another, and some things are more worth knowing than others. Surely a man cannot be considered educated unless he has at least some under-standing of science. "It is not at all necessary that the average man should be acquainted with the latest theory of the universe or the newest hormone," George Sarton, the most distinguished historian of science, argued, "but it is very necessary that he should understand as clearly as possible the purpose and the methods of science." Nor can a man be considered educated unless he has some knowledge of the past, some understanding of the human condition ("A sense of tragedy and triumph achieved through the study of literature," Jerome Bruner writes, "is surely as important to modern man as a sense of the struc-ture of matter achieved through the study of physics"), some knowledge of the nature and dynamics of human society, and some knowledge of language and of the arts.

Certain skills or abilities are also essential to the educated man: the ability to learn for himself, to take hold of a subject and "work it up" for himself, so that he is not dependent upon his teacher's direction; the ability to think for himself, "to ask the right critical questions and to apply rigorous tests" to his hunches, so that he is not dependent upon the ideas and opinions of others; the ability to respond to beauty, the beauty of nature as well as the art made by his fellow man; and the ability to communicate his ideas and feelings to others. The fact that there is no one curriculum to be specified for everyone does not mean, therefore, that there should be no curriculum at all. "The most dangerous intellectual aspect of the contemporary scene," as Robert A. Nisbet suggests, is the inability of so many of the young (and so many of the would-be young) to distinguish be-tween authority and power.

What is crucial so far as the schools are concerned is that authority resides not only in individuals and institutions, but in the culture as well. In Nisbet's words, "There is the authority of learning and taste; of syntax and grammar in language; of scholarship, of science, and of the arts. In traditional culture there is an authority attaching to the names of Shakespeare,

Montaigne, Newton and Pasteur in just as sure a sense of the word as though we were speaking of the law. There is the authority of logic, reason, and of genius. Above all, there is the residual authority of the core of values around which Western culture has been formed."

The greatest and most frightening manifestation of the generation gap, moreover, is the new generation's rejection—at times, its inability even to understand—the authority of culture and the responsibilities that follow from it. "Their lack of a sense of history is bewildering," Paul Goodman says of the students he knows. "They do not really understand that technology, civil law, and the university are *human* institutions, for which they too are responsible"; they do not understand "that these institutions, works of spirit in history, are how Man has made himself and is." But "if they treat them as mere things, rather than being vigilant for them," Goodman worries, "they themselves become nothing. And nothing comes from nothing."[14]

It is absolutely crucial, therefore, to bring the young into contact with, and possession of, their culture. To do this, high schools must offer more than just a potpourri of courses. This is not to say that they should provide a single curriculum or sequence that every student must follow, come what may; given the mood of the present generation, nothing would be more self-defeating, more likely to turn students away from the culture. Since the time of Socrates, at the very least, it has been a truism that a teacher must start where his students are if he is to take them someplace else. For this generation of students, it means starting with more freedom than previous generations have enjoyed.

But the teacher, as Plato's *Dialogues* illustrate so beautifully, must do more than simply start where his students are; he must also take them somewhere else. To do that, he must have some convictions about where they should go, convictions, that is to say, about what is worth learning. The real conflict, therefore, is not between "freedom" and "restraint"; it is between rival judgments about what is most worth knowing. The conflict need not be resolved: it is not essential that teachers and students share the same educational goals, only that they *have*

---

[14] Paul Goodman, "The New Reformation," *The New York Times Magazine,* September 14, 1969. Cf. also "The Present Moment in Education," *New York Review of Books,* XII, No. 7, April 10, 1969.

educational goals—goals that can be articulated into some coherent structure. For education, as Daniel Bell argues, "is a
confrontation with a discipline, a confrontation with a teacher."[15]

Education is also a confrontation with oneself. "In fact, there
is only one process," the philosopher Marjorie Grene writes,
"that is ourselves trying to make sense of things, trying to find
significance in what would else be chaos. . . . Learning is a
transformation of the whole person."[16]

All the more so during adolescence, whose "central developmental task," as Edgar Friedenberg puts it, "is self-definition.
Adolescence," he writes, "is the period during which a young
person learns who he is, and what he really feels. It is the time
during which he differentiates himself from his culture, though
on the culture's terms."[17] For this to happen, adolescents need
a good deal of freedom—what Erik Erikson calls a "psycho-
social moratorium"—for personal exploration and growth, for
a "search for something and somebody to be true to."[18]

The kind of education we have been talking about is a necessary part of this process of growth and exploration, for the
adolescent passion for self-definition is a product of cognitive,
not just sexual and physiological, maturation. It is, indeed, the
mental structures that emerge during adolescence, and that a
well-conceived curriculum is designed to enhance, that make
self-definition possible, for they enable young people to think
abstractly—to reflect on the meaning of their own thoughts,
experiences, and feelings, and to conjure up the full range of
alternatives for the future. "Such cognitive orientation," Erik
Erikson points out, "forms not a contrast but a complement to
the need of the young person to develop a sense of identity, for,
from among all possible and imaginable relations, he must make
a series of ever narrowing selections of personal, occupational,
sexual, and ideological commitments." Or as Piaget succinctly

[15] Daniel Bell, "Social Change in Education and the Change in Educational Concepts," in Clarence H. Faust and Jessica Feingold, eds., *Approaches to Education for Character*, New York: Columbia University
Press, 1969. Cf., also Daniel Bell, *The Reforming of General Education*,
Columbia University Press, 1966.
[16] Marjorie Grene, *The Knower and the Known*, New York: Basic
Books, 1966.
[17] Edgar Z. Friedenberg, *The Vanishing Adolescent*.
[18] Erik H. Erikson, "Youth: Fidelity and Diversity," in E. H. Erikson,
ed., *The Challenge of Youth*.

puts it, "affectivity is nothing without intelligence. Intelligence furnishes affectivity with its means and clarifies its ends."[19]

In short, the proper kind of education gives meaning and direction to the search for identity, preventing it from being a mere exercise in narcissism. Indeed, the school has a special obligation in this regard: more than any other institution, it has the capacity, and therefore the obligation, as Friedenberg puts it, "to clarify for its students the meaning of their experience of life in their society." It does this by helping students develop the knowledge and skills they need to make sense out of their experience—their experience with themselves, with others, with the world—not just during adolescence, but for the rest of their lives.

II

For this to happen, it is not just the curriculum that will have to change, but the entire way in which high schools are organized and run. As we have seen in Chapters 4 and 5, students at present are hardly permitted, let alone encouraged, to confront either their teachers or themselves. They are given little opportunity, and no reason, to develop resolute ideas of their own about what they should learn, and in most schools they are actively discouraged from trying to test those ideas against their teachers'. By and large they are expected to learn what the faculty wants them to learn in the way the faculty wants them to learn it, and no nonsense, please. Freedom to explore, to test one's ideas as a means of finding out who one is and what one believes—these are luxuries a well-run school cannot afford. As one student summed it up, "It's all a question of what they want to produce, not what we want to become." The result, at best, is to persuade students that knowledge has no relation to them, no relevance for the kinds of lives they will lead; at worst, it produces the kind of alienation, the rejection of authority, the rejection of the whole notion of culture, of discipline and of learning, with which we are now contending.

Fortunately, there are signs of change, in part as a response to student dissent, in part as a result of the growing distaste a number of teachers and administrators feel for the way schools are run, and their conviction that schools can be more humane, that students can handle and benefit from greater freedom and

[19] *Six Psychological Studies*, p. 69.

responsibility. Whatever the reasons, there would appear to be a growing ferment in high schools around the country.

The changes now going on fall into three broad categories:

• Modest changes in school regulations designed to create a freer and more humane atmosphere outside the classroom;

• Somewhat bolder attempts to humanize the schools as a whole—for example, by cutting the number of required classes, leaving students with a third or more of their time unscheduled, to be used for independent study, for taking more elective courses, for fulfilling some course requirements outside the classroom, or for relaxation and leisure;

• Radical experiments involving changes of the most fundamental sort—reordering the curriculum and indeed the entire teaching-learning process, and in some instances broadening the very concept of what constitutes a school.

Most of the changes are of the first sort, in response to the growing student hostility to arbitrary or demeaning rules and regulations. Schools all over the country—some voluntarily, some in response to court orders—are abandoning codes governing dress and appearance, codes that usually are as inane as they are unenforceable. (Schools with dress codes, for example, may forbid girls from wearing slacks on the grounds that they are provocative, while permitting the mini-est of mini-skirts; schools that forbid boys from sporting beards have bearded teachers.) Inane or not, the codes are resented, and properly so, as invasions of the students' privacy and as exercises in arbitrary power. It is hard to persuade students that a school respects their rights and values their individuality when its rules specify, as does one fairly typical suburban school's, that "Whatever, in the judgment of the faculty, is considered bizarre, unusual, eccentric or careless in personal appearance and dress will not be tolerated."

A good many schools, moreover, from Maine to Florida and from New York to California, are dropping the demeaning requirement that students must have a pass to go to the toilet or get a drink of water, along with the insane regulation that forbids them from using the library without first getting a library pass. Some schools are going further, permitting students to use their unscheduled time as and where they see fit, instead of requiring them to be in a study hall or other specified place during so-called "free" periods, and in the cafeteria during the lunch hour. (One of the stranger school traditions is the one that treats first graders, but not high school students, as capable of going home for lunch.) Here and there, schools are turning over some of the responsibility for formulating rules of conduct to the students themselves or to student-faculty committees. Some are even experimenting with freedom of the press, placing the responsibility for maintaining minimum standards, e.g., avoiding offensive language or illustrations, on the student editors.

Like it or not, more and more high schools are going to have to make more and more changes of these sorts. In California, New York, and Connecticut, for example, as well as in a number of other states, schools that have tried to enforce codes governing dress and grooming in the traditional way—suspending the offending student or denying him "class privileges"—have had their codes overruled by the courts on the grounds that dress and personal adornment are a form of self-expression subject to the same constitutional guarantees as any other. Any regulations a school makes, California Superior Court Judge W. G. Watson stated in expressing the court's decision in the case of *Myers v. Arcata Union High School,* "must reasonably pertain to the health and safety of the students or to the orderly conduct of school business. In this regard consideration should be given to what is really health and safety . . . and what is merely personal preference. . . . In a society as advanced as that in which we live," the judge added, "there is room for many personal preferences . . ."

To be sure, a good many teachers, principals, and parents question the advisability of relaxing the rules in any way. There is too much freedom already, they argue. As evidence, they point to high schools where there is a flourishing traffic in narcotics, with students using drugs freely in the bathrooms, cafeterias, and even the classrooms themselves. (In some schools, a boy can hardly go to the bathroom without seeing other students "mainlining," i.e., injecting, or sniffing, heroin.) Or they point to schools where authority has broken down altogether, with students disrupting classes, vandalizing or stealing school property, and generally terrorizing both teachers and students. For schools of this sort, it would be irresponsible as well as naïve to suggest that freedom is a panacea.

Whether or not it is a panacea, however, freedom happens to

be a constitutional right; as the Supreme Court has put it, "neither the Fourteenth Amendment nor the Bill of Rights is for adults alone." Moreover, the notion that students have constitutional rights which the school cannot infringe is no whim of the moment; it is firmly rooted in the law. As far back as 1943, the Supreme Court made it clear that compulsory school attendance did not mean that students surrendered their rights at the schoolhouse door. The Fourteenth Amendment, the Court declared, "protects the citizen against the State itself and all of its creatures—the Board of Education not excepted. These have, of course, important, delicate and highly discretionary functions, but none that they may not perform within the limits of the Bill of Rights. That they are educating the young for citizenship is reason for scrupulous protection of Constitutional freedoms of the individual, if we are not to strangle the free mind at its source and teach youth to discount important principles of our government as mere platitudes."[20]

Now, as a result of a series of test cases, many of them brought by the American Civil Liberties Union and its various affiliates, schools are being forced to recognize the Constitution, and in some cases to recognize their own state education codes, which they have also been violating in wholesale fashion. It seems clear, for example, that the almost universal practice of "denying class privileges," suspending, or expelling students without any kind of due process simply will not stand. As a minimum, a student has a right to receive advice in writing of the charges against him, with a summary of the evidence on which the charges are based, along with a formal hearing at which (he and his parent or guardian) may be represented by counsel, with the right of cross-examination, and a reasonable time in which to prepare the defense. It seems equally clear that students have the right to peaceful protest, as well as the right to distribute their own publications.[21]

School officials who have freedom forced upon them may discover that it is a better solvent of disorder than repression. "The thing that frightens me about the modern intelligentsia," George Orwell wrote in 1940, "is their inability to see that human society must be based on common decency." Orwell might just as well have been talking about teachers, principals, superintendents, and school board members, and the apparent in-

[20] *West Virginia Board of Education v. Barnette,* 319 U.S. 624 (1943).
[21] *Academic Freedom in the Secondary Schools,* New York: American Civil Liberties Union, September 1963.

ability of so many to see the need for common decency in the human society that is the school. Certainly it is clear that repression does not work, that "cracking down" serves only to breed more defiance and disruption, which breeds more repression, and so on ad infinitum. And all the more so when "cracking down" is accompanied by the kind of arbitrariness, racial prejudice, assumption of student guilt, and general disregard of individual rights that characterizes "difficult" schools. In a war between faculty and students, the students are bound to win; there are more of them, and when put to the test, they can be disruptive in the most ingenious ways.

Since repression fails anyway, it may be worth trying freedom. There is evidence that it can work—that even "difficult" and "disruptive" students can respond to an atmosphere of trust, particularly if administrators do not confuse trust and confidence in the students with sentimentality about them.

ITEM: A large (3,000 students) comprehensive high school in a suburban city wracked by racial and ethnic conflict had posted uniformed guards throughout the school in a futile attempt to maintain order. A new principal removes the guards, telling the students, in a series of meetings on the first day of the school year, that he has done so out of respect for their maturity and confidence in their ability to maintain order. While conveying empathy and affection for them, his manner at the same time makes it clear that he is no sentimental pushover. The principal also goes to great pains to win the respect and confidence of the leaders of the black and dominant white ethnic student groups, asking them to report instances of racial and ethnic slurs and tension so that he can take prompt action. The self-fulfilling prophecy works: despite enormous tension in the adult community, the school remains calm. Over Easter vacation, the students return the compliment, deluging a local radio station with some two and a half million postcards to elect the principal "principal of the year" in an area-wide contest.

III

Recognizing that a freer and more humane atmosphere is educationally sound as well as constitutionally necessary, high schools in a number of communities around the country—among them, Melbourne, Florida; Abington, Pennsylvania; Silver Spring, Maryland; New York City; Troy, New York; Green Bay, Wisconsin; Decatur, Illinois; Fullerton, California—have taken a variety of measures to humanize the school as a whole, and to put more of the responsibility for their learning on the students themselves. As the John F. Kennedy High School in Silver Spring, Maryland, one of the more innovative of these schools, states its goals, "The purpose of the program . . . is to provide an environment which will focus on the individual—a climate where student responsibility is emphasized, where conformity is not imposed, where learners solve problems important to them, where interest is high, and where there is an active commitment to discovery and learning."

One of the ways in which high schools are finding it possible to inch toward greater freedom and responsibility for their students is through the adoption of so-called flexible modular scheduling, a technique first developed, and advocated with missionary zeal, by Professor Robert Bush of the Stanford University Graduate School of Education and Dr. Dwight Allen, formerly of Stanford, now dean of the University of Massachusetts' School of Education. In most high schools, the day is divided into a fixed number of periods of equal length (usually forty to fifty minutes), so that every meeting of every class lasts the same amount of time. Flexible scheduling uses a shorter time module—typically sixteen, eighteen, or twenty minutes— which makes it possible to provide class periods of varying length—forty minutes, say, for a lecture or demonstration, sixty or eighty minutes for a seminar or small group discussion. The technique makes it easier for teachers to adapt their teaching style to the purpose at hand.

What should be emphasized, however, is that flexible scheduling is simply an administrative technique that makes possible, but in no way guarantees, a freer and less restrictive atmosphere. All too often, in fact, the technique turns out to be a kind of gimmickry in which nothing much changes but the length of the periods (and not always that) and the vocabulary with which the program is described.

ITEM: "I charge you with the responsibility of becoming your own man or woman," the principal of a California high school, well publicized for its early adoption of "flexible modular scheduling," tells his students in the opening sentence of the school's student handbook. Becoming your own man or woman does not extend, however, to deciding how to dress or look; the handbook contains a dress code with *sixteen* separate regulations, governing such matters as the length of a boy's sideburns ("no longer than the bottom of the ear"), the length of his hair ("no longer than the top of the normal dress-shirt collar in back"), whether or not he can sport a beard (he cannot), the use of sunglasses ("may be worn inside school building only upon a physician's recommendation"), the length of a girl's skirt ("Skirts shall allow freedom of movement and shall not be more than three inches above the top of the knee cap when standing"), and the styling of their footwear ("Sandals or shoes must have back or heel straps").

ITEM: "Our school philosophy commits us to the development of the inquiring, creative mind and the self-directed individual," a Wisconsin high school—also a user of flexible modular scheduling—declares in its statement of principles. But the school's "self-directed individuals" are placed in detention if they chew gum, come late to class, or violate what the school calls its "Alight Policy," which reads as follows:

> No student should be in the corridors after the 4 minute passing time unless he has an approved pass. Students must plan their day in such a manner as to remain in each classroom or study area for the entire length of the mod. Once a student has "alighted" he must remain in that room until the end of the mod. Violators will be assigned detention make-up duty. Although some movement in the corridors will occur at the termination of each module, students are not to use the occasion to take a 4 minute rest every 20 minutes. During unscheduled time students are expected to stay in one area or room as much as possible. Students who have consecutive modules of unscheduled time should plan to spend at least 2 mods in a given location before moving to another area.

However, a number of schools *are* using flexible modular scheduling to break out of the usual rut. A fairly common practice, for example, is to arrange programs so that scheduled lectures, discussions, and classes occupy only part of each student's week, with a substantial portion of his time— generally 30 to 40 percent—left unscheduled. In some such schools, students are free to use the time in any way they wish— for recreation and leisure, for independent study projects, or to complete assignments. In others, students are technically free but are expected to use the time mainly to complete work assigned by their teachers or to probe more deeply into some aspect of a course. In most, teachers and administrators find it hard to let go of the traces. Even so, such schools are a lot more humane than most, since students have the freedom of the building during their free time, i.e., they can work in the library, a study hall, a lounge, or what have you, instead of being herded into a supervised study hall where talking is forbidden and a pass required to go to the john or get a drink of water.

ITEM: At Abington, Pennsylvania High School's North Campus, students have about 30 percent of their time unscheduled. During these periods, students may use the library, which includes a typing area and audio-visual room, or one of two "study centers"; or they may go to a "learning resource center," one for each of the major subject areas (English, foreign languages, math, science, and social studies), which has specialized collections of books, magazines, and journals, as well as a good bit of technological gadgetry, e.g., videotape lectures and science demonstrations, tape recorders, 8-mm. cartridge loop viewers. Students may also use the gym, the photography dark room, or greenhouse; they may just relax in the student lounge or the "talking commons"; or they may take a short noncredit course which they or the faculty may devise. (The reduction in the number of scheduled classes gives teachers the time to offer such courses, as well as the time to confer with colleagues or students, to prepare their lectures, to take in-service courses, or even to relax.)

To make sure that they use their "free" time "productively," students attend a weekly "freshman orientation seminar during the first of the two years (ninth and tenth grades) they spend at the North Campus. The seminar aside, the school keeps fairly close tabs on how and where students spend their time. Nearly half the time, officials report, is spent in the library and learning centers and about one-third in the study centers, with little more than 10 percent of the time spent in the areas set aside for relaxation. Students who seem unable to use their time productively—never more than 3 percent of the enrollment of 2,000, according to school records—are required to spend their unscheduled time in carefully supervised study halls for a two-week interval, repeated as deemed necessary.

ITEM: Lakeview High School in Decatur, Illinois, encourages students to use their unscheduled time for a variety of activities, distinguishing carefully between individual study and independent study. If students are working by themselves but doing work a teacher assigned, the process cannot honestly be called independent. Hence the faculty distinguishes four "levels" of activity students may engage in during their unscheduled time.

Level I is conventional homework—a specific assignment that is due on a specific date, usually the next day or two. Level II— "Project Work"—is homework in which students have some discretion in the choice of topic, and generally a somewhat longer period of time in which to complete it. Level III—"Contract Work"—involves proceeding through a course at the student's own rate; class attendance is optional, and the student takes tests as he is ready for them, with the teacher, however, remaining responsible for evaluation of the work that is done. Level IV is true independent study—work that a student initiates, plans, and evaluates on his own, drawing on the faculty for advice or evaluation as he sees fit.

A happy by-product of this kind of flexibility is its tendency to stimulate examination of a good many other school practices. One of the most deeply embedded traditions, for example, one that James B. Conant reinforced with his studies of the American high school, is the notion that educational quality can be measured in terms of time rather than knowledge. "Improvement would come about almost automatically in most schools," Dr. Conant declared, "if seven years of English and social studies were required and if, instead of a two-year course in a foreign language, a sequence of four years of at least one foreign language were offered . . ."[22]

Maybe; but students can be, and usually are, as illiterate in a foreign language after four years as they are after two; it would make eminently better sense to judge the quality of a school's language offerings by some measure of competence in reading, writing, and speaking the language. And whether a school is improved by offering another year or two of English and social studies depends, of course, on what it is that students learn during that extra time. Neil Postman and Charles Weingartner call this tradition "The Vaccination Theory of Education," since it implies that "a subject is something you 'take' and, when you have taken it, you have 'had' it, and if you have 'had' it, you are

[22] James B. Conant, *The American High School Today*, New York: McGraw-Hill, 1959. Cf. also James B. Conant, *The Comprehensive High School: A Second Report to Interested Citizens*, New York: McGraw-Hill, 1967.

immune and need not take it again."[23] One of the more encouraging aspects of the current ferment, therefore, is the fact that here and there schools are questioning this tradition and are trying to shift the emphasis from time served to knowledge gained.

ITEM: Students at John F. Kennedy High School in Silver Spring, Maryland, may elect to fulfill course requirements on their own, outside the classroom; in the 1968–69 school year, some 40 percent of the student body chose to do so for at least one course. The student is expected to take the initiative; he and his teacher then determine how he will satisfy the requirement— whether he will simply cover the assigned material on his own, or whether—the more usual approach—he will make a more intensive study of some concept or problem that interests him. Student and teacher also decide in advance what materials will be covered; whether or not the student will come to class, and how often; and how frequently, and in what ways, his work will be evaluated, e.g., via research papers, essays, oral reports, discussions, etc. When agreement is reached, a "contract" is drawn up which the student, his parents, and the teacher sign.

Some schools are also questioning the notion that a course has to last a minimum of one semester, offering "mini-courses" of varying lengths, particularly in areas of special interest to the students:

ITEM: At the Hamilton-Wenham Regional High School in Hamilton, Massachusetts, thirty miles north of Boston, all classes for seniors were suspended for a two-week period at the end of the 1968 school year, to provide time for courses sponsored, organized and in many cases, run by the seniors themselves. (The faculty was agreeable, since the last few weeks of senior year are thrown away anyway.) A member of the student council sent seniors a questionnaire asking them what they would like to study during the period, and then circulated the tabulations among the faculty, many of whom discovered that students wanted to study subjects they had always wanted to teach, but had never been able to fit into the curriculum. Departmental lines were crossed as teachers began volunteering their services for the various mini-courses—such things as film criticism, filmmaking, poetry writing, the plays of Eugene O'Neill, and marine

[23] *Teaching as a Subversive Activity,* New York: Delacorte Press, 1969.

ecology, along with more mundane courses in "Home Mechanics for Girls," "Cooking for Boys," and the like.

The program was a success, affecting the faculty as much as the students. Teachers were surprised to find that students they had regarded as slow or apathetic appeared bright and eager when they were free to study what interested them. "Freed from the stigma of homogeneous grouping," Robert R. Hayward, a member of the English Department, writes, "many of our not-bound-for-college seniors elected the more intellectual mini-courses. (Used to their apathetic performance in general classes, we were amazed by their sophisticated handling of difficult subjects in mixed discussion groups. They sometimes outdid the brightest seniors in their penetrating observations about Bergman's *The Virgin Spring* or his *Smiles of a Summer Night*.)"[24] As a result, the school has continued the program for seniors and expanded it to other students, bringing in volunteer experts from the community—several ministers, an artist, a disc jockey, assorted psychiatrists, lawyers, social workers—to teach part or all of a number of the courses. Now the experience is seeping into the regular curriculum: teachers are beginning to involve students in planning courses and are starting to question the wisdom of homogeneous grouping, letter grades, and other school practices.

The question of grades and their impact on the teaching-learning process is receiving increasing attention, with a growing number of students and teachers proposing modification of the present system, or its elimination altogether.

ITEM: In the high school equivalency program he runs for high school dropouts—mostly Negroes from the streets of Portland and other Northwest cities, Mexican-American and Anglo migratory workers, and Indian Americans—Professor Arthur Pearl of the University of Oregon has dropped the usual grading system altogether. Teachers and students share a mutual responsibility, he argues. If a student does not learn, the teacher may be to blame as well as the student; both should hold themselves accountable. Hence teacher and student negotiate a contract at the beginning of the course, setting target dates at which the student will take the exam for each unit of work. If a stu-

---

[24] Robert R. Hayward, "Maximum Results from Mini-Courses," *Today's Education*, September 1969.

dent feels that he is not ready for the test when the date comes around, he can renegotiate the contract with the instructor—after discussing why he's not ready.

When he does take the exam, the student receives one of two grades—"pass," or "have not passed yet," in which case the contract is again renegotiated. The grade itself can also be appealed if a student feels he has been marked unfairly. Once there is a means of adjudicating grievances, Pearl argues, the student-teacher relationship can change from the usual adversary relationship to one of partnership—essential, in his view, if students are to become responsible, self-directed learners.

Teachers and administrators retain their authority; "it would be the cruelest of deceptions," Pearl says, "to suggest to students that they have unlimited decision-making powers." But that authority, he insists, must be exercised responsibly, which means that no more rules should be promulgated than are absolutely necessary, and that those promulgating rules must be willing to defend them in terms of their purpose.

Only a handful of schools (discussed in Sections IV, V, and VI below) have been willing to go this far, fearing that any drastic modification of the traditional grading system would handicap their students in the battle for college admission. Some, however, are trying to tinker with the system in an effort to offset or reduce some of its adverse effects, awarding grades for required courses but not for electives. This kind of tinkering fails to come to grips with the real problem: how to make evaluation serve the ends of education, instead of being the end itself. Indeed, by continuing the traditional system for the required courses and dropping it for electives, schools obscure the real issue. What is wrong with the present system is not the use of grades per se, but the fact that the awarding of a grade has been divorced from the larger function of evaluation, thereby preventing it from fulfilling its proper educational purpose.

And evaluation *is* an important part of the teaching-learning process. Tests, examinations, term papers, projects, etc., are useful to students, teachers, and administrators alike. They provide teachers, for example, with a means of determining the degree to which they are achieving their objectives. A well-constructed examination enables the teacher to judge the effectiveness of his teaching, since it reveals—sometimes traumatically—just what it is that students have learned, and what they have not learned or have misunderstood. A good exam may also reveal weaknesses in the curriculum, and suggest ways by which it, too, can be improved. Exams can be useful to school administrators as well, providing a means of evaluating the effectiveness of the institution and the soundness of the assumptions on which its curriculum is based.[25] But teachers and administrators rarely view examinations in these lights; if students do poorly, the reflection is on them, not on the teacher or the school.

Evaluation is even more important, of course, to the student himself. Tests should warn him when he is falling below minimum standards of performance. More important, examinations should make it possible for a student to test his knowledge and competence by giving him an opportunity to apply it in a new way or to a new situation or problem. This in turn can help the student discover what he knows and what he has failed to understand or to learn. The feedback must be prompt, however; the student must learn quickly where he went wrong if an exam is to help him improve his performance. Since students will have to judge their own performance after they leave school, it is important, too, to provide as much experience as possible in self-evaluation.[26]

Schools rarely use tests for these purposes, either, except, perhaps, as a storm signal. It is a rare high school, for example, in which a student ever sees his final examination paper again, once he has handed it in; in most schools, there is no feedback at all. (If evaluation were the goal, teachers would give their final exams well before the end of the semester, to allow time to return the exams to the students with detailed comments and suggestions.) The procedure thus makes it clear to students that the purpose of testing is not evaluation but rating—to produce grades that enable the school to rank students and sort them in various ways for administrative purposes. The result is to destroy any interest in learning for its own sake; what is worth learning, the students quickly realize, is what will be asked for on the exam. Hence the inevitable question that chills the conscientious teacher's soul: "Will we be responsible for this on the final?"

[25] Eugene R. Smith, Ralph W. Tyler, et al., *Appraising and Recording Student Progress,* New York: Harper & Row, 1942 (*Adventure in American Education,* Volume III). Cf. also E. F. Lindquist, ed., *Educational Measurement,* Washington, D.C.: American Council on Education, 1951, especially essay by Ralph W. Tyler.
[26] Lee J. Cronbach, *Educational Psychology,* New York: Harcourt, Brace & World, second edition, 1963, Chapter 16.

IV

One of the measures of how far we have to go in reforming the American high school is the fact that the changes we have been discussing can be described as major steps forward. They are— if one measures them against the high school as it now is. Compared to the repressive, almost prison-like atmosphere of most high schools, the ones we have been talking about are bastions of freedom and trust. And to the extent to which they have put more of the responsibility for learning, for seeking out, for probing, on the students themselves, they are affecting a basic part of the educational process.

For the most part, however, these schools have not addressed themselves to the basic questions of educational purpose. Indeed, the changes they have introduced, important and welcome as they are, sometimes have the effect of avoiding the really hard questions. Independent study, for example, is an important means; it is not an end in itself. "Schools have got to stand for something," Charles E. Brown insists. Or as Wilford M. Aikin, who directed the Eight-Year Study, wrote in 1942, "It is not enough to create better conditions for learning. It is equally necessary to determine what American youth most need to learn." That necessity remains; the high school, in Aikin's phrase, must "rediscover its chief reason for existence."

Only a handful of schools are engaged in that kind of an attempt—among them, the Parkway Program in Philadelphia, the Newton, Massachusetts, High School, in its Murray Road Annex, and John Adams High School in Portland. None as yet can be judged a success; they are still too new and too tentative and experimental (the oldest, at this writing, is in its third year of operation, the youngest, in its first) for any such judgments to to be made. They demand close study nonetheless, because of the seriousness with which they are raising fundamental questions about both the means and the ends of education.

The architects of the Parkway Program in Philadelphia—the "school without walls," as it is sometimes called—are questioning virtually every one of the traditional assumptions about what constitutes a school, and what constitutes an education. The starting point, in fact, is the conviction, expressed by the program's director, John Bremer, a forty-two-year-old Englishman, that "It is not possible to improve the high school; it has reached the end of its development. We need a new kind of educational institution."[27] Under the auspices of the Philadelphia Board of Education, and with funding from the Ford Foundation, Bremer is attempting to do precisely that—to fashion an almost totally new kind of institution.

Parkway departs from tradition in a number of respects. One of the most striking is the absence of any building or campus. "Learning is not something that goes on only in special places called classrooms, or in special buildings called schools," Bremer writes; "rather, it is a quality of life appropriate to any and every phase of human existence, or, more strictly, it is human life itself." Hence "the spatial boundaries of the educational process in the Parkway Program are co-terminous with the life space of the student himself." The program is designed to "help the student to live learningly within his present life space," and to help him expand that space.

In a sense, then, the "school" is the city of Philadelphia itself. Parkway has its own faculty, to be sure, composed of teachers transferred from other Philadelphia high schools, plus a number of university interns. It also has its own headquarters on the second floor of an old building in downtown Philadelphia, three blocks from City Hall, with offices for the faculty, study rooms, and a general area for students to hang out in during their spare time. Learning is not confined to classrooms, however, or to the conventional school day or school year. The courses offered by the regular faculty may be held almost anywhere—in a meeting room in a public library, a museum, a "Y," a university or research institute laboratory, a school building, or a teacher's home.

ITEM: A Spanish class meets in a building in Spring Garden, the Spanish-speaking section of Philadelphia. After an hour or so of classroom instruction, the students walk around the neighborhood, practicing the language by striking up conversations with storekeepers or passers-by. "It's really amazing because you realize how many flaws you make in your speech patterns much better than any record could give you," one student, who had been failing in Spanish in his former school, observes. "You don't have to sit in the classroom and fold your hands and say

[27] *The Parkway Program,* The School District of Philadelphia, May 1969 (mimeographed). The quotations from Bremer that follow come either from that pamphlet, his article, "The Good of the Curriculum," *The Center Forum,* Vol. 3, No. 5, March 1, 1969, or conversations with him by the writer and a member of the Carnegie Study staff.

you will not learn. You learn by experiencing, by doing different things, by really going out."

ITEM: A geometry class learns "by really going out," too. The students meet in the teacher's apartment for formal instruction, then go about the city, trying out what they've learned. "We had one class in Logan Circle, where we tried to figure the diameter of the circle itself," a student reports. "That's something new; you know you have to get certain measurements and everything—not just that you're told you have a circle of such and such a distance. You couldn't waste your time finding irrelevant facts, because you were going to get soaked by the big fountain there if you did. You actually learn by going out and doing what you're learning in theory, which is something I never did before."

In addition to the courses offered by the Parkway faculty, students are expected to choose at least one "institutional offering"—a course or activity offered by one of the many scientific, business, cultural, and journalistic institutions concentrated along and around the Benjamin Franklin Parkway, from which the program's name derives. The offering may be a formal course, a work-study program, a research-assistantship or apprenticeship, or simply a chance to hang around and watch, or to participate in the institution's activities in any way the student or the cooperating "teacher" may see fit. Cooperating institutions include the Philadelphia Zoo, which offers a course on "The Animal Kingdom"; the Franklin Institute, one of the best science museums in the United States; the Museum of Art; the Insurance Company of North America, which offers a course called "What's the Risk?"; Smith, Kline & French, a leading drug manufacturer, which gives a course in "The Modern Corporation"; a local television station (KYW) and newspaper publisher (*The Philadelphia Bulletin* and the *Inquirer*); the Police Department and District Attorney's office, members of which teach a course on law enforcement; and the Philadelphia Chapter of the American Civil Liberties Union, where students take a "course" in "Law and Civil Rights" by helping the director in investigating complaints and preparing cases. The object is to reconnect the schools with the larger community, not through the conventional field trip, but through some continuing experience. What matters, in Bremer's view, is less where the student is than that he "have enough time to find out what it is like to live in that place, to be a real part of it, and for it to be a real part of him."

Students are also encouraged to work in one of these institutions—for some, as a means of social service, for others, as a source of income, for still others, as a means of clarifying their thinking about a career after school, and for all, as a way of testing some of the skills acquired in the classroom. "The skills acquired should always be tested by something outside the educational system," Bremer argues. "If a student cannot do something—in an office, on a train, at the airport—somewhere, that he could not do before, it is highly doubtful that he has learned anything; it is certain that he has not learned anything useful. To incorporate this kind of 'reality-testing' is very important because it helps the student to develop his own feedback system."

In effect, then, students plan their own education, subject to the constraints of the state education law, which specifies minimum "Carnegie units" in English, math, social studies, language, etc., for a high school diploma. They are helped in doing so by assignment to a "tutorial group"—fifteen or sixteen students, a teacher, and a university intern—which meets for two hours, three times a week. The tutorial group is responsible for counseling and support and for continuing evaluation of the student's program and performance; while students receive only two grades, pass or fail, evaluation is regarded as an integral part of the educational process. "Our students have to learn to be responsible for their own education, to make choices, and to face the consequences of those choices," Bremer believes. Hence students are also involved in running the school, through "town meetings" of the entire student body and through participation in smaller "management groups." Bremer's purpose, as he puts it, is "to make the school's organization and administration part of the educational process, instead of being a precondition to it."

The tutorial group is also responsible for giving students a mastery of the basic skills of language and mathematics; given society's growing dependence on symbols, mastery of these "intellectual virtues," as Bremer calls them, is essential. To that degree, therefore, there is a prescribed curriculum; but each tutorial group decides the specific content. "I assume the students need intellectual virtues," Bremer says. "What I don't assume is that I happen to know what they are, or that I can force students into acquiring them." To set up a list of topics or subjects is both silly and arrogant, he maintains, when, "given any student, you do not know—you cannot know—where he is in his learning process, what he needs to learn right now, or what he ought to be learning now." Hence the program is designed to provide the maximum opportunities for students to learn what *they* want to learn. As Bremer sees his function, it is to find and establish "starting points for learning"—to help the student discover where he can begin to learn, so that he can take over the responsibility for his own education. What he then learns is his business.

What Bremer *hopes* the student will learn is how to live—with others as well as with himself. To define the purpose of the curriculum, Bremer quotes Whitehead ("There is only one subject-matter for education, and that is Life in all its manifestations") and Socrates ("For our conversation is not about something casual, but about the proper way to live"). Everything that is done in education, he argues, must be judged in the light of this search for "the proper way to live"; everything that is done must *itself* be an appropriate way to live. This means placing great emphasis on the quality of the relationships among students, teachers, and administrators, which means keeping the "learning community" small. "Since learning is a human activity," Bremer writes, "the problem of how to enter into the learning process, or to be a learner, can be restated in terms of group membership—how to be a member of a learning community." And that "learning community" is intended to be one in which teachers as well as students are learning,[28] and in which students and teachers as well as administrators are involved in planning and evaluating the curriculum. "Every school should have, as part of its curriculum, the continuing re-creation of its own curriculum," Bremer writes.

It is too early to make any firm judgments about the Parkway Program and its applicability to other situations; more experience is needed at Parkway itself, and in other cities. One has to wonder, for example, whether the program is *sui generis* to Philadelphia; as the Parkway Program's introductory booklet

[28] For that reason, Bremer did not give his teachers any in-service training before the program began. "It seems to me that if you need in-service training or staff development programs or whatever you want to call them," he says, "what you're really saying is that the structure of your educational program is not itself educational. What we try to do here is to so structure things that we all have to learn. We should not, as it were, think of learning as something to be carried on only by the students, or think that if the faculty or I are going to learn, that we do it in a special situation cut off from the rest of the activity."

observes, "the unique and specific importance of the Parkway institutions lies in the unparalleled wealth of material and human resources which they bring to a very small area of the city"—a wealth and a concentration that few cities can match.

One has to wonder, too, whether museums, newspapers, business firms, universities, and social service agencies would be willing to cooperate if a substantial proportion of Philadelphia's high school students were enrolled in something like the Parkway Program, as Bremer proposes. Since the program is experimental, it began with only 143 students in the spring of 1969, expanding to five hundred in the 1969–70 school year.[29] Each cooperating institution, therefore, has had to accommodate only a relative handful of students. If they were asked to find room for hundreds or thousands of students, the institutions might very well change their minds.

Bremer himself believes that these resources are not critical, and that the program could be duplicated anywhere. What *is* critical, in his view, is the absence of a central building, not the presence of museums and other cooperating institutions, for it is the lack of a traditional school building that forces the creation of a distinctive social structure.

Evaluation is difficult, too, because there was a certain intellectual flabbiness in a great many of the courses being offered during the first semester, when our visit was made. Bremer hopes the flabbiness will be temporary; there is a tendency, observable in other programs, for teachers, once they are released from the rigidities of the traditional curriculum and school organization, to swing to the opposite extreme, turning classes into extended "rap sessions." Usually, both students and teachers tire of this fairly rapidly and return to some more structured curriculum or approach. At Parkway, however, the temptation may have been even greater, in view of the fact that the tutorial groups are responsible for guidance and support, as well as for instruction in language and math—functions Bremer believes can and should be combined, but which the faculty has tended to see as separate. The flabbiness may also be encouraged by Bremer's insistence that only "starting points" should be prescribed, and not goals—an insistence which the students translate to mean that school is defined as the place where everyone does "his thing." There is a certain irony, indeed, in Bremer's latitudi-

[29] The students, who were chosen by lot from a much larger number of applicants, represented a cross-section of the city's high school population in terms of race and academic ability.

narian approach to curriculum; he himself teaches a course in Greek and another on Plato, and draws freely on his rigorous, somewhat classical education (the universities of Cambridge and Leicestershire and St. John's College) to argue the case for an absence of rigor and an emphasis on the here and now. One wonders whether his students will have the same qualities of intellect.

And yet the visitor cannot help but be impressed by the excitement Parkway has generated among its students, and the seriousness with which they seem to be thinking about their education.

ITEM: An eleventh-grade student, asked how Parkway differs from the school she had been attending, said, "First of all, the pressure. I used to put a lot of pressure on myself—to get good grades. I never had any problems, I really didn't need to put the pressure on. But I didn't know I was even putting the pressure on myself. Here you begin to realize, you know, Why am I doing this? What do you want? Why are you getting an education? You're not getting it for anybody else, you're getting it for yourself. I think that's the biggest difference. Before, I used to get the grades, I used to study. If I had a particularly nice teacher, I'd try to please him or whatever. And here, you know, I don't feel I have to show anybody that I am, you know . . . if I want to learn something, nobody else is responsible for my education except myself, and nobody's going to come up and pat you on the back and say, 'You're not doing your best and you're not going to get an education.' It's up to me now."

ITEM: A sixteen-year-old boy, asked if he felt he had learned more than usual at Parkway: "I really think so, because now I'm finally starting to pay attention." Why? "It's become more interesting, it's more of a personal thing like an impartation of knowledge from one person to another, instead of, 'You'll learn this, that's it, put it down on the test paper, I'll mark it, you'll pass.' But now the teachers are concerned: 'I'll help you, you know; if you're not doing well, we'll see what we can do; if we can work out an arrangement, I'll tutor you.' . . . It's the way I think school should be. You don't come from nine to three and sit there and listen to the teacher blah, blah, blah, put the answers down on the test sheet, get up and walk out and forget it. Here it's made interesting enough for you to want to know. On the bad weather days here I fought my mother to come;

she'd say, 'You're not going to school today,' and I'd get up and walk out—whereas I had the worst attendance record on record at the old school; I was absent 112 days last year."

The significance of the Parkway Program, in short, lies in the kinds of questions it is asking, and not necessarily in the answers it has tentatively suggested.

V

At least two other schools are asking the same kinds of questions, but in an attempt to reform the high school rather than to create an entirely new kind of institution. In its small experiment in the Murray Road Annex, for example, the Newton, Massachusetts, High School is trying to find out how far students can go in accepting responsibility for their own education, and how far students and teachers together can go in jointly creating and managing their own educational program.

In its original conception, interestingly enough, the Murray Road Annex experiment was not very different from some of the programs described previously, for example, John F. Kennedy High School in Silver Spring, Maryland, and Lakeview High in Decatur, Illinois. When the program began in September 1967, the 107 juniors—Newton High students who had volunteered for the experiment—were expected to take a minimum of four and one half majors. These courses—English, math, social studies, French, and physical education—were rigidly scheduled into three mornings, leaving students and teachers free to use the rest of the week for additional work in these subject areas, or to pursue other interests. During their free time, students had the use, without supervision, of any space in the building not being used for a class and, with parental permission, could leave the building to work anywhere else—to use a library, take a course somewhere else, etc. In the major subjects, however, students were to do homework, take exams, receive grades, and be given regular Newton High credits; students and faculty were free to decide on methods of evaluation and other rules and procedures only in the elective areas.

This initial approach was modified soon after the program began, when the Murray Road faculty decided that awarding grades in the major subjects was incompatible with their goal of encouraging students to take responsibility for their own education. Self-education, they argued, involved a number of processes: self-assessment of one's strengths and weaknesses and interests and needs; consideration of alternative goals and of alternative ways of meeting them; choice of a course of action; and self-evaluation of one's progress. Awarding grades would undermine all of them, encouraging students to direct their energies toward pleasing the teacher rather than setting and meeting their own goals and evaluating their progress toward them. At the same time, the faculty recognized that high school students may not yet know enough about the subject in question, or may not yet be able to see themselves in a sufficiently objective light, to rely solely on their own evaluation. Hence Murray Road students' records contain two written evaluations, one by the student and one by the teacher, as well as a brief description of the course content.

Students took responsibility from the beginning. They formed a committee to sound out colleges on their receptivity to this kind of unconventional program; using this information, as well as information gleaned from soundings taken among students and faculty, another committee reviewed the curriculum and suggested a number of changes for the second year, to permit students to meet the subject-major requirements in a variety of ways. They proposed and organized committees to develop friendly relations with the local residents, and to develop an afternoon program for children in the neighborhood, who had been creating problems by running through the building and occasionally damaging property. (The Murray Road Annex is housed in an old elementary school that had been vacant for some time.) They worked with the faculty in creating and running a tutoring program in a number of Newton elementary schools; nearly three-quarters of the students participated. They worked with the faculty too, in discussing the program with parent and other community groups, as well as in evaluations of the program. And they proposed and organized, and in some cases taught, a number of new courses. These electives, many of which are taught by parents, university students from the area, or other volunteers from the community, frequently are held in the evening or on a weekend; they may meet in a student's home, the home of the person offering the course, a library, or what have you. As one student puts it, "We have a course wherever there is a floor we can sit on. All this meeting in teachers' homes, kids' homes, and the like," he adds, "has blurred the distinction between school and life."

The emphasis throughout is on developing and maintaining

an atmosphere of mutual trust, respect, and concern. "You can't give personal freedom," Barry Jentz, a young Murray Road English teacher observes. "You have to create an environment where people learn to make themselves free; that environment is one of trust."

It wasn't easy for the students to "learn to make themselves free"; discovering that freedom is more than the absence of restraint and developing the self-discipline that would enable them to use their freedom were slow and sometimes painful. At first, for example, the multiplicity of choices presented a problem. Unaccustomed either to the freedom or the richness of the offerings, some students tended to bound from course to course and seminar to seminar. As one student later described the process, "Instead of finding out what we were interested in, we tried to be the winner of a game called 'How many courses can you take at Murray Road?'" As a result, some students loaded themselves down with more work than they could do, and some never finished anything, dropping one course as they took up another. Other students were simply paralyzed by the need to make a choice; most had difficulty learning how to organize their time, and themselves. But by and large they *did* learn—not only how to discipline their time, but also how to set realistic goals when they found they had made unwise choices.

ITEM: From a student's evaluation of his first year's experience. "Last year I had problems of self-discipline in various areas such as math and history. My other self-discipline problems were my attitude and lack of organization of my time. I did not know exactly what I wanted to do so I couldn't organize my time to suit any particular goals. I wanted to practice the piano and to write music. I wanted to do something interesting in my subjects, but I didn't know what that was exactly. The result was that I let things evolve; some things turned out better than I expected (music) and some things went terribly. (In math I started in honors, dropped it, and eventually I ended up hurriedly learning enough to pass the Curriculum I exam.) I also wasted an abominable amount of time complaining and listening to complaints about the world, school, and a multitude of things."

ITEM: From another student's evaluation. "When it comes to improving on discipline, we have two choices: we can either change the structure so that it leaves less room for misbehavior, or we can continually struggle day by day to improve our self-discipline. To do the former—to make Murray Road a more structured school with greater disciplinary action—goes completely against the basic premise on which we have been working all year—that we want to learn to discipline ourselves. The only alternative I see is to continue as we have been—arguing, getting frustrated, learning slowly how to discipline ourselves. I see no way of changing the structure to help us in this kind of collective personal struggle."

ITEM: From a parent's evaluation. "When my son was unhappy at Newton High School and doing poorly I could never decide whether he was the problem or if perhaps he was right when he said that much of the school did not teach him anything. I feel now he was sincere. This year he cannot get enough of all he is learning—he spends every minute singing the praises of Murray Road, but he does *not* talk about freedom, bull sessions, fooling around and indifference but downright, genuine desire to make papers perfect, an absolutely amazing love for every teacher, an incentive which has focused his every bit of energy toward doing better today than yesterday and suddenly a hunger for many tomorrows which will enable him to do more. . . . With less pressure from school routine that was so great at Newton High, my son has pressured himself more, putting study first and working to conclusions. I believe his scope has broadened—his desire to absorb more and more. . . . If he had stayed at Newton High School, I see the possibility of his wings never spreading. I had no idea so much could unfold in so short a time."

The students learned to handle feelings, too, and to view feeling as an aspect of thought. "Feelings are important at Murray Road," one student remarked, in explaining how the school differed from the regular high school. "Even in a subject like math it becomes harder and harder to separate feelings from thinking." "Yeah," another student chimed in. "I remember hearing myself say in class, 'Now I know what I'm about to say is emotional, so don't take it too seriously'—and suddenly I thought, 'Who says we shouldn't take emotion seriously? Who says that a reaction to a situation is only valid if it is cerebral?' *Sure,* feelings are important and there's no reason to delegate them to some sort of second place. So now I don't, and I don't think many others do, either."

As a result of this concern with feeling, as well as the emphasis on freedom and responsibility, students also learned a great deal about themselves—about their strengths and weaknesses, their beliefs (their *real* beliefs), their ability to take responsibility, to work with others, and so on. They also learned a great deal about their teachers, for the first time seeing them as human beings with strengths and weaknesses and feelings of their own.

ITEM: From a student's self-evaluation. "I haven't done all the things I wanted to do, but just by not doing them I learned about myself. I learned how much I didn't know about all those ideals I'd been advocating. . . . I've changed in that I will tell you all this too, because I know there was a time when I wouldn't have."

ITEM: From another student's evaluation. "Unfortunately, I succeeded at Newton High without a great deal of work. Without really pursuing things and without really doing excellent work. It's much harder being at Murray Road, and it took me a while to really discover this. At the high school I was able to do a great many things, not really as well as I could have, and still pull A's, etc. When I arrived at Murray Road I was very excited by all the options and became rapidly overextended. The standards here, which are self-imposed, are much harder to fulfill. To really fulfill them, one must do a few things excellently rather than many things fairly. . . . At first, I thought I was destined to another hell-raising year in French. But soon I realized that teachers need cooperation from the class, and that teachers have feelings as well—which must sound over-obvious, but I never considered teachers' feelings before."

One of the principal ways in which the Murray Road students have learned how to handle freedom and responsibility—one of the principal means by which they have learned to respect and trust their teachers—has been through the teaching they have done, in the tutoring program, or in the courses they have taught for their fellow students.

ITEM: From a student's self-evaluation. "I gave tutoring all I had and I learned so much from it—more about revising my expectations than anything else. I had to learn to be flexible in teaching and in dealing with kids. I learned photography in order to teach it. I learned mostly through failure, but now I know something about what kids want, what they need and the timing of an activity. . . ."

ITEM: From another student's evaluation of the tutoring program. "Before I began teaching for myself I never thought about how a teacher might feel about things. I guess I always took my teachers' role for granted, and more times than not I suppose I thought they were all very comfortable. One thing my teaching experiences have taught me is that this is not true. Teachers can be different inside, just like I fluctuate inside as a student. Sometimes there is comfort and security, but in a teacher there can also be fear and insecurity. Many of these things are unrecognizable to students perhaps because they already have the teacher role stereotyped in their minds."

ITEM: A student, evaluating a course he had taught in comparative religion. "This course was a barren enthusiasm course, meaning I was really excited about studying different religions, but I didn't know why I wanted to study them or what specific areas I wanted to study. The course failed—for the above reasons and for others. First the course was organized at the very beginning of the year when all the students were running around trying to take as many courses as they could. . . . Secondly, it didn't have a teacher. Although Murray Road aims toward more student-oriented, student-directed courses, a teacher has to be present for nearly every one of the classes. There has to be an authority figure, older and exerting influence over a group studying a whole new field. For these reasons the course failed, and I learned from my failure."

The teachers, too, have learned a great deal—about themselves and about their students. For the most part, the teachers were as unused to freedom as their students, and they, too, have had to struggle to answer some of the hard questions about freedom: what it is; how much is too much; how much is not enough. Some teachers had to learn how to let go of the reins. "I didn't realize until the end of the year that students could handle more freedom than they already have," one teacher confessed. "For a long time I distrusted the students' ability to take responsibility or follow it through. Now I think the students are very able to take on all sorts of responsibility." Other teachers had to learn that there are times when students want and need direction, that freedom is not merely the absence of restraint. They had to learn that <u>freedom and structure are quite compatible</u> with each other—that indeed, a certain minimum of structure may be a prerequisite to freedom.

ITEM: Seeing freedom and structure as antithetical, several teachers refused to give their students any direction when the first semester began. They simply sat back in class, waiting in silence for the students to take over; the frustrated students, not knowing how to proceed, sat in equally stony silence, waiting for the teacher to begin. In time, the teachers realized that they were being overly rigid, that the students, especially at the very beginning, needed some structure and direction, and that complete teacher passivity was not the only alternative to the traditional teacher-dominated classroom they had rejected. The students, in turn, realized that they were also being too passive, and they gradually took on more responsibility. "Teachers and students are really working together here," one student remarked, in recalling the frustration of those first few days. "The teachers are changing and developing with us."

At times, the process of "changing and developing" was as painful for the teachers as it was for the students. "You have to be willing to be hurt, criticized, evaluated, and to see the truth of how others see you," one teacher explains, observing that before teaching at Murray Road, she would not have been able to "open up" to a hundred students. There were times, indeed, when teachers found themselves as exposed and vulnerable as the students—for example, when a teacher offered an elective course, and had to withdraw it when there were no takers. Nonetheless, the teachers are as enthusiastic about the program as the students. "When a teacher can *see* how he makes a difference in his student's life," one explains, "he is more willing to expend his time and energy." "In the conventional school," another teacher adds, "most teachers don't begin to realize their teaching potential because they don't feel they will make a difference in the institution." At Murray Road, teachers know they make a difference. In part because of the program's small size, but in part also because of its basic character, there is no gulf between teachers and administrators; the teachers handle both functions. "I used to think that teachers should teach and administrators should administer," one teacher says. "Now I feel that determining schedules, arranging class offerings, and teaching are all part of one whole; I wouldn't want to give up any of it."

One of the most important, and sobering, lessons to be learned from the Murray Road experiment, however, is that freedom frightens both students and teachers—that many who clamor for freedom are afraid to try it when the opportunity arises. "Familiarity breeds contempt," Dewey wrote in *The Child and the Curriculum*, "but it also breeds something like affection. We get used to the chains we wear, and . . . through custom we finally embrace what at first wore a hideous mien."

So it was at Newton when the Murray Road program was announced in the spring of 1967. With nearly 1,000 students eligible—applications were invited from the entire sophomore class at Newton High—school officials expected a flood of applications and planned to select a representative sample of 150. The flood turned out to be a trickle; only 107 students—forty-seven boys and sixty girls—applied, all of whom were accepted. The faculty was equally cautious; fewer teachers volunteered for the program than had been expected, with some of those who had been most vocal in calling for greater freedom holding back when they heard what was being planned. They, too, preferred the security of the known.

Neither the program's apparent success, moreover, nor the evident enthusiasm of both students and teachers, have produced any stampede to get into Murray Road, although the number of applicants has exceeded the number of places. In the second year, enrollment rose to 115—ninety seniors, who chose to remain for a second year, and twenty-five juniors, selected by the faculty from a somewhat larger number of applicants. Enrollment remained the same in the 1969–70 school year, with twenty-five seniors, forty-five juniors, and forty-five sophomores. The hesitation stems from several factors, in addition to fear of the unknown and a preference for the security that the traditional structure seems to provide. Going to Murray Road, as the students attending it explain, requires more than opposition to the traditional school; it demands a commitment to one's own education, and it takes more effort and may cause more pain, albeit of a different sort than in the conventional school. Many students are reluctant to make that commitment.

Other students held back because of their fear, or their parents', that attending Murray Road might hurt their chance of getting into college. (This is the reason fewer boys than girls applied.) The fear is understandable; it is also greatly exaggerated. Colleges are a good deal more flexible in their admission

requirements than students and parents—or high school principals and guidance counselors—realize; and for the most part,
the more prestigious the college, the more flexible it tends to be.
Parents were particularly concerned, for example, about the
absence of grades and therefore of class rankings at Murray
Road, but only two colleges refused to accept applications on
that account.[30] More to the point, students in the first graduating
class, who were accepted in such schools as Harvard, Barnard,
Wisconsin, and Johns Hopkins, had no more difficulty gaining
admission than students in the regular Newton High program.

VI

Both Parkway and Murray Road, it should be emphasized, are
limited experiments designed to test a number of ideas about the
nature and purposes of education. Their small size, together with
the fact that their students and their faculties are both self-
selected volunteers, makes it difficult to know the degree to which
their various approaches can be applied in other circumstances.
Many of the Newton teachers and administrators who are most
enthusiastic about Murray Road, for example, question its
applicability to Newton High, with its student body of 2,700;
this degree of freedom and flexibility, they argue, can work only
in a very small, intimate environment. Charles E. Brown, under
whose aegis the experiment was conceived and begun (he was
superintendent at the time) disagrees sharply. "If we can't create
a sense of community with 2,700 students," he asked a group of
Newton teachers and administrators, "how can New York City
survive?" Nonetheless, Newton officials are moving very cautiously in the attempt to apply some of the Murray Road experience elsewhere.

The most important experiment in secondary education,
therefore, may well be the one being tried in Portland, Oregon's
new John Adams High School. The kinds of fundamental questions being raised at Murray Road and at Parkway are also being raised at Adams—not in the rather precious, hothouse
atmosphere of those two schools, but in what Adams' principal,
Robert Schwartz, accurately describes as "a classic urban high
school." Unlike Parkway and Murray Road, there is no self-

---

[30] Both schools had recently turned to computer analysis of applicants'
records to simplify the admissions officers' decision-making; the computers couldn't handle applications without certain kinds of data.

selected student body at Adams; it is a district high school to which all students living in its district are assigned. The great majority of the 1,280 students come from working-class or lower-middle-class families; 25 percent are black, and based on past experience, only a third or so are likely to go to college.

What makes Adams so important is not only the size and nature of its student body, however, but the fact that it is also the most comprehensive and systematic, and perhaps the most carefully thought-out, attempt to create a new kind of secondary school. How successful that attempt will be remains to be seen; since Adams did not open its doors until September 1969, we can do no more here than indicate what Schwartz and his colleagues hope to do. What is clear is that the school is a real testing ground; if radical reform succeeds at Adams, it can succeed elsewhere, too.

Curiously enough, the Adams experiment had its genesis some three thousand miles to the east of Portland. In the fall of 1967, a group of secondary school teachers in their final year of doctoral study at the Harvard Graduate School of Education began meeting regularly to discuss the possibility of establishing a new kind of high school, whose principal objective, as they defined it, "would be to find better ways of helping adolescents to learn."

Their thinking was influenced by a number of sources, apart from their own experiences and their work at Harvard. One was their fascination with the way in which teaching hospitals like Massachusetts General combined the diverse, and sometimes contradictory, functions of patient care, education and training of new doctors, re-education of experienced doctors, and basic and applied research. Another was Robert J. Schaefer's Deweyan notion of "the school as a center of inquiry." "The school must be more than a place of instruction," Dean Schaefer argued forcefully in his little volume, published as the Harvard group was formulating its plans. "It must also be a center of inquiry— a producer as well as transmitter of knowledge." For one thing, our ignorance about teaching and learning is so massive that university scholars cannot produce the necessary knowledge working alone; they need the help of the schools as well. But the schools also need the university. "When divorced from appropriate scholarship," Schaefer writes, "teaching resembles employment as an educational sales clerk." Thus, schools must be made into centers of inquiry for teachers as well as students if they are to attract teachers as well as students to the life of the mind.[31]

The result was a formal proposal by Schwartz and his colleagues for the creation of what they called a "clinical high school" in which "the instruction of children and youth, pre-service and in-service teacher education, basic and applied research, and the development of curriculum materials" would all take place, with senior faculty members holding university appointments.[32] With the help of Dean Theodore Sizer and several other members of the Harvard faculty, the proposal was circulated widely among school superintendents and deans of education schools throughout the country. After talks in five cities, the group decided on Portland, which was in the process of building a new comprehensive high school intended to be a center for curricular innovation. The superintendent, Dr. Melvin Barnes, and the board of education offered the new school the setting for the experiment, and Oregon State University, the Northwest Regional Education Laboratory, and the Teaching Research Division of the Oregon State System of Higher Education offered joint appointments to the senior members of the clinical school faculty. In August 1968, therefore, Schwartz and three other members of the Harvard group moved to Portland to begin planning for the clinical school, which opened in September 1969.

In a sense, then, Adams High is really two schools: a comprehensive high school; and a professional school concerned with the education of teachers, its own and others, as well as with educational research. The pre-service and in-service teacher education aspects will be discussed in Chapter 11, when we turn to the problem of teacher education. Our concern here is with the way in which the high school function itself is being handled.

The school resembles the ones we have been describing in a number of respects. For example, students are scheduled for only half of each day. During the other half, they may receive tutoring in math, reading, writing, or some other basic skill, work on an independent study project, participate in a tutoring program or a "work experience" program, take one or more

[31] Robert J. Schaefer, *The School as a Center of Inquiry*, New York: Harper & Row, 1967.
[32] "The Clinical School," A Proposal Prepared by the Members of the Clinical School Collaborative, Cambridge, Mass., October 30, 1967 (mimeographed).

elective courses, or just relax. The electives include a full range of vocational training courses as well as a traditional college preparatory program. And students, in conjunction with their parents, may decide whether to receive conventional letter grades in their required and elective courses, or to take them on a credit–no credit basis. In short, the freedom to be conventional is respected, along with the freedom to experiment.

The most important part of the Adams High day, however, is the scheduled half, in which every student takes a required three-year sequence in general education. The high school is subdivided into four "houses," each containing 320 randomly assigned students, a guidance counselor, a guidance intern, an administrative aide, and its own instructional staff. The staff consists of interdisciplinary teams of teachers, drawn from English, social studies, math, and science, who design, implement, and evaluate a general education program for their house. Since each team is autonomous, it must grapple with the gut question of what ought to be learned, as well as deciding how it should be learned. While the program varies from house to house, it tends to be problem-oriented; the curriculum for the opening week, for example, was created by racial incidents that occurred on opening day. Schwartz's hope is that students and teachers will move from the problems that evoke their interest to a study of the intellectual disciplines needed to illuminate and deal with them—that the general education course, in short, will have serious intellectual content.

The risks are large. For the moment, at least, Adams is committed to heterogeneous grouping in the general education program; one of the questions being tested is how—or whether—the entire spectrum of student ability and interest can be contained in a single class. The answers are unknown. There is a risk, moreover, of intellectual flabbiness; the young, swinging teachers pride themselves on their ability to relate to their students, and at the beginning tended to pander to them, turning "general education" into a three-hour daily bull session. "I hope the intellectual bankruptcy of that approach will become apparent," Schwartz confessed early in the first semester.

He is relying on more than hope. One of the things that distinguishes Adams from the experiments just described is the hard-headed recognition that structural changes are a means to a larger end and not only an end in themselves. "The critical issues in secondary education have less to do with free time," Schwartz argues, "and more with reordering the curriculum itself, and with involving both teachers and students in the process." It is not a question of either/or; both are essential if a school is to find some tenable middle-ground between the Bruners and Schwabs, on the one side, and the Holts and Friedenbergs on the other. "Admittedly we found it much easier to abolish hall passes, give kids more free time, and in general create a reasonably humane climate than to figure out the essentials of a new curriculum," Schwartz confided midway through the school year. "But without the kind of climate we are creating," he added, "no curriculum would make much difference; the environmental issues must be dealt with before we can wrestle with the what-knowledge-is-of-most-worth kind of question."[33]

What gives reason for hope that the school will come to grips with all the questions is the fact, as the school's senior researchers have written, that "Adams is committed to becoming an experimental school with more than its own intuitive claims to substantiate its value." That commitment in turn means that the school must create and maintain a climate that encourages the teachers themselves, as well as outside scholars, to engage in the systematic study of the processes of teaching and learning and to use such study as a basis for revising the curriculum, the teaching strategies, and the school organization. "Given the publicly stated goals, aims, or objectives of Adams," the researchers continue, "the entire staff has the obligation to confront certain kinds of questions, and the responsibility of seeking personally convincing answers to those questions."

The questions go to the heart of what the school is about:

1. In what ways do you want people to be different after their contact with you than they were before?
2. What would you be willing to accept as evidence that you had succeeded?
3. What would you regard as undeniable evidence that you had failed and therefore should make changes?
4. How might you go about finding some kinds of evidence, however tenuous, for determining either success or failure?

---

[33] Not that Schwartz is under any illusion that the environmental questions have been answered, either. "We know very little about the educational ramifications of a policy which allows students to assume control and responsibility for basic educational decisions in a school," he says. The policy raises a number of questions that need to be studied systematically.

5. How can you gather evidence in a way that is meaningful to someone else?[34]

Asking, of course, is not enough; teachers need help in trying to find the answers. Hence the teaching teams work under the guidance of a staff of "curriculum associates" holding joint university and public school appointments. These senior men are expected to "bring a combination of professional competence and skills in scholarly inquiry" that will enable them to provide a kind of leadership and guidance not usually found in secondary schools. Moreover, the school's clinical character—its attempt to combine the instruction of adolescents, the education of teachers, research on pedagogy, and development of new curricula in a single institution—means that a number of tensions and conflicts are built into its basic structure. Senior staff are responsible to at least two constituencies, the university and the community, which have conflicting interests. The expectation, at least, is that the conflicts will be quite fruitful—that "the university will keep the school intellectual and serious, and that the community will keep it relevant and honest." Anyone concerned with reforming secondary education will want to watch the Adams High experiment with the closest interest and attention.

[34] Jerry Fletcher and John Williamson, *Research and Evaluation at John Adams High School,* October 1969, mimeographed.

IV

The Education of
Educators

9

The Liberal Education
of Teachers

The great men of culture are those who have a passion for diffusing, for making prevail, for carrying from one end of society to the other, the best knowledge, the best ideas of their time; who have laboured to divest knowledge of all that was harsh, uncouth, difficult, abstract, professional, exclusive; to humanize it, to make it efficient outside the clique of the cultivated and learned, yet still remaining the best knowledge and thought of the time, and a true source, therefore, of sweetness and light.

—MATTHEW ARNOLD
Culture and Anarchy, *1899*

I

In the end, we come back to the teacher. "Our most pressing educational problem," as Philip Jackson keeps reminding us, is "learning how to create and maintain a humane environment in our schools." Technological aids—film strips, programmed instruction, instructional television, computer-assisted instruction—"may help in the process, but they will not substitute for a firm sense of direction and a commitment to the preservation of human values. Only people come equipped with these qualities."[1] Hence the teacher's indispensability.

And hence the indispensability of a thorough-going reform

[1] Philip W. Jackson, *The Teacher and the Machine*, Pittsburgh, Pa.: University of Pittsburgh Press, 1968.

of teacher education, to make sure that teachers are equipped with a firm sense of direction and a commitment to the preservation and enlargement of human values, as well as with the ability to transmit that commitment and sense of direction to their students. "Education is too significant and dynamic an enterprise to be left to mere technicians," Lawrence Cremin writes, urging that we "begin now the prodigious task of preparing men and women who understand not only the substance of what they are teaching but also the theories behind the particular strategies they employ to convey that substance. A society committed to the continuing intellectual, esthetic, and moral growth of all its members can ill afford less on the part of those who undertake to teach." If, as we argued at the beginning of this volume, it is fruitless to reform teacher education without simultaneously trying to reform the schools in which the teachers will teach, the reverse is also true. The remaking of American public education requires, and indeed will not be possible without, fundamental changes in the education of teachers—without, in a sense, the creation of a new breed of teacher-educator, educated to self-scrutiny and to serious thought about purpose.

The task is huge: it is not possible to reform the education of teachers without reforming higher education as a whole. For one thing, three-quarters of the nation's colleges and universities are in the business of preparing teachers. Only a handful of teachers now receive their education in single-purpose normal schools or teachers colleges. On the basis of data collected for James Conant's study of teacher education, Merle Borrowman, dean of the School of Education at the University of California at Riverside, estimates that 90 percent now receive their education in multi-purpose institutions—municipal, private, and state colleges and universities—each of which prepares more than one hundred teachers a year.[2] Borrowman's estimate may be somewhat high, since he classifies an institution as multi-purpose if 20 percent or more of its graduates are prepared for a field other than education.

But changing the definition would not alter the order of magnitude or change the basic point, namely, that the overwhelming majority of teachers now receive their education in colleges and universities for which teacher education is only one of a number of educational missions. Many of these institutions, to be sure,

[2] Merle L. Borrowman, "Liberal Education and the Professional Preparation of Teachers" in M. L. Borrowman, ed., *Teacher Education in America.* New York: Teachers College Press, 1965.

began as normal schools or single-purpose teachers colleges, and some remain teachers colleges in function and spirit, if not in title. Most, however, have become, or are rapidly becoming, full-fledged colleges and universities. Of the twenty-five largest "producers" of teachers, for example, half began as single-purpose institutions. But as Table 2 indicates, eighteen of the twenty-five now award more than half their degrees to students preparing for fields other than education.

As the figures in Table 2 also suggest, teacher education is a gigantic enterprise. (There were another 98 colleges and universities which prepared 500 or more teachers each.) In 1967, for example, the nation's colleges and universities turned out nearly 207,000 students eligible for initial certification as teachers, 192,000 of them recipients of bachelor's degrees, the rest receiving Master of Arts in Teaching (M.A.T.) degrees or its equivalent. This represented 35 percent of all bachelor's and first professional degrees—a ratio that has been remarkably stable in recent years. Since the number of college graduates is increasing, the number of graduates certified for teaching rose to nearly 260,000 in 1969, and may exceed 300,000 by 1975. Not all of these graduates, of course, go on to teach. In recent years, between 70 and 75 percent of those completing their preparation for teaching have entered the classroom in the year following graduation; of the remainder, some continue their studies, some enter the armed services, some get married and stay out of the labor force, some take other jobs; many simply are not accounted for.[3]

The public colleges and universities account for the bulk of the teacher education. According to an American Council on Education study of freshmen entering college in the fall of 1967, 22.4 percent of the freshmen at *all* institutions, but 42.2 percent of those at public four-year colleges, were planning to go into elementary or secondary teaching (for female students only, the corresponding ratios were 36.4 percent at all institutions and 59.4 percent at public colleges). Fewer than half of these students, however—10.5 percent of the students at all institutions,

[3] National Education Association, *Teacher Supply and Demand in Public Schools,* 1968, Washington, D.C.: NEA Research Report 1969–R4; U.S. Office of Education, *Education in the Seventies,* U.S. Government Printing Office, 1968 (U.S. Department of Health, Education and Welfare Planning Paper 68–1); The American Association of Colleges for Teacher Education, *Teacher Productivity—1967,* Washington, D.C.: The American Association of Colleges for Teacher Education, 1968.

Table 2

Number of Initially Certified Teachers, 1967

Institution	Total Certified	Proportion of Total Degrees Granted
Michigan State University	2,102	27.7
Western Michigan University	1,837	48.7
Indiana University	1,661	26.1
Arizona State University	1,441	44.4*
Ohio State University	1,426	20.4
Illinois State University	1,358	68.0*
University of Puerto Rico	1,354	43.8*
Eastern Michigan University	1,338	56.2
Pennsylvania State University	1,302	23.5
Wayne State University	1,290	28.8
Bowling Green State University (Ohio)	1,179	56.9
Kent State University (Ohio)	1,171	53.1*
University of Michigan	1,153	14.1
East Carolina University (North Carolina)	1,139	83.8
Ball State University (Indiana)	1,133	43.7
Central Michigan University	1,132	64.9
Boston University	1,124	28.2*
Brigham Young University (Utah)	1,064	33.0
Miami University (Ohio)	1,054	46.7*
Mankato State College (Minnesota)	1,026	59.4
Morehead State University (Kentucky)	1,026	n.a.
Southern Illinois University	1,019	34.5
CUNY—Brooklyn College	993	30.0
CUNY—Queens College	993	40.5
San Jose State College (California)	983	23.2

Source: American Association of Colleges for Teacher Education, *Teacher Productivity—1967.*

Note: * means proportion estimated by the author, from Otis A. Singletary, ed., *American Universities and Colleges,* 10th Edition (Washington, D.C.: American Council on Education, 1968). n.a. — not available

18.2 percent of those at public four-year institutions—were planning to major in education, a division roughly corresponding to the proportions interested in elementary versus secondary school teaching. The typical (though by no means invariant) pattern is that only students planning to teach at the elementary level major in education and/or register in the school of education. Students planning to teach at the secondary level, on the other hand, typically major in an academic subject and register in the appropriate liberal arts college or department, although they are generally required to take some specified minimum number of courses in the school or department of education.

Thus, teacher education is a major responsibility of the academic departments of most colleges and universities, and not just their schools or departments of education.

ITEM: At Michigan State University, some 2,000 students are enrolled in the College of Education, all of them students planning to become elementary school teachers. Twice as many undergraduates are enrolled in the College of Arts and Letters—students majoring in history, English, philosophy, Romance languages, music, and art. Curious as to what its students did after graduation, the College of Arts and Letters made a survey which turned up the startling fact that 70 percent of its students went on to become secondary school teachers.

The situation varies, of course, from institution to institution. But whether students major in education or in an academic subject, they take the bulk of their course work—as a rule, two-thirds to three-quarters—in the academic departments. This is true whether they attend a teachers college or a large university. In comparing the requirements of a group of prestigious colleges and universities with a group of teachers colleges, for example, Dr. Conant could not find any differences in the time allocated to academic as opposed to professional or technical education courses. Some teachers colleges, in fact, required more academic preparation than some of the liberal arts institutions.[4]

Thus, if American schoolteachers are poorly educated it is the liberal arts professors, not just the educationists, who are to blame. Scholarly critics of the schools have not always acknowledged this fact, preferring to place the blame on that easy, if

[4] James B. Conant, *The Education of American Teachers,* New York: McGraw-Hill Paperbacks, 1964.

well-deserved, target, the professor of education. Addressing the 1966 annual meeting of the Council for Basic Education, for example, Dr. Glenn T. Seaborg of the California Institute of Technology (at the time, chairman of the Atomic Energy Commission), described the state of science instruction in the schools at the beginning of the decade of curriculum reform:

> Although there were prominent weaknesses in our instructional materials and facilities, perhaps the greatest deficiencies were due to our programs for teacher training and our somewhat one-sided philosophy of education. In educating our teachers we had emphasized courses on pedagogy and method to the detriment of preparing them in the subjects they were supposed to teach. Often it seemed that school science had been swallowed up by the prevalent goal of "life adjustment." There had grown up—regrettably—a rigid estrangement between scientists and science educators, so that science courses for prospective teachers were commonly taught in departments or colleges of education, while professors in the scientific departments often tended to discourage their better students from considering careers as school science teachers.[5]

But "science courses for prospective teachers" are *not* "commonly taught in departments or colleges of education"—nor were they in the 1930s or 1940s. To be sure, elementary school teachers in that period frequently did receive a limited education, but this is hardly relevant to Seaborg's point; before the middle or late 1950s, science was not taken seriously in the elementary schools, nor did any scientist propose that it should be. If Seaborg's critique has any point of reference, it can only be the high school curriculum. But the "life adjustment" movement, which began around the end of World War II, had no impact on the preparation of high school science teachers. On the contrary, the high school physics or chemistry teacher typically took his bachelor's degree in physics or chemistry, not education; in all probability, he would have twenty courses in physics or chemistry, several courses in other sciences, and perhaps a half-dozen courses in education, together with some practice teaching. If he didn't know his chemistry, it was the chemistry department's, not the education department's, fault.

[5] Glenn T. Seaborg and Jacques Barzun, *The Sciences and the Humanities in the Schools After a Decade of Reform,* Washington, D.C.: Council for Basic Education, Occasional Paper No. 13.

Lest there be any misunderstanding, let this point be made clear: to insist that the academic departments bear a large part of the blame for what James Koerner referred to as "The Miseducation of American Teachers" is in no way to exonerate the departments and schools of education. On the contrary, they deserve most of the approbrium which critics like Koerner, Seaborg, and Arthur Bestor have heaped upon them. But they deserve praise as well, for fulfilling, however imperfectly, a responsibility which the liberal arts faculties simply refused to accept and indeed disparaged. As Seaborg concedes in the passage just quoted, the arts and sciences faculties not only refused responsibility for teacher education, they actively discouraged their students from careers in the public schools. Thus, Arthur Bestor, one of the severest but fairest critics of teacher education, writes: "The training of teachers for the public schools is one of the most important functions of the American university. It ought always to be treated as a function of the university as a whole. In recent decades it has not been so treated. The blame rests squarely upon the faculties of liberal arts and sciences, who have simply abdicated their responsibilities. By refusing to take seriously the problem of setting up sound and appropriate curricula for the education of teachers, scholars and scientists have left a vacuum into which the professional educationists have moved."[6]

II

The problem runs deeper still. As we have argued repeatedly throughout the book, what is wrong with elementary and secondary education—or for that matter, higher education, journalism, television, social work, and so on—has less to do with incompetence or indifference or venality than with mindlessness.

If this be so, the solution must lie in infusing the schools, and the other educating institutions, with purpose—more important, with thought about purpose, and about the ways in which techniques, content, and organization fulfill or alter purpose. Given the tendency of institutions to confuse day-to-day routine with purpose, to transform the means into the end itself, the infusion cannot be a one-shot affair. The process of self-examination, or "self-renewal," must be continuous. We must find ways of stim-

[6] Arthur Bestor, *The Restoration of Learning*, New York: Alfred A. Knopf, 1955.

ulating educators—public school teachers, principals, superintendents, and school board members, as well as college professors, deans, and presidents; radio, television, and film directors
and producers; newspaper, magazine, and TV journalists and
executives—to think about what they are doing, and why they
are doing it. There is a measure of romantic exaggeration, to be
sure, but a larger measure of truth, in Harold Taylor's insistence
that "preparing to become a teacher is like preparing to become
a poet. The preparation begins in a decision to become something, a commitment made about one's own life and the purpose of it."[7]

But that commitment is rarely made, for the sense of purpose
is rarely cultivated. What is wrong with the way teachers and
administrators (or journalists, filmmakers, TV directors, et al.)
are educated has less to do with the fact that they are given inadequate mastery of the techniques of teaching (or writing,
directing, filmmaking, etc.) than with the fact that they are not
trained to think about either the purposes or the processes, the
ends or the means, of education. Men or women who are going
to be teaching elementary school children need some preparation
that is different from those who will be teaching graduate students; and prospective journalists or TV directors need some
preparation different from those who will teach.

They all need an education that equips them to ask why, to
think seriously and deeply about what they are doing—which is
to say that they all need a liberalizing and humanizing education. "Men are men before they are lawyers, or physicians, or
merchants, or manufacturers, and if you make them capable
and sensible men," John Stuart Mill observed in his Inaugural
Address at the University of St. Andrew, "they will make themselves capable and sensible lawyers or physicians"—or teachers.
"The education of teachers," Mark van Doren has written (and
his words apply equally well to the education of journalists,
lawyers, college professors, et al.), "is an education in the liberal
arts. When this education is good and falls on the right ground,
it produces persons with usable intellects and imaginations who
know both what and why they are teaching."

In short, the weakness of teacher education is the weakness of
liberal education as a whole; if teachers are educated badly, that

[7] Harold Taylor, *The World and the American Teacher*, Washington,
D.C.: The American Association of Colleges for Teacher Education,
1968.

is to say, it is in large measure because almost everyone else is educated badly, too. For in the last analysis, we are *all* educators—of our wives or husbands, our children, our friends and colleagues—and ourselves. "The purpose of education at Chicago," the catalogue of that university's College states, "is to free students to explore, for a lifetime, the possibilities and limits of the human intellect. Though we cannot promise to produce educated men and women, *we do endeavor to bring each student . . . to a point beyond which he can educate himself.*" [Emphasis added] And this, after all, is what liberal education is all about—what liberal education has always been about.

This much we have argued before, and we have attempted at several points (e.g., Chapters 4 and 8) to indicate of what the capacity to educate oneself consists. What distinguishes education at the college level from that which precedes it is not simply its greater complexity and intensity, but its greater self-consciousness as well. To be educated to the point where one can educate himself, or others, means not only to think seriously about the means and ends of education (one's own, and others'), but about the *consequences* of education as well—about the way education shapes and molds the people being educated.

This in turn means that to be educated—to be an educator—is to understand something of how to make one's education effective in the real world. It means to know something of how to apply knowledge to the life one lives and the society in which one lives it—in a word, to know what is relevant—and how to make knowledge relevant, which is to say, effective.

And the most direct and immediate way of finding out what it is one really knows and how it can be applied—of finding the purpose and testing the human relevance of what one has learned—is to teach it to someone else. In this sense, teaching is the ultimate liberal art—something many of the rebellious college students understand better than many of their professors. One of the ways in which some college students have sought relevance and purpose in recent years, one of the ways they have tried to relate education to life, has been to go out and teach—in the urban slums and ghettos, in the underdeveloped nations of Africa, Asia, and Latin America or the underdeveloped rural areas of the United States.

What these students are discovering is what the faculty should have known: that while one cannot be an educator without having received a liberal education, the converse is also true—

one cannot be liberally educated without becoming an educator —of others, as well as of oneself. For if one cannot teach a subject to others without really knowing it, neither does he really know it unless he can teach it to others. The "art of the utilization of knowledge," which Whitehead calls the aim of education, means, as a minimum, knowing how to communicate what one knows to others, especially to those less informed than oneself.

The capacity and, equally important, the desire, to educate— to translate what one knows into a form that makes it available to others—is increasingly important in an increasingly specialized society. "Almost everybody in this society of ours is a specialist of some sort, whether biochemist or cost accountant," Peter F. Drucker has written. "Almost everybody therefore speaks his own language and uses his own jargon. But no one in this society, least of all the great majority who work in large organizations, is productive within his own specialty alone. Everyone depends on somebody else (who necessarily is a layman in all areas except his own specialty) to make his output truly effective, to convert his information into knowledge, to turn his efforts into results. Everyone therefore is dependent upon being understood by a great many laymen who themselves are specialists in their own areas."[8]

An increasingly interdependent world economy and polity imposes the same requirement. "The growing need for wisdom, for versatility of judgment, and for wide and sophisticated communication remains obvious," F. Champion Ward, a former University of Chicago dean, now a Ford Foundation vice-president, says after ten years in India and other developing nations. "To be a business executive, a scholar or scientist, or a civil servant, diplomat, or politician requires a range of informed response that grows wider daily." Thus, "if East and West, North and South, are to meet rather than collide," Ward continues, the university in every country must provide "a common education in principles permitting communication and rational progress to occur among citizens otherwise variously expert and occupied."[9]

This does not necessarily mean special courses or training in "communication skills." It does mean persuading students (and

---

[8] *The Age of Discontinuity.*
[9] F. Champion Ward, "Returning Coals to Newcastle," in Wayne C. Booth, ed., *The Knowledge Most Worth Having,* University of Chicago Press, 1967.

before them, the faculty) that the responsibility of the man of knowledge is to make himself understood. Otherwise, he runs the risk of producing information rather than knowledge—of being ineffective or irrelevant.

What this means is that the education of educators should be a central purpose of the college or university. The first step would be to incorporate what the students are discovering for themselves into the curriculum—to make teaching a normal part of the undergraduate experience for every student, not just those who plan to teach. This would represent a major step toward reforming the education of everybody, educators and laymen alike. The teaching might take a wide variety of forms: in the classroom, teaching fellow students, or youngsters in the public or private schools; in Peace Corps- or Vista-like programs; or perhaps in work experience related to a student's career interests.

Several university educators are urging precisely that. Jerrold Zacharias of MIT, who has been broadening his activities from curriculum reform to the reform of education as a whole, argues that college and professional school students of every sort, not just teacher education candidates, would learn more if teaching were made a regular part of their education. "Not only would the student get a feel for teaching and learn the problems, possibilities, and pitfalls of the classroom," Zacharias writes, "but he would also learn a great deal about his subject matter. He can't help learning more when he has to know both his own and his pupil's understanding."[10] Harold Taylor reached the same conclusion in the course of a study of teacher education he made for the American Association of Colleges for Teacher Education. "To study education from the point of view of the education of teachers raises a different set of questions from those involved in the study of education as that term is generally used," he writes in *The World and the American Teacher*. "I was continually made conscious of one very important educational difference—the difference between possessing knowledge

[10] Jerrold Zacharias, "A Portmanteau Proposal," paper given to the Tri-University Project in Elementary Education, New Orleans, February 1–3, 1968 (mimeographed). This view of Zacharias' stems directly from his experience in developing the PSSC high school physics course in the 1950s. Both Zacharias and his collaborator, the late Professor Francis Friedman of MIT, a distinguished theoretical physicist, told this writer in 1960 that they had learned more about physics in the process of "trying to get the subject right" for presentation to high school students than they had in years of university teaching and research.

384 THE EDUCATION OF EDUCATORS

and using it." Hence the central idea Taylor advanced was "that the best way to learn something is to teach it, that this applies to students as well as to teachers, that the best way to teach teachers is to have them teach—themselves, each other, and children in the schools."

There is nothing new in the notion that the educated man should take responsibility for making himself understood. In classical antiquity, as Werner Jaeger points out, rhetoric was the point from which education began.[11] The idea continued in the Middle Ages and after. Walter Ong may be exaggerating when he argues that the medieval universities "were in their origins normal schools," and that "from the very beginning, the very heart of the university has been concerned with the arts of communication." But he is on solid ground in insisting that "throughout the history of learning and research there has been more preoccupation than we might suspect with techniques and theories of communication. We often fail to recognize this preoccupation because it is not labeled educational theory, but it is there nevertheless."[12]

In addition to teaching itself, the study of education should also be put where it belongs: at the heart of the liberal arts curriculum, not at its margins. For the study of education is the study of almost every question of importance in philosophy, history, and sociology. Our concept of education reflects our concept of the good life, the good man, and the good society; and as already argued, there can be no concept of the good life or the good society apart from a concept of the kind of education needed to sustain it.

To do all this would be to return the college or the university to its most authentic tradition: as Merle Borrowman has put it, "that teacher education is the central responsibility of institutions of higher learning, and that the liberal arts and literature constitute the ideal curriculum for teacher preparation. In these traditions to be liberally educated and to be prepared to teach are equivalent."[13]

[11] Werner Jaeger, *Paideia: The Ideals of Greek Culture,* New York: Oxford University Press, Second Edition, 1945, Vol. I, pp. 291–3.
[12] Walter J. Ong, S.J., "Educationists and the Tradition of Learning," in *The Barbarian Within,* New York: Macmillan, 1962.
[13] Merle L. Borrowman, "Liberal Education and the Professional Preparation of Teachers," in M. L. Borrowman, ed., *Teacher Education in America,* New York: Teachers College Press, 1965.

III

To return to the tradition that to be liberally educated is to be prepared to teach still leaves open the question of what "to be liberally educated" really means. It is easier to say what it does *not* mean than to say what it does mean.

One thing it does not mean is that all students should receive a classical education, as academic conservatives of the Robert Hutchins variety sometimes seem to imply. Hutchins, for example, would cut the size of colleges and universities sharply by eliminating most professional and vocational studies, restricting entry to "those professors who wanted to lead the life of the mind and who had the capacity for it and to those students who were able to associate themselves with the enterprise . . ." Those students who wanted preparation "to enter upon any of the multifarious occupations of life"—teaching, business, engineering, perhaps even law—would go not to a college or university but to a technical training school, or would be taught on the job. And those professors interested in the advancement rather than the transmission of knowledge would be assigned to research institutes. By eliminating the vocationalism of students and faculty alike, Hutchins would thus return the university to its "true" mission, that of contemplating the life of the mind.[14]

It would be hard to imagine a more profound misreading of the history of the university. Indeed, the students' demand for relevance, of which vocationalism is one form, is more authentic to the spirit and historic role of the university than Hutchins' call for concentration on "pure learning." "At no time have universities been restricted to pure abstract learning," Whitehead pointed out in 1927, in addressing a convention of American business school professors and administrators. "The University of Salerno in Italy, the earliest of the European universities, was devoted to medicine. In England, at Cambridge, in the year 1316, a college was founded for the special purpose of providing 'clerks for the King's service.' Universities have trained clergy, medical men, lawyers, engineers. Business is now a higher intellectualised vocation, so it well fits into the series."[15]

It is necessary, to be sure, to find the right balance between involvement in the affairs of society and detachment from them.

[14] Robert M. Hutchins, *The Learning Society,* New York: Frederick A. Praeger, 1968. The writer is also drawing on Hutchins' other writings, and on a long conversation with him.
[15] "Universities and Their Function," in *The Aims of Education.*

It is necessary, that is to say, to find the means by which some parts or members of the university can give society the information, knowledge and advice it needs and demands while, as Robert A. Nisbet puts it, "at the same time nourishing and protecting those fragile, life-giving activities within the university that are not primarily concerned with giving advice to society" and that require some degree of autonomy if they are to remain creative.

Where that balance is is by no means obvious, and men are bound to disagree over the relative weight to be attached to involvement and detachment. What is obvious, however, is that Hutchins' call for almost total detachment—as Nisbet puts it, his call for "a monastic retreat to organizations of a type so opulently exemplified by his Center for the Study of Democratic Institutions in Santa Barbara"—is not the right solution. Certainly Hutchins is wrong in suggesting that such an organization is more closely related to the great tradition of the Western university than is the contemporary American "multiversity." Hutchins is thinking not of the university tradition, Nisbet continues, but of the monastic tradition, "one which—whatever its pietistic graces, its value as a haven for the tender-minded, its role in the ritual perpetuation of texts and ideas—has been generally sterile in furthering intellectual advancement." As Nisbet points out:

> The odium under which the words "monk" and monkish" lay for many hundreds of years in the minds of intellectuals in Western society had almost nothing to do with the fact of religious identification and almost everything to do with the monastery's sequestration from the powerful currents which were altering European thought and life. The university, in contrast to the monastery, beginning with the great Bologna in law and Padua in medicine and Paris in theology, has ever been in the thick of things; ever related to the professional needs of society, be these legal, medical, and theological, as they were in the beginning, or scientific, administrative, and industrial as they have come also to be in our age.[16]

Thus, for the university to retreat from active engagement in and service to society would be to retreat from a tradition of nearly a thousand years.

[16] Robert A. Nisbet, "Conflicting Academic Loyalties," in Calvin B. T. Lee, ed., *Improving College Teaching,* Washington, D.C.: American Council on Education, 1967.

Those who mourn the decline of classical studies and see in it the triumph of vocationalism or grubby materialism also misunderstand the history of the university. When the classics reigned supreme in higher education, it was not because of any inherent superiority—not because they formed the mind or shaped the character more successfully than other studies—but because they were vocationally useful. As Peter Drucker states:

> In 1700 or 1750, no one would have argued that teaching Latin taught anything but Latin. No one spoke of it as "forming the mind," no one praised it as a "discipline," no one asserted that knowing Latin was the key to learning the other European languages more easily. One learned Latin because Latin was the "communications medium" of educated people. Until the mid-eighteenth century when French cultural imperialism tried unsuccessfully to put the language of Louis XIV into place of the language of Augustus, books for the educated and documents of importance were normally written in Latin. Latin was taught as a tool of high utility without which a scribe could not properly function. When this came to an end—in the early nineteenth century—all the other virtues of Latin were suddenly discovered. Now, for the last fifty or a hundred years, Latin is being defended because it has no usefulness whatever; that is, it is an ornament. An "educated man," it is argued, should not learn subjects of utility but subjects such as Latin which are "liberal" . . . precisely because no one can do anything with them.[17]

In short, classical studies are not inherently more liberal than other, more vocationally or professionally oriented studies. There is an inherent contradiction, in fact, in the notion of "pure learning," or learning for its own sake. Those, like Hutchins, who espouse this view also argue that all knowledge is not of equal worth—that some kinds of learning are more important than others. But more important in what sense? To argue that some learning is more important than others is to argue, in effect, that learning has some external purpose, some objective outside itself. "Pedants sneer at an education that is useful," Whitehead observed. "But if education is not useful, what is it? Is it a talent, to be hidden away in a napkin? Of course education should be useful, whatever your aim in life. It was useful to Saint Augustine

---

[17] *The Age of Discontinuity*, p. 315. Cf. also A. N. Whitehead, "The Place of Classics in Education," in *The Aims of Education*.

and it was useful to Napoleon. It is useful, because understanding is useful."

What determines whether a particular study is liberal, then, is the way it is taught, and even more, the purpose to which it is taught—whether its purpose is to enlarge the student's humanity and his understanding of the role and purpose of knowledge. "The question of what it is to be a man, of what it is to be fully human," Wance C. Booth argues, "is the question at the heart of liberal education."

Taught with this question in mind, many technically or vocationally oriented college and university courses can be liberal as well. "Is it possible," John Dewey asked the Association of American Universities in 1917, "that training in law, medicine, or engineering when informed by adequate recognition of its human bearing and public purpose should not be genuinely liberal?" There is nothing inherent in these careers, he went on to argue, that "confers upon preparation for them that sense of narrowness and selfishness carried by the ordinary use of the words 'professional' and 'technical,' " but only the neglect of the public interest that has characterized professional education.

There are ample examples of the correctness of Dewey's thesis. At the hands of a Willard Hurst, for example (see Chapter 2, Section IV), the study of law can be as liberalizing and humanizing as any other. So can engineering, when studied under a Harvey Brooks, the dean of the Division of Engineering and Applied Physics at Harvard, who argues that "the professional is much more than a man with knowledge. Rather he must be thought of as the middle-man or intermediary between a body of knowledge and society—a lay society. To the professional," Dean Brooks argues, "belongs the responsibility of using both existing and new knowledge to provide services that society wants and needs."[18] He cannot fulfill that responsibility without a deep concern for human values—a concern his education can and must evoke and cultivate.

No less a humanist than Paul Goodman, in fact, now argues that "technology is a branch of moral philosophy."[19] The foremost contemporary exponent of this idea, particularly as it affects the nature of higher education, is Sir Eric Ashby, vice-chancellor of Cambridge University. Technology, he argues, "could become

---

[18] Harvey Brooks, "The Dilemmas of Engineering Education," unpublished speech.
[19] Paul Goodman, "Can Technology Be Humane?", *New York Review of Books*, Vol. XIII, No. 9, November 20, 1969.

the cement between science and humanism. Far from being an unassimilated activity in universities, it could become the agent for assimilating the traditional function of the university into the new age. For technology," he continues, "is inseparable from men and communities. . . . The technologist is up to his neck in human problems whether he likes it or not. Take a simple example: the civil engineer who builds a road into a new territory in tropical Africa. He may assert that it is not his business to take into account the effect his road will have on primitive villages up country; but his road is in fact a major experiment in social anthropology. He does not need to be a professional anthropologist, but he cannot afford to be utterly ignorant of the implications of his work. He is a technologist, not a pure scientist: the social consequences of his work are therefore an integral part of his profession."[20] In our terms, he is an educator, and must be educated accordingly.

The problem, however, is less that technical courses are taught in a technical and illiberal way than that liberal courses are taught in the same technical and illiberal way. All too often, the so-called liberal courses—courses in history, philosophy, the social sciences, the humanities, music and art, the natural and physical sciences—are taught with a narrowly professional and technical purpose in mind—to train professional historians, sociologists, literature professors, physicists, etc. Many history courses, David Riesman says—and his strictures apply to a great many other departments—"are efforts to show that one 'school' of historiography is better than another, chiefly by putting down the latter." Riesman further observes:

The extent of intra-mural discourse in the typical middle-level undergraduate course is astonishing to the neophyte. Someone who really wanted to understand the history of this country might find many history courses devoted entirely to questions about so-and-so's sloppy historiographic methods, or so-and-so's poor use of documents. And while a certain amount of this dwelling on the sources of evidence is desirable, so as to engender skepticism in the otherwise innocent, this dwelling on intra-mural issues which were being agitated when the instructor was in graduate schools turns all American history into a backdrop for academic narcissism. This may put it too strongly, but the idea that courses in the History Department—

[20] Eric Ashby, *Technology and the Academics,* London: Macmillan, 1963.

or in any department in the Humanities—are generally liberal would be a surprise to many students.[21]

And yet it need not be. A course in historiography, for example, could be the most liberalizing of courses, if taught so as to show students how knowledge is developed, how historians differ in their approaches, and so on, rather than as a means of putting down the instructor's rivals. The same is true in every field.

There is an important, perhaps critical, difference, however, between an individual course or set of courses that is liberal and liberalizing, and an *education* that is liberal and liberalizing. An education, and a curriculum, involve more than just a set of courses taken at random. If liberal education—the education of educators—is not to be merely an occasional happy by-product of other activities, there must be some conception of what liberal education is about—what its purposes are, and what its substance is.

That conception is sadly lacking at most colleges and universities; few faculty members seem willing or able to think about the purposes and consequences of their own individual courses, let alone the larger problem of the curriculum as a whole. Consider, for example, Martin Trow's savage strictures about undergraduate education at Berkeley:

> Berkeley, as an institution, has no conception of the educated man, nor any plan for liberal education. This is not to say that there is no liberal education at Berkeley: in the hundreds of courses offered by the forty-odd departments of Berkeley's College of Letters and Sciences, many students lose their provincialism, and gain an understanding of the role of values in inquiry, of the social source of ideas, of the nature of conceptual innovation. Yet admittedly it happens haphazardly; there is no common learning, and no one knows how many students pass through the University without any substantial experience of liberal education.[22]

Not even the Berkeley student uprising succeeded in forcing the Berkeley faculty to think about education; four years after

[21] In a letter to the writer.
[22] Martin Trow, "Bell, Book and Berkeley: Reflections Occasioned by a Reading of Daniel Bell's *The Reforming of General Education*," in *The American Behavioral Scientist,* June 1968.

the Free Speech movement exploded on campus, the educational pattern had not changed in any fundamental way. Indeed, if the revolt had any effect on education, it was to *reduce* the proportion of the budget spent on instruction.[23]

To be sure, the faculty *talked* about education, and a "Select Committee on Education" of the Berkeley Faculty Senate produced a lengthy report on *Education at Berkeley,* the so-called Muscatine Report, named after the committee chairman. But the report devoted no more than ten or twelve rather perfunctory pages to the undergraduate curriculum; its main thrust was a series of proposals which would free individual instructors from faculty constraints, but leave the curriculum essentially unchanged, except for the addition of new courses from time to time. As Trow observes, *"Education at Berkeley* has the one (for Berkeley surely the highest) virtue of not affecting anybody who does not want to be affected by it. . . . The Report leaves people alone to get on with their work. That is what the Berkeley faculty wants of an undergraduate program—that it not interfere too much with the real business of academic men."

It is what all too many other faculties want as well. The tendency to think about thinking, which is one of the characteristics of the scholar, Joseph Schwab, of the University of Chicago, writes, is "notably uncommon and invisible in the one place which matters most to the collegiate community—its curriculum. As far as students are allowed to see," Professor Schwab continues, "the curriculum is not a subject of thought; it merely is. In many cases, indeed, thought about the curriculum is not merely invisible; it barely occurs. Single courses are sometimes the outcome of single happy thoughts but are rarely accorded the reflexive, critical scrutiny we give as a matter of duty and right to our 'scholarly' productions. Their origins are left obscure and their outcomes only occasionally examined. Sequences and groupings of courses are sustained by tradition and inertia and only rarely examined. Least of all do we worry about our sins of omission, the courses we do not give, the outcomes we do not seek.[24]

Wayne Booth writes in much the same vein, suggesting that "There is something irrational in our contemporary neglect of

[23] Nathan Glazer, " 'Student Power' in Berkeley," *The Public Interest,* No. 13, Fall 1968; Christopher Jencks and David Riesman, *The Academic Revolution,* New York: Doubleday, 1968, p. 542.

[24] Joseph J. Schwab, *College Curriculum & Student Protest,* University of Chicago Press, 1969.

systematic thought about educational goals." The irrationality is all the greater in view of the fact that any curriculum involves judgments about goals, and the priorities attached to them, however unconscious those judgments may be. As Dean Booth adds, "we regularly make choices that are based on implied standards of what is worth knowing. We set degree requirements, we organize courses, we give examinations and we would scarcely want to say that what we do is entirely arbitrary. We conduct research on this rather than that subject, and we urge our students in this rather than that direction. . . . And yet we seem to be radically unwilling to discuss the ground for our choices; it is almost as if we expected that a close look would reveal a scandal at the heart of our academic endeavour."

As indeed it might—the scandal of not thinking seriously, and to a degree, not really caring, about that most serious of the university's functions, education. Few instructors have ever asked why they are teaching what they are teaching. It may be just as well; if the question were to be asked, the answer might prove embarrassing. In many large universities, faculty members acknowledge privately that the real reason many freshman and sophomore courses are given is that they provide employment for the department's graduate students; the more graduate students, the more status and power the department has within the university. This is most notoriously the case, perhaps, with required freshman English courses.

ITEM: In one large state university, the required composition course is given in three hundred sections; even so, the sections are so large that the instructors—all, or virtually all, of them graduate T.A.'s (teaching assistants)—cannot spend enough time to read, correct, and discuss the students' papers to make the course meaningful.

ITEM: Another university has abolished all "distribution requirements"—the requirement that students take a specified minimum number of credits in the sciences, humanities, physical sciences, etc.—except for foreign languages. The reason, admitted privately if not publicly, is not that the faculty feels more strongly about the importance of language than any other area, but that eliminating the language requirement would eliminate most of the language department's enrollment and thus leave the university with a number of unemployed but tenured professors.

Few faculty members, moreover, have thought about what in recent years has become their central educational problem: how to provide a liberal and liberalizing education to kinds of students who have not previously gone to college—students coming from a culture alien to that of the university, students who arrive at the university with no conception of what the life of the mind is like. "What strikes me most in reading books like Alfred Kazin's haunting poetic reminiscences of boyhood in an immigrant Jewish neighborhood in the East, is the vast gulf which separates that kind of growing up and the childhood and adolescence of those of us who came out of the towns of the American South and Southwest a generation later," Willie Morris, wrote in his magnificent autobiography, *North Toward Home.*

> With the Eastern Jewish intellectuals . . . the struggle as they grew up in the 1930s was for one set of ideas over others, for a fierce acceptance or rejection of one man's theories or another man's poetry . . .
> But for so many of us who converged on Austin, Texas, in the early 1950s, from places like Karnes City or Big Spring or Abilene or Rockdale or Yazoo City, the awakenings we were to experience, or to have jolted into us, or to undergo by some more subtle chemistry, did not mean a mere finishing or deepening, and most emphatically did not imply the victory of one set of ideologies over another, one way of viewing literature or politics over another, but something more basic and simple. This was the acceptance of ideas themselves as something worth living by. It was a matter, at the age of eighteen or nineteen, not of discovering *certain* books, but the simple presence of books, not the nuances of ideas and feeling, but ideas and feeling on their own terms. . . . If places like City College or Columbia galvanized the young New York intellectuals already drenched in literature and polemics, the University of Texas had, in its halting, unsure, and often frivolous way, to teach those of us with good minds and small-town high school diplomas that we were intelligent human beings, with minds and hearts of our own that we might learn to call our own, that there were some things, many things—ideas, values, choices of action—worth committing one's self to and fighting for, that a man in some instances might become morally committed to honoring every manifestation of individual conscience and courage.[25]

[25] Willie Morris, *North Toward Home,* Boston: Houghton-Mifflin, 1967.

The problem is how to have this impact without at the same time destroying the student's roots or his sense of self. Too many professors practice a kind of intellectual colonialism as they set about their task of rescuing the natives from their ignorance and savagery. "As higher education continues to expand," Dr. Allan M. Cartter, chancellor of New York University, has written, "a larger proportion of the students who come to us are *without the family and community background which would provide them with intellectual curiosity and a strong moral sense.* We are expected to give them a purpose to live for and standards to live by, *to encourage those attributes of being which are associated with the cultured gentleman . . .*"[26] [Emphasis added]

Cartter's air of moral superiority is hardly new; he is only repeating the noblesse oblige that generations of academics have displayed when confronted with the democratization of their student body. "While doubtless the old New York stock will always be represented, Columbia is not likely ever again to be a fashionable college *per se,*" Dean Frederick Keppel of Columbia College wrote in 1914. "One of the commonest references that one hears with regard to Columbia," he continued, "is that its position at the gateway of European immigration makes it socially uninviting to students who come from homes of refinement. The form which the inquiry takes in these days of slowly dying race prejudice is, 'Isn't Columbia overrun with European Jews who are most unpleasant persons socially?' " The college, Keppel went on to explain, was not "overrun with Jews," whose admission he defended on the grounds that Columbia had a public duty to help the bright and ambitious but socially backward immigrant children. "What most people regard as a racial problem is really a social problem," he explained. "The Jews who have had the advantages of decent social surroundings for a generation or two are entirely satisfactory companions. . . . There are, indeed, Jewish students of another type who have not had the social advantages of their more fortunate fellows. Often they come from an environment which in any stock less fired with ambition would have put the idea of higher education entirely out of the question. Some of these are not particularly pleasant companions, but the total number is not large, and every repu-

---

[26] Allan M. Cartter, "University Teaching and Excellence," in Calvin B. T. Lee, ed., *Improving College Teaching,* Washington, D.C.: American Council on Education, 1967.

table institution aspiring to public service must stand ready to give those of probity and good moral character the benefits which they are making great sacrifices to obtain."[27]

What colleges are going to have to confront—what they are being forced to confront as a result of the admission of black students—is that "those attributes of being which are associated with the cultured gentleman," as Cartter terms it, involves a strong if unconscious ethnic and class bias. "The demand being made on me as a student of Western Culture," Norman Podhoretz has written of his days at Columbia College, "was seductively abstract and idealized: 'Become a gentleman, a man of enlightened and gracious mind!' It is not that Columbia was being dishonest in failing to mention that this also meant 'Become a facsimile WASP!' In taking that corollary for granted, the college was simply being true to its own ethnic and class origins; and in nothing did this fidelity show itself more clearly than in the bland unconsciousness that accompanied it." The result, in any case, was to destroy Podhoretz's roots. "To wean me away from Brownsville," he adds, "all Columbia had to do was give me the superior liberal education it did: in giving me such an education it was working a radical change in my tastes, and in changing my tastes it was ensuring that I would no longer be comfortable in the world from which I had come."[28]

Like many students of his, and previous, generations, Podhoretz saw no choice but to surrender his roots, if only temporarily, in exchange for "the superior liberal education" Columbia offered. Many of the new generation of black students refuse to pay that price. To some degree, their refusal may be naïve and unrealistic; if education does *not* force a student to question his background, if it does not give him the means to live comfortably in cultures other than his own, it is not really education. In a sense, the pain black students feel in predominantly white colleges—the agony they experience when they discover how rapidly they have been alienated from their family and friends—is an exaggerated version of what the young Willie Morris experienced when he returned to Yazoo City from the University of Texas, or what the young Thomas Wolfe experienced when he discovered that "You Can't Go Home Again." And yet what makes *North Toward Home* so moving is that

[27] Quoted in Daniel Bell, *The Reforming of General Education,* New York: Columbia University Press, 1966.
[28] Norman Podhoretz, *Making It,* New York: Random House, 1967.

Morris *was* able to go home again. Somehow or other, he found the means to keep his roots without surrendering what he learned in Austin and New York; he was able to continue loving and accepting his family even while rejecting their values and life-style. If North became his home, the South was where his roots remained.

But the black experience, while like that of other ethnic groups in some regards, is profoundly different in other respects. What ultimately distinguishes the black student from white students of whatever ethnic or religious group is that he is black; he does not have the option of changing his name or altering his nose and disappearing in the crowd. What was pain for previous generations of students, therefore, is agony for the black student.[29]

And so the black students' demands cannot—must not—be ignored, or sloughed off by pointing to the experience of other ethnic groups. Behind the sometimes exaggerated rhetoric in which their demands are phrased, there is, as a rule, an insistence on the reality of group identity in the United States, along with a sometimes plaintive plea for help in maintaining that identity and giving it dignity and meaning. What most black students want is to enter the mainstream of American life and culture without surrendering their sense of identity as blacks.[30] The result is to force colleges and universities to seek answers to what is surely one of the central questions of American life: how to create and maintain a sense of community when that community is composed of groups as well as of individuals.

Black militancy, however, is only one of a number of forces demanding that the Academy think through anew what it means by such terms as "liberal education," "culture," and "gentleman." The larger problem with which colleges and universities are grappling—more precisely, perhaps, the problem with which they *should* be grappling—is how to provide a liberalizing, humanizing education not just for a social elite, nor for an intellectual elite, but in effect, for everyone.

Reordering the curriculum is not the only problem with

[29] For an analysis of the differences between the experience of blacks and of other ethnic groups in the United States, and their significance, see C. E. Silberman, *Crisis in Black and White,* especially Chapters 3 and 4.

[30] Not always, of course. At some campuses—most notably San Francisco State College—black militance and separatism can be understood only as a political, indeed revolutionary, movement.

which colleges and universities are grappling; they face equally pressing problems of internal governance, as well as of their relations with the communities in which they are located, with trustees and regents, and in the case of municipal and state institutions, with legislatures, mayors and governors, and the public at large. Many if not most of these difficulties, Martin Trow of Berkeley argues, reflect the strains involved in transforming what was a system of *mass* higher education into one of *universal* higher education. "That development," Professor Trow writes, "clear in trends and projections, is obscured by the fact that currently only about half of all high school graduates across the country go directly from high school to some form of higher education. But in the upper middle classes, and in states like California, the proportion of youngsters going on to some form of post-secondary education is already over eighty percent. For youngsters in those places and strata, universal higher education is here: nearly everybody they know goes on to college. And those strata and areas are growing inexorably."[31] As indeed they are!

Our concern here, however, is with curriculum—with the weakness of liberal or general education, especially in the first two years of college. At the moment, the problems of structure, governance, and relations with trustees and constituencies outside the university, are more urgent—more immediately pressing —than those of educational policy in the narrower sense. If they lead to populist assaults on academic freedom, as events in California and elsewhere suggest may well happen, they could prove more important as well; if faculty appointments have to pass tests of political loyalty, the resulting blandness or fear could make liberal education impossible.[32]

Be that as it may, the challenge to educational policy is clear enough. The shift toward universal higher education is compounding the problem the colleges and universities have been facing since the early postwar period, when the shift from elitist to mass higher education became pronounced. In different form, it is the problem that, earlier in the century, confronted, and in

[31] Martin Trow, "Reflections on the Transition from Mass to Universal Higher Education," *Daedalus,* Winter 1970.
[32] In addition to the paper by Trow already cited—in the writer's judgment, the best single analysis of the problem—the reader is directed to the following sources: Christopher Jencks and David Riesman, *The Academic Revolution;* "Governance of the Universities," Parts I and II, *Daedalus,* Fall 1969.

large measure, overwhelmed, the high schools: in Lawrence Cremin's phrase, how to humanize or popularize knowledge without vulgarizing it—to "resynthesize and reorder" knowledge so as to make it teachable to the mass of men, not just the few who, in the past, had had a monopoly on what, for want of a better phrase, we call culture.[33]

There is comfort, perhaps, in the fact that there is little precedent for what is being attempted. "Many societies," F. Champion Ward observes, "have believed that some knowledge is of most worth, but that most learners were not worthy of it. So far as higher education is concerned, they have accepted the contention of Nietzsche that to speak of a 'common good' is to contradict oneself. The idea of a common *lower* learning is accepted even among robins, who teach all their young to fly. All modern societies also accept the idea of higher uncommon or specialized learning. It remained for America to press home the idea of a higher common learning extending beyond the level of schooling, and, theoretically, to everyone."[34]

The task is complicated by the fact that this great extension of "the higher common learning" is occurring at a point in time when some of the most thoughtful educators are less and less sure in their own minds as to what a liberal education consists of, what knowledge is of most worth, or whether a common learning is possible or even desirable in the contemporary world, given the exponential growth of information and knowledge.

There is a tendency, however, to see the present situation as unique in ways that it is not. In arguing that the "knowledge explosion" makes a common learning impossible in today's college, for example, scholars frequently exaggerate the degree to which a common learning existed in the recent past. "The possession of a common body of knowledge, and the existence of an intellectual class, involved in essentially the same inquiry— this may have been the situation in a remote past," the historian Stephen Graubard of Brown University writes; "it is not one that has prevailed for some time"—certainly not since the eighteenth century. "The notion that intellectuals met on the basis of shared intellectual competences would be difficult to demonstrate," he continues.

---

[33] Lawrence A. Cremin, *The Genius of American Education.* Cf. also Martin Trow, "The Democratization of Higher Education in America," *European Journal of Sociology,* Vol. III, 1962, pp. 231–2.
[34] F. Champion Ward, "Returning Coals to Newcastle" in Wayne C. Booth, ed., *The Knowledge Most Worth Having.*

In the nineteenth century, the philologist cannot have expected the political economist to know his work, and neither can have looked to the botanist for particular intellectual insights. They met on another basis which had little to do with specific learning, but involved a shared set of values, attitudes, and experiences. . . . If they learned from each other, it was not because they were involved in inquiries less complex than those which presently engage us, but that the pace of life permitted a certain sort of communication which is now difficult to achieve, and also, that their number was small enough for them to form fairly compact societies.[35]

Alfred North Whitehead made much the same point half a century ago. "There is a curious illusion that a more complete culture was possible when there was less to know," he observed in 1917, in his Presidential Address to the Mathematical Association of England. "Surely the only gain was that it was more possible to remain unconscious of ignorance. It cannot have been a gain to Plato to have read neither Shakespeare, nor Newton, nor Darwin. The achievements of a liberal education have in recent times not been worsened," he continued. "The change is that its pretensions have been found out."[36]

Serious thought about the nature of liberal education is impaired, too, by a tendency to exaggerate both the extent and the impact of the knowledge explosion. "Despite the fact that a subject taught to college freshmen may have altered basically by the time the same students are seniors," Margaret Mead has written, in a statement quoted approvingly by Robert M. Hutchins, "it is still said that colleges are able to give students 'a good education'—finished, wrapped up, and sealed with a degree . . ."[37]

But change is *not* that rapid except perhaps in some advanced areas of biology; there are no subjects in which knowledge becomes obsolete between the freshman and senior years. Indeed, to talk this loosely about "obsolescence" is to confuse knowledge with information. There has not been any knowledge explosion, except perhaps in biology and physics. There *has* been an *information* explosion, which together with an explosive increase

---

[35] Stephen Graubard, "Notes on Contemporary Culture," mimeographed.
[36] A. N. Whitehead, "Technical Education and Its Relation to Science and Literature," in *The Aims of Education*.
[37] Margaret Mead, "Is Education Obsolescent?", *Harvard Business Review*, November–December 1963, reprinted in Ronald Gross, ed., *The Teacher and the Taught*, New York: Dell Publishing, 1963.

in the volume of publications and in the speed of communication, has produced an information glut. But that is a different affair and does not mean rapid obsolescence of knowledge, only lack of the concepts and theories needed to handle the glut of information. The result, as Whitehead foresaw, is that "we are left with no expansion of wisdom and with greater need of it."[38]

The steady expansion of information and knowledge, and the proliferation of new disciplines and sub-disciplines from which it springs have been posing problems for education since at least the turn of the century. "The accumulation has become so great that the educational system is disintegrating through the wedges of new studies continually introduced," John Dewey complained in 1896. "While there is an almost constant cry that the curriculum is being too diversified, that students are distracted and congested by the wealth of material forced upon them, the demand for more studies and for more time for each of these studies never ceases. The pressure began in the college and high school. It is now finding its way into the primary school . . . "[39]

IV

Unlike Dewey and some of the other giants of his period, and unlike the professors, college deans, and university presidents of the 1920s, '30s, and '40s, who developed courses in "general education" as a means of solution, most contemporary scholars have tended to throw up their hands in despair over the difficulty of redefining liberal education.

The reasons are several. One of the most important, and most frequently overlooked, is that the crisis of authority has affected faculty members as well as students. In the college years which we now call the stage of youth, as Erik Erikson has written, "the tables of childhood dependence begin slowly to turn: no longer is it merely for the old to teach the young the meaning of life, whether individual or collective. *It is the young who, by their responses and actions, tell the old whether life as represented by the old and as presented to the young has meaning;* and it is the young who carry in them the power to confirm those who con-

[38] Alfred North Whitehead, *Science and the Modern World*, New York: Macmillan, 1925.
[39] John Dewey, "Pedagogy as a University Discipline," *University Record* (University of Chicago Press), Vol. 1, No. 25, September 18, 1896.

firm them and, joining the issues, to renew and to regenerate, or to reform and to rebel."[40] [Emphasis added]

What has happened, then, is that the new generation's rejection of the authority of scholarship, knowledge, and culture has shaken their professors' confidence in their own intellectual and moral authority. If in some academicians, confidence in their intellectual and moral authority leads to arrogance and cultural imperialism, in others loss of confidence has led, in effect, to abdication of responsibility. As Martin Trow puts it, "Many academic men no longer really believe they have a right to define a curriculum for their students, or to set standards of performance, much less to prescribe the modes of thought and feeling appropriate to 'an educated mind.' Indeed the very notion that there are qualities of mind and sensibility to be gained from experience in a college or university is often treated with amusement or contempt, as merely a reactionary expression of middle class prejudices."[41]

The result is the intellectual and moral void which Yeats described:

> *Things fall apart; the centre cannot hold;*
> *Mere anarchy is loosed upon the world . . .*
> *The best lack all conviction, while the worst*
> *Are full of passionate intensity.*

Thus, many colleges which had required all students to follow a program of general education in their first two years are scrapping it in favor of "distribution requirements"—so many credits in the humanities, so many in the natural sciences, so many in the social sciences, with little or no specification as to which courses may be taken to fulfill the requirement. And many colleges that have had distribution requirements are, in turn, abolishing those requirements, leaving students free to take what they wish. But if students are simply turned loose to "do their own thing," as Harris Wofford, president-elect of Bryn Mawr College, suggests, the college is not likely to be free to do *its* thing—or to have a thing to do. "It is a liberal education we

[40] Erik H. Erikson, "Youth: Fidelity and Diversity," in Erikson, ed., *The Challenge of Youth,* Garden City, N.Y.: Doubleday Anchor Books, 1963.
[41] "Reflections on the Transition from Mass to Higher Education," *Daedalus,* Winter 1970.

must expound," Wofford argues, "and this means a college with a curriculum, with a view of what liberal education is, with something to say about how to get it; a college that respects its students enough to assume that they are ready to listen, and that they will respond. It is the cluttered and empty colleges, with nothing to say, that diminish the dialogue" that lies at the heart of liberal education.[42]

What is crucial is the dialogue. To suggest that a college must have something to say is not to imply that there must be only one curriculum. There are many routes to a liberal education; given the temperament of this generation of students, a college would be wise to offer a number of routes from which they may choose, and to give them considerable leeway in deciding how to follow them. But each of the routes—each of the curricula— must have coherence and purpose, each must reflect some conviction about what is worth knowing and doing and being. Students are not likely to be able to learn how to choose, how to decide for themselves between the better and the worse, if their teachers convey the notion that the choices do not matter. If students "see in the four years ahead of them in college no large horizons, no anticipations of delight, no promise of an opening up of their lives, but only duties to be borne and trivial tasks to undertake," Harold Taylor writes, "they are unlikely to find the inner energies through which to infuse their own education with a sense of purpose. The curriculum, whatever it is, must start with the intention of creating a situation in which the student can honestly commit himself to what he is asked to do . . ."[43]

What made undergraduate education so exciting at Columbia and Chicago in the thirties and forties, certainly, was not that those colleges had defined liberal education "correctly" either for that period or for all time, but that they had conceptions that shaped the students' and faculties' lives outside the classroom as well as in. The conception was not one that every faculty member shared; much of the excitement, in fact, stemmed from the faculty members', and students', disagreements over what should be studied. What the faculty did share, however, is critical to liberal education: a concern for the possibilities and character of education, a conviction that the shape and content of the curriculum really matters, that some kinds and sequences

---

[42] Harris Wofford, Jr., address to the Union for Research and Experimentation in Higher Education, July 11, 1967 (mimeographed).
[43] Harold Taylor, *The World and the American Teacher.*

of courses are better than others, and that the curriculum, consequently, should be shaped by educational conviction rather than
by administrative convenience.

The decline of general education at Chicago and Columbia
helps explain the weakness of undergraduate education elsewhere. It was not lack of interest or rebellion on the part of
students that caused the general education courses to be dropped
at Chicago and reduced and weakened at Columbia; it was their
abandonment by the faculty.[44] And the abandonment came
about less because the faculty lost faith in what they had been
teaching than because they lost interest. Teaching undergraduates, and in particular, teaching general education courses to
freshmen and sophomores, came to be seen more and more as
an interference with the real business of academic men, which
is defined as carrying on research and the ancillary consulting
and advising activities that have sprung up around research.

What happened, in large measure, was that the expanding
market for college professors—a function of the accelerating
increase in enrollments—brought about a profound shift in the
balance of power within the prestigious private and public universities and colleges. In a national sellers' market for professors,
young men frequently could advance their careers more easily
by moving from institution to institution than by rising within a
single one. What determined advancement, in any case, was
the man's reputation as a scholar rather than as a teacher. The
result is that academic departments have greatly increased their
power vis-à-vis the college or university as a whole, with a consequent shift in allegiance among professors, from fealty to the
institution to fealty to the academic discipline, which is institutionalized in the department. "From being primarily and essentially a university member whose field was, more or less incidentally, sociology," Robert Nisbet explains, "one is today a
sociologist whose job is, more or less incidentally, in a university." Indeed, the university tie is more or less incidental—
"more a matter of housing than of umbilical tie."[45] And under-

44 In the early 1940s, for example, when the writer was a student at
Columbia College, most of the senior faculty—men like Ernest Nagel,
Lionel Trilling, Mark van Doren, John Herman Randall, Jr., Gilbert
Highet, James Gutmann, Harry Carman—taught one or more sections
of the Humanities or Contemporary Civilization courses. Today, most
senior faculty refuse to teach either, and junior faculty resent the burden.
45 Robert A. Nisbet, "Conflicting Academic Loyalties," in Calvin B. T.
Lee, ed., *Improving College Teaching,* American Council on Education,

standably so, for in many fields—perhaps most fields, outside the humanities—the demand for scholars is as great outside the university as inside; half of all those receiving Ph.D. degrees, in fact, now take jobs outside academic life.

It is too simplistic, of course, and a bit unfair, to attribute this change to scholarly opportunism. Scholars and scientists have never been immune to personal ambition; the image of the disinterested scientist, concerned with nothing but the advancement of knowledge, has always been a myth, and one that has obscured our understanding of the way knowledge advances. "Scientific inquiry, like human action generally," Robert Merton writes, "stems from a variety and amalgam of motives in which the passion for creating new knowledge is supported by the passion for recognition by peers and the derivative competition for place."[46] The creation of a national sellers' market for professors made recognition easier and so intensified the "competition for place." It has also contributed to a shift in the ethos of academic life, in which the professor's professional obligation is defined more and more as contributing to the advancement of knowledge rather than to its transmission or humanization.

That the process is understandable, however, does not make its consequences any less undesirable. If continued too long, as William Arrowsmith of the University of Texas warns, quoting Nietzsche, the emphasis on research and graduate training may result in "the advancement of learning at the expense of man."[47]

The changes we have been talking about directly affect only a relative handful of institutions—the great private and state universities like Berkeley, Harvard, Columbia, Wisconsin, Chicago, Michigan, Cornell—in which undergraduate education is subordinated to graduate education and research, and in which professors' advancement and status depend more on their research productivity than on their teaching. If the teaching is bad in the great majority of colleges and universities, it is less because professors are subordinating teaching to research, than because they do not know how to teach. Of the 350,000 or

---

1967. For a detailed analysis of the change and its implications, cf. Christopher Jencks and David Riesman, *The Academic Revolution*.
[46] Robert K. Merton, "Behavior Patterns of Scientists," *The American Scholar*, Vol. 38, No. 2, Spring 1969.
[47] William Arrowsmith, "The Future of Teaching," in Calvin B. T. Lee, ed., *Improving College Teaching*. The paper is contained also in *The Public Interest*, No. 6, Winter 1967.

so full-time college and university teachers, the great majority—85 percent, according to one estimate—do not publish or carry on research.[48]

And yet the "academic revolution," as Jencks and Riesman call it, has exerted a profound, if indirect effect on most colleges and universities. The prestigious universities—the ones in which graduate training and research predominate—are remarkably uniform in their outlook and values, and they exert a powerful leverage on the other institutions of higher education. For one thing, they are a major source of faculty: a mere fifty universities account for 90 percent of the Ph.D.'s who enter college and university teaching each year.[49] Equally important, they represent the model to which other institutions aspire. The values of the Academy—which is to say, the values of the leading graduate schools—are becoming more and more the values of higher education as a whole. The result is a well-defined and well-recognized, if unwritten, hierarchy in which each institution is trying, sometimes desperately, to become more like the institution on the next highest rung of the ladder.

The second-echelon universities, for example—among them, some of the largest producers of teachers—are now striving to become first-echelon. "The recent successes of the academic revolution have generated rising expectations all over the country," Jencks and Riesman write; "and there are now perhaps 150 Avis institutions hoping to become Hertz." To "become Hertz," of course, means to gain recognition for the graduate departments and schools, not the undergraduate. And so re-oources are poured into expanding graduate faculty and students, frequently at the expense of the undergraduate. Equally important, an effort is made to alter the nature of the student body—the term is "upgrade"—by turning down the present clientele and attracting academically abler students from elsewhere. The process is cumulative: attracting academic "stars" makes it easier to attract able students, and able students make it easier to attract the academic stars. The result is a tremendous pressure toward uniformity and conventionality in undergraduate programs.

[48] Ann M. Heiss, "The Preparation of College and University Teachers," and "The Utilization of the College and University Teacher," Berkeley, California: Center for Research and Development in Higher Education, mimeographed.
[49] Ann M. Heiss, "The Preparation of College and University Teachers."

ITEM: Asked if he could define his institution's goals, the provost of a large state university answered yes, without hesitation. The goal: to be ranked in the middle of the Conference to which his university belongs, instead of near the bottom, the next time the American Council on Education publishes "An Assessment of Quality in Graduate Education." As a result, the university is pushing hard to expand its graduate programs, and is trying to "upgrade" the quality of its student body by drawing on a national rather than statewide pool.

ITEM: Asked to define his institution's goals, the president of another large state university answered, "We intend to be no different than thirty or forty other universities"—the thirty or forty most prestigious, of course.

Not every administrator is as frank or as precise. But the pressures to uniformity—and to lack of thought about how this particular institution can best educate *its* particular student body —are evident in every part of the system. If the "Avises" try to become "Hertz," others try to become "Avis." Thus, state colleges try to become universities; the junior colleges try to become four-year institutions; and so on. In all these cases, energy and thought are directed to changing the institution's character, or at least its prestige and status, rather than to figuring out how best to educate the students who are already there.

ITEM: The Dean of Faculty Planning of a large state college would like to drop the freshman and sophomore classes altogether, to permit the college to concentrate on upper classmen and, more important, expand its graduate program, now offering only a master's degree, into a full-fledged doctoral program. "The community colleges around the state give lower classmen as good a general education as we provide," the dean claims. Five or ten minutes later, however, by way of illuminating the necessity of expanding the graduate program, he explains that limiting graduate study to the master's degree condemns most of the college's graduate students to teaching at community colleges. "They're too good to settle for that," he says.

ITEM: "Not long ago," Professor Arthur M. Cohen, director of the Junior College Teacher Preparation Program at UCLA, writes, "I received a query from the president of a new junior college in a small southern town. He wanted the names of people 'with Ph.D.'s' whom he might be able to entice to serve on his staff. My reply was to send him a few names along with the admonition that it might be possible for him to build a good program with non-doctoral people. Only later, when I received a set of public relations releases from the college, did I realize I had misinterpreted his question. I thought he had been asking, 'How can I find people to help me create a viable post-secondary educational program in an area where there was none before?' But his question actually had been, 'How can I gain prestige in my district most rapidly?' The matter became clear when I saw that, regardless of its topic, each release was careful to note that the college 'had nine Ph.D.'s on the staff—more than any other junior college in the state!' "[50]

V

Fortunately, there are signs of change. For one thing, the long dearth of serious discussion of, and debate over, the ends and means of liberal or general education has been ended. In 1966, for example, Wayne Booth spoke of the university faculties' radical unwillingness to discuss the grounds for their choices about curriculum. "The journals are full, true enough, of breast-beating and soul-searching, especially since 'Berkeley,' " he wrote. "But you will look a long while before you find any discussion of what is worth knowing. You will look even longer before you find anything written in the past ten years worthy of being entered into the great debate on liberal education."

Not any more; the volume Booth edited—the papers given at a Liberal Arts Conference sponsored by the undergraduate college of the University of Chicago as part of the university's seventy-fifth anniversary celebration—was an early and important entry in that debate. Other important contributions include Daniel Bell's *The Reforming of General Education,* Joseph Schwab's *College Curriculum and Student Protest,* Franklin Patterson's *The Making of a College,* Christopher Jencks and David Riesman's *The Academic Revolution,* and a variety of essays, papers, book reviews, and speeches by such scholars as William Arrowsmith, Henry David Aiken, and Martin Trow.

If there is a dominant theme in these writings, it is that the

[50] From Arthur M. Cohen, *Dateline '79: Heretical Concepts for the Community College,* Beverly Hills, Calif.: Glencoe Press, 1969.

way to reconcile the old tradition of liberal education and the new tradition of specialization in the disciplines is through an emphasis on the means of communication and the conduct and strategy of intellectual inquiry. "The distinctive function of the college," Daniel Bell argues, "must be to teach modes of conceptualization, explanation and verification. . . . The distinctive function of the college is to deal with the grounds of knowledge: not *what* one knows but *how* one knows. . . . The task of education is metaphysics, metasociology, metapsychology, and, in exploring the nature of its own communications, metaphilosophy and metalanguage." Indeed, language and communication are so important, Bell suggests, that in the future, "a course in *language*—dealing with the nature of symbolism, communication theory, psycholinguistics (and computer languages), structural linguistics—should be a basic course, required of *all* students, as the foundation for many different lines of study."[51]

Bell's argument is impressive, both in what he says and how he says it; the book shows evidence throughout of both wit and learning, characteristics that are lacking in many writers on education, whose style makes one wonder whether they themselves are educated men. Bell *is* an educated man, and he writes with passion as well as wit and learning. And yet the book leaves this reader a trifle uneasy. In the last analysis, an emphasis on method, language, and communication can take us only so far. Ultimately we stumble on the question of what it is that we want to know or to communicate, and to what end— more important, what it is that we want to be and to do.

Much as educators may try, there is no avoiding the question of purpose. And that means that there is no way of avoiding the question of values, of the kind of man and society education is designed to produce; for education involves the molding of men, not just the transmission of knowledge. To be sure, Bell acknowledges the essential unity of thought, feeling, and action, but he nonetheless appears uncomfortable with the new concern for feeling.

In any case, his emphasis on method, on the strategies of inquiry and the modes of communication, runs the risk of reinforcing the scholarly tendency to distinguish between, and indeed to exalt, thought above feeling or action. "Knowledge of forms of scholarly inquiry and learning will serve at best only to relate those same investigations to each other," Henry David

51 Daniel Bell, *The Reforming of General Education.*

Aiken writes in a thoughtful, if sometimes unfairly critical, review of Bell's book. "But the contemporary university student needs and demands something else as well. To be sure, he wants help toward an understanding of the connections between, say, the methods of physical science and those of sociology or between the findings of the economic historian and those of the historian of English literature. He wants also to know the wisdom that may lie in the study of such connections. He wants not only to tie the academic strands together, but to tie his knowledge of them and their methods back into his developing experience as a human being. He wants to know what they portend as forms of life, both for him and for his kind."[52] Or as Jencks and Riesman write (without reference to Bell), the best contemporary students do not "demand flashy lectures by professional showmen, nor easy answers to recalcitrant questions. But they do insist that there be a visible relationship between knowledge and action, between the questions asked in the classrooms and the lives they live outside it."[53]

The fact that students are asking these kinds of questions and making these kinds of demands makes it likely that the revival of thought and debate about curriculum will continue. When the student protest movement first erupted at Berkeley, and for some time thereafter, educational policy was the least of its concerns. At Berkeley, for example, discussion of the Muscatine Report was as desultory among students as among faculty; much the same was true at Columbia, where Bell's book evoked remarkably little interest and discussion. Student protest was concerned, rather, with political ends: the university's involvement in the war in Vietnam, in racial discrimination, in the "military-industrial complex," and so on. If the students addressed themselves to educational questions at all, it was to the political issues involved in the governance of the university.

On a number of campuses, however, students seem to be turning their attention to the curriculum as well. Brown University provides the most striking example: a group of students prepared a detailed and thoughtful critique of the undergraduate curriculum and a proposal for its radical modification. Their skillful lobbying to force faculty attention to the document (initially, the faculty ignored it) led the university to revise the

---

52 Henry David Aiken, "The University, II: What Is a Liberal Education?", *New York Review of Books,* November 3, 1966.
53 Christopher Jencks and David Riesman, *The Academic Revolution.* Cf. also William Arrowsmith, "The Future of Teaching."

curriculum, in good measure (though not entirely) along the lines the students had proposed.

This is not to suggest that students have a monopoly on wisdom about curriculum; they do not, although a few occasionally act as though they do. "The moral imperialism of the so-called Movement," Harris Wofford writes, from sometimes bitter experience as president of the experimental State University of New York College at Old Westbury, "tends toward a conformity as oppressive as any the non-conformists criticize." At Old Westbury, where the first students were given a major role in planning the curriculum, this moral imperialism "has already made it difficult for those students and teachers who differ,"[54] for example, treating as pariahs those who opposed a demand that the college establish a 50 percent nonwhite quota for admissions.

At Old Westbury, and at a great many other colleges and universities, some students have tended to view liberal education as nothing more than the exploration of their psyches or a crusade against injustice, regarding disciplined inquiry as a cop-out, or worse; they accept the false dichotomy between thought and feeling, celebrating the latter and derogating the former. They make the mistake, too, of thinking that the world can be changed without understanding it, or that understanding can be acquired by experience alone, unmediated by reflection or thought. Many students, moreover, in understandable reaction against the competition for grades in which they have been enmeshed since childhood, confuse grading with evaluation and so press for the elimination of all evaluation, which is to say all standards, as well as for the "let everyone do his own thing" anarchy of no requirements.

When all these qualifications have been made, however, the fact remains that the new student interest in curriculum reform is the most hopeful development on the academic scene. Indeed, in most of the institutions with which the writer has had firsthand contact, the students interested in curriculum reform have been a good deal more serious and more thoughtful than the faculty, and a lot harder-working as well.

In any case, a growing number of college and university faculties and administrations are now addressing themselves to

[54] Harris Wofford, Jr., "Case Study of an Experiment: The New College at Old Westbury," paper given to the Danforth Foundation Workshop on Liberal Arts Education, July 7, 1969 (mimeographed); republished in the *Educational Record,* Winter Issue, 1970.

the basic questions of educational purposes and processes, whether in response to student pressure or to the promptings of their own consciences. The range of institutions involved—small, old liberal arts colleges like Haverford, Swarthmore, and Trinity; large state universities like the University of Oklahoma, the University of Michigan, and Wayne State University; private universities like Northwestern and Stanford; new colleges and universities like New College in Sarasota, the University of California branch at Santa Cruz, the State University of New York College at Old Westbury—suggests that the revival of discussion and debate about education will continue for some time. Indeed, while it is obviously too early to make definitive judgments, there is reason to think that we are at the beginning of a period of rich and thoughtful innovation in higher education.

10

The Teacher as Student: What's Wrong with Teacher Education

The present divorce between scholarship and method is as harmful upon one side as upon the other—as detrimental to the best interests of higher academic instruction as it is to the training of teachers.

—JOHN DEWEY,
"The Relation of Theory to
Practice in Education," *1904*

I

Liberal education is necessary but not sufficient; teachers need professional education as well. This is not to deny that one may be a good teacher without professional preparation; some of the greatest teachers have never taken a single education course. Nor is it to suggest that people be denied the right to teach without having had such training. The issue was stated clearly in 1888 by Charles Kendall Adams, the president of Cornell University, when he urged the members of the New England Association of Colleges and Preparatory Schools to accept responsibility for teacher education. "It would be flying in the face of all observation and experience," he declared, "to deny that many of the best teachers have come up to their present condition with no other helps than the gifts of nature and opportunity; but this important fact no more proves the inutility of training than the successes of

Washington and Franklin and Lincoln prove the inutility of a collegiate education. We must, in judging of every subject of this kind, eliminate the exceptional examples of genius, and form our opinion from results on the great uninspired masses of mankind."[1]

Adams' argument applies equally well to the present situation. With 190,000 beginning teachers entering the schools in the 1970–71 school year, and the number expected to increase by about 10,000 a year over the next five years,[2] it is clearly impossible to rely upon native talent alone as the means to improve teaching. If the schools are to be remade—if the quality of teaching is to be raised—average people must be educated to teach well.

The question, then, is not whether teachers should receive special preparation for teaching, but what kind of preparation they should receive. That the preparation should be substantially different from what they now receive seems hardly open to debate; there is probably no aspect of contemporary education on which there is greater unanimity of opinion than that teacher education needs a vast overhaul. Virtually everyone is dissatisfied with the current state of teacher education: the students being educated, the teachers in the field, the principals, superintendents, and school board members who hire them, the liberal arts faculties, and the lay critics of education.

Dissatisfaction is even beginning to penetrate the inner sanctum of the educationist "establishment" itself.

ITEM: A 1969 report on teacher education sponsored and published by the American Association of Colleges for Teacher Education (AACTE), speaks of "smugness where there should be concern" and complains that "The moderate and the mild control the destiny of education. . . . They desire change but the change is only some modest tinkering."[3] Tinkering, however, will not be enough. "Education is beyond repair!" the authors

---

[1] Charles Kendall Adams, "The Teaching of Pedagogy in Colleges and Universities," in Merle L. Borrowman, ed., *Teacher Education in America,* New York: Teachers College Press, 1965.

[2] U.S. Office of Education, *Education in the Seventies,* Table 14, Washington, D.C.: U.S. Government Printing Office, 1968.

[3] B. Othanel Smith in collaboration with Saul B. Cohen and Arthur Pearl for the Task Force of the NDEA National Institute for Advanced Study in Teaching Disadvantaged Youth, *Teachers for the Real World,* Washington, D.C.: The American Association of Colleges for Teacher Education, 1969.

go on to declaim. "What is needed is radical *reform*. This reform is to include the nature of the schooling process, the systems which control educational policy, and the institutions which prepare people to be teachers." [Emphasis in original]

This call for "radical reform" of the entire educational system is the outgrowth, interestingly enough, of what had started out to be a much more limited study by a task force of the NDEA National Institute for Advanced Study in Teaching Disadvantaged Youth. What happened, the principal author, Professor B. Othanel Smith of the University of Illinois College of Education, explains in his preface, was that "In the course of its deliberations, the Institute Task Force came to consider teacher education more and more as a whole, to attribute failures and inadequacies of education for the disadvantaged to defects in the education of teachers"—of *all* teachers. "In consequence, the Task Force undertook to explore the issues in teacher education and to set forth the outlines of a plan of education to prepare teachers for all children, regardless of their cultural backgrounds or social origins." While the plan falls far short of what this writer, at least, would call radical reform, it is surely significant that the authors' criticisms of the existing system is couched in a rhetoric heretofore employed only by the AACTE's severest critics.[4]

This is not the first time the call for reform has been issued. Teacher education has been the subject of heated and frequently acrimonious debate since the early nineteenth century, and it has been the object of recurrent investigation since the end of World War I; indeed, the preparation of teachers has been studied as frequently as the plight of the black man in America, and with as little effect. Since 1920, in fact, ten major studies of teacher education have been published, one of them running to six, another to eight volumes.[5] In addition, the National Society for the

[4] To be sure, the Associate Executive Secretary of the AACTE was careful to point out in a foreword to the volume that its criticisms and proposals reflect the opinions of the authors and the other members of the Task Force and "do not necessarily represent the points of view" of the AACTE, or of the U.S. Office of Education, which funded the study. But neither has the AACTE disavowed the volume; on the contrary, discussion of it formed a major part of the formal program at the 1969 AACTE annual meeting.

[5] William C. Bagley and William S. Learned, *The Professional Preparation of Teachers for American Public Schools*, New York: Carnegie

Study of Education, the American Association of Colleges for Teacher Education, the John Dewey Society, and the Association for Student Teaching have each devoted one or more of their annual yearbooks to the question, and the past two decades have seen a plethora of conference reports, serious critical studies, polemical attacks and counterattacks, and announcements of "revolutions" and "breakthroughs."[6]

More important, the debate about teacher education has, from the beginning, followed a single script, with much the same arguments being repeated in only slightly different form in each generation. In essence, the argument has raged between advocates of what Merle Borrowman calls the liberal and the technical views of teacher education. Advocates of the former would make professional preparation for teaching incidental to the liberal education they see as central; advocates of the latter stress the need for specialized professional training, with all or most instruction to be judged by its contribution to professional competence. There is, of course, a third position, which seeks to combine the two views, and in some cases to organize instruction so that it serves both liberal and professional and technical ends. But since most of the advocates of this middle ground differ

---

Foundation for the Advancement of Teaching, 1920; U.S. Office of Education, *National Survey of the Education of Teachers,* U.S. Government Printing Office, 1933–35 (six volumes); William S. Learned and Ben D. Wood, *The Student and His Knowledge,* New York: Carnegie Foundation for the Advancement of Teaching, 1938; American Council on Education, *The Improvement of Teacher Education: A Final Report by the Commission on Teacher Education,* Washington, D.C.: A.C.E., 1946 (this volume summarizes the eight volumes published in all); Donald P. Cottrell, ed., *Teacher Education for a Free People,* Washington, D.C.: AACTE, 1956; James D. Koerner, *The Miseducation of American Teachers,* Houghton-Mifflin, 1963; James B. Conant, *The Education of American Teachers,* McGraw-Hill, 1963 and 1964; Harold Taylor, *The World and the American Teacher,* AACTE, 1968; B. Othanel Smith, et al., *Teachers for the Real World,* AACTE, 1969.

[6] Cf. Seymour B. Sarason, Kenneth S. Davidson, and Burton Blatt, *The Preparation of Teachers,* New York: John Wiley, 1962; Lindley J. Stiles, ed., *Teacher Education in the United States,* New York: Ronald Press, 1960; G. K. Hodenfield and T. M. Stinnett, *The Education of Teachers,* Englewood Cliffs, N.J.: Prentice-Hall, 1961; Paul Woodring, *New Directions in Teacher Education,* New York: Fund for the Advancement of Education, 1957; James C. Stone, *Breakthrough in Teacher Education,* San Francisco: Jossey-Bass, 1968; Elmer R. Smith, ed., *Teacher Education: A Reappraisal,* New York: Harper & Row, 1962.

sharply over the relative emphasis they would give to liberal and professional education and the point at which the latter should begin, they tend ultimately to fall into either the liberal arts or the teachers college camp.

To understand why teacher education is in such a parlous state, therefore, and to thread one's way through the thicket of attack and counterattack, proposal and counterproposal, and panacea and failure, some understanding of how teacher education developed in the United States is essential. (The general reader may wish to skip directly to Chapter 11.)

II

The view that liberal education provides all the preparation a teacher needs derives from the eighteenth and early nineteenth centuries, when, as Professor Borrowman points out, "the course of the liberal arts college probably contained the best available knowledge relevant to the education of teachers." It was the best available, however, not because the educationists of that day believed that teachers needed no professional training, but because there was no professional training other than the content of the liberal arts curriculum. Works such as Plato's *Republic,* Aristotle's *Ethics,* Cicero's *Orator,* and Quintilian's *Institutes of Oratory*—the backbone of the liberal arts curriculum—contained the best available statements of pedagogy as well as of educational purpose. What this meant was that the prescribed curriculum prepared the student for teaching as well as he could be prepared prior to an actual apprenticeship. "The beauty of it, from the classical point of view," Borrowman writes, "was that he received this preparation without being led, through an emphasis on specific vocational goals, to narrow his concerns to matters of professional technique or to see his professional interest as separate from his need for liberal culture."[7]

The weakness, however, was that this same harmony of vocational and cultural goals meant that students did not develop any commitment to teaching as a profession or a career. Most col-

[7] M. L. Borrowman, "Liberal Education and the Professional Preparation of Teachers," in Borrowman, ed., *Teacher Education in America.* For a more detailed analysis of the different traditions of, and controversies over, teacher education, cf. M. L. Borrowman, *The Liberal and Technical in Teacher Education,* New York: Teachers College Press, 1956.

leges, after all, were sectarian institutions, formed initially to train ministers and, later on, lawyers and other community leaders as well. Teaching in any case was not an attractive career for men with the ability or social status to attend college—in the early 1800s, colleges enrolled only one-half of 1 percent of the men of college age, or roughly one in 1,500—since schooling itself was not regarded as very important. For the bulk of the population, as Abraham Lincoln described the America of his youth, "there were some schools, so called, but no qualification was ever required of a teacher beyond readin', writin', and cipherin' to the Rule of Three." Certainly taxpayers saw no reason to pay a premium to hire college graduates when in their judgment any literate man would do as well. Since not every college graduate was able to find a pulpit, some did end up as teachers; for the most part, however, they regarded it as only a temporary, and generally undesirable, expedient.

Sparked by men like Horace Mann, however, the conviction that everyone ought to be educated began to spread. By the third or fourth decade of the nineteenth century, therefore, it was apparent that the existing secondary schools and colleges had neither the desire nor the capacity to train the number of teachers required for the common schools that were beginning to spring up all over. For one thing, the colleges admitted only men, and it seemed clear that to recruit the number of teachers that would be needed at the modest salaries communities were willing to pay, a female teaching corps would have to be created.[8] The colleges also required applicants to have more than an elementary education, that much education seemed unnecessary for elementary school teachers, and in any case would have eliminated too many prospects. Moreover, most colleges were still sectarian institutions for which public financial support was becoming harder to obtain; yet public subsidy seemed essential

---

[8] Since teaching was almost the only respectable white-collar occupation open to them in the nineteenth century, women received substantially less pay than men. Although there are still occupations in which women are paid less than men for the same work, this is no longer true of teaching; today, male and female teachers receive the same salaries for the same kinds of positions. But the comparatively low salary scale and social status of teaching vis-à-vis other occupations reflects the fact that American society still defines teaching as a female occupation. Cf. Chapter 7; and Dan C. Lortie, "The Balance of Control and Autonomy in Elementary School Teaching," in Amitai Etzioni, ed., *The Semi-Professions and Their Organization,* New York: The Free Press, 1969.

if the requisite number of students, few of whom could afford to
pay tuition, were to be trained.[9]

The result was the creation of a new, publicly financed institution, the normal school, which in this period recruited women
at the end of eight years of elementary schooling. For the most
part, the women came from social classes that did not then receive advanced education. For them, a career as a teacher was a
decided move up the social ladder, a fact that caused many right-
thinking people to oppose the creation of normal schools.

ITEM: "Many thought it was an error to educate girls above
their station in life," a New York City journalist wrote in 1870,
commenting on the reaction to the establishment of the Female
Normal and High School (now Hunter College), "because superior education made them discontented and caused them to
look down on their less-informed parents. Some thought the
higher education of girls would greatly lessen the supply of
servants, and others thought that teachers in elementary schools
needed to know very little more than the children they taught."

To their generally eager students, the normal schools offered
training designed to produce competence in the classroom. As
Cyrus Pierce, principal of the first public normal school, defined
the role in 1851, "The art of teaching must be made the great,
the paramount, the only concern."

And so a second tradition, emphasizing professional or technical training rather than liberal education, was established. It
took firm root after the Civil War, the number of state normal
schools jumping from thirty-five in 1865 to 103 in 1890 and
perhaps twice that number just after the turn of the century.
The normal schools never were able to devote themselves
exclusively to professional education, however. Students entered
with so many gaps in their own education that the normal
schools were forced to offer academic instruction as well; how
teach someone how to teach reading or arithmetic when he
himself could barely read or multiply? But given the brevity of
the training period—anywhere from six weeks to two years—
the normal schools had little choice but to gear their academic instruction exclusively to the requirements of the elementary school classroom. The rapid adoption of the Quincy

[9] Christopher Jencks and David Riesman, *The Academic Revolution*,
New York: Doubleday, 1968, pp. 231–6.

Plan of graded classrooms made it possible to narrow that instruction to what teachers needed to know for the specific grade they were to teach. Thus, the normal schools could not hope to do more than give their students some knowledge of subject matter, along with a bag of tricks—the so-called "art of teaching"—with which to teach it. Their function was as narrow as it was explicit: to turn out competent technicians for the schools as they were, not educational leaders or innovators. It was simply taken for granted that the leadership role would remain where it was and had always been—in the hands of talented amateurs like Horace Mann.[10]

This narrow view of the teacher's role was not regarded as a weakness at the time; events proved otherwise. School attendance grew far more rapidly than anyone could have anticipated, as a result of mass immigration, a high rate of natural population growth, and the spread of compulsory attendance laws. In the last three decades of the century, school enrollment more than doubled, from 6,872,000 to 15,503,000, as the proportion of school-age population enrolled in school rose from 57 percent to 72 percent. Equally important, individual school systems became much larger and more complex as a result of rapid urbanization; by 1900, 40 percent of the population lived in urban areas—four times the proportion in 1840, when the normal school movement was beginning.

These changes produced a whole new set of problems. It was one thing to advocate universal public education, the lay leaders discovered, and quite another to provide it. Faced with sky-rocketing enrollments and dangerously overcrowded facilities, large school systems required a new species of educational leader, the professional administrator, to take over the day-to-day task of running the schools—a task grown too complicated and too time-consuming for local school boards to handle. The urban schools also needed new kinds of teachers, armed with new curricula and new teaching methods. Providing any kind of meaningful education to the hordes of poverty-stricken and frequently non-English-speaking children who filled the classrooms to overflowing—superintendents spoke wistfully of re-

[10] Cf. Lawrence A. Cremin, "Horace Mann's Legacy," in Cremin, ed., *The Republic and the School: Horace Mann on the Education of Free Men,* New York: Teachers College Press, 1957; and Robert W. Lynn, *Protestant Strategies in Education,* New York: Association Press, 1964; Jencks and Riesman, *The Academic Revolution.*

ducing class size to sixty children per teacher—was simply beyond the capacity of most normal school graduates.[11]

But where were these teachers to come from? Who was to develop the new curricula and the new teaching methods, and who was to train teachers in their use? Where were the administrators to come from, and who was to educate them, and in what way? Only one source seemed possible—the university, which was itself undergoing an enormous expansion in size and a metamorphosis in organization, outlook, and quality. For a time—roughly speaking, from about 1885 to 1905, a brief but critical period in the history of public education—it looked as though the university would take on this new leadership role. Some of the most distinguished university presidents, for example —men like Charles Eliot of Harvard, Daniel Coit Gilman of Johns Hopkins, and Frederick A. P. Barnard of Columbia— worked closely with superintendents of schools, professors of education, and the National Education Association to devise new approaches to public education.

So did a number of the most distinguished university scholars. In February 1887, for example, Nicholas Murray Butler, who had been attracted to the study of education by Barnard, assumed the presidency of the Industrial Education Association. Two months later the Association established the New York College for the Training of Teachers—what a few years later became Teachers College—and Butler became its president and principal professor.[12]

Butler was joined in the study of education by such men as the psychologist G. Stanley Hall and the philosopher John Dewey. "A distinct division of labor is indicated as regards training in the science and art of education," Dewey wrote in 1896. "There must be some schools whose main task is to train the rank and file of teachers—schools whose function is to supply the great army of teachers with the weapons of their calling and direct them as to their use." But such schools were no longer enough, he went on to argue. There was a need as well for new kinds of schools concerned with the education "not of the rank

---

[11] Cf. Lawrence A. Cremin, *The Transformation of the School,* Chapters 1–5.
[12] Cf. Cremin, *The Transformation of the School,* Chapter 5; and Lee J. Cronbach and Patrick Suppes, *Disciplined Inquiry for Education,* New York: The National Academy of Education, 1968, Chapter 2.

and file, but of the leaders of our educational system—teachers in normal and training schools, professors of pedagogy, superintendents, [and] principals of schools in our large cities."

What Dewey proposed was that universities create schools of education devoted "to the work of pedagogical discovery and experimentation" at an advanced level. It was "obvious, without argument," that this was a responsibility the universities could and indeed had to fulfill. The schools desperately needed expert guidance and direction, and there was no centralized governmental bureau to provide it. Hence it was up to the universities "to gather together and focus the best of all that emerges in the great variety of present practice, to test it scientifically, to work it out into shape for concrete use, and to issue it to the public educational system with the imprimatur, not of governmental coercion, but of scientific verification."[13]

Unfortunately, the rigorous and systematic study of education that Dewey urged never took hold. If it had, the liberal and technical traditions of teacher education would have merged within the university, giving the professional preparation of teachers a broad philosophic and humanistic cast. Instead, a rift between academicians and educationists developed after 1905, or thereabouts, with the result that the technical tradition took hold in the universities as well as in the normal schools.

What happened, in part, was that the newly created university departments and schools of education were overwhelmed by the unexpected need to train huge numbers of high school teachers, as the extension of free public schooling to the secondary level produced an explosive rise in the number of high school students.

ITEM: In 1890, there were only 203,000 students enrolled in secondary school, out of a total enrollment of 12,520,000. But the number of high school students increased two and a half times by 1900, and doubled again in each of the next two decades. By 1920, therefore, some 2,200,000 students were attending high school—ten times the number in 1890, when the university study of education was just beginning. By contrast, the number of elementary students increased 30 percent in the same period.

13 John Dewey, "Pedagogy as a University Discipline," *University Record* (University of Chicago Press), September 18, 1896, and September 25, 1896.

Only the universities, and to a lesser degree, the liberal arts colleges could attempt to meet the resulting demand for high school teachers, since most normal schools still admitted students who had no more than an elementary education themselves. Since most of the new public high schools simply took over the traditional academic curriculum of the private academies, it was taken for granted that high school teachers needed a degree in the subject or subjects they were going to teach, along with some training in pedagogy. In most universities, however, the academic departments wanted no part of this latter function, and they gladly delegated it to the department or school of education. By World War I, therefore, most major universities—private ones like Chicago, Columbia, Harvard, and Stanford, as well as public universities like Michigan, Wisconsin, and Illinois—had schools of education, some of them quite large.

But universalizing high school attendance forced the normal schools to change as well. For one thing, the spread of free local high schools cut into their clientele by giving girls a chance to get a secondary education while living at home; until the turn of the century or thereabouts, most girls wanting a free secondary education had no alternative but to attend a normal school. The incentive to attend a normal school was reduced still more by the fact that new kinds of respectable white-collar jobs were opening up for girls—as clerical workers, secretaries, telephone operators, retail sales clerks, and so on. The growth of public high schools also challenged the normal schools' near-monopoly of the market for elementary school teachers: high school graduates were at least as old and well-educated as normal school graduates, and considered themselves just as well qualified to teach the three R's.

At the same time, however, the growing number of female high school graduates enabled the normal schools to raise their admission standards, thereby becoming more like the colleges and universities. One by one, the normal schools began to require a high school diploma for admission, and then to lengthen their course of study to three years and later to four. This attempt to make normal schools more like colleges was strongly encouraged by their faculties, more and more of whom were university graduates. In time, as normal schools won permission to award the Bachelor of Arts or Bachelor of Sciences degree, their new status became legitimized by a change of name from "State Normal School" to "State Teachers College."

This change was only the beginning. Once they became colleges, the normal schools felt obliged to hire university men with doctorates, which made them dependent for their faculties on university graduate programs in education. As Jencks and Riesman observe, these new faculty members, most of whom sported Ed.D. rather than Ph.D. degrees, "often had little idea what academic research was about, much less how to do it, but they did have a fairly clear idea how the academic pecking order was organized and what constituted respectability in the university world."

The result was pressure from within as well as without to imitate the more prestigious liberal arts colleges and universities. The first step usually was to expand into training teachers for secondary as well as elementary schools. This meant broadening the curriculum to permit students to "major" in the academic subjects taught in high schools, which in turn meant recruiting faculty members who had Ph.D.'s in these academic subjects. Equally important, it meant admitting large numbers of male students; then, as now, the majority of high school teachers were male, the majority of elementary teachers female. But many of the male students decided at some point during their education, or after graduation, that teaching was not the career they wanted; some were attracted initially to the teachers college less by the idea of becoming a teacher than by the chance to earn a B.A. at a lower cost than elsewhere.

This change in student body created a new set of opportunities for the state teachers colleges: instead of being tied to the teaching profession, they could expand their size, and hopefully also their prestige, by attaching themselves to more prestigious occupations. Most of the state teachers colleges, therefore, have evolved into state colleges through the addition of programs for students headed for business, engineering, social work, journalism, and a host of other careers besides teaching. Many have taken a further step, becoming regional universities, through the addition of graduate programs, e.g., Western Michigan University, Arizona State University, Southern Illinois University, and Kent State University. The result has been the virtual elimination of the single-purpose teachers college in the United States, and a considerable blurring (though by no means the elimination) of the differences among the various institutions that prepare teachers.[14]

[14] The 297 state colleges and regional universities affiliated with the American Association of State Colleges and Universities (AASCU),

III

Despite all these changes, the rift between academicians and educationists that developed after the turn of the century has never healed. For the most part, the education faculties have remained isolated from the faculties of arts and sciences, and their relations have generally been characterized by mutual suspicion and distrust, at times bordering on outright hostility. The intensity of the rift, and the speed with which it came about, is reflected in Nicholas Murray Butler's changing attitudes. Butler had waxed eloquent over what he termed his "vigorous and enthusiastic service" to the National Education Association during the 1890s. "It is difficult to convey my sense of the real distinction of the men who in so great numbers adorned our educational system at that time," he later recalled. "They were certainly a most extraordinary group. They were not all philosophers by any means, but they were almost without exception scholars. They were admirable administrators and, what is more important, they were powerful personalities."[15] But after 1905 or thereabouts, he complained, what had been an organization of educational statesmen concerned with ideas and institutions degenerated into "a large popular assembly dominated by a very inferior class of teachers and school officials whose main object appeared to be personal advancement."[16]

Notwithstanding Butler's strictures, the academicians bore a large share of the blame; most arts and sciences faculties simply refused to accept responsibility for teacher education. "In the nineteenth century they had been quite ready to leave to the normal schools the task of preparing teachers for the elementary schools. When social changes in this century transformed the nature of the high school, the typical college professor himself was viewing with disgust and dismay what was happening in the schools," Dr. James B. Conant writes, adding parenthetically that he is "reporting on personal observations of fifty years." Hence "with few exceptions, college professors turned their backs on the problem of mass secondary education and eyed

most of which began as normal schools, enroll just over 20 percent of the nation's college students but account for nearly half the annual crop of new teachers. Cf. E. Alden Dunham, *Colleges of the Forgotten Americans: A Profile of State Colleges and Regional Universities,* New York: McGraw-Hill, 1969.

[15] Quoted in Koerner, *The Miseducation of American Teachers.*

[16] Quoted in Cronbach and Suppes, *Disciplined Inquiry for Education.*

with envy Great Britain and the Continent, where such problems did not exist."[17]

They turned their backs for several reasons. Some were genuinely skeptical about whether education was a proper subject for university study. Others were simply hostile, viewing the creation of departments or schools of education as a form of academic *lèse majesté*. With familiar academic hauteur, they regarded schooling (especially schooling for the masses) as a subject not worthy of the concern of genuine (and gentlemanly) scholars. More than snobbery was—and is—involved, however. For an academic professor to accept the legitimacy of the educationist's claim is to admit the possibility that his own teaching, or that of his graduate students, might be improved by the study of pedagogy—or that he should take his own teaching seriously. Some academicians are reluctant to make that admission because of the pride they take in their own teaching ability. Others were, and are, reluctant because of their lack of interest in teaching.

ITEM: "I resent having to leave my reading or writing to teach," a political science professor told me.

ITEM: "I went to graduate school to become an anthropologist, not a teacher," an anthropology professor observed. "I'd resent taking time out from my work to study teaching."

Whatever the reasons, the result has been the same: few scholars have been willing to be bothered with what they considered the pedestrian job of educating teachers for the public schools.

If academicians look down their noses at professors of education, however, it is at least in part because the educationists all too often have given them cause for disdain. They are notable exceptions, of course, and always have been; yet James D. Koerner's acerbic criticism is all too close to the mark. "It is an indecorous thing to say and obviously offensive to most educationists," he writes, "but it is the truth and it should be said: the inferior intellectual quality of the Education faculty is *the* fundamental limitation of the field . . ."[18]

[17] James B. Conant, *The Education of American Teachers,* New York: McGraw-Hill, 1964.
[18] James D. Koerner, *The Miseducation of American Teachers,* Baltimore, Md.: Penguin Books, 1964.

The study of education began in a promising enough way, as a branch of philosophy, which until the late nineteenth century embraced almost every aspect of the study of man and society. But this was the period in which the social sciences were breaking away from philosophy and establishing themselves as separate academic disciplines. Educationists wanted the same status within the university that psychologists, economists, and sociologists had just acquired, insisting that education was (or was about to become) a science in its own right. But they also demanded the same administrative independence and autonomy that the professional schools of law and medicine had acquired, arguing that education was a profession as well as a science.[19]

Wanting the best of two worlds, the educationists managed only to get the worst of both. They gained autonomy, but not academic recognition or status; with few exceptions, they have remained where they began, at the bottom of the academic pecking order. The reason, in large measure, was that the educationists failed to understand the profound difference between a science or academic discipline and a profession, a mistake that has haunted both teacher education and educational research to this day.

The point is that education is *not* a science or discipline, and cannot be made into one. The mark of a discipline is a distinctive mode of inquiry, a conceptual framework which defines the way questions are asked and answered, thereby defining and limiting the subjects to be investigated. "In spite of their strident assertions that they were creating a discipline," Michael Katz writes, the early educationists "developed no distinctive mode of inquiry and refused to limit their territory. They claimed to be renaissance men." The result was that "by their own actions educationists became the outcasts of the academic community. They would not adopt the badge of specialized competence within a distinctive area of inquiry, the mark of status within the university."[20]

They would not because they could not: teaching is a profession, or if you will, an art. Like other professions, especially law,

[19] Cf. Michael B. Katz, "From Theory to Survey in Graduate Schools of Education," *Journal of Higher Education,* XXXVI, 1966.
[20] Michael B. Katz, "From Theory to Survey in Graduate Schools of Education." Cf. also Cronbach and Suppes, *Disciplined Inquiry for Education;* and Israel Scheffler, "University Scholarship and the Education of Teachers," *Teachers College Record,* Vol. 70, No. 1, October 1968.

medicine, and engineering, teaching can and should draw on a number of sciences and disciplines; but it must go beyond them. The professional, as Harvey Brooks puts it, "must be thought of as the middle-man or intermediary between a body of knowledge and society—a lay society. To the professional belongs the responsibility of using existing and new knowledge to provide services the society wants and needs. This is an art because it demands action as well as thought, and action must always be taken on the basis of incomplete knowledge."

Professionals must act on incomplete knowledge because science does not, and as a rule, cannot directly generate rules of practice, and certainly not rules to cover the almost infinite variety of behavior a teacher will experience in the classroom. "You make a great, a very great mistake," William James told the teachers of Cambridge, Massachusetts, in 1892, in a passage we have already quoted in Chapter 6, "if you think that psychology, being the science of the mind's law, is something from which you can deduce definite programmes and schemes and methods of instruction for immediate classroom use. Psychology is a science, and teaching is an art; and sciences never generate arts directly out of themselves. An intermediary inventive mind must make the application, by using its originality." James went on to say:

> The science of logic never made a man reason rightly, and the science of ethics (if there be such a thing) never made a man behave rightly. The most such sciences can do is to help us catch ourselves up and check ourselves, if we start to reason or to behave wrongly; and to criticize ourselves more articulately after we have made mistakes. A science only lays down lines within which the rules of the art must fall, laws which the follower of the art must not transgress; but what particular thing he shall positively do within those lines is left exclusively to his own genius . . . And so everywhere the teaching must *agree* with the psychology, but need not necessarily be the only kind of teaching that would so agree; for many diverse methods of teaching may equally well agree with psychological laws.[21]

The philosopher Josiah Royce advanced much the same argument. "Teaching is an art," he argued in a famous essay in the

[21] William James, *Talks to Teachers on Psychology and to Students on Some of Life's Ideals,* New York; Dover Publications, 1962.

first issue of the *Educational Review*. "There is indeed no science of education. What there is, is the world of science furnishing material for the educator to study." The educator who turns to that world "for exact and universally valid direction" will fail to get it, and deservedly so, for that is not the business of science. The teacher who turns to science for insight and illumination, on the other hand, will be much the better for it.[22]

Dewey understood this well, and urged that the study of education be grounded thoroughly in at least half a dozen academic disciplines. The educator, he argued, needed a thorough knowledge of psychology, philosophy (especially ethics, to illuminate the discussion of educational purpose), history (both the history of human thought and the history of education), and sociology and economics (to understand the complex and changing relations of school and society).

In their determination to establish education as a separate discipline as well as a separate profession, however, most educationists ignored Dewey's insistence that the study of education be rooted in philosophy and the social sciences. In the process, they both alienated and allowed themselves to become separated from their academic friends and supporters, and from the disciplines they represented. Teacher education still suffers as a result.

What happened, in part, was that the departments and schools of education came to maturity at a time when scholarly inquiry began to be dominated by the empirical and the statistical; quick to notice a trend and hungry for academic status, the educationists tried to follow suit, with unfortunate results. Giants like Dewey and Hall were at home in both theoretical and empirical investigation and saw the two as inextricably related; but most of their followers lacked the capacity or the interest to handle both modes of inquiry. "We lived in one long orgy of tabulation," Harold Rugg wrote of his pre–World War I work at the University of Illinois. "Mountains of facts were piled up, condensed, summarized and interpreted by the new quantitative technique. The air was full of normal curves, standard deviations, coefficients of correlation, regression equations."[23]

The result was empiricism gone wild, in which the survey became the foundation on which the entire study of education and

[22] Josiah Royce, "Is There a Science of Education?", *Educational Review*, I (January–February 1891), reprinted in Borrowman, *Teacher Education in America.*
[23] Quoted in Cremin, *The Transformation of the School.*

training of teachers was built. "The true basis for the final organization of the School of Education," Charles Judd, dean of the
University of Chicago's School of Education, wrote in 1923, "is
to be found in a complete survey of education." By surveying
what was—by analyzing the way in which the school system
was organized and run, breaking it down into its most minute
subdivisions—it would be possible, Judd argued, to "lay out all
the lines of inquiry which must be taken up if the schools of this
country are to be organized on a basis of fact rather than a basis
of tradition and opinion."[24]

ITEM: Shortly before Judd assumed the deanship, the University of Chicago's Graduate School of Education replaced its
general course in public school administration with separate
courses in school finance, the administrative management of
pupils, and the organization and supervision of the teaching
staff. On his accession, Judd dropped all courses in the philosophy of education and sharply reduced the offerings in the history
of education, while boasting that "there are now formulated and
offered in the School more detailed and specific courses . . .
than in any institution in the country."

Judd was merely following a trail that others had blazed. As
early as 1916, for example, Columbia's Teachers College was
offering specialized diplomas in no fewer than fifty-five separate
teaching and administrative positions.

The triumph of the survey approach brought the normal
school tradition of technical education into the university. The
educationists' outspoken eclecticism and empiricism and their
failure to develop any conceptual apparatus—their failure even
to develop any criteria by which the mounds of data they collected could be organized—made it impossible for them to
develop any coherent conception of what education was all
about. More important, it destroyed the normative orientation—
the sense of what education can and should be, the concern for
ends as well as means—that had distinguished the early study of
education at the university level from the technical approach of
the normal schools. Almost everywhere, in consequence, teacher

[24] Michael B. Katz, "From Theory to Survey in Graduate Schools of
Education." Cf. also Cronbach and Suppes, *Disciplined Inquiry for
Education,* Chapter 2.

education was geared to preparing teachers and administrators to be technicians in the schools as they were.

This general mindlessness—the failure, indeed the refusal, to organize teacher education around any conception or conceptions of what education could and should be, and the accompanying lack of interest in philosophy, history, sociology, and the other academic foundations of pedagogy—was intensified in the 1920s and '30s, when the second generation of education professors began taking over. For all their faults, the first generation had received their own education in the academic disciplines; there was no other kind of education when they had been students. The best of them, moreover—men like Paul Monroe, E. L. Thorndike, Lewis Terman—had been recruited from the academic disciplines and remained important figures in them; they saw themselves, in the main, as psychologists, philosophers, historians, with a deep interest in and commitment to education.

Their students, however, who began to occupy influential chairs in education in the 1920s, saw themselves as educationists with an interest in psychology, philosophy, or history. Having been trained by education professors rather than by academicians, the second generation of educationists felt little or no allegiance to the academic disciplines; and *their* students, who in turn formed the faculties of the rapidly growing state colleges and universities, were even more estranged. This inbreeding among education faculties served to dilute still further the intellectual and scholarly component in teacher education and to increase the isolation of the educationists from the faculties of arts and sciences, with whom they felt less and less comfortable.

IV

We are all the victims of this history. Certainly much of what is wrong with teacher education, and to a degree with the schools themselves, stems directly from this divorce between the faculties of education and the faculties of arts and sciences.

One of the most unfortunate consequences of the educationists' isolation from the mainstream of academic life and of the academicians' abdication of responsibility for teacher education is that it left control of both teacher education and the schools in the hands of an informal and largely self-perpetuating educationist "establishment." The main components are the state departments of education, the associations of education professors, public school teachers and administrators, and teachers colleges and education schools, and the national and regional accrediting agencies. They constitute an establishment by virtue of their shared outlook and community of interest; the latter is reinforced by a series of interlocking directorates in which all roads somehow lead to the National Education Association.[25]

The establishment's power stems directly from its control over the teacher certification machinery—the rules and procedures which in each state determine who can hold a teaching certificate or license. In most states, certification is limited to those who have completed a prescribed program of studies, including a minimum number of courses in education, or to those who have received a degree from a college or university whose teacher education program has been accredited by NCATE. The requirements for certification are nominally set by the fifty state departments of education, which have ultimate control over all aspects of schooling. In most states, however, the departments work closely with, and are heavily influenced by, the local TEPS affiliate and the NEA-affiliated state teachers association, which usually is one of the largest and most influential lobbies in the state. Although only about half of all public school teachers belong to the NEA itself, the great majority belong to the state associations, in part because they are expected (or think they are expected) to do so by their administrative superiors.[26]

[25] For example, the powerful National Council for the Accreditation of Teacher Education (NCATE) makes its influence felt through its close relations with the National Association of State Directors of Teacher Education and Certification and with the state affiliates of the NEA's National Commission on Teacher Education and Professional Standards (TEPS). Of NCATE's nineteen members, six are appointed by TEPS, which Conant describes as "the political arm of the NEA in achieving state acceptance of NCATE accreditation," and seven by the American Association of Colleges for Teacher Education (AACTE), which is an NEA department supervised by the same NEA official who serves as the TEPS director. (TEPS and AACTE also provide the bulk of NCATE's budget.) Two more NCATE members are appointed by the Council of Chief State School Officers and the National Association of State Directors of Teacher Education and Certification, ostensibly independent organizations that occupy rent-free space provided by the NEA. Cf. James B. Conant, *The Education of American Teachers*, Chapters 1 and 2; James D. Koerner, *The Miseducation of American Teachers*, Chapter 7, and *Who Controls American Education?*, Boston: Beacon Press, 1968.

[26] The NEA and its state affiliates traditionally have been dominated by administrators, despite the fact that teachers comprise the bulk of the membership. This is beginning to change, however. To protect itself

A close alliance between the education faculties and the coalition of teacher and administrator groups and state officials was natural, for a variety of reasons. One of the differences between professional schools and graduate schools of arts and sciences is that the faculties of the latter derive their status almost entirely from within the Academy, whereas professional school faculties also look outside the university, to their own professional peers, for recognition and support. For educationists, there was no alternative; their low status within the academic world and the evident contempt in which their academic colleagues held them forced them to look elsewhere for recognition and support. Since many of them had been teachers, principals, or superintendents before joining a college or university faculty of education, they felt comfortable with the schoolmen, many of whom, after all, had been their students.

The educationists have been dependent upon the schoolmen as well. For one thing, they need the goodwill of superintendents and principals if their current or future students are to find jobs. They need the schoolmen's goodwill too, if their students are to have any practice-teaching experience. Few schools of education, if any, have a laboratory school large enough to provide teaching practice for all their students; most need the cooperation of a number of schools or school districts. The education professors also need the schoolmen's political leverage to establish and maintain certification requirements for new teachers, without which they might have far fewer students.

The notion that there should be some form of control over who may be permitted to teach emerged simultaneously in the late medieval period with the growth of schooling itself.[27] In the United States, local secular authorities assumed control of the certification machinery from the beginning, using two devices—character witnesses and an oral or written examination —to screen teachers for their tax-supported schools. But since most local school boards had difficulty finding *any* teachers,

---

against inroads by the more militant American Federation of Teachers, the NEA has had to become much more militant on behalf of its teacher members; this new militancy has created strains between classroom teachers and the associations of principals and superintendents, with predictions that the latter groups may have to pull out of the NEA.
[27] *The Education of American Teachers.* Cf. Walter J. Ong, S.J., "Educationists and the Tradition of Learning," in Ong, *The Barbarian Within,* New York: Macmillan, 1962; and Borrowman, *Teacher Education in America.*

their tendency often was to tailor the examinations to suit the candidates that happened to be available. In many districts, moreover, especially those in rural areas, the examiners were themselves too unschooled to develop or evaluate academic standards, and local ethnic or religious prejudices, personal favoritism, or simple graft frequently were the determining factors.

As state supervision of public schooling took hold in the 1830s and after, the newly emerging state education departments began taking over the certification function.[28] The growth of state licensing paralleled the rapid expansion of public schools and the creation of public normal schools to train teachers for them. Since most of the public normal schools were operated by, or under the supervision of, the state education departments, the departments tended to accept completion of the normal school course of study as a basis for certification, with teachers receiving their education elsewhere being required to pass an examination. As a result, the normal school emphasis on technical training in how to teach carried over into state certification requirements, and state education department personnel developed close working relationships with educationists well before the creation of the NEA and the various state and national associations of teachers and administrators.

Those relationships stood the educationists in good stead after the turn of the century, when the states began to depend on academically oriented colleges and universities as well as normal schools for their supply of teachers. The result was the development of new regulations which required candidates for certification to take a series of specified courses in education, it being assumed that the colleges and universities would make sure that their graduates were adequately prepared in the subjects they were preparing to teach. When it became clear that the liberal arts faculties were unwilling to accept that responsibility, and even more unwilling to tailor their curricula to the needs of prospective teachers, the state departments began adding specific requirements for a teaching "major" as well.

Increasingly, therefore, certification came to depend not on an

---

[28] Control has never been complete. Although the states have clear sovereignty over the schools, the strength of the tradition of local control has been such that most states have delegated operation to the various localities. As a result of this ambiguity, a number of large cities, most notably New York, Chicago, Philadelphia, and St. Louis, still maintain their own certification machinery, separate from that of the state.

examination, but on the completion of a set of courses specified by the state. Not surprisingly, the new requirements—imposed on the colleges and universities by a coalition of educationists, schoolmen, and state education department personnel—increased the hostility between the education and the arts and sciences faculties. Forgetting their own refusal to accept responsibility for teacher education, the academicians increasingly came to feel, with considerable justification, that their colleagues in the education faculty would have far fewer students, and indeed might not have been hired at all, had it not been for the fact that the courses they taught had been mandated by the state.

In recent years, moreover, as attacks on the educationists have been stepped up, with laymen and academicians demanding more academic and less pedagogical training for teachers, education faculties, especially in the state universities, have looked to the schoolmen's political muscle for support in maintaining their separate identity.

ITEM: In discussions growing out of the search for a new dean, the president of a large midwestern state university suggested the desirability of a closer association between the college of education and the university's college of arts and sciences. Though couched in the most tentative and gingerly fashion, the mere suggestion touched off a storm. Members of the education faculty were united in opposition, for fear that they would become a mere department within the larger arts college. Their insecurity reflected years of debate between the two faculties over questions ranging from who shall train the school psychologists (the department of psychology or the department of educational psychology) to who shall decide the curriculum for a prospective high school English (or history, mathematics, or science) teacher.

The president might have been able to resolve the education faculty's fears or override their objections. What stopped him, at least for the moment, was the reaction from what he describes as "the educational establishment within the state, that is, the principals and superintendents," most of whom are graduates of the state university. No threats were made—but the president quickly learned that the superintendents and principals would regard any merger between the education and arts and sciences faculties "as an indication that the University was no longer interested in 'professional education,'" and that they would, in consequence, transfer their allegiance and support to other state institutions maintaining a traditional program. Such a transfer not only would dry up the job market for the university's teacher graduates but might also jeopardize the university's financial support in the state legislature. "I naturally anticipated adverse reactions," the president observes, "but I am surprised by its intensity."

The alliance between the educationists and the schoolmen is not a one-way street, however; the schoolmen look to the educationists as often as the educationists look to them. For one thing, the alma mater tie works both ways; the tie is particularly close in the case of school superintendents and state education department and NEA officials, most of whom have doctorates from, or have done graduate work at, some graduate school of education. One of the main functions of graduate study in any field is to instill a professional ethic and point of view—what sociologists call the process of socialization into the profession. The process is particularly intense in education because of the defensiveness most educationists feel about their status in the university and in society at large. Hence it is natural and inevitable that the schoolmen look to their former teachers, i.e., to the education faculties, for guidance and support.

They need the educationists' support for other, more subtle reasons. One of the marks of a profession is its ability to control entry—to decide who may practice the profession. In the case of medicine and law, the criteria for licensing are set by the professional associations, which have considerably greater power, and use it more arbitrarily, than the educationist establishment, a fact which critics like Koerner and Bestor tend to ignore. (They sometimes write as though the educationists' attempt to control entry to, and education for, their profession was a phenomenon unique to education.) The states have delegated the licensing power to the medical and legal associations, along with the power to revoke licenses, out of a conviction that the practice of medicine and law requires esoteric knowledge which laymen do not, and perhaps cannot, possess. Whether this is so or not is beside the point. What is crucial, as Dan C. Lortie of the University of Chicago argues, is not the actual state of professional knowledge, but whether the relevant publics—clients and governmental agencies—*believe* that knowledge to be both essential and arcane. If they do—if they believe that professional knowledge is the monopoly of the members of the profession—they are likely to accord those members a large degree of autonomy, not only in controlling entrance to the profession, but in defining the way in which the profession is to be practiced.[29]

Teachers have always wanted, but have never had, this kind of autonomy and control, for laymen have refused to recognize their professional knowledge as either essential or esoteric. For all the importance attached to public education, Americans, particularly those of the upper middle class, who comprise the bulk of school board membership, have been unwilling to put teachers on any kind of pedestal. As Lortie points out, the familiar quip that "no one ever died of a split infinitive" reflects the popular view that the teacher's knowledge, unlike that of the doctor, is something less than vital. More important, perhaps, while virtually no laymen have attended medical school or law school, almost every school board member (and every taxpayer) has been to public school, and most feel themselves competent to decide matters of educational policy—an outlook dating back to the eighteenth and nineteenth centuries, when little more than bare literacy was expected of elementary school teachers.

Thus, the tradition of lay control has been too strong to permit the kind of delegation of the licensing power to the professional associations of teachers or administrators that has characterized medicine and law.[30] The same tradition has prevented teachers and administrators from gaining the power over their own curriculum and teaching methods that English schoolmen traditionally have had, or that American college professors now exercise.

A superintendent of schools, for example, has no policy-

---

[29] Dan C. Lortie, "The Partial Professionalization of Elementary Teaching, in Amitai Etzioni, ed., *The Semi-Professions and Their Organization,* New York: The Free Press, 1969. Cf. also Howard M. Vollmer and Donald L. Mills, eds., *Professionalization,* Englewood Cliffs, N.J.: Prentice-Hall, 1966; A. M. Carr-Saunders and P. A. Wilson, *The Professions,* London: Oxford Press, 1933; Nelson B. Henry, ed., *Education for the Professions,* The Sixty-first Yearbook of the National Society for the Study of Education, Part II, 1962.

[30] That difference is narrowing rapidly, however, in response to a growing realization that medicine is too important to be left to the doctors. Recent experience has made it abundantly clear, for example, that a radical reorganization of medical practice and medical education is essential if Americans, and especially poor Americans, are to receive adequate medical care—and that such a reorganization will not be possible unless the medical profession's almost total control of medical practice is broken and a large measure of lay control introduced. Much the same is true in law, where advocates of expanded legal services to the poor have had to fight the various state and national bar associations.

making powers of his own. Policy is set by the school board, whose authority and responsibility is usually set forth in state law. The superintendent is the chief executive officer of the board, charged with implementing its policies; while he may recommend different policies to the board, he is expected to avoid substantive disagreements in public. Since the demarcation between policy and its implementation is not always sharp and clear, a strong or politically sophisticated superintendent frequently makes policy through the exercise of his administrative discretion; he may also influence the board's policy decisions through force of personality, or by shaping the agenda for board meetings. But the usual situation for superintendents is "one of tenuous rather than assured possession of position."[31]

If there is some ambiguity surrounding the superintendent's professional status, there is none at all where teachers are concerned; they are employees, pure and simple. They have a measure of protection as a result of tenure regulations, although imaginative superintendents can usually persuade tenured teachers or principals to leave. But whether they have tenure or not, teachers have no official power to govern their own operations; unlike universities, school systems do not have faculty senates or other devices through which teachers can participate in academic decision-making.[32]

It has always been thus. As we have already seen, the normal school movement viewed teachers as technicians rather than as autonomous professionals, and trained them accordingly. This view was solidified in the first few decades of this century, when superintendents of school were caught up in the national fervor for "Scientific Management." Slavishly imitating the way they (sometimes mistakenly) thought corporate executives operated, superintendents tried to control the most minute details

[31] Lortie, "The Balance of Control and Autonomy in Elementary School Teaching." Cf. also Neal Gross, *Who Runs Our Schools?*, New York: John Wiley, 1958; John M. Foskett, *The Normative World of the Elementary School Principal*, Eugene, Oregon: Center for the Advanced Study of Educational Administration, University of Oregon, 1967.

[32] Some of the local units of the American Federation of Teachers, most notably the United Federation of Teachers, the powerful New York City chapter, have begun to demand teacher participation in decisions about curriculum and related matters. This represents a major shift in direction; in contrast to the NEA's traditional concern for professional status, the AFT, until now, at least, has insisted on defining relations between teachers and their superiors in traditional employer-employee terms.

of school operation, from the number of paper clips and pieces of chalk used to the curriculum and the way it was taught; teachers were production-line workers whose every move had to be controlled and checked. The schools still bear the marks of this "cult of efficiency," as it has been called.[33] Witness the fact that most teachers still punch time clocks and are still expected to submit daily lesson plans for their principal's approval.

Understandably, therefore, teachers and administrators have been engaged in a long and wistful, and sometimes desperate, search for professional status. If they could not persuade state legislatures to give them the same policing powers that the medical and bar associations enjoy, they could insist that the state itself restrict entry to men and women who had mastered the art of teaching or of educational administration. To do so, however, they had to argue that there was in fact a body of essential professional knowledge that they—not laymen, and not academicians—possessed.

Enter the education professor! For if teachers and administrators possessed some expertise that set them apart from laymen whose general education was equal, and in many cases, more extensive than theirs, they could only have acquired it in the course of their professional education. To argue that they had gained their expertise in the field would have served them badly, for it would have confirmed what most academicians and most laymen had been claiming all along—namely, that anyone with a college education could learn to teach on the job. The only body of esoteric knowledge to which teachers and administrators could point as distinguishing them from other well-educated people, therefore, was that provided in professional education courses. Hence they have insisted that prospective teachers, like aspiring doctors and lawyers, must first complete a prescribed course of professional study. With the aid of their allies in the state education departments and the college and university schools and departments of education, they have succeeded in embodying this insistence in state certification requirements.

The professional teacher and administrator associations thus have expended a large part of their political capital in the effort to establish and maintain these certification requirements, for

[33] Raymond E. Callahan, *Education and the Cult of Efficiency,* University of Chicago Press, 1962.

they have served their members well. If there were no requirements, school boards might hire anyone with a college degree,
whether out of conviction, convenience, economy, or patronage;
the result might be to flood the market, and thus to hold down
teachers' salaries. Requiring all teachers to have a special type
of training, on the other hand, restricts the supply of teachers
and thus makes it easier for their leaders to negotiate higher
salaries and better working conditions. Certification requirements
provide important psychic benefits as well. They make teaching
seem more like a profession, by guaranteeing that not just anyone
can become a teacher; in this sense, certification, along with the
professional education courses they require, serve an important
symbolic function. They also provide a protective shield for
teachers and administrators in their dealings with parents or
other laymen, making it possible for them to justify their decisions on the grounds of superior knowledge.

v

Certification requirements have provided even more protection
to the faculties of education, guaranteeing them a large and
steady demand for their course offerings. The results have been
stultifying; while there are notable exceptions, of course, the
intellectual level of most education courses and programs borders on the scandalous. Indeed, the ever-charitable Dr. Conant,
who shuns controversy and generalization, leaning over backward to find *some* good wherever he goes, is almost acerbic when
he describes teacher education programs. "One would like to
look at the education of future teachers in terms of a free market
of ideas," he writes in *The Education of American Teachers,*
"and this I endeavoured to do in my visits to teacher-training
institutions during this study. But I came to the conclusion that
such an inquiry lacks reality. The idea of state certification is so
thoroughly accepted that I have found it hard to get a serious
discussion of the question, 'What would you recommend if there
were no state requirements?'"

Serious discussion was difficult in part because certification
requirements have saved educationists from the necessity of
having to justify—or even think about—their programs. Certainly, few of them have asked themselves why they are doing
what they are doing, or how it affects the kind of students they

turn out. Indeed, this kind of question is almost discouraged by certification requirements, which make licensing depend not on a student's ability as a teacher but on whether he has taken the requisite number of courses.

ITEM: In visiting schools of education around the country, I made a point of asking the deans why it mattered that a student was educated in his school of education rather than some other; we asked in what way their graduates differed from teachers coming from other schools of education, and what, if anything, in their program accounted for the difference. Few deans were able to answer the questions; with a handful of exceptions, to be discussed in Chapter 11, the overwhelming majority had never even considered the question before.

ITEM: From an interview with the dean of the school of education at a Midwestern university.

> Q. Do you have some conception of what kind of teacher you're trying to turn out?
> A. Right. That's exactly right. Now we have decided that we would do a kind of job analysis and say, "Now, in the next four years, here are experiences you ought to get, here is knowledge you'll need in some way to get a hold of. And knowledge about learning; for example, you ought to know how to use audio-visual aids."

ITEM: From an interview with the Director of Secondary Teacher Education at a major Southern college of education.

> Q. Do you have any model or conception of what a secondary teacher should be?
> A. No, I wouldn't say that we did have. It's a trite thing to say, but we just try to turn out the best that we can.
> Q. Your catalogue makes it seem as though you value academic success. . . .
> A. No, we don't emphasize any particular item in either the preparation or in the actual and direct experience. . . .

But Dr. Conant found discussion impeded by the educationists' sensitivity as well as by their mindlessness. "There is too much resentment of outside criticism, and too little effort toward vigorous internal criticism," he writes, adding that he "found the establishment's rigidity frightening."

ITEM: In order to carry through the reorganization of the elementary schools of North Dakota along the informal lines described in Chapter 7, the University of North Dakota felt it necessary to by-pass its own School of Education entirely. Instead of turning to the existing faculty, it established a completely new unit, the aptly named New School for Behavioral Studies in Education, to educate both undergraduates and experienced teachers in the new approach.

ITEM: The Charles F. Kettering Foundation's IDEA division sponsored a symposium on teacher education in early 1968 at which the participants were all first-year elementary school teachers. They were selected by asking a number of the leading schools of education to recommend one or more outstanding graduates. A number of institutions flatly refused to recommend anyone. "While they may have had reasons which they failed to make clear," the Conference Report explains, "their responses indicated that they might be fearful of what their graduates would say about their preparation."

And no wonder; few of the graduates who did attend the IDEA Conference had anything good to say about their training —an attitude that Conant found to be almost universal. "To be sure, by no means all students I interviewed were critical," he writes; "so many were, however, that I could not ignore their repeated comments that most of the educational offerings were 'Mickey Mouse' courses. There can be no doubt that at least in some institutions the courses given by professors of education have a bad name among undergraduates, particularly those intending to be high school teachers."

The bad name is well earned. Conant was particularly appalled, for example, by the stultifying introductory courses in the "foundations of education" which students were required to take in most of the schools he visited. At the hands of a philosopher and social critic like James E. McClellan of Temple University, to be sure, the "foundations" course can provide an intellectually exciting and rewarding insight into, and critique of, American education and society.[34] But most "foundations" courses, as Conant writes, consist of "scraps of history, philosophy, political theory, sociology, and pedagogical ideology"

[34] James E. McClellan, *Toward an Effective Critique of American Education,* New York: J. B. Lippincott, 1968.

patched together by instructors who "are not well trained in any one of the parent disciplines" and whose teaching style he found to be "far too reminiscent of the less satisfactory high school classes" he had visited. Although a growing number of educationists believe these courses should be dropped from the curriculum altogether, certification requirements in many states make their elimination impossible.[35]

Dr. Conant's unflattering assessment of teacher education is widely shared. "Course work in Education deserves its ill-repute," writes James D. Koerner, who does *not* lean over backward to be kind. "It is most often puerile, repetitious, dull, and ambiguous—incontestably so. Two factors make it this way: the limitations of the instructor, and the limitations of subject-matter that has been remorsely fragmented, sub-divided, and inflated, and that in many cases was not adequate in its uninflated state. That some teachers and courses in education can be found to equal the best in any of the academic areas is a happy fact," Koerner continues; "but it does not change the basic fact that the intellectual impoverishment of the course work remains a major characteristic of the field."[36]

The intellectual puerility of most foundation courses is matched by most courses in educational psychology, history, philosophy, and sociology. Yet there are notable exceptions— more so, in fact, than in foundations courses. Indeed, the past two decades have seen something of a renaissance in the study of the history, philosophy, sociology, and economics of education. In faculties of arts and sciences, distinguished scholars such as Robert K. Merton, David Riesman, James S. Coleman, Everett C. Hughes, Howard Becker, Martin Trow, Bernard Bailyn, Richard Hofstadter, Jerome Bruner, George Miller, Harry Levin, Herbert Simon, Theodore Schultz, Clark Kerr, Jerrold Zacharias, and the late Francis Friedman have turned their attention to problems of education. And within schools of education themselves, philosophers such as Israel Scheffler, Philip H. Phenix, and Maxine Greene, historians such as Lawrence A. Cremin, Merle Borrowman, and Robert W. Lynn, sociologists such as Edgar Z. Friedenberg, Fred L. Strodtbeck, and Alan B. Wilson, or psychologists such as Lee J. Cronbach, Benjamin S. Bloom, Lawrence Kohlberg, and Jerome Kagan

---

[35] Cf. James J. Shields, Jr., "Social Foundations of Education: The Problem of Relevance," *Teachers College Record,* Vol. 70, No. 1, October 1968.

[36] James D. Koerner, *The Miseducation of American Teachers.*

are turning out research and teaching courses that equal anything to be found in graduate or undergraduate schools of arts
and science.[37]

The wasteland of teacher education, virtually unrelieved by
hopeful exceptions, is the course work in "methods of teaching." "Those terrible methods courses," as Conant calls them,
tend to be both intellectually barren and professionally useless.
Some are so abstract as to have no contact with reality; what
passes for theory is a mass of platitudes and generalities. Some
courses focus entirely on the "how to" of teaching, presenting
a grab-bag of rules of thumb, unrelated to one another or to
any conception of teaching. Still other courses are glorified bull
sessions in which teacher and students exchange anecdotes.
Rarely do any of the courses make any effort to relate the
discussion of teaching methods to what the students may have
learned in their work in psychology, philosophy, or anything
else. More often than not, the professors teaching the courses
contradict their own dicta—for example, delivering long, dry
lectures on the importance of not lecturing. Indeed, there can
be no greater demonstration of the irrelevance of most methods
courses than the way the methods professors teach.

ITEM: The dean of a liberal arts college in a large Eastern
university arranges a short course in teaching methods for his
faculty, to be given by senior members of the faculty of the
university's graduate school of education. The course confirms
all the prejudices the liberal arts professors had had about educationists and adds a few more. At the first session, for example,
the educationist—the ed. school's most distinguished authority
on adult education—tells the assembled faculty that it is important for a teacher to see things from the learner's perspective
as well as his own. While he realizes that it may not always be
possible for them to do so, he goes on to say, it is nonetheless
essential that they try their very best to learn at least one new

[37] Schools of education pay a certain price, however, for the growing
emphasis on scholarship: scholars on education school faculties tend
to look to their colleagues in the arts and science faculty more than to
the teaching profession for recognition and status. The result is to subtly
downgrade the importance of public school teaching, and therefore of
teacher education, in favor of research and the education of what
Lawrence Cremin calls "second-level educators," i.e., those who will go
on to teach in schools of education. This, in turn, tends to draw the best
students away from public school teaching and into college and university
teaching.

thing about their subject each year, so that they can recapture, however fleetingly, the learner's perspective. (The second session is devoted in large measure to an exposition of the superiority of yellow chalk vis-à-vis white chalk.)

ITEM: A graduate course in "Methods for Teaching the Disadvantaged" at a West Coast school of education. The instructor asks the students, most of whom are experienced teachers, why it is important for them to understand the cultural background of their students and the social and political structure of the community in which their school is located. A physical education teacher eagerly responds, "That way, you know who to turn to when you need more baseballs or footballs or other supplies." The professor nods approvingly and moves on to the next topic for discussion.

What is wrong with teacher education, in short, is less that too much time is devoted to "how to" courses than that the "how to" courses do not teach anyone how to do anything, except perhaps bore a class of students. The shortcomings are most dramatic in the case of teachers going into lower-class schools, especially those with a predominantly black, Mexican-American, or Puerto Rican population.

ITEM: Midway through her first year of teaching in a Spanish Harlem junior high, a young graduate of the Harvard Graduate School of Education wrote Dean Theodore R. Sizer to complain about the inadequacy of her training.

> In your attempt to uplift the quality of teaching and materials you have us take courses from assistants and Ph.D. candidates who have had little teaching experience. And although they were extremely bright and charming people, their lack of experience "in the field" was a significant handicap. . . .
> How to tell you about JHS 45 . . . ?
> At 8:40 A.M. I am meant to be standing in the hall outside my classroom, welcoming my children, preventing them from running down the halls, killing each other, passing cigarettes, etc.; however, I can't make it to the hall because I haven't mastered the taking of attendance. Each day I have four separate attendance sheets to fill out (twice, needs to be done after lunch). A crisis and then a cross in blue or black ink. Red pen for mistakes. About eight different kinds of notations for different sorts of lateness.

Postcards home for those who were absent . . . "T-slip" for probation for those who are absent five days. At the end of each week there's the fifth attendance form, which involves averages. . . .

The whole place is mad and absurd; going to school is going to war. My classes are devoted to trying to get the kids to open their notebooks, stay seated, stop talking, stop fighting. . . .

We have not started to *learn* yet, I am afraid. When I admit this to my colleagues, they retort, "Miss Kovner, you must learn to keep your classroom door closed when you're having trouble." . . .

My suggestions: please to God, if you are going to send HGSE students into urban schools, prepare them a bit more than I was prepared. The dynamics of the classroom situation are overwhelming; they must be studied and solved before *anything* can be taught and learned. For me the idea of trying to teach any normal academic curriculum is absurd at the moment. . . . As to teacher training, expose future "slum" teachers to the killing fact that they have a war on their hands. . . . Whether I'll be able to last out more than a year at [JHS] 45, I don't know.[38]

As things turned out, the young lady was not able to "last out" even her first year at JHS 45; she left her post at the end of only one semester of teaching—to join the faculty of the Harvard Graduate School of Education!

While the inadequacies of teacher education are more serious for teachers going into urban slum schools, I have yet to meet a teacher in a middle-class suburban school who considered his preparation even remotely adequate. On the contrary, the great majority agree with the judgment of Seymour Sarason of Yale, that "the contents and procedures of teacher education frequently have no demonstrable relevance to the actual teaching task."[39]

One reason they have no relevance is that many educationists are as far removed from the public schools as they are from the arts and sciences faculties. This sounds paradoxical, to say the least, in view of what we have said about the close collaboration

---

[38] Quoted in Bernard Bard, "The Classroom Combat Zone," *The New York Post,* January 28, 1967.
[39] Seymour B. Sarason, Kenneth S. Davidson, and Burton Blatt, *The Preparation of Teachers,* New York: John Wiley, 1962.

between educationists and schoolmen to maintain control over certification requirements. But that collaboration has been political rather than educational, engineered by the leaders of the professional associations of educationists and of teachers and administrators, with the aim of controlling the market for teachers. The leaders of teacher education have used the power they have gained thereby to create a demand for more extensively trained—but not necessarily more effective—teachers.

A certain tension between educationists and public school teachers and principals is to be expected, since it obtains in every profession. "The voice of the aggrieved alumnus is always loud in the land," Professor Cyril O. Houle of the University of Chicago has written, "and no matter what the profession, the burden of complaint is always the same."

> In the first five years after graduation, alumni say that they should have been taught more practical techniques. In the next five years, they say they should have been given more basic theory. In the tenth to fifteenth years, they inform the faculty that they should have been taught more about administration or about their relations with their co-workers and subordinates. In the subsequent five years, they condemn the failure of their professors to put the profession in its larger historical, social, and economic contexts. After the twentieth year, they insist that they should have been given a broader orientation to all knowledge, scientific and humane. Some time after that, they stop giving advice; the university has deteriorated so badly since they left that it is beyond hope.[40]

Up to a point, tension between professional school faculties and the practitioners in the field is to be desired, since it reflects a kind of division of labor between the faculty, concerned with how the profession *should* be practiced, and the ordinary practitioners, who tend to be overwhelmed by the here and now. Without a certain distance—what Martin Trow calls "educating *against* the profession"—professional schools are likely to turn out technicians to fill existing job slots rather than potential leaders committed to a conception of what the profession ought to be.[41] Indeed, the genius of professional education in the

[40] Cyril O. Houle, "The Lengthened Line," *Perspectives in Biology and Medicine,* Vol. 11, No. 1, Autumn 1967.
[41] One reason for the relative backwardness of English industry, Trow argues, is that English engineering and business schools have been tied

United States is that it has tended to be far enough ahead of the profession to stimulate change, but not so far ahead as to lose contact, and therefore influence. In general, professional practice in the United States has tended to follow changes in professional education with about a ten-year lag.

From time to time, schools of education have played a similar role vis-à-vis the schools, e.g., San Francisco State under Frederick Burk's presidency, and Teachers College in the heyday of the progressive movement. By and large, however, education faculties have given their students the worst of both worlds. On the one hand, they have failed to develop any conception of what education should be—of how schools should be organized, how teachers should teach, and to what ends—and thus have been unable to turn out leaders with the desire or the capacity to improve the schools. (Most of the innovations in elementary education described in Chapter 7, for example—and some of the most exciting experiments in secondary education described in Chapter 8—have had their origins outside the school of education.) On the other hand, the educationists have been so removed from the schools—so uninformed about what life in the classroom is really like—that they have also failed to prepare their students for the schools as they now are. To be sure, many education professors began their careers as public school teachers. But given their own desire for status together with the Academy's disdain for schooling, they tend to give the schools a wide berth once they join an education faculty.

ITEM: The educational psychology department in the school of education at a large university in the Southwest voted to abandon a program which had each of the two hundred students in a required course in child development spending one morning a week working with an individual child in a local elementary school. Working with children, the educational psychologists explained, took too much time away from the academic content of the course.

Until the racial crisis erupted into violence in the mid-1960s, moreover, most education faculties went about their business as

---

too closely to the industries their graduates enter, and thus have not exerted pressure for change.

if the public schools catered to nothing but an upper-middle-class white clientele.

ITEM: A widely used textbook, *An Introduction to Education in American Society*, published in 1960, contains not a single index listing for Negro, Puerto Rican, or civil rights. Another widely used text, *Foundations of Education*, published in 1967, has only one citation each for civil rights, "culturally disadvantaged," and the American Federation of Teachers, and no citation at all for compensatory education.[42]

Even now, educationists' naïveté about urban schools, and their impotence when asked for help, borders on the cosmic—and the comic.

ITEM: With a great deal of fanfare, the School of Education at New York University announced a bold new program, whereby it "adopted" a junior high (JHS 57) in the all-black Bedford-Stuyvesant section of Brooklyn. With the aid of a $350,000 grant from the Ford Foundation and another $100,000 from the New York City Board of Education, members of the N.Y.U. faculty were to spend a substantial portion of their time at the school, working with students, faculty, and administration to turn one of the worst junior highs in the city (of New York's 118 junior highs, JHS 57 ranked 104 in reading achievement) into a model school.

"We got the hell kicked out of us by the situation," Professor John C. Robertson, the N.Y.U. faculty member in charge, confessed a year later. "We've abandoned our efforts to change the school. Our staff has been through a shattering experience. It's a defeat for the university and for the school system."

In Professor Robertson's view, the defeat was caused by intransigence on the part of both the principal, who gave "administrative difficulties" as the reason for not implementing the N.Y.U. team's proposals, and the teachers, who resisted the proposed changes because they were "preconditioned to what the system demands of them." The principal, on the other hand, blamed what he called the "dilettantist approach" on the part of the N.Y.U. group for the failure. "The forces brought in by this project just didn't sit down long enough to comprehend what they were walking into," he said. "They were dabbling with

[42] James J. Shields, Jr., "Social Foundations of Education: The Problems of Relevance."

our children. We were simply a training ground for N.Y.U."
The project was abandoned before the end of the second year.

ITEM: In May 1969, twelve members of the faculty of the Ohio
State University College of Education traded places for a week
with the principals of twelve schools in a midwestern city. Although the college and the school system had enjoyed a "long-
time collaboration . . . in the preparation of teachers," the
educationists apparently were completely unprepared for what
they found, and none more so than Dean Luvern L. Cunningham, who was assigned to a junior high regarded as the most
difficult in the system. Writing in *Phi Delta Kappan* magazine,
Dean Cunningham, whose college is the fifth-largest producer
of teachers in the United States, describes the exchange as an
experience for which he was totally unprepared:

> This is a report. It is as objective as I can make it. The
> remarks that follow are based on a few days' experience as
> principal of an inner-city junior high school—a problem-
> saturated place.
> I want it known that although what I say here is critical, it
> is not intended to be critical of any person or group of per-
> sons. But it is an indictment of us all—educators and laymen,
> critics and the criticized.
> The notion of an exchange cropped up out of the wood-
> work. Someone had an idea that this would be a good thing to
> do. The big-city people agreed and we agreed and so we were
> off and running. We didn't have the luxury of much advanced
> planning time. Had we had a chance to contemplate the event
> in Columbus (in the peace and quiet and solitude of the ivory
> tower) we could have lost our courage and copped out on the
> whole deal. We didn't have that time, so we did appear at our
> respective schools at the appointed hour, Monday, May 5. On
> that fateful morning (like little kids going to kindergarten) we
> picked up our pencil boxes and marched off to the school
> house.

As the dean describes the experience, he was even less prepared than "little kids going off to kindergarten."

> . . . My first several minutes as the new helmsman were
> exciting, to say the least. I walked in through the front door
> and introduced myself to the regular principal's secretary. She
> was most cordial and smiled knowingly. I think she chuckled
> to herself, thinking that this guy is really in for an education.
> If those were her feelings she was quite right.

I walked into the office and was about to set my briefcase down. I looked up and there must have been 20 faces, most of them black, all around. And others were coming in through the office door. Some were students, some were faculty members with students in tow, others were clerks who wanted me to make some monumental decision about events of the day.

They weren't even in line. They were all just kind of standing around there competing for attention. And to make life more exciting a little black fellow with a flat hat and a cane about two feet long came up to me. He whipped that cane around on his arm and stuck it in my stomach and said, "Hey, man, you our principal?" I began thinking longingly of Columbus and said, "Well, no, I'm not. But I'm here for a week and I am going to be taking his place." I was backpeddling and trying to think of some answer that would make sense to this eighth-grade student.

And so it went throughout the week, as Dean Cunningham discovered, to his amazement, that "life at this junior high is a charade" in which neither teaching nor learning takes place, and in which violence is endemic. At the end, he was simply overwhelmed.

What to do about this school? And other similar junior highs in other places? An archaic building, a largely uncaring community, an irrelevant program of studies, a student population that is out of hand, an underprepared, overpressed staff, a sympathetic but essentially frustrated central administration, a city that wishes such schools would go away. A proposal from the staff and administrators was to burn the school down. Destroy it. Get the symbol out of the neighborhood. This was more than a half-serious proposal. Short of that, what can be done? The question haunted me during my stay. What could be done? Only a few feeble proposals occurred to me.

Some of the proposals in fact were radical: abolition of compulsory attendance, complete autonomy for the principal in selecting faculty without regard to state certification requirements, in allocating his budget, and in establishing his own curriculum. None of them, however, involved direct assistance from the College of Education; all, in fact, involved giving the men on the firing line the freedom to devise their own solutions. As the dean writes in conclusion:

It is clear that we have no experts in this sort of urban education anywhere. The most expert may be those professionals who are there every day engaging in the fray. But they are reaching out, and it is for this reason [not because the universities have any answers] that some kind of liaison with universities and other sources of ideas is critical. Refined, umbilical relationships need to be developed. We are just scratching the surface at Ohio State . . .

There are many schools in America like the one I have described. . . . And we educators stand impotent, frightened, disheveled in the face of such tragedy.[43]

Dean Cunningham spent the following year on leave, as a fellow at the Center for Advanced Study in the Behavioral Sciences in Stanford, California.

VI

To the extent to which they value any aspect of their professional education, teachers generally cite practice teaching as the most valuable—sometimes the *only* valuable—part. Critics of teacher education, too, all agree that whatever else might be dispensable, practice teaching is not. But these judgments provide no basis for complacency, or even satisfaction. Compared with the kind of clinical training teachers should and could receive, practice teaching falls woefully short of the mark.

In some respects, in fact, practice teaching may do more harm than good, confirming students in bad teaching habits rather than training them in good ones. "There is instilled into teacher education," Professor Arthur Pearl of the University of Oregon writes, "the idea that observation and participation (little as it is) are effective learning devices. Ignored, by and large, is the truth that Thorndike discovered in his test of the 'law of exercise.' He found that no matter how much a person 'practiced' at dart throwing, he got no better when the target was hidden from his view and he received no feedback on how he was doing." Students receive incredibly little feedback on their performance, for supervision tends to be sporadic and perfunctory. More important, the target is usually hidden from the students' view; they, their supervisors, and the teachers in whose classrooms they practice usually have no conception of education from which to criticize and evaluate their teaching. There are some notable exceptions, of course, to be discussed in Chapter

[43] Luvern L. Cunningham, "Hey, Man, You Our Principal? Urban Education as I Saw It," *Phi Delta Kappan,* November, 1969.

11, when we turn to the question of how teacher education *should* be organized. By and large, however, student teaching is in as dismal a state as the rest of teacher education.

There is general agreement, for example, that supervision is something less than adequate, the most common complaint being that supervisors either have never taught the subject in question or have been out of the public school classroom so long that they've forgotten what it is like to teach. To meet this objection, the school of education at a Midwestern university has adopted James Conant's proposal that supervision be handled by "clinical professors"—high school teachers who continue to spend half their time teaching, in the employ of the public schools, and the other half supervising student teachers, in the employ of the school of education. It is doubtful, however, whether the change represents much of an improvement; a Carnegie Study researcher discovered that many students did not even know who their clinical professor was.

ITEM: From a transcription of a taped interview with a group of students, most of them in their senior year.

> Q. Did you ever see your clinical professor?
> A. I did because my junior year the clinical professor was the head of the English department at the school where I was teaching . . .
> Q. Did you see yours?
> A. Not my sophomore year. Was it Miss _____? [asked of another student]
> A. She never visits anyone, I don't think.
> A. [another student] Whoever my clinical professor is now, I've never seen one in my classroom until this year. [her senior year] He watched me teach twice, I guess. He never made any comments, though.
> A. [another student] They're very busy people. They've got two things to do.

And indeed they are busy people! The clinical professor just referred to, for example, was responsible for supervising no fewer than twenty-two student teachers, in addition to his own half-time high school teaching job. (At schools of education where supervision is a full-time job, loads are commensurately higher.) Supervisors rarely have time to observe their students more than a few times; to reduce their loads to the point where they could observe student teachers more frequently would cost more than schools of education are willing or able to spend. For supervision is inherently expensive—a supervisor can observe only one student at a time—and teacher education is done on the cheap in the United States.[44]

The problem is compounded by the fact that supervisors rank at the bottom of the educationists' totem pole, rarely being given full faculty status. With budgets tight to begin with, therefore, education schools are reluctant to allocate more for supervision of student teaching than the minimum required by state certification requirements. Indeed, a number of educationists are now proposing to turn the entire responsibility for student teaching over to the public schools. They offer a seemingly plausible and superficially tempting argument, until one realizes that their motive is to cut their deficit rather than to improve teacher education. Far from improving matters, turning practice teaching over to the schools might make them worse, for schools would tend merely to reproduce the kinds of teachers they already have. If necessary changes are to come about, they will require the kind of cooperative effort that the University of North Dakota has developed with the elementary schools of that state. (See Chapters 7 and 11.)

More money and lower case loads for supervisors would not necessarily improve matters, however. What is wrong with supervision has less to do with its frequency than with its nature. Lacking any conception of teaching, and without having thought seriously about the ends or means of education, supervisors of student teaching tend to focus on the minutiae of classroom life,

---

[44] Teacher education is under-financed for two reasons: the nature of the institutions at which teachers are educated, and the allocation of funds within those institutions. More than one-third of the annual crop of new teachers, for example, receive their education at colleges and universities that fall at the D level or below on the American Association of University Professors' rating of faculty salaries; costs per student at these institutions rarely exceed more than $800 per year. Another third or thereabouts come from institutions at the C level, where the annual cost of educating students may run anywhere from $800 to $2,000. (More are near the bottom than the top.) About 30 percent are educated at A and B institutions, where costs per student run considerably higher. But since many of the prestige colleges and universities allocate proportionally less of their budgets to education schools than to the other undergraduate colleges—teaching loads are heavier, and there are fewer research grants to faculty and scholarships to students—expenditures per education student probably do not run much above $2,000 a year. Cf. B. Othanel Smith, et al., *Teachers for the Real World*, AACTE, 1969, Chapter 13.

e.g., the fact that a child in the third row was chewing gum, rather than on the degree to which the student teacher was able to achieve his teaching objective, or relate to the students, or evoke their interest, or what have you. Without any conception of teaching, moreover, the supervisors frequently disagree among themselves as to what constitutes good or bad teaching. Indeed, individual supervisors frequently are unable to agree even with themselves, applying different criteria to different student teachers, or to the same student on different days.

ITEM: Researchers at one graduate school of education asked high school students to rate the student teachers. Their evaluations were then compared with those made by the supervisors of student teaching. To their surprise, the researchers found that students' evaluations were more consistent than those of the supervisors.

A good many colleges and universities are attempting to remedy or offset the mindlessness of supervision by training both supervisors and prospective teachers in the use of "interaction analysis." (See Chapter 4, page 149, especially footnote 40.) This is a technique for analyzing the number and kinds of verbal interchanges between teacher and students: how much of the time the teacher talks, how much the students; how much of the teacher's talk is in the form of questions, how much in the form of lecturing and giving directions and orders; how frequently the teacher responds to a student with praise, how often with criticism; and so on. Armed with a set of categories for classifying the interchanges and a code for recording them rapidly, the supervisor has a more or less objective basis for evaluating and criticizing each student teacher's performance and for sensitizing him to behaviors that are a priori bad. At some schools, e.g., the College of Education of the University of Texas at Austin, student teachers may have a few of their sessions videotaped. The supervisor than analyzes the tape with the student watching it, stopping the tape from time to time to elaborate on some weakness or suggest what the student-teacher might have done instead.

ITEM: Using a form of interaction analysis, researchers at Hofstra University found that teachers tend to call on boys far more often than on girls, the reason being that calling on a student is a means of keeping him "under control." One needs no grand theory of instruction to conclude that calling on boys so much more often than girls is undesirable—or that using questions as a disciplinary device is questionable pedagogy.

Since the technique of interaction analysis can be mastered fairly easily, moreover, it gives the student teacher a means of monitoring his own performance, simply by tape recording a class session and analyzing it afterward. (Where videotape equipment is available, students may analyze the videotape as well as the audio.)

ITEM: In one of the most widely used systems, that developed by Professor Ned A. Flanders of Temple University, formerly of the University of Minnesota—there are now any number in use around the country—teacher-student interchanges are broken down into ten categories, as follows:

Teacher Talk: Indirect Influence

1. *Accepts Feeling:* accepts and clarifies the feeling tone of the students in a non-threatening manner . . .
2. *Praises or Encourages:* praises or encourages student action or behavior . . .
3. *Accepts or Uses Ideas of Student:* clarifying, building or developing ideas suggested by a student. As teacher brings more of his own ideas into play, shift to category five.
4. *Ask Questions:* asking a question about content or procedure with the intent that a student answer.

Teacher Talk: Direct Influence

5. *Lecturing:* giving facts or opinions about content or procedure; expressing his own ideas, asking rhetorical questions.
6. *Giving Direction:* directions, commands, or orders to which a student is expected to comply.
7. *Criticizing or Justifying Authority:* statements intended to change student behavior from non-acceptable to acceptable behavior; bawling someone out; stating why the teacher is doing what he is doing . . .

Student Talk

8. *Student-Talk-Response:* talk by students in response to teacher. Teacher initiates the contact or solicits student statement.
9. *Student-Talk-Initiation:* talk by students which they initi-

ate. If "calling on" student is only to indicate who may talk next, observer must decide whether student wanted to talk. If he did, use this category.

Other

10. *Silence or Confusion:* pauses, short periods of silence and periods of confusion in which communication cannot be understood by the observer.

Unfortunately, the greatest strength of interaction analysis is also its greatest weakness. The simplicity that makes it possible for almost anyone to analyze his own or someone else's teaching, that is to say, encourages a one-dimensional and in some ways distorted view of what teaching is all about. The fourth category in Flanders' system, for example, records the fact that the teacher has asked a question; it does not indicate the *kind* of question the teacher has asked. A "what's the capital of Colorado" question is recorded in the same way as one whose answer calls for serious analysis and thought. Much the same is true of other categories in the Flanders system. Category 3—teacher accepts or uses ideas of students—does not indicate the quality of the student's idea or the subtlety with which the teacher uses it. Category 5—lecturing—does not indicate whether the teacher is simply reciting a series of facts, reading from the textbook, or developing some concept or conceptual structure. Nor does Category 9—student-talk-initiation—indicate whether the student has raised a probing question or simply asked, "Are we responsible for that on the test?"

The problem runs deeper still. Most, if not all, systems of interaction analysis take the conventional formal classroom as given. To be sure, many of those using interaction analysis for teacher training believe strongly that the less indirect a teacher is, i.e., the less he lectures and the more he solicits student response, the better his teaching, and there is some evidence that teachers trained in this way do teach in a less directive way. But while it is in what this writer, at least, would call the right direction, the change nonetheless is modest. The teacher, after all, remains the focal figure, standing in the front of a room filled with rows of desks, teaching twenty-five or thirty youngsters as though they all were interested in the same thing at the same time. If the teacher is less directive, it is because he lectures less and asks more questions and not because he tries to evoke learning from the students' interests; the teacher still dominates the classroom, deciding what the learning should be, when it should start, and when it should end.

To be sure, some interaction analysts have recognized this limitation, and have tried to remedy it by developing more complex and complicated systems of analysis that get at the nature of the questions and answers both teachers and students raise. The late Professor Hilda Taba of San Francisco State College, for example, whose main concern was improving children's ability to handle abstract and conceptual thinking, constructed an interaction analysis system that distinguished between different kinds of conceptual thought. In the nature of things, however, the system involved so many categories that only someone with Taba's sophistication is able to use it. Hence the dilemma: if the analytic system is sophisticated enough to reflect the varieties and complexities of classroom interchange, it is too cumbersome to use (and certainly too cumbersome to be easily mastered); if it is simple enough to be easily used, it provides a simplistic picture of classroom interchange.

Nothing in interaction analysis suggests that there are entirely different ways of organizing a classroom, in which the emphasis is on learning rather than on teaching. On the contrary, the approach assumes that the teacher initiates and directs all the learning that occurs; and since it can deal only with verbal exchanges, it implies that verbal learning is the only kind that counts. Thus, in Flanders' system, which is representative of most, seven of the ten categories involve conversation on the teacher's part, with only two categories—both verbal—reserved for students.[45] The bias in favor of what is, is inherent in the approach; interaction analysis developed originally not as a device for teacher training, but as a method by which scholars could analyze what goes on in the classroom as it is now organized.

A number of schools of education are trying to improve student teaching in still another way, through the use of what is called "micro-teaching," a technique first developed at the Stanford University Graduate School of Education. As it is typically used, the student teacher, having been instructed in the use of a particular teaching technique—how to lecture, how to ask questions, how to get students to ask questions, how to reinforce

[45] At least one system of interaction analysis codes only teacher conversation, ignoring students altogether.

students' answers, and so on—practices the technique by teaching a five to ten minute lesson to a mini-class of four students. The supervisor videotapes the session and plays it back for the student teacher immediately after, analyzing and evaluating the way he handles the skill in question. After a fifteen-minute pause, the student teacher re-teaches the same lesson, with the videotape analyzed a second time, again focusing only on the one skill. (At some schools, the procedure is repeated a third time.)

Micro-teaching is a promising technique, but the promise is as yet unfulfilled: analysis of the changes in the student teachers' behavior indicate that the changes are disappointingly small, and that they tend to wash out fairly quickly. The reason, in all probability, is that a powerful technology is being used in a mindless way; neither the techniques the student teachers practice nor their supervisors' analysis of their videotaped performance are related to any concept of education or any theories of teaching or learning. Thus, there is no structure to the micro-teaching sessions themselves, no attempt to develop a hierarchy of skills. On the contrary, the education students are merely taught to use various teaching techniques that are not related to one another, still less to any conception of what teaching is about or any notion of which strategies are most appropriate for which teaching objectives, or with which kinds of students or which subject matters. What *is* conveyed, however, is the notion that one need not (perhaps should not) teach any differently to a small class than to a large one, since students learning to teach conventionally sized classes do their initial practicing with classes of four. Indeed, part of the stated rationale for micro-teaching—the argument used to convince those who doubted that practicing before a mini-class of only four students would prepare someone for teaching in the real world—was the demonstration that teachers teach no differently to four students than to thirty-five!

Perhaps the weakest link in the chain of practice teaching, and the one that is most difficult to correct, is the public school teacher in whose classroom the student teacher does his practice teaching. A large body of experience, corroborated by some research, indicates that this teacher exerts considerably more influence on the student teacher's style and approach than do his supervisor or the education professors under whom he has studied. With inadequate supervision, and unarmed with any theories of teaching or learning or any philosophy of education by which he can judge and criticize the teacher with whom he is placed, the student teacher naturally and inevitably tends to imitate him.

All too often, the classroom teacher affords anything but a proper model of how to teach. The sheer number of education students means that many, if not most, will be placed with teachers who are dull or harsh or both—teachers of the sort described in Chapters 3 and 4. In all probability, moreover, the student teachers studied under the same kinds of teachers when they were public school students themselves. After twelve years of dull, repressive, formal public schooling and three and a half years of uninspired formal college teaching, six months of practice teaching in the same kind of classroom is almost bound to convince the student teacher that that is the way teaching is— worse, that that is the way teaching has to be. Almost inevitably, therefore, that is the way he tends to teach when he finishes his training and takes over his own classroom.

Remarkably little has changed, in fact, since 1904, when John Dewey described the unhappy consequences of the failure to relate theory and practice in teacher education. The teacher coming out of the usual teacher training school, he wrote, has not received "the training which affords psychological insight— which enables him to judge promptly (and therefore almost automatically) the kind and mode of subject-matter which the pupil needs at a given moment to keep his attention moving forward effectively and healthfully. He does know, however, that he must maintain order; that he must keep the attention of the pupils fixed upon his own questions, suggestions, instructions, and remarks, and upon their 'lessons,' " for that, after all, was the way he was taught. The result, Dewey continued is that

> the student adjusts his actual methods of teaching, not to the principles which he is acquiring, but to what he sees succeed and fail in an empirical way from moment to moment; what he sees other teachers doing who are more experienced and successful in keeping order than he is; and to the injunctions and directions given him by others. In this way the controlling habits of the teacher get fixed with comparatively little reference to principles in the psychology, logic, and history of education . . . Here we have the explanation, in considerable part at least, of the dualism, the unconscious duplicity, which is one of the chief evils of the teaching profession. There is an enthusiastic devotion to certain principles of lofty theory in the abstract—principles of self-activity, self-control, intellectual

and moral—and there is a school practice taking little heed of the official pedagogic creed. Theory and practice do not grow together out of and into the teacher's personal experience.[46]

In some respects, moreover, the way practice teaching is usually structured gives the student teacher the worst of two worlds. On the one hand, he never experiences "the real thing" —never gets the feel of what teaching is actually like. Because the regular classroom teacher remains responsible for everything that goes on in his room, the student teacher cannot feel the full impact of that responsibility. Neither can he experience the full authority of being a teacher. He is, after all, a visitor in someone else's classroom, and visitors are not welcome to rearrange their host's furniture, alter his schedule, revise his curriculum, or change the atmosphere he has labored to create. Nor is the student teacher likely to be able to make these kinds of changes if he wanted to.

Even with an able and cooperative classroom teacher, practice teaching rarely gives the student teacher the experience of teaching in the real world. For one thing, student teachers rarely spend more than a half-day at a time in the classroom, yet there is something different in kind, not just in degree, about teaching a whole day. For another, the brevity of the student-teaching assignment, and the fact that it generally begins in the middle of a semester, means that the student teacher has little option but to follow the cooperating teacher's lesson plan. The fact that practice teaching begins after the public school semester has started has a further disadvantage, for what a teacher does in the first few days of the semester may be decisive in setting the tone of the class for the rest of the year. Thus, new teachers almost invariably experience a shock on the day they begin their teaching career, as they suddenly realize that no one had ever suggested to them (nor had they thought to ask) what to say or do in those first few awesome moments.

And yet student teachers rarely enjoy the advantages that a more synthetic environment might provide. Instead of plunging into a regular classroom, for example, the novice might learn

---

[46] John Dewey, "The Relation of Theory to Practice in Education," National Society for the Scientific Study of Education, *The Relation of Theory to Practice in the Education of Teachers*, Third Yearbook, Part I, Bloomington, Ill.: Public School Publishing Co., 1904 (reprinted in M. L. Borrowman, ed., *Teacher Education in America*).

a great deal more if practice teaching were structured in order to enable him to move from simpler to more complex kinds of teaching. But because he practices in a regular, and formal, classroom with a curriculum to cover, what the student teacher does his first day of practice all too often tends to be essentially the same as what he does the last day. In many classrooms, the only differentiation he experiences is that he may hang fewer bulletin-board displays and perform fewer clerical chores toward the end of the practice-teaching period than at the beginning.

The fact that most education schools delay practice teaching until the student's senior year is another serious, and sometimes fatal, weakness, for it denies students the chance to discover whether they like teaching or not until the end of their course of study.

ITEM: A graduate summer session course at a West Coast school of education. The instructor asks the students, all of them teachers with some years of experience, to talk about whether they feel fulfilled or frustrated in their teaching. One woman, a ten-year veteran, replies that she has hated it since her first day of practice teaching. Asked why she took a job in the first place, she explains that her practice teaching didn't come until the second half of her senior year. "I couldn't afford to change majors and start all over again, so I decided to make the best of it." One suspects that her students have had the worst of it.

Schools of education, it should be understood, have no monopoly on ignorance, confusion or failure, which are, in fact, diffused throughout the university. Every professional school is wracked by controversy and plagued by doubts concerning how professional practitioners should be educated, and to what ends; in just about every profession, the existing modes of education are being attacked as out of touch with the changing roles the professional, be he doctor, lawyer, engineer, minister, social worker, businessman, journalist, or teacher, now has to play.[47]

47 Whether each of these vocations can properly be called a profession is a question that exercises some sociologists, but does not concern us in this volume. "In my own studies," Professor Everett C. Hughes, perhaps the leading American student of professionalization, has written, "I passed from the false question, 'Is this occupation a profession?' to the more fundamental one, 'What are the circumstances in which people

Yet each profession tends to act as though its educational problem were unique, a phenomenon which Robert Merton calls "pluralistic ignorance."

Medical schools have been the first to break out of this mold. In the 1950s, a number of medical educators, eager to renew (or restore) their profession's concern with the patient as a person affected by his social environment, began working with sociologists who were themselves interested in the sociology of medicine.[48] More recently, as the crisis in medical care has taken on increased urgency, medical educators have sought the help of educators from almost every part of the university—every part, it seems, except the school of education—in devising new patterns of medical education and of medical care.[49]

Educationists could learn a great deal, therefore, by studying the ways in which medical schools—and law schools and engineering schools—have been responding to what Harvey Brooks calls "the crisis of the professions," a crisis brought about by the "fact that both ends of the gap [the professional] is expected to bridge with his profession are changing so rapidly—both the

---

in an occupation attempt to turn it into a profession, and themselves into professional people?' " (Quoted in Howard M. Vollmer and Donald L. Mills, eds., *Professionalization,* Englewood Cliffs, N.J.: Prentice-Hall, 1966.) Cf. also A. M. Carr-Saunders and P. A. Wilson, *The Professions,* Oxford: The Clarendon Press, 1933; Amitai Etzioni, ed., *The Semi-Professions and Their Organization,* New York: The Free Press, 1969; Nelson B. Henry, ed., *Education for the Professions, The Sixty-first Yearbook of the National Society for the Study of Education,* Part II, University of Chicago Press, 1962.

[48] Cf. especially Robert K. Merton, George Reader, and Patricia L. Kendall, *The Student Physician: Introductory Studies in the Sociology of Medical Education,* Cambridge, Mass.: Harvard University Press, 1957; and Howard S. Becker, Blanche Geer, Everett C. Hughes, and Anselm Strauss, *Boys in White: Student Culture in Medical School,* University of Chicago Press, 1961.

[49] Cf. Oliver Cope, *Man, Mind & Medicine: The Doctor's Education,* Philadelphia, Pa.: J. B. Lippincott Company, 1968; Oliver Cope and Jerrold Zacharias, *Medical Education Reconsidered,* J. B. Lippincott Company, 1966; *The Crisis in Medical Services and Medical Education,* Report of an Exploratory Conference, February 1966, Fort Lauderdale, Florida, sponsored by Carnegie Corporation of New York and The Commonwealth Fund (unpublished); *The Graduate Education of Physicians,* The Report of the Citizens Commission on Graduate Medical Education, Chicago, Ill.: Council on Medical Education, American Medical Association, 1966. In addition to sources cited, I am relying, throughout this section, on memoranda prepared by Mrs. Sybil Pollet of the Carnegie Study research staff.

body of knowledge which he must use, and the expectations of the society he must serve." John Dewey urged such a study on schools of education two-thirds of a century ago. "I doubt whether we, as educators, keep in mind with sufficient constancy the fact that the problem of training teachers is one species of a more generic affair—that of training for professions," he wrote. "Our problem is akin to that of training architects, doctors, lawyers, etc."

Not that educationists have entirely ignored Dewey's advice; for some fifty years or more, they have been pointing out analogies between the education of teachers and doctors, urging schools of education to adopt the terminology and forms of medical education. But they have done so from a distance, without seeking the advice of medical educators and without bothering to examine how doctors are in fact educated. This tradition is so strong that in the past decade or two, the critics of teacher education have fallen into the same trap, erecting their proposals for change on simplistic and misleading analogies with medical education. The result has been a series of expensive "reforms" whereby schools of education have been persuaded to adopt precisely those educational practices that medical schools were abandoning.

The most important proposal that Dr. James B. Conant advanced in *The Education of American Teachers,* for example, was that practice teaching—"the one indisputably essential element in professional education," as he termed it—be given the central role in the preparation of teachers. (Conant urged state education departments to drop all other requirements for certification.) But despite his sweeping criticism of the way practice teaching is generally handled, Dr. Conant offered only one prescription for improvement—that "the professor from the college or university who is to supervise and assess the practice teaching should have had much practical experience. *His status should be analogous to that of a clinical professor in certain medical schools."* (Emphasis added.) Which medical schools, however, he did not say—yet there are enormous variations in the way medical schools structure their students' clinical experience.

Similarly, Dr. Conant attempted to solve the knotty problem of how—or whether—the study of the history, philosophy, psychology, and sociology of education should be incorporated into teacher education programs by urging education schools to imitate the way medical schools incorporate the so-called preclinical sciences into medical education. Yet no aspect of medical education is quite so controversial, or is changing quite so dramatically!

The Ford Foundation has used misleading medical analogies, too, in its attempts to reform teacher education. "A revolution is under way in the education of teachers," the Foundation announced in 1962. As a result of its activities, it continued, "the path to the teaching profession is changing as dramatically as the path to the medical profession changed following the historic Flexner Report on medical education in 1910":

> The most serious shortcoming of American physicians, [the Flexner Report] charged, was their lack of grounding in the basic medical sciences; their schooling had emphasized medical practice at the expense of education in the underlying substance of medicine. Today's revolution in teaching education . . . seeks to redress an imbalance. Under the new pattern, the prospective teacher devotes less of his undergraduate time to courses on how to teach and considerably more to the academic subjects he is preparing to teach. His graduate work consists of even further grounding in academic subject matter, plus studies of the underlying disciplines of teaching: history, psychology, and philosophy. The new teacher's entrance into full-time professional service, like the physician's, is preceded by an internship, which gives him supervised, first-hand experience in teaching a subject he knows.[50]

But no one who had actually looked at what was happening to medical education could have suggested the 1910 Flexner Report proposals as a model to be followed today for the education of either teachers or doctors. However relevant it may have been in 1910—a matter of some controversy in its own right—the "Flexner Model" is seriously out of touch with contemporary needs. For one thing, Flexner regarded quantity and quality as incompatible. Indeed, his central thesis was "that the country needs fewer and better doctors; and that the way to get them better is to produce fewer."[51] The current serious

[50] *The New Teacher: A report on Ford Foundation assistance for new patterns in the education of teachers,* New York: Ford Foundation, 1962.
[51] Abraham Flexner, *Medical Education in the United States and Canada,* New York, Carnegie Foundation for the Advancement of Teaching, Bulletin Number Four, 1910.

shortage of doctors stems directly from the pattern of medical education that Flexner proposed and to which medical schools faithfully clung for too long.

More important to an understanding of where both Conant and Ford went wrong: the sharp distinction between education in "medical practice" and in "the underlying substance of medicine" that Flexner imposed upon medical education is no longer viable. The dichotomy stemmed from the need, in 1910, to incorporate both the findings and the methods of the biological and physical sciences into medical practice and research. This could only be done, Flexner felt, if medical schools gave instruction in the basic sciences, since few students had had any previous exposure to them. Just as, in the nineteenth century, students entered normal school after no more than an elementary school education, many, if not most, students in Flexner's day entered medical school directly from high school. Hence Flexner proposed that the course of study be lengthened so that students could spread their first two years learning the "preclinical" laboratory sciences—anatomy, physiology, pharmacology, pathology, and bacteriology—with the last two years devoted to clinical work in medicine, surgery, and obstetrics.

For some time, however, the most thoughtful medical educators have been arguing that this dichotomy between the preclinical and clinical years must be scrapped, just as many of those concerned with teacher education believe that education students should begin their clinical, i.e., classroom, work as early as possible. The medical reformers' arguments have gained wide and rapidly growing acceptance. For one thing, the Flexner Model wastes precious time. Students now enter medical school after at least three, and usually four, years of college. Most, therefore, have already had the grounding in the biological and physical sciences that the preclinical years were intended to provide.

There is a growing concern, moreover, that the sharp distinction between preclinical and clinical studies tends to dissipate or even destroy the medical school's most valuable instrument— the interest, enthusiasm, and idealism with which students begin their studies. As in teacher education, the students' interest and enthusiasm evaporate when they spend two years studying basic sciences without any indication of how these sciences may contribute to their needs and activities as a practitioner.

More important, the two-year deferment of the students' basic objective, that of helping sick people, also tends to erode their initial idealism. Attitudinal surveys show medical school students scoring lower on "idealism" and higher on "cynicism" each year they are in medical school—so much so that many medical professors refer to the preclinical and clinical years as the "precynical" and "cynical" years.

Medical schools, consequently, have been moving away from the Flexner Model in a number of respects. A majority of schools, for example, now give students at least some contact with patients well before the end of the second year. Some schools have gone further, scrapping the distinction between the preclinical and clinical years altogether.

ITEM: At Case-Western Reserve, which as long as fifteen years ago pioneered in the reform of many aspects of medical education, each student is assigned to a family early in his first year, and generally follows the family through the entire four years of medical school. At the time the student is assigned to the family, the wife is pregnant and under the care of a staff physician, but the family members have no serious or long-standing medical problems. (Seeing patients only in hospital context tends to focus attention on the acute and the abnormal, with doctors, and therefore students, tending to treat the illness rather than the patient.) Initially, of course, the Western Reserve medical students are expected only to observe their "patients." But this observation continues during pregnancy and delivery, and then during the child's early growth and development. As the students' knowledge grows, they take on more and more responsibility, helping all the members of the family cope with whatever medical problems arise and acting as its contact and spokesman (and sometimes its ombudsman) in the complex medical school–medical care system.

At the same time that the student is assigned to his family, moreover, he is also assigned to a group of eight or nine other students; under the guidance of a "clinical preceptor," this group meets regularly to discuss the families the students have been following and to relate their observations to their work in the basic sciences. If a question on which the preceptor lacks expertise arises, he calls on the appropriate specialist for help. The basic sciences themselves are taught in an integrated, semi-clinical manner, with the various departments—physiology, anatomy, biochemistry, pathology, and so on—cooperating in the study of one organ at a time.

Internships and residencies are also under fire, for reasons that again illuminate the debate over teacher education. One of the recurrent themes in the literature on teacher education is the notion that education schools should turn over to the public schools the responsibility for supervising practice teaching. But medical reformers want to move in the opposite direction. What is wrong with medical internships and residencies, they argue, is in large measure a result of the very division of responsibility educationists are proposing—specifically, the fact that supervision of medical interns and residents has always been the responsibility of hospitals rather than of medical schools. Just as public schools are not organized or run to provide instruction to teachers in training, so hospitals are not organized to provide instruction to young doctors; their function—the reason they exist—is to provide medical care to their patients.

There is at least as much ferment over *what* should be taught in medical school as over *how* it should be taught. "The primary purpose of medical education in the past was to impart a closed body of knowledge or identifiable content requisite for a physician's education," Dr. Charles G. Child III and Dr. Ralph J. Wedgewood write. "This is no longer true."[52] It simply is not possible for doctors, any more than for teachers, to learn in professional school more than a fraction of what they will need to know for careers that will extend into the twentieth century.

As with teacher education, the biggest obstacle to reform is the profession's lack of understanding of the nature of medicine and of the processes by which doctors learn to practice it. "Learning to practice medicine competently is a highly complex process," the Millis Commission declared in its report, "and not enough is known about the learning process to justify any hope for easy answers." For all their scientific grounding, the Commission continues, "the good primary physicians now in practice have acquired much of their skill and wisdom from experience, or from intuition."[53] What medical schools lack and must now develop, the Millis Commission argued, in terms

52 Charles G. Child III and Ralph J. Wedgewood, "Our Primary Purpose," Appendix E in Oliver Cope, *Man, Mind & Medicine,* Philadelphia, Pa.: J. B. Lippincott, 1968.
53 *The Graduate Education of Physicians,* Report of the Citizens Commission on Graduate Medical Education, Chicago, Ill.: Council on Medical Education, American Medical Association, 1967.

remarkably evocative of the literature on teacher education, is "an intellectual framework into which the lessons of practical experience can be fitted."

The problem is complicated by the need to educate doctors to a new conception of their role. To view the doctor as educator— to try to shift the focus of medicine from curing disease to maintaining health—is to substantially enlarge his role, which in turn means broadening his education. Consequently, medical schools must add a whole new body of knowledge to the curriculum at the same time that they are being called upon to reduce sharply the material covered in the traditional courses. The debates over how to introduce the social and behavioral sciences illustrate the subtlety of the relation between theory and practice in the education of professionals. They demonstrate, therefore, how ingenuous it is to suggest that the school of education would solve its curriculum problem if only professors of the history, philosophy, psychology, and sociology of education were to play the same "intermediary role" in teacher education that professors of the preclinical sciences play in medical schools. As Dr. Oliver Cope describes the 1966 Swampscott Study in Behavioral Science in Medicine, for example, the participants disagreed "about almost everything, including definitions and what to do. About all the study could agree upon was that behavioral science was important somehow in medicine."[54]

Most of the arguments centered on where the behavioral sciences should be studied, e.g., in the medical school itself, or in the graduate departments of psychology, sociology, and anthropology. But it is chimerical to expect to transform doctors' conceptions of themselves and their role merely by rearranging the courses they take in medical school. Certainly, introducing them to the behavioral sciences (or, as at Penn State, to the humanities) will not per se make them more sensitive and humane, more interested in and responsive to their patients' feelings and emotional and social needs. Neither the behavioral sciences nor the humanities are inherently more humane than the physical sciences or any other field of study; to incorporate them into the medical curriculum is an administrative procedure that might very well leave students' attitudes and values unchanged. Medical educators—and teacher educators—might ponder Felix Frankfurter's recollection of how values were shaped in his student days at Harvard Law School:

[54] Oliver Cope, *Man, Mind & Medicine,* Philadelphia, Pa.: J. B. Lippincott Company, 1968.

There weren't any courses on ethics, but the place was permeated by ethical presuppositions and assumptions and standards. . . . It was the quality of the feeling that dominated the place largely because of the dean, James Barr Ames. We had no course on ethics, but his course on the law of trusts and fiduciary relations was so much more compelling as a course in ethics than any formal course in ethics that I think ill of most courses in ethics.[55]

So it is in medical school: attitudes and values are shaped far more by the so-called invisible or informal curriculum than by the formal curriculum. Learning to be a physician—or a teacher, lawyer, engineer, or journalist—is a function of the social as well as intellectual environment. The social environment of most medical schools has not been conducive to turning out doctors with a deep concern for their patients as people.

To create more sensitive doctors, therefore, or doctors who take a broader view of the nature and purpose of medical practice, medical schools will have to change more than the curriculum or administrative arrangements. Faculty attitudes toward teaching and research, the medical school's status and reward system, the manner in which faculty members and staff physicians treat patients, the nature of students' clinical experience, the degree to which the faculty encourages students to assume responsibility and the ways they respond to error, the nature of the student subculture—these and similar factors shape attitudes and values far more profoundly than the formal curriculum itself. The same is true, needless to say, in the education of teachers.

[55] Quoted in Cope, *Man, Mind and Medicine*, Appendix F.

11

The Education
of Educators

The antithesis between a technical and a liberal education is fallacious. There can be no adequate technical education which is not liberal, and no liberal education which is not technical: that is, no education which does not impart both technique and intellectual vision. In simpler language, education should turn out the pupil with something he knows well and something he can do well. This intimate union of theory and practice aids both.

ALFRED NORTH WHITEHEAD, *1917*

I

How, then, *should* teachers be educated?

As the preceding chapter has made clear, teacher education has suffered too long from too many answers and too few questions. After all the dashed hopes of the postwar period—after all the "revolutions" that failed, the "breakthroughs" that never occurred, the "new directions" that led nowhere—it may be time to worry less about finding the right answers and more about asking the right questions.

Not that I am without answers: far from it. As I did in Chapters 6, 7, and 8, dealing with the reform of the public schools, I shall, in this chapter, indicate how teacher education can be improved by describing programs that are in operation now. But anyone who hopes to find a checklist or "how to" manual will be disappointed; there is no cheap or easy way to reform teacher education. I have no panacea or master plan to offer, and know of none worth following—least of all the fancy "models" now being sponsored by the U.S. Office of Education, which use the grating jargon of systems analysis ("performance criteria," "cost-effectiveness," "instructional modules," and the like) to mask an absence of serious thought or substantive change.[1] Reading the descriptions of programs such as METEP (the University of Massachusetts Model Elementary Teacher Education Program) or ComField (A Competency Based, Personalized and Field-Centered Model of an Elementary Teacher Education Program, the brainchild of the Northwest Regional Educational Laboratory), one is reminded of the warning John Dewey delivered in the disillusionment of old age: "The real danger is in perpetuating the past under forms that claim to be new but are only disguises of the old."[2]

The starting point for thinking about how teachers should be educated is recognition of the fact that teaching, as Dan C. Lortie writes, is "the occupation whose tasks are best known to American adolescents." Lortie's studies indicate that a majority of the students entering law school have "a wildly romantic and inaccurate conception" of what being a lawyer entails; much the same is true of students entering medical school. Students planning to become teachers, on the other hand, "approach their education with a *relatively* accurate picture of what teachers do." Their picture is relatively accurate because they have spent some 10,000 hours in direct contact with elementary and secondary school teachers by the time they begin their first year of college. The preparation of teachers begins not in college but in kindergarten or first grade.[3]

And that is precisely why teachers require special preparation at the college or university level. While teachers-to-be start out with a relatively accurate picture of what most teachers do, what most teachers do is not what they *should* be doing. Unless prospective teachers are given alternative pictures of what teaching and learning can be, along with the techniques they

[1] For a description of seven such models, see *Journal of Research and Development in Education,* Vol. 2, No. 3, Spring 1969.

[2] John Dewey, Introduction to *The Use of Resources in Education* by Elsie Ripley Clapp, New York: Harper & Row, 1952 (reprinted in Martin Dworkin, ed., *Dewey on Education,* New York: Teachers College Press, Classics in Education No. 3, 1959).

[3] Dan C. Lortie, "Teacher Socialization: The Robinson Crusoe Model," in *The Real World of the Beginning Teacher,* Report of the Nineteenth National TEPS Conference, Washington, D.C.: National Education Association, 1966.

need to implement them, they are almost bound to teach in the same way as their teachers taught them.

The central task of teacher education, therefore, is to provide teachers with a sense of purpose, or, if you will, with a philosophy of education. This means developing teachers' ability and their desire to think seriously, deeply, and continuously about the purposes and consequences of what they do—about the ways in which their curriculum and teaching methods, classroom and school organization, testing and grading procedures, affect purpose and are affected by it. "To place the emphasis upon the securing of proficiency in teaching and discipline," Dewey warned two-thirds of a century ago, *"puts the attention of the student-teacher in the wrong place, and tends to fix it in the wrong direction. . . .* For immediate skill may be got at the cost of the power to keep on growing. The teacher who leaves the professional school with power in managing a class of children may appear to superior advantage the first day, the first week, the first month, or even the first year. But later 'progress' may with such consist only in perfecting and refining skills already possessed. Such persons seem to know how to teach, but they are not students of teaching." Unless a teacher is also a student of teaching, "he cannot grow as a teacher, an inspirer and director of soul-life."[4] [Emphasis in original]

As our discussion of medical education has made clear, purpose in this sense cannot be transmitted by a single course, or group of courses; it must be the product of a program of studies that is itself infused with purpose. "The deepest criticism which can be made of the present system of teacher education," Harold Taylor observes, "is that it does not touch the life of its students, it does not arouse in them a delight in what they are doing, it does not engage them in action through which their own lives may be fulfilled."[5]

Faculties of education will not be able to touch the lives of their students unless their own lives have been touched—unless

[4] John Dewey, "The Relation of Theory to Practice in Education," National Society for the Scientific Study of Education, *The Relation of Theory to Practice in Education,* Third Yearbook, Part I, Bloomington, Ill.: Public School Publishing Co., 1904. Reprinted in M. L. Borrowman, ed., *Teacher Education in America.*
[5] Harold Taylor, *The World and the American Teacher,* Washington, D.C.: The American Association of Colleges for Teacher Education, 1968.

their conception of education is reflected in the way they teach as well as in what they teach. "If students see around them in the colleges the cynicism of teachers who care little for the art of teaching, whose own true lives are lived elsewhere, or whose talents ill-equip them for the task they have accepted," Taylor continues, they will be "unable to respond and unlikely to create their own conceptions of what it means to be a teacher."

It is unreasonable, of course, to expect every educationist to be an inspiring teacher, let alone an inspiring human being; inspiration will always be in short supply. It is not unreasonable, however, to expect education faculties to take their job seriously—to expect them to think about educational purpose, and to arrange a curriculum that reflects their thought. If schools of education are to turn out men and women who not only know how to teach but who are, as well, "students of teaching," their programs must have far greater coherence than most now have. Instead of an educational cafeteria, there must be a curriculum, which means that the courses and programs that are offered must grow out of and reflect some carefully considered conceptions of education. To provide coherence in this sense, the faculty must continually ask itself the question few faculties have asked: what difference does it make that a teacher is educated here, rather than somewhere else?

Faculties of education will have to do more than that. The remaking of American education requires, and will not be possible without, a new kind of relationship between colleges and universities, on the one side, and public schools, on the other. While the schools cannot be transformed unless colleges and universities turn out a new breed of teacher educated to think about purpose, the universities will be unable to do this unless they, working with the schools, create classrooms that afford their students live models of what teaching can and should be. At the moment, painfully few such classrooms exist, and painfully few schools of education are trying to create them.

The most notable exception is the University of North Dakota's two-year-old New School for Behavioral Studies in Education, which is developing what is easily the most exciting teacher education program in the United States. As the New School's statement of purpose declares, "The New School has as its major task the preparation of a new kind of elementary teacher. It strives to educate students to acquire the qualities of mind and behavior which will assist them in nurturing the creative tendencies in the young, and in introducing a more individualized mode of instruction into the schools of North Dakota"—two of the qualities most strikingly absent in most American public schools.

This purpose is the raison d'être for the New School's existence; it was created specifically to be the principal instrument for reorganizing the elementary schools of North Dakota along individualized and informal lines. A Statewide Study of Education had found that a majority—59 percent—of the state's elementary school teachers lacked a college degree; certification requirements established as recently as 1953 had required no more than two years of college for a teaching certificate. The Statewide Study proposed a program not only to bring the state's teachers up to the minimum educational level by 1975, but to reorganize the elementary schools along informal lines in the process. (See Chapter 7, Section III.) Persuaded that the state's existing teacher-training institutions—four state colleges and a regional university in addition to the School of Education at the University of North Dakota—were not equipped to educate a new breed of teacher for a new kind of school, the members of the Statewide Study of Education recommended the creation of a new kind of institution.

Thus, the New School came into existence with a mandate to do what schools of education throughout the country as well as in North Dakota have generally failed to do. "Seldom do teacher education programs, even those that are considered most innovative, have a significant impact upon public education in the regions they serve," Dean Vito Perrone and his colleagues observed in a paper delivered before the 1969 annual meeting of the American Association of Colleges for Teacher Education. "Typically, institutions of higher learning are isolated from the communities in which they reside," with "that portion of a university committed to the preparation of teachers" tending to be the most isolated of all. If they are to carry out their mandate, Perrone and Co. declared, the New School must "bridge the isolation that traditionally exists between the University and local communities."

The principal bridge is a teacher exchange program, under which cooperating school districts send their "less-than-degree teachers" to the New School for as much undergraduate work as they need to earn a B.A. degree. The New School in turn sends its master's degree candidates to these school districts to take over the vacant classrooms; the year-long teaching internship comprises the bulk of their work for the degree. The internship is preceded and followed by summer sessions at the New School, and the interns are closely supervised by "clinical professors" assigned to each region, as well as by Dean Perrone and members of his administrative staff.[6] At the New School, meanwhile, experienced teachers, many of them in their forties and fifties, are attending classes with young undergraduate teachers-to-be. Taking older teachers away from their classrooms would be pointless unless the experience were to change the way they, as well as the more impressionable undergraduates, teach. The program is intended to do both.

But how?

The answer, the New School faculty suggests, is to teach its students the same way it would have them teach. "An institution of higher learning, if it is to be effective in contributing to a change in the educational fabric of its society, must itself become a model of the kind of educational environment it is promoting," Dean Vito Perrone states. "The New School in all its educational endeavors will strive to be such a model."

Thus, the faculty eschews lectures, compulsory reading lists, and large group instruction of all kinds in favor of "student-oriented instructional activities," i.e., independent study and small classes and seminars in which each student is expected to initiate his own program of study, with the instructor providing guidance as needed. Dean Perrone hopes that by putting the responsibility for learning on the students, they "will be better prepared to inculcate a spirit and capacity for inquiry and discovery" among their own elementary school students.

To develop its students' capacity to nurture rather than squelch the creative tendencies of their elementary school children, moreover, the New School gives them a two-year sequence in "Creative Expression," which includes work in drama, dance, writing, painting, sculpting, and any other forms of expression individual students may want to pursue. The faculty has no illusions about uncovering great talent; many students, perhaps most, will remain uncreative no matter how many haiku poems

[6] In the summer of 1969, the New School also conducted a summer program for the principals of the cooperating schools, to give them some understanding of what their teaching interns were up to, and what their experienced teachers would be up to when they returned to their classrooms. By the end of the program, the principals, many of whom had been hostile or indifferent to informal education, asked Perrone to arrange workshops for them at intervals throughout the school year.

and one-act plays they write or pictures they paint. "But if we cannot make every teacher personally creative," Vito Perrone argues, "we can at least make every teacher sensitive to the creativity in her children, so that she will nourish *their* attempts."

Thus, teachers who have answered the question "Why aren't we all one color?" by painting a picture, or who have created a collage or "junk" sculpture on the theme "Would you believe . . . ?" are less likely to insist that their own students draw identical-looking pumpkins for Halloween or turkeys for Thanksgiving. Teachers who have struggled to evoke a mood within the constraints of haiku poetry and to capture a person's personality in a 250-word character sketch are likely to be more concerned with their children's imaginative use of language and less with their spelling and punctuation. And teachers who have struggled over a painting only to see it ruined when the paint dripped, or who have forgotten their lines in a play when they froze with stage fright, are more likely to appreciate their children's fumblings and mistakes and to respond more sensitively to their inhibitions and fears.

ITEM: "I'm just beginning to appreciate the hang-ups some of my kids used to have when I asked them to participate, now that I have experienced butterflies in the stomach myself," one less-than-degree teacher explained. "Actually doing the things we ask our children to do gives you a special understanding."

In short, "Creative Expression" is intended to help teachers become more open, flexible human beings, not just to give them a tool kit for classroom use. The "Creative Drama" segment of the sequence plays a major role in that process; students write their own skits and short plays, create their own costumes, sound effects, and props, and then perform for children in neighboring schools, which in North Dakota means anything within a radius of 100 miles. (During the first year of the New School's operations, the students became known locally as "The Burlap Bag Players," after the burlap bag in which each "actress" carried her props, accessories, and basic costume consisting of black slacks, black sweater, and black ballet slippers.)

ITEM: "I lost some inhibitions and learned to loosen up, to get a little open and free," a less-than-degree teacher with some thirty or forty years' experience reported. Had she had a choice, she would have dropped the course the first day—"and what an experience I would have missed," she wrote in her self-evaluation. "I lost some inhibitions and learned to loosen up, to get a little open and free."

> That first class meeting when the instructor presented her ideas to us, I could not possibly imagine myself doing things such as she suggested. And as for me wearing slacks, that could never be! I had never worn a pair in my life! Well, I got slacks, I wore them, and do you know, they are comfortable, and I wear them a great deal now. If we were to have presented our skits to the _____ school I think I would have refused—or at least wanted to. However, we did have the skits to do; we did have to present them; we did—and do you know, it wouldn't bother me to go to _____ now, and if the principal wanted the entire school to watch (I have taught all of these students) I could do that, too.

ITEM: "It's made us all more flexible," another veteran teacher remarked. "If something doesn't go over with the kids when you're putting on a skit, you have to learn to change it or scrap it altogether. After you've laid an egg a few times, you can't go on insisting that the kids *should* like it."

The "Do as we do, not just as we say" approach to teacher education extends to almost every aspect of the New School program, including the way in which the faculty itself is organized. For example, there are no departments or divisions, which reflects (and hopefully also conveys) the faculty's conviction that knowledge cannot be compartmentalized. The New School is organized instead as a single unit in which faculty members from a variety of fields—psychology, philosophy, English, religion, sociology, music, speech, education—jointly shape the total academic and professional program.[7] This attempt to reunite teacher education with liberal education has evoked an extraordinary response from the arts and science faculty; departments which had given the old School of Education a cold

[7] The relatively small size of the New School—the student body will reach its maximum size of 300 in the 1970–71 academic year—makes it easier, of course, for the faculty to operate in this manner. But there is no a priori reason why larger schools of education could not be broken up into smaller "cluster colleges," as many large universities and colleges, e.g., the University of California at Santa Cruz, the State University of New York College at Old Westbury, are doing.

shoulder are cooperating eagerly with the New School. Thus, the chairman of the university's psychology department teaches quarter-time in the New School; the chairman of the English department has released several of his best faculty members for joint appointments with the New School and spends a fair amount of his own time meeting with New School faculty and students; and so on.

The curriculum also reflects and conveys the concern for seeing teacher education whole. In the conventional teacher education program, the curriculum institutionalizes the dichotomy between liberal and professional education by distinguishing sharply between subject matter, which students study in the college of arts and sciences, and "method," which they study in the school of education. The New School is trying to erase that distinction by integrating content and methodology in most of the courses it offers. Students gain a deeper understanding of a subject, Perrone argues, when they pursue the question of how it can best be taught to children. And since there is a big difference between knowing how something should be done and actually being able to do it—since teachers have to make the connection between what they have learned and what they do in the rapid give-and-take of the classroom—New School students are given frequent contact with children from the beginning of their studies. "Clinical experiences," some quite brief, some lasting as long as four weeks, are built into the required courses in "Modes of Communication" and "Nature and Conditions of Learning."

The network of schools involved in the New School's teacher exchange program provides a particularly advantageous setting in which to give students a step-by-step introduction to teaching, for it means that they can be placed in classrooms that reflect the approach they are supposed to be learning. Thus, undergraduate students are placed with the teaching interns who have taken over the classrooms vacated by the less-than-degree teachers; both work under a clinical professor's supervision. To make sure that a gap does not open up between the New School and the cooperating elementary schools, administrators, starting with Dean Perrone himself, as well as the clinical professors, spend time in the elementary classrooms working with both the children and the interns and undergraduate student teachers.

Clinical experiences of a different sort are provided in the

New School's own premises. A large demonstration room, equipped as an English infant schoolroom would be, shows students how a number of separate interest areas can be integrated into a single classroom. There is a math corner, for example, filled with concrete materials of all sorts—sticks, rods, pebbles, geoboards and rubber bands, mathematical games—in which the students learn math in the same style in which, hopefully, their students will be learning it. Thus, the New School students go through the unsettling experience of deciding what to do with all this richness, which materials to use first, how to make sense of it all. There is, in addition, a reading corner, a science center, a Wendy House—the whole setup is there for them to play in, work in, live in, until they get the gut feeling of how open and alive and exciting an elementary classroom can and should be.

It is not surprising, therefore, that New School graduates turn out to be far more imaginative, creative, and sensitive than the great majority of American teachers, as the detailed descriptions of their classrooms in Chapter 7 makes clear. Skeptics can dismiss this impact, of course, by attributing it to the so-called "Hawthorne effect," whereby participants in an experiment display the behavior the experimenters desire, their new behavior being the result of the experimental situation itself, rather than of the changes the experimenters have introduced. The fact remains that one can walk into any school in which New School graduates are teaching and determine, within five minutes, which teachers have been to the New School and which have not; no teacher education program in the United States, with the possible exception of New York's Bank Street College of Education, has that impact.

This is not to suggest that the New School is an unqualified success; far from it. In good measure, the program displays the weakness that Dewey warned against in his 1904 paper on the relation of theory to practice; New School graduates are superior teachers, but they are not "students of teaching." They have not acquired the grounding in theory or the intellectual disciplines they need in order to set their own goals or understand the reasons behind the teaching methods they use so competently. This is a serious shortcoming, and one of which Vito Perrone is aware; he has no illusions about having found the ultimate answers to teacher education, and indeed views his program with an honesty that is as rare as it is refreshing. At the same time, however, it should be pointed out that graduates of most other schools of education lack the New School graduates' competence in the classroom without having gained any greater mastery of the intellectual tools of their profession.

This weakness stems from the same factors that give the New School program its strength—particularly the faculty's desire to teach in the same informal, individualized, non-directive manner it would like its students to use. Forcing students, so to speak, to develop and shape their own programs of study, to decide what books to read and what projects to do, the New School faculty believes, will make them better able to experiment and innovate, indeed to create their own classroom environments, as well as better able to let learning evolve out of their students' interests.

But students—college students no less than elementary school students—cannot choose what they have never experienced, heard of, or imagined. And many New School students lack the intellectual experiences that are a prerequisite to making intelligent and useful choices about their own professional education—understandably so, in view of the inadequate elementary and secondary schooling that the New School was created to correct. The typical University of North Dakota student, for example, was graduated from a high school with a total student body of eighty and a faculty of six; the median ACT (American College Testing Program) score of entering freshmen places them in the thirtieth to fortieth percentile, which means their score is exceeded by 60 to 70 percent of the nation's college freshmen. Two years of general education is hardly enough background to enable such students to create their own course of study without any direct assistance.

Yet a number of New School faculty members insist that the students do precisely that. "If it is going to be the New School, it cannot be pseudo-new," Professor Jeanne Frein adamantly maintains. "Thirty pages read with genuine interest and from internal motivation is worth more than 3,000 read under coercion. I believe in approaching the undergraduates in elementary education the same way we are asking them to approach their pupils." Hence the goals for Mrs. Frein's humanities course "are whatever each individual student sets for himself." But this of course is *not* the way elementary school teachers approach their students; as we have seen, the teacher in an informal classroom cannot avoid setting goals, for they are embedded in the myriad ways he structures the classroom environment.

The result, in any case, is that few students in the humanities course—part of the two-year sequence on "Creative Expression"—read deeply or widely; given freedom to choose, Mrs. Frein admits, most students flounder. In her judgment, this is a necessary part of the educational process. "There is no such thing as a sudden switch from external to internal learning," she maintains, and most students have experienced nothing but "external learning" until they enter the New School. "What they face now is a void," Mrs. Frein explains. "I think it is very important that they talk to someone and admit that they are unable to follow through because they lack self-discipline. From that void," she hopes, "students will build very slowly to some positive motivation."

This kind of latitudinarianism involves faculty members in some curious inconsistencies. Few of the faculty members who refuse to assign any specific books for their students to read, or who oppose, on the grounds of "coercion," a proposal that the course in "Nature and Conditions of Learning" include a common core of required readings, object to the fact that every junior is required to take the course in "Creative Drama" and to perform student-written skits before elementary school audiences. That kind of experience is essential, they explain, if the New School is to turn out teachers able to nurture creativity in their own students. But certain kinds of intellectual experiences are equally necessary if students are to understand *why* they are doing what they are doing.

The dilemma is real: how directive can or should a teacher-training institution be if one of its goals is to turn out non-directive teachers? Putting it this way, however, suggests that the answer is not, and cannot be, either/or; it is a matter of degree, of "how much" or "how little." There is no such thing as *no* structure; there are different kinds of structure which provide different kinds of choices. If a teacher training institution has goals of its own and is serious about reaching them—if the institution really stands for something—it cannot simply turn every student loose to do his own thing.

Certainly the New School does stand for something; it has goals to which it is seriously committed and which indeed provide the justification for its existence. These goals rule out certain kinds of choices and make others possible. "We wouldn't think of allowing an elementary school teacher the option of not knowing anything about elementary arithmetic," Professor Ralph Kolstoe, the University of North Dakota psychology department chairman who also teaches in the New School, pointed out to his New School colleagues. Why, then, give students the option of knowing only those fragments of psychology and child development that happen to catch their fancy? To require every student to develop his own program without faculty guidance, Professor Kolstoe argued, is in a sense to deny the very individuality the New School is trying to encourage, "for some students are ready for 'self-actualization' as soon as they enter the New School, while others have needs that have to be met first." What is crucial is that the New School's goals be clear, which can happen only if students and faculty discuss them. "We must talk about goals, about what the end product of the New School should be like." If that is done, then each student is free to make his most important decision—whether he shares the institution's goals, and if not, whether the New School is the place for him to be.

II

To some degree, of course, the New School is a special case; with the notable exception of Vermont, I know of no other state that is even considering a complete reordering of its public schools. But education faculties do not have to wait for changes as far-reaching as those North Dakota is instituting in order to furnish their students with live models of what schooling should be. We have already described how Professor Lillian Weber of the City College of New York provided suitable practice teaching experience for her students in early childhood education by creating an informal program in the corridor outside five classrooms in a Harlem elementary school (Chapter 7, Section IV). The results demonstrate the catalytic effect that schools of education can have when they work closely with the public schools. The "corridor program" expanded from a single hour three times a week to an hour and a half a day in the school in the original school, and has spread to four other schools, at the request of concerned parents and teachers. Now there is a long waiting list of other public and private schools eager to have Professor Weber train their teachers for informal education; the interest is so great that Mrs. Weber worries that schools will try to move too quickly and thereby jeopardize the program's success.

In other cities, education faculties have ready-made opportunities growing out of the fact that the public schools are themselves experimenting with informal approaches. Philadelphia provides the most striking example. Faculty members at the University of Pennsylvania and Temple University have placed undergraduate and graduate students in Lore Rasmussen's "learning centers" program. (See Chapter 7, Section V). And some thirty or so internes from colleges and universities in Philadelphia and elsewhere get their practice teaching experience at Parkway High School (Chapter 8, Section V).

At the University of Connecticut, Professor Vincent R. Rogers, head of the Department of Elementary Education, has created another option: he sends his students to England for first-hand observation of, and experience in, informal primary schools. Professor Rogers' first exposure to English education came in 1966, when as a Fulbright scholar studying the teaching of social studies in England, friends took him to see three informal primary schools in Oxfordshire. As Rogers puts it, "I have not been quite the same since. Seventy-two schools later I still find myself wondering if what I saw was real, if such schools and teachers do exist."[7a]

It was not until he returned to the United States, however, and his children, after a year of informal schooling, had to adjust to better-than-average formal American schools, that Rogers felt the full impact of his English experience. His admiration of the British school had been tempered by a number of weaknesses he had also seen; but in the face of the harsh reality of American primary schools, these weaknesses loomed smaller and smaller. "There is so much that seems magnificently 'right' in the British primary schools," he writes in the final paragraph of his descriptive volume, "that criticisms of them need to be put in perspective. At their best, these schools are nothing short of superb. They do, in fact, offer 'another way' to those of us who are willing to listen and examine our own practices—however agonizing such a reappraisal might be."

For the last three years, therefore, Rogers has been exposing a group of elementary education majors to this "other way." Each summer, some thirty students, most of whom have completed their junior year, spend seven weeks in England. (The group comprises about a third of the junior class.) The first week is spent at Keswick Hall College of Education in Norwich, where members of the faculty provide an orientation to English

[7a] Vincent R. Rogers, *Teaching in the British Primary Schools,* New York: The Macmillan Company, 1970, p. v.

culture and society, as well as to English education. The students then fan out to various parts of England, living with English families and working as teacher aides in informal schools for some four to five weeks. They reassemble at Keswick Hall at the end of the period for a week or two of seminars designed to help them assess the significance of what they have experienced.

This summer program has affected students so profoundly— they return with an almost unanimous refrain of "it was the only meaningful thing that's happened to me during my education"—that Rogers is now sending students to England to do their practice teaching as well. The program is beginning in a modest way, with six students spending the 1970 fall semester teaching in schools in London and Oxfordshire. If the program succeeds, Rogers plans to enlarge it substantially, setting up a University of Connecticut center in London, manned by one or more faculty members. (At Rogers' instigation, most of the members of his department have spent at least a summer studying the informal English approach.)

Even students who do not go to England are likely to get some exposure to the informal approach, since an effort is made to place them in one of several schools in the area that are trying to move in that direction. To encourage these, and other, schools, moreover, Rogers has brought English heads over to the University of Connecticut campus to run six-week summer workshops in informal education. And in the summer of 1970, he took a group of experienced Connecticut teachers to Oxfordshire for a three-week round of seminars and school visitations.

At the same time, Rogers is careful to avoid forcing the informal approach on students who feel uncomfortable with it. "Some kids are just not right for informal education," he says; "they need something else." Hence University of Connecticut students have their choice of several other programs designed to open them up to different cultural and educational perspectives; students learn as much from having to adjust to a different culture and set of values, Rogers believes, as they do from the schools themselves. (Having to understand new ways of doing things forces them to adopt a questioning attitude, to become genuine learners in a way that does not happen when they remain in their own culture, where they understand the language, the customs, the currency.) Thus, there is a summer program in Denmark, which includes a two-week stint in government-run recreational camps as well as a brief exposure to Danish schools, which shut down for vacation much earlier in the summer than do the English schools. Students may also do their practice teaching in the Virgin Islands, in an exchange program with the College of the Virgin Islands, or at the Rough Rock Demonstration School in northeastern Arizona. (Located on a Navaho reservation, Rough Rock is the only Indian-run school in the U.S.)

Because so few colleges and universities are offering this kind of educational experience, school systems and associations interested in informal education have filled the vacuum by organizing their own in-service programs. Thus, the National Association of Independent Schools has taken to sponsoring summer workshops designed to acquaint both public and private school teachers with the philosophy of the informal English schools and to give them mastery of some of the techniques. The first such workshop was held at the Shady Hill School in Cambridge, Massachusetts, the month of July, 1968.[8] The program proved so successful that the Association ran three workshops (in Philadelphia, New York, and Cambridge) in the summer of 1969, all of them oversubscribed—and nine workshops in 1970, in such diverse places as Atlanta, Georgia; Rochester, N.Y.; Cleveland, Ohio; Bloomfield Hills, Michigan; and Chicago, as well as Cambridge, Massachusetts.

The success these workshops have enjoyed stems from the fact that they have been largely staffed by English teachers, heads, advisers, inspectors, and educationists who have followed much the same approach they use for in-service courses in England. It would be hard to exaggerate the impact even a brief encounter with this approach can have on both new and experienced teachers, especially in forcing them to break through the mold in which they had always viewed teaching and learning. "The quality of the experience differed from that of an ordinary teachers' workshop," Charles H. Rathbone of the Harvard Graduate School of Education has written, in a report of his experience in a week-long residential in-service course for primary school teachers conducted by the Leicestershire County Advisory Center in the spring of 1968.[9] The course, an annual affair, was conducted at Loughborough University, some twenty

[8] For a sensitive description of the 1968 program, see Edward Yeomans, *The Wellsprings of Teaching,* Boston, Mass.: National Association of Independent Schools, 1969.
[9] Charles H. Rathbone, "A Lesson from Loughborough," *This Magazine Is About Schools,* Vol. 3, No. 1, February 1969. Cf. also "Discovering a Context for Growth," *Froebel Journal,* Summer 1969.

miles north of the city of Leicester. Some seventy "students," mostly infant and junior school teachers, but including a half dozen heads and a sprinkling of people from outside the Leicestershire County schools, were enrolled. The "faculty" included ten or twelve members of the Leicestershire Advisory Center and about as many from outside the County—curriculum specialists from the Nuffield Foundation and several teacher training colleges plus some experienced teachers and heads who were about to become HMI's or members of local advisory groups.

The course was organized much the same way an informal primary school is organized, but with differences appropriate to the maturity of the students enrolled. There were six workshop rooms or areas—for art, natural science, math, English, physical education, and music—which students were free to use from after breakfast until nine or ten at night. Except for the scheduled meals and morning and afternoon breaks for tea and coffee, students were free to use the workshops as they saw fit. They could flit from workshop to workshop, they could spend all their time in one or two—or they could congregate, to relax or to talk shop, in either of the two bars on the premises.

There were group activities as well, although these were also voluntary. A "visiting professor," present for only two days, offered a "course" in "Physical Education to Music." Because of the limited time, the instructor had carefully planned every aspect of the morning's activity, putting the students through a set assignment which, nonetheless, permitted them to respond each in his individual way. Other group activities—lectures, discussions, field trips, films—were made available in response to a particular interest a student or group of students had expressed, and evolved as the participants' interests evolved.

Rathbone describes one such experience as follows:

> One day a notice appeared advertising a field-trip, organized by the natural science staff man. The following morning a number of participants went out to visit a nearby stream. They returned, bearing literally hundreds of living creatures, which they proceeded to identify and classify, transplant and encapsulate. But it was from an apparently peripheral incident that the most exciting study evolved. On their way to the stream, the bus had passed a field where there were some badger holes. No one on the bus had ever seen a badger, it seemed, and as the conversation continued, interest mounted. Someone recalled hearing of a local gentleman reputed to be knowledgeable on

the nocturnal, hard-to-see animals. A phone call followed; a lecture was arranged. It turned out that the man was one of the foremost badger experts in all Europe; his talk and excellent slides were enthusiastically received, especially those parts concerned with baiting—that is, with the techniques of luring the animal from his lair in order that he can be seen and studied. Needless to say, for the next three or four afternoons, just at dusk, badger-baiting parties went forth into the surrounding country-side, armed with field-glasses and ripe, uncooked ham.

"The lesson of the badger incident," Rathbone suggests, is that the teacher, given (and giving) this context of freedom, cannot predetermine what will be learned. He can be prepared for numerous eventualities, he can—on the basis of past performance and enthusiasm—predict the possibilities, but he never will be able, with certainty, to say what will happen next."

But the lessons were more profound than that. Forced to confront the "stuff" with which the workshops were filled—forced to decide what to do first, what stuff to work with and how, what specific goals to set for themselves—the students, many of them for the first time, began to understand the agony of indecision that can afflict a child in an informal classroom if the teacher remains too passive, or if the teacher fails to respond to that child's individual needs. "At Loughborough I was constantly confronting neutral material—classroom stuff that displayed no attitude whatsoever towards me," Rathbone writes. "Yet time and time again I found myself unable to accept what was there—either I would seek some pre-packaged 'lesson' or I would look to the teacher for clues on how I was 'supposed' to define and solve some predetermined 'problem.' The difficulty lay in feeling free to ask my *own* question, yet this is precisely the possibility the Loughborough experience made me aware of."

More important, perhaps, the students at Loughborough began to understand how the quality of the human relationships in the classroom can encourage learning or prevent it from occurring. For learning involves a commitment, a commitment of oneself, and such a commitment involves the risk of exposing oneself to others, and even more, to oneself. "I found myself having difficulty with certain materials," Rathbone reports, "not because my fingers fumbled or because I was stupid, but because of a fundamental inability to release myself to the learning situation," to take the "bold act of commitment" that the situation requires. "This type of situation is scary, and the temptation is great to beat a quick retreat"—especially when the learner feels less than confidence in his own ability.

> Consider how I felt when I finished my first linoleum block. As someone else said about *his* attempt in this medium, he hadn't done a lino block for nearly twenty years, and during the interval there had been little progress in either style or accuracy; his 1968 effort reminded him above all else of the work of a third-grader.
>
> For me it was horribly difficult to admit being connected to that drab little print; it required real humility before I was prepared to own up and accept, without embarrassment, full responsibility for this thing which I had created. For to discover where you are in respect to lino blocks and to find that you are still at the third-grade level is discomforting. It means first, admitting that the work you do is an indication—of who you are. In the second place, it means an admission that in terms of this particular competency, in respect to this particular part of you, you stink.

But the enormous range of stuff that was available made it almost impossible for a student to see himself from a single perspective; almost inevitably, he would discover that he was among the most competent in some activities, run-of-the-mill in others, and among the least competent in still others. And the different ways in which teachers responded to different students—the different ways a single teacher related to a single student according to the activity that student was pursuing—illuminated the complexity of the learning process and demonstrated the truth of Dewey's insistence that we cannot distinguish what the student learns from things and from other people. "I knew, for instance, that what the art teacher offered me as I was painting was quite different from what she offered me when I was fumbling with the linoleum-cutting tools," Rathbone writes. "Likewise I knew the counsel she offered to competent craftsmen contrasted sharply with her advice to novices. I could see that she was constrained at each intervention to take into account the particular context of each student's work, and in my case that differed radically as I moved from task to task."

And so the Loughborough course had a profound effect on its participants, the most profound being to give them new insights into themselves as students, and as people. "Successful learning does mean change," Rathbone writes, "including change in one's own estimation of oneself; to be able to adapt swiftly and without anguish to a new notion of self" is crucial to learning. Loughborough made him see himself more clearly with respect to three relationships—the relationship of himself to the materials, to the teachers, and to his own image of himself as a learner—and these insights in turn made it possible for him to change. "So in the end the lesson I took from Loughborough was a lesson about learning," he concludes, "a lesson, finally, about the education of teachers, but a lesson, first, about myself."

III

"The tendency of educational development to proceed by reaction from one thing to another, to adopt for one year, or for a term of seven years, this or that new study or method of teaching, and then as abruptly to swing over to some new educational gospel," John Dewey wrote in 1904, "would be impossible if teachers were adequately moved by their own independent intelligence. The willingness of teachers, especially of those occupying administrative positions, to become submerged in the routine detail of their callings, to expend the bulk of their energies upon forms and rules and regulations, and reports, and percentages, is another evidence of the absence of intellectual vitality. If teachers were possessed by the spirit of an abiding student of education, this spirit would find some way of breaking through the mesh and coil of circumstances and would find expression for itself."

If this be so, teachers need more than a knowledge of subject matter and a little practice teaching experience before they enter the classroom. They need knowledge *about* knowledge, about the ramifications of the subject or subjects they teach, about how those subjects relate to other subjects and to knowledge—and life—in general. They need insights into their purposes as a teacher—why they are teaching what they are teaching, and how these purposes relate to the institutional setting of the school and to the values of the local community and the society at large. They need understanding of the processes of growth and development and of the nature of mind and thought. Most important, perhaps, they need to know that they need to know these things—they need to understand the kinds of questions their teaching will raise and to have some sense of where to turn for further understanding.

If colleges and universities were as they should be, teachers would acquire much of that knowledge and insight in the process of learning subject matter itself. One of the significant differences between education for teaching and for other professions is that every subject a student takes in the course of his liberal education can and should be a professional course as well. Any course, that is to say, be it in history, literature, chemistry, physics, or mathematics, should also be a course in teaching methods, epistemology, and the philosophy of education. "The body of knowledge which constitutes the subject-matter of the student-teacher," as Dewey argued, "must, by the nature of the case, be organized subject-matter. It is not a miscellaneous heap of separate scraps. Even if (as in the case of history and literature) it be not technically termed 'science,' it is none the less material which has been subjected to method—has been selected and arranged with reference to controlling intellectual principles. There is, therefore, method in subject-matter itself—method indeed of the highest order which the human mind has yet evolved." Hence "there is something wrong in the 'academic' side of professional training, if by means of it the student does not constantly get object-lessons of the finest type in the kind of mental activity which characterized mental growth and, hence, the educative process."[10]

Of course, something *is* wrong in the academic side of professional education—and in the academic side of liberal education as well, as we have seen in Chapter 9. But even if liberal education were all that it should be, teachers-to-be would not begin to learn all they need to know in the course of majoring in the subject they are to teach. "Basic education" advocates like James Koerner and Arthur Bestor frequently write as though, to paraphrase Gertrude Stein, a subject is a subject is a subject. It is not; the "subject" taught in one college or by one professor may have little resemblance to that same "subject" as taught in another college or by another professor in the same college. There is even less correspondence between a subject, be it history, mathematics, literature, or physics, as it is taught in college and as it is taught in elementary school, junior high, or even high school.

No course, moreover—indeed, no sequence of courses—can

[10] John Dewey, "The Relation of Theory to Practice in Education."

present more than a fragment of what is known in the field. A "subject" is not something handed down from Mount Sinai; it reflects some individual's, or some group's, selection, from the almost infinite range of possibilities, of what he, or they, consider most worth knowing by this particular group of students at this particular stage of their education and at this particular moment in time. If the elementary or secondary school teacher is to be more than a technician, he must have the capacity to make that selection himself, or at the very least, to understand the basis on which it has been made by others.

That basis lies only partly within the subject itself. The "controlling intellectual principles," to use Dewey's phrase, by which material is selected and arranged to form a "subject" are themselves subject to question and change as new knowledge develops.[11] And if one talks about the curriculum as a whole rather than about what should be taught in a single course, it is clear that such decisions cannot be made apart from judgments about what is most worth knowing—judgments which in turn reflect and depend upon judgments about the purposes of education and about the most appropriate means to achieve them.

It is at least as important that prospective teachers learn to make these kinds of judgments as that they gain mastery of subject matter per se. No one, after all, can "master" a subject in the course of his education; the best that college can do is give him a solid foundation and the knowledge of how to learn whatever else he needs to know as he goes along. The clearer a teacher's view of his purposes, the greater his understanding of the strategies he might employ to achieve them, and the deeper his insight into the relations or conflicts between his own purposes and those of the school as an institution, the better able he will be to pick up what he needs to know on his own, and the more likely he will be to do so.

Hence the study of the history and philosophy of education must occupy a central place in teacher education, rather than the marginal role which Dr. Conant assigned them and which the New School and most other schools of education have given them. None of these studies will *directly* improve a teacher's performance in the classroom; to expect that they will is to misunderstand the nature of theory and its relation to practice. They are crucial nonetheless. While the study of history, philos-

[11] See Chapter 8, pp. 323–336. Cf. also Thomas S. Kuhn, *The Structure of Scientific Revolutions,* University of Chicago Press, 1962.

ophy, sociology, and psychology "do not directly enhance craftsmanship," Israel Scheffler states, "they raise continually the sorts of questions that concern the larger goals, setting, and meaning of educational practice"—the kinds of questions that teachers need to think seriously about if they are to shape the purposes or processes of education. "To link the preparation of teachers with such questions," Professor Scheffler adds, "is the special opportunity of the university."[12]

It is its special responsibility as well. Many critics have suggested that teachers would be better prepared if teacher education were a function of the public school, or of special training institutions, rather than of the colleges and universities. The most important reason for keeping teacher education in the university is to enlarge the intellectual context within which the teacher views his work—to give him the intellectual tools with which to analyze and understand, and therefore ultimately to improve, the education of the young. "A curious quality of education," Theodore R. Sizer, dean of the Harvard Graduate School of Education, observes, "is that, while most persons experience it intimately, few study it in any serious way at all":

> In our hurry to purvey or consume it, we pause infrequently to question what we are up to. We are alternately too brash and too reactionary and always, it seems, too busy to decide which and why. More importantly, we are too caught up with pressing numbers and immediate crises to decide what we should be doing in the first place. So we stumble on, giving and receiving schooling without full reflection on the truly sophisticated and ethical practice it involves.[13]

To urge more emphasis on the systematic study of education and less on subject matter is not to suggest that liberal education be subordinated to professional education. It is, rather, to argue that one's liberal education is not ended—and should not be ended—when his professional education begins. A subject is not any less liberal because it is also useful; as we have already argued, what determines whether a subject is liberal is the way

---

[12] Israel Scheffler, "University Scholarship and the Education of Teachers," *Teachers College Record,* October 1968.
[13] Theodore R. Sizer, Foreword to *The Graduate Study of Education: Report of the Harvard Committee,* Cambridge, Mass.: Harvard University Press, 1966.

it is taught and, even more, the purpose to which it is taught—whether it is designed to enlarge the student's humanity and his understanding of the nature and role of knowledge. Few courses are more liberalizing and humanizing in this sense than courses of the sort Lawrence Cremin and Israel Scheffler teach in the history and philosophy of education. As Harold Taylor writes, "To be involved in one or another kind of education, formal or informal, is the universal experience of man, and the study of education is the study of every question of importance in philosophy and history, from the question of how should one's life be lived to the question of how things came to be as they are."[14] Hence it would be a "strange sort of narrow-mindedness," as Merle Borrowman puts it, to postpone such study until the graduate or postgraduate years merely because it has professional relevance.

Needless to say, philosophy and history are not the only means by which a college can enlarge the intellectual context within which a teacher views his work. The study of literature can be used in the same way; the psychiatrist Robert Coles, for example, gives a course on the novel in the Harvard Graduate School of Education, designed to show how some of the dominant themes of contemporary literature can be used to illuminate the problems, purposes, and processes of education. And it would be hard to find courses anywhere that give teachers a deeper understanding of what education is all about than the two which Martin Dworkin of Teachers College offers in "Aesthetics and Education" and "Education, Ideology, and Mass Communication," or Professor Maxine Greene's course in "The Arts and American Education." What makes literature and art so useful is that they confront students with the concrete; the genius of the artist is to present the problems and experiences of life in personal, concrete terms, to make the reader experience them, if only vicariously.[15] Hence the study of literature can be used to illuminate the problems of any profession.

The study of psychology, sociology, and anthropology also deserves a central place in teacher education. Even Dr. Conant, who would postpone the study of the philosophy, psychology, and sociology of education to a master's program, not to be begun until a teacher has had several years of teaching experi-

---

14 Harold Taylor, *The World and the American Teacher.*
15 For an example of how the study of literature can throw new light on the history of American education, see Maxine Greene, *The Public School and the Private Vision,* New York: Random House, 1965.

ence, concedes that *some* knowledge of psychology is essential for beginning teachers. "I have come to the conclusion that there are perhaps a few principles of psychology—as well as a considerable amount of purely descriptive material—which are relevant," he writes. "Despite the present limitations on the scientific aspect of psychology as applied to teachers, *I have been convinced, largely by the testimony of students and teachers, that for those who teach children, psychology has much to say that is so valuable as to warrant the label 'necessary', at least for elementary teachers.*"[16] [Emphasis in the original]

Certainly a teacher needs to know something of the psychology of learning and cognition. But a teacher has just as much need for some knowledge of developmental psychology; one of the factors that most distinguishes teacher training in England from its counterpart in the United States is the emphasis the English give to the study of child development and to experience with children of different ages. If a teacher is to be able to respond to each child's individual needs, he also needs some insight into individual differences in personality and aptitude; and he needs to see and understand his students as individuals with lives outside the classroom as well as inside—lives that are affected by their family, ethnic, religious, and socioeconomic backgrounds. If a teacher is to turn the classroom to maximum educational advantage, he needs some understanding of the dynamics of group behavior in general and of the sociology and anthropology of the school and the classroom in particular.

As with the history and philosophy of education, the study of psychology combines liberal and professional education. "The purpose of studying psychology, whether as a professional or liberal arts course, is to enrich the student's knowledge of the qualities and character of human nature," Harold Taylor writes. "In this, the study of psychology is no different from the study of literature, philosophy, anthropology, or theater." The same is true for the study of the sociology and anthropology of education; "to study a school," Taylor suggests, "is to study the entire culture of man."

All of these studies, moreover, are important as a means of helping the prospective teacher understand *himself*—perhaps the most neglected aspect of teacher education. The beginning teacher, after all, is thrust into a situation fraught with anxiety

16 *The Education of American Teachers.*

and fear, anxieties and fears that do not necessarily evaporate with experience. He sees himself as on trial before his pupils, his colleagues and superiors, and, above all, himself. The less self-assured a teacher is, the more dependent he is likely to be on the approval of others, and the more vulnerable he therefore will be. Since most of a teacher's contacts are with his students, his need for their approval—his desire to be liked—can place him at their mercy. And some youngsters, as Arthur Jersild points out, "have an almost uncanny gift for showing dislike or what seems to be dislike in subtle ways."[17] To some degree, in fact, the more sensitive the teacher, the more likely he is to be thrown or even destroyed by students' expression of hostility, anger, and aggression, expressions that in many cases may be directed less against the teacher himself than against the school as an institution, with the teacher simply serving as the handiest target.

Some of the most basic problems the teacher faces, in short, may be personal and subjective rather than professional or academic. "If teachers are to meet these problems," Professor Jersild argues, "it is essential for them to grow in self-understanding."

A handful of teacher training institutions are trying, therefore, to give their students knowledge of themselves, as well as of their students, their subject matter, and their teaching techniques. The most elaborate effort of this sort, in all probability, and certainly the one of the longest duration, is that carried on by New York's Bank Street College of Education, a small independent graduate institution whose roots lie deep in the progressive education movement. After student teaching, the most important part of the Bank Street curriculum is the counseling program, and the most important figure in the Bank Street student's education is the guidance counselor, who serves as advisor, supervisor, friend, therapist, and mother confessor. The guidance counselor sees each student weekly in a conference group with about five other students, bi-weekly in an individual conference, and monthly in the classroom in which the

---

[17] Arthur T. Jersild, "Behold the Beginner," in *The Real World of the Beginning Teacher,* Report of the Nineteenth National TEPS Conference, Washington, D.C.: National Commission on Teacher Education and Professional Standards, National Education Association, 1966. Cf. also Arthur T. Jersild, *When Teachers Face Themselves,* New York: Teachers College Press, 1955.

student is doing her student-teaching.[18] The guidance counselors are selected ostensibly because they are mature, sensitive,
caring human beings; in the Bank Street view, as Professor
Charlotte Winsor puts it, teaching is an act that involves
"succor" as well as the transmission of knowledge. Besides their
meetings with their students, the counselors also meet once a
week with a psychiatrist or psychiatric social worker to improve
their counseling techniques and, more important, gain a deeper
understanding of themselves and of their reactions to their own
advisees.

Thus, the Bank Street advisors combine a psychological
counseling role, at times bordering on the therapeutic, with the
traditional role of supervisor of student teaching. In both the
group conferences and the individual interviews, students and
counselors discuss and try to deal with the various problems
that arise in the course of student teaching, or in the course of
the students' private lives.

Some problems are universal, or nearly so. Most students, for
example, suffer anxiety about how to exercise authority as a
teacher: some fear that direct methods of control will be interpreted as domination, and thus will cost them the children's
affection; others worry that methods of indirect control are
really disguised, and therefore dishonest, forms of manipula-
tion. Many students, too, are troubled by supervising teachers'
tendency to treat them as menial aides rather than as mature
teachers-to-be; and many students are distressed when they find
themselves less knowledgeable than their own students in some
areas, fearing that they will lose status in the children's eyes as a
consequence. More important, middle-class students tend to get
upset or frightened when they first encounter anger, aggression,
or profanity in the classroom; they need help in understanding
the offending child's behavior, and even more, in understanding
and coping with their own reactions of anger or revulsion.

Other problems are specific to a particular student, who may
have difficulty getting along with her peers or finishing class
assignments, or specific to a particular classroom.

ITEM: From a Bank Street manual.

A competent student finds herself unable to act or relate to a
group of six-year-olds, after a very successful period with nine-

---

[18] Since Bank Street prepares students only for nursery and elementary
schools, virtually all its students are female, as are most of its faculty.

year-old children to whom she was a gay, youthful spirit, in contrast to their older, more somber teacher. Her anxiety is increased by her feelings of retaliatory dislike to these children and her shocked surprise at these feelings in herself. Through counseling she is able to see how much she has been depending on being liked in order to teach, to recognize the transitory nature of the attributes for which she was being liked, and to connect this experience with the more general patterning of her relations to people.

The advisor's role is not supposed to end, however, with bringing the student to some understanding of the specific situation at hand, nor even with leading the student on to a deeper understanding of her own reactions. Rather, the advisor is expected to use the experience and the understanding that has come from it to deepen the student's understanding of the nature of teaching in general and of her own teaching patterns in particular. In the instance cited, "it was important for the advisor to supplement the student's knowledge about six-year-oldness as a period in child-adult relations, to supply background information about what the children in this particular school expect from teachers and student-teachers, to stimulate direct observations, to prime the student's groping efforts for new ways of getting into action and reaction."[19] The advisor is also expected to act as a master teacher, demonstrating how to deal with one or another situations by taking over the class herself in the course of her monthly visit. Students find it somewhat easier to accept criticism when it comes from someone playing a supportive as well as supervisory role, seeing the corrections and suggestions as a way of being strengthened rather than being chipped away at.

The College of Education at the University of Texas has been experimenting with an analogous, yet different approach developed by Professors Robert F. Peck, Oliver H. Brown, and Frances Fuller. Education students are given a battery of personality tests to serve as the basis of what Peck calls "assessment-feedback counseling," whereby the test results are used to explore with each student his strengths and weaknesses, particularly as they bear on teaching. While no student is excluded from the teacher training program because of the tests alone,

[19] Barbara Biber, Elizabeth Gilkeson, and Charlotte Winsor, *Basic Approaches to Mental Health: Teacher Education at Bank Street,* New York: Bank Street College of Education, 1966.

"selective career counseling" is given those who need it. The counseling is also offered to all students; a third or more now seek it voluntarily.[20]

The psychological assessment is used in other ways as well. Perhaps the most important use is as a guide in selecting the particular public school classrooms to which students are assigned for their practice teaching; the aim is to place each student, so far as possible, with the teacher who can best facilitate his or her growth. Thus, a student who is "cold" or who has trouble relating to other people may be assigned to a motherly first-grade teacher; a non-stop talker may be placed with a teacher who is particularly adept at indirect teaching; and so on. The psychological-test results are also used for "videotape feedback counseling," i.e., an analysis of the student's videotaped teaching, in which the goal is to help the student understand not only what he was doing wrong, but why he was doing it, and how he might develop an effective teaching style consistent with his own personality strengths and weaknesses.

The problem with both the Bank Street and University of Texas approaches is that they require people with an extraordinary combination of expertise. The advisers or counselors must be expert clinical psychologists, as at Texas, or expert guidance counselors, as at Bank Street; in either case, they also must have a thorough understanding of how schools and classrooms operate if they are to relate their psychological insights to the specific problems of teaching. Such people are rare, at best; the University of Texas program, one of its developers ruefully concedes, is something like a fire department that is so exclusive it maintains an unlisted telephone number. Certainly it is unlikely that enough people with these combinations of expertise can be found to counsel more than a small fraction of the annual crop—some 260,000 in 1969—of new teachers. And even if they could be found, the costs would be prohibitive, unless substantial amounts of new money were made available for teacher training. Even with research funds from the foundations and the federal government, for example, the Texas group can afford to give students in the experimental counseling program only an hour and a half each of "assessment feedback

[20] Robert F. Peck and Oliver H. Brown, *The R&D Center for Teacher Education*, Austin, Texas: The Research and Development Center for Teacher Education, University of Texas at Austin, R & D Report Series No. 1. A briefer version of this paper appears in the *Journal of Research and Development in Education*, Vol. 1, Number 4, Summer 1968.

counseling" and "videotape feedback counseling"—far too little to exert any significant impact on them.

Costs and available people aside, moreover, the Bank Street design is not readily transferable to state colleges and universities, where the bulk of teachers receive their education; the counseling program, like Bank Street itself, may be sui generis. For one thing, Bank Street's size—only about 100 full-time matriculated master's degree candidates and no undergraduates at all—permits an intimacy that is rare. Because of this intimacy and a self-consciousness about the Bank Street tradition, with roots in both Dewey and Freud, the school attracts and maintains a faculty whose members share a common outlook and approach. The students are self-selected in much the same way; a college graduate is not likely to apply to Bank Street unless he or she already has some orientation to its psychological approach. Thus, Professor Charlotte Winsor, perhaps the most distinguished and influential member of the faculty, calls Bank Street "a convinced society"—not a term one would apply to any other teacher training institution except North Dakota's New School.

Understandably, therefore, a growing number of educationists and school administrators are turning to "sensitivity training" as the means of giving both prospective and experienced teachers a greater awareness of themselves and of others. The term "sensitivity training" is a loose one, embracing a wide variety of approaches to human relations and group dynamics —T-groups (i.e., training groups), encounter groups, confrontation sessions, Gestalt awareness training, sensory awareness, applied human relations training, and so on; the very looseness of the terms and the vagueness of their underlying concepts have helped sensitivity training gain wide acceptance and use.

In general, however, the T-group is the heart of the approach as it is most often used, especially in pre-service or in-service teacher education. As originally developed and refined by the National Training Laboratory of Bethel, Maine (a division of the NEA, the National Training Laboratory now has branches at Cedar City, Utah, and Lake Arrowhead, California, in addition to the Bethel headquarters), a T-group consists of a small group of people—ten to sixteen is considered ideal—who meet in a residential setting for approximately two weeks. "The objectives of the T-group," as Professor Max Birnbaum, director of the Boston University Human Relations Laboratory, defines them, "are to help individual participants become aware of why both they and others behave as they do in groups." The objectives are realized, with the help of a "trainer," by "creating an atmosphere in which the motivations for typical human behavior, of which individuals are often unaware, are brought to the surface in an exaggerated form."

> Once they are made clear and explicit, they can be discussed and analyzed. Thus, the individual participant can observe both his own behavior and that of others in the group, discover sources of different kinds of behavior, and identify the effect they have upon the functioning of the group. The effort to stimulate exaggerated behavior in order to get at the motivation behind it more explicitly is an uncomfortable experience for many people, but the experience is usually transitory. The emotional component of the experience makes it appear to verge on therapy, but there is a significant difference between therapy that is focused on the problems of emotionally disturbed people and training that aims at the improvement of human relations skills of normal people.[21]

A great many variants of this traditional form have now been developed, in part reflecting varying objectives. In the early years of T-grouping, the emphasis was on the sociology of groups rather than on their psychology; the "founding fathers"—social psychologists of the Kurt Lewin persuasion—were primarily interested in improving individuals' capacity to work as leaders and/or members of an organization, rather than in their personal growth and development. The emphasis began to shift toward the latter in the 1950s, when "the movement" started to attract people with training or interest in clinical psychology and psychiatry. Now, T-group sessions may range from a single day or weekend to as long as three weeks, with an equally wide range of objectives.

However much advocates of sensitivity training may disagree over terminology and approach, they are pretty well united in their faith in its efficacy. "By whatever name it is known," Max Birnbaum declares, "human relations training is capable, if properly employed, of producing substantial educational change. It holds tremendous potential for improving education by dealing with its affective components, reducing the unnecessary friction between generations, and creating a revolution in

[21] Max Birnbaum, "Sense About Sensitivity Training," *Saturday Review,* November, 15, 1969.

instruction by helping teachers to learn how to use the classroom group for learning purposes."

Sensitivity training also holds tremendous potential for harm. "The most serious threat to sensitivity training," Birnbaum complains, "comes first from its enthusiastic but frequently unsophisticated school supporters, and second from a host of newly hatched trainers, long on enthusiasm or entrepreneurial expertise, but short on professional experience, skill, or wisdom." A few sessions as a trainee, topped by a two-week session for trainers at Bethel, frequently is enough to qualify a person as a trainer.

Even with qualified trainers, sensitivity training can be dangerous; the human psyche is too fragile and too personal to be casually probed by professional or amateur psychologists. To insist that an individual expose his psyche for someone else's purposes—for example, to improve the efficacy of the organization in which he works—is, at the least, a gross invasion of privacy. More seriously, sensitivity training can have seriously adverse, even disastrous, consequences on the mental health of the people involved. What Birnbaum calls "the effort to stimulate exaggerated behavior in order to get at the motivation behind it" is, after all, a form of psychological probing for which neither the trainee nor the trainer may be prepared. The risk of psychological damage is compounded by the brevity of the experience and its residential nature, which inject an extraordinary and abnormal intensity into personal relationships; even at its most benign, sensitivity training tends to be a "shocking and bruising experience." The risk is compounded still more by the usual training technique, which is to break through the defenses with which people normally cloak their attitudes, feelings, and motives. As the film *Bob and Carol and Ted and Alice* illustrated with devastating humor, most trainers are doggedly persistent in the attempt, for part of the creed of sensitivity training is that people should be "open," "honest," and uninhibited in their relations with others. "Sensitivity training may come as a liberation to the inhibited lower middle-class," David Riesman warns, but "it is often conducted in such a way as to manipulate the inhibited for the benefit of the sophisticated, the intrusive, and the sadistic. Of course this need not happen," he adds "but it is no tool to be blithe or casual about."[22]

[22] David Riesman, "Commentary," in E. Alden Dunham, *Colleges of the Forgotten American,* New York: McGraw-Hill, 1969, p. 173.

It is ingenuous, therefore, for a trainer to argue that "there is a significant difference between therapy that is focused on the problems of emotionally disturbed people and training that aims at the improvement of human relations skills of normal people." Certainly there is such a difference—but the trainer has no way of knowing which of the people he is training are "normal" and which are "abnormal," if indeed so stark and simplistic a dichotomy has any meaning at all. Meeting them for the first time when they enter the training session, a trainer would have to be the greatest diagnostician of all time to assess the nature and degree of each of his trainees' neuroses and psychoses. He has no way of knowing, therefore, why a particular individual may resist his, or other trainees', probings, or what the consequences might be of breaking through that resistance—whether that individual's defenses are crusts that can be easily tossed away, for example, or whether they are the foundation on which a once-sick individual has made his adjustment with himself and the world. It may be easy to destroy that foundation; once destroyed, it may take a lifetime to replace it.

In short, sensitivity training is too dangerous to be used very widely, however laudable its goals. Some teacher training programs are trying to develop their own adaptations, therefore, in attempt to gain some of the benefits without the dangers and risks. Professor Alan F. Westin, director of the Center for Research and Education in American Liberties at Columbia University and Teachers College, has been experimenting with a non-residential variant of the T-group as one component of a summer workshop program for the in-service education of teachers. The object is to give teachers insight into the authoritarian nature of the typical public school; unless teachers provide a more democratic atmosphere in the classroom, with greater respect for the students' individuality, students are not likely to develop any deep commitment to a democratic society. By maintaining a mix of different races and colors among the teacher participants, Westin also hopes to give them greater insight into their own attitudes about racial, religious, and ethnic differences. With the assistance of Professor Louis Levine of San Francisco State College, a sensitivity trainer who is aware of the risks of the approach, Westin and his workshop staff try to avoid the extreme intensity of the usual T-group with its deep psychological probing and its attempt to break down each member's defenses; they try instead to keep the sessions focused on the specific questions at hand.

Another approach might be to change the way courses in psychology and child development are taught—to use the principles and insights these disciplines provide to give prospective teachers an understanding of themselves as well as of the students they will be teaching. This is rarely done; the "breach of continuity between learning within and without the school," Dewey wrote in his essay on "The Relation of Theory to Practice in Education," "is the great cause in education of wasted power and misdirected effort." One of the great weaknesses of teacher education, in fact, is that, as Dewey wrote, "it throws away or makes light of the greatest asset in the student's possession—his own direct and personal experience. There is every presumption (since the student is not an imbecile) that he has been learning all the days of his life, and that he is still learning from day to day."

If psychology instructors did use their students' own experiences as source material for their courses in learning, cognition, and child development, they would give the students a deeper understanding of child psychology as well as a deeper insight into themselves as people and as teachers. But this is rarely done; in the typical course, Seymour Sarason, Kenneth Davidson, and Burton Blatt write, educational psychology "is viewed as something which has to do with how children learn and not with how teachers learn. The student in the process of becoming a teacher is not made acutely aware of how he is learning"; he is not required, or shown how, to "utilize himself as a source of understanding of the learning process."[23]

When educational psychology is taught this way as something having to do only with children, Dewey pointed out, the prospective teacher "comes unconsciously to assume that education in the class-room is a sort of unique thing, having its own laws." Hence he comes to rely in his own classroom on "materials, methods, and devices which it never occurs to him to trust to in his experience outside of school." And hence, as Sarason, Davidson, and Blatt put it, the teacher tends "to function as a technician who applies rules which are contradicted both by her own learning experiences and her pupils' unproductive learning." Few things prevent teachers knowing themselves more effectively than this myopia that the mindlessness of their own education

---

[23] Seymour B. Sarason, Kenneth S. Davidson, and Burton Blatt, *The Preparation of Teachers: An Unstudied Problem in Education,* New York: John Wiley & Sons, 1962.

instills in them. And few things would give teachers clearer insight into themselves as teachers than an education that would "illuminate the nature of *their* learning process and how this relates to and affects the learning process of their pupils."

These strictures apply equally well to the prospective teacher's study of philosophy. If a teacher is to know himself, he must know what he wants to be; "self-realization" is pointless if the individual does not know what self it is that he wants to realize. This, in a sense, is what educational philosophy is all about; it is, as Professor Maurice Friedman of Temple University puts it, "an integral part of man's search to understand himself in order to become himself."[24]

It is not enough, therefore, for a course in the philosophy of education to give students some knowledge of what Plato, Comenius, Rousseau, Froebel, Dewey, et al., had to say about the ends and means of education. It must be taught in such a way as to give students a deeper understanding of themselves as educators. "Every society has an image of man it wishes to educate in its young," Professor Friedman writes, "and the teacher properly represents the society in this task. Yet he does not fulfill his task through imposing an image but through confronting his student with it and through allowing him to develop in free dialogue with it. Nor will the image the student develops ever be identical with that of the teacher or of the society he represents. It can at best be a creative response to that image." A teacher will be unable to develop that kind of dialogue with his students unless he has been engaged in the same kind of dialogue with *his* teachers. And that means that the philosophy of education cannot be taught in large lecture halls; if it is to serve its function, it must be taught in classes small enough and intimate enough to permit the kind of dialogue that would enable prospective teachers to develop their own "images of man."

Taught this way, philosophy, and indeed literature, history, and the humanities as a whole, can arm students with the means to deal with at least some of the anxieties that are bound to arise in the course of their own teaching. "To teach in the American school today is to undertake a profoundly human as well as a professional responsibility," Professor Maxine Greene of Teachers College writes in an illuminating introduction to her

[24] Maurice Friedman, "Education and The Image of Man," *Teachers College Record*, Vol. 70, No. 3, December 1968.

volume, *Existential Encounters for Teachers*. "The teacher in the present age is asked to undertake the rigorous task of enabling students to develop concepts in a range of subject matter fields. Only as they learn to conceptualize, he is told, can they deal effectively with the complexities of the world. And why must they conceptualize? Why must they learn to function effectively? So that they may make competent choices . . . when they confront the situations of 'real life.' They are to be educated, in other words, to make their own way as persons . . . they are to be educated so that they may create themselves."[25]

To accept this view of teaching is to accept an enormous burden; the teacher "must engage himself fully in his classroom life so that he can deal with each student as an individual with his own peculiar structure of capabilities." And this means that the teacher is constantly taking the risk of making decisions about how to deal with each student, decisions that may affect that student for good or for ill. "Confronting his own freedom, his own need to choose," the teacher "is bound to suffer from disquietude. Engaged as he must be, he is bound to move into himself from time to time—exploring his own consciousness of what it is to choose, to act, to be." Existential philosophy and literature can help the teacher understand the disquietude and anxiety his decisions inevitably evoke in himself, Professor Greene argues, for the great existential writers have been "concerned with the problem of freedom, with men's sometimes desperate efforts to create identities for themselves." While they have not been explicitly concerned with children or schools, they have been concerned with education in its broader sense, "as it refers to the multiple modes of becoming, of confronting life situations, of engaging with others, of reflecting, forming, choosing, struggling to be."

IV

School administrators—principals, superintendents, curriculum coordinators, guidance counselors, and so on—need the kind of education we have been talking about even more than classroom teachers, for they have the responsibility of thinking about the means and ends of education for an entire school or school

[25] Maxine Greene, ed., *Existential Encounters for Teachers,* New York: Random House, 1967.

system, rather than for a single classroom. They are not now being educated in this manner.

There is considerable ferment among those concerned with the education of school administrators. Unfortunately, the main thrust of most new programs is in the wrong direction: toward an emphasis on developing broad skills of administration, rather than on the study of education. The new emphasis is understandable and, up to a point, desirable. In part, it reflects the growing recognition that administration is an art which cuts across institutional lines and that, within certain limits, the able administrator has skills that are transferable to any kind of organization.

In some universities, therefore, schools of public administration and schools of business administration are offering joint programs or are exchanging students and courses. At Massachusetts Institute of Technology, which has no school of public administration, the Sloan School of Industrial Management has dropped the word "industrial" from its title; as the Sloan School of Management, it now enrolls city managers, church administrators, and students preparing for a variety of careers in government and non-profit organizations, as well as in business itself. Columbia University's graduate schools of journalism and business have developed a joint program in "media management," Temple University's School of Business Administration is working closely with the university's medical school and affiliated hospital to develop a new breed of hospital administrator; and so it goes.

With all this going on, it is not surprising that some graduate schools of education are interested in developing joint programs with schools of public administration, or as Stanford has done, with the school of business. In part, their interest reflects a desire to broaden the pool of talent from which public school systems can draw, in part a recognition that superintendents are being called upon to play an increasingly political, which is to say public, role. To be sure, superintendents have always had to be political animals if they were to effectively manage school systems responsible to, and ultimately controlled by, the public. But the superintendent's political role has come to the fore as a result of the acrimonious public debate over school desegregation and integration and the widespread taxpayers' revolts over school budgets and bond issues.

What is wrong with the administration of the public schools has far less to do with the fact that principals and superintendents are poor administrators or poor politicians, however, than with the fact that they are poor educators. This is in no way to denigrate the skills of administration or of politics; it is to argue that they are not ends in themselves but rather means to an end. The function of the executive is to be effective—to make the organization he manages effective. But "it is not possible to be effective unless one first decides what one wants to accomplish," Peter F. Drucker, perhaps the most distinguished contemporary management theorist reminds us. "It is not possible to manage, in other words, unless one first has a goal. It is not even possible to design the structure of an organization unless one knows what it is supposed to be doing and how to measure whether it is doing it."[26]

The first responsibility of the manager, therefore, is to ask what the organization's goals are, and to make sure that the question is studied and answered—to keep asking the question, for organizational goals change from time to time. "That the question is so rarely asked—at least in a clear and sharp form—and so rarely given adequate study and thought," Drucker writes, "is perhaps the most important cause of business failure."[27] It is surely the most important single cause of educational failure, as we have argued repeatedly throughout this book. But the manager cannot be content with merely asking the question, however much he may believe in democratic or participatory management. He must play an active leadership role in helping define the objectives, for there is no "scientific" way of doing so; deciding an organization's objectives—a business firm's no less than a school system's—involves value judgments, which means that the decisions are political in the most fundamental sense of that much-abused term.

To be sure, the manager is also responsible for making sure that the objectives are realized. To do so, he must keep firmly in mind the difference between "effectiveness"—getting the right things done—and "efficiency"—getting things done right. The effectiveness approach places the emphasis on results, its hallmark being vitality. The efficiency approach places the emphasis

---

[26] Peter F. Druker, *The Age of Discontinuity*, New York: Harper & Row, 1969. Cf. also Peter F. Drucker, *The Effective Executive*, Harper & Row, 1967, *Managing for Results*, Harper & Row, 1964, and *The Practice of Management*, Harper & Row, 1954; Chester I. Barnard, *The Functions of the Executive*, Cambridge: Harvard University Press, 1947.
[27] *The Practice of Management*, p. 50.

on procedure, on the assumption that results will be achieved automatically if the proper procedures are followed; its hall-mark, therefore, is order. Both are essential. Too much emphasis on efficiency turns procedures into ends that are worshipped for their own sakes—a familiar phenomenon in the schools and in government and many large corporations. Too little emphasis on efficiency runs the risk, as Drucker puts it, "of being tripped up by the slighted routine." A certain degree of efficiency, that is to say, is a precondition for effectiveness: "Battles are not won because horses are properly shod; but as the old nursery rhyme for the junior accountant reminds us, 'for want of a nail, the kingdom was lost.'"[28]

A school administrator is not likely to be able to ask probing questions about educational purpose, and almost certainly will be unable to provide or even judge the answers or the usefulness of the means proposed to achieve them, unless his education has equipped him to think seriously and systematically about educa-tion. He needs to be equipped with a great deal more, of course. A man is not likely to be an effective superintendent of schools, for example, unless he understands the politics and social structure of his community, unless he can persuade the school board and community of the correctness of his purposes and programs, and unless he can persuade and motivate the princi-pals and teachers under his jurisdiction to carry out that program. But all these skills will be of no avail if the purposes are "wrong," or if the purposes are "right" but the teaching methods and modes of classroom and school organization are ill-suited to achieve them.

What is crucial is the way in which the principal or superin-tendent conceives himself—whether he sees himself as a "school executive," to use Raymond E. Callahan's derisive term, or an educator or educational philosopher.[29] Schools of education have a major role to play in developing the latter conception in their graduate programs for school administrators. This means changing the emphasis from "how-to" courses in administrative technique (a leading graduate school offers no fewer than four separate courses in "school plant planning" and "school plant administration") to advanced studies in the history,

---

[28] *The Age of Discontinuity,* p. 198.
[29] Raymond E. Callahan, *Education and the Cult of Efficiency.* For a less jaundiced view of the development of educational administration, see Lawrence A. Cremin, *The Transformation of the School,* especially Chapters 2, 4, and 5.

philosophy, sociology, and psychology of education. It means, as well, teaching courses in administration in a liberal, humanistic way, to illuminate the ways in which different administrative and organizational approaches affect educational purpose, and vice versa. Most important of all, perhaps, since professional education is preeminently a means of socialization into a profession, it means exposing students in administration to administrators and professors of administration who themselves exemplify the conception of the administrator as educator.

v

One of the strangest and strongest traditions of American higher education is the one that holds, implicitly if not explicitly, that those who teach students below the age of eighteen require special preparation for teaching, whereas those who teach students eighteen or older do not. The notion is patently absurd; nothing magical occurs at age eighteen to suggest or justify this kind of dichotomy. If there is any case at all for giving educators some preparation for teaching over and above an education in the liberal arts—and clearly there is—it applies to those who teach in colleges and universities no less than to those who teach in the public schools. Some medical schools are beginning to recognize this fact, as we have already seen; so are a few graduate departments of arts and sciences.

Most graduate professors, however, still bristle at the suggestion that their doctoral candidates take time away from "their education" to receive preparation for teaching. Yet, because of the prevalence of teaching assistantships, most Ph.D. candidates spend a considerably greater proportion of their time in practice teaching than do prospective secondary school teachers.[30] The real issue, therefore, is not whether time should be spent learning how to teach, but whether the time should be spent productively or not. The experience students now receive via the teaching assistantship is unproductive—the least valuable aspect of graduate study, in the opinion of both faculty and students.

The problem, in large measure, is that the debate over the value of preparation for college teaching generally turns on a narrow view of what preparation for teaching consists of. Most

[30] Bernard Berelson, *Graduate Education in the United States,* New York: McGraw-Hill, 1960. Cf. also W. Max Wise, "Who Teaches the Teachers?", in Calvin B. T. Lee, ed., *Improving College Teaching,* Washington, D.C.: American Council on Education, 1967.

of those who call for special preparation, and most of those who oppose it, talk in terms of the usefulness or uselessness of a course in pedagogy, a pedagogy conceived of solely in terms of technique, of imparting a bag of teaching techniques. A good many graduate departments, for example, now require their teaching assistants, and in a few instances, all students, to take a seminar in teaching methods, in most instances with indifferent results.

Understandably so; a bag of tricks is the least of what most teaching assistants need. Many T.A.'s see themselves as mere cogs in a huge, impersonal instructional machine; all too often, they are expected to be technicians carrying out someone else's instructional design—the infantrymen or assembly-line workers of mass higher education. What they need most is to understand what they are doing—to understand why they are teaching what they are teaching, and how it relates to the larger discipline they are studying, as well as to knowledge in general. Senior faculty members who take their own teaching seriously do this as a matter of course, meeting with their T.A.'s—informally in some institutions, in others in a seminar for which the T.A.'s receive credit—to discuss the purposes of the course, the reasons why it is organized the way it is, and the teaching techniques that might be effective in the sections which the T.A.'s handle.

But such faculty members are all too rare; and in any case, teaching assistants need more systematic study of education if they are to develop into thoughtful teachers in their own right. The idea seems not to have occurred to most university presidents, provosts, and graduate deans—not even to those expressing deep concern over their graduate students' lack of preparation for teaching. For example, when I suggested to administrators complaining about the inadequacy of the usual seminar in teaching methods that T.A.'s might learn more from the study of education as a humanistic subject, I was met with blank stares and a surprised, "Why, that's an interesting idea; it had never occurred to me."

The problem transcends the curriculum: merely adding a required course or two in the history and philosophy of education would have little impact on existing graduate programs, for the weakness of graduate education lies far less in the curriculum than in its overall tone and purpose. At the elite universities which turn out the bulk of the nation's Ph.D.'s—90 percent of the Ph.D.'s who enter academic life receive their degrees from fifty universities—graduate education involves a process of socialization into a professional model which does not prize and indeed frequently scorns communication to anyone other than fellow specialists. The process continues when graduate students go on to teach. "The big university," as Martin Trow writes, "does not whip or seduce an unwilling body of teachers into research and publication; it recruits research-minded men, and then rewards them for doing what it hired them to do, thus reinforcing their inclination toward research."[31]

Critics of college teaching have been aiming their fire at what William James called "the Ph.D. Octopus" ever since the turn of the century, when the prestigious universities began emphasizing graduate education. Indeed, no one has yet improved upon the critique that that great philosopher-psychologist provided in 1903:

> To interfere with the free development of talent, to obstruct the natural play of supply and demand in the teaching profession, to foster snobbery by the prestige of certain privileged institutions, to transfer accredited value from essential manhood to an outward badge, to blight hopes and promote invidious sentiment, to divert attention of aspiring youth from direct dealings with truth to the passing of examinations—such consequences, if they exist, ought surely to be regarded as drawbacks to the system, and an enlightened public consciousness ought to be keenly alive to the importance of reducing their amount . . .
>
> Is not our growing tendency to appoint no instructors who are not also doctors an instance of pure sham? Will anyone pretend for a moment that the doctor's degree is a guarantee that its possessor will be successful as a teacher? Notoriously his moral, social and personal characteristics may utterly disqualify him from success in the classroom; and of these characteristics his doctor's examination is unable to take any account whatever . . .
>
> The truth is that the Doctor-Monopoly in teaching, which is becoming so rooted in American custom, can show no serious grounds whatsoever for itself in reason. As it actually prevails and grows in vogue among us, it is due to childish motives exclusively. In reality it is but a sham, a bauble, a dodge, whereby to decorate the catalogues of schools and colleges . . .
>
> The more widespread becomes the popular belief that our

31 Martin Trow, "Undergraduate Teaching at Large State Universities," in Calvin B. T. Lee, ed., *Improving College Teaching*, Washington, D.C.: American Council on Education, 1967.

diplomas are indispensable hallmarks to show the sterling metal of their holders, the more widespread those corruptions will become. We ought to look to the future more carefully, for it takes generations for a national custom, once rooted, to be grown away from.[32]

In the generations that have passed, the Ph.D. Octopus has become so deeply rooted that many critics of higher education have despaired of ever eliminating it. They have concentrated their efforts instead at developing an alternative program of graduate education, leading to a different kind of degree, to prepare those teachers whose careers will be devoted to teaching undergraduate, and especially freshmen and sophomore, students. Within ten years, according to some predictions, some three to four million students who do not intend to go beyond the sophomore year will be enrolled in junior colleges. "Are we making teachers who are both willing and professionally equipped to teach effectively these freshmen and sophomores?" Roger H. Garrison, of Westbrook (Maine) Junior College, asked at an annual meeting of graduate deans. "Are we preparing them, both intellectually and temperamentally, to do this job at a reputable professional level? Are we preparing them, for instance, to teach—and teach well—general courses, with four or five sections of 25 to 30 students each . . . students whose abilities range from the brilliantly competent to the unaroused illiterate?" Garrison thinks not. Graduate programs in English, he argues, utterly fail to prepare prospective junior college teachers for the harsh realities of their job: "for students who hate to read; for students who wouldn't know a run-on sentence from a three-gaited horse; for students whose language habits have long since been distorted by the verbal barbarities of the rock-'n-roll disc jockey, the TV commercial, the peer group jargon; yet for students who, if they realistically saw the need to write clearly, would eagerly learn to do so. Or try to learn." And the same is true in every field.

Recognition of these realities is beginning to overcome the traditional opposition to creating a second track for college teachers. The demand for teachers stemming from the explosive increase in attendance at community colleges and municipal and state colleges and regional universities has already opened a number of alternative routes to a college teaching position. A small but significant, and rapidly growing, number of professors

[32] Quoted in Bernard Berelson, *Graduate Education in the United States.*

at these institutions have received their advanced training at graduate schools of education; these Ed.D.'s are in strong demand, too, to fill positions teaching lower-division students at some of the large state universities. And community colleges have been drawing their faculties from a variety of sources.

A number of colleges and universities are experimenting, therefore, with new programs to prepare college teachers. In general, the programs reflect one of two approaches. The first would retain the traditional graduate program aimed at the Ph.D. Recognizing that many students will not, and do not necessarily need to, continue through the writing of the dissertation, however, they would award a new intermediate degree reflecting academic attainment substantially beyond that of the traditional master's degree, but substantially short of the Ph.D. Yale University, for example, has begun awarding a new degree of Master of Philosophy to students who have completed all the requirements for the Ph.D. except for the dissertation; the new degree requires at least a year of study beyond that required for the traditional Master of Arts degree. Other universities, e.g., Michigan and Berkeley, prefer calling the new degree by a new name—the Candidate's Degree—to distinguish it clearly from the M.A. and thus give it more status. The hope, as Stephen H. Spurr, dean of the University of Michigan's Horace Rackham School of Graduate Studies, expresses it, is that the Candidate's or Master of Philosophy degrees will be regarded "not as a consolation prize, but rather as the positive attainment of a major step in graduate study." The fact that some recipients of the degree will cease their formal education at that point, while others will continue on to the doctorate, "is entirely appropriate," he insists, "and not derogatory in any sense."[33]

But of course it *is* derogatory; it is hard to believe that the intermediate degree, whatever it is called, will be regarded as anything other than a consolation prize for those without the stamina to stay the course. More important, however, the approach accepts existing graduate programs as desirable. But if the traditional doctoral program is an inappropriate means of preparing teachers, and it is, it makes little sense to propose a "reform" that leaves the program intact and merely awards a new degree to those who do not finish it.

Hence the second group of reformers urge the development

[33] Stephen H. Spurr, "The Candidate's Degree," *Educational Record*, Spring 1967.

of an entirely new kind of graduate program designed to pre-pare students for teaching rather than research and leading to a new kind of doctorate.

ITEM: Carnegie-Mellon University has taken the lead in de-veloping a three-year program, leading to a new Doctor of Arts degree, to prepare students for careers as college teachers or high school teachers or curriculum specialists. The program requires two years of graduate study beyond the bachelor's degree, about three-quarters of which is in a subject area, such as history or English. The remainder is devoted to a course in cognitive processes, a course in "methods and materials of in-struction," and an internship in a curriculum project involving both practice teaching and curriculum development. The third year is devoted to a dissertation in which the student may either write a thesis relating scholarship in his field to the teaching of the field, or develop new curricular material which he tries out in a teaching situation similar to the one in which he expects to make his career.

Those who urge this approach hope that the new degree will gain a status equal to that of the Ph.D. "Just as the Ph.D. is recognized as the appropriate research degree regardless of academic department," E. Alden Dunham of the Carnegie Corporation writes, "so I would hope that the doctor of arts (D.A.) might likewise become recognized as a teaching degree cutting across all academic departments."[34] To hope for any basic change in Ph.D. programs is unrealistic, Dunham argues —resistance is simply too strong, as six decades of unsuccessful reform efforts have demonstrated—and may in any case be unwise. "The academic revolution has brought with it much that is undesirable," he writes, "but it has also made American scholarship second to none in the world." Hence no institution should mount a doctor of arts program unless it is fully com-mitted to it, the test of commitment being "the willingness of the institution not only to hire graduates of its own program but to promote them and give them tenure as well." Since the major universities are not likely to meet this test—all experience suggests that they will continue to give preference to Ph.D.'s—

[34] E. Alden Dunham, *Colleges of the Forgotten Americans,* New York: McGraw-Hill, 1969, Chapter 10. Cf. also Everett Walters, "Trends toward a Degree for College Teachers," *Educational Record,* Spring 1967.

the new programs should be located in universities which do not already have a doctoral program.

The argument has much to commend it, yet it leaves this writer more than a little uneasy. Precisely because the Ph.D. is so firmly entrenched, Christopher Jencks and David Riesman argue, a teaching doctorate "would have less status and attract less talented students than one aimed at training scholars. Its graduates would have difficulty getting good jobs, even in colleges that claim not to be concerned with whether their faculty do research." The result would be to "scare away able students interested in teaching, simply because they would not want to settle for a degree that kept many academic doors closed to them."[35]

But the separate teaching doctorate would not only institutionalize the status differences between the "Hertz" and "Avis" colleges and universities; more important, it would validate and institutionalize the false dichotomy between teaching and research that is the bane of American higher education. The existence of separate doctoral programs for men interested in teaching would encourage and indeed justify the subordination of teaching to research at the elite colleges and universities. It thus would further distort graduate education for the Ph.D., which is as inappropriate for the education of research scholars as it is for teachers. "A large proportion of the research published in the disciplines we know best," Jencks and Riesman write, "exhibits no genuine concern with answering real questions or solving important problems; it is simply a display of professional narcissism. Instead of recording a struggle with methodological and substantive issues that actually matter to either teachers or students, it is simply a roller coaster ride along a well-worn track. A man who does research of this kind may at times perform a useful service to his colleagues," they add, "simply because he collects data somebody else can put to use. But such a man is a menace in the classroom, for he reenforces the anti-academic prejudices of his students."

The problem is especially serious among the best students at the best universities. These are not mostly students who demand flashy lectures by professional showmen or easy answers to recalcitrant questions. But they do insist that there be a visible relationship between knowledge and action, be-

[35] Christopher Jencks and David Riesman, *The Academic Revolution,* Garden City, New York: Doubleday, 1968, p. 535.

tween the questions asked in the classroom and the lives they
live outside it. Confronted with pedantry and alienated erudi-
tion, they are completely turned off. All too often the job of
turning them back on goes by default to critics of higher
education who encourage the students to believe that all systematic and disciplined intellectual effort is a waste of time
and that moral assurance will suffice not only to establish their
superiority over their elders but to solve the problems their
elders have so obviously botched.

The solution is to impose a unity of teaching and research—
to subject research to the test of human relevance by training
the researcher to be an educator as well. "Do you want your
teachers to be imaginative?" Whitehead asked. "Then encourage
them to research. Do you want your researchers to be imaginative? Then bring them into intellectual sympathy with the young
at the most eager, imaginative period of life, when intellects are
just entering upon their mature discipline. *Make your researchers explain themselves to active minds,* plastic and with
the world before them." This, indeed, is the reason—the justification—for the university's existence. "The universities are
schools of education, and schools of research," Whitehead went
on to argue. "But the primary reason for their existence is not
to be found either in the mere knowledge to be conveyed to the
student or in the mere opportunities for research afforded to the
members of the faculty":

> Both these functions could be performed at a cheaper rate,
> apart from these very expensive institutions. Books are cheap,
> and the system of apprenticeship is well understood. So far
> as the mere imparting of information is concerned, no uni-
> versity has had any justification for existence since the popu-
> larization of printing in the fifteenth century. . . .
> The justification for a university is that it preserves the con-
> nection between knowledge and the zest of life, by uniting the
> young and old in the imaginative consideration of learning.[36]

Thus, both the doctoral candidate who is not planning to teach
at all—barely half of those receiving the Ph.D. now enter
academic life—and the prospective academician whose main in-

[36] Alfred North Whitehead, "Universities and Their Function," in *The
Aims of Education and Other Essays,* New York: New American Library, Mentor Books, 1949.

terest is research, need preparation for teaching at least as much as the student planning to devote himself entirely to teaching. For if it is true that one cannot teach a subject unless he knows it, it is equally true that one never really knows a subject until he has tried to communicate it to others. Hence graduate students who are educated as educators—who have studied education as a human process and who have subjected their knowledge to the test of communication, which is to say, to the test of human relevance—will make better scholars, better scientists, better economists, etc., as well as better professors. The term "doctor," as we have emphasized, *means* teacher. If the degree of Doctor of Philosophy means anything, therefore, it should certify its holder's ability to teach, to communicate to others the knowledge he has acquired and the new knowledge he may develop.

The remaking of American education thus requires a new kind of relationship within the university between the faculties of education and the faculties of arts and sciences, law, medicine, journalism, social work, and so on, as well as new kinds of relationships between universities and public schools. If they are to turn out educated men and women—men and women capable of educating themselves and others—our institutions of higher education can no longer relegate the study of education to those who happen to teach or study in the school of education. As we have already argued (page 384), the study of education must be put back where it belongs, at the heart of the college or university, rather than at its margin, for no man can be considered truly educated unless he has thought seriously about education in general and his own education in particular.

VI

To say this is to leave a great many questions unanswered— questions that appear urgent to deans, provosts, and presidents, but that affect students and faculty as well. Where, for example, should the study of education be carried on—in the school of education, or in the undergraduate colleges or graduate schools or arts and sciences? Should the courses be taught by educationists, or, as Dr. Conant suggests, by "intermediaries," i.e., by historians, philosophers, sociologists, and psychologists with an interest in public education and a commitment to its improvements? Should these subjects be taught as separate disciplines, or should they be integrated into some kind of core curriculum?

518   THE EDUCATION OF EDUCATORS

The questions cannot be answered in any categorical way. As we have seen in the case of medical education, the relationship between a professional school and the rest of the university involves a series of dilemmas that are not easily resolved. On the one hand, professional practitioners lack the necessary depth of knowledge of the scholarly disciplines—but on the other hand, the academic disciplines have their own agendas, which are not the same as those of the professional school. In the case of teacher education, the problem is exacerbated by the seventy-year-old split between the education and liberal arts faculties, which has tended to define the study of education as something to be delegated to and, in a sense, fit only for the education faculty. The result is that many departments of history, philosophy, sociology, and psychology, including some of the most distinguished, quite literally do not have a single member with any interest in the problems of the schools.

The fact remains that the more closely the education and arts and sciences faculties cooperate, the better off they both will be. "Cut off from its natural links with developments in pure research and scholarship," Harvard's Scheffler Committee warned, "professional study tends to wither"—as indeed it has. Conversely, the Committee continued, pure learning, "when cut off from problems of professional practice, is diminished in relevance and power"—as it, too, has been.[37]

Closer relationships are developing in a number of colleges and universities. "We feel that the School of Education has a responsibility for improving teaching, curriculum, and learning throughout the university, not just in our own school," says B. J. Chandler, dean of the School of Education at Northwestern University. Hence, Dean Chandler is seeking funding to establish a Center for the Teaching Profession, which would train and supervise Teaching Assistants in collaboration with interested academic departments, and help departments and professional schools improve their curricula and their faculties' teaching ability. A start has already been made: a professor from the Ed School is advising the Dental School in a complete overhaul of its curriculum, and a recent Ph.D. in education is serving as Assistant Dean of the Medical School, with responsibility for curriculum and evaluation of the school's teaching.

[37] *The Graduate Study of Education: Report of the Harvard Committee,* Cambridge, Mass.: Harvard University Press, 1966.

Resistance to creation of the Center proved to be considerably less than Dean Chandler has expected; "we already have more requests for help than we can begin to accommodate," he told a Carnegie Study researcher in the spring of 1969.

The relationship is not entirely unilateral; as is the case in a good many universities, Northwestern has an all-university committee on teacher education. Like most such committees, however, Northwestern's is more window-dressing than anything else, since the committee is merely "an idea group" with little or no responsibility for setting or implementing policy. To the extent to which control of teacher education is shared, the sharing comes about through joint faculty appointments with other departments. (But only nine of the forty-nine members of the education faculty have joint appointments.)

Merely putting educationists and academicians on an all-university committee will not, by itself, improve the education of teachers or of anyone else, a fact amply illustrated by New York State's so-called Five College Project. The project was designed to test two major proposals of the Conant Report: that state education departments drop all requirements for teacher certification except for a mandated period of practice teaching, delegating responsibility for deciding what constitutes adequate preparation for teaching to each individual college and university; and that institutions receiving such a broad franchise take an "all-university approach," whereby decisions about teacher education are made jointly by education and academic departments. Five institutions—Brooklyn College, Colgate University, Cornell University, the State University College at Fredonia, and Vassar College—participated in the experiment, with funding from the Danforth Foundation and the New York State Legislature, and an almost unlimited charter for experimentation from the State Education Department.

The results were disappointing, to say the least. While "Several colleges reported serious faculty conflicts in the all-university committee deliberations," A. Jean Kennedy, the State Education Department's Project Consultant reported, "the colleges offered scant evidence that such faculty dialogues resulted in improved teacher education programs." On the contrary, the new programs looked remarkably like the old ones—except that in several cases, the number of required courses was increased rather than reduced. "The college administrative structure may be so cumbersome, or the faculty interest so diverse," Dr. Kennedy concluded, "as to render the all-university approach difficult, if not impossible, to implement."[38]

The University of Notre Dame has been more successful in moving toward what its president, Father Theodore M. Hesburgh, calls "a total institutional commitment to education." A 1968 review of all the university's activities had revealed that Notre Dame was more deeply involved in teacher education and educational research and service than either faculty or administrators had realized.

ITEM: The university had had a department of education for half a century, but its enrollment was small and its programs were all on the graduate level, in recent years focusing on doctoral studies for scholars and prospective leaders of church-related schools. No fewer than nine academic departments, however, were offering summer (and in some cases, year-long) programs for experienced teachers, for the most part under National Science Foundation or U.S. Office of Education sponsorship. And rapidly growing numbers of Notre Dame undergraduates were developing an interest in teaching careers, an interest reflected in mushrooming enrollments in the undergraduate education courses offered at St. Mary's College, a neighboring girl's school with which Notre Dame has an exchange relationship.

Instead of centralizing all these activities in a school of education, a move which might have isolated the study of education from the rest of the university's programs, Notre Dame instead has created an Institute for Studies in Education, to coordinate the various education programs and to symbolize the total institutional commitment to education.

In most universities, change will be more difficult to come by. "Few institutions are so conservative as the universities about their own affairs while their members are so liberal about the affairs of others," Clark Kerr has written; "and sometimes the most liberal faculty member in one context is the most conservative in another."[39] Yet change *is* possible. Those who argue that the university is impervious to change tend to forget how rapidly it has already changed in their own lifetime. The domina-

[38] *The Five College Project: Report of Final Conference*, Albany, N.Y.: The State Education Department, 1968.
[39] Clark Kerr, *The Uses of the University*, New York: Harper & Row, Harper Torchbook edition, 1963, p. 99.

tion of the graduate school, with its subordination of undergraduate teaching to research, is a phenomenon of the postwar period. Only ten years before World War II began, Abraham Flexner complained that "the graduate school is in imminent danger of being overwhelmed" and bitterly attacked the leading American universities for subordinating research and graduate education to undergraduate education and service to the larger society.[40] An institution that can change so rapidly in one direction ought to be able to change in other directions as well.

From at least one standpoint, the prospects for change have never been more propitious. A new generation of academicians is already visible, a generation that in good measure rejects the scholarly careerism of its teachers. It is too soon to know precisely what impact the younger academicians will have, of course. Some of the new generation, as Jencks and Riesman write, "seem so anti-organizational in outlook that it is difficult to imagine their having any significant influence on the institutional forms of academic life. Their attitudes could, indeed, alarm their elders and their more moderate age-mates, accentuating adult fears that any change in the established order will mark the beginning of a descent into youthful self-indulgence." But many of these young men are committed to teaching and to a more humanistic view of the role of scholarship. And "in the long run," as Jencks and Riesman conclude, "the young always displace the old, and they seldom completely resemble them." If they mean what they say—if they really want to build a different, a better world—they will have the power to do so.

VII

No amount of reform of colleges and universities will suffice if the schools themselves are left unchanged. "It is trivial to argue about the degree of knowledge necessary to begin teaching," Robert J. Schaefer argues, "while we ignore the crucial question of how teachers can continue to learn throughout their careers."[41] Trivial and pointless: most efforts to reform teacher education have been doomed by the reformers' myopic concentration on preservice education, as if teachers' education ended when they entered the elementary or secondary school classroom.

[40] Abraham Flexner, *Universities,* New York: Oxford University Press, 1930 (paperback edition, 1968). See also Chapter 2, Section I.
[41] Robert J. Schaefer, *The School as a Center for Inquiry,* New York: Harper & Row, 1967, p. 14.

But of course it does not! On the contrary, almost any teacher will testify that his education—his *real* education for teaching—began the day he took over his first class. The education that counts is the informal education that goes on in the classroom every Monday through Friday from nine to three. This "in-service education" is far more powerful and effective than anything teachers receive in college, in schools of education, or in the traditional in-service teachers' workshop or course. The tragedy is that it is education to the wrong ends and to the wrong means. Teachers, no less than students, are victimized by the way most schools are organized and run.

It need not be! As we have seen, schools can facilitate the education of teachers as well as of children. When the emphasis is shifted from teaching to learning—when schools become "centers for inquiry" rather than buildings for the one-way transmission of information—teachers become learners along with their students; in Dewey's phrase, they become "students of teaching." And when schools become warm and humane, teachers grow as human beings as well as as teachers. The lesson is clear; Dewey stated it two-thirds of a century ago. What is needed, he wrote, "is improvement of education, not simply by turning out teachers who can do better the things that are now necessary to do, but rather by changing the conception of what constitutes education."

Afterword

But to all doubters, disbelievers, or despairers, in human progress, it may still be said, there is one experiment which has never yet been tried. It is an experiment which, even before its inception, offers the highest authority for its ultimate success. Its formula is intelligible to all; and it is as legible as though written in starry letters on an azure sky. . . . But this experiment has never yet been tried. Education has never been brought to bear with one hundredth part of its potential force, upon the natures of children, and through them, upon the character of men, and of the race.

HORACE MANN, 1848

"It is one of the complaints of the schoolmaster that the public does not defer to his professional opinion as completely as it does to that of practitioners in other professions," Dewey wrote in one of his last published works. While this might appear to be a defect in the way education is organized, he argued, it in fact is not, for the relation between professionals and the public is different in education than in any other profession. "Education is a public business with us, in a sense that the protection and restoration of personal health or legal rights are not." The reason is simple: "To an extent characteristic of no other institution, save that of the state itself, the school has the power to modify the social order. And under our political system, it is the right of each individual to have a voice in the making of social policies as, indeed, he has a vote in the determination of political affairs. If this be true," Dewey concluded, "education is primarily a public business, and only secondarily a specialized vocation. The laymen, then, will always have his right to some utterance on the operation of the public schools."[1]

This, of course, is why I have addressed this book to laymen and educators alike. The remaking of American education will not be possible without a new kind of public dialogue in which all interested parties join. It will not be possible, moreover, unless we go beyond dialogue. Students, parents, teachers, administrators, school board members, college professors, taxpayers—all will have to act, which means that all will have to make difficult decisions; the road to reform is always uphill.

Legend has it that Rabbi Schneur Zalman, one of the great Hasidic rabbis of the late eighteenth and early nineteenth centuries, was imprisoned in St. Petersburg on false charges. While awaiting trial, he was visited by the chief of police, a thoughtful man. Struck by the quiet majesty of the rabbi's appearance and demeanor, the official engaged him in conversation, asking a number of questions that had puzzled him in reading the Scriptures. Their discussion turned to the story of the Garden of Eden. Why was it, the official asked, that a God who was all-knowing had to call out when Adam was hiding and ask him, "Where art thou?"

"You do not understand the meaning of the question," the rabbi answered. "This is a question God asks of every man in every generation. After all your wanderings, after all your efforts, after all your years, O man, where art thou?"

It is a question asked of societies as well as of individuals. One is almost afraid to ask it of this society at this moment in time; the crisis in the classroom is but one aspect of the larger crisis of American society as a whole, a crisis whose resolution is problematical at best. It does no good, however, to throw up our hands at the enormity of the task; we must take hold of it where we can, for the time for failure is long since passed. We will not be able to create and maintain a humane society unless we create and maintain classrooms that are humane. But if we

[1] John Dewey, *Moral Principles in Education,* New York: Philosophical Library, 1959, pp. v–vi.

succeed in that endeavor—if we accomplish the remaking of American education—we will have gone a long way toward that larger task, toward the creation of a society in which we can answer the question "Where art thou?" with pride rather than with dread.

Index

Index

D

H

Z

CHARLES E. SILBERMAN is both journalist and scholar. *Crisis in the Classroom* was named one of the twelve best books of the year by the *New York Times Book Review* and was on the American Library Association's Notable Books list for 1970. It has received many awards, including the John Dewey Society Award for Distinguished Service to Education in Recent Years, the National Conference of Christians and Jews special award, and the National Fellowship Award. His previous national best seller, *Crisis in Black and White,* received the Four Freedoms Literary Award and the National Conference of Christians and Jews Superior Merit Award, and was selected as one of the 50 Notable Books of 1964 by the American Library Association.

Currently a Field Foundation Fellow, Mr. Silberman was on the editorial staff of *Fortune Magazine* from 1953 to 1971. Between 1966 and 1969, while on leave from *Fortune,* he served as Director of the Carnegie Study of the Education of Educators, a $3,000,000 study of American education commissioned and financed by the Carnegie Corporation of New York; this present book is the result of that study. Mr. Silberman has also taught at Columbia University, the College of the City of New York, and the Training Institute of the International Ladies' Garment Workers' Union.

Mr. Silberman was born in Des Moines, Iowa, in 1925; he was educated in the New York public schools and at Columbia College and the Graduate Faculty of Political Science, Columbia University. He currently lives in Mount Vernon, New York, with his wife and four sons.

VINTAGE POLITICAL SCIENCE
AND SOCIAL CRITICISM